Basic Skills in English

10

Contents of the Teacher's Edition

Components of *Basic Skills in English*

Student Texts

 **Red Level Grade 7**

 **Green Level Grade 8**

 **Orange Level Grade 9**

 **Blue Level Grade 10**

 **Yellow Level Grade 11**

 **Purple Level Grade 12**

Teacher's Editions

Practice Books/Duplicating Masters

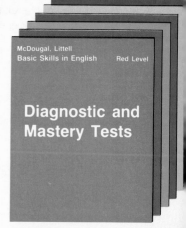

Diagnostic and Mastery Tests

The only English series for students reading *below* grade level . . . with content that is *on* grade level!

Ever since its introduction, *Basic Skills in English* has been the only series of its kind—a composition/grammar series for students reading below grade level. It's a program designed to teach all essential skills while helping students learn with confidence and achieve success.

The 1985 edition maintains the tone, format, and clear instruction that teachers praised in the earlier edition. It then builds on this success with more practice exercises, greatly expanded instruction in the process of writing, and new material on study and research skills, speaking and listening, critical thinking, and more. *Basic Skills in English* provides:

Clear, readable presentation for below-level readers

The series offers a controlled reading level, a one-step-at-a-time approach, and success-directed lessons. As a result, students read with ease and master skills gradually, gaining confidence as they progress (see pages T4–T5).

Comprehensive coverage of on-level skills

Students reading below grade level need the same skills and preparation that average students do. That's why *Basic Skills in English* provides thorough instruction in all the language basics: composition, grammar, and related language skills (see pages T6–T7).

So complete, you can be sure your students will learn all essential English skills.

All students need the same skills, regardless of their reading abilities. That's why *Basic Skills in English* teaches all of the essential concepts and skills that students are expected to master at their grade level. It's a comprehensive program that provides instruction in *all* the language basics: composition; grammar, usage, and mechanics; and related language skills.

Composition

In-depth writing instruction teaches students the skills and techniques they'll need to write effectively:

Process of Writing
Students learn the three stages of the process of writing . . . pre-writing, writing, and revising . . . then use the process consistently throughout the program.

Types of writing
The series teaches students the various elements and techniques that characterize narrative, descriptive, and explanatory writing.

Forms of writing
Students learn and practice the different forms of writing that they will use in school and in everyday life. Lessons on sentences, paragraphs, compositions, reports, and research papers give students the essential skills they need.

Part 5 **Return to the Scene**

Revising Your Descriptive Paragraph

Part 4 **Put It There!**

Writing the First Draft

Part 3 **A Certain Feeling**

Pre-Writing: Creating Mood

Here's the Idea Have you ever read a really scary mystery novel or ghost story? What scared you? Was it just the story, or was it also the way the writer described what was happening? Most writers, especially when they are describing someone or something, try to suggest a certain feeling to the reader. This feeling is called **mood.**

Writers suggest mood through the language they use. Suppose a writer is describing the park in winter. The writer wants the reader to feel that the park is a pleasant place, alive with happy people. The writer might fill his description with words like these:

Nouns	Adjectives	Verbs	Adverbs
couples	crisp	skate	merrily
flurries	smiling	stroll	gently
snowballs	sunny	frolic	excitedly

Now suppose that the writer wants to suggest a different mood to the reader. The writer wants the reader to feel that the park is a cold, dead place. In that case, he or she might use words like these:

Nouns	Adjectives	Verbs	Adverbs
slush	biting	howled	harshly
clouds	frozen	stung	terribly
storm	bare	whipped	miserably

Think about the kind of mood you want to suggest in your description. Make lists of nouns, adjectives, verbs, and adverbs that will help you to suggest that feeling.

122

Grammar, usage, and mechanics

Basic Skills in English offers exceptionally clear, to-the-point instruction in grammar, usage, and mechanics. A flexible handbook format allows for developmental teaching, skills review, and student reference. And each section includes a wealth of varied exercises that are both fun and instructive. The series pays special attention to problems of usage and speech that often present difficulties for less able students.

Possessive Pronouns and Contractions

Some contractions are formed by joining a pronoun and a verb, omitting one or more letters. The apostrophe shows where letters are left out.

it's = it + is   they're = they + are
you're = you + are   who's = who + is

The possessive forms of the pronouns *its, your, their,* and *whose* sound the same as these contractions: *it's, you're, they're,* and *who's.* Because they sound alike, the contractions and possessives are sometimes confused.

Wrong: The groundhog saw it's shadow.
Right: The groundhog saw its shadow.

Right: You're (You are) late for your appointment.
Right: They're (They are) planning to show their slides.
Right: Who's (Who is) favored to win?

Exercise A   Write the correct word from the two in parentheses.

1. (They're, Their) going to pick up the uniforms.
2. Have you made up (you're, your) mind?
3. (You're, Your) idea might work.
4. Are you sure that (they're, their) coming?
5. (Who's, Whose) going to the Eagles concert?
6. (They're, Their) glad (its, it's) Friday.
7. (Who's, Whose) going to remove the spider?
8. The amusement park gave free passes to (it's, its) first 500 entrants.
9. (Who's, Whose) bike is chained to the tree?
10. (Who's, Whose) got a dime that I can borrow?

Exercise B   Write the words for which the contractions in these sentences stand.

1. It's twenty miles from this tow
2. The book is called *Who's Who*

444

Related language skills

Separate chapters teach the related skills students need for effective communication and for successful learning in every subject area:

Critical thinking
Topics include distinguishing fact and opinion, avoiding errors in reasoning, and drawing conclusions.

Vocabulary
The series develops skills such as discovering word meaning from context and recognizing word parts.

Levels of language
Students learn about standard and nonstandard English, slang, jargon, regional language, and more.

Life skills
Letters, forms, applications, résumés, and interviews are a few of the topics taught throughout the program.

Study and research
Students learn skills such as following directions, completing research, and preparing for tests.

Speaking and listening
Skills include presenting formal and informal speeches, evaluating speeches, and participating in group discussions.

Part 4

Wanted!

Reading Help-Wanted Ads

Here's the Idea   An important step in looking for a job is finding out what jobs are available. You can do this by checking the help-wanted ads in your local newspaper. These ads are organized alphabetically by job title. Ads for full-time jobs are usually listed separately from ads for part-time jobs. A help-wanted ad may contain any or all of the following information:

1. Job title
2. Job description
3. Skills or experience required
4. Days or shifts to be worked
5. Number of hours per week
6. Salary or wages to be paid
7. How to contact the employer

Read the help-wanted ads carefully. Note details such as those listed above. Decide whether your skills and experience match those required for the job. Also decide whether you are available at the times given in the ad.

Check It Out   Read the following help-wanted ads.

OFFICE—Filing Clerk. Full-time days, M-F. Filing for busy medical office. Some scheduling of appts. Exper. preferred. Start at $5.20 hr. Call Dr. Plessas, 555-1263.

RETAIL SALES, bakery. Christmas holiday only. Full-time, evenings. Weekends included. Mature, experienced person pref. Call Sandi, 555-2800.

STOCK & CLEAN UP work. 15 hrs./wk., after school and wknds. Apply in person. Melinke Auto Supply, 253 Warrington Rd.

333

T5

As students progress, they build on the success they've already achieved.

Success-directed lessons, a controlled reading level, and a one-step-at-a-time approach combine to make concepts more accessible to students. As a result, they read with ease and master skills gradually, gaining confidence as they progress.

Success-directed lessons

The short, highly-structured lessons are fail-proof . . . every student can achieve success.

Here's the Idea
The main idea of the lesson is presented in a clear, concise manner. Explanations are especially easy to understand.

Check It Out
High-interest examples and models illustrate the main idea of the lesson. Questions help students focus on key points.

Try Your Skill
These highly-structured, success-directed exercises allow students to apply the skill they have learned.

Keep This in Mind
For further reinforcement, a boxed summary highlights the main idea of the lesson.

Now Write
The second exercise is a writing application that gives students independent practice in using the skill.

Part 9 **Top It Off**

The First Draft: Ending a Paragraph

Here's the Idea Have you ever watched a television show and waited for a thrilling ending, only to find that the episode would be continued the next week? It is not a very satisfying experience. That is why you must include a good ending when you write a paragraph.

A good ending sentence is important to a paragraph. It sums up, or ties together, the ideas of the paragraph. It may also explain the importance of the ideas presented.

An ending sentence should not introduce any new information. A good ending makes a clear, final statement that works well with the other sentences in the paragraph. In fact, an ending sentence often restates the idea of the topic sentence in a slightly different way.

A good ending sentence should also be interesting. Whenever you write a paragraph, try to express your idea in an ending sentence that is memorable as well as clear.

Check It Out Read the following paragraph.

New highway lights, not flying saucers, are responsible for a recent wave of UFO sightings. At about the same time that new highway lights were installed on Route 31 in our town, people began reporting UFO sightings. The highway lights are bright orange disks that light up the night sky in an eerie way. However, when a group of residents studied several photographs taken of these lights, they agreed that the lights resembled the UFO's they had reported. Our town's close encounter turned out to be much closer than we thought.

· Does the ending sentence tie together the ideas of the paragraph?

92

Try Your Skill Read these three paragraphs with poorly written ending sentences. Then rewrite the endings. Make your endings clear and interesting.

1   We trudged through the swamp, jars held ready. Each time one of us saw a frog or tadpole, a cry went up. Then all of us would come sloshing to where the sighting had been made, ready to lunge with our jars. Usually, we turned around and around without success. *This was the second field trip for our biology class.*

2   Television news coverage is different from newspaper reporting. The best stories for TV news are those having strong visual elements. Such visible events often deal with violence, death, or disaster. Newspapers, on the other hand, rely more on words than on pictures to tell stories. Therefore, newspapers usually have a better balance of stories than television stations do. *It is better to read a newspaper.*

3   Pike, the superintendent in our building, lets me use the tools in his basement workshop. I go down to the basement whenever I have free time. I gather my tools from the pegboard panel on the prickly cement wall behind the workbench. As I cut, sand, and hammer, time passes quickly. I enjoy the whine of the saw and the smell of freshly cut wood. *I can even taste the sawdust in the air.*

Keep This in Mind

· A good ending sentence should sum up the main idea of a paragraph. It should also be interesting.

Now Write Now you are ready to write a strong ending for your own paragraph. Review what you have written. It is a good idea to read your work aloud, at least to yourself. Then write an ending that sums up your idea in an interesting way. Save your paragraph in your folder.

93

Controlled reading level

While the content of each text is on grade level, the readability has been carefully controlled so that it does not interfere with the concepts.

The language and tone of the instruction is encouraging and conveys confidence in the student's ability. To further motivate students, the text uses lively, high-interest models and exercises.

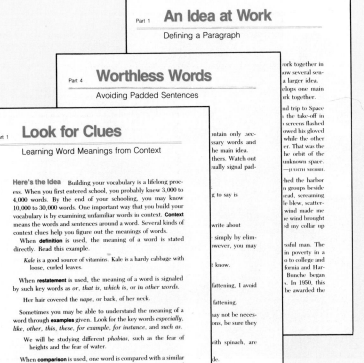

One-step-at-a-time approach

Each lesson follows a consistent, manageable format that focuses on one . . . and only one . . . topic at a time.

Single-concept lessons

So that students master skills gradually, lessons focus on a single skill and develop it. Later lessons review and build on the concept, helping students retain what they've learned.

Developmental sequence

Instruction moves logically from the word, to the sentence, to the paragraph, and on to longer types of writing.

Using the Teacher's Edition

The Teacher's Edition for each level provides step-by-step teaching strategies for presenting, developing, reinforcing, and reviewing each lesson.

Full-size student pages
Student pages are reproduced full size for ease in reading.

Objectives
Knowing what the objectives are can make your teaching more directed and purposeful.

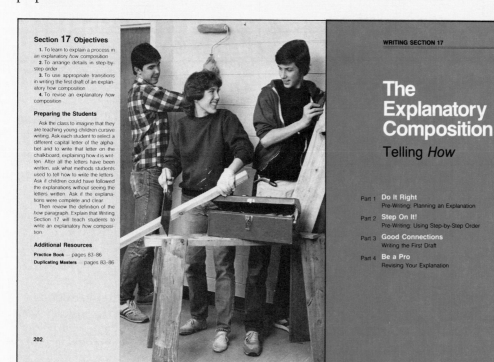

Preparing the students
The Teacher's Edition suggests ideas for motivating and preparing students prior to every new section.

Additional resources
A detailed list directs you to extra practice, review, and tests.

Teaching special populations
At the beginning of each writing section and at the end of each handbook, the Teacher's Edition explains difficulties faced by the special student. Strategies are presented for helping students for whom English is a second language, students with learning disabilities, and students who speak nonstandard dialects.

esson objectives

bjectives are clearly stated in terms of udent performance.

resenting the lesson

eaching suggestions stress points to emhasize, possible areas of difficulty, and ays to use the exercises effectively.

Answers

For your convenience, exercise answers are printed on or beside the student page.

Optional practice

Additional ideas are provided for drill, review, or reinforcement.

Part 7

Objective
To revise a report

Presenting the Lesson

1. Have students read **Here's the Idea.** Outline the revision questions on the chalkboard as you discuss them.
2. Have students examine the revised paragraph in **Check It Out.** Help the class recognize that the paragraph's overall organization has been revised to more effectively introduce the topic.
3. Assign **Try Your Skill.**
4. Read **Keep This in Mind.**
5. Assign **Now Write.** Point out that first drafts tend to be messy when they are revised, as in the sample in **Check It Out.** Students should not worry about neatness at this point as long as their revisions are legible.

Individualizing the Lesson

Less-Advanced Students

After students have made major revisions in their reports, devote one class period to proofreading for errors in grammar and mechanics. Note on the chalkboard any points of punctuation, grammar, capitalization, and spelling that the class has found troublesome. Urge students to keep an eye out for errors that they have made in the past. Instruct them to look up questionable items in the dictionary or Handbook. Finally, have students exchange papers near the end of the period and help their classmates proofread.

250

Part 7   **Check Up**

Revising a Report

Here's the Idea   Now that you have a first draft, you're almost finished. However, you have a few more steps to complete. Revising your report is the first of these steps.

As you revise your work, remember that a report depends on an accurate presentation of facts. Check the accuracy of dates and figures. Make sure that special words and names are spelled correctly. You may have to go back and check your sources.

Try reading your report aloud to yourself. Sometimes your ears will catch mistakes that your eyes have missed. As you read your report, ask yourself these questions.

1. Does my introduction tell the reader what my report will be about? Is the introduction interesting and informative?
2. Does the report follow my outline?
3. Are all of the facts and dates accurate? Do they develop my topic thoroughly?
4. Have I used quotation marks when copying a writer's work word for word?
5. Is each paragraph about one main idea? Does each fact in a paragraph develop that main idea?
6. Have I used effective transitions between sentences and paragraphs?
7. Does my conclusion summarize the main ideas?

Proofreading is the last step in revising. Read your paper carefully. Look for and correct any errors in grammar, capitalization, punctuation, and spelling. Once again, check dates, figures, and the spelling of special words and names.

Check It Out   Read this revised introductory paragraph.

250

A hero is a person who is known for special achievements. The names of such heroes are honored. However, there are also lesser known people who have performed acts of bravery. The Carnegie Hero Fund honors these heroes. Americans have respected men and women who have excelled in government, the arts, sports, and the sciences.

· What has the writer done to improve the paragraph?

Try Your Skill   This concluding paragraph has been revised, but it has not been proofread. The paragraph has five errors in grammar and mechanics. Find and correct these errors.

Today, the carnegie Hero Fund is more than seventy-five years old. During its existance, it has considered more than 50,000 heroic acts. It has awarded more than thirteen million dollars, to more than 6,300 winners. It is visable evidence that there is a deep admiration of people who help others. In this Democratic spirit, brave human beings—Whatever their sex, race, age, or background—become honored heroes.

· for organization, and for word choice.
· Proofread your report to correct errors in grammar, capitalization, punctuation, and spelling.

Now Write   Using the guidelines in this lesson, revise your report. Then proofread it. Save your revised work.

251

Advanced Students

After students have revised their reports, duplicate one paragraph from each of several revised drafts, each illustrating a different item that has been revised. Point out the improvements that have been made and have the class suggest further improvements. Then give students a chance to further revise their reports.

Optional Practice

Have the class revise the following paragraph from the body of a report, which does not stick to one main idea.

A great variety of dinosaurs existed. Some were vegetarians and some were meat-eaters. There were horned dinosaurs such as triceratops and duck-billed dinosaurs like corythosaurus. The name "dinosauria" means "terrible lizard." There were even bird-sized dinosaurs.

Extending the Lesson

Invite students who wrote especially good reports to read them to the class. Just as the class learned about the Carnegie Hero Fund from the textbook, they can also learn about their classmates' topics. A similar exercise is to read a few good reports yourself. After a report is read, ask what the class especially liked about the report.

251

On-page teaching suggestions

The text provides ideas for motivating the student, presenting the lesson, and providing enrichment.

Individualizing

Each section provides approaches for adjusting the basic lesson to different levels of ability or skill development.

Extending the lesson

An enrichment lesson or exercise suggests way students can apply the concepts outside of the English classroom.

Guidelines for evaluating composition

Special pages offer guidelines for teaching and evaluating student writing, including an evaluation form.

T9

Other McDougal, Littell Programs

Building English Skills

Building English Skills is the only complete, developmental grammar and composition program for grades 1–12. Skills are developed sequentially from one grade to the next, with each level reinforcing and extending the skills learned earlier.

The McDougal, Littell Literature Series

The *McDougal, Littell Literature* Series for grades 7–12 provides an in-depth presentation of literary types at every level to give students a strong grasp of the possibilities of each genre.

Reading Literature Series

Reading Literature is a new literature program for grades 7–12 that combines high-quality literature selections with developmental instruction in reading skills. The program builds skills in comprehension, reading literature, vocabulary, and writing. In addition, related skills such as study and research, speaking and listening, and critical thinking are reinforced throughout.

Teaching Special Populations

Many classrooms in our society include students with special language needs. Some of these students may have learning disabilities (LD). Others may be learning English as their second language (ESL). Still others may speak a nonstandard dialect of English (NSD). These students are likely to encounter special difficulties in mastering some of the concepts and acquiring some of the skills presented in *Basic Skills in English.*

The purpose of this section is to make the classroom teacher aware of these students and the learning difficulties they may face. A teacher who understands the special needs of these students can make certain that they are not penalized for learning deficiencies beyond their control. At the same time, the teacher will be better equipped to help these students fulfill their potential.

The text for *Basic Skills in English* has been reviewed by consultants whose areas of expertise include the problems faced by LD, ESL and NSD students in the English classroom. Our consultants' general suggestions for adapting *Basic Skills in English* to the special needs of these students are provided on the following pages. Additionally, specific suggestions for teaching special populations are presented at the beginning of each writing section and at the back of this book.

Special Consultants

Rebecca Benjamin, Educational Consultant, Albuquerque, New Mexico

Grace Massey Holt, Instructor of English as a Second Language, California State University, Sacramento, California

Dr. Eleanor Wall Thonis, District Psychologist, Wheatland School District, Wheatland, California

Karen Bustelo Wehle, S.L.D. Teacher, Leon County School District, Tallahassee, Florida

Virginia Woods, Secondary Resource Teacher, Dripping Springs Independent School District, Dripping Springs, Texas

Following are some general strategies for modifying lessons and assignments to help LD, ESL, and NSD students overcome some of their difficulties.

Learning Disabled Students

LD students typically have average or above average potential. However, specific areas of deficiency, which vary from student to student, can make the processing of information and the acquisition of skills difficult. There are many learning problems that can be included under the general heading "learning disabilities."

Specific areas of dysfunction include auditory memory, auditory discrimination, visual memory, visual discrimination, fine motor coordination, gross motor coordination, written expression, and oral expression.

It is important for the teacher to realize that these learning difficulties are beyond the students' control. Learning disabilities may be the result of brain damage, central nervous system dysfunction, mild cerebral palsy, or other physical impairment. Therefore, what may appear to be inattentiveness or an uncooperative attitude on the part of a student may actually be a sign of his or her inability to learn through conventional methods. Nevertheless, learning disabled students can compensate for their handicaps and overcome their problems. This is most likely to occur when teachers understand their students' strengths and limitations and are willing to adjust assignments and the presentation of material to maximize the chances for success.

Whenever possible, the teacher should work with counselors and special education teachers to determine the specific nature of a student's disability. This will allow the teacher to devise strategies for circumventing the disability. Some general strategies that apply to many kinds of learning disabilities are presented here. How-ever, the teacher is encouraged to improvise new methods and to modify material as necessary for individual students.

General Areas of Difficulty

Whatever the nature of a student's disability, there are certain predictable problems that will impede his or her efforts to learn:

1. short attention span
2. poor memory
3. difficulty in generalizing
4. hyperactivity
5. distractability
6. low motivation
7. poor motor coordination

These problems of concentration and memory are usually compounded by low levels of acquired skills:

1. low reading level
2. inability to organize work and ideas
3. laborious and illegible handwriting

General Strategies

There are several strategies the teacher can use to counter learning disabilities.

1. Seat the students in the front of the classroom where there are no obstructions to sight or hearing.
2. Present essential information both orally and in writing. Reinforce written material in the text with oral explanation or with tape recordings made by the teacher, the student, or the student's parents. Write oral instructions and assignments on the board, and provide a written study guide that highlights the key points of oral presentations.
3. Supply visual aids whenever possible, to reinforce

material from the text. Simple charts, diagrams, photographs, and other illustrations may help to clarify the relationships among ideas.

4. Repeat important ideas frequently and begin each lesson with a summary of the material covered the previous day. This will help students to compensate for poor short- and long-term memory. Repeat assignments more than once, and give them both orally and in writing.

5. Demonstrate the correct way to complete an assignment. Work one or more problems on the board, showing the students how to go about answering them. Break down the assignment into steps, and be sure that the order of the steps is clear.

6. Give two grades for written work, one for content and another for mechanics. This two-grade system rewards students for good ideas despite mechanical shortcomings. Do not penalize students with visual disabilities for misspellings.

7. Allow students to answer test questions orally, either directly to the teacher or into a tape recorder. This can help to eliminate the anxiety caused by the prospect of writing under the pressure of time.

8. Help the students find shortcuts so that they can avoid writing long or difficult words repeatedly. When complete words or sentences are unnecessary, devise abbreviatons. For example, use *D., Int., Imp.,* and *E* instead of *Declarative, Interrogative, Imperative,* and *Exclamatory* for completing exercises on the types of sentences. Allow LD students to print rather than write if printing is easier and more legible. You might also suggest that students with writing difficulties learn to type.

Modification of Material

The teacher may find that some modification of the course material in *Basic Skills in English* will be necessary so that learning disabled students can keep pace with the rest of the class.

1. Break long-term assignments into shorter, individual tasks that can be assigned on a step-by-step, short-term basis.

2. Shorten and simplify all regularly assigned work; these students must put extra time and effort into completing their work. When possible, allow the students to select one, or a few, of several questions, topics, or exercises.

3. Simplify the assignments for written paragraphs and compositions, and allow students to work with partners or to put first drafts on tape.

4. If the reading level of a Section is too advanced, explain important vocabulary words and concepts before asking the students to read it.

5. Either supplement or replace difficult terms from the text with simpler ones. For example, when teaching the types of sentences, supplement or replace the terms *Declarative, Interrogative, Imperative,* and *Exclamatory* with words like *Statement, Question, Command,* and *Strong Feeling.*

6. Review "Study and Research Skills" with LD students several times during the year. This chapter will help them to overcome their difficulties in organizing work and ideas.

English as a Second Language

Students whose first language is not English face a number of challenges. These vary in difficulty depending on their native language and culture and their familiarity with American language and culture. In general, speakers of Indo-European languages, such as German and Spanish, will probably have fewer problems learning English grammar and adapting to American culture than will, for example, speakers of Oriental languages. However, most ESL students share one distinct disadvantage: they lack their classmates' years of experience with the English language, experience which is necessary to the thorough understanding of most standard textbooks. For these students, the problems of using textbooks fall into two categories: difficulty with the complexity of language and unfamiliarity with cultural references.

The Sections of *Basic Skills in English* are written at a level that may be difficult for many ESL students. Moreover, the exercises and assignments require students to analyze and manipulate a language that many ESL students will not yet have acquired fully. Once a teacher is aware of these problems, he or she can implement certain techniques for reducing the difficulties ESL students face.

General Strategies for Countering Language Barriers

To help students overcome these difficulties posed by an unfamiliar language, the following strategies may be employed:

1. Introduce new topics at a slower pace, and provide guided practice with increased feedback and monitoring.
2. Read aloud the essential parts of each Section, allowing time for explanation, examples, and the answering of questions.
3. In explaining any abstract concept such as "unity," it is better to go to the specific example first, pointing out the elements that show unity before giving the definition. Beginning from the concrete and particular enables ESL students to follow to the general or abstract.
4. Shorten assignments for these students and allow extra time for the acquisition of concepts.
5. Simplify all activities and exercises linguistically

whenever possible. Exercises from intermedia ESL books would be helpful.
6. Build into the activities as many visuals, mani ulatives, and concrete experiences as possible. Th teacher may have to illustrate and demonstra meanings as if with small children. However, the aids should not be presented in a condescendin manner—the age and intelligence of the studen must be respected.
7. Suggest that students work as a group whenev possible. Allowing each student to go through a tivities with the group before having to do it ind vidually gives him or her enough concrete practic and confidence to try it alone.
8. Correct written exercises and compositions car fully so that students will not continue to practic mistakes.
9. Precede *every* writing activity for ESL studen with a similar oral activity; these students mu have opportunities to speak and express themselve *before* writing. This procedure provides studen with an opportunity to separate the tasks of clarify ing ideas and translating them into correct writte form.
10. Encourage ESL students to keep journals in En lish, recording thoughts and impressions withou concern for grammar, spelling, and pronunciatio It will help them to develop fluency and buil confidence and enjoyment in their writing, and will free them from anxieties about absolute co rectness.
11. To reduce the demands on the teacher's tim recruit advanced students to help the ESL studen understand written materials and to monitor the practice.

General Strategies for Countering Culture Diffe ences

The other major problem area for ESL students will b

the many cultural references that appear in the text. Some ESL students will have trouble determining gender from proper names alone. They may also have difficulty understanding references to national holidays, sports, individual teams, famous people, geography, foods, and popular culture. Slang, jargon, and idiomatic expressions are tied directly to a specific culture and are often impossible to translate. The following approaches could alleviate these problems:

1. Encourage class discussion to clarify cultural references and provide general information to the whole class. This and other oral work will greatly facilitate the ESL student's acquisition of English.
2. Encourage discussion of differences and similarities between ESL student's language and English. In covering verb tenses, for example, ask the ESL student to explain how his or her language expresses ideas of time. Such comparisons would benefit the American students by exposing them to aspects of language that are not part of their own linguistic experience.
3. Encourage ESL students to write about their native customs, holidays, geography, celebrities, and foods.
4. Encourage ESL students to read material, at an appropriate level, about specifically American people, places, and events. You might even provide these students with newspapers and popular magazines to read and discuss. This will help them acquire the common stock of information familiar to most Americans.

Speakers of Nonstandard Dialects

Everyone speaks some sort of dialect. The speech of Americans in one section of the country differs in at least some aspects of pronunciation, vocabulary, and grammar from the speech of people in other sections.

In addition, certain social, ethnic, and racial groups share a distinct way of speaking. Sometimes, however, the dialect common to a particular group departs so much for the most widely used and accepted dialects that it is termed "nonstandard." It is with students who speak such a dialect that this section is concerned.

Teachers must be aware that nonstandard dialects are legitimate language variations. These dialects follow regular phonological and semantic rules and serve the needs of the speech communities that use them. Speakers of "nonstandard" dialects are not necessarily careless speakers of English, nor should the variant features of these dialects be considered "errors." On the other hand, speakers of these dialects should be led to recognize that they cannot participate fully in mainstream American culture and society without understanding and effectively employing its language, standard English.

General Strategies

The teacher of NSD students should bear in mind that one need not, and indeed should not, eradicate one dialect in order to teach another. Instead, the teacher should implement the following strategies:

1. Encourage students to learn the patterns and usages of standard English for use in contexts where it is considered more appropriate: for academic writing and speech; in job applications and interviews; at work, if co-workers or superiors use standard English.
2. Encourage students to use the dialect that sounds natural both to speaker and listener in informal, casual, and family settings.
3. Tape-record samples of speech from various settings: playing fields, family gatherings, classrooms, committee meetings. Guide students in analyzing the vocabulary, sentence patterns, and grammar

used in these different contexts. This practice will make them see that various forms exist within a single language, each form being appropriate in a certain setting. It has proven to be a non-threatening way to increase all students' awareness of linguistic variation and to demonstrate that shifting from one form of speech to another does not involve a loss of identity.

4. When covering the Writing Sections have the NSD students keep journals, in whatever dialect is natural and comfortable, of thoughts, feelings, impressions, and experiences. Read the journals periodically and comment in writing about potential uses for the material in later compositions. Do not "correct" variations from standard usage or point out misspellings. Such nonjudgmental reading, discussion, and subsequent use of the journal entries will reinforce the lesson that writing in standard English is not abandoning one's identity but communicating it to a wider audience.

5. Establish small-group "workshops" consisting of four or five students, and have them collaborate in making suggestions for revision of written work. This strategy educates all of the students about the various dialects spoken in class.

6. Take note of the areas of grammatical variation that appear in the NSD students' written work, and be prepared to help the students with any problems that arise from these differences. Speakers of so-called Black English, for example, may have trouble with verb usage, for some of the principles of standard grammar and usage do not match their speech patterns. For similar reasons speakers of Hawaiian dialect may encounter difficulties with articles and pronouns. Other groups may have trouble with word order in sentences. Provide extra coaching, more details explanations, and additional practice, until the students have mastered the unfamiliar parts of standard dialect.

Specific suggestions for teaching composition to special populations appear at the beginning of each Composition Section of this book.

Specific suggestions for teaching grammar, usage, and mechanics to special populations appear at the end of this book.

Basic Skills in English

Purple Level

Yellow Level

Blue Level

Orange Level

Green Level

Red Level

THE McDOUGAL, LITTELL ENGLISH PROGRAM

Basic Skills in English

Blue Level

Joy Littell, EDITORIAL DIRECTOR

McDougal, Littell & Company

Evanston, Illinois
New York   Dallas   Sacramento

AUTHORS

Joy Littell, Editorial Director, McDougal, Littell & Company

The Editorial Staff of McDougal, Littell & Company

Kraft and Kraft, Developers of Educational Materials, Newburyport, Massachusetts

CONSULTANTS

Carole B. Bencich, Coordinator of Secondary Language Arts, Brevard County School Board, Rockledge, Florida

Dr. Sheila F. S. Ford, Coordinator for Secondary Language Arts, Spring Branch Independent School District, Houston, Texas

Marietta H. Hickman, English Department Chairman, Wake Forest-Rolesville High School, Wake Forest, North Carolina

Mary Evans Roberts, Supervisor of English and Language Arts, Savannah-Chatham Public Schools, Savannah, Georgia

ISBN: 0-86609-496-2   TE ISBN: 0-86609-497-0

Acknowledgments

Simon & Schuster: for entries on pages 25, 27, 28, 30, 31, 418, and 464 from *Webster's New World Dictionary,* Students Edition; copyright © 1981 by Simon & Schuster, Inc. Macmillan Publishing Company: the Handbook section contains, in revised form, some materials that appeared originally in *The Macmillan English Series, Grade 8,* by Thomas Clark Pollock et. al., © 1963 by Macmillan Company. Used by arrangement. (Acknowledgments are continued on page 711.)

Composition

Handbook

HANDBOOK SECTION 13

Capitalization

HANDBOOK SECTION 14

Punctuation

Section 1 Objectives

1. To understand the use of context clues in learning word meanings

2. To gain skill in using inference as a means of understanding words

3. To learn the importance of using synonyms and antonyms

4. To use a knowledge of base words to understand the meanings of new words

5. To understand the meanings and use of common prefixes

6. To understand the meanings and use of common suffixes

7. To understand the meanings and use of common root words

8. To understand the importance of using sensory words in description

9. To understand the meaning of new words from scientific and technological fields

Preparing the Students

Discuss with students how their own vocabulary has grown since they were toddlers. Encourage them to share recollections of their "baby talk," as well as terms they have acquired recently. Ask them to reflect on the ways that they have learned new words (conversation, reading, the media, schoolwork). Explain that Section 1 will help them to gain a wider, more precise vocabulary through the use of context, word analysis, and their senses.

Additional Resources

Mastery Test — pages 11–12 in the test booklet

Practice Book — pages 1–9

Duplicating Masters — pages 1–9

Building Vocabulary

Teaching Special Populations

LD Students with learning disabilities will benefit from additional exercises, both written and oral. Create new exercises or alter the ones provided to meet the needs of your students.

Have students memorize definitions for listed prefixes, suffixes, and roots. Help them do so by providing flashcards, lists, and worksheets.

To help LD students differentiate between synonyms and antonyms, hold "bees" in which students match words and their synonyms. Oral reinforcement is especially important for students with motor problems.

ESL The exercises in this Section will be difficult for many ESL students with limited vocabularies. Give these students assignments well in advance. ESL students may also have a difficult time understanding inferences, synonyms and antonyms, and the ways words are built from suffixes, prefixes, and roots. Discuss with them the primary meaning of each word, and help them to create sentences that use these words in context.

NSD Help students learn the standard words that are similar to the nonstandard words with which they are familiar. Encourage NSD students to keep a list of important standard English words they must use correctly. Help NSD students with the proper pronunciation of these words.

Objective

To understand the use of context clues in learning word meanings

Presenting the Lesson

1. Read aloud **Here's the Idea** and discuss the meaning of the word *context.* Discuss with students the different kinds of context clues: definition, restatement, examples, comparison, and contrast.

2. Read aloud and discuss **Check It Out.** Have students identify each context clue and point out the key words used.

3. Assign **Try Your Skill.** Have students underline the key words that they use and write the context clues next to their sentences.

4. Read **Keep This in Mind.**

5. Assign **Now Write.** Have students write the context clues next to the words they define. Ask students to share their new words and definitions with the class.

Individualizing the Lesson

Less-Advanced Students

Add the following sentences to **Check It Out.**

1. Unlike Ann's room, which was covered with papers, books, and clothes, Jody's room was *immaculate.*
2. The little boy *lamented,* or mourned, the death of his dog.
3. Norway has many *fjords,* which are narrow sea inlets bordered by steep cliffs.
4. *Hematologists* are interested in diseases of the blood such as leukemia.

Look for Clues

Learning Word Meanings from Context

Here's the Idea   Building your vocabulary is a lifelong process. When you first entered school, you probably knew 3,000 to 4,000 words. By the end of your schooling, you may know 10,000 to 30,000 words. One important way that you build your vocabulary is by examining unfamiliar words in context. **Context** means the words and sentences around a word. Several kinds of context clues help you figure out the meanings of words.

When **definition** is used, the meaning of a word is stated directly. Read this example.

> *Kale* is a good source of vitamins. Kale is a hardy cabbage with loose, curled leaves.

When **restatement** is used, the meaning of a word is signaled by such key words as *or, that is, which is,* or *in other words.*

> Her hair covered the *nape,* or back, of her neck.

Sometimes you may be able to understand the meaning of a word through **examples** given. Look for the key words *especially, like, other, this, these, for example, for instance,* and *such as.*

> We will be studying different *phobias,* such as the fear of heights and the fear of water.

When **comparison** is used, one word is compared with a similar word. Look for the key words *as, like, in the same way,* and *similar to.*

> Jack's *version* of the game is similar to your account.

When **contrast** is used, one word is contrasted with an opposite word. Look for the key words *although, but, unlike, while, on the contrary,* and *on the other hand.*

Our house was untouched by the tornado, but the house across the street was *devastated*.

By using context clues to understand unfamiliar words, you will be able to add many words to your vocabulary.

Check It Out   Read the following sentences.

1. Like other hounds, a *basset* is a good hunting dog.
2. The magician had an *enigmatic*, or mysterious, smile.
3. The story mentioned a griffin. A *griffin* is a mythical animal that is part lion and part eagle.
4. The rain stopped for a while, but now it has *resumed*.

   • What is the meaning of each of the italicized words? What context clue is used in each sentence?

Try Your Skill   Choose four of these words: *glider, cantaloupe, jeep, graceful, robin, captured, expensive*. Write a sentence for each that explains the word in context. Use key words to signal the context clues you use.

Keep This in Mind

   • You can often learn the meanings of unfamiliar words from clues in their context. Helpful context clues are definition, restatement, example, comparison, and contrast.

Now Write   Using any of your textbooks, find five words that are new to you. Copy the words as they appear in context. Using the context clues, write a definition for each of the words. Then check your meanings in a dictionary. Label your paper **Look for Clues.** Keep your work in your folder.

Advanced Students

1. Discuss the fact that using context clues is often done unconsciously. Polishing skills in using context clues will help students find meaning even more automatically as they read.

2. Have students find five unfamiliar words in the newspaper and copy them in context. After writing their own definition of each word, they can look the word up in the dictionary. They can then bring the words to class and share them.

Optional Practice

Have students define each of the following italicized words and tell what context clue is used in each sentence.

1. Aluminum foil is *opaque*, unlike plastic wrap, which you can see through.
2. Gloria was preparing for her first *marathon*, which is a 26-mile run.
3. Anthony read an interesting article about *arachnids*, such as spiders and scorpions.
4. Like a four-leaf clover, the rabbit's foot is a traditional *talisman*.
5. The biology class visited the *arboretum*. An arboretum is a park where trees and shrubs are exhibited.

Extending the Lesson

Write these nonsense words on the chalkboard: *treep, lunxious, glarky,* and *moonfrous*. Ask students to make up definitions and write sentences that give context clues to the meanings of the words. Afterwards, have each student read a sentence aloud. Let the rest of the class guess the intended definition.

Objective

To gain skill in using inference as a means of understanding words

Presenting the Lesson

1. Read aloud and discuss **Here's the Idea.** Read the paragraph containing the word *pandemonium* and point out how, with careful reading, it is not difficult to infer the meaning of many words.

2. Read the paragraph in **Check It Out.** Have students identify key words and expressions that help the reader infer the meaning of *melancholy*.

3. Assign and discuss **Try Your Skill.**

4. Read **Keep This in Mind.**

5. Assign **Now Write.** Allow students to use dictionaries for their sentences about *peace*. Have students share their sentences with the class.

Individualizing the Lesson

Less-Advanced Students

Students may need extra practice learning definitions through context clues and inference in their everyday reading. Have students keep a journal for one or two weeks in which they record unfamiliar words from their reading. If a word's definition is clear through context clues or inference, students should write their own definition of the word. Otherwise, they should write the dictionary definition of the word. Students can share their words with the class.

Take the Hint

Inferring Meaning from Context

Here's the Idea   The context in which an unfamiliar word appears does not always give direct clues to the meaning of the word. The context may only hint at the meaning. You may have to work to discover the meaning by putting clues together. From all the clues, you can draw a conclusion about the meaning of the word. This process of reading between the lines to draw a conclusion is called **inference.**

The main idea of an entire paragraph may center on the meaning of an unfamiliar word. As you read the following paragraph, for example, try to **infer** the meaning of the word *pandemonium.*

> When Carlos scored the winning goal with one minute left to play, the stadium seemed to explode. Shouting fans ran out onto the field and surrounded the players. People tossed programs and hats into the air. Strangers hugged each other and jumped up and down. Wendy hollered, "Have you ever seen such *pandemonium?*"

From this example you can infer that *pandemonium* means wild disorder, noise, and confusion.

Check It Out   Read the following paragraph.

> There are some days when I cannot help feeling *melancholy*. Usually I am a very cheerful person, but dark, rainy days bring on my melancholy mood. Then I start thinking about how much work I have to do, and all my problems seem to grow. Luckily, when the sunshine chases away the clouds, it also chases away my melancholy mood.

- What can you infer about the meaning of *melancholy?*

Try Your Skill As you read these paragraphs, try to infer the meanings of the italicized words. Then write definitions for them.

1. Nora's musical tastes are *eclectic*. She shares her mother's love for classical music, her father's passion for jazz, and her brother's affection for rock.

2. Many house fires are caused by *spontaneous combustion*. Someone may leave oily rags in a closed place. The oil and the rags react chemically with each other. The reaction gives off heat, which builds up inside the closed area. When the temperature rises high enough, the rags burst into flame.

3. Every seat in the *ampitheater* was full. The arena was cleared. Then on the far side of the arena, four messengers in costumes stood up out of the crowd and blew a blast on their trumpets. The band played, and from the entrance on the far side of the ring four horsemen in black velvet rode out into the white glare of the arena. Behind the four horsemen came the procession of the bull fighters.
— ERNEST HEMINGWAY

Keep This in Mind

- Inference is the process of putting clues together to draw a conclusion about the meaning of a word. Inferences can be drawn from the main idea of a paragraph.

Now Write Suppose that you are writing a story about a country that is at *peace*. You want to hint at the meaning of the word without defining it directly. Write three or four sentences about *peace*. Label your paper **Take the Hint** and put it into your folder.

Advanced Students

After students have written definitions for the words in **Try Your Skill**, have them compare their definitions to those in the dictionary.

Optional Practice

Add the following paragraph to **Try Your Skill.**

The mood of my grandparents' farm is pleasantly *pastoral*. In the farmyard a large collie sleeps through the warm summer afternoons. Some ducks and geese glide easily on the surface of the small pond. Sheep graze peacefully on the large green field beyond the pond.

Extending the Lesson

Write the following words on the chalkboard:

courage	generosity
beauty	anger
jealousy	sadness
cowardice	sickness
hate	conceit

Have each student select one word and write three or four sentences about a person who possesses that quality. Tell them not to define the word directly. Collect the sentences, read them to the class, and see if everyone can guess the qualities implied.

Part 3

Objective

To learn the importance of using synonyms and antonyms

Presenting the Lesson

1. Before you begin **Here's the Idea,** ask the class if they know the difference between *synonym* and *antonym*. Often students confuse these terms. Sometimes it helps if they can equate *synonym* with *same;* they both begin with the letter *s.* Students can also equate *antonym* with *anti,* meaning "against"; both words begin with the letter *a.*

Read aloud **Here's the Idea** and have students study the synonymy. Tell them that *SYN.* stands for *synonym* and *ANT.* stands for *antonym.*

2. Read and discuss **Check It Out.** If students have difficulty answering the first question following the examples, have them refer to the synonymy on page 6.

3. Assign **Try Your Skill.** Ask students to complete this exercise individually, without the aid of a dictionary; however, if they need to check their work in the dictionary, they may do so.

4. Read **Keep This in Mind.**

5. Assign and discuss **Now Write.**

Individualizing the Lesson

Less-Advanced Students

Provide practice in using a thesaurus. Look up the word *little* in a thesaurus and point out each item in the entry. Then have students use a thesaurus to find a synonym for each of the italicized words in the following sentences. Answers will vary.

6

Say What You Mean

Using Synonyms and Antonyms

Here's the Idea   Words with nearly the same meaning are **synonyms.** There may be only a shade of difference in meaning, but the difference is usually important. For example, the words *childlike* and *childish* are synonyms meaning "like a child." However, *childlike* means having the favorable qualities of a child, such as being honest and trusting. *Childish* means having the unfavorable qualities, such as being immature and self-centered.

In a dictionary, such important shades of meaning are often explained in a synonymy. A *synonymy* (si nän′ ə mē) is a list of synonyms.

Look at this symonymy given at the end of the entry for *new.*

> **SYN.—new** is applied to that which has never existed before or which has only just come into being, possession, use, etc. *[a new coat, plan, etc.];* **fresh** is used of something so new that it still has its original appearance, quality, strength, etc. *[fresh eggs; a fresh start];* **novel** implies a newness that is very strange or unusual *[a novel idea, combination, etc.];* **modern** and **modernistic** refer to that which is associated with the present time rather than an earlier period and imply up-to-dateness, with **modernistic** sometimes being used to suggest contempt as well *[modern dance; a modernistic painting];* **original** is used of that which not only is new but is also the first of its kind *[an original plan, melody, etc.]* —**ANT. old**

Synonyms are also given in a book called a *thesaurus* (thi sôr′ ə s). A thesaurus gives many synonyms for a word. A thesaurus also lists antonyms. **Antonyms** are words with opposite meanings. For example, the words *good* and *bad,* or *positive* and *negative* are antonyms. Antonyms help you to point out contrasts. For example, "Bob's attitude was so *positive* that even the delay of the race did not have a *negative* effect on him." Antonyms may be listed in some dictionaries. Notice that the antonym *old* is listed at the end of the synonymy for *new.*

When you write, decide exactly what you want to say. Use synonyms and antonyms to express your ideas more precisely.

6

Check It Out   Read the following sentences.

1. The Lee's kitchen has many *new* conveniences.
   fresh   <u>modern</u>   novel   original
2. The library is a quiet place, but the cafeteria is *loud*.
   exciting   confusing   <u>noisy</u>   disagreeable

- Which is the best synonym for *new*? Why? Is *loud* the best antonym for *quiet*? Can you explain your answer?
- Look up the words *new* and *loud* in a dictionary or thesaurus.

Try Your Skill   In each of the following sentences, the italicized word does not fit the context. Below each sentence are four words. One of the choices is a better synonym for the italicized word. Another choice is an antonym. Rewrite each sentence using the appropriate <u>synonym</u>. At the end of each sentence, write the <u>antonym</u>. Use a dictionary if you need help.

1. I want you to be *true* with me, even if it hurts me.
   <u>dishonest</u>   realistic   right   <u>honest</u>
2. My father was extremely *rigid*, but he was fair.
   <u>strict</u>   tough   <u>lenient</u>   bad
3. The two tug-of-war teams pulled the rope *tight*.
   <u>slack</u>   <u>taut</u>   hard   tense

Keep This in Mind

- Synonyms are words with similar meanings. Antonyms are words with opposite meanings.
- Use a dictionary or thesaurus to check synonyms and antonyms. Learn to use words precisely.

Now Write   Choose two of the italicized words in **Try Your Skill** and the antonym of each given below it. Use each word correctly in a sentence. Write two more sentences using the antonyms. Label your paper **Say What You Mean.** Put it in your folder.

1. The Chinese dinner that Kay prepared was *delicious*.
2. Art said the book about Russia was very *interesting*.
3. The tourists *walked* slowly down Fifth Avenue.
4. The students ate a quick snack in the *restaurant*.

Advanced Students

Discuss connotation (the implied meanings of words). Point out that the examples in **Here's the Idea,** *childish* and *childlike,* have different connotations. Connotation must be taken into account when students look up synonyms in the dictionary or a thesaurus. Have students name three synonyms for each of the following words and discuss their connotative differences. Answers will vary.

car   road   store

Optional Practice

Have students find a synonym and an antonym for each of the following words and use each word in a sentence. Answers will vary.

fresh   cheerful   clear

Extending the Lesson

Divide the class into groups of five and give each group a word that has several synonyms, such as *glad, bright, serious, pity, friend,* or *cruel.* Ask each group to use dictionaries to find five synonyms for the word. Then each student in the group should write a sentence using one of these synonyms. After each group reads its sentences aloud, discuss how the synonyms differ in meaning. Repeat the exercise, using antonyms for the words.

Objective

To use a knowledge of base words to understand the meanings of new words

Presenting the Lesson

1. Discuss **Here's the Idea,** writing *base word* and its definition on the chalkboard. Ask students for additional examples of two base words combined to create a new word, such as *bookmobile* or *homework*.

2. Have students read the groups of words in **Check It Out.** Help students recognize the dropping of the final e in the spelling of *judging* and in combining the base word *imagine.*

3. Assign **Try Your Skill.** Ask volunteers to spell each base word.

4. Read **Keep This in Mind.**

5. Assign **Now Write.** Have an informal contest to see who can create the most new words from each base word.

Individualizing the Lesson

Less-Advanced Students

Have students see how many words they can create by combining the following base words (example: *workbook*). Answers will vary.

1. book
2. trade
3. work
4. pocket
5. house
6. mark

Advanced Students

For **Try Your Skill,** have students create one new word for each base word they discover.

The Heart of the Matter

Using Base Words

Here's the Idea   Many English words are made of smaller units called **word parts.** One type of word part is the base word. A **base word** is a complete word to which another word part can be added. By adding a new word part to a base word, you create a new word. For example, the following new words can be created by adding parts to the base word *taste.*

> **dis** + taste = distaste
> taste + **ful** = tasteful
> taste + **ing** = tasting

Notice that the spelling of a base word sometimes changes when a new word part is added. In the third example above, the silent *e* in *taste* was dropped before adding *-ing.*

Sometimes you may be able to add more than one word part to a base word. For example, by adding *dis-* and *-ful* to the word *taste*, you can create a new word, *distasteful.*

Occasionally, new words are created by adding one base word to another. For example, the base words *foot* and *ball* can be joined to create the word *football.* The base words *space* and *walk* can be combined to create the word *spacewalk.*

One simple way to improve your vocabulary is to learn new words that are made from base words that you already know. In Parts 5 and 6 of this section, you will learn about two types of word parts, prefixes and suffixes. You can use these word parts to turn familiar base words into new words in your vocabulary.

Check It Out   Read the following groups of words.

finally	misjudge	humanity	imagination
finalist	judgment	inhuman	imaginable
finality	judging	inhumanity	unimaginable

- What is the base word in each group?
- Did the spellings of any of these base words change when a word part was added?
- Are any of these words new to you? Which ones?

Try Your Skill   Read the following list, and write the base word or base words in each word. You may wish to check the spellings of these base words in a dictionary.

1. un<u>think</u>able
2. mis<u>spell</u>
3. ir<u>regular</u>
4. non<u>poisonous</u>
5. pre<u>paid</u>
6. extra<u>ordinary</u>
7. <u>wisdom</u> wise
8. <u>historical</u> history
9. <u>cat</u>like
10. <u>friend</u>ly

> ### Keep This in Mind
>
> - New words can be created by adding word parts to base words.
> - The spelling of a base word may change slightly when a word part is added.
> - Sometimes more than one word part can be added to a base word.
> - Sometimes two base words can be joined together.

Now Write   Make a list of the new words you can create by adding word parts to the following base words.

    act   just   back   place

Label your list **The Heart of the Matter.** Save it in your folder.

Optional Practice

Add the following words to **Try Your Skill.**

1. bi<u>annually</u>
2. <u>mysterious</u> mystery
3. <u>child</u>hood
4. <u>obedient</u> obey
5. un<u>known</u>

Extending the Lesson

Have each student make a list of five base words that can be changed to new words by adding word parts. Students can then exchange word lists and create as many new words as possible from the base words.

Part 5

Objective

To understand the meanings and use of common prefixes

Presenting the Lesson

1. Before you begin the lesson, ask students if they know the meaning of the prefix *pre-*. If they know that *pre-* means *before*, they might not confuse the words *prefix* and *suffix*. Read aloud and discuss **Here's the Idea**. Discuss the list of nine common prefixes. Ask students if they can think of other words containing the prefixes listed.

2. You may have the students complete **Check It Out** orally or write out the answers individually. In either case, make certain that the students know both the prefixes and the base words.

3. Ask the students to do **Try Your Skill** individually. Do not allow them to confer with each other while finding the three words without prefixes. They may refer to the preceding page in order to find the meanings of the prefixes.

4. Read **Keep This in Mind.**

5. Each student should use his or her own dictionary while completing **Now Write.** If you have an insufficient number of dictionaries, borrow them from classrooms nearby. Have students share the new words.

Individualizing the Lesson

Less-Advanced Students

Give students extra practice recognizing prefixes. Have them write

First in Line

Using Prefixes

Here's the Idea   One way to determine the meaning of an unfamiliar word is to examine the word and its parts. In English, many words are made up of parts that work together. By learning a few common word parts, you will be able to add many new words to your vocabulary.

A **prefix** is a word part added to the beginning of a base word. A prefix has its own meaning. For example, the prefix *un-* means "not," as in the word *uneven*. The prefix *non-* also means "not," as in *nonviolent*. You can see how the prefixes *un-* and *non-* change the meaning of the base words *even* and *violent*.

Here is a list of some common prefixes, their meanings, and examples of words that contain them. Notice that some prefixes have more than one form and that some have more than one meaning. Study this list.

Prefix	Meaning	Examples
in- (also **il-, im-,** and **ir-**)	"not"	incomplete, illegal imperfect, irregular
mis-	"wrong, bad"	mislead, misfortune
pre-	"before"	pretest
re-	"again" or "back"	reuse, return
sub-	"under" or "less than"	subsoil, subcompact
super-	"above" or "more than"	superstructure, superstar

Not all words have prefixes, however. Some words that appear to have a prefix really do not. To determine if a word contains a prefix, check the word and its history in a dictionary.

Check It Out   Read these words and their definitions.

inactive—"not active, idle"
illogical—"not logical"
impossible—"not possible"
irresponsible—"not responsible, unreliable"
misjudge—"to judge wrongly or unfairly"
preview—"to show beforehand"
rewrite—"to write again, to revise"
substandard—"below the standard set by law or custom"
superhuman—"greater than normal for a human being"

- What is the prefix in each example? What is the base word?

Try Your Skill   Most of the words below have prefixes. Three do not. For each word that has a prefix, write the meaning of the prefix plus the base word. For example, for the word *incomplete* you would write: not + complete.

1. subhuman   *less than + human*
2. mispronounce   *wrong + pronounce*
3. inadequate   *not + adequate*
4. reason
5. preheat   *before + heat*
6. supermarket   *large + market*
7. press
8. subatomic   *less than + atom*
9. superfine   *extra + fine*
10. rerun   *again + run*
11. remarry   *again + marry*
12. irresistible   *not + resistable*
13. prepay   *before + pay*
14. mistreat   *wrong + treat*
15. mission

Keep This in Mind

- A prefix is a word part added to the beginning of a base word. Each prefix has its own meaning.

Now Write   Using a dictionary, find six words containing each of the six prefixes you have learned. List the words and define them. Finally, study the prefixes. Label your paper **First in Line** and keep you work in your folder.

the following words and underline the five that have prefixes.

preschool	submarine
rewind	independent
missile	misinform
regular	pretty

Advanced Students

Have students add the following prefixes to those in **Here's the Idea.** Students should look up the definition of each prefix and find two words in which it is used.

1. un-   *not*
2. de-   *away from; off*
3. inter-   *between or among*
4. extra-   *outside; beyond*

Optional Practice

Have students write the meaning of the prefix plus the base word for each word below (example: for *endanger, cause to be + danger*). Instruct the class to find the definitions of the prefixes in the dictionary.

endanger
anteroom   *in front of + room*
monotone   *single + tone*
befriend   *treat as + friend*

Extending the Lesson

1. Review meanings of the nine prefixes. Then hold a definition match, with the same rules as a spelling bee. Ask members of the two teams for definitions of words having the prefixes covered in this part. For a list of words, you might use those generated by students in **Now Write.**

2. Divide the class into teams. Make a game of using dictionaries to find the three prefixes that can be added to each of these base words: *match, heat, enforce, urban, change.* After the new words are announced, instruct students to write definitions.

Objective

To understand the meanings and use of common suffixes

Presenting the Lesson

1. Read aloud **Here's the Idea** and have the students study the list of eight suffixes. Ask students if they can add to the list of examples containing these suffixes.

2. Read the directions for **Check It Out.** You may have students complete this assignment orally or write it individually.

3. Students may need to refer to dictionaries for the assignment in **Try Your Skill.** Have students complete this assignment individually. Students may also refer to the preceding page for meanings of suffixes.

4. Read **Keep This in Mind.**

5. Assign **Now Write.**

Individualizing the Lesson

Less-Advanced Students

Have students draw a line between the base word and the suffix in each word below.

1. plentiful
2. colorless
3. reliable
4. writer
5. cartoonist
6. famous
7. believable
8. mysterious

Advanced Students

Have students add the following suffixes to those listed in **Here's the Idea.** Students can look up the definition of each suffix and find two words in which it is used.

In Last Place

Using Suffixes

Here's the Idea   A **suffix** is a word part added at the end of a base word. A suffix, like a prefix, has its own meaning and changes the meaning of the base word. For example, the word part -*ness* is a suffix that means "the state or quality of being." Thus, *sadness* means "the state of being sad."

Sometimes when a suffix is added, the spelling of the base word is changed. A letter may be dropped from a base word. For example, *sense* becomes *sensible.* Sometimes the final letter of the base word may be changed. For example, *envy* becomes *envious.* Sometimes the final consonant of the base word may be doubled. For example, *plan* becomes *planner.* If you add a suffix to a word, it is a good idea to check the spelling of the word in a dictionary.

Here is a list of some common suffixes, their meanings, and examples of words that contain them. Notice that a suffix, like a prefix, may have more than one form. Study this list.

Suffix	Meaning	Example
-able or **-ible**	"can be, having this quality"	agreeable, forcible
-er or **-or**	"a person or thing that does something"	dancer, elevator
-ist	"a person who does something"	artist, typist
-less	"without"	restless
-ful	"full of, having"	beautiful
-ous	"full of, having"	joyous

Check It Out   Read these words and their definitions.

enjoyable—"giving enjoyment, pleasurable"
  sensible—"having sense"
amplifier—"a thing that amplifies, or strengthens"
counselor—"a person who counsels or advises"
  alarmist—"a person who spreads alarm, expects the worst"
effortless—"without effort, easy"
   tactful—"having a sense of the right thing to say"
gracious—"having kindness, courtesy, charm"

- What is the suffix in each example? What is the base word?

Try Your Skill   Number your paper from 1 to 15. Find the suffix in each word below. Check the spelling of the base word, if necessary. Write the base word and the meaning of the suffix for each word. For example, for the word *forcible* you would write: force + having this quality.

care + without
1. careless
race + one who does
2. racer
biology + one who does
3. biologist
comfort + state of
4. comfortable
tear + full of
5. tearful

courage + having nature of
6. courageous
over + without
7. powerless
manage + able to
8. manageable
doubt + full of
9. doubtful
terror + one who believes in
10. terrorist

operate + person who does
11. operator
pity + full of
12. pitiful
religion + full of
13. religious
accept + able to
14. acceptable
glory + having
15. glorious

Keep This in Mind

- A suffix is a word part added at the end of a base word. Each suffix has its own meaning. Use a dictionary to check the spelling of a word when you add a suffix.

Now Write   Use a dictionary to find six words containing each of the six suffixes you have learned. List the words and define them. Finally, study the suffixes. Label your paper **In Last Place** and put it into your folder.

1. -ish of or belonging to
2. -ness state, quality or instance of being
3. -like like, characteristic of
4. -ment a result or product

Optional Practice

Have students write the base word plus the meaning of the suffix for each word below (example: for *boyish*, *boy* + *like*). Instruct students to find the definitions of the suffixes in the dictionary.

1. childlike child + like
2. boyish
3. patriotism patriot + qualities of
4. sadness sad + state of

Extending the Lesson

Write these pairs of words on the chalkboard: Answers will vary.

joyful—joyless
restless—restful
converter—convertible
humorist—humorless
odorous—odorless

Using their knowledge of suffixes, ask students to define these pairs of words formed from the same base words. Have them check definitions in a dictionary and then write a sentence for each word.

Objective

To understand the meanings and use of common root words

Presenting the Lesson

1. Read aloud and discuss **Here's the Idea.** Point out that base words and roots are not necessarily the same. Often a root is not a complete word. Have students study the list of Latin roots on page 14. You may wish to ask your students for additional words that are formed from these Latin roots.

2. Check It Out should be a class activity. Write each word on the chalkboard and ask the class to tell you the letters that comprise the Latin root. Underline the root. Discuss how the meaning of the root relates to the meaning of the whole word.

3. Have students complete **Try Your Skill** individually. Ask the students to avoid using dictionaries if possible. However, if they are uncertain of the meanings or if they have difficulty writing coherent definitions, they should refer to dictionaries. Discuss the Latin roots and the meanings of the words after all students have finished this exercise.

4. Read **Keep This in Mind.**

5. Assign **Now Write.** Write some of the students' new words on the chalkboard and discuss the meanings and the roots. Have students copy the words and their meanings and keep them in their folders. Remind the students that they may not use words already listed in the lesson.

Take Root

Using Roots from Latin

Here's the Idea   You have seen that word parts can be added to base words. You have seen that a prefix like *mis-*, meaning "wrong," can be added to a base word like *judge*. The new word, *misjudge*, means "to judge wrongly or unfairly." You have also seen that a suffix like *-less*, meaning "without," can be added to a word like *effort*. The new word, *effortless*, means "without effort, easy." In each of these examples the base words have clear meanings of their own. What are the base words in *misfit*, *weightless*, and *unforgettable?*

Some words are formed from a different kind of word part, called a **root.** A root is not often an English word by itself, but it is a part of a word and has a meaning. Since almost half of the words in English come from Latin, many roots also come from Latin.

Here are four common Latin roots listed with their meanings and examples of words in which they appear. Study this list.

Latin Root	Meaning	Example
dic, dict	"speak, say"	*predict*, meaning "to say what one believes will happen"
port	"carry"	*portable*, meaning "something that can be carried"
scrib, script	"write"	*scribble*, meaning "to write carelessly or hurriedly"
vis	"see"	*visit*, meaning "to go to see"

Check It Out   Read the following words and their definitions.

> dictate—"to speak aloud for someone else to write down, or to command"
> contradict—"to speak against a person, or to deny a statement"
> export—"to carry or send goods to another country"
> report—"to carry and repeat a message"
> inscribe—"to write on or engrave a surface"
> prescription—"a doctor's written direction for the use of medicine"
> invisible—"that cannot be seen"

- What is the Latin root in each example? How is the meaning of the root related to the meaning of the whole word?

Try Your Skill   Write the following words. Underline the Latin root in each word. Use the meaning of the root to help you figure out the meaning of the word. Then check each meaning in the dictionary.

dictionary	import	script	visual
dictator	transport	describe	television

Keep This in Mind

- A root is a part of a word with a meaning of its own. Many common roots come from Latin. By learning some Latin roots, you will have clues to the meanings of many unfamiliar words.

Now Write   Use a dictionary to find four words, each containing one of the four Latin roots you have learned. List the words and define them. Finally, study the roots. Label your paper **Take Root** and put it into your folder.

Less-Advanced Students

Review the etymology part of a dictionary listing. Have students look up two or three of the words in **Check it Out.** Point out how the Latin root is indicated.

Advanced Students

Add the following Latin roots to the list in **Here's the Idea.** Have students look up their meanings and find another word using each root.

anima   life principle; soul
liber   free
grat   thank or favor

Optional Practice

Have students first look up the following words and find the meanings of their Latin roots. Then have them list another word with the same root.

1. involve   in + volvere, to roll
2. perfect   perficere, through + do
3. inspect   inspicere, to look
4. include   claudere, close
5. secede   se + cedere, apart + to go

Extending the Lesson

Bring in a newspaper and give each student a page. Ask them to see how many words with Latin roots they can find. Write the words on the chalkboard, underlining the roots. Have students try to figure out the meaning of each word and then check the meanings against the definitions in a dictionary.

Objective

To understand the importance of using sensory words in description

Presenting the Lesson

1. Before reading aloud **Here's the Idea,** discuss the difference between a description that does not use the senses and one that does. Give the students these descriptions: "stopping car," "amazing waves," and "good food." Compare them with the more vivid descriptions in the first paragraph of **Here's the Idea.** Ask students why they need to be aware of their senses when they choose words for descriptions.

2. Read aloud the words in **Check It Out.** If students do not understand some of the words, have them use dictionaries. Review the use of the thesaurus. Show the students that by looking for the word *hit,* for example, they can find synonyms ranging from *poke* to *clobber.* Remind students that although a word may have many synonyms, there is usually only one word that is most effective in a particular context.

3. Read and assign **Try Your Skill.** As students select sensory words to describe the places, they may refer to a thesaurus and to the lists on pages 18–19.

4. Read **Keep This in Mind.**

5. Have students take out a sheet of paper and list four places where they would like to be. Next, have them select one of those places. Discuss and assign **Now Write.**

16

Part 8 # It's Sensational!

Building a Vocabulary of the Senses

Here's the Idea   Your five senses tell you about the world around you. You may see the sudden flash of brake lights on a car ahead of you. You may hear the roar of waves pounding a rocky shore. You may feel the spongy earth under your feet after a spring rain. You may smell the sweetness of freshly baked apple pie and enjoy its warm, rich taste. From these few examples, you can see how important your five senses are in making you more aware of your surroundings.

When you write, you can also bring your experiences to life for a reader. By using details gathered by your senses, you can create a vivid picture of the experience for your reader to share.

To learn how to use sensory details effectively, you should do three things. First, train yourself to be aware of your senses. For example, close your eyes for a moment. What do you hear, feel, or smell around you? Wherever you are, try to notice the details of your surroundings.

Second, build a vocabulary of the senses. Try to become familiar with as many sensory words as you can. Read and think about the sensory words listed on pages 18 and 19 at the end of this lesson. Try to add your own words to these lists.

Third, use your sensory vocabulary effectively. Be specific. Choose sensory words with care. For example, what sensory words would best describe the room you are in now?

When you write, appeal to as many senses as possible. Use vivid details. Try to let a reader see, hear, feel, taste, and smell what you have experienced.

16

Check It Out   Read the following examples of sensory words.

Sight: scarlet, transparent, feathered, flowery
Hearing: crash, bray, bleat, drawl, guffaw
Touch: elastic, satiny, gritty, pulpy, tepid
Taste: hearty, savory, bland, gingery, bittersweet
Smell: aromatic, dank, acrid, rancid

- Which of these sensory words are new to you? What do these words mean?

Try Your Skill   Choose two of the places or scenes below and list them on your paper. Under each, write as many sensory words as you can think of that describe your place. Try to use all of your senses. Be specific.

a certain street
your favorite room
a snowy morning
a particular beach
your favorite holiday meal

Keep This in Mind

- Use your senses to tell you about your surroundings. Build a vocabulary of the senses. When you write, use vivid sensory details to make your experience come to life.

Now Write   Think of a place where you would like to be. It may be a familiar place, such as your kitchen, or a park, or a nearby store. List as many sensory details about your place as you can. Test each sense. Be as specific and precise as possible. You may want to refer to the sample lists on the following pages. Label your paper **It's Sensational!** Keep your work in your folder.

Individualizing the Lesson

Less-Advanced Students

Show a variety of photographs from *National Geographic, Life* magazine, or a photography book. Have students write their visual impressions. Encourage them to seek exact, precise words such as those listed on page 18.

Advanced Students

Ask students to suggest specific pleasant smells, such as the odor of roses, home-baked cookies, homemade soup, or toast. Choose five, and make columns on the chalkboard. Ask for vivid sensory words to describe each smell. Start with the list on page 19 to see if any words apply. Then ask students for more words of their own. Finally, have students use a thesaurus to find appropriate synonyms. List all these words on the board.

Optional Practice

1. Ask students to choose one of the following scenes to describe to a deaf friend. Remind them to describe sounds precisely.

a horse stable   school halls
a subway   a construction site
a fire   a playground full of
a circus   children

Discuss the scenes thay have created, commenting on vivid sensory words.

2. Review the list of taste words on page 19 before you begin. Give each of four groups of students one of these words: apple, jelly bean, pretzel, raisin. Ask each group to make a list of phrases describing the taste. Then have groups exchange lists, and see if they can add more taste details, such as how the taste and texture change as the item is chewed.

Extending the Lesson

Collect five or six objects such as a brush, a Christmas tree ornament, a stapler, and a shoe lace, and place each into a separate paper bag. Have students form groups of five and hand a paper bag containing an item to one student in each group. Have that student put his or her hand into the bag and, without identifying the item, describe its feeling to the other students in the group. Next, have the other members of the group draw the item on pieces of paper. The paper bags should be passed to different groups with each student taking his or her turn at describing one item to the other members of the group. At the end of this exercise, show the items and discuss some of the words used to describe them.

A List of Sight Words

colorless	round	dotted	tidy
white	flat	freckled	handsome
ivory	curved	wrinkled	tall
yellow	wavy	striped	lean
gold	ruffled	bright	muscular
orange	oval	clear	sturdy
lime	angular	shiny	healthy
green	triangular	sparkling	fragile
turquoise	rectangular	jeweled	pale
blue	square	fiery	sickly
pink	hollow	sheer	small
red	wide	muddy	tiny
maroon	narrow	drab	large
purple	lumpy	old	immense
gray	swollen	worn	attractive
silver	long	messy	perky
hazel	wiry	cluttered	showy
brown	lopsided	fresh	lacy
black	shapeless	clean	elegant

A List of Hearing Words

crash	squawk	crackle	chime
thud	whine	buzz	laugh
bump	bark	clink	gurgle
boom	bleat	hiss	giggle
thunder	bray	snort	guffaw
bang	blare	bellow	sing
roar	rumble	growl	hum
scream	grate	whimper	mutter
screech	slam	stammer	murmur
shout	clap	snap	whisper
yell	stomp	rustle	sigh
whistle	jangle	whir	hush

A List of Taste Words

oily	rich	bland	raw
buttery	hearty	tasteless	medicinal
salty	mellow	sour	fishy
bitter	sugary	vinegary	spicy
bittersweet	crisp	fruity	hot
sweet	ripe	tangy	burnt

A List of Smell Words

sweet	piney	acrid	sickly
scented	pungent	burnt	stagnant
fragrant	spicy	gaseous	musty
aromatic	gamy	putrid	moldy
perfumed	fishy	spoiled	dry
fresh	briny	sour	damp
earthy	sharp	rancid	dank

A List of Touch Words

cool	wet	silky	sandy
cold	slippery	velvety	gritty
icy	spongy	smooth	rough
lukewarm	mushy	soft	sharp
tepid	oily	wooly	thick
warm	waxy	furry	dry
hot	fleshy	feathery	dull
steamy	rubbery	fuzzy	thin
sticky	bumpy	hairy	fragile
damp	crisp	leathery	tender

Objective

To understand the meaning of new words from scientific and technological fields

Presenting the Lesson

1. Read and discuss **Here's the Idea.** Hold a class discussion about why it is important for students, even those who do not plan to work in a scientific or technological field, to keep abreast of current scientific language. To emphasize how wide-spread technical terms are, bring in an edition of a newspaper or news-magazine with scientific and technological terms circled in red.

2. Read the list of computer-related words in **Check It Out.** Most students will have some familiarity with these words. If there are any computer "experts" in the class, they can briefly explain the more difficult words and mention other frequently used ones.

3. Assign **Try Your Skill.** Call attention to the fact that a good dictionary lists the meanings of scientific words as they apply to various fields.

4. Assign **Now Write.** Students may need to find words from more than one chapter.

Individualizing the Lesson

Less-Advanced Students

Help students feel comfortable with the use of the language of science and technology. Point out that new technical terms are often used in newspapers and magazines for

20

Words for Tomorrow

New Language for Special Fields

Here's the Idea   English has more words than any other language. English contains over six hundred thousand words, and it is still growing. Today, much of this growth comes from the fields of science and technology. New ideas, discoveries, and inventions require new words to describe them. For example, during the past fifty years, scientists have discovered several new types of stars. Scientists have had to find new words to describe these discoveries.

A *giant* or *supergiant* is a star that is more than three times the size of our sun.

A *dwarf* is a star of average size.

A *supernova* is a star that has exploded.

Sometimes new words are created. The word *supernova*, for example, is altogether new. At other times, old words are given new meanings. The words *giant* and *dwarf* have been around for a long time, but they have had different meanings.

To understand the world of tomorrow, you will have to understand many newly-created words. For this reason, you should begin now to learn any new science or technology words that you read or hear. When you come across one of these words, always copy the word into your notebook. Then, check the definition of the word in a dictionary. Finally, write the definition of the word and a sentence using the word. This will help you to remember its meaning.

Check It Out   Read the following list of words from the field of computer science.

program	software	bug
memory	printer	input
language	terminal	disk

- What are the meanings of these words? How can you find out?
- Which of these words have other meanings outside the world of computers?
- Which of these words is used only in the world of computers?

Try Your Skill Using a dictionary, answer the following questions.

1. What does the word *nucleus* mean in astronomy? in biology? in chemistry and physics? What do these meanings have in common?
2. What is a *formula* to a chemist? to a mathematician?
3. What does the word *dissect* mean to a biologist?
4. What does *psycho-* mean in the word *psychology*?

Keep This in Mind

- The English language is constantly growing.
- Many new words come from the fields of science and technology.
- Somtimes new words are created. Sometimes old words are given new meanings.

Now Write Look through a chapter in a science textbook. Make a list of ten new terms that you find. Check each term in a dictionary. Then, write the meaning of each term and use each term in a sentence. Label your paper **Words for Tomorrow.** Save it in your folder.

the general public; they are not used only by professional experts. Have students keep an ongoing list of new words they encounter from science and technology.. Plan to spend a few minutes in class each week sharing new words.

Advanced Students

Have students choose one scientific or technological field that interests them and write a list of important words and their definitions. Students can then share their lists with the entire class, in small groups, or by creating a bulletin board featuring words from their chosen fields.

Optional Practice

Have students tell from what field each of the following terms comes and define each one by referring to a dictionary or to current materials at the library.

1. clone botany
2. hologram photography
3. microchip computer science
4. behaviorism phychology
5. artificial-intelligence computer science
6. thermonuclear physics

Extending the Lesson

Mention some fields with growing vocabularies that are often discussed in the news: biology, medicine, astronomy, space exploration, environmental science. Have students read the newspaper for one week and record any words pertaining to these or other scientific fields that they discover.

Section 2 Objectives

1. To recognize the basic characteristics of a dictionary
2. To understand the information contained in dictionary entries
3. To gain skill in using context to determine the correct definition of a word

Preparing the Students

Bring to class as many different types of dictionaries as you can. For example, ask to borrow the unabridged dictionary from the school library. Try to collect enough dictionaries so that each student can use one. If you cannot find enough, have students share.

Have students turn to the table of contents of the dictionary. Ask volunteers to identify the different sections in their dictionaries. Point out that while some dictionaries have special sections about population, others have sections about geographical names. Note that a few dictionaries have sections on colleges; others have sections on foreign words and phrases.

Point out that while many students think that dictionaries contain only words and definitions, dictionaries actually have far more to offer. Ask students to think of other possible uses for dictionaries. Explain that Writing Section 2 will help students to use dictionaries efficiently.

Additional Resources

Mastery Test — pages 13–14 in the test booklet
Practice Book — pages 10–12
Duplicating Masters — pages 10–12

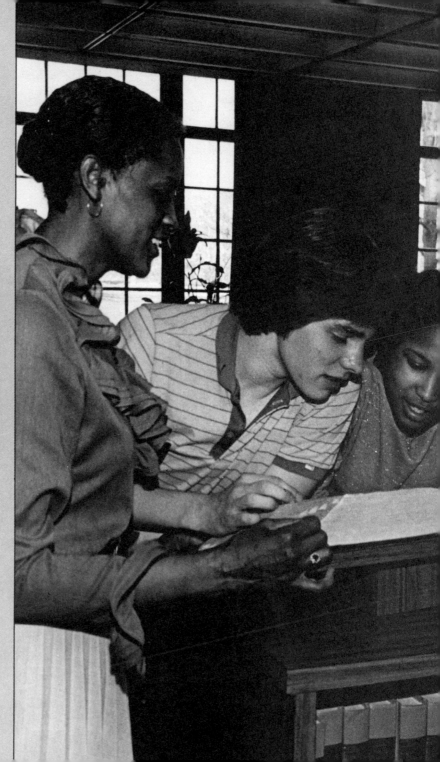

Using a Dictionary

Teaching Special Populations

LD Pretest LD students to ascertain their alphabetizing skills. Prepare additional exercises as needed. Work with students individually as they look up words in a dictionary. Review with students the concept of syllables. Have students restate dictionary definitions in everyday language.

ESL These students will have difficulty finding words in a dictionary according to pronunciation. Explain how sounds are pronounced, and emphasize phonemes with which students may not be familiar. Review with students how words are broken up into syllables.

Determine ESL students' knowledge of parts of speech (See Handbook Sections 3–8). Explain that not all languages permit multiple functions for particular words. Give many examples of words that have multiple functions.

Allow sufficient time for students to complete the exercises

NSD Tell students to look up the meaning and pronunciation of unfamiliar words they encounter. As an additional exercise, ask students to list and look up frequently mispronounced words in the dictionary.

Objective

To recognize the basic characteristics of a dictionary

Presenting the Lesson

1. Read aloud **Here's the Idea.** Show students the difference between an unabridged dictionary and an abridged dictionary. Compare the number of words and pages each contains. Next emphasize the purpose of guide words. Tell students they can save time by looking at the guide words rather than at words elsewhere on the pages.

2. Read and discuss **Check It Out.** Write the special symbols on the board and have students try to identify what each one stands for. If students have dictionaries, have them study the key to abbreviations and labels used in the dictionary.

3. Assign **Try Your Skill.** Have one student read the alphabetized list to the entire class.

4. Read **Keep This in Mind** and then assign **Now Write.**

Individualizing the Lesson

Less-Advanced Students

Students may need extra practice in looking up words in the dictionary. Have them look up the following words and copy the words' pronunciation with symbols and accent marks.

From A to Z

How To Use a Dictionary

Here's the Idea   A dictionary is a useful reference book containing lists of words and information about the words. It is probably the best and most convenient source of information you have available.

When you look for a dictionary you will find that there are several kinds. An abridged, or shortened, dictionary contains almost all the information that you will usually need. An unabridged dictionary contains nearly every word in the language, including specialized or rare words. A specialized dictionary lists words used in one subject area only, such as medicine.

Different dictionaries present information in slightly different ways. For instance, some include biographical or geographical information in the main part of the book, but others have an appendix for this kind of information. Dictionaries may use their own special symbols and abbreviations. Check the front of the dictionary for explanations of such symbols. Become familiar with the dictionary you use.

All dictionaries, however, have two things in common. They list words in alphabetical order. That is, words starting with *a* come before words starting with *b*, and so on through the alphabet. If two words begin with the same letter, they are alphabetized by the second letter. If the first two letters are the same, look at the third letter, and so on.

In addition, all dictionaries have two **guide words** in large, bold print at the top of each page to help locate words listed on the page. The left guide word is the same as the first word on the page. The right guide word is the same as the last word on the page. To find a word you are looking for, flip through the dictionary until you find the page where your word comes alphabetically between the guide words.

Check It Out   Look at this top portion of a dictionary page.

- How is each column of words listed? What special symbols are used? What words are new to you?
- What are the guide words? Would you find the word *between* or the word *beware* on this page?

Try Your Skill   List these words in alphabetical order.

note	northeast	nose	notice	notion
northwest	nothing	northern	notebook	not

Keep This in Mind

- A dictionary is a reference book that lists words alphabetically and explains each word. Become familiar with the dictionary you use.

Now Write   If you were writing a report about weather, you might want to look up the following words: *barometer, cyclone, humidity, hurricane, meteorologist, tornado.* Find each word in the dictionary, and list the guide words on the page where it is found. Choose four of the words, and use them in sentences. Label your paper **From A to Z.** Put it into your folder.

Advanced Students

Have students go to the school library or public library and find the titles of five specialized dictionaries.

Optional Practice

List the following guide words on the chalkboard:

pen/paper	ear/echo	love/loyal
third/three	curtain/cut	siren/skate

Have each student write three words that would appear on the page headed by each set of guide words. Ask students to share their answers.

Extending the Lesson

Ask each student to give a sales pitch for buying a dictionary. In preparation, instruct the class to list as many uses for the dictionary as they can think of. Encourage your students to use a clever style by including slogans and catchy intro-ductions in their sales talks.

Objective

To understand the information contained in dictionary entries

Presenting the Lesson

1. Point out that the word *entry* means not only the word that students are looking for, but also everything that is written about the word. Read aloud and discuss **Here's the Idea.** You may wish to discuss one concept at a time and refer immediately to the sample entry in **Check It Out.**

Write these terms on the chalkboard: *entry word, pronunciation, part of speech, special forms, origin, definition, synonym,* and *antonym.* Make sure students can define these terms.

2. Read the entry in **Check It Out.** As you read it, whenever you approach a symbol, ask students what it means. Have students answer the questions at the end of this entry.

3. Assign **Try Your Skill.** Have students consult with you if they see symbols that they cannot identify. When students have finished, ask volunteers to read the answers aloud.

4. Read **Keep This in Mind.**

5. Distribute dictionaries and assign **Now Write.** You may find that you need to review terms such as *syllable* and *part of speech.*

Individualizing the Lesson

Less-Advanced Students

Emphasize the fact that if students do not note a word's part of

A Word to the Wise

How To Read a Dictionary Entry

Here's the Idea   You know that a dictionary entry explains the meaning of a word. However, are you aware of how much additional information a single entry contains?

The **entry word** itself appears in bold print and is divided into syllables. For instance, the word *generous* is entered as **gen·er·ous.** When you are writing, you may have to divide a word at the end of a line. Use a dictionary to find the correct syllable division.

The **pronunciation** of a word is usually given within parentheses. Special symbols and accent marks help you to sound out the word. The word *knowledge,* for instance, appears as (näl′ij). An explanation of some of the special symbols used is often given at the bottom of the page. A complete pronunciation key is usually given at the front of the dictionary.

The **part of speech** is indicated by an abbreviation in bold print. For example, *noun* is abbreviated **n.** and *adjective* is abbreviated **adj.** A complete list of abbreviations used is usually presented in the front of the dictionary.

Some words can be used as more than one part of speech. In an entry for such a word, the other parts of speech will be given elsewhere in the entry, often at the end.

If a word has **special forms** or **endings,** they will be presented next in the entry. For example, the entry for the irregular verb *give* includes the forms **gave, given, giving.** Plural endings of some nouns are also included. For the noun *tomato,* for example, the plural ending **-oes** is shown.

The **origin,** or **history,** of a word is given next, usually in brackets. The symbol < means "came from." Abbreviations, like *L.* and *Sp.,* stand for the languages from which words came, like "Latin" and "Spanish."

Definitions are given next. Often, the most common definition is given first. If a word has a special meaning in a certain field, that meaning will be included. For example, one definition of *round* says "*Boxing:* any of the timed periods of a fight."

A word may have a meaning used in conversation and informal writing. This is called a *colloquial* meaning. The dictionary may indicate this. For example, one definition of *bounce,* as a noun, is "[Colloq.] energy; zest." A dictionary also indicates slang—very informal, popular language. Another definition of *bounce,* as a verb, says "[Slang] to put a person out by force."

Synonyms and **antonyms** may also be indicated in a dictionary entry. Some dictionaries may include a *synonymy*—a group of synonyms with their shades of meaning. Sometimes, the notation "*see SYN. at*" directs you to another entry.

You can see how much useful information is contained in a dictionary. In order to find such information easily, become familiar with the dictionary you use most often.

Check It Out   Examine this dictionary entry.

sec·tion (sek′shən) *n.* [< L. < pp. of *secare,* to cut: for IE. base see SAW¹] **1.** a cutting or separating by cutting; specif., an incision in surgery **2.** a part separated by cutting; slice; division **3.** *a*) a division of a book, newspaper, etc. *b*) a numbered paragraph of a law, etc. **4.** any distinct or separate part [a bookcase in *sections*] **5.** a segment of an orange, grapefruit, etc. **6.** *a*) a part of a city, country, etc.; district or region [a hilly *section;* the business *section*] ☆*b*) a division of public lands that is a mile square (640 acres)' **7.** a drawing, etc. of a thing as it would appear if cut straight through in a given plane **8.** any of the distinct groups of instruments or voices in an orchestra or chorus [the woodwind *section*] ☆**9.** any one of two or more buses, trains, or airplanes used for a particular run or flight ☆**10.** *Railroading* several miles of track maintained by a single crew —*vt.* **1.** to cut or divide into sections **2.** to show in sections —see **SYN.** at PART

- How many syllables are there in *section?* Where is its pronunciation given? What parts of speech is *section?* From what language did the word come? Which definition is most familiar to you? Is there a meaning used in a special field? Are there synonyms given?

speech when they look it up in the dictionary, they may not use the word correctly in a sentence. Have them look up the definition of each of the following words, noting the word's part of speech, and then use the word correctly in a sentence.

multitude	lucid
decorous	apprise
askance	progeny
noun	adj.
adj.	verb
adv.	noun

Advanced Students

Have students look up and briefly note the origin of each of the following words:

patio	umbrella
library	shampoo
priest	magazine
Sp.	It./Lat.
OFr.	Hindi
OE	Fr.

Optional Practice

Have groups of four students investigate the origins, pronunciations, parts of speech, and definitions of these words: *extort, corsage, fender, salary, strategy,* and *volcano.* Afterward, ask groups to compare their findings.

Extending the Lesson

Allow each student to write four dictionary entries for current slang or colloquial words, such as *jock* or *nerd.* Instruct them to follow dictionary form, including the entry word, pronunciation, imaginary origin, part of speech, and definition. You might compile the best entries into a dictionary of current slang.

Try Your Skill   Read the following dictionary entry and answer the questions.

drum (drum) *n.* [< Du. *trom*]   **1.** a percussion instrument consisting of a hollow cylinder or hemisphere with a membrane stretched tightly over the end or ends   **2.** the sound made by beating a drum, or any sound like this   **3.** any drumlike object; specif., *a)* a metal cylinder around which cable, etc. is wound in a machine   *b)* a barrellike metal container for oil, etc.   ☆**4.** any of various fishes that make a drumming sound   **5.** *Anat.* *same as:* *a)* MIDDLE EAR *b)* EARDRUM   —*vi.* **drummed,** **drum′ming**   **1.** to beat a drum   **2.** to beat or tap continually, as with the fingers   —*vt.*   **1.** to beat out (a tune, etc.) as on a drum   **2.** to beat or tap continually   **3.** to assemble by beating a drum   **4.** to put (ideas, facts, etc. *into*) by repeating again and again   —☆**beat the drum for** [Colloq.] to try to arouse enthusiasm for   —**drum out of** to expel from in disgrace   —**drum up**   **1.** to summon as by beating a drum   **2.** to get (business) by asking or appealing

1. As what parts of speech can *drum* be used?
2. What endings does the verb *drum* have?
3. From what language does *drum* come?
4. In the field of anatomy, to what does *drum* refer?
5. What does the informal expression "beat the drum" mean?

Keep This in Mind

- A dictionary entry contains the meanings of a word and other helpful information. An entry may differ in different dictionaries.

Now Write   Use a dictionary to find words with these characteristics. Each word should have one characteristic. Label your paper **A Word to the Wise** and put it into you folder.

1. four syllables
2. two pronunciations
3. two parts of speech
4. has come from Latin
5. meaning in a special field
6. an informal meaning
7. an antonym
8. a synonym

What Do You Mean?

How To Find the Meaning of a Word

Here's the Idea   As you read, you may see an unfamiliar word now and then. Usually, you can look up the word in a dictionary to find its meaning. However, what can you do if the word has more than one meaning? If you read through all the meanings, you will probably find the one that fits the context of the word as you find it.

For example, the simple word *set* has a surprising variety of meanings. *Webster's New World Dictionary, Students Edition,* gives twenty-seven meanings for *set* as a verb. The same entry gives nine meanings for *set* as an adjective, eight for *set* as a noun, and fourteen phrases that include the word. Notice in the following examples how the context helps you to determine the appropriate meaning.

　　1. Dr. Taylor *set* my broken arm.
(In this context, *set* means "put the bone in a normal position.")
　　2. Please *set* the alarm clock for six thirty.
(Here, *set* means "adjust, regulate.")
　　3. I borrowed a *set* of tools to work on my bike.
(Here, *set* means "a group of things belonging together.")
　　4. We painted the *set* for the class play.
(Here, *set* means "scenery for a movie or play.")
　　5. Everyone agreed to meet at a *set* time.
(Here, *set* means "fixed in advance.")
　　6. The runners are all *set* for the race.
(Here, *set* means "ready, prepared.")

From these examples, you can see how many different meanings can be contained in a single entry.

Sometimes the same word seems to be shown in more than one entry. For example, you will find the word *bark* entered

29

Part **3**

Objective

　To gain skill in using context to determine the correct definition of a word

Presenting the Lesson

　1. Ask the class if they have ever had difficulty in finding the right meaning for a word in a certain context. Read **Here's the Idea**. Ask a student to read the first sentence using the word *set*. Discuss the meaning. Follow this procedure with the remaining five sentences. If students have dictionaries, you might ask them to locate other words with many meanings.

　Write *homograph* on the chalkboard and explain its definition. If students have dictionaries, have them look up the word *bark* and find the origins of the three homographs. See if students can point out other homographs in the dictionary.

　2. Read and discuss **Check It Out.** As you read aloud, review what the symbols mean. You might have students make up sentences for each meaning of *stem*.

　3. Assign and discuss **Try Your Skill**. Have students work in pairs. Advise them to decide first on the part of speech of the word *spell* in each sentence. Have students share their answers.

　4. Read **Keep This in Mind** and then assign **Now Write**.

29

Individualizing the Lesson

Less-Advanced Students

Make sure students understand the distinction between a homograph and a word that simply has several different definitions. Also discuss the role that a word's part of speech plays in determining its context. Have students use each of the following words in a sentence as specified, referring to a dictionary when necessary.

part as a verb
glow as a noun
well as an adjective
promenade as a verb

Advanced Students

Students can look up the following homographs in the dictionary, copy the pronunciation and origin of each word, and then use each homograph in a sentence.

hatch   hach< ME, OE, OF
lead   led or lĕd<OE
stoop   stoop; OE
desert   Du dez' ərt<OF or
         di zurt'<Fr

Optional Practice

Have students look up the following homographs in the dictionary and use each word in a sentence.

rack   slip   strain   post

Extending the Lesson

Using the dictionary, have students find two fairly common words that have more than one meaning. Have students write both words on a scrap of paper. Collect these and have each student draw a paper from a bag or shoebox. Then ask students to look up the two words, list two definitions for each word, and write sentences using each meaning. Have students share their definitions and sentences.

30

three times: *bark¹*, a noun, means "the outside covering of trees"; *bark²*, a verb, means "to make the sharp cry of a dog"; *bark³*, a noun, means "a kind of sailing vessel." In each of these three entries, *bark* has a different meaning and a different origin. Such words are called *homographs*. Each homograph has the same spelling, although it may have a different pronunciation from the others. If you see a word with more than one entry, read all the entries to find the meaning you want.

Check It Out   Read the following dictionary entries.

> **stem¹** (stem) *n.* [OE. *stemn*] **1.** the main stalk or trunk of a tree, shrub, or other plant, extending above the ground and bearing the leaves, flowers, etc. **2.** any stalk supporting leaves, flowers, or fruit **3.** a part like a stem; specif., *a)* the slender part of a tobacco pipe attached to the bowl *b)* a narrow supporting part above the foot of a wineglass, goblet, etc. *c)* the shaft projecting from a watch, with a knob for winding the spring *d)* the thick stroke of a letter, as in printing *e)* the vertical line of a musical note **4.** the forward part of a ship; bow **5.** a branch of a family **6.** the part of a word to which inflectional endings are added —*vt.* **stemmed, stem'ming 1.** to remove the stem from (a fruit, etc.) **2.** to move forward against [to row upstream, *stemming* the current] —*vi.* to originate or derive [all her troubles *stem* from her illness] —**from stem to stern 1.** from one end of a ship to another **2.** through the length of anything — **stem'less** *adj.* —**stem'like'** *adj.*
> **stem²** (stem) *vt.* **stemmed, stem'ming** [ON. *stemma*] **1.** to stop or check by or as if by damming up [to *stem* the flow of water] **2.** to turn (a ski) in stemming —*vi.* to stop or slow down in skiing by turning the tip of the ski(s) inward —*n.* an act of stemming on skis

- Which definition of *stem* fits the context of the following sentence? Don's fear *stems* from his accident.
- From what languages did *stem¹* and *stem²* come? What meanings of *stem¹* and *stem²* are most familiar to you?

Try Your Skill   Read the following dictionary entries. Then read the five sentences. Describe which meaning of *spell* fits the context of each sentence and write your answer.

30

spell¹ (spel) *n.* [OE., a saying] **1.** a word or words supposed to have some magic power **2.** power or control that seems magical; charm; fascination —**cast a spell on** to enchant or charm by or as by magic —**under a spell** held in a spell or trance
spell² (spel) *vt.* **spelled** or **spelt, spell′ing** [< OFr. *espeller,* to explain < Frank. *spellōn*] **1.** to say, write, or signal in order the letters of (a word, etc.) **2.** to make up, or form (a word, etc.): said of specified letters **3.** to mean [red *spells* danger] —*vi.* to spell words, etc. —**spell out 1.** to read letter by letter or with difficulty **2.** to make out or recognize as if by close reading ☆**3.** to explain in detail [the supervisor *spelled out* his duties]
spell³ (spel) *vt.* **spelled, spell′ing** [OE. *spelian*] [Colloq.] to work in place of (another) while he rests; relieve —*n.* **1.** a turn of working in place of another **2.** any period of work, duty, etc. [a two-year *spell* as reporter] **3.** a period (*of* being in some state) [a *spell* of gloom] **4.** a period of specified weather [a cold *spell*] **5.** [Colloq.] a period of time that is indefinite, short, etc. **6.** [Colloq.] a period of some illness ☆**7.** [Dial.] a short distance

1. The hot *spell* lasted for two weeks.
2. The music seemed to cast a *spell* on me.
3. Mom *spelled* out exactly what our duties were.
4. Do we lose points if we don't *spell* the words correctly?
5. I'll take a *spell* at raking the leaves for you.

Keep This in Mind

- When you look up an unfamiliar word in the dictionary, decide which meaning fits the context.
- Sometimes a word has more than one entry, with a different origin and meaning for each. Again, use context to help you determine the meaning.

Now Write   Look up two of the following words in the dictionary: *bat, plane, pound, skate.* If the word appears more than once, read all the entries. Write three definitions for each of your two words. Then write sentences using each of the meanings you have written. Label your paper **What Do You Mean?** Keep it in your folder.

Section **3** Objectives

1. To recognize standard and nonstandard English and to use standard English in speaking and writing

2. To recognize slang and to use it only in casual conversation or dialogue for stories and plays

3. To recognize jargon and to use it only when it is appropriate

Preparing the Students

Read the following sentences to the class:

I ain't never seen a machine like that before.

Those wheels are awesome, for sure!

The batter stroked a letter-high fastball into short left field.

Help students recognize that the language in these sentences has one thing in common: it is used in casual conversation and may not be understood by everyone. Then discuss the particular kind of language in each sentence, helping students label the sentences as nonstandard English, slang, and jargon respectively. Tell students that Section 3 will teach them to recognize the uses and misuses of these kinds of language.

Additional Resources

Mastery Test — page 15 in the test booklet

Practice Book — pages 13–15

Duplicating Masters — pages 13–15

The Right Language at the Right Time

Teaching Special Populations

LD Simplify and explain instructions for **Check It Out, Try Your Skill,** and **Now Write.** Stress the importance of using language that is clear to the listener. Provide additional practice as needed.

ESL Many students will not be familiar enough with English to determine what is standard usage and what is not. Stress that slang is not usually acceptable, even though it is often heard on television and in informal situations. Also explain that double negatives, though acceptable in many languages, are not correct in English.

Consider using native English speakers to demonstrate appropriate and inappropriate usage.

NSD This is an important Section for NSD students. Emphasize that no pronunciation or usage is "wrong" or "bad." Explain that the purpose of conforming to a standard dialect is to communicate with the greatest number of people. Tell students that there are always many nonstandard dialects of a language; although people who speak each dialect communicate well with each other, they may not communicate clearly with speakers of other dialects.

Encourage students to suggest examples of slang that is dated, or that is understood by a small group. Explain that slang is often inappropriate because it is not understood by everyone speaking the language.

Objective

To recognize standard and non-standard English and to use standard English in speaking and writing

Presenting the Lesson

1. Discuss the example in the first paragraph of **Here's the Idea.** Read and discuss the chart, "Using Standard and Nonstandard English," encouraging students to see standard English as language that is understood and accepted by everyone. Discuss the purpose of language—to communicate through speaking and writing. Avoid terms like right/wrong, correct/incorrect, focusing instead on the fact that standard English helps students to communicate more efficiently and effectively than nonstandard English.

2. Discuss the examples in **Check It Out.** Encourage students to explain the grammatical errors in the nonstandard sentences.

3. Assign **Try Your Skill.** Have students explain how each nonstandard sentence varies from standard English.

4. Read **Keep This in Mind** and then assign **Now Write.** Have students share their examples of nonstandard English in small groups. Or each student may read one or two examples to the entire class.

Individualizing the Lesson

Less-Advanced Students

Students who are in the habit of using nonstandard English may find it difficult to recognize nonstandard

Language You Choose

Standard and Nonstandard English

Here's the Idea   Suppose you were asked to choose music for a dance at your school. What kind of music would you select? Would it be march music? Would it be old English ballads? Of course not. You would look for music that is popular and that people can dance to. In other words, you would choose music to suit the occasion.

Similarly, when you speak and write, you must choose language that is right for the audience and occasion. Two types of language from which you can choose are **standard English** and **nonstandard English.** These are described on the following chart.

Using Standard and Nonstandard English	
Definition and Use	**Examples**
Standard English is language that follows the rules of good grammar and usage. Standard English is acceptable in all situations.	1. Jim and I went to the planetarium. 2. I don't know anything about it.
Nonstandard English is language that does not follow the rules of good grammar and usage. Nonstandard English is acceptable only in very casual conversation. It is not acceptable in class discussion, in talks, or in most writing.	1. Me and Jim went to the planetarium. 2. I don't know nothing about it.

Notice that nonstandard English is rarely acceptable. Therefore, whenever you speak and write, use standard English.

Check It Out Read the following pairs of sentences.

Standard English	Nonstandard English
1. Are you the captain of the team?	1. Is you the captain of the team?
2. Are you feeling sick?	2. Do you be feeling sick?
3. Those are my pictures.	3. Them is my pictures.

- Why is the second sentence in each pair nonstandard?

Try Your Skill Choose the sentences written in standard English.

1. I saw her there myself.
   I seen her there myself.
2. Sandi plays tennis real good.
   Sandi plays tennis really well.
3. The teacher hasn't learned us about business letters yet.
   The teacher hasn't taught us about business letters yet.
4. Them books belongs to me.
   Those books belong to me.

Keep This in Mind

- Use standard English when you speak and write.
- Avoid nonstandard English.

Now Write Draw two columns on a sheet of paper. Label one column *Standard English* and the other *Nonstandard English.* Whenever you hear an example of nonstandard English, write it in the column labeled *Nonstandard.* Then, in the other column, rewrite the example in standard English. Label your paper **Language You Choose.** Save it in your folder.

35

language in their own speech. Bring a cassette recorder to class and have students tape a short, informal talk about their family, a pet, or a trip they have taken. Allow students to replay their tapes privately and write down examples of nonstandard English and revisions of these.

Advanced Students

For the examples of nonstandard English in **Check It Out** and **Try Your Skill,** have students look up the appropriate rules in the Handbook and copy them in their notebooks.

Optional Practice

Have the students revise the following examples of nonstandard English. Answers below.

1. It seem like people don't bake homemade bread no more.
2. Joe ain't never been to the circus before.
3. We be walking home from school and we seen three fire trucks.
4. Anita and me went to see *Annie.*

1. It seems like people don't bake homemade bread anymore.
2. Joe has never been to the circus before.
3. We were walking home from school and we saw three fire trucks.
4. Anita and I went to see *Annie.*

Extending the Lesson

Discuss the fact that young children often use nonstandard English. Have students record examples of nonstandard English used by younger brothers and sisters or neighbors for a week. Students can then bring their examples of children's language to class to share. Point out that children outgrow their nonstandard language usage.

35

Part 2

Objective

To recognize slang and to use it only in casual conversation or dialogue for stories and plays

Presenting the Lesson

1. Read and discuss **Here's the Idea.** Have students name some current slang words; write these on the chalkboard. List some dated slang, such as *jalopy* or *groovy*, on the chalkboard. Explain that these terms were once as up-to-date as students' current slang. Look up a slang term such as *swell* in the dictionary to show the class how its slang definition is listed.

2. Read the slang terms in **Check It Out.** Discuss the questions, helping students realize how quickly most slang becomes outdated.

3. Assign **Try Your Skill.** Have students read their revised sentences, making sure everyone understands the meanings of the slang expressions.

4. Read **Keep This in Mind.**

5. Assign **Now Write.** Encourage students to be imaginative in thinking of language used by themselves and their friends every day.

Individualizing the Lesson

Less-Advanced Students

If students have trouble thinking of slang that they use, tell them to jot down all the slang expressions that they and their friends use for a period of one day. They will probably be surprised at the richness of their informal vocabularies.

Skidoo, Scram!

Using and Misusing Slang

Here's the Idea   In this section you are learning when to use different types of language. One type of language that is right to use only in very informal situations is slang. **Slang** is made up of fad words and phrases that have not become accepted as standard English. Slang usually lives a brief, colorful life. Then, it disappears and is replaced by newer slang. The following slang terms have been used at various times to mean "a person who dresses in fancy clothes."

> *macaroni* (used in the 18th century)
> *sport* (used from the late 1800's to the mid 1900's)
> *swell* (used from the 1920's to the mid 1940's)
> *dude* (used in the 20th century, especially in the American West)

As you can see, one problem with slang is that it soon becomes outdated. Another problem with slang is that it is not understood by everyone.

Most people use an occasional slang word or phrase. You probably know many slang words and phrases that are popular today. You hear these slang terms from your friends, on television, in the movies, and in popular songs. Slang, however, is considered nonstandard English. Because of this, slang is not appropriate for most writing. Never use slang in compositions, reports, business letters, or speeches. Use slang only in very casual conversation with friends or in dialogue in a short story or play.

If you are unsure about whether a word is slang, look it up in a dictionary. If the word is not in the dictionary, or if the word is labeled *slang*, do not use it in formal situations.

Check It Out   The following slang terms and expressions are very similar in meaning. However, each term was popular at a different time during the twentieth century. Read this list.

fly the coop   make yourself scarce   light out
hightail it   scram   skiddoo
hit it   skedaddle   beat it

- What meaning is shared by these terms?
- Are any of these terms popular today? Which ones?
- How many of these terms are not used much today? What does this tell you about the nature of slang?

Try Your Skill   Find the slang in the following sentences. Then, rewrite each sentence. Replace each slang expression with a standard word or phrase.

1. The spy refused to sell out to the enemy.
2. That pitch was a real hummer. It was so fast that the batter didn't even see it.
3. This restaurant is a real pit.
4. I'm tired. I think it's time to hit the hay.
5. These new fashions are out of sight!

Keep This in Mind

- Slang is made up of fad words and phrases that are not accepted as standard English.
- Use slang only in casual conversation with friends or when writing dialogue for a short story or play.

Now Write   Suppose that you have a pen pal in Brazil. Your pen pal has studied English for many years. However, he or she has not learned any English slang. Write a letter to your pen pal. Explain the meanings of five slang words and phrases used by teenagers in the United States. Label your paper **Skidoo, Scram!** Save it in your folder.

Advanced Students

As a group project, students can write a short skit using as many current slang expressions as possible. Discuss how the use of slang helps characterize characters in a play or story.

Optional Practice

1. Give students the following list of old and current slang terms with similar meanings. Discuss the terms, using the study questions in **Check It Out.**

cool   swell
groovy   far out
keen   awesome
neat   heavy

2. Add the following sentences to **Try Your Skill.** Answers will vary.

1. Losing the last football game was a real drag.
2. Patrick pulled an all-nighter before the chemistry test.
3. Mr. Perez advised his students to get on the stick and do their homework.
4. The new disc jockey is really with it.

Extending the Lesson

Have students ask parents and grandparents for slang that was popular when they were young. Students can compile a list of previous generations' slang and discuss which words and phrases are still used today. The class may want to create a bulletin board showing slang of the past and present.

Part 3

Objective

To recognize jargon and to use it properly

Presenting the Lesson

1. Read and discuss **Here's the Idea.** Have students list fields that have their own specialized vocabularies; some examples are computer science, psychology, and baseball. Ask the class if they can list any medical or police jargon they may have gleaned from television programs. Emphasize that misuse of jargon detracts from effective communication.

2. Discuss **Check It Out.** In addition to the football jargon listed, use the study questions for these jargon words from filmmaking:

wrap   set
take   location

3. Assign **Try Your Skill.** Point out the difficulty in understanding the carpenter's jargon if one is unfamiliar with carpentry.

4. Read **Keep This in Mind** and then assign **Now Write.** Encourage students to find an article about a field that interests them.

Individualizing the Lesson

Less-Advanced Students

Help students find articles for **Now Write.** You might bring five or six appropriate articles to class and let students choose one to read. Then have them complete the assignment in class.

Words That Work

Using and Misusing Jargon

Here's the Idea   Workers in many fields use special words and phrases to describe their work. These words and phrases are known as **jargon.** The following are some jargon words used by sailors to describe parts of a ship:

bilge keel	casemate
bollard	conning tower
bulwarks	mizzenmast

Sailors can use these words when talking to one another because they all know what these words mean. However, a sailor would not use these words when talking to someone who is not familiar with ships. Such people would not understand the jargon of sailing.

Jargon allows workers in specialized fields to talk to one another quickly and easily. However, jargon is appropriate only with certain audiences. Whenever you are writing or speaking about a specialized activity, ask yourself the following questions.

Is my audience familiar with this activity?
Will my audience understand the jargon of this activity?

If your answer to these questions is "No," avoid using jargon. If you must use a jargon word, be sure to define it so that your audience will understand what you are saying.

Check It Out   Read the following words from the jargon of football.

goal post	fourth down
halfback	receiver
hike	offensive line

- How many of these words do you know?
- Which of these words would only be understood by someone who knows a great deal about football?
- Which of these words have other meanings outside of football?

Try Your Skill The following words are from the jargon of carpentry. Look up each word in a dictionary. Find out how each word is used by carpenters. Write the definition of each word. Then, use each word in a sentence.

1. miter box
2. joist
3. plane
4. square
5. plumb line

Keep This in Mind

- Words and phrases used to describe specialized activities are called jargon.
- Use jargon only when it is appropriate for your audience.

Now Write Find a magazine article that deals with a specialized activity. This activity can be a hobby, a job, or a sport. Make a list of jargon words used in the article. Define each word. Then, use each word in a sentence. Label your paper **Words That Work.** Save it in your folder.

Advanced Students

Have each student make a list of the jargon of a particular field they are familiar with. Some possibilities are music, chess, and ballet. Have students meet in small groups and read their jargon, letting the other students identify the fields in which the words are used.

Optional Practice

The following sentences contain words taken from the jargon of various sports. Have students point out the jargon words, tell what sport they are from, and define them, looking the words up in a dictionary if necessary.

1. Barbara served three aces in a row. tennis
2. The left-hander threw a slider on the inside corner. baseball
3. Jeffrey got his first hole-in-one on the ninth hole last Saturday. golf
4. Rudy's teammates skated up to congratulate him on his hat trick. hockey

Extending the Lesson

Have students write a paragraph summarizing the article they found for **Now Write.** Instruct students to use some of the article's jargon words and define them when necessary.

Section 4 Objectives

1. To identify and use clear, interesting sentences

2. To include only related details in sentences

3. To avoid writing sentences that are repetitive or that state unsupported opinions

4. To avoid sentences padded with useless words

5. To avoid overloading sentences with too many ideas

Preparing the Students

Write the following groups of words on the chalkboard:

1. a large woman with a large purse she
2. was that had everything in it
3. but a hammer and nails

Ask students why the groups of words do not make sense. Then instruct them to write one complete sentence using all the words in the three fragments. ("She was a large woman with a large purse that had everything in it but a hammer and nails."—LANGSTON HUGHES) Compare the fuzziness of the fragments with the clarity of the composite sentence.

Tell students that this Section will help them to write precise, clear sentences.

Additional Resources

Mastery Test — pages 16–17 in the test booklet

Practice Book — pages 16–20

Duplicating Masters — pages 16–20

Improving Your Sentences

Teaching Special Populations

LD LD students will require additional drill and practice with this Section. Simplify instructions for the exercises. As an example, present the **Now Write** exercise as follows.

Write three sentences:

1. one that tells something that happened, *or*
2. one that tells what something looks like, *or*
3. one that explains one step of a process, *or*
4. one that explains an opinion, *or*
5. one that tells what something is.

When you finish writing your sentences, read them over. Make sure they are clear, complete, and correct. Correct your sentences before handing them in.

ESL Stress the definitions of "empty sentences" and "padding." Give ESL students additional examples of these kinds of sentences. Explain that it is not the number but the content of words that is important. Assign this chapter well in advance so ESL students have time to read and understand the lessons before class discussions. If possible, pair ESL students with native English speakers and have them work the exercises together.

NSD NSD students can learn standard English from exposure to well-formed sentences. Present many examples of clear, standard-English sentences, and ask these students to write examples of their own.

Power Play

Using Sentences

Objective

To identify and use clear, interesting sentences

Presenting the Lesson

1. Read aloud **Here's the Idea.** Emphasize the definition of *sentence.* Ask what makes each of the sample sentences powerful. For example, help students notice how the second sentence is brief and to the point and yet contains both humor and truth.

2. Discuss **Check It Out.** Write the first sentence on the chalkboard, leaving out the word *raced:* "Neil _____ up the path after the stranger." Have students supply different verbs to see how the meaning of the sentence changes. Point out how word choice helps make these sentences vivid.

3. Assign and discuss **Try Your Skill.** Have students revise their sentences until they are clear and direct.

4. Read **Keep This in Mind.**

5. Assign **Now Write.** Have students brainstorm in order to find three original topics for their sentences. For example, ask students to think about the two most important things in their lives. After they have written original sentences, encourage students to revise their sentences for clarity.

Individualizing the Lesson

Less-Advanced Students

For **Try Your Skill,** encourage students to use original wording and

Here's the Idea   Through your study of vocabulary, you know how important it is to choose words carefully. You know that you should use words that are specific and vivid, words that say what you mean. Usually, you express an idea by putting those words into a sentence. A **sentence** is a group of words that expresses a complete thought.

A good sentence expresses an idea in a clear and original way. It appeals to your reader's senses and imagination. In fact, a single sentence can be powerful. Read these examples of powerful, original sentences.

> What is now proved was once only imagined.
> —WILLIAM BLAKE
> Experience is a hard teacher because she gives the test first, the lesson afterwards.—VERNON LAW
> Dreams are necessary to life.—ANAIS NIN
> Friendship is like money, easier made than kept.
> —SAMUEL BUTLER
> He who has courage and faith will never perish in misery.
> —ANNE FRANK

Sentences like these have been remembered because they express ideas in precise and imaginative ways. The sentences express observations, advice, and humorous thoughts. The sentences you write may not be famous. However, when you write a sentence, you will also want to express an idea in a direct and lively way.

Check It Out   Read the following sentences.

1. Neil raced up the path after the stranger.
2. Great-Aunt Clara held out her small, wrinkled hands.

3. You can make a light and delicious meal with fresh fish.

4. Fresh fruits and vegetables and whole grains are essential to a healthy diet.

5. A shark is a large ocean fish that has been on earth more than 350 million years.

- Does each sentence express a single complete thought?
- Is each sentence clear and interesting?

Try Your Skill   Number your paper from 1 to 7. Write one sentence in response to each of the directions below. Make your sentences direct and interesting. Use details from your memory or from your imagination.

1. Tell about one event from your childhood.
2. Describe your favorite flower.
3. Explain how to shoot a basketball.
4. Explain why you like music.
5. Tell one event that happened in this class.
6. Explain why friends are important.
7. Describe a person you see every day.

Keep This in Mind

- A sentence is a group of words that expresses a complete thought. A good sentence is clear and interesting.

Now Write   Think of ideas for three original sentences. You may want to express an opinion, make an observation, or describe something. You may want to tell part of a story or explain something. In any case, state your ideas in a clear, direct, and original way. Choose your words carefully. Write the best sentences you can. Read your sentences. Do you like them? Have you said exactly what you wanted to say? Make revisions if necessary. Label your paper **Power Play** and put it into your folder.

ideas in each sentence. For example, instruct students not to begin sentence 6, "Friends are important because. . . ." You might use this sentence as a sample and write the class's responses for it on the chalkboard. Then have the class revise one sample sentence until it is as direct and interesting as possible. Instruct students to revise each sentence they write until it is clear and original.

Advanced Students

Add the following directions to **Try Your Skill.** Answers will vary.

1. Describe your favorite holiday.
2. Explain why you like (or dislike) going to movies.
3. Explain why exercise is important.
4. Describe your favorite relative.

Optional Practice

Have the students write the names of five of their favorite television shows, past or present. Then have the students select only one of these shows to describe in one sentence. Instruct them to make specific statements that will distinguish the TV show from all others. Have students read their sentences aloud, without saying the title of the show. See if the other students can identify the show.

Extending the Lesson

Have students start a collection of lively, original sentences such as those in **Here's the Idea.** Instruct the class to be on the lookout as they read newspapers, magazines, and books for sentences that express an idea in an especially original and interesting way.

Part 2

Objective

To include only related details in sentences

Presenting the Lesson

1. Read aloud and discuss **Here's the Idea.** Point out the three sentences beginning with the word *Frank.* Discuss their differences. Read the sentences beginning with the words *In Washington.* Contrast related and unrelated details.

2. Discuss **Check It Out.** Have students point out the unrelated details. Ask for interesting related details that might be added.

3. Assign and discuss **Try Your Skill.** Have volunteers share their revisions with the class.

4. Read **Keep This in Mind.**

5. Assign **Now Write.** It may be difficult for the students to find examples of sentences that do not keep to the point. You might suggest that the students review their own writing contained in their folders. Another possibility is to suggest that students write two sentences about a state or city they have visited. Then they should add related details to make the sentences clear and interesting.

Individualizing the Lesson

Less-Advanced Students

Give students extra practice in recognizing unrelated details with the following sentences.

1. Clue, which I got for Christmas two years ago, is a board game that requires deductive logic.

Stay with It

Keeping to the Point

Here's the Idea   You know that a well-written sentence states one idea. Read the sentences below.

> Frank swam sixty feet underwater.
>
> In Washington, the Smithsonian Institution displays famous national treasures.

Related details may be added to a sentence. Details add meaning to a sentence and make it more interesting. Related details support the main idea of a sentence. Look at the examples below.

> Frank, our diving champion, swam sixty feet underwater.

The added detail is related to Frank's ability as a swimmer.

> In Washington, the Smithsonian Institution, sometimes called our nation's attic, displays famous treasures.

The added detail is related to the idea of the Smithsonian as a museum.

However, sometimes unrelated details are included in a sentence. They interrupt the meaning of a sentence.

> Frank, a boy with red hair, swam sixty feet underwater.

The added detail tells us about Frank, but it has nothing to do with Frank's ability as a swimmer.

> In Washington, our nation's capital, the Smithsonian Institution displays famous national treasures.

The sentence is about the Smithsonian, not Washington. The added detail is unrelated to the main idea of the sentence.

Whenever you write a sentence, keep to the point. Do not include any unrelated details that interrupt the meaning.

Check It Out   Read the following sentences.

1. When Sally was eight, her family lived in Ohio, and Columbus is the capital.

2. My brother, who has a new girlfriend, works at Dan's Market after school.

3. In Africa, which is a huge continent, zebras are among the most striking animals.

4. Jason left his biology book at the town library, which was built two years ago.

- In each sentence what unrelated detail should be omitted? Are there any related details that you would add?

Try Your Skill   Below are four sentences with unrelated details. Rewrite these sentences. Leave out the unrelated details.

1. Owls can see well at night, which is when I study.

2. Abraham Lincoln, who was born in Kentucky, delivered the Gettysburg Address in 1863.

3. My grandfather, who is six feet tall, said that he could remember a time when there were few cars.

4. New York City, where Central Park is, is one of the world's most important centers of business and culture.

Keep This in Mind

- Use related details to add meaning and interest to the main idea of a sentence. Leave out unrelated details that interrupt the main idea of a sentence.

Now Write   Find or write two examples of sentences that do not keep to the point. Underline the unrelated details that interrupt the meaning of the sentences. Then write two original sentences on any subject. Add a related detail that adds to the meaning of each sentence. Rewrite your improved sentences. Label you paper **Stay with It** and keep your paper in your folder.

2. The Beatles, whom my sister saw on *The Ed Sullivan Show* in 1964, broke up in 1970.

3. Richard Burton, who appeared on the *Today* show several times, was a great Shakespearean actor.

Advanced Students

Have each student write five sentences, purposely inserting unrelated details. Students can exchange sentences and rewrite them, omitting unrelated details.

Optional Practice

Have students add interesting related details to the following sentences. The class can share their revisions to make sure the new sentences keep to the point.

1. Reading magazines can keep you well informed.

2. Shopping malls are great places for people-watching.

3. Science fiction is a popular kind of literature.

Extending the Lesson

Distribute copies of these sentences to your students:

1. Luis piled three scoops of ice cream on top of the banana slices. Luis works part-time.

2. Jeanne took the subway to Wilson Stadium. The game between the Phillies and the Cardinals was being played at Wilson Stadium.

3. Melinda ran in the women's marathon. Melinda was pleased that she had finished the race.

Discuss which pairs of sentences have related ideas. Ask students to combine the sentences with related ideas into single sentences.

Answers will vary.

Objective

To avoid writing sentences that are repetitive or that state unsupported opinions

Presenting the Lesson

1. Read aloud and discuss **Here's the Idea.** Differentiate between the empty sentence that states the same idea twice and the empty sentence that gives an unsupported opinion.

2. Divide the class into groups of three to discuss **Check It Out.** Have the groups revise the sentences. Ask one student from each group to read that group's improved sentences. Comment on details used.

3. Assign and discuss **Try Your Skill.** Have volunteers share their revisions with the class. Point out the specific ideas that the revised sentences contain.

4. Read **Keep This in Mind.**

5. Assign **Now Write.** Ask the students to bring to class two examples of each kind of empty sentence. If they cannot find examples in newspapers or magazines, you may suggest that they write their own sentences about the following topics: a favorite car design, a favorite TV star, a favorite sport, a vacation, a good friend. Stress that each sentence should be revised carefully.

Individualizing the Lesson

Less-Advanced Students

Have students discuss why the following sentences are empty and how they could be improved.

Answers will vary.

46

Nothing Doing

Avoiding Empty Sentences

Here's the Idea   A good sentence says something. It contains a complete thought and keeps to a point. A poor sentence says little or nothing. One kind of poor sentence is the **empty sentence.** There are two kinds of empty sentences.

The first kind of empty sentence states the same idea twice.

Marty is extremely popular, and almost everyone likes him.

If a person is said to be popular, it is understood that he or she is well liked. The sentence above repeats an idea unnecessarily.

You can improve an empty sentence by avoiding repetition. You may want to make the sentence simpler. Sometimes you may want to add more information.

Marty is extremely popular.

Marty is extremely popular and is class president.

Watch for repeated words or ideas in sentences that you write. Revise this kind of empty sentence by eliminating repetition.

The second kind of empty sentence gives an unsupported opinion. A strong or startling statement is made, but no facts, reasons, or examples are offered to explain it.

Teenagers should have summer jobs.

Such a strong statement is empty of meaning for a reader unless it is explained. The supporting evidence may be given in the same sentence or in another sentence.

Teenagers should have summer jobs in order to learn special skills and earn extra money.

Teenagers should have summer jobs. These jobs will help them learn special skills and earn extra money.

46

Sometimes a strong opinion may be developed in a longer piece of writing, such as a paragraph or a composition.

Check for unsupported opinions in your writing. Look for sentences that raise questions but do not answer them. Revise this kind of empty sentence by supplying facts or reasons.

Check It Out   Read the following empty sentences.

1. Everyone should learn to cook.
2. I like loud music, and I always turn up the volume.
3. A dog makes the best pet.
4. High schools should teach driver's education.

- Which sentence repeats an idea? Which sentences offer an unsupported opinion? How would you improve these empty sentences?

Try Your Skill   Rewrite each of these empty sentences.

1. Food should not be wasted.
2. I enjoy playing the piano because it is fun for me.
3. People should drive smaller cars.
4. Fishing is the most enjoyable hobby.

Keep This in Mind

- Sentences that repeat an idea or offer an unsupported opinion are empty sentences. Improve a sentence that repeats an idea by making it simpler or by adding information. Improve a sentence with an unsupported opinion by adding reasons or facts that explain the opinion.

Now Write   Label your paper *Empty Sentences*. Find or write two examples of each kind of empty sentence. Improve the sentences by avoiding repetition or by including reasons or facts. Keep your work in your folder.

---

1. We should help the starving people in Africa.
2. Needlepoint is an enjoyable craft and it is fun to make needlepoint items.
3. Typing is an important skill.

Advanced Students

Add the following sentences to **Try Your Skill.** Answers will vary.

1. Christmas shopping is for the birds.
2. Writing poetry is a creative activity requiring imagination.
3. Everyone should read *Romeo and Juliet*.

Optional Practice

Pair students to take turns interviewing each other. Have them ask these questions:

1. What is your opinion of pro football?
2. What kind of friend are you?
3. How do you feel about salsa music?
4. What do you think of sports cars?

Instruct them to write each other's responses in sentence form and to place a check mark in front of any repetitive statement or unsupported opinion. Have them rewrite any empty sentences.

Extending the Lesson

Have students write three or four sentences supporting one of the following opinions. After careful revision of each sentence, students can exchange papers to check for empty sentences.

1. Swimming is an excellent form of exercise.
2. Everyone should have a vegetable garden.
3. There are many worthwhile programs on television.

Objective

To avoid sentences padded with useless words

Presenting the Lesson

1. Read aloud **Here's the Idea.** Review the common phrases used for padding on page 48. Ask the students why these phrases are used frequently. Stress that they are unacceptable in writing even though they are common in speaking. As you read the examples of padded sentences and the improved sentences, point out how the improved sentences express the same idea more concisely.

2. Discuss **Check It Out.** Ask students to explain what is wrong with each sentence and how it can be improved.

3. Assign and discuss **Try Your Skill.** Have volunteers share their improved sentences with the class.

4. Read **Keep This in Mind.**

5. Read aloud the directions for **Now Write.** Specifically, tell your students to be aware of the words *you know.* Have them listen for padded sentences used at the lunch table, in classes, at work, or at home.

Individualizing the Lesson

Less-Advanced Students

Discuss in detail the list of common wordy phrases in **Here's the Idea.** Distinguish between the phrases that can usually be replaced with a single word, and those that can often be left out altogether. For example, the first three

48

Part 4

Worthless Words

Avoiding Padded Sentences

Here's the Idea Well-written sentences contain only necessary words. **Padded sentences** have unnecessary words and phrases. The useless words and phrases hide the main idea.

Some expressions pad sentences more than others. Watch out for the common phrases listed below. They usually signal padding and should be avoided in your writing.

because of the fact that	what I think is
due to the fact that	what I'm trying to say is
on account of the fact that	what I want is
the point is	you see
the reason is	you know
the thing is	I am going to write about

Usually you can improve a padded sentence simply by eliminating the useless expressions. Sometimes, however, you may have to rewrite a sentence completely.

Padded: What I mean to say is that I don't know.

Improved: I don't know.

Padded: Because of the fact that they are fattening, I avoid desserts.

Improved: I avoid desserts because they are fattening.

Groups of words using *that, which,* or *who* may not be necessary in a sentence. When you use such expressions, be sure they add to the meaning of a sentence.

Padded: The noodles, which are made with spinach, are homemade.

Improved: The spinach noodles are homemade.

48

Check It Out Read these padded sentences.

1. What I'm trying to say is that I do not have enough money.
2. Jackie had to work late because, you know, the restaurant was very busy.
3. Because of the fact that I enjoy photography, I bought a new camera.
4. Due to the fact that our cat likes to prowl, sometimes it disappears for several days.

- How would you improve each of these padded sentences?

Try Your Skill Improve the following padded sentences. Either eliminate the unnecessary words and phrases or rewrite the sentence completely.

1. The thing was that Sheila needed a ride.
2. Every morning I drink orange juice which is made by the Sunshine Company.
3. Due to the fact that Paul missed the beginning of the movie, he did not understand the ending.
4. I am going to write about my first view of the ocean.

Keep This in Mind

- Sentences containing unnecessary words are padded sentences. Improve a padded sentence by eliminating the useless expressions or by rewriting the sentence completely.

Now Write Label your paper *Padded Sentences*. Find or write four examples of padded sentences. Improve the sentences by omitting any unnecessary words. Rewrite the entire sentence if necessary. Put your paper into your folder.

phrases can usually be replaced with the word *because*.

Advanced Students

Have students revise the following padded sentences and then compare the number of words in the original and revised sentences. Emphasize that padded sentences contain *unnecessary* words; a good sentence may be long if every word and phrase adds to the main idea. Answers will vary.

1. On account of the fact that Leslie had seen the Picasso exhibit, she reported on it to the class.
2. I am going to write about the importance of students taking an interest in local and national elections.
3. What I think is that cooking is a creative hobby.

Optional Practice

Add the following sentences to **Try Your Skill.** Answers will vary.

1. The reason Diana wrote about Michigan is that her family goes there every summer.
2. A woman who is an illustrator of children's books spoke to the art class.
3. The thing is, you know, that many people rely on public transportation to get to work and school.

Extending the Lesson

Divide the class into groups of five. Give each group one sentence from a newspaper editorial. Ask each member of the group to add a different phrase from page 48 or to add a padded phrase of their own to the sentence. Have each group exchange the sentences they have written with another group. Ask groups to discuss how the sentences should be revised.

Part 5

Objective

To avoid overloading sentences with too many ideas

Presenting the Lesson

1. Read aloud **Here's the Idea.** In the first example, ask students how many *and's* were used. Ask which *and's* connect unrelated thoughts. Point out the changes made in the revision.

2. Discuss **Check It Out.** Point out the words used to begin the sentences in the revision.

3. Assign and discuss **Try Your Skill.** Allow students to use only one *and* in each of the three sentences.

4. Read **Keep This in Mind.**

5. Assign **Now Write.** Have students check their own folders containing past writings. If they find overloaded sentences, they may revise them.

Individualizing the Lesson

Less-Advanced Students

Have student volunteers read aloud the sample overloaded sentences in this Section. To dramatize the crowded, confusing quality of overloaded sentences, instruct the readers not to take a breath until they come to a period. Then have volunteers read the revised sentences, again taking a breath at the end of each sentence.

Advanced Students

Add the following sentences to **Try Your Skill.**

1. Some new houses are being built on the cornfield behind the school,

50

Avoiding Overloaded Sentences

Here's the Idea You have learned some important ideas about writing sentences. You have learned that you must express a complete thought, keep to a point, and avoid unnecessary words. You must also limit the number of ideas that you express in a single sentence. A sentence that contains too many ideas is called an **overloaded sentence.**

> The subway roared past one station after another, and the people in the train looked as surprised as the people on the platforms, and Jack and I exchanged worried glances, and just then the lights flickered, and the brakes screeched.

From this example, you can see that an overloaded sentence is confusing. Which idea is the main one? It is difficult to tell.

If you look closely at the overloaded sentence, you will see the repetition of the word *and*. The word *and* is used correctly only when it joins related ideas, as it does in these two examples.

> Lee *and* Veronica are talented musicians.
> Willy sanded the doors, *and* Tina painted them.

The word *and* is often used incorrectly. Wherever it is used to join unrelated ideas, it should be replaced by a period. Separate the overloaded sentence into several shorter sentences.

> The subway roared past one station after another. The people in the train looked as surprised as the people on the platform. Jack and I exchanged worried glances. Just then the lights flickered, and the brakes screeched.

In your writing, be sure that a sentence contains only one main idea or related thoughts that belong together.

50

Check It Out   Read this overloaded sentence.

Overloaded: The runners and high jumpers moved out onto the field and began their exercises and the stands began to fill up and just before the meet began the officials checked their stopwatches.

Improved: The runners and high jumpers moved out onto the field. As they began their exercises, the stands began to fill up. Finally, just before the meet began, the officials checked their stopwatches.

- How has this overloaded sentence been improved?

Try Your Skill   Improve the following overloaded sentences.

1. In my uncle's garage are several old license plates, some bald tires, a lot of junk, and his trash barrels, and he cannot fit his car into the garage.

2. With the score tied 103 to 103, Jones brought the ball up the court and passed to Russo, and there were only three seconds left to play, and Russo took a jumpshot and scored the winning basket right at the buzzer.

3. We ran into the water, and I knew right away the undertow was strong, and I shouted to Ben and Betty, and both of them told me not to worry.

Keep This in Mind

- Sentences that contain too many ideas are overloaded sentences. Improve an overloaded sentence by breaking it into several shorter sentences.

Now Write   Label your paper *Overloaded Sentences*. Find or write four examples of overloaded sentences. Improve the sentences by separating them into several shorter sentences. Put your work into your folder.

and the old farmhouse has been boarded up, and the barn has been knocked down by bulldozers.

2. I've been going to the public library since I was very small and before I started school I went there for story time and in grade school I would check out books to read and now I go there to find information.

Optional Practice

Copy the following passage on the chalkboard. Tell students that you have altered a passage from a short story by Isaac Bashevis Singer to make overloaded sentences. Ask them to revise the paragraph.

Somewhere, sometime, there lived a rich man whose name was Kadish, and he had an only son who was called Atzel, and in the household of Kadish there lived a distant relative, an orphan girl, called Aksah, and Atzel was a tall boy with black hair and black eyes, and Aksah was somewhat shorter than Atzel, and she had blue eyes and golden hair, and both were about the same age, and as children, they ate together, studied together, played together, and Atzel played the husband; Aksah, his wife, and it was taken for granted that when they grew up they would really marry.

Extending the Lesson

Have students begin by writing one sentence about something that they remember from grade school. Then have all students pass their papers to their right. Ask each student to add *and* or *but* and to continue the story with another sentence. Rotate two more times. Then ask students to rewrite the overloaded sentences that have been created. Have volunteers read "befores" and "afters" aloud.

Section 5 Objectives

1. To combine short sentences whose main ideas are closely related with *and, but,* and *or*

2. To combine related sentence parts with *and, but,* and *or*

3. To combine sentences by adding a single word from one sentence to another sentence

4. To use sentence-combining skills in revising

Preparing the Students

Duplicate and distribute the following paragraphs.

1. Joanna was telling a story to some children. The children were in kindergarten. Joanna was nervous. She was also excited. She told a story about Peter Rabbit. She used puppets to dramatize the story. At the end of Joanna's performance, the children clapped. They were enthusiastic. The children enjoyed their story time very much. Joanna enjoyed the story time very much.

2. Joanna was telling a story to some kindergarten children. She was nervous but excited. She told a story about Peter Rabbit and used puppets to dramatize the story. At the end of Joanna's performance, the children clapped enthusiastically. The children and Joanna all enjoyed the story time very much.

Have the students compare and discuss the two paragraphs. Which one has more variety in its sentence structure? How was the second paragraph revised? Tell students that this Section will teach them to combine sentences in their own writing to add variety and show how ideas are related.

Sentence Combining

Additional Resources

Mastery Test — page 18 in the test booklet

Practice Book — pages 21–24

Duplicating Masters — pages 21–24

Teaching Special Populations

LD LD students will need practice using the coordinating conjunctions properly. Give additional sentences that use the coordinating conjunctions, and ask students to explain why a particular conjunction is best in each case. Duplicate sets of short, related sentences, and have students combine those sentences. List on the chalkboard the steps required for each exercise.

ESL Be sure students understand the meaning of each sentence in the exercises. Remind students as they combine sentences that some words can function as several parts of speech. Explain that the sentences being combined are logically related, and that none of the meaning is lost by combining sentences. Provide examples of sentences that should not be combined, as well as extra examples of sentences that should be combined.

NSD Explain to students that by combining sentences, they can add variety to their writing. Keep in mind that nonstandard dialect sometimes uses nonstandard conventions to express relationships between sentence parts. Explain that students can communicate more clearly by using the proper coordinating conjunctions and punctuation.

Two-Part Harmony

Combining Sentences

Objective

To combine short sentences whose main ideas are closely related with *and*, *but*, and *or*

Presenting the Lesson

1. Read and discuss **Here's the Idea,** asking students to read aloud the sample sentence combinations. Stress the correct punctuation: a comma precedes *and*, *but*, and *or* when they are used to join complete sentences.

2. Read the sentences in **Check It Out** and help students recognize how ideas are combined in each sentence. Have students write on the chalkboard the two uncombined sentences for each example.

3. Assign **Try Your Skill.** Remind students to combine complete sentences and not sentence parts. Have volunteers write their combined sentences on the chalkboard; check for correct comma placement.

4. Read **Keep This in Mind** and then assign **Now Write.** Once again, have students write their sentences on the board.

Individualizing the Lesson

Less-Advanced Students

For **Now Write,** help students decide which conjunction should join each pair of sentences.

Advanced Students

Have each student write three pairs of short sentences whose main ideas are closely related: one

Here's the Idea Sometimes you write short sentences whose main ideas are closely related. Often you can make the relationships between such sentences clearer by joining them together. If two sentences state similar ideas of equal importance, you can usually join them with a comma and the word *and*.

> Monica plays the harmonica. Toby plays the tuba.
>
> Monica plays the harmonica, **and** Toby plays the tuba.

If two sentences state contrasting ideas of equal importance, you can usually join them with a comma and the word *but*.

> Jill enjoys tennis. I prefer racquetball.
>
> Jill enjoys tennis, **but** I prefer racquetball.

If two sentences offer a choice between ideas of equal importance, you can usually join them with a comma and the word *or*.

> Will you compete in the track meet on Saturday?
>   Is your ankle still bothering you?
>
> Will you compete in the track meet on Saturday, **or** is your ankle still bothering you?

Check It Out Read the following sentences.

1. Parachuting is fun, **but** it is also dangerous.
2. The weather turned cold, **and** the leaves began to fall.
3. You can paint in oils, **or** you can paint in watercolors.

- Which sentence combines similar ideas of equal importance?
- Which sentence combines contrasting ideas of equal importance?

- Which sentence combines ideas of equal importance and offers a choice between them?

Try Your Skill   Combine each pair of sentences. Follow the directions in parentheses.

1. Would you like dessert now? Will you wait until later? (Join with **, or.**)
2. An owl swooped through the barn door. The mice scampered to safety. (Join with **, and.**)
3. The subway was crowded. Mark still found a seat. (Join with **, but.**)
4. Yount hit a home run. The Brewers won the game. (Join with **, and.**)
5. A train was derailed near Pittsburgh. No one was injured. (Join with **, but.**)

Keep This in Mind

- Combine sentences that state similar ideas of equal importance with a comma and *and*.
- Combine sentences that state contrasting ideas of equal importance with a comma and *but*.
- Combine sentences that offer a choice between ideas of equal importance with a comma and *or*.

Now Write   Combine each pair of sentences using **,and** or **,but** or **,or.** Label your paper **Two-Part Harmony.** Save it in your folder.

1. Did you see the meteor shower? Were you sleeping?
2. Marvin Hamlisch wrote the music. Edward Kleban wrote the lyrics.
3. Marian's hands were very cold. They were not frostbitten.
4. The band took the stage. The audience cheered wildly.
5. The painting was beautiful. No one bought it.

55

that can be combined with *and*, one with *but*, and one with *or*. Students can then exchange papers and combine each pair of sentences.

Optional Practice

Add the following sentences to **Now Write.** Answers below.

1. Did you put the tent up yourself? Did your sister help you?
2. John did not think he would like *The Nutcracker*. He enjoyed it immensely.
3. The village's big Christmas tree was beautifully decorated. The colored lights were strung along the main street.
4. Sharon tried to open her front door. The door was locked.
5. You can wrap the gift yourself. The department store will wrap it for you.

1. Did you put the tent up yourself, or did your sister help you?
2. John did not think he would like *The Nutcracker*, but he enjoyed it immensely.
3. The village's big Christmas tree was beautifully decorated, and the colored lights were strung along the main street.
4. Sharon tried to open her front door, but it was locked.
5. You can wrap the gift yourself, or the department store will wrap it for you.

Extending the Lesson

Have students find three sentences in the newspaper: one that combines two independent clauses with *and*, one with *but*, and one with *or*. Have them separate each sentence into two short, unjoined sentences.

55

Part 2

Objective

To combine related sentence parts with *and*, *but*, and *or*

Presenting the Lesson

1. Read and discuss **Here's the Idea.** As you read the sample combined sentences, ask students if they can name the sentence parts that are combined. For example, the first sample sentence combines direct objects.

2. Read and discuss **Check It Out.** Again ask students to identify the sentence parts being combined.

3. Assign **Try Your Skill.**

4. Read **Keep This in Mind.**

5. Assign **Now Write.** Remind students to combine only sentence parts and not independent clauses (for example, sentence 5 should not be "The movie had a clever plot but it was much too long.").

Individualizing the Lesson

Less-Advanced Students

If students have difficulty completing **Now Write,** lead them through a step-by-step combination of each pair of sentences. First have students decide whether the sentences have similar parts, contrasting parts, or parts that offer a choice. The class should then combine the complete sentences with the appropriate conjunction. Next, direct the students to underline the repeated words in the second part of the combined sentence and write the sentence again, leaving out the repeated words.

Words of a Feather

Combining Sentence Parts

Here's the Idea   In Part 1 you learned how to join complete sentences. It is also possible to join related sentence parts.

Sometimes sentence parts state similar ideas of equal importance. Such parts can usually be joined with *and*.

> The band plays country music. *The band* plays rock and roll.
>
> The band plays country music **and** rock and roll.

Notice that the repeated words were dropped when the sentences were combined.

At times sentence parts state contrasting ideas of equal importance. Such parts can usually be joined with *but*.

> The workers went on strike. *The workers* didn't receive a raise.
>
> The workers went on strike **but** didn't receive a raise.

Occasionally two sentence parts offer a choice between ideas of equal importance. Such parts can usually be joined with *or*.

> Will you go to the movie? *Will you* stay at home?
>
> Will you go to the movie **or** stay at home?

Check It Out   Read the following groups of sentences.

1. Are you leaving today? Are you leaving tomorrow?
Are you leaving today or tomorrow?

2. The diver bumped his head on the bottom of the pool. The diver wasn't seriously hurt.
The diver bumped his head on the bottom of the pool but wasn't seriously hurt.

3. The bird gathered leaves. The bird placed them in its nest.
The bird gathered leaves and placed them in its nest.

- Which sentence combines similar parts of equal importance?

- Which sentence combines contrasting parts of equal importance?
- Which sentence combines parts that offer a choice between ideas of equal importance?

Try Your Skill   Combine each pair of sentences by following the directions in parentheses. Leave out the italicized words.

1. The paramedics rushed to the scene of the accident. The police *rushed to the scene of the accident.* (Join with **and.**)
2. Have you studied auto mechanics? *Have you studied* body repair? (Join with **or.**)
3. The engine sputtered. *The engine* continued running. (Join with **but.**)
4. The Chinese invented paper. *The Chinese invented* gunpowder. (Join with **and.**)
5. The Senators discussed the bill. *The Senators* didn't pass it. (Join with **but.**)

Keep This in Mind

- Sentence parts that state similar ideas of equal importance can be joined with *and.*
- Sentence parts that state contrasting ideas of equal importance can be joined with *but.*
- Sentence parts that offer a choice between ideas of equal importance can be joined with *or.*

Now Write   Combine each pair of sentences. Use **, and** or **, but** or **, or.** Label your paper **Words of a Feather.** Save it in your folder.

1. Central High School won the sectionals. Central High School lost the regionals.
2. Would you prefer a canoe? Would you prefer a raft?
3. The girls changed the oil. The girls replaced the air filter.
4. The rabbit had long ears. The rabbit had a white tail.
5. The movie had a clever plot. The movie was much too long.

Advanced Students

For **Now Write,** have students note what sentence parts are joined in each pair of sentences.

Optional Practice

Add the following sentences to **Now Write.** Answers below.

1. Tom got a subscription to *Popular Mechanics* for his birthday. Tom got a record album for his birthday.
2. Did you have pancakes for breakfast? Did you have oatmeal for breakfast?
3. *War and Peace* is a long book. *War and Peace* is a fascinating book.
4. Melanie went to the Joe Jackson concert. Alicia went to the Joe Jackson concert.

1. Tom got a subscription to *Popular Mechanics* and a record album for his birthday.
2. Did you have pancakes or oatmeal for breakfast?
3. *War and Peace* is a long but fascinating book.
4. Melanie and Alicia went to the Joe Jackson concert.

Extending the Lesson

Have students write three pairs of sentences with parts that can be combined, one with *and,* one with *but,* and one with *or.* Then have students exchange papers and combine the sentences.

Part 3

New Additions

Combining by Adding Single Words

Objective

To combine sentences by adding a single word from one sentence to another sentence

Presenting the Lesson

1. Read **Here's the Idea.** Discuss the first example of combining sentences by adding one word. Read the subsequent examples, discussing the fact that the words that have been added are modifiers. In the first two sets of sentences, the words *crackling* and *wrinkled* modify nouns. In the last set of sentences, the word *bravely* modifies a verb. Point out that, generally, modifiers ending in *-ing* and *-ed* modify nouns; those ending in *-ly* modify verbs.

2. Read and discuss the sentences in **Check It Out.** Have the students point out the new modifier and the word being modified in the combined sentence of each example.

3. Assign **Try Your Skill.**

4. Read **Keep This in Mind** and then assign **Now Write.** You may want to have students discuss the important word to be combined in each pair of sentences.

Individualizing the Lesson

Less-Advanced Students

If students have difficulty deciding how to change word endings to combine sentences by adding single words, briefly discuss adjective and adverb modifiers. Explain that the endings *-ing* and *-ed* are used on adjectives (which modify nouns) and *-ly* is used on adverbs (which

Here's the Idea   Occasionally you may write a sentence that states a main idea, followed by a second sentence that repeats much of this idea. If the second sentence contains only one word that adds new information, this word can be added to the first sentence in the pair. The remaining words in the second sentence can then be dropped.

The new plaza is paved with brick. *The brick is* red.

The new plaza is paved with **red** brick.

Notice that only the word *red* was added to the first sentence. The words in italics were dropped.

Sometimes you must change the form of a word before adding it. You may have to change the ending to *-ing*, *-ed*, or *-ly*.

We cooked dinner over a fire. *The fire* crackled.

We cooked dinner over a **crackling** fire.

Rick ironed the shirt. *The shirt had some* wrinkles.

Rick ironed the **wrinkled** shirt.

Beth announced her decision. *Her announcement was* brave.

Beth **bravely** announced her decision.

Check It Out   Read the following groups of sentences.

1. A tornado struck the city. The tornado struck suddenly.
A tornado suddenly struck the city.

2. We returned the record. The record had a scratch.
We returned the scratched record.

3. An astronaut emerged from the shuttle. The shuttle gleamed.
An astronaut emerged from the gleaming shuttle.

4. Charlotte told us the news. The news was good. Charlotte told us the good news.

- What words were added to each sentence?
- Which words were changed before they were added?

Try Your Skill Combine each pair of sentences by adding the important word. Leave out the italicized words.

1. Mark squinted in the sunlight. *The sunlight* glared. (End the important word with **-ing**.)
2. Rosa discovered a letter inside the book. *The letter had turned* yellow. (End the important word with **-ed**.)
3. Otters have fur. *The fur is* shiny.
4. Bert played the piano. *His playing was* beautiful. (End the important word with **-ly**.)
5. You can make this casserole with tuna. *The tuna comes in* cans. (End the important word with **-ed**.)

Keep This in Mind

- One sentence may state a main idea. Another sentence may add only one important word to that idea. Combine such sentences by adding the important word from the second sentence to the first.
- Before you add a word to a sentence, you may have to change the ending of the word to *-ing*, *-ed*, or *-ly*.

Now Write Add the important word from the second sentence to the first sentence. You may have to change the ending of the added word. Label your paper **New Additions.** Save it.

1. Crack the egg into the water. The water must be boiling.
2. This telephone answering machine can store twenty messages. The messages are on tape.
3. In the distance we heard a coyote. The coyote howled.
4. Nancy agreed to help. Her agreement was enthusiastic.
5. Moonlight shimmered on the water. The water had ripples.

59

Part 4

Objective

To use sentence-combining skills in revising

Presenting the Lesson

1. Read and discuss **Here's the Idea.** Stress that sentence combining is a skill that can improve students' writing. Review the skills as summarized in the chart.

2. Have volunteers read the two paragraphs in **Check It Out** aloud. As they compare the paragraphs, help students notice that paragraph 2 reads more smoothly than paragraph 1.

3. Assign **Try Your Skill.**

4. Read **Keep This in Mind.**

5. Assign **Now Write.** Instruct students to look for repeated words and phrases in determining which sentences to combine.

Individualizing the Lesson

Less-Advanced Students

Before assigning **Now Write,** discuss with the students which sentences should be combined. If necessary, also discuss how to combine each set of sentences.

Advanced Students

Have each student write a paragraph composed of short sentences that can be combined according to the guidelines in this Section. The students can then exchange paragraphs and revise them by combining the sentences.

Stick Together

Using Combining Skills in Writing

Here's the Idea   Use your sentence-combining skills whenever you revise your writing. These skills will help you to add variety to your sentences. These skills will also enable you to show how your ideas are related. The following chart summarizes the sentence-combining skills you have learned.

Combining Ideas in Sentences

1. Combine sentences by using a comma and the words *and, but,* or *or.*

2. Combine parts of sentences by using the words *and, but,* or *or* without a comma.

3. Add a single word from one sentence to another. If necessary, change the form of the word by changing the ending to *-ing, -ed,* or *-ly.*

Check It Out   Read the following paragraphs.

1.   Maria opened the carton. Maria looked inside. The carton was full of padding. The padding was made of foam. Had the padding done its job? Had the vase broken in shipment? A layer of padding was on top. Maria removed the layer of padding. She smiled. She looked at the vase. The vase was unharmed. The vase was antique.

2.   Maria opened the carton and looked inside. The carton was full of foam padding. Had the padding done its job, or had the vase broken in shipment? Maria removed the top layer of padding. Smiling, she looked at the vase. The antique vase was unharmed.

- In which paragraph are related ideas combined?
- How are the ideas combined in that paragraph?

Try Your Skill Revise the following paragraph by combining each pair of sentences. Follow any directions given in parentheses. Leave out the words given in italics.

1. All beetles have outer wings. *The outer wings are* thick. (Add the important word.) 2. They also have inner wings. *The inner wings are* thin. (Add the important word.) 3. When flying, beetles open their outer wings. *When flying, beetles* beat the air with their inner wings. (Combine the sentence parts with the word *and*.) 4. When they land, beetles close their hard outer wings to protect their soft inner wings. *They are* quick *about doing this*. (Change the form of the word *quick* by adding *-ly*. Then, add this word to the first sentence.) 5. Some beetles have bright dots on their outer wings. Others have wings that are decorated with stripes or splotches. (Join the two sentences with a comma and the word *and*.)

Keep This in Mind

- Use combining skills to revise your writing.
- You may combine related sentences or sentence parts.
- You may also combine sentences by adding single words. You may have to change the form of these words by adding *-ing*, *-ed*, or *-ly*.

Now Write Improve the following paragraph by combining its sentences. Write the paragraph in its revised form. Label your paper **Stick Together.** Save it in your folder.

The library was vast. The library was empty. The only sound was a clock. The clock ticked. Before me on a table was a book. The book was large. I opened the book. I read a couple of pages. It was a book about my life. It was also about my times. I turned to the chapter on the 1990's. The pages were blank. My heart leaped in my chest. Then I realized that these pages have yet to be written.

61

Section 6 Objectives

1. To understand that a paragraph is a group of sentences dealing with one main idea

2. To recognize and write unified paragraphs

3. To recognize and write topic sentences of paragraphs

4. To identify and use three kinds of paragraph development

5. To identify the three kinds of paragraphs: narrative, descriptive, and explanatory

Preparing the Students

Read the following passage to your students:

> The lieutenant looked up. He had a face that once had been brown and now the rain had washed it pale. The rain had washed the color from his eyes and they were white, as were his teeth, and as was his hair. He was all white. Even his uniform was beginning to turn white, and perhaps a little green with fungus.—RAY BRADBURY

Ask students what picture the passage conveys to them. Ask them what feeling they get from the passage. Point out that in paragraphs like the one just read, single sentences work together for a certain purpose. Tell students that in this Section they will learn how sentences combine to form paragraphs.

Additional Resources

Mastery Test — pages 19–20 in the test booklet

Practice Book — pages 25–29

Duplicating Masters — pages 25–29

What Is a Paragraph?

Teaching Special Populations

LD Provide LD students with a visual demonstration of paragraph unity. List the sentences of a paragraph in sequence on the chalkboard. Join them with arrows, and ask students what each sentence adds to the main idea.

Simplify the instructions for **Now Write** and other exercises as necessary. Write a paragraph on the board, and have students identify the sentences that do not belong.

Provide LD students with additional examples of each type of paragraph.

ESL Go through this Section carefully and slowly; it sets the foundation for future writing by ESL students. It is necessary that ESL students understand all parts.

Read examples of each type of paragraph aloud. Students will better understand the differences between the types of paragraphs by your inflections and tonal changes in each reading.

NSD Give students extra exercises for this Section. Many NSD students create "paragraphs" by extensive use of run-on sentences. Point out that paragraphs aren't created by stringing together sentences. Demonstrate on the board or with an overhead projector how the unity and coherence of a paragraph can be improved. Encourage students to add relevant details and examples to their paragraphs.

Objective

To understand that a paragraph is a group of sentences dealing with one main idea

Presenting the Lesson

1. Read aloud and discuss **Here's the Idea.** Emphasize the definition of *paragraph*. Read each of the three paragraphs to the class. Then have the students read each one silently. Ask them what main idea connects all the sentences in each paragraph. Discuss how each sentence contributes to the main idea.

2. Discuss **Check It Out.**

3. Assign **Try Your Skill.** Divide the class into groups of three. Have the groups decide which group of sentences is a paragraph and state its main idea. Encourage the groups to explain their answers to the rest of the class. If there is disagreement among the students, refer them to the definition of a paragraph.

4. Read **Keep This in Mind** and then assign **Now Write.**

Individualizing the Lesson

Less-Advanced Students

Discuss in detail paragraph 2 in **Try Your Skill.** Help students recognize that the first sentence states the paragraph's main idea; sentences 5 and 6 do not develop the paragraph's main idea.

Ask students how they recognize paragraphs when they are reading. Students should realize that indentation gives them a visual clue that a group of sentences is a paragraph.

An Idea at Work

Defining a Paragraph

Here's the Idea   You have seen how words work together in a sentence to express an idea. Now you will see how several sentences work together in a paragraph to express a larger idea.

A **paragraph** is a group of sentences that develops one main idea. See how the sentences in these groups work together.

1   Half a million people actually made the round trip to Space Station One that day. They wanted to watch the take-off in person. Back on Earth a hundred million video screens flashed the picture of Captain Melnick. The screens showed his gloved hand waving a dramatic farewell at the port, while the other hand slowly pressed down the all-important lever. That was the lever that would fire the ship out beyond the orbit of the satellite, past the Moon and the planets, into unknown space.

—JUDITH MERRIL

2   Standing at the foot of Dock Street, I watched the harbor begin to come to life. Dockworkers gathered in groups beside two towering freighters. Gulls wheeled overhead, screaming and squawking in the pale light. A steam whistle blew, scattering the gulls with its shrill blast. A stinging wind made me shiver and thrust my hands into my pockets. The wind brought with it the sharp smell of salt and oil. I turned my collar up against the wind and headed for home.

3   Ralph Bunche was a determined and successful man. The grandson of a slave, he spent his childhood in poverty in a Detroit ghetto. Nevertheless, he managed to go to college and earn degrees from both the University of California and Harvard. After teaching at Howard University, Bunche began working as a diplomat for the United Nations. In 1950, this American statesman became the first black to be awarded the Nobel peace prize.

Check It Out   Look again at the three groups of sentences. Notice that the first group tells part of a story. The second group describes a city scene. The third group tells about a person.

- Are these groups of sentences paragraphs? Does each group of sentences develop one idea?

Try Your Skill   Read these groups of sentences. One of them is a paragraph. One is not. For the group that is a paragraph, write the <u>main idea</u>. For the group that is not, explain why.

1   Some animals are experts at camouflage. Arctic foxes have grayish fur in summer and snow-white fur in winter. The wings of some moths look amazingly like the tree bark they rest on. Snakes have skins colored like the lights and shadows of undergrowth. Flatfish blend so well into the ocean bottom that it is almost impossible to pick them out.

2   The planets in our solar system are quite different from one another. Pluto is the smallest and the farthest from the sun. The biggest planet is Jupiter. It is over 88,000 miles in diameter. Jupiter was the Roman god of light. He was the husband of Juno. Some planets are fairly smooth, like Mars and Earth. Others are pitted with craters, like Mercury.

Keep This in Mind

- A paragraph is a group of sentences that develops one main idea.

Now Write   Look again at the group of sentences in **Try Your Skill** that is not a paragraph. Rewrite it so that it is a paragraph. Label your paper **An Idea at Work**. Put it into your folder.

Remind the students to indent the first line of each paragraph they write.

Advanced Students

Find a three- or four-paragraph newspaper or magazine article and type it with no paragraph indentations. Distribute the article and have students determine the paragraph divisions. The students may have difficulty separating the article into its original paragraphs; the exercise can lead to an interesting discussion of how each paragraph deals with one aspect of one main idea.

Optional Practice

Have students decide which sentence states the main idea in the following paragraph. Then have them determine which sentences do not develop the main idea.

Some scientists believe they have located a planet in a solar system outside our own. The large ball of gas is twenty-one light-years from the earth. Astronomers use extremely powerful telescopes. Other scientists say that the discovery is actually a star. Still other scientists say that the body is a brown dwarf, a small star that failed to develop fully.

Extending the Lesson

Hand out current magazines such as *Sports Illustrated*, *Seventeen*, and *Car and Driver*. Have each student randomly select a paragraph and check to see that it deals with one main idea. Then ask students to write down the main idea and note how each sentence supports that idea. Have students read their paragraphs to the class and share their conclusions.

Part 2

Objective

To recognize and write unified paragraphs

Presenting the Lesson

1. Read aloud and discuss **Here's the Idea.** Ask students to state the main idea of the paragraph about the Great Barrier Reef. Point out how each sentence relates to the main idea.

2. Discuss **Check It Out.** Ask how each sentence relates to the main idea. Point out that whether a paragraph explains, tells a story, or describes, it should be unified by one main idea.

3. Assign and discuss **Try Your Skill.** After students copy the main idea on their papers, ask what the key words are in the main idea.

4. Read **Keep This in Mind.**

5. Assign **Now Write.**

Individualizing the Lesson

Less-Advanced Students

Read the following main idea and have the students decide which of the sentences listed below it say something about the main idea.

Main idea: Many important scientific discoveries have been made by accident. 1, 3, 4

1. Louis Daguerre of France discovered the chemical to develop the image on a photographic plate when he stored an exposed plate in a cabinet containing various chemicals.

2. The first photographs were called daguerrotypes.

With One Voice

Recognizing Unity in a Paragraph

Here's the Idea   A paragraph is the basic unit for organizing ideas in writing. A paragraph should develop one idea. All the sentences in a paragraph should say something about that main idea. When they do, a paragraph has **unity.**

Notice how each of these sentences develops a description.

> The Great Barrier Reef, off the coast of Australia, could be described as an underwater paradise. The reef supports an enormous variety of sea life. Sea anemones of every color and size sway back and forth with the ocean currents. Brightly painted fish, some spotted and others striped, weave among the fine seaweed. Perhaps the most striking creatures are the sea-snails, which tumble and float through the water like great butterflies. Most people would agree that the Great Barrier Reef is one of wonders of the natural word.

Check It Out   Now read these two paragraphs.

1   Birds that cannot fly have developed other means to survive. The cassowary, a large Australian bird, has a razor-sharp nail on the innermost of its three toes. This unusual bird gives trouble-makers a deadly kick. Penguins are well equipped to survive in the sea. They are completely unable to fly. However, they have layers of blubber and close-set feathers, which make them excellent divers and swimmers. All flightless birds such as these have developed special or unusual features.

2   I will never forget the night that Jean, my only sister, was born. I was awakened by my parents on their way to the hospital. My four younger brothers and I shuffled sleepily into the kitchen. We munched boxfuls of crackers while we waited during the night for any news. At 6:00 A.M. the phone rang. My father told us that our family now had a girl. We finally had a sister!

• In each paragraph, do all of the sentences say something about one main idea? Does each paragraph have unity?

Try Your Skill   The main idea listed below is followed by several sentences. Some say something about the main idea. Some do not. Copy the main idea on your paper. Below it, write only those sentences that are related to the main idea.

Main idea: The Galápagos Islands are home to mysterious and unusual animals.

1. These volcanic islands lie in the Pacific Ocean 600 miles off the northwest coast of South America.

2. The unusual animals that live on the islands include four-foot-long lizards called *iguanas*.

3. Pirates buried treasure on these islands.

4. Politically, the islands are part of the country of Ecuador.

5. These strange islands take their name from the Spanish word for the huge turtles that live there.

6. In 1881, Charles Darwin described these turtles as able to carry several people on their backs.

7. The group of fifteen islands was once known as the Enchanted Isles.

8. Darwin's study of animals led to his theory of evolution.

Keep This in Mind

• Each sentence in a paragraph should say something about the main idea. Then a paragraph has unity.

Now Write   Write the name of a place that you know well. Then write one sentence that expresses the main idea of your thoughts about the place. Below your sentence, list five more sentences that give more information about your topic. Label your paper **With One Voice.** Keep your work in your folder.

3. Charles Goodyear accidentally melted India rubber and sulfur to create vulcanized rubber.

4. Sir Alexander Fleming accidentally contaminated an experimental bacterial culture and discovered penicillin.

5. Some of our rubber products today still carry the name Goodyear.

Advanced Students

Have students find and cut out three paragraphs from magazine articles. Have them bring the paragraphs to class and write the main idea of each paragraph.

Optional Practice

Make copies of the following paragraph. Ask students if the paragraph is unified. Have them cross out any unrelated sentences and write the main idea.

An abrupt sound startled him. Off to the right he heard it, and his ears, expert in such matters, could not be mistaken. Again he heard the sound, and again. He enjoyed music of all kinds. Somewhere, off in the blackness, someone had fired a gun three times. In Westerns, cowboys always ride horses and have gunfights.

—RICHARD CONNELL

Extending the Lesson

Assign students to work in pairs. Tell each student to write a sentence answering this question: Would you rather live in the city, the suburbs, or the country? Ask them to write five sentences explaining their choices with specific reasons. Then have partners exchange papers and check that all sentences are related to the main idea.

Part 3

In Control

Using a Topic Sentence

Objective

To recognize and write topic sentences of paragraphs

Presenting the Lesson

1. Read aloud and discuss **Here's the Idea.** Emphasize the definition of a *topic sentence*. Point out that a topic sentence has three important functions in a paragraph. For examples of topic sentences, you might refer to page 66 and discuss the first sentence in each of the three sample paragraphs.

2. Discuss **Check It Out.** Ask for a show of hands to see if the students can identify which sentence is the topic sentence. Point out how all the other sentences relate to the topic sentence.

3. Read the instructions for **Try Your Skill.** Read each paragraph twice for the class. Then give the students time to write the topic sentence for each paragraph. Discuss their answers. If there are disagreements, remind students that all the other sentences should support the topic sentence.

4. Read **Keep This in Mind.**

5. Assign **Now Write.** If the students have difficulty thinking of topics, suggest that they state what they like to do on holidays, what their favorite pet is, or how to make their favorite foods. Remind them that their topic sentence can describe, explain, or tell a story.

Here's the Idea   A **topic sentence** states the main idea of a paragraph. Because it tells what the paragraph is about, it often begins the paragraph. Wherever it appears in a paragraph, a topic sentence does several important things.

First, a topic sentence helps the writer control unity in a paragraph. The main idea is before the writer's eyes. Each supporting sentence can be checked to make sure it is related.

Second, the topic sentence tells the reader what to expect in the paragraph. It acts as a guide. It serves as a general introduction to the main idea.

Third, a good topic sentence arouses a reader's curiosity. For example, a topic sentence might say, "Rangers have learned that it can be helpful to start fires in a crowded forest." The reader will want to read the rest of the paragraph to find out how or why a controlled fire can be of help to a crowded forest.

Check It Out   Read the paragraph below.

Scheduling city buses is a difficult job because there are so many factors to consider. First, the number of riders on any given route is different at different hours during the day. Second, the traffic on each route is heavier at some times than at others. Third, a certain number of buses must always be reserved to take over for those that break down. Schedulers have to try to meet the needs of riders on every bus route in the city. The best job of scheduling is the one that, with the fewest buses, meets the needs of the most people.

• What is the main idea of this paragraph? Which is the topic sentence?

Try Your Skill   Read the three paragraphs below. Decide which is the topic sentence in each. On your paper, write the topic sentence for each paragraph.

1   We surprised my sister Diane on her sixteenth birthday. I had invited four of her closest friends to a dinner party. While Diane was out of the house, I decorated the living room and cooked her favorite meal. I made lasagna and salad, and a chocolate cake. Diane's friends and I were waiting to surprise her when she walked in. Diane's friends had also planned another surprise. They had bought tickets to a rock concert for all of us that night. After we ate, we took our party to the concert. That was one of the best birthdays *I* ever had!

2   A breed of dog that is not commonly seen as a pet is the Afghan hound. This type of hunting dog comes from northern Afghanistan. It has a long, narrow head, a long neck, long legs and tail, and long, silky hair. The Afghan is a good hunting dog especially suited to hilly country where it leaps and runs easily.

3   Begin making popcorn by pouring one-quarter cup of vegetable oil into a large pan. Heat the oil. Then pour in one-half cup of popcorn and quickly cover the pan. Shake the pan over the heat from the time the popping begins until the noise stops. Pour the popped corn into a bowl. Add melted butter and salt if you wish. Popcorn is a quick and easy snack to make.

Keep This in Mind

- A topic sentence states the main idea of a paragraph. Often, a topic sentence begins a paragraph.

Now Write   Think of three topics that you might want to write a paragraph about. What would be the main idea of each paragraph? Write a topic sentence for each paragraph that states your main idea. Label your paper **In Control.** Put it into your folder.

Less-Advanced Students

Have students discuss the kinds of information they would expect to find in paragraphs with the following topic sentences:

1. Although the British won the Battle of Bunker Hill in 1775, it was a morale booster for the Americans.
2. Artificial snowmaking is a common practice at many ski resorts.
3. All drivers should obey the 55-mile-per-hour speed limit.
4. Bonsai is the Japanese art of growing dwarf trees.

Advanced Students

For **Now Write,** have students revise each topic sentence they write by reviewing the points about topic sentences in **Here's the Idea.** They may wish to focus especially on writing a sentence that captures a reader's interest.

Optional Practice

Have students choose a subject and write three different topic sentences for it. Have the students share their sentences and discuss how a paragraph's main idea would change according to its topic sentence.

Extending the Lesson

Distribute copies of a short newspaper editorial on a current topic of interest. After you have read the editorial aloud, ask students to underline the topic sentence in each paragraph. Have students share their answers.

Objective

To identify and use three kinds of paragraph development

Presenting the Lesson

1. Read aloud the first paragraph in **Here's the Idea.** Explain that details are "specifics" that make a subject come alive. Read aloud the paragraph using sensory details. Ask the class to identify the details, and also the topic sentence. Next read the paragraph using examples. Ask what the topic sentence is and what examples are used to develop it. Next, read aloud the paragraph using facts and statistics. Have the students name the topic sentence and the facts and statistics used to support it. Finally, read aloud the paragraph using an anecdote. Have the class identify the topic sentence.

2. Discuss **Check It Out.** Ask students to identify the topic sentence. Ask which words and phrases support the topic sentence. If the students have difficulty discerning between examples and facts and statistics, refer to the paragraphs on the preceding page.

3. Assign and discuss **Try Your Skill.**

4. Read **Keep This in Mind.**

5. Assign **Now Write.** Read the directions and note that they call for only three details, three examples, or three facts and figures. Students should not combine details, examples, and facts and figures at this time.

What a Buildup!

Ways of Developing a Paragraph

Here's the Idea Sentences that follow a topic sentence should develop the main idea of the paragraph. Use sensory details, specific examples, facts and statistics, or incidents or anecdotes to develop your topic.

Sensory details make a description seem real.

> The black stove, stoked with coal and firewood, glows like a lighted pumpkin. Eggbeaters whirl, spoons spin round in bowls of butter and sugar, vanilla sweetens the air, ginger spices it; melting, nose-tingling odors saturate the kitchen, suffuse the house, drift out to the world on puffs of chimney smoke. In four days our work is done. —TRUMAN CAPOTE

Use **specific examples** to develop a general statement.

> Most tempting of all at Lombardo's Foods are the salads. There is a beautiful pasta primavera—pasta and crisp vegetables enveloped in a pale green basil sauce. My favorite salad is thin slivers of carrots and zucchini squash in sweet vinegar.

Use **facts and statistics** to support an opinion or make an idea clear.

> Basketball was the most popular team sport at our school this year. Season attendance at the boys' games was 20,155. The total figure for the girls' games was even higher at 22,415.

Incidents or anecdotes (very short stories) can illustrate a point.

> The British soldier T. E. Lawrence was a master of self-control. Once while his fellow soldiers watched, Lawrence lit a match and held it until it burned completely out. One of the soldiers asked how Lawrence could hold the match so long without hurting himself. "The trick," Lawrence replied, "is not minding that it hurts."

Check It Out   Read this paragraph about music.

Today's music reflects several influences of the 1950's. Bill Haley and the Comets introduced the rock beat with such hits as "Rock Around the Clock" and "Shake, Rattle, and Roll." Buddy Holly and the Crickets paved the way for the music of the 1960's, especially that of the Beatles. Individual hits, such as "Chantilly Lace" by The Big Bopper and "Duke of Earl" by Gene Chandler, were re-recorded in the 1970's and 1980's.

• What kinds of details develop the topic sentence?

Try Your Skill   Tell what kinds of details develop the main idea of this paragraph.

One of the most unforgettable faces of ancient Greek myths belonged to Medusa, the Gorgon. Medusa had hissing, poisonous snakes growing from her head. She had burning eyes that turned anyone who looked into them to stone. Medusa also had sharp fangs for teeth.

Keep This in Mind

• The main idea of a paragraph may be developed by sensory details, by specific examples, by facts and statistics, or by incidents or anecdotes.

Now Write   Take out the paper labeled **In Control.** Select one of your three topic sentences. List three sensory details, three specific examples, three facts and statistics, or one incident or anecdote that you could use to develop the main idea of that topic sentence. Label your paper **What a Buildup!** and put it into your folder.

71

Less-Advanced Students

Before assigning **Now Write,** discuss how a paragraph's topic sentence helps to determine its method of development. Have the students decide whether other methods of development would have worked for the paragraphs in **Here's the Idea.** If so, would the other methods have been as effective as the one used? Then, for **Now Write,** help the students determine which method of development is most appropriate for their particular topic sentences.

Advanced Students

Have students turn back to the sample paragraphs in this Part. Ask them to identify the way that each paragraph is developed.

Optional Practice

Have students choose one of the following topic sentences and write three sentences that develop it with either sensory details, specific examples, facts and statistics, or an incident or anecdote.

1. The winter weather in my hometown is wonderful (or terrible).
2. Having a summer job can be an educational experience.
3. The job of a television newscaster is more difficult than it seems.

Extending the Lesson

Select articles from a few weekly magazines. Ask students to locate paragraphs that are clearly developed by either details, examples, or facts and figures. Have volunteers read their paragraphs and identify the topic sentence and method of development.

Objective

To identify the three kinds of paragraphs: narrative, descriptive, and explanatory

Presenting the Lesson

1. Read aloud **Here's the Idea.** Emphasize the definitions of narrative, descriptive, and explanatory paragraphs. Ask the class to give examples of times when they have used these three kinds of paragraphs in their writing.

2. Discuss **Check It Out.** Point out that the three paragraphs deal with the same topic in three different ways. Ask students what the purpose of each paragraph is and what makes the first paragraph narrative, the second one descriptive, and the third one explanatory.

3. Assign and discuss **Try Your Skill.** Encourage students to defend their answers and convince others who disagree with them.

4. Assign **Now Write.**

Individualizing the Lesson

Less-Advanced Students

Have students tell whether the following paragraph is narrative, descriptive, or explanatory. Discuss the fact that narrative and explanatory paragraphs often include descriptive details.

A few years ago, my friends and I played a practical joke on our good friend Kay. We threw a birthday party for her one September evening. A beautifully frosted sheet cake sat on the table as Kay opened her gifts. Our friend Chris said, "Kay, I made this

72

Nameplates

Recognizing Three Kinds of Paragraphs

Here's the Idea   When you write a paragraph, you may want to tell a story. Sometimes you may want to describe something. At other times, you may want to explain something. For each of these times you would use one of the three kinds of paragraphs.

A **narrative** paragraph tells a story about something that happened. It is usually told in the order that it happened.

A **descriptive** paragraph is a word picture that appeals to the senses. A detailed description often creates a certain mood.

An **explanatory** paragraph explains something. It may explain *how* to do something or *how* something happens or works. It may also explain *why* something should be done, or *what* something is.

Check It Out   Notice how one topic is presented in three different ways in three different kinds of paragraphs.

1   As Tai and I rounded a bend in the forest path, we heard a low growl. We looked up and froze in terror. Ahead of us, about twenty yards away, stood a black bear with her two cubs. The bear stared at us, unmoving, as if wondering whether to attack. Suddenly she dropped onto all fours and charged. We threw down our packs and raced back along the path. Satisfied that she had chased us away, the she-bear returned to her cubs.

2   The black bear stood tall on her powerful legs. She was a beautiful animal. Her thick cinnamon fur glistened in the sunlight. Two rounded ears stood straight up on the top of her head. She bobbed her head slowly, tasting the air with her nostrils and sliding a bright-pink tongue around her muzzle. Occasionally, a low growl came from her throat.

72

3   The black bear is one of the most common species of bear. These animals grow to about five feet in length. Most adult black bears weigh between two hundred and three hundred pounds. They range in color from black to cinnamon to creamy white. Some are even bluish in color. Black bears can be found in the forests of North America. There are about 75,000 of them in the United States.

- Which paragraph is narrative? Which is descriptive? Which is explanatory?

Try Your Skill   Write whether this paragraph is *Narrative, Descriptive,* or *Explanatory,* and explain your answer.

Thousands of prehistoric tools exist today. This fact seems amazing, but it is logical. The early tools were made of stone, one of the hardest, most long-lasting substances on earth. These tools were small enough to remain unbroken during the huge changes in the earth's surface. A tool could fall into mud or be buried in a cave and remain unchanged for a million years. These important tools can show us the progress made long ago by our human ancestors.

Keep This in Mind

- A narrative paragraph tells a story or relates an event.
- A descriptive paragraph creates a word picture.
- An explanatory paragraph tells *how* to do something or *how* something happens or works, *why* something should be done, or *what* something is.

Now Write   From your folder, take out the paper labeled **What a Buildup!** Review what you have written. Write which of the three kinds of paragraphs you would use for this topic. Explain why it is the best kind to use for your topic. Label your paper **Nameplates.** Keep your work in your folder.

sponge cake just for you. Why don't you cut it?" Kay, who was very polite and reserved, started to cut the cake. Her face reddened and her knuckles grew white as she tried to cut into her special cake. Then she looked in amazement as the rest of us burst out laughing—and Chris took the cake apart to show Kay the two sponges she had used to put it together.

Advanced Students

Give students the following topic sentence: *The rocket lifted off in a burst of flames.* Ask one-third of the students to write three sentences developing the topic sentence as part of a descriptive paragraph, one-third for a narrative paragraph, and the rest for an explanatory paragraph.

Optional Practice

Copy this list on the chalkboard:

handbook on plant care
front-page newspaper story
travel brochure
cookbook
sports story
letter from a friend

Ask students which of these would be likely sources for narrative, descriptive, or explanatory paragraphs and have them explain why. Point out that each could have different types of paragraphs.

Extending the Lesson

Divide the class into three groups. Make each group responsible for one type of paragraph: narrative, descriptive, or explanatory. Have the groups look through their other textbooks to find at least three examples of their assigned type of paragraph. Ask each group to share these paragraphs with the class.

Section 7 Objectives

1. To recognize the three stages—pre-writing, writing the first draft, and revising—in the process of writing

2. To choose a topic for a paragraph

3. To narrow a topic for a paragraph

4. To consider the purpose and audience for a piece of writing

5. To write a direct and interesting topic sentence for a paragraph

6. To gather details to develop a paragraph

7. To organize the details in a paragraph

8. To write the first draft of a paragraph

9. To write an effective concluding sentence to end a paragraph

10. To revise the ideas, organization, and word choice in a paragraph

Preparing the Students

Explain to students that they will now apply what they have previously learned about paragraphs. Point out that effective paragraphs need to be planned in advance. This Section will teach them skills for planning and writing paragraphs of their own.

Additional Resources

Mastery Test — pages 21–22 in the test booklet

Practice Book — pages 30–39

Duplicating Masters — pages 30–39

74

Writing a Paragraph

Teaching Special Populations

LD LD students will need much guidance and reinforcement as they go through Writing Sections 7–20. Go over the process with students carefully and slowly. Learning disabled students may have a difficult time learning revision skills. Help students with this step individually.

Students with motor or attention difficulties might be more successful if they can work with another student who serves as a recorder, or if they are allowed to record their "first drafts" on a tape recorder.

Offer students interesting material to write about, such as magazine articles, posters, short films, or interesting current events. Have students first respond verbally to this material.

Students will need extra help learning to narrow topics. Give them additional exercises for this purpose.

ESL Help students gain confidence by conducting some exercises as group activities. Brainstorming is a prewriting step that can be conducted in this manner. Students who have trouble writing in English might be encouraged if you assign a native English speaker to write down what they express orally. Offer additional help as necessary.

NSD Explain that many writers use nonstandard dialects, abbreviations, and other nonformal forms of expression in their first draft. Tell students that they can write their first thoughts in their own dialects. Explain that they can standardize their language when they revise.

Step Right Up

Objective

To recognize the three stages—pre-writing, writing the first draft, and revising—in the process of writing

Presenting the Lesson

1. Read **Here's the Idea.** Ask students for examples of activities that consist of a process. Then write on the chalkboard the three steps in the process of writing, discussing each step.

2. Read the list of activities in **Check It Out** and have the class answer the questions that follow the list. Students may need to refer to **Here's the Idea** to do so.

3. Use **Try Your Skill** as a classroom activity. Have students read and study the list. The class can then discuss the question. Emphasize the preliminary quality of the pre-writing notes.

4. Read **Keep This in Mind.**

5. Assign **Now Write.** Explain that students will perhaps not write in their journals every day; the journal is an ongoing project that can contain thoughts and ideas on reading, movies and television, conversations, classes, current events, etc. Plan to devote a few minutes of class time at regular intervals to journal writing. You may want to stimulate writing by asking a question or suggesting a topic.

Individualizing the Lesson

Less-Advanced Students

If students have difficulty getting started in their journal writing, hold a

Writing as a Process

Here's the Idea Writing is a process. The process of writing has three stages: pre-writing, writing the first draft, and revising. Each step is necessary for you to create a good piece of writing.

Pre-writing is the first stage of the process. Pre-writing includes all of the planning you do before you actually begin writing. This includes choosing and narrowing a topic and thinking about your purpose and your audience. Pre-writing also includes gathering ideas and putting those ideas into a logical order.

Writing the first draft is the second stage of the process. During this stage, you write your ideas in sentence form. First, you write a topic sentence to present the subject of your paragraph. Then you use the ideas in your pre-writing notes to develop your subject. Let your thoughts and ideas flow freely. Don't worry about mistakes.

Revising is the third part in the process. Your goal is to improve what you have written. You want all of your ideas to support your topic sentence. You also want to see that your ideas are well organized. Look at the language you have used. Are all of your words vivid and precise? Proofread your paragraph. Correct any errors you have made in grammar, capitalization, punctuation, and spelling.

Check It Out Here is a list of activities a writer does.

> writing a topic sentence
> writing sentences from details and ideas
> choosing a topic
> gathering details and ideas
> correcting punctuation
> checking to see that the paragraph makes sense

- Which of these activities are part of pre-writing? writing the first draft? revising?

Try Your Skill   At what stage of the process of writing would you write a list like the one below? Explain your answer.

Pre-writing
How To Bake a Chicken

Ingredients: a fresh chicken, salt, pepper, garlic, and oregano, half a stick of butter, baking dish

Preparation: preheat oven to 400 degrees, rinse chicken in cold water, sprinkle the spices over chicken, cut butter into small cubes and put them into baking dish, put chicken into baking dish

Baking: bake chicken for one hour at 400 degrees

Keep This in Mind

- Writing is a process that has three stages: pre-writing, writing the first draft, and revising.
- *Pre-writing* includes all of the planning you do before you write.
- *Writing the first draft* is the stage where you write a rough version of your paragraph.
- *Revising* is the stage where you work to improve your writing.

Now Write   Have you ever kept a journal? In a journal you can write about events, feelings, thoughts, or ideas that you've had. You can also write about something you've read in a book or magazine.

Keep a notebook that you can use as a journal. Try to write in it as often as possible. By keeping a journal, you can practice your writing skills. Your journal can also become a storehouse of ideas for future writing projects.

For today, write about something interesting that you read about recently. Label your paper *Journal*. Save your work.

series of five-minute free writings. These are strictly-timed writings, the only rule of which is that pencil and pen should be on the paper, writing, the entire time. Encourage the students not to worry about what they write; the physical act of writing often stimulates ideas.

Advanced Students

Have the students find diaries or journals of well-known writers such as Anne Frank, Sylvia Plath, and Virginia Woolf. Students can look up "diaries and journals" in the card catalog in the library and find one or two volumes to browse through; they can then report on their findings to the rest of the class.

Optional Practice

Have students write a journal entry on one of the following topics:

a good friend	high school
poetry	the U.S. President
the climate in your area	reading for fun
	vacation

Extending the Lesson

Help students recognize that all writers go through the steps discussed in this lesson through one of the following activities:

1. Invite a writer (e.g., a local newspaper writer, a college or graduate student, or a teacher) to class to discuss the steps he or she performs in the process of writing.

2. Bring to class pre-writing notes or a revised first draft that you have written.

3. Bring to class an example of a first draft and revised version of a poem or part of a short story or novel. Some published examples include poems by Yeats, Keats, and Blake.

Part 2

Objective

To choose a topic for a paragraph

Presenting the Lesson

1. Read and discuss **Here's the Idea.** Show the class as many examples as possible of the methods of choosing a topic. For example, hold a class brainstorming session by using one of the sample topics—*sports* or *cooking*—and writing the students' responses on the chalkboard. Show the class how brainstorming can produce a topic such as "my first Vietnamese meal."

2. Have students read the sample journal entry in **Check It Out.** Help students to recognize the wide-ranging writing topics, such as television violence, realism on television, or the effects of television rating methods, to be found in the entry.

3. Assign **Try Your Skill.** Encourage the class to let their imaginations roam freely. Show the class how numerous topics, such as *ballet, break dancing*, and *ballroom dancing*, may occur to someone brainstorming the topic *dancing*.

4. Read **Keep This in Mind** and then assign **Now Write.**

Individualizing the Lesson

Less-Advanced Students

Have students meet in small groups to brainstorm topics for writing. One member of each group should take notes as the group

Pre-Writing: Choosing a Topic

Here's the Idea   Do you ever complain that choosing a topic to write about is the hardest part of writing? Sometimes you have so many ideas, it is hard to choose just one. At other times, you may not be able to think of a single good subject.

A good topic is something that interests you and that is important to you. The best subjects are the things right around you. When you write about people, write about your friends and family. When you describe something, describe places and things that are familiar to you. When you write about activities, write about things *you* enjoy, such as your hobby or your favorite sport.

Here are some good places to look for interesting topics.

Journal Keep a journal of your ideas, feelings, and personal experiences. Write in your journal whenever you can. You will be surprised at the number of good writing ideas that you will find there.

Brainstorming Brainstorming is another way to discover topics. Start with a general idea, such as *sports* or *cooking*. Then write down whatever comes into your mind about the general idea. As your list grows, you will see many ideas you can use.

Interviews and Discussions Often you will find that people you know can be good sources for writing ideas. For example, you might talk with your grandmother about what school was like when she was your age. You might talk with a classmate who is from another country about his or her culture. Listen carefully and ask questions.

The things you talk about in class or with your friends can give you writing ideas, too. Did you agree or disagree with what you heard? Did you discover new ideas? Did you hear stories you would like to retell?

Reading You can find interesting writing ideas by reading magazines, books, and newspapers. Make notes in your journal about interesting things that you read.

Check It Out Read this excerpt from one student's journal.

> Why are there so many T.V. programs about doctors and police officers? Why doesn't someone come up with something different for T.V.? I would like to see a show about farmers or about high school students.
>
> I also think that there is too much violence on T.V. My little brother watches T.V. all night. It seems all he sees are car crashes, shootings, and fist-fights.

- What ideas in this journal entry might make good topics for a paragraph?

Try Your Skill Read the general topics below. Choose one, and spend five or ten minutes brainstorming on it. Write your ideas on a piece of paper. See if you can find three or four good topics for a paragraph. Write these topics in your journal.

| your family | hobbies | music |
| dancing | animal stories | vacations |

Keep This in Mind

- A good topic is one that interests you and is important to you.
- There are many ways to find a good topic. You can look in your journal, brainstorm, interview people, discuss ideas with friends and classmates, and read.

Now Write Make a list of possible topics for a paragraph. Use one or more of the methods described in this lesson. Then, choose one topic that you'd like to write about in a paragraph. Write your choice on a piece of paper, and save it in your folder.

brainstorms one of the following topics:

| travel | childhood |
| careers | animals |

Advanced Students

Hold discussion groups to generate topics for writing. Tell students to bring at least one interesting topic, from their journals or reading, to discuss in a small group. Groups can then discuss each student's topic in turn, with students taking notes to stimulate their own writing.

Optional Practice

Have students find two writing topics from each of the following sources:

1. a current newspaper
2. a current newsmagazine such as *Time* or *Newsweek*
3. a specialized magazine such as *Seventeen, Sports Illustrated,* or *Scientific American*

Extending the Lesson

Have students conduct interviews as sources of possible writing topics. Each student should interview someone with an interesting perspective, take notes on the interview, and then list two or three possible writing topics suggested by the interview. Possible interview subjects are:

1. a grandparent or older person in the community
2. someone with an interesting job or hobby
3. someone who has traveled to or lived in an interesting place

Objective

To narrow a topic for a paragraph

Presenting the Lesson

1. Read and discuss **Here's the Idea.** Have students explain why the sample paragraph on winter sports is uninteresting. Point out that asking *who, what, when, where, why,* and *how* about a topic is a form of brainstorming.

2. Have a volunteer read the paragraph in **Check It Out.** Help the class recognize that the writer writes from personal experience, as discussed in the previous lesson. In addition, the paragraph is detailed and specific, unlike the one about winter sports.

3. Assign **Try Your Skill.** Instruct students to choose a general topic that interests them.

4. Read **Keep This in Mind.**

5. Assign **Now Write.** Remind students that their topic should be sufficiently narrow to be covered well in one paragraph.

Individualizing the Lesson

Less-Advanced Students

Emphasize the differences in interest between the paragraph on winter sports and the one on the writer's personal experience. Then check each student's topic to be sure it is narrow enough for an interesting paragraph. Alternatively, have students work in pairs to narrow their topics.

A Closer Look

Pre-Writing: Narrowing a Topic

Here's the Idea   A student wanted to find his street on a map. He looked at a map of the United States, but he couldn't find his street. Then he looked at a map of his state. Again, he had no luck. Next, he looked at a map of his city. Finally, the student had found a map that was specific enough to give him what he was looking for.

The same is true when you choose a topic for a paragraph. You must find a topic that is narrow enough to give you what you're looking for: an interesting, informative paragraph.

For example, the topic "winter sports" is too general. This topic might lead you to write a vague, dull paragraph.

> Americans enjoy many different winter sports. Skiing is popular. Ice skating is also popular. Other good winter sports are cross-country skiing, ice fishing, and sledding.

However, if you narrowed this topic, you could write an interesting, informative paragraph. One simple way to narrow a general topic is to ask questions about it. These questions might begin with *who, what, when, where, why,* and *how.*

For instance, you could ask *what?* about the general topic "winter sports." You might get a list like this one.

> skating, skiing, hockey, tobogganing

Now you would choose the sport that you enjoy the most. You might choose "skating." Then ask questions like these:

When?	Winter in Oregon, November in Dallas
Who?	me, Ricky and Tom, Gail, other friends
Where?	Oregon (Tree Lake, Robertson Park), Dallas (Love Field)

While you write your notes, you might remember the time you went ice skating in Dallas, right after you moved there. You went to an indoor rink. You thought it was strange to be ice skating when the temperature outside was almost 70 degrees. Now you've got a topic that is narrow enough to be covered well in a paragraph: ice skating in the heat.

Check It Out   Read this paragraph.

> I went ice skating in Texas. Last year we moved to Dallas from Portland, Oregon. In November, I discovered an indoor skating rink at the Love Field entertainment center. It felt strange to be lacing up my skates on days when the temperature averaged sixty-five degrees, but that's exactly what I did. The rink was smooth and fast, and I was happy to be skating.

- Why is this paragraph more interesting than the one about "winter sports?"

Try Your Skill   Choose one of these general topics. Ask *Who? What? When? Where? Why?* or *How?* about it. Use your answers to write a narrowed topic. Be sure the topic is one that can be covered well in one paragraph.

hobbies	music	famous women
gardening	food	dreams

Keep This in Mind

- Narrow a general topic by asking *who, what, when, where, why,* and *how* questions. Be sure that your topic can be covered well in one paragraph.

Now Write   You are now ready to begin narrowing the topic you chose in the last lesson. Ask yourself *who, what, when, where, why,* and *how* questions about your topic. Use the answers you get to narrow your topic. Save your narrowed topic.

81

Advanced Students

Have students choose an additional topic from **Try Your Skill** to narrow by asking the questions *who, what, when, where, why,* and *how.*

Optional Practice

Select three or four one-paragraph articles from the "People" section of *Time* magazine. Duplicate them and give copies to your students. For each paragraph, have students explain how the following questions are answered: *who, what, when, where, why,* and *how.* Mention that not all of the questions will be answered in every paragraph.

Extending the Lesson

Ask each student to bring a paragraph from a newsmagazine to class and exchange it with a classmate. Each student should then write down the general topic and the specific topic of his or her paragraph.

81

Objective

To consider the purpose and audience for a piece of writing

Presenting the Lesson

1. Read and discuss **Here's the Idea,** emphasizing the words *purpose* and *audience* by writing them on the chalkboard. In general, encourage students to consider their purpose in writing as more than just fulfilling an assignment, and their audience as wider than just their teacher.

2. Have a volunteer read the paragraph in **Check It Out.** As students discuss the paragraph's descriptive purpose, ask them to point out its sensory words and phrases.

3. Assign **Try Your Skill.** After they have written their paragraphs, have the students discuss the ways they would adjust their writing to fit their audiences.

4. Read **Keep This in Mind.**

5. Assign **Now Write.** Review the possible purposes of writing: to narrate, to describe, to explain, to persuade, to define. The audience for class writing may often be simply classmates and the teacher.

Individualizing the Lesson

Less-Advanced Students

Emphasize the concept of writing for different audiences. Have students discuss the kinds of differences they would take into account when considering different audiences for the following subjects:

For What and Whom?

Pre-Writing: Finding Purpose and Audience

Here's the Idea   Before a writer actually begins to write, he or she should ask two important questions: "What is the purpose of my paragraph?" and "For whom am I writing?"

Everything you write has a **purpose.** Your purpose is what you hope to accomplish with your writing. Is your purpose to tell a story, describe someone or something, or explain an idea? When you know your purpose, you know what your paragraph is supposed to do. This knowledge will help you to understand your subject more clearly and to write a better paragraph.

Your **audience** is the people who will read your writing. If you want your work to be appreciated and enjoyed by your audience, you must first determine just who your readers are. Ask yourself some questions about your audience. How old are your readers? Knowing this will help you to choose language that your readers will understand. How much do your readers know about your subject? The answer to this question will tell you how detailed your information should be. What are your audience's interests and opinions? Knowing this will help you to select a topic that your audience will enjoy.

Check It Out   Read the following paragraph.

One morning I was pounding some red chillies into powder. *Cho-chup!* went the pestle into the mortar, crushing the brittle chillies and the seeds in them. Each time it fell, a fine red dust rose up, spreading a rich, acrid smell in the air. It was a pleasant smell, hot and pungent, which made my nostrils water and squirted tears into my eyes, so that every few minutes I had to stop to wipe them. It was a fine, peaceful morning, not a sound from the tannery, which for one blessed day in the week closed down completely. Each time I paused I could hear sparrows twittering, and the thin, clear note of a mynah bird.

—KAMALA MARKANDAYA

- What is the writer's purpose in this paragraph? How do you know?

Try Your Skill Suppose you were asked to help prepare two pamphlets describing your high school. One pamphlet will be sent to eighth graders. The other pamphlet will be sent to the parents of the eighth graders.

Write a description of the pamphlet sent to the students. Then write a description of the pamphlet sent to their parents.

Keep This in Mind

- Your purpose is what you want to accomplish in your writing.
- Your audience is the people who will read your writing.
- Knowing your purpose and your audience will help you to write a better paragraph.

Now Write Write the purpose of the paragraph you are planning. Then decide who your audience is. Write a short description of your readers. Save your notes in your folder.

camping: a) elementary school children b) a Boy Scout or Girl Scout troop your age

television: a) your classmates b) students from South America

French cooking: a) a cooking class b) your classmates in English

Advanced Students

Have students discuss the characteristics of the audiences for the following kinds of writing:

1. an article about fire hazards to be used in elementary schools
2. an article about a medical breakthrough in a newsmagazine
3. a record review in the school newspaper

Optional Practice

Have students pretend they are writing two letters: one to a good friend their own age and one to a grandparent or aunt or uncle. Instruct the students to write one paragraph from each letter describing their studies and extracurricular activities. Students can then read their paragraphs and discuss the differences in style and content due to the different audiences.

Extending the Lesson

Have students find examples of the same subject matter in writings for different purposes and audiences. The class can then share and discuss their examples. Some possible examples are:

1. an event discussed in an elementary school history book and the same event in a high-school textbook
2. literature about a college for prospective students and literature about the college for alumni

Part 5

A Good Start

Pre-Writing: Creating Good Topic Sentences

Objective

To write a direct and interesting topic sentence for a paragraph

Presenting the Lesson

1. Have students read **Here's the Idea.** Read aloud the sample dull topic sentence and compare it to the two direct, interesting topic sentences. You may write the words *direct, interesting,* and *informative* on the chalkboard to stress these traits of a good topic sentence.

2. Have student volunteers read the sentences in **Check It Out.** Then ask the class to tell whether each one is well written or not. Point out that a well-written topic sentence such as number 4 contains key words—*bizarre* and *fascinating*—that help the writer decide on supporting details for the paragraph.

3. Assign **Try Your Skill.** Call attention to the unnecessary introductory words that make these sentences uninteresting.

4. Read **Keep This in Mind** and then assign **Now Write.** Students may exchange papers to check for unnecessary introductory phrases.

Individualizing the Lesson

Less-Advanced Students

Students may often begin paragraphs with an uninteresting personal statement; help them avoid this by comparing the two topic sentences in each pair below. Which sentence in each pair is more interesting and informative?

Here's the Idea   When you narrowed the topic for your paragraph, you were able to see your subject more clearly. To help your readers see your subject just as clearly, you must write a good topic sentence. The topic sentence states the main idea of your paragraph. It should tell your audience exactly what your paragraph is about.

A topic sentence should be direct and interesting. To make a topic sentence direct, get to the point quickly. Avoid using unnecessary phrases or statements that introduce you as the writer. Such statements make dull topic sentences.

> This paragraph will tell about what subways are like for those of us passengers who ride them regularly.

Notice how direct a good topic sentence is.

1. In 1863, London became the first city to have a subway.
2. Many major cities in the United States have unique subway systems.

These topic sentences are also interesting. A reader will want to know what the first London subway was like. A reader will also want to know what makes some city subway systems unique. In other words, these topic sentences make the reader want to continue reading.

A topic sentence should also be informative. It should give some specific information about a paragraph. Each of the two topic sentences above gives an interesting fact about subways.

Check It Out   Read the following topic sentences.

1. Fire department paramedics often take part in dramatic rescues.

2. My paragraph is going to be about flying saucers.
3. I would like to tell you about a stock car race I saw.
4. Australia is home to many bizarre and fascinating animals.

- Which of these topic sentences are well written? Which are not? Explain your answers.

Try Your Skill   Rewrite these six weak topic sentences. Make each one direct, interesting, and informative. Use real or imaginary details.

1. This paragraph is about movies.
2. I really want to tell you about the poster contest.
3. Now I'll explain surfing.
4. This is my story about Uncle Harry.
5. My paragraph is about a funny mistake.
6. I think I can tell you how to build a box kite.

Keep This in Mind

- A topic sentence states the main idea of a paragraph.
- A well-written topic is direct, interesting, and informative.

Now Write   Think about the topic you chose and narrowed for your paragraph. Write several possible topic sentences that state the main idea of your paragraph. Be sure each sentence is direct, interesting, and informative. Save your topic sentences in your folder.

1. For this assignment I am going to tell how to make guacamole. Guacamole is a Mexican dish that is a simple and nourishing snack.
2. I went to Williamsburg, Virginia, last summer, and this paragraph will describe my trip. Williamsburg, Virginia is a reconstructed town that brings colonial America alive.
3. I read an interesting article about artifical hearts, which I will discuss in this paragraph. Artificial hearts can prolong the lives of some people stricken with serious heart disease.

Advanced Students

Add the following topic sentences to **Try Your Skill.** Answers will vary.

1. I would like to write about my hobby, photographing butterflies.
2. My favorite kind of music is country and western, and this paragraph will tell why.
3. I'm going to try to explain why I like the comic strip *Doonesbury*.

Optional Practice

Have students write an interesting and informative topic sentence for each of the following topics:

1. summer evenings
2. movies for teenagers
3. talking on the telephone

Extending the Lesson

Ask students to bring in several one-paragraph letters to the editor of a local newspaper. Have the students underline the letters' topic sentences and discuss whether they are well written as specified in this lesson.

Objective

To gather details to develop a paragraph

Presenting the Lesson

1. Have students read **Here's the Idea.** Outline on the chalkboard the kinds of details that can be used to develop a paragraph. Then outline the ways to gather details. Emphasize that the kinds of details used depend on the writer's topic and purpose.

2. Ask a student volunteer to read the paragraph in **Check It Out.** Discuss the question that follows, helping students recognize that more than one kind of detail is used to develop the paragraph.

3. Assign **Try Your Skill.**

4. Read **Keep This in Mind.**

5. Assign **Now Write.** Remind students to use descriptive, sensory words if they are developing their paragraphs with sensory details. If facts and statistics are used, students may need to consult reference books in the classroom or in the library.

Individualizing the Lesson

Less-Advanced Students

Work with students individually to help them determine how to develop their paragraphs. Or students can work in pairs to help each other.

Advanced Students

Add the following sentences to **Try Your Skill.** Answers will vary.

1. New Wave is one kind of music that has developed from rock-and-roll.

Building Blocks

Pre-Writing: Developing a Paragraph

Here's the Idea When an architect designs a building, he or she must decide whether to use wood, concrete, bricks, or steel as building material. A good architect will choose materials that suit the type of building he or she is designing.

When you are planning your paragraph, you must decide what kinds of details you will use as the building blocks of your paragraph. The type of details you use will depend on your topic and your purpose.

Sensory details describe the way things look, sound, taste, feel, and smell. Use sensory details when you want to describe someone or something. **Specific examples** are helpful when you want to explain a general idea or statement. **Facts and statistics** are statements and numbers that can be proven true. They can help to make an idea clear or to support an opinion. **Incidents and anecdotes** are very short stories. They serve as examples or illustrations.

There are many ways you can gather details for your paragraph. You can gather details through **observation.** You can find details by **brainstorming** your topic and by doing **research** in books, magazines, and newspapers. You can gather details through **interviewing** and **discussion.** Your **personal experiences** can also be a rich source of detail for your writing.

Check It Out Read the following paragraph.

Second Street was peaceful. There was no traffic at that hour of the morning. Steve stood out in the deserted street looking up at the rows of apartment windows with their shades still drawn. The sky was still dark, but the air was sharp and fresh. Steve began bouncing the basketball he had been carrying. A few minutes later, he heard a shout from an eighth-floor window. "Be right down," Chris hollered.

- Is the topic sentence developed by sensory details, by specific examples, by facts and statistics, or by incidents or anecdotes?

Try Your Skill   What kind of detail is used in each of the following sentences?

1. In 1961, Roger Maris hit 61 home runs, a record that still stands. facts and statistics

2. The strange fruit tasted slightly bitter and tangy, like an unripened grapefruit.   sensory details

3. Seashells have many uses, including jewelry and other decorations. specific examples

Keep This in Mind

- A paragraph can be developed with sensory details, specific examples, facts and statistics, or incidents and anecdotes.
- You can gather details through observation, brainstorming, research, interviewing, discussion, and personal experience.
- The type of details you look for depends on your topic and your purpose.

Now Write   Begin gathering details for your paragraph. First, review your topic and your purpose. Decide what types of details you need to develop your paragraph. Use one or more of the methods described in this lesson to gather those details. Save your pre-writing notes in your folder.

A Sense of Order

Objective

To organize the details in a paragraph

Presenting the Lesson

1. Have the students read **Here's the Idea.** Write on the chalkboard each type of order and the kind of writing in which the order is used. Stress the point that the paragraph's purpose will dictate its organization.

2. Read and discuss **Check It Out.** Help the students recognize that the paragraph's purpose is to narrate events. Ask the students to list the paragraph's transitional words and phrases and tell how they help to make the paragraph coherent.

3. Assign **Try Your Skill.** Advise the students to first write the purpose of each topic.

4. Read **Keep This in Mind** and then assign **Now Write.** Instruct students to first write the purpose of their paragraph at the top of their pre-writing notes.

Individualizing the Lesson

Less-Advanced Students

Help the students make charts that match each type of order with the type of writing it is used for. Instruct the students to keep their charts in their folders for easy reference.

Advanced Students

Add the following topics to **Try Your Skill.**

Pre-Writing: Organizing a Paragraph

Here's the Idea   Your pre-writing notes should include all of the details you want to use in your paragraph. There are several ways to organize details. The method you choose will depend on the type of paragraph you are planning.

If you are telling a story or explaining a process, you will use **chronological order.** This is the order in which events happen or should happen.

When you write a description of someone or something, you will arrange your details in **spatial order.** Spatial order presents details in the order in which the writer wants the reader to notice them.

When you write a paragraph that states an opinion, you should organize your supporting details in the **order of their importance.** This method organizes your details so that the strongest ideas are presented last. This leaves your audience with the most important idea fresh in their minds.

When you write a paragraph that defines something, arrange your details from the **general to the specific.** Begin with details that give a general, familiar definition. Then add more specific details to further develop the definition.

Another way to organize details that define or explain is called **comparison and contrast.** This method allows you to show how things are alike and how they are different.

Check It Out   Read this paragraph.

At seven in the morning the alarm clock clicked—that's all—and Homer McCauley sat up. He adjusted the clock so that the alarm would not go off. He then got out of bed and brought out his body-building course from New York and began reading the instructions for the day. His brother Ulysses watched, as he always did, awakening with Homer at the click just before the alarm, which Homer never allowed to go off. The body-building course from New York consisted of a printed booklet and an elastic stretcher. Homer turned to Lesson 7 while Ulysses crowded his arm to be nearer the mysterious stuff. After some ordinary preliminary exercises, including deep breathing, Homer lay flat on his back and lifted his legs stiffly from the floor.   —WILLIAM SAROYAN

- What is the purpose of this paragraph?
- What kind of organization has the writer used?
- Does the organization suit the purpose? Explain your answer.

Try Your Skill   Here is a list of topics for paragraphs. For each topic, write down the kind of organization that would best fit the topic. Be prepared to explain your choices.

1. how to sew a needlepoint picture
2. how hurricanes differ from tornadoes
3. the view from the north edge of the Grand Canyon
4. a story about the school track meet
5. why we should demand better programs on television

Keep This in Mind

- The details in a paragraph can be arranged in any one of these orders: chronological order, spatial order, the order of importance, general to specific order, and comparison and contrast.
- Choose the method of organization that best suits the purpose of the paragraph you are writing.

Now Write   Take out your pre-writing notes. Organize them according to one of the methods described in this lesson. Be sure to use a method that suits the purpose of your paragraph. Save your organized notes in your folder.

89

general to specific
1. a definition of jealousy
comparison and contrast
2. the differences between theatrical movies and TV movies
spatial order
3. the way your school looks and sounds first thing in the morning

Optional Practice

Have students decide what kind of order is appropriate for the following details for a paragraph. They can number the details to indicate their order.

2 —then I hear children running to buy an ice cream bar

4 —as the sun finally sets, I hear the insects begin their nightly concert

1 —from inside my house I hear the bells of the ice cream truck

3 —later I hear the children groaning as their parents call them in for the night

Extending the Lesson

Divide the class into five groups and assign each group one of the orders studied in this lesson. Give each group two or three magazines and have the students find one or more paragraphs using the order they have been assigned. The students can then share one or two of their paragraphs with the rest of the class.

Objective

To write the first draft of a paragraph

Presenting the Lesson

1. Have students read **Here's the Idea.** Point out how much work has been devoted to the pre-writing stage of the writing process; only after much preparation is it time to write a first draft. Emphasize the fact that this is a *first* draft, helping students feel comfortable with the idea of rewriting a paragraph several times if necessary.

2. Have students read the notes and first draft in **Check It Out.** Discuss the sample writing according to the questions that follow it.

3. Assign **Try Your Skill.** Encourage the class to be imaginative in revising the paragraph.

4. Read **Keep This in Mind.**

5. Assign **Now Write.** Students should find that their pre-writing work has paid off and that the first draft comes easily. Remind students that they should make any changes they like in the material from the pre-writing stage.

Individualizing the Lesson

Less-Advanced Students

Students who have difficulty writing their first drafts may not have done sufficient work in the pre-writing stage. Urge them to go back and fill in the details in their pre-writing notes and then transfer their notes into sentence form as directly as possible. They can then improve their writing in the revision stage.

Free Flowing

Writing the First Draft

Here's the Idea   The second stage of the process of writing is called **writing the first draft.** At this stage of the process, you use your organized pre-writing notes as a plan for your paragraph.

Begin your paragraph with a good topic sentence. Then simply write to get the ideas from your pre-writing notes down on paper. Let your thoughts and ideas flow freely. Don't worry about such mechanical details as spelling and punctuation at this point. You can correct your mistakes later.

Experiment in your first draft. Don't be afraid to add new details. Take out details that don't develop your main idea. You may decide to change some of your ideas. You may discover completely new ideas. Just be sure that any new details or ideas will work well with your topic sentence.

You may also want to change the order of your details. A new way of arranging your ideas may make your paragraph clearer.

The important thing to remember as you write your first draft is that this is just one version of your paragraph. A first draft is not a final copy. You can change your first draft as much as you need to.

Check It Out   Read the following notes and first draft.

Notes: main idea—Times Square on New Year's Eve
  details—people crushed together, shouting and laughing
  —people blowing into plastic horns
  —lots of shops, restaurants
  —neon lights, searchlights
  —everyone caught up in holiday spirit
  —theaters on Broadway

First Draft: Times Square on New Year's Eve is fun. The streets are filled with people dancing and shouting and having fun. Plastic horns make noise and confetti comes down from the windows. Neon lights shine and searchlights are in the skies. Everyone and everything comes to life with the spirit of the holiday.

- How is the first draft different from the pre-writing notes? What ideas were added to the first draft? What ideas were left out?
- What is the topic sentence of this paragraph?

Try Your Skill Rewrite the paragraph in **Check It Out**. Try experimenting with the details and ideas in the paragraph. Invent some details of your own. Improve the word choice. Compare your draft with those of your classmates.

Keep This in Mind

- The first draft is the first written version of your paragraph.
- Use your organized pre-writing notes as a plan for writing your first draft.
- Write to get your ideas down on paper. Let your thoughts and ideas flow freely. Don't be afraid to make changes as you write.

Now Write Take out your topic sentence and organized pre-writing notes. Use them to guide you as you write the first draft of your paragraph. Remember, let your ideas flow freely. Don't worry about mistakes in grammar, capitalization, punctuation, or spelling at this point. When you have finished your first draft, save it in your folder.

Advanced Students

Urge students to review and use the sentence combining skills studied in Writing Section 5 both in completing **Try Your Skill** and in writing the first drafts of their own paragraphs.

Optional Practice

Have students organize the following sample pre-writing notes and use them to write the first draft of a paragraph.

Main Idea: Students should join at least one extracurricular group in high school
Details: School groups need student support
Students can gain experience and widen interest
Colleges look at applicants' extracurricular activities
School clubs are fun

Extending the Lesson

Have students make pre-writing notes on one of the following topics. Then have the students exchange papers and write the first draft of a paragraph based on the notes they have been given. Point out that the ease in writing a first draft depends in large part on the thoroughness of the pre-writing notes. Remind students to organize the notes before they write the first draft.

1. children's belief in Santa Claus
2. the length of professional football and baseball seasons
3. the best way to spend a summer vacation

Objective

To write an effective concluding sentence to end a paragraph

Presenting the Lesson

1. Have the students read **Here's the Idea.** Discuss the idea that every piece of writing should have a beginning, a middle, and an end. The students have so far written a beginning (the topic sentence) and a middle (supporting details). Emphasize the importance of an interesting, definite ending to the students' paragraphs.

2. Have the class read the paragraph in **Check It Out** and discuss its ending sentence. Help the students recognize how the paragraph's conclusion lets the reader know in an interesting way that the paragraph is finished, and does not introduce any new ideas that could leave questions in the reader's mind.

3. Assign **Try Your Skill.** You may want to have students read the paragraphs aloud and discuss why each concluding sentence needs improvement.

4. Read **Keep This in Mind** and the assign **Now Write.** Guide students in writing interesting concluding sentences that do not simply restate the paragraph's topic sentence.

Individualizing the Lesson

Less-Advanced Students

Guide the students in rereading the concluding sentences of the sample paragraphs in this Part. Have the class discuss how each conclusion sums up its paragraph's

---

Top It Off

The First Draft: Ending a Paragraph

Here's the Idea   Have you ever watched a television show and waited for a thrilling ending, only to find that the episode would be continued the next week? It is not a very satisfying experience. That is why you must include a good ending when you write a paragraph.

A good ending sentence is important to a paragraph. It sums up, or ties together, the ideas of the paragraph. It may also explain the importance of the ideas presented.

An ending sentence should not introduce any new information. A good ending makes a clear, final statement that works well with the other sentences in the paragraph. In fact, an ending sentence often restates the idea of the topic sentence in a slightly different way.

A good ending sentence should also be interesting. Whenever you write a paragraph, try to express your idea in an ending sentence that is memorable as well as clear.

Check It Out   Read the following paragraph.

New highway lights, not flying saucers, are responsible for a recent wave of UFO sightings. At about the same time that new highway lights were installed on Route 31 in our town, people began reporting UFO sightings. The highway lights are bright orange disks that light up the night sky in an eerie way. However, when a group of residents studied several photographs taken of these lights, they agreed that the lights resembled the UFO's they had reported. Our town's close encounter turned out to be much closer than we thought.

- Does the ending sentence tie together the ideas of the paragraph?

Try Your Skill Read these three paragraphs with poorly written ending sentences. Then rewrite the endings. Make your endings clear and interesting.

1   We trudged through the swamp, jars held ready. Each time one of us saw a frog or tadpole, a cry went up. Then all of us would come sloshing to where the sighting had been made, ready to lunge with our jars. Usually, we turned around and around without success. *This was the second field trip for our biology class.*

2   Television news coverage is different from newspaper reporting. The best stories for TV news are those having strong visual elements. Such visible events often deal with violence, death, or disaster. Newspapers, on the other hand, rely more on words than on pictures to tell stories. Therefore, newspapers usually have a better balance of stories than television stations do. *It is better to read a newspaper.*

3   Pike, the superintendent in our building, lets me use the tools in his basement workshop. I go down to the basement whenever I have free time. I gather my tools from the pegboard panel on the prickly cement wall behind the workbench. As I cut, sand, and hammer, time passes quickly. I enjoy the whine of the saw and the smell of freshly cut wood. *I can even taste the sawdust in the air.*

> ## Keep This in Mind
>
> • A good ending sentence should sum up the main idea of a paragraph. It should also be interesting.

Now Write Now you are ready to write a strong ending for your own paragraph. Review what you have written. It is a good idea to read your work aloud, at least to yourself. Then write an ending that sums up your idea in an interesting way. Save your paragraph in your folder.

93

main idea. The students may work in pairs to critique their concluding sentences when they have completed **Now Write**.

Advanced Students

Have students write two possible concluding sentences for their paragraphs and meet in pairs to discuss the best ending.

Optional Practice

Distribute this paragraph to students or write it on the chalkboard:

> On the first warm day of spring, people gather to enjoy the weather together. Beaches that have been empty all winter are suddenly jammed with sun-seekers. Newly green parks come alive with children's laughing and shouting. The hum of bikes and roller-skates, and the buzzing of motorcycles invades the quiet landscape.

Ask your students to provide an ending sentence that will tie the paragraph together in an interesting way. Have volunteers read their sentences aloud, and comment on strong sentences.

Extending the Lesson

Find three one-paragraph articles from a magazine or newspaper. Divide the class into three groups and distribute copies of a different paragraph to each group. Have the students work together to write two alternate concluding sentences for their paragraphs. Then each group can read its paragraph and its three endings to the rest of the class. The class can discuss the ending sentences and choose the best one.

Part 10

Objective

To revise the ideas, organization, and word choice in a paragraph

Presenting the Lesson

1. Have the students read **Here's the Idea.** Outline the revision process on the chalkboard as you discuss it. Review the definitions of *unity* and *coherence.* Stress the fact that revision is much more than a correction of grammar and mechanics; in fact, proofreading of punctuation, spelling, etc. is the last step in the revision process.
2. Have the students read and discuss the paragraph in **Check It Out.** Guide the class in recognizing and analyzing the changes in content that the writer has made.
3. Assign **Try Your Skill.** Remind the students that for this exercise they need only make changes in grammar and mechanics.
4. Read **Keep This in Mind** and then assign **Now Write.**

Individualizing the Lesson

Less-Advanced Students

Lead the class in a step-by-step revision of their paragraphs, using the points in **Here's the Idea** as a guide. Help students see that sometimes an entire sentence must be added, omitted, or changed. Also, remind the students to consider their audience and purpose throughout the revision process.

Advanced Students

Collect the paragraphs completed in the **Now Write** activity.

Revising a Paragraph

Here's the Idea   Revising is the last stage in the writing process. When you revise your paragraph, your goal is to improve your writing. Because there are so many things to look for when you revise your paragraph, carefully read over what you have written. Read it more than once.

First, you must read your first draft for content. **Content** refers to the ideas and details you have presented. You want your paragraph to have **unity.** Unity means that all the details and ideas in your paragraph relate to the main idea. Ask yourself these questions as you review the content of your paragraph: Is my topic sentence direct, interesting, and informative? Are all of the details related to the topic? Have I presented enough details to develop my topic fully?

Next, you must review your presentation. **Presentation** refers to the way you have organized your ideas. The presentation of your ideas should have **coherence.** Coherence means that you have arranged your sentences in a logical order. Ask yourself these questions: Do my ideas flow smoothly from one idea to the next? Is my organization clear? Does my method of organization suit the purpose and topic of my paragraph?

Then, read your paragraph aloud for style. **Style** refers to the way you have chosen and presented the words you have used. Make sure that your language is lively and interesting. Replace any dull sentences and phrases that you find. Check to see that your verbs, adjectives, and adverbs are strong and specific. Be sure your language suits your audience.

Finally, you need to proofread your paragraph for errors in grammar and mechanics. *Mechanics* is another way of saying capitalization, punctuation, and spelling.

Check It Out   Read the following revised paragraph.

~~I like~~ the harbor in ~~san~~ Francisco. *has always been a special place for me.* My favorite time to go there is in winter. *The tourists have all gone, and* Nobody is there then. There is a *special* silence to the place. The fog *rolls* ~~comes in.~~ *blanketing* ~~It gets into~~ the coves and valleys. Sometimes the silence is broken by the *shrill cry* ~~call~~ of a seagull, *or* ~~Also,~~ the *distant moan* ~~sound~~ of a foghorn. Yet these sounds add to the peace*fulness* of the scene. ~~Winter is not the same in other places.~~ I can sit on the pier for hours, ~~I~~ think*ing,* and daydream*ing, and letting* The fog*,* covers, me. *wrap me in its cool, grey*

- What kinds of changes has the writer made in the paragraph? Has the writer improved the paragraph?

Try Your Skill   Proofread the following sentences for errors.

1. Ricardo ~~triped~~ *tripped* over a rock and fell into the Street.
2. Nobody ever ~~gone in~~ *went into* that ~~Cemetry~~ *cemetery* after dark.
3. ~~Youv'e~~ *You've,* been gone too long, Bill Bailey!
4. The ~~Solderes~~ *soldiers* told us to wait ~~right~~ here.

Keep This in Mind

- Revise your paragraph for content, presentation, and style. Then proofread it for errors in grammar and mechanics.

Now Write   Revise your paragraph. Follow the guidelines in this lesson. When you are satisfied that your paragraph is the best it can be, make a neat final copy. Save your paragraph in your folder.

Compile these paragraphs into a booklet. Duplicate the booklet and give students time to look it over. Then ask them to point out well-narrowed topics, good topic sentences, especially effective paragraph development, and lively ending sentences.

Optional Practice

Add the following sentences to **Try Your Skill.**

1. Dana's new bedspread was decorated with ~~daisys~~ *daisies* and morning ~~glorys.~~ *glories.*
2. ~~Me and~~ Laura *and I have* ~~had~~ been best friends since kindergarten.
3. I was born in ~~sacramento~~, which is the capitol of ~~california~~.
4. The Statue of Liberty is the most impressive sight I've ever ~~saw~~ *seen*.

Extending the Lesson

The following paragraph lacks unity. Have the students revise it to correct this problem.

It is amazing how a snowstorm can slow down a big city. I like snow, but not when it's April and I'm ready for spring. First of all, snow-covered roads are difficult to drive on, and traffic often comes to a standstill. People who would normally drive to work or school take pubic transportation, so buses and trains are crowded and behind schedule. One January, school was canceled for two days due to snow. And slow transportation delays people's arrival at school or work, delaying people who depend on their presence. Mother Nature can really play tricks on a major city with a few snowflakes!

Section 8 Objectives

1. To understand the three main stages of the writing process: pre-writing, writing the first draft, and revising

2. To understand and correctly use proofreading symbols

Presenting the Section

In Writing Section 7, your students used the process of writing to produce a paragraph. Writing Section 8 presents an overview of the process and gives students a chance to see how one student used the process to write a narrative paragraph about a music competition.

When you discuss pre-writing, be sure the students are familiar with all the activities that are part of this stage of the process of writing: selecting and limiting a topic, considering purpose and audience, gathering ideas and details, and evaluating and organizing information. Refer the students to the illustration of pre-writing notes on page 99.

Also be sure the students know the different methods for gathering ideas and details (brainstorming, observation, and library research) and the different methods of organizing information (chronological order, spatial order, order of importance, comparison and contrast, and general to specific order). Review all of these methods with your students.

Stress the importance of a first draft. Remind students that a first draft is an opportunity to experiment with language and ideas. Be sure that students understand that it is all right to change their ideas and or-

The Process of Writing

ganization during this stage of the process.

Also, stress the importance of revising to your students. Be sure they understand that revising is more than just fixing misspellings or adding missing punctuation. Revising is a chance to improve the entire paragraph or composition, including ideas and organization. Look over the revised paragraph on page 102 with your students. Ask them to tell you how it is different from the first draft on page 100.

You may want to introduce your students to the following techniques for revising their work.

Peer evaluation—In pairs or small groups, students critique each other's writing.

Conference—Oral evaluations by the teacher concentrate on both strengths and problems.

Editorial group—Students assigned the roles of author, editor, and proofreader work together on an assignment.

Group questioning—After one student in a group reads a piece of writing aloud, the other students ask questions focusing on what they still want to know about the subject.

Clinics—In workshops, students with similar writing problems receive instruction from the teacher.

Tutoring—A student who is weak in some area is paired with a student who is stronger in the same area.

Review the proofreading symbols on page 101 with your students. Tell them to use these symbols when they revise their work.

The Process of Writing

From this point on, you will be learning and practicing the skills of writing. You will be writing stories, descriptions, and explanations. As you do so, you will be writing about things that are important to you.

Although there will be a great deal of variety in your writing experiences, one thing will never change. You will always use the **process of writing** to guide your efforts. The process of writing has three stages: **pre-writing, writing the first draft,** and **revising.** As you work your way through these you will discover that good writing doesn't just happen. It is the result of careful planning and thoughtful work.

Pre-Writing What do you do when you're given a writing assignment? If you are like many students, you probably take out a sheet of paper and write your name at the top. Then you rest your chin on your hand, stare off into space, and try to think of some ideas. Sometimes the ideas come. Sometimes they don't. When the ideas don't come, writing can become a frustrating experience.

You can avoid this frustration by doing some planning before you start to write. This planning is called pre-writing. Pre-writing is the first stage of the process of writing.

Unless you've been assigned a topic, your planning should start with choosing something to write about. Always select subjects that you find interesting. Also, choose subjects that you know something about. Experienced writers agree that familiar things are the easiest to write about.

You can find subjects to write about in a number of ways. You can try brainstorming and interviewing. Reading books, magazines, and newspapers is another way to get writing ideas. Your journal is also a source of stories, opinions, and observations. Discussions with your classmates can help, too.

When you've chosen a subject, focus it. Narrow the subject so that you can cover it in a paragraph or short composition.

Next, consider your purpose for writing about your subject. Do you want to inform, persuade, or entertain your readers? Think about your audience, too. How old are your readers? What are their interests and opinions?

Now you are ready to gather details. These details might include sensory details, specific examples, facts and statistics, or incidents or anecdotes. You can gather these details through observation, brainstorming, research, and interviewing.

The final pre-writing step is to organize the details you have gathered. Be sure to choose an order that suits the type of writing you are doing. You might use chronological order, spatial order, the order of importance, general to specific order, or comparison and contrast.

Use of Writing Folders

Throughout this series, students are asked to keep their independent **Now Write** assignments in folders. Depending on your school's policy, you may issue these folders to students or ask them to purchase their own. Both you and your students need to keep track of writing assignments in separate writing folders for reasons that are as practical as they are educationally sound:

1. Students should be encouraged to write in the classroom and to keep assignments there.

2. Both you and your students need a permanent record of assignments completed. Assignments can be compared in order to see measurable progress, and in order to determine grades.

3. As students see a growing body of material that reflects their own ideas and interests, writing folders become special, personal collections. In this way, writing becomes a more positive experience.

Pre-Writing

the Bruins game
spraining my ankle
moving to Denver

my job interview
the music competition

① City School of Music
H2 contestants
six-string guitar
scholarship money
audition panic
⑤ five years of practice
② Ms. O'Brien, teacher

dark auditorium
④ fingers numb
rehearse chords
③ pacing, waiting
⑥ alone on stage
⑦ a dream—I won!

Writing the First Draft As you write your first draft, concentrate on turning your details into sentences and your sentences into paragraphs. Use your organized pre-writing notes as a writing plan. Don't worry about the mechanics of writing.

Writing the First Draft

You write a paragraph about your topic.

It was the day of my audition for a scholarship to the city school of music. Ms. O'Brien, my music teacher, had finally persuaded me to enter the competition. I tried real hard to relax. As I paced backstage, I moved my numb fingers a lot. I had spent about five years preparing for this moment. I had practiced for so long. Finally my turn came, I sat alone on the empty stage. The stage was quite large. I forced myself to concentrate only on the music I was playing. When the scholarship winners were announced, my name was announced. I was very happy as you can imagine. What a day! Now it was over.

Revising   The third and final stage of the process of writing is called revising. Revising is the key to good writing. During this stage of the process you must work carefully and thoughtfully. Look closely at what you have written. Do you like it? Is it interesting? As you read over your first draft, ask these questions.

1. Does each paragraph I've written have a good topic sentence? Is the topic sentence direct, informative, and interesting?

2. Have I included enough details to develop my topic?

3. Have I arranged my details in a logical order? Does the order suit the kind of writing I am doing?

4. Have I used lively, vivid language?

5. Is my language well suited to my audience?

6. Have I written a good ending? Does it bring my writing to a satisfactory conclusion?

7. Have I fulfilled my purpose for writing?

Proofreading   The last step in revising is called proofreading. Read your first draft carefully. Find and correct any errors you made in grammar, capitalization, punctuation, and spelling. As you revise your first draft, use the following proofreading marks to show your corrections and changes.

Proofreading Symbols

Symbol	Meaning	Example
∧	add	would ∧ gone *(have)*
≡	capitalize	United states
/	make lower case	our club President
∾	reverse	thier
℘	take out	finished the the race
¶	make new paragraph	....be over. ¶New ideas
⊙	period	....and stop⊙Before we
∧	add comma	Red, blue ∧and green are

Notice how the paragraph has been revised.

Revising

~~It was the day~~ *Friday, May 20th, turned out to be one of the happiest days of my life.* of my audition for a scholarship to the city school of music. Ms. O'Brien, my music teacher, had finally persuaded me to *test my talent in* ~~enter the~~ *this citywide* competition. *took deep breaths, trying* ~~I tried real hard to relax.~~ As I paced *nervously* backstage, I *flexed* ~~moved~~ my *cold, stiff* ~~numb~~ fingers a lot. I had spent about five years preparing for this moment. I had practiced *several hours each day* ~~for so long~~. Finally, my turn came. I sat alone on the empty stage. ~~The stage was quite large.~~ I forced myself to concentrate only on the music I was playing. *Hours later,* When the scholarship winners were announced, my name was *among them* ~~announced~~. *No music has ever sounded so sweet.* ~~I was very happy as you can imagine.~~ What a day! ~~Now it was over.~~

Making the Final Copy Finally, when you are satisfied that your writing is clear and correct, write it in its final form. Write carefully. Make your work as neat as possible.

When you have finished your final copy, proofread your work one last time. Neatly correct any errors you find.

Final Copy

> Friday, May 20th, turned out to be one of the happiest days of my life. It was the day of my audition for a scholarship to the city school of music. Ms O'Brien, my music teacher, had finally persuaded me to test my talent in this citywide competition. As I paced nervously backstage, I flexed my cold, stiff fingers. I took deep breaths, trying to relax. I had spent five years preparing for this moment. I had practiced several hours each day. Finally, my turn came. I sat alone on the empty stage. I forced myself to concentrate only on the music I was playing. Hours later, when the scholarship winners were announced, my name was among them. No music has ever sounded so sweet.

Now you are ready to begin your writing adventures. Whenever and whatever you write, follow all the stages of the process of writing. Each time you write, you will be learning something about writing and about yourself.

Section 9 Objectives

1. To select and limit a topic and to select details for a narrative paragraph

2. To use chronological order to organize a narrative paragraph

3. To understand three points of view in narrative writing: first-person, third-person limited, and third-person omniscient

4. To use appropriate transitions in writing the first draft of a narrative paragraph

5. To revise a narrative paragraph by checking for specific details, chronological order, consistent point of view, and clear transitions

Preparing the Students

Have two or three students briefly tell what happened in a movie or television show they have seen recently. Explain that these are narratives told in chronological order and that this Section will teach them how to write a clear, interesting narrative paragraph.

Additional Resources

Mastery Test — page 23 in the test booklet

Practice Book — pages 42–46

Duplicating Masters — pages 42–46

The Narrative Paragraph

Teaching Special Populations

LD See **Teaching Special Populations,** page 75.

ESL ESL students may have trouble with transitional words and phrases related to time. Prepare additional exercises to emphasize these words and phrases. Also present additional point of view exercises in which students must change first-person constructions to third-person, and vice versa. Stress the change of form in third-person singular present tense verbs.

Encourage students to write narratives based on their personal experiences.

NSD See **Teaching Special Populations,** page 75. Have students check their paragraphs carefully for pronoun agreement. Have them underline each pronoun in their first drafts, and then identify each antecedent.

Objective

To select and limit a topic and to select details for a narrative paragraph

Presenting the Lesson

1. Have students read **Here's the Idea.** Make sure they understand that a narrative paragraph tells a story and that it uses specific events and details to answer the questions *who, what, when, where, why,* and *how.* Note the details about a roller coaster ride in paragraphs 4 and 5.

2. Read **Check It Out,** asking students to name the sensory details included in the pre-writing notes.

3. Assign **Try Your Skill.** Encourage students to include sensory details in their pre-writing notes, as in **Check It Out.**

4. Read **Keep This in Mind.**

5. Assign **Now Write.** Suggest the following general topic for a narrative paragraph: a funny, exciting, embarrassing, or frightening experience. You might stimulate a pre-writing discussion by telling of an experience you have had and ask students to do the same.

Individualizing the Lesson

Less-Advanced Students

When assigning **Now Write,** tell students to write at least one sensory detail for each question about their topic. Remind them that they need not use every detail when they write their first draft.

Tell a Tale

Pre-Writing: The Narrative Paragraph

Here's the Idea   The next four writing sections will teach you how to write different kinds of paragraphs. As you study each type of paragraph, notice that the process of writing is always the same. However, each type of paragraph is developed and organized differently. In this section, you will learn how to develop and organize a **narrative paragraph.**

A narrative tells a story. When you write about an experience at the state fair or your first trip in an airplane, you are writing a narrative. A narrative does not have to be a true story. For example, Rudyard Kipling wrote about a mongoose called Rikki Tikki Tavi, who saves his human and animal friends by slaying two evil cobras. Kipling's story is an imaginary narrative.

When you choose a topic for your narrative paragraph, select a story you can tell well in this length. To help you limit your story, ask questions about it. Ask *who? what? when? where? why?* and *how?* The answers you get will give you the details you need to zero-in on your topic.

After you have selected and limited your topic, think about it. How will you develop your story? Any story, even one brief enough to be told in a single paragraph, is made up of many small incidents or events. Suppose you decided to write about your first ride on a roller coaster. This story would be made up of many events. First, you buy your ticket. Then you wait in line. Finally, it's your turn. You board the roller coaster. These are the kinds of specific details that will help you to tell your story.

A good story also contains sensory details. There are screams as the roller coaster descends. There are the colored lights that decorate the amusement park. There is the smell of popcorn and hot dogs. Details will bring your narrative to life.

Check It Out   Here are some pre-writing notes for a narrative paragraph.

Who?   my brother Jack
What?   found a corked bottle—message inside—bottle was light green.
When?   last summer—hot day in July
Where?   Near Charleston, S.C.
How?   He was swimming—surf crashing on the beach
Result?   He has a new friend in Providence, R.I.

- Do you see how asking questions about a topic can make that topic more specific?

Try Your Skill   Imagine that the following entry is from your journal. Ask questions about it as the writer did in **Check It Out.** Use your personal experience as a guide, or invent some details. Make a list of pre-writing notes for a narrative paragraph based on this journal entry. Your notes can be for a real or an imaginary narrative.

Today I lost my best friend for the worst reason.

Keep This in Mind

- A narrative paragraph tells a brief story. It can be a true story or an imaginary one.
- Zero-in on your topic by asking the questions *who? what? when? where? why?* and *how?*
- Develop your narrative paragraph by using specific and sensory details.

Now Write   Refer to your journal, your memory, or another source to find an interesting topic for a narrative paragraph. In a few words, write down the topic. Then write questions and answers that will help to limit your topic. Gather specific and sensory details to develop your story. Save your notes.

Advanced Students

For **Try Your Skill,** have students write a second set of pre-writing notes, using the following imaginary journal entry.

Redecorating my bedroom turned into a minor disaster.

Optional Practice

Distribute this paragraph and read it aloud to your students:

Across the sky, very high and beautiful, a rocket burned on a sweep of orange fire. It circled and came down, causing all to gasp. It landed, setting the meadow afire here and there. The fire burned out, the rocket lay a moment in quiet, and then, as the silent crowd watched, a great door in the side of the vessel whispered out a breath of oxygen. The door slid back, and an old man stepped out.

—RAY BRADBURY

Ask students if the six questions are answered in this paragraph and how they are answered. Within the paragraph have them underline details that they think are especially vivid. Let students discuss their responses.

Extending the Lesson

Have students look at copies of your school newspaper. You can probably obtain old copies from the journalism teacher at your school. Have each student take a different news article and see if the first paragraph answers all six questions. Point out that good news articles usually answer *who, what, when, where, how,* and *why* early in the story. Ask students to share their conclusions with the rest of the class.

Part 2

Objective

To use chronological order to organize a narrative paragraph

Presenting the Lesson

1. Read aloud **Here's the Idea.** Write the word *chronological,* along with its definition, on the chalkboard. Read the paragraph by Frank Bonham and point out the step-by-step order of the narrative. Have students note the sensory details, particularly in the first sentence.

2. Read and discuss the paragraph in **Check It Out.** Help the class see that the first three sentences briefly provide background information and then the events are narrated in time order.

3. Read aloud the directions for **Try Your Skill.** Have students complete this assignment and compare answers. Ask one student to read the events in chronological order.

4. Read **Keep This in Mind** and then assign **Now Write.** Instruct students to provide brief background details if necessary as in the paragraph in **Check It Out.**

Individualizing the Lesson

Less-Advanced Students

Discuss in detail the confusing paragraph in **Here's the Idea.** Explain that although people sometimes tell a story in this manner when speaking, faulty chronological order can be easily corrected in the pre-writing stage.

Pre-Writing: Using Chronological Order

Here's the Idea   Have you ever heard someone tell a story like this?

> John was coming down the beach and it looked like he was mad. So I . . . wait a minute, before I saw John, I was talking to Greg and John saw us. Anyway, John was walking toward me and . . . oops, I forgot, I was supposed to call John before I left for the beach, but I was in a hurry so I just left. Anyway, John is coming down the beach. . . .

Stories like this are confusing. The events are all mixed up. To make sure your story is clear, you must organize your details in the order that they actually happened. This type of arrangement is called **chronological order.** *Chronological* means "arranged in the order of time."

Read this narrative paragraph. Notice that the events are arranged in chronological order.

> The sun woke them early, bursting in glory over the mountains behind the canyon. They ate breakfast, then they spent an hour hunting more ladybug colonies. They realized at last how lucky they had been to find the one they did. All their searching turned up only a few more small clusters. Uncle Baron let them play for an hour. Then everything was loaded into the bus; the trash was burned in the fire ring, and the embers were doused with water. They headed back down Sierra Molina Canyon.
>
> —FRANK BONHAM

Check It Out   Read this narrative paragraph. It is based on an actual event in someone's life.

> My fourteenth summer was the worst one of my life. It began with a family weekend vacation to Starved Rock State Park. My

cousin Gary isn't afraid of anything. While the rest of us hiked the wooded trails, he explored the cliffs and ravines above the river. As I watched, he scrambled down a steep cliff. When he reached the bottom, he yelled at me to follow. I said no, but he kept calling me chicken. So I started down. I slipped and slid on leaves, and soon I was crashing downhill, out of control. Suddenly I tripped over a tree root and fell. That's how I got to spend a month in traction in the hospital and the rest of the summer in a body cast. What a lousy summer vacation!

- Are the events of this narrative arranged in chronological order? Explain your answer.

Try Your Skill Below is a list of events for a narrative paragraph. As you read them, you will notice that they are not in chronological order. On your paper, write the events in chronological order.

3 (a) The newspaper published my letter.
4 (b) My state congresswoman phoned to say that she had read my letter and would do what she could to save the trees.
2 (c) I wrote a letter of complaint to the editor of the newspaper.
1 (d) I read in the local newspaper that the city planned to cut down the trees along our street.
5 (e) So far, the trees are still standing.

Keep This in Mind

- Organize the events of a narrative paragraph in chronological order.

Now Write Take out the pre-writing notes you wrote in the last lesson. Arrange the notes in chronological order. You may want to add some additional details to your notes. Save the notes in your folder.

Advanced Students

Discuss the use of flashbacks in longer narratives. Explain that an event from the past may temporarily interrupt the chronological flow but that the event flashed back to is itself narrated in chronological order.

Optional Practice

Divide the class into groups of three. Have the groups put these sentences in chronological order and then write a strong opening sentence for the paragraph:

4 Although we searched the apartment and the entire neighborhood, we couldn't find Waffles, so we had to leave without him.

2 Then we labeled each carton.

6 To our surprise, from out of the carton marked *food* jumped Waffles.

5 When we arrived at our new apartment, we unpacked the cartons.

1 On moving day we packed all of our belongings into huge cartons.

3 After we had loaded all the cartons onto the van, we noticed that our dog Waffles was missing.

When the groups have finished, ask one student to read the sentences in chronological order. Ask for volunteers to read sample opening sentences.

Extending the Lesson

Have students write a narrative summary of a movie they have seen recently. Students can then exchange papers to check for clear chronological order.

Part **3**

Objective

To understand three points of view in narrative writing: first-person, third-person limited, and third-person omniscient

Presenting the Lesson

1. Have students read **Here's the Idea.** Then write the name of each point of view on the chalkboard, emphasizing the pronouns used in each. Explain to students that the third-person limited point of view is their usual stance as they observe the actions of those around them. To use the third-person omniscient point of view, writers must imaginatively project themselves into the minds and emotions of others.

2. Read Toni Cade Bambara's paragraph in **Check It Out.** Students should quickly recognize the first-person point of view by the use of the pronoun *I.*

3. Assign **Try Your Skill.** Guide the students in changing the paragraph's point of view: for first-person they must narrate from one character's viewpoint, using the pronoun *I;* for third-person omniscient they must imagine what each character thinks and feels as he or she performs the narrated action.

4. Read **Keep This in Mind.**

5. Assign **Now Write.** Remind students that the most effective point of view depends on the particular story they are telling.

Who Says?

Pre-Writing: Choosing a Point of View

Here's the Idea   Every story has a storyteller. The storyteller is called the **narrator.** You can choose the person who will tell your story. Do you want to be the narrator yourself? Do you want the narrator to be a character in the story? Do you want the narrator to be an outsider? All of these are possibilities.

When you choose a narrator, you are also choosing a point of view. **Point of view** means the eyes and mind through which something is written. There are several types of point of view.

One type of point of view is called the **first-person point of view.** When you choose this point of view, the narrator is identified by the first-person pronoun *I. I* tells what he or she sees and hears. *I* can also tell what he or she is thinking. However, *I* cannot tell what anyone else in the story is thinking.

A second type of point of view is called **third-person point of view.** The third-person pronouns *he* and *she* are used. The narrator is not a character in the story. He or she is an outsider. This narrator can tell everything that the characters say and do. Because this narrator cannot report what other characters are thinking or feeling, this point of view is called **third-person limited.**

If you want to tell what the characters in a story are thinking or feeling as well as what they are saying or doing, you should use the **third-person omniscient point of view.** *Omniscient* means "all knowing." This point of view allows the reader to see into the hearts and minds of the characters.

Decide which type of narrator can best tell your story. The first-person narrator is more personal than a third-person narrator. However, using a third-person narrator, especially an omniscient one, allows you to tell more about your characters. Whichever type of narrator you choose, be consistent. Do not switch from one point of view to another in your paragraph.

Check It Out   Read this paragraph.

I don't have much work to do around the house like some girls. My mother does that. I don't have to earn my pocket money. George runs errands for the big boys and sells Christmas cards. Anything else that's got to get done, my father does. All I have to do in life is mind my brother Raymond, which is enough. —TONI CADE BAMBARA

- Which point of view is used in this narrative? first-person

Try Your Skill   The following paragraph is written from a third-person limited point of view. Change the point of view to either third-person omniscient or first-person.

The kitchen was warm now. A fire was roaring in the stove. Arnold's mother was spooning eggs from a pot of boiling water and putting them into a bowl. His sister Nora was lifting a frying pan full of trout from the stove. His father had just come in from bringing the cows from the north pasture to the barn. He was sitting on the stool, unbuttoning his plaid jacket.

—GINA BERRIAULT

Keep This in Mind

- Point of view shows through whose eyes a story is told. With the first-person point of view, the narrator, *I*, reports what the characters say and do.
- With the third-person limited point of view, the narrator reports what the characters say and do, but not what they think or feel.
- With the third-person omniscient point of view, the narrator is "all-knowing." The narrator reports what the characters say, do, think, and feel.

Now Write   Choose a point of view for your narrative paragraph. Write *first-person*, *third-person limited*, or *third-person omniscient* on your pre-writing notes. Save your notes.

111

Less-Advanced Students

Have students identify the point of view used in each sentence below.

third-person ominiscient
1. The dance number went smoothly; Jill felt more confident with each step, and Maria was thrilled at performing for an audience.

first-person
2. I performed my first dance number, stricken with stage fright at first but more confident as I sensed the audience's enjoyment.

third-person limited
3. The two girls danced as gracefully as birds on the dimly lighted stage.

Advanced Students

Before deciding on a point of view for their narratives, students should write three preliminary topic sentences, each using a different point of view.

Optional Practice

Have students write two different topic sentences—one from the first-person point of view and one from the third-person limited or third-person omniscient point of view—for each of the following narrative topics:

1. playing a chess game
2. watching a World Series baseball game
3. learning to ice skate

Extending the Lesson

Have the class find short stories written from the three different points of view studied in this lesson. You may want to divide the class into three groups and assign one point of view to each group. A spokesperson for each group can then read a paragraph or two from the chosen short story.

Objective

To use appropriate transitions in writing the first draft of a narrative paragraph

Presenting the Lesson

1. Read aloud **Here's the Idea.** Emphasize the definition of *transitions.* Have students copy the list of transitions to keep in their folders for referral. They may label their papers *Transitions in a Narrative.*

2. Read aloud and discuss **Check It Out.** Emphasize that the function of transitions in a narrative is to show chronological order. As students find transitions, list them on the chalkboard. Point out that Woody Guthrie used his different ages to show the passing of time.

3. Assign and discuss **Try Your Skill.** Remind students to choose a variety of transitions. After students finish rewriting the paragraph, ask them to share their revisions with others. If students chose different periods of time, comment on the options that writers have.

4. Read **Keep This in Mind** and then assign **Now Write.** Refer students to the list of transitions on page 112 as well as Section 8, **The Process of Writing.**

Individualizing the Lesson

Less-Advanced Students

Instruct students to use at least four different transitions from the list on page 112 in writing the first draft of their narrative paragraph. Also ask students to underline each transitional word or phrase.

Time Will Tell

Writing the First Draft

Here's the Idea You have finished your pre-writing notes for your narrative paragraph. You have a list of details organized in chronological order. You also have selected a point of view. Now you are ready to write your first draft. As you start to tell your story, think about how you can make the order of events clear to the reader.

Words and phrases that can help you to make chronological order clear are called **transitions.** Using transitions will also allow you to show how much time has passed between events. Study this list of transitions.

first	now	when	at the same time
then	before	soon	by the time
next	earlier	suddenly	at the beginning
while	after	immediately	in the middle
last	later	finally	at the end

This list shows some of the most common transitional words and phrases. There are many others you may want to use, such as *for a few minutes, at noon, tomorrow, in June,* or *by next year.*

Check It Out Read this narrative paragraph.

I was thirteen when I went to live with a family of thirteen people in a two-room house. I was going on fifteen when I got a job shining shoes, meeting the night trains in a hotel up in town. I was a little past sixteen when I first hit the highway and took a trip down around the Gulf of Mexico. I spent my time picking grapes, helping carpenters and well drillers, cleaning yards, chopping weeds, and moving garbage cans. Then I got tired of being a stranger. I stuck my thumb in the air again and landed back in my old home town.—WOODY GUTHRIE

- Point out the transitions. Do they help to make the order of events clear?

Try Your Skill Read the following paragraph. Is the subject an illness that lasted for months, for a few days, or for a single day? Without transitions, you cannot tell. Rewrite the paragraph. Add transitional words and phrases to show a clear order of time.

I felt really bad. I could hardly lift my head off the pillow. I felt better. I could eat a little. I felt terrific and ready for action.

Keep This in Mind

- Transitional words and phrases make the order of events clear.
- In a narrative, use transitional words and phrases to show chronological order.

Now Write Write the first draft of your narrative paragraph. Use your organized pre-writing notes as a guide while you write. Use transitional words and phrases to make the order of events clear. Save your first draft in your folder.

Advanced Students

After students have completed their first drafts, have them exchange papers and check for transitions that clarify and emphasize chronological order.

Optional Practice

Have students revise the following paragraph to show a clear time order, using a variety of transitional words and phrases. Answers will vary.

I was taught always to use my seat belt when riding in a car. I used my seat belt all the time. I got careless and stopped using my seat belt on short trips. My brother and I were driving home from the grocery store. Another motorist ran a stop sign and hit our car. I suffered a broken arm and couldn't play baseball for six weeks. I always wear my seat belt when riding in an automobile.

Extending the Lesson

Stage an event in your classroom that your students can report in the form of a narrative paragraph. For example, have a fellow teacher or a student from another class enter your classroom, shake hands with you, write on the chalkboard, and remove your chair from the room. Afterward, ask your students to write one paragraph telling what happened by using specific details and effective transitions. Have volunteers read their paragraphs aloud. Comment on good details and transitions.

Part 5

Objective

To revise a narrative paragraph by checking for specific details, chronological order, consistent point of view, and clear transitions

Presenting the Lesson

1. Have students read **Here's the Idea.** Outline on the chalkboard the four main points to check for in revising a narrative paragraph. Discuss using strong verbs and avoiding the overuse of the verb *to be.* Explain that a descriptive verb such as *chatter* takes the place of a weaker verb + adjective.

2. Read the paragraph in **Check It Out.** Help the class recognize that verbs like *jumped, strode, dropped,* and *gesturing* help the reader more clearly appreciate the sense of the narrated experience.

3. Assign **Try Your Skill.** After students have completed the exercise, you might compile on the chalkboard a list of the class's strong, vivid verbs.

4. Read **Keep This in Mind.**

5. Assign **Now Write.** Instruct students to proofread only after they have revised their paragraph according to the questions in **Here's the Idea.**

Individualizing the Lesson

Less-Advanced Students

Lead the class through a step-by-step revision of their paragraphs. Read each question in **Here's the Idea,** pausing to allow students to

114

Replay

Revising Your Narrative Paragraph

Here's the Idea   After you have written the first draft of your narrative paragraph, set it aside for a while. Then return to it with a fresh eye for how it can be improved. You may want to revise the ideas, the organization, and the language. As you revise your paragraph, ask yourself these questions:

1. Have I developed my narrative with specific details?
2. Are my events and details presented in chronological order?
3. Did I stick with just one point of view?
4. Have I used transitional words and phrases to make the order of events clear?

As you revise your paragraph, pay special attention to the language you have used, especially your choice of verbs. Try to avoid using too many state-of-being verbs like *is*, *seems*, or *become*. They are weak. Use strong verbs like *races*, *sings*, or *bakes*. For example, "He races sports cars" is a stronger sentence than "He is a sports car racer."

Also, try to replace general verbs with specific verbs. For example, what specific verbs could you substitute for the general verb *walk?* You could say *sauntered*, *shuffled*, *strolled*, or *paced*, to name just a few. As a writer, you must decide which verb best expresses the action you are describing.

When you finish revising the ideas, organization, and word choice in your paragraph, proofread it. Correct any errors in grammar, capitalization, punctuation, and spelling.

Check It Out   Read the following paragraph from a narrative.

Blajeny jumped lightly down from the rock. Despite his height and girth he moved, Meg thought, as though he were

114

used to heavier gravity than earth's. He strode lightly halfway across the pasture to where there was a large, flat rock where the children often went with their parents to watch the stars. He dropped down onto the rock and lay stretched out on his back, gesturing to the others to join him.

—MADELEINE L'ENGLE

- What specific verbs does this paragraph contain?
- How do the verbs help to make the narrative more exciting?

Try Your Skill   Each of the following sentences contains a general verb and a modifier in italics. Revise each sentence by replacing the general verb and modifier with one vivid, specific verb. Compare your revised sentences with those of your classmates.

1. Rich *talked excitedly* about his trip down the Mississippi.
2. The detective *wrote quickly* in her notebook.
3. An old man *walked slowly* through the park.
4. Marta *quickly drank* the cool spring water.
5. A mouse *moved suddenly* across the kitchen floor.

Keep This in Mind

- Revise your narrative paragraph to make it livelier and more interesting.
- Include enough specific details to tell the story well.
- Use the same point of view throughout the story.
- Use clear chronological order and good transitions.

Now Write   Revise your own narrative paragraph. Proofread it, then make a final copy. Save your completed paragraph in your folder.

check their drafts for the appropriate points. Also have students underline each verb and replace it with a stronger verb if necessary.

Advanced Students

Discuss using a thesaurus to find vivid verbs for narratives. Explain that after finding a synonym in a thesaurus, students should look the new word up in a dictionary to be sure of its exact definition. Have students use a thesaurus in revising their narrative paragraphs.

Optional Practice

Have students think of a strong, descriptive verb that can be used in place of each of the following common verbs. Students can then use each vivid verb in a sentence.

1. eat
2. talk
3. work
4. defeat
5. run

Extending the Lesson

Ask students to observe a sports event, write and organize some prewriting notes, and then write a narrative paragraph summarizing the game or meet. Remind them to include vivid details, to use clear transitions, and to revise their first draft according to the questions in this lesson.

Section **10** Objectives

1. To gather sensory details to develop a descriptive paragraph

2. To use spatial order to organize a descriptive paragraph

3. To use language to create a specific mood in a descriptive paragraph

4. To use transitions in the first draft of a descriptive paragraph to indicate spatial order

5. To revise a descriptive paragraph by checking for vivid sensory details, spatial order, effective transitions, and language that creates a specific mood

Preparing the Students

Ask your class to tell you what they know about descriptive paragraphs. Then read the following selection aloud.

> He opened his eyes again many hours later because he was cold. His head ached and he shivered. The lamp still burned, but its light seemed to have paled. He looked around the room and saw that a hesitant daylight was filtering through the curtains. The room, with the window shut and the lamp burning, was very stuffy. He crawled out of the chair, yawning, and went on unsteady legs to the window. Pulling back the curtains he flung it open. The day had come. A white, shadowless light showed an empty street, blank windows, and shut doors.
> —JOAN PHIPSON

Ask students how this person must have felt. Also ask them how they felt as they heard the passage. Ask what details account for these feelings. Tell your students that descriptions such as this one by Joan Phipson arouse images and feelings. Note that Section 10 will show

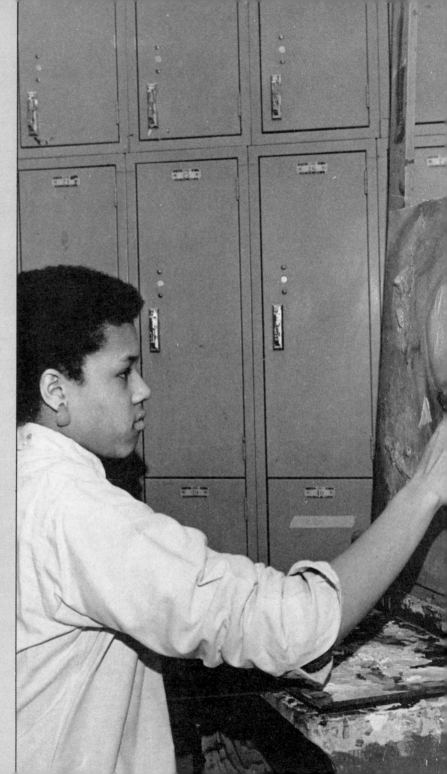

The Descriptive Paragraph

them how to write good descriptive paragraphs.

Additional Resources

Mastery Test — page 24 in the test booklet

Practice Book — pages 47–51

Duplicating Masters — pages 47–51

Teaching Special Populations

LD See **Teaching Special Populations,** page 75. Provide additional exercises in using words that indicate spatial order.

ESL Students will have to increase their vocabularies to write effective descriptive paragraphs. Discuss sensory vocabulary in detail. Provide specific examples of textures, smells, sounds, and foods.

Discuss with students the ways different cultures classify experiences. For example, people in warm climates have few words for *snow* while others in colder areas have many.

Prepare additional exercises that use words that indicate spatial order. Reinforce these exercises by having students describe rooms or scenes in photographs or posters.

NSD See **Teaching Special Populations,** page 75. Remind students to avoid slang in their descriptions.

Objective

To gather sensory details to develop a descriptive paragraph

Presenting the Lesson

1. Before you read aloud **Here's
the Idea,** review the vocabulary of
the senses on pages 18–19. Explain
that sensory details describe specific sights, sounds, textures, tastes,
and smells. Encourage students to
be aware of all their senses when
they experience something.

2. Read **Check It Out.** Then pair off
students to list the sensory details
and write which senses each detail
appeals to.

3. Assign and discuss **Try Your
Skill.** You might allow students to
describe a different place. Have volunteers read their lists of details.

4. Read **Keep This in Mind.**

5. Assign **Now Write.** After reading
the instructions aloud, suggest some
possible topics: a family member, a
teacher, a place where they work,
an art object, or a favorite park.

Individualizing the Lesson

Less-Advanced Students

Have students look up the pronunciation and definition of each of
the following words from the descriptive paragraph in **Check It Out:**
trench, rhododendrons, suffocated,
and *acrid.*

Advanced Students

Have students list the active
verbs in the paragraph in **Check It
Out.** Discuss with the class how
verbs such as *gurgled* and *suffo-*

Common Senses

Pre-Writing: Gathering Sensory Details

Here's the Idea   A descriptive paragraph uses words to
create a picture in the reader's mind. The purpose of a descriptive paragraph is to describe a person, place, or thing as clearly
as possible. That way the reader will feel that he or she has
"been there," too.

The best way to develop a descriptive paragraph is to use
sensory details. Sensory details describe things that can be *seen,
heard, felt, smelled,* or *tasted.* If you want to use good sensory
details in your description, you must learn to observe things
carefully.

Suppose you want to describe a dentist's office. As you look
around, you would make some pre-writing notes. What do you
see when you enter the office? You might notice the plush
waiting room furniture, the shining metal dental equipment,
and the space-age dental chair. What sounds do you *hear?* Is
there music in the background? What does the drill sound like?
How does the office *smell?* Does it smell like antiseptic? Is your
sense of *taste* awakened? What does the tooth polish taste like?
Do the examining tools have a taste? What does it *feel* like to sit
in the dentist's chair? How do the instruments feel on your
teeth? Details like these can make your readers feel that they,
too, have been in that office.

You may also use your memory to recall sensory details. Try
to picture the person, place, or thing that you want to describe.
Jot down as many sensory details about your subject as you can
remember.

Check It Out   Read the following descriptive paragraph.

The fire crackled musically. From it swelled light smoke. Overhead the foliage moved softly. The leaves, with their faces turned toward the blaze, were colored shifting hues of silver, often edged with red. Far off to the right, through a window in the forest, could be seen a handful of stars lying, like glittering pebbles, on the black level of the night.   —STEPHEN CRANE

- What sensory details does this description use?

Try Your Skill   Choose two of the following places to describe. List sensory details about each place. Try to use all of your senses. Refer to pages 18–19 for a list of words appealing to the different senses.

a restaurant	a gas station	a subway station
a museum	a park	a doughnut shop

Keep This in Mind

- Use sensory details to create a vivid description.
- Gather sensory details through observation or from memory.

Now Write   Choose a person, place, or object to describe. Observe your subject carefully. Make a list of sensory details to describe it. You may also want to gather details from your memory. Save your pre-writing notes in your folder.

cated appeal to the reader's senses.

Optional Practice

Have students list sensory details for two of the following objects. Instruct students to try to use all the senses.

a horse	a peach
a rose bush	a sweater
the inside of a refrigerator	a new pair of shoes

Extending the Lesson

Have each student bring a small object such as a marble, a coin, or an apple to class. Students can then exchange objects and list sensory details to describe them, using as many senses as possible.

Objective

To use spatial order to organize a descriptive paragraph

Presenting the Lesson

1. Discuss **Here's the Idea.** Review the definition of *chronological order* and define *spatial order*. Read and discuss the example of spatial order in describing a fish market.
2. Read **Check It Out.** Help students recognize that the description moves from bottom to top and that it emphasizes the man's face and hair because these are described last.
3. Read and assign **Try Your Skill.** Emphasize that a logical and effective order depends on the particular house being described.
4. Read **Keep This in Mind.**
5. Assign **Now Write.**

Individualizing the Lesson

Less-Advanced Students

Have the class write a group description of the classroom. After listing descriptive details, students can choose a spatial order for the description. The class may want to order their details in two or three ways and decide which order is the most effective.

Advanced Students

Discuss in further detail the paragraph in **Check It Out.** Ask students what would be lost if the man were described in reverse order, i.e. from top to bottom.

Patterns

Pre-Writing: Using Spatial Order

Here's the Idea Sensory details can make a description seem real. However, a writer must be sure to organize the sensory details well. That way the reader will get an accurate picture of the person, place, or thing being described.

In a narrative paragraph, the details are organized in chronological order. They are presented in the order that they happened. In a descriptive paragraph, however, the writer can choose a number of different ways to arrange the details that describe the topic. The person, place, or thing may be described from top to bottom, bottom to top, or front to back. The subject may also be described from near to far, left to right, or in any other logical way that the writer wants the reader to see the subject.

This type of order is called **spatial order.** The writer selects the detail that he or she wants the reader to notice first. Then the remaining details are presented in the order that the writer wants the reader to see them.

Suppose you want to describe a fish market. The first detail you want the reader to notice might be the overpowering fishy smell of the shop. Then you might describe from left to right the items in the baskets on the top of the refrigerated display case. Next you might move down and describe from right to left the kinds of fish in the display case. Lastly, you could describe the different kinds of breads piled on the shelf in front of the cooler.

When you write a description, remember that there is no single correct spatial order. Arrange the details in the order that *you* want the reader to see them.

Check It Out   Read the following description.

I looked from his hands to his sand-stained khaki pants; my eyes traveled up his thin frame to his torn denim shirt. His face was as white as his hands, but for a shadow on his jutting chin. His cheeks were thin to hollowness; his mouth was wide; there were shallow, almost delicate indentations at his temples, and his gray eyes were so colorless I thought he was blind. His hair was dead and thin, almost feathery on top of his head.

—HARPER LEE

- How does this description use spatial order?

Try Your Skill   Suppose you were asked to describe the rooms in your house. How would you organize your description? Would you begin at the front door and work your way through the house to the back door? Would you start in the basement and lead your reader up to the second floor? Perhaps you would first describe your favorite room and then describe the rooms around it.

Make a list of the rooms in your house. Then arrange the items on the list in spatial order. In other words, list the rooms in the order that you would want a reader to notice them. Be sure the order that you choose is logical. Write a few sentences explaining why you chose that order.

Keep This in Mind

- Use spatial order to organize the details for your descriptive paragraph.
- Arrange your details in the order that you want your reader to notice them.

Now Write   Use spatial order to organize your pre-writing notes. Arrange your details in the order that you want the reader to notice them. Save your organized notes in your folder.

121

Objective

To use language to create a specific mood in a descriptive paragraph

Presenting the Lesson

1. After students have read **Here's the Idea,** discuss the concept of *mood* in writing. Tell students that the word *atmosphere* also describes this quality. Just as movies and television programs often create a particular mood, so does effective descriptive writing. Have students read aloud each list of descriptive words to emphasize how the choice of words affects a description.

2. Ask a student volunteer to read the paragraph in **Check It Out.** Help students recognize that the mood of fear and tension is achieved through words such as *richly, decorated, elaborately,* and *silken.*

3. Assign **Try Your Skill.** Have students refer to the lists in **Here's the Idea** to review the parts of speech.

4. Read **Keep This in Mind.**

5. Assign **Now Write.** Instruct students to describe in one or two words the mood they want to create before making their lists of descriptive words.

Individualizing the Lesson

Less-Advanced Students

List on the chalkboard some moods that writing can create: happy, sad, depressing, poignant, frightening, humorous, exciting, etc.

Part 3

A Certain Feeling

Pre-Writing: Creating Mood

Here's the Idea Have you ever read a really scary mystery novel or ghost story? What scared you? Was it just the story, or was it also the way the writer described what was happening? Most writers, especially when they are describing someone or something, try to suggest a certain feeling to the reader. This feeling is called **mood.**

Writers suggest mood through the language they use. Suppose a writer is describing the park in winter. The writer wants the reader to feel that the park is a pleasant place, alive with happy people. The writer might fill his description with words like these:

Nouns	Adjectives	Verbs	Adverbs
couples	crisp	skate	merrily
flurries	smiling	stroll	gently
snowballs	sunny	frolic	excitedly

Now suppose that the writer wants to suggest a different mood to the reader. The writer wants the reader to feel that the park is a cold, dead place. In that case, he or she might use words like these:

Nouns	Adjectives	Verbs	Adverbs
slush	biting	howled	harshly
clouds	frozen	stung	terribly
storm	bare	whipped	miserably

Think about the kind of mood you want to suggest in your description. Make lists of nouns, adjectives, verbs, and adverbs that will help you to suggest that feeling.

Check It Out   Read this paragraph.

A file of forty or fifty state barges drew up to the steps. They were richly gilt, and their lofty prows and sterns were elaborately carved. Some of them were decorated with banners and streamers, some with cloth of gold and arras embroidered with coats of arms, others with silken flags that had numberless little silver bells fastened on them which shook out tiny showers of joyous music whenever the breezes fluttered them . . . .

—MARK TWAIN

- What mood is Mark Twain trying to suggest?
- What words help to suggest that mood?

Try Your Skill   Imagine you are going to write two different paragraphs describing an old man walking down the street. In the first paragraph you want to suggest that the man is happy and carefree. In the second paragraph you want to suggest that the man is deeply troubled.

Make two lists of words you could use to suggest mood in these two paragraphs. Each list should include nouns, adjectives, verbs, and adverbs. Compare your lists with those of your classmates.

Keep This in Mind
- Mood is the feeling suggested by a piece of writing.
- Express mood in your writing through the language you use.

Now Write   What mood do you want to suggest in the descriptive paragraph you have been planning? Make a list of nouns, adjectives, verbs, and adverbs you could use to express that mood. Save this list in your folder. Refer to it often as you write the first draft of your description.

Ask students for examples they recall of writing that created a particular mood.

Advanced Students

Have students create two group paragraphs describing a park in winter based on the two lists of descriptive words in **Here's the Idea.**

Optional Practice

After students have made two lists of words for **Try Your Skill,** have them write two descriptive paragraphs using the words on their lists.

Extending the Lesson

Have students write a paragraph for a raisin advertisement. First, give each student a raisin and tell the class to list ten sensory details that describe it. Then tell students to revise their lists, using only details and words that create a positive, appealing mood. Encourage them to use a dictionary or thesaurus to choose vivid words. Finally, instruct students to combine the sensory details with a topic sentence and an ending sentence and write a descriptive paragraph.

Part 4

Objective

To use transitions in the first draft of a descriptive paragraph to indicate spatial order

Presenting the Lesson

1. Read aloud and discuss **Here's the Idea.** Have students write the list of transitions shown on page 124 and keep it in their folders. Ask them to label the list "Transitions in Description." Students will be using this list all year. Ask your students to point out the transitions in the descriptive paragraph.

2. Read aloud and discuss **Check It Out.** Ask the class to identify the transitions used in the paragraph to show spatial relationships.

3. Assign and discuss **Try Your Skill.** Have the class review the list of transitions on page 124. After the students complete the assignment, ask them to read their paragraphs to the class.

4. Read **Keep This in Mind** and then assign **Now Write.** Encourage the class to use a variety of transitions.

Individualizing the Lesson

Less-Advanced Students

Emphasize the importance of transitions in making a description clear to readers. Have students exchange the first drafts of their paragraphs and suggest ways to improve clarity with transitions.

Put It There!

Writing the First Draft

Here's the Idea   You have learned how one kind of transitional word shows chronological order in narrative paragraphs. You need to use a different kind of word to show spatial order in descriptive paragraphs. You need to use transitional words and phrases that will show where things are in relation to other things.

Here are some of the **transitional words and phrases** used often in description.

above	beside	in the center	over
against	between	low	side by side
ahead of	by	near	south
alongside	down	next to	throughout
at the end of	east	north	to the left
at the top	facing	on	to the right
around	high	on the bottom	toward
behind	in	on the corner	under
below	in back of	on the edge	up
beneath	in front of	outside	west

Transitional words and phrases that show spatial order often begin sentences. They may also be used effectively in the middle or at the end of sentences. Notice the use of transitional words and phrases as you read the following description.

I saw a shiny steel trash can at the corner of Maple and Ridge this morning. On the sidewalk near the can were several piles of cardboard boxes that looked as if they were about to topple over. Leaned up against the can were four threadbare cushions, torn and soiled with age. A scrawny yellow cat had scrambled up the biggest cushion and was peering into the open trash can.

Check It Out   Read the following paragraph.

A man stood upon a railroad bridge in northern Alabama, looking down into the swift water twenty feet below. The man's hands were behind his back, the wrists bound with a cord. A rope closely encircled his neck. It was attached to a stout beam above his head and the slack fell to the level of his knees. Some loose boards supplied a footing for him and his executioners—two private soldiers directed by a sergeant. At a short distance from this temporary platform was an officer in a captain's uniform, armed. At each end of the bridge stood a sentinel with his rifle over his left shoulder.   —AMBROSE BIERCE

- How does this descriptive paragraph use transitional words and phrases to show spatial order?

Try Your Skill   Look at this list of objects for a descriptive paragraph about a city intersection. Using transitional words and phrases, write four sentences that show a logical spatial order. Add other details of your own if you wish.

Main Street	large clock	pedestrians
newsstand	pigeons	City Hall
traffic light	National Bank	pothole
Smith's Drug Store	patrol car	North Avenue

Keep This in Mind

- In a description, use transitional words and phrases that show spatial order.

Now Write   Write the first draft of your descriptive paragraph. Follow your original pre-writing notes as you write. Use transitional words and phrases that make the spatial order clear. Include words from the list you wrote in Part 3 to express mood. Save your first draft in your folder.

Have students revise the following descriptive paragraph by adding transitions that show spatial order. Students can then compare their paragraphs.

Our school gym is a busy place, and it is ingeniously set up to adapt to many different uses. Two basketball goals are set up for practice games. A net is stretched for volleyball and tennis practice. There is a small track for jogging. One area is devoted to gymnastics and includes mats, parallel bars, and a balance beam.

Optional Practice

Bring an interesting photograph or slide to class and have each student write a paragraph describing what they see. Emphasize the need for transitions that show spatial order. Tell the class to refer to the list on page 124. The paragraphs should have transitions, sensory details, and a specific mood.

Extending the Lesson

Draw a pattern using geometric shapes. Allow only one student to look at the drawing, and have that student describe it for the class. As the student describes it, have the class try to duplicate the drawing on their own papers. Afterward, let students compare drawings. Discuss how transitions helped to show them the spatial order of the pattern.

Objective

To revise a descriptive paragraph by checking for vivid sensory details, spatial order, effective transitions, and language that creates a specific mood

Presenting the Lesson

1. Discuss **Here's the Idea,** reading aloud the questions to consider when revising a descriptive paragraph. In addition to reminding students of the elements of description discussed in this chapter, discuss the topic sentence of a descriptive paragraph. Tell students that it should mention the subject of the paragraph and introduce the mood of the description.

2. Have a student volunteer read the paragraph in **Check It Out.** Help students recognize that the paragraph includes good sensory details; have the class identify the mood of the description.

3. Assign **Try Your Skill.** After the class has completed the assignment, several students can read their revisions and comment on their improvements of the paragraph.

4. Read **Keep This in Mind.**

5. Assign **Now Write.** Remind students to proofread their spelling and punctuation only after they have revised sensory details and transitions.

Individualizing the Lesson

Less-Advanced Students

Help students revise their topic sentences so that they accurately and interestingly reflect the topic

126

Return to the Scene

Revising Your Descriptive Paragraph

Here's the Idea   Careful revision will make your descriptive paragraph clearer and more interesting. Read your first draft. Think about your ideas, your organization, and your word choice. You may want to add details to paint a clearer picture of your subject. You might reorganize your details so that they make better sense for the reader. You may need to add some transitional words and phrases. You might also want to look for words that better express the mood you are trying to create.

As you revise your paragraph, ask yourself these questions.

1. Is my topic sentence interesting and informative?
2. Did I include enough details to develop my description? Will the reader almost be able to see, hear, taste, smell, or feel what I am describing?
3. Did I arrange my details in clear spatial order?
4. Have I included transitional words and phrases to make the order of my details clear? Do these words and phrases lead the reader from one detail to the next?
5. Have I used specific nouns, adjectives, verbs, and adverbs to suggest a particular mood?

When you feel your description is as clear and as interesting as you can make it, proofread your paragraph. Look for and correct any mistakes in grammar and mechanics.

Check It Out   Read this descriptive paragraph.

On the windowsill of my bedroom stands the magic unicorn. He is hand-cut from crystal. His forefeet are prancing, and his neck arches high. His mane and tail are delicately carved, each facet catching the sunlight. Most exquisite of all is his long, twisted horn. The light bouncing off him throws little rainbows onto the walls of my room. He seems to have leaped from the pages of a fairy tale. My physical science teacher would call my unicorn a prism. I call him magic.

- What are the strong points of this description? Explain your answers. Be specific.

Try Your Skill   Revise this descriptive paragraph. Follow the guidelines in this lesson.

The homecoming half-time show was really good. The marching band played. There were introductions of the parents of all the players. The cheerleaders performed. They did some tumbling stunts. At the beginning, the queen was introduced. She looked beautiful. Riding in a convertible and holding flowers. Everyone enjoyed the show.

Keep This in Mind

- Include strong sensory details in your description.
- Arrange your details in the order that you want your reader to notice them.
- Use transitional words and phrases to show spatial order.
- Select nouns, adjectives, verbs, and adverbs to suggest mood.

Now Write   Use the guidelines in this lesson to revise your descriptive paragraph. Proofread it. Then write a neat final copy. Save your paragraph in your folder.

and mood of their paragraphs. Remind students that a descriptive topic sentence should get the reader's interest immediately by using sensory, mood-evoking details.

Advanced Students

Students may tend to be too easily satisfied with the first drafts of their paragraphs. Tell them that one can never have too many vivid details in a descriptive paragraph. Instruct students to deliberately put in two or three "extra" descriptive details; these can be deleted in the final revision, but few students will find it necessary to do so.

Optional Practice

After revising their descriptive paragraphs, students can exchange papers and identify the moods that their fellow students have created. Students can then revise their paragraphs further to clarify or emphasize a particular mood.

Extending the Lesson

Have students combine their narrative and descriptive writing skills. Instruct them to write a narrative paragraph that creates a mood through descriptive, sensory details. Some possible topics are a frightening, happy, or sad experience.

Section **11** Objectives

1. To list the steps in a process for an explanatory *how* paragraph

2. To organize pre-writing notes for an explanatory *how* paragraph in step-by-step order

3. To use transitions to show step-by-step order

4. To revise an explanatory *how* paragraph by checking for completeness of steps; logical, step-by-step order; and clear transitions

Preparing the Students

Give the class the following problem to solve:

> You have a younger brother who is five years old. His kindergarten teacher told him that he must learn to tie his shoelaces. How would you teach him this simple task?

Have students work in pairs with one student assuming the role of the younger brother and the other student the role of the older sibling. Have the groups act out this teaching/learning experience. They probably will find that it is not easy to explain this task.

Afterward, tell them that the older siblings' words were explanatory. Ask what directions seemed to work best for explanations. Announce that in Section 11 students will learn how to write a paragraph that explains *how*.

Additional Resources

Mastery Test — page 25 in the test booklet

Practice Book — pages 52–55

Duplicating Masters — pages 52–55

The Explanatory Paragraph

Telling *How*

Teaching Special Populations

LD See **Teaching Special Populations,** page 75. Review the concept of step-by-step order.

ESL Suggest additional topics that reflect the ESL students' cultural backgrounds and experience. Allot extra time to explain the transitional words and phrases related to the concept of time. Give special help to those students whose native language doesn't include such words.

NSD See **Teaching Special Populations,** page 75. Tell students that standard English is the clearest way to communicate a process. Pair students with fluent speakers of standard English, and have them discuss ways of translating nonstandard dialect into explanatory paragraphs that use standard English.

Part 1

Objective

To list the steps in a process for an explanatory *how* paragraph

Presenting the Lesson

1. Read and discuss **Here's the Idea.** Help students recognize the difference between a *how* paragraph that instructs and one that informs. Emphasize that in both types of *how* paragraphs, the steps must be presented thoroughly and logically.

2. Read the paragraph in **Check It Out.** Ask students if they could make sun tea after reading the paragraph.

3. Assign **Try Your Skill.** This may be done as a class activity.

4. Read **Keep This in Mind.**

5. Assign **Now Write.** Instruct students to determine first whether they are explaining a process to instruct or to inform their readers. Some possible general instructional topics are how to play a particular game or sport, how to prepare a particular dish, or how to prepare for a test. Some topics to inform are how water is piped into homes or how a jet engine works.

Individualizing the Lesson

Less-Advanced Students

Hold a discussion about some everyday examples of explaining how to do something or following directions: giving a friend directions to one's home, following a recipe, following instructions for putting together a toy or model.

Pre-Writing: Explaining a Process

Here's the Idea   You already know how to write narrative and descriptive paragraphs. In this section, you will learn how to write an explanatory paragraph. An explanatory paragraph explains something. One kind of explanatory paragraph explains a process. This kind of paragraph is called an explanatory *how* paragraph.

There are two types of *how* paragraphs. The first type explains how to do something. In this type of paragraph you might explain how to make yogurt or how to develop a black-and-white photograph.

The second type of *how* paragraph explains how something happens or how something works. In this type of paragraph you might explain how fog develops or how a printing press works.

Both types of explanatory *how* paragraphs must be clear, detailed, and accurate. When you have chosen a subject to explain, ask yourself, "What does my reader need to know?" In your pre-writing notes you will list all of the steps in the process you are going to explain. Each step should be expressed clearly and simply. No important step should be left out. Then your explanation will be easy to understand.

Check It Out   Read the following explanation.

Do you like to drink iced tea in the summer? If you do, you can save time and energy by making sun tea. First, on a sunny morning, fill a one-quart glass pitcher with cold water. Second, add four tea bags. Then, cover the container with a lid or plastic wrap. Finally, set the pitcher outdoors in a sunny spot, such as a back step or window ledge. Let the sun do the rest. When you return in the afternoon, simply add ice and enjoy your sun-brewed tea.

- What process is explained? Are the steps explained clearly and simply? Have any steps been left out?

Try Your Skill   Here are some pre-writing notes for an explanatory *how* paragraph. Make changes and additions to the list. Include every step a reader needs to know. Leave out any steps that are not necessary to the process.

How To Get a Driver's License

1. Complete a driver's education course.
2. Practice driving the family car.
3. Wash and wax the car.
4. Fill out an application.
5. Show proof of your age.
6. Pay the license fee.
7. Pass the vision test.
8. Cross your fingers.
9. Pass the road test.

Keep This in Mind

- An explanatory *how* paragraph explains how to do something or how something works.
- An explanatory *how* paragraph should include all of the steps in the process being explained.
- Each step should be explained clearly and simply.

Now Write   Think of a process you would like to explain to someone else. It might be how to do something, or how something happens or works. Choose a process that you find interesting and that you know something about. List the steps that are involved in this process. Be sure to include all of the steps. Save your pre-writing notes in your folder.

131

Ask a volunteer to name the steps explaining how something happens or how something works. This could be a scientific explanation such as photosynthesis or a mechanical process such as how an internal combustion engine works.

Optional Practice

Choose a simple topic such as preparing a salad or making a sandwich. Have the class name the steps involved in the process. Write the steps on the chalkboard and then ask students to make additions, changes, or deletions to the pre-writing notes.

Extending the Lesson

Have students find and bring to class two explanatory *how* paragraphs: one that instructs the reader how to do something and one that informs the reader how something happens or how something works. The paragraphs can be exchanged and discussed in class.

Part 2

Objective

To organize pre-writing notes for an explanatory *how* paragraph in step-by-step order

Presenting the Lesson

1. Read **Here's the Idea,** defining step-by-step order. Emphasize the importance of putting the steps of a process in the correct order; for example, suppose student cooks were instructed to preheat the oven to 350 degrees after being told to put the cake in the oven.

2. After reading the paragraph in **Check It Out,** discuss the logical sequential order that it follows. Explain that the steps could not be placed in any other order. Ask students if they used a step-by-step order in the shoelace exercise in the introduction to this Section.

3. Read the directions for **Try Your Skill.** Have students complete this exercise on their own. Then have a volunteer read the steps in logical sequence. Ask the class if the steps are clear.

4. Read **Keep This in Mind** and then assign **Now Write.**

Individualizing the Lesson

Less-Advanced Students

Ask several students to name, in random order, the steps involved in preparing for a test. Write the steps on the chalkboard and then have the class arrange the steps in logical step-by-step order.

Follow Through

Pre-Writing: Using Step-by-Step Order

Here's the Idea   Your pre-writing notes should include every step in the process that you want to describe. Before you can begin writing about that process, however, the steps must be organized. To present a clear explanation to your reader, the steps should be arranged in **step-by-step order.** This is the natural time order in which a process occurs.

Arranging your pre-writing notes in correct step-by-step order is important. Suppose that you were explaining how to build a charcoal fire. What would happen if you told the readers to arrange the coals in a pyramid shape *after* you told them to light the fire?

Organize your notes carefully. Ask yourself, "What is the first step in the process I am explaining?" Write this step down. Then list the rest of the steps in the order in which they should happen. Be sure you do not leave out any steps. If you do, your reader will not understand your explanation.

Check It Out   Read the following paragraph.

Making maple syrup is a simple but time-consuming process. First, holes are drilled into the trunks of maple trees. Then metal spouts are fitted into the holes. Covered buckets are hung on the spouts to catch the sap as it flows from the trees. The buckets must be emptied several times a week. The sap from all the trees is stored in a vat. From the vat it flows into an evaporator. The sap is boiled in the evaporator, and it becomes thicker. At the end of that process, the sap has become maple syrup.

- What process is explained in this paragraph?
- Are all the steps in this process presented in the order that they happen? Explain your answer.

Try Your Skill Can you do a push-up? Read this confused list of instructions. Write the directions in their correct order.

5 1. Support your weight with your palms.
1 2. Lie face down on the floor.
3 3. Keep your back straight and your feet in place.
2 4. Position your hands directly under your shoulders.
4 5. Push yourself up until your arms are straight.

Keep This in Mind

- In an explanatory *how* paragraph, explain a process step by step.
- Organize the steps of the process in the order that they take place or should be done.

Now Write Reread your pre-writing notes for the process you plan to explain. See if the steps are in correct step-by-step order. If any step is out of order, rearrange your notes. Save your organized notes in your folder.

Objective

To use transitions to show step-by-step order

Presenting the Lesson

1. Read aloud **Here's the Idea,** and review the kinds of transitions the students have learned. Have students copy the list of transitions, label it "Explanatory *How* Transitions," and put it into their folders.

2. Read the paragraph in **Check It Out.** Help students recognize transitions such as *first, then,* and *after that.*

3. Assign **Try Your Skill.** After the class has completed the assignment, ask several students to read their paragraphs. Emphasize the various transitions that can clarify the paragraph's step-by-step order.

4. Read **Keep This in Mind.**

5. Assign **Now Write.** Remind students to write a topic sentence that states the paragraph's topic, attracts the readers' attention, and lets them know that the paragraph will explain *how.*

Individualizing the Lesson

Less-Advanced Students

Explain to students that every sentence in their explanatory paragraph need not start with a transition. Encourage students to experiment with various transitions in different positions until their step-by-step order is clear.

Smooth the Way

Writing the First Draft

Here's the Idea   Now it is time to write the first draft of your paragraph. Begin with a strong topic sentence that presents the process you are explaining. Then turn the list of steps in your pre-writing notes into supporting sentences.

As you write your first draft, try to make your explanation as clear as possible for your readers. One way to do this is by using transitional words and phrases.

You have learned about transitions used in a narrative paragraph. They show chronological order. You have also learned about transitions used in a description. They show spatial order. Now you will learn about transitions you can use in an explanation. These will show step-by-step order.

Study this list of transitional words and phrases often used in explanatory *how* paragraphs.

first	as	at first	wait until
second	then	to start with	finally
third	when	after that	the next step
next	while	at the same time	the last step

Use these transitional words and phrases and others like them when you write your first draft.

Check It Out   Read this paragraph.

You can observe the passing of time by making your own clock. You will need a piece of cardboard about twelve inches square, an empty spool of thread, a pencil, and glue. First, glue the spool to the middle of the cardboard. Then put the pencil into the hole in the spool. At nine o'clock on a bright morning, put your clock outdoors in a sunny spot. Notice how the pencil makes a shadow. Write the number nine on that spot where the shadow ends. After that, do the same thing at ten, eleven, twelve, and so on. By the end of the day, you will have clocked the movement of the sun.

- Does this explanatory *how* paragraph explain a process step by step?
- Which transitional words and phrases show step-by-step order?

Try Your Skill   In the following explanatory *how* paragraph, all the steps are in the correct order. However, the paragraph lacks transitions. Use several of the transitional words and phrases listed in this lesson to make this explanation as clear as possible. You may use other transitional words and phrases also.

If you have ever seen a dinosaur in a museum, you may have wondered how it was rebuilt from a heap of bones. The work begins when a dinosaur skeleton is unearthed. As much dirt is removed as possible. Great care is taken to avoid disturbing the bones. Photographs are taken. Every bone is carefully dug up. They may have to be coated with resin or plaster if they are fragile. In the museum, plaster casts are made of each bone. Wire and metal rods are used to fit the casts together. It's not easy to build a dinosaur!

Keep This in Mind

- In an explanatory *how* paragraph, use transitions that show step-by-step order. These will help you to make your explanation as clear as possible.

Now Write   Write the first draft of your explanatory *how* paragraph. Start out with an interesting and informative topic sentence. Use transitional words and phrases to help show step-by-step order. Save your first draft in your folder.

Advanced Students

Ask students to use at least three different transitions in writing the first drafts of their explanatory *how* paragraphs.

Optional Practice

Have groups of three students put these steps in order and add transitions to show step-by-step order.
Answers will vary.

4   a. Water and weed the garden.

6   b. Enjoy the taste of home-grown vegetables.

1   c. Choose a sunny spot for a vegetable garden.

3   d. Sow seeds in rows.

5   e. Pick vegetables.

2   f. Prepare the ground by turning the soil and raking it.

Extending the Lesson

Have students write paragraphs explaining how to make paper airplanes or paper hats. Remind them to include transitions that show step-by-step order. Ask volunteers to read their paragraphs as the rest of the class follows their instructions. Discuss how logical and complete the explanations are.

135

Objective

To revise an explanatory *how* paragraph by checking for completeness of steps; logical, step-by-step order; and clear transitions

Presenting the Lesson

1. Discuss **Here's the Idea,** reading aloud the questions to ask in revising an explanatory *how* paragraph. Emphasize the importance of clarity in an explanatory *how* paragraph.

2. Read the paragraph in **Check It Out.** Have students discuss ways they would improve the topic sentence and the clarity of the paragraph.

3. Read the directions for **Try Your Skill.** Have the class discuss the specific problem in each example. Then assign the exercise as individual work.

4. Read **Keep This in Mind** and then assign **Now Write.** Have students refer to the questions for revision in **Here's the Idea.** Again emphasize clarity through step-by-step order and transitions.

Individualizing the Lesson

Less-Advanced Students

Discuss in detail the beginnings for explanatory *how* paragraphs in **Try Your Skill.** Instruct students not just to state the purpose of their paragraph, as in examples 1 and 3. Have students work in pairs or groups on topic sentences that are both informative and attention-getting.

How's That Again?

Revising Your Explanatory *How* Paragraph

Here's the Idea   The goal of an explanatory *how* paragraph is to explain a process so that the reader will understand it as well as you do. Once you have written your first draft, you must read it to see if it reaches that goal. If it does not, you must revise the paragraph. Examine your ideas, your organization, and your word choice. Ask yourself these questions as you revise.

1. Does my topic sentence present the process I am going to explain? Is my topic sentence interesting?
2. Have I included every important step in the process?
3. Have I arranged the steps in the order that they happen?
4. Have I explained each step simply and clearly?
5. Have I included transitions to help show the order of the steps in the process? Do these transitions guide the reader from one step in the process to the next?

When you have revised the ideas, organization, and word choice in your paragraph, proofread it. Correct any errors in grammar, capitalization, punctuation, and spelling.

Check It Out   Read this paragraph.

The *Readers' Guide to Periodical Literature* is important. You must find the volume that you want to use. There are also cross-references to help you continue your research. The entries are arranged in alphabetical order by topic. Note the title and author of each article. Then you are ready to find the magazine articles themselves. Also jot down the names of the magazines, the dates of publication, the volume numbers, and the page numbers. Find the page on which your topic appears.

- Does this paragraph have an interesting and informative topic sentence? Explain your answer.
- Is this paragraph organized in clear step-by-step order?
- What would you do to improve this paragraph?

Try Your Skill   Here are the beginnings of three explanatory *how* paragraphs. Each beginning lacks an interesting and informative topic sentence. Write a topic sentence that presents the subject of the paragraph and that captures the reader's interest.

1. In my paragraph, I'm going to write about how a caterpillar becomes a butterfly. It's really beautiful. And amazing. First . . .

2. This is how to make a pizza. Start out by . . .

3. I want to tell you in my paragraph about letters and how they get from the mailbox to the place they are supposed to go. It's kind of complicated. And sort of interesting. It takes a lot of people, too. Anyway, first of all . . .

Keep This in Mind

- When you revise an explanatory *how* paragraph, include every necessary step, in clear step-by-step order.
- Explain each step clearly and simply.
- Use transitional words to help your reader follow the steps.

Now Write   Use the guidelines in this lesson to revise your explanatory *how* paragraph. When you have revised and proofread it, make a neat final copy. Save your paragraph in your folder.

Section **12** Objectives

1. To state an opinion clearly in the topic sentence of an explanatory *why* paragraph

2. To list reasons and facts to support the opinion

3. To organize the reasons and facts that support an opinion from the least important to the most important

4. To write a strong opening sentence and use good transitions in writing the first draft of a *why* paragraph

5. To check for clarity and logic in supporting facts when revising a *why* paragraph

Preparing the Students

Present the following opinions to the class:

Tickets for professional baseball and football games are terribly overpriced.

The movies being made for teenagers today insult high-school students' intelligence.

Explain that these opinions should be backed up with facts in order to be convincing. This Section will teach students how to state an opinion in an explanatory paragraph and support it with strong reasons.

Additional Resources

Mastery Test — page 26 in the test booklet

Practice Book — pages 56–59

Duplicating Masters — pages 56–59

138

The Explanatory Paragraph

Telling *Why*

Teaching Special Populations

LD See **Teaching Special Populations,** page 75.

ESL Since many ESL students have never written their opinions before, they may need extra help with this Section. To help students develop confidence in stating opinions, assign or suggest non-controversial subjects first. Explain that it is not impolite in this case to disagree with the teacher or with classmates.

Many languages express modals in the inflection of the verb. Some ESL students will therefore be unaware of the need for separate words.

NSD See **Teaching Special Populations,** page 75.

Objectives

1. To state an opinion clearly in the topic sentence of an explanatory *why* paragraph

2. To list reasons and facts to support the opinion

Presenting the Lesson

1. Discuss **Here's the Idea.** Encourage students to consider the sample opinions and start developing opinions of their own on the subjects mentioned in paragraph 2. Emphasize that for a *why* paragraph, opinions must be supported by facts and reasons.

2. Read the paragraph in **Check It Out,** and have students discuss the questions. Help the class see that the paragraph states a clear opinion and offers supporting reasons; it could be better organized and improved with transitions.

3. For **Try Your Skill,** have a class discussion about one or two topics to stimulate students' opinions. Or divide the class into four groups and assign one topic for each group to discuss. Remind students to narrow their topics sufficiently when writing a topic sentence.

4. Read **Keep This in Mind.**

5. Assign **Now Write.** Instruct students to use the library if necessary to find supporting facts.

Individualizing the Lesson

Less-Advanced Students

During class or group discussions on the topics in **Try Your Skill,** urge students to take a strong stand

What Do You Think?

Pre-Writing: Developing an Opinion

Here's the Idea   As you know, an explanatory paragraph can explain a process. It can also tell *how* something is done, happens, or works. An explanatory paragraph can be used to explain an opinion. It can tell *why* a person feels as he or she does about a subject. The purpose of an explanatory *why* paragraph is to present an opinion and to give reasons that support the opinion.

It is easy to find a topic for a *why* paragraph. Think about your family, your school, your neighborhood, and your town. What things do you like? What things should be changed? How do you feel about the government, about other countries, or about the business world? What frustrates you? What do you approve of or disapprove of? By asking yourself these kinds of questions, you can discover opinions to develop in your writing.

Begin your pre-writing notes for a *why* paragraph with a sentence that states your opinion. Make sure that the statement is clear and direct. This statement of opinion can become the topic sentence when you write the first draft. Look at these statements of opinion.

1. Everyone should have three aerobic workouts a week.
2. The athletic department should have a videotape recorder.
3. Some advertising is misleading.

Once your opinion is stated clearly, you must list reasons and facts that develop and support your opinion. The reasons must be logical and clear. The facts must be accurate. Ask yourself if the reasons and facts you have listed will make the reader understand *why* you feel the way you do.

Check It Out   Read this paragraph.

The abandoned reservoir south of town should be made into a recreational area. It's just going to waste now. We need a lake for water sports. If the reservoir were also stocked, it would be perfect for fishing. Sailing and water skiing would be great, too.

- Does this paragraph present an opinion? What is it?
- Is the opinion well-supported with facts and reasons? How could it be improved?

Try Your Skill   Develop an opinion about one of the general topics below. Write a good topic sentence that expresses your opinion. Then list several reasons or facts that support your opinion.

cities   computers
movies   holidays

Keep This in Mind

- An explanatory *why* paragraph presents and supports an opinion.
- Use logical reasons and accurate facts to support your opinion.

Now Write   Think of a topic about which you have a strong opinion. Write a sentence that states your opinion clearly and directly. Then make a list of reasons and facts that support your opinion. Be sure your reasons are logical and your facts accurate. Save your pre-writing notes in your folder.

on an issue that interests them and to state the opinion firmly. Assist students individually with their topic sentences as much as possible.

Advanced Students

Have students develop two opposing viewpoints about one of the topics in **Try Your Skill** and debate the issue.

Optional Practice

To provide practice in developing opinions, have students write an opinion on each of the following topics:

television
the legal driving age
part-time jobs for students

Extending the Lesson

Tell your students that you will present them with an imaginary situation to which they will have to respond. Tell them that you have just spoken to the principal and that he or she reported that all extracurricular sports and activities will be cancelled this year because of lack of funds. Ask students to write one-paragraph letters to the principal stating reasons why the school's extracurricular program should or should not be cancelled.

Part 2

Here's Why

Objective

To organize the reasons and facts that support an opinion from the least important to the most important

Presenting the Lesson

1. Read **Here's the Idea.** Read the sample reasons for a *why* paragraph, having students discuss each reason and its relative importance.

2. Have a volunteer read the paragraph in **Check It Out.** Briefly list on the chalkboard each supporting reason in the paragraph and have students discuss whether the reasons are thorough and specific and whether their order is effective.

3. Assign **Try Your Skill.** Have a volunteer read the details in their order of importance.

4. Read **Keep This in Mind** and then assign **Now Write.**

Individualizing the Lesson

Less-Advanced Students

Help students individually as much as possible to organize their reasons in order of importance. Help students first make sure their reasons are varied, specific, and thorough.

Advanced Students

Students who have no difficulty organizing their pre-writing notes may do this assignment: choose a specific product to advertise, and

Pre-Writing: Organizing an Opinion

Here's the Idea   As you learned from studying narrative, descriptive, and explanatory *how* paragraphs, a strong organization can help you to get your message across to the reader. This is true with explanatory *why* paragraphs, too.

A *why* paragraph always begins with a statement of opinion as a topic sentence. That tells the reader *what* you believe. Then you must explain *why* you believe as you do by presenting logical reasons and accurate facts. The most convincing way to present these reasons and facts is to organize them in the order of their importance. You begin with the least important idea and move toward the most important idea. By doing this, you leave your readers with the most important evidence fresh in their minds.

For example, in a paragraph about why jumping rope is good exercise, you might include the following reasons.

1. Jumping rope is inexpensive and can be done anytime.

2. Jumping rope takes only a short time and requires no special training.

3. Jumping rope is a good, all-around exercise for the arms, legs, and heart.

Notice that the reasons have been listed in order, from the least important to the most important. Organized in this way, the reasons are convincing.

Check It Out   Read the following paragraph.

All high school students should learn to type. First, if students can type their own compositions and reports, they will be more satisfied with the neat, easy-to-read results. Second, students who choose to go on to college will discover that instructors require that most work be typed. Students who type well will meet that requirement easily. Finally, students who are able to type can qualify for a variety of full-time jobs after their graduation.

- Does the topic sentence state an opinion directly?
- Is the opinion supported by specific reasons or facts? Is the supporting evidence organized in order of importance?

Try Your Skill   Here are some pre-writing notes for an explanatory *why* paragraph. Read the opinion. Then organize the supporting details in the order of their importance. Start with the least important reason, and end with the most important.

Opinion: Everyone should learn to play a musical instrument.

   2 1. Learning to play a musical instrument teaches an appreciation of different types of music.

   1 2. Playing a musical instrument is fun.

   3 3. Knowing how to play a musical instrument could lead to an exciting career in music.

Keep This in Mind

- In an explanatory *why* paragraph, organize your evidence in order of importance. Present your reasons from the least important idea to the most important.

Now Write   Organize the list of reasons or facts that you gathered for your explanatory *why* paragraph. Arrange them in the order of their importance. Save your organized notes in your folder.

list convincing reasons why consumers should buy it, listing the reasons from least important to most important.

Optional Practice

Have students organize the following pre-writing notes for the sample opinion in order from least important to most important.

Opinion: All students should learn to speak a foreign language.

  3 1. Many people in European countries speak two or three languages fluently.

  2 2. Understanding another language helps you understand another country's people and culture.

  1 3. You may travel to another country some day and need to know how to communicate with the people there.

Extending the Lesson

Have each student find a letter to the editor of a local newspaper and comment on the order of supporting facts and the effectiveness of that order.

Objective

To write a strong opening sentence and use good transitions in writing the first draft of a *why* paragraph

Presenting the Lesson

1. Read and discuss **Here's the Idea.** Explain that if a writer sounds unsure of his or her opinions, readers will certainly not be convinced by the argument. Ask students which of the following opinions is stated more effectively:

It seems to me that people should try to vote in national elections.
Everyone of legal voting age should vote in national elections.

Have students study the transitional words and phrases useful for a *why* paragraph.

2. Have a volunteer read the paragraph in **Check It Out.** Write the transitional words and phrases on the chalkboard as students list them; have the class tell what purpose each transition serves.

3. Assign **Try Your Skill.** Write the transitions used by students on the chalkboard.

4. Read **Keep This in Mind.**

5. Assign **Now Write.** Remind students not to end their paragraphs with their last supporting reasons but to write a summarizing concluding sentence.

Individualizing the Lesson

Less-Advanced Students

Students may tend to overuse the word *because* as a transition. En-

---

Thus and Therefore

Writing the First Draft

Here's the Idea When you write the first draft of your explanatory *why* paragraph, remember that your purpose is to explain your opinion to the reader. The way you present your case is as important as the reasons and facts you give. There are several ways that you can make your composition clear and convincing.

First, be sure your topic sentence states your opinion directly. Do not use phrases like "I think" or "In my opinion." Openers like these actually weaken a statement of opinion. Compare these sentences. Notice which sounds better.

1. If you ask me, I think that a vegetarian diet is a healthy diet.

2. A vegetarian diet is a healthy diet.

Another way to make your paragraph more effective is to use good transitional words and phrases. There are two main types of transitions that you can use. One kind helps you to state reasons or facts. The other kind shows their order of importance. Study these examples of transitional words and phrases.

To State Reasons or Facts:	because, so, since, if, therefore, as a result
To Put in Order of Importance:	the first reason, second, more important, most important, finally

Finally, end your paragraph confidently. Write a strong ending sentence that summarizes your opinion and your reasons.

Check It Out Read this paragraph:

The U.S. government should spend more money to improve our nation's train lines. First of all, existing trains are slow and uncomfortable, and the tracks are worn and dangerous. Money is needed to repair these trains. More important, if trains were made safer and more comfortable, more people will ride them. These trains will then make money and provide new jobs. As a result of increased dependence on public transportation, the United States will save a great deal of the fuel now used for travel in private cars.

- What transitional words and phrases show the readers the reasons and their order of importance?

Try Your Skill   Read these pre-writing notes. The reasons are arranged in the order of their importance. If you were going to write a first draft from these notes, what transitional words and phrases could you use? Make a list of appropriate transitions. Compare your list with those of your classmates.

Opinion: Aretha should be class president.
Reasons: She speaks well, she knows everyone, she's actively involved in school

Keep This in Mind

- In an explanatory *why* paragraph, state your opinion in the topic sentence.
- Use transitional words and phrases that show reasons and their order of importance.
- Sum up your argument in a concluding sentence.

Now Write   Write the first draft of your explanatory *why* paragraph. Use transitional words and phrases to present your reasons and to show the order of their importance. Be sure your paragraph has a direct and informative topic sentence. Also, give your paragraph a strong ending sentence. Save your first draft in your folder.

courage students to use at least three different transitions from the list in **Here's the Idea.**

Advanced Students

Have students write three different concluding statements for their *why* paragraphs and then choose the most effective. One statement should restate the main idea, one should summarize, and one should draw a final conclusion from the information presented.

Optional Practice

Have students write a concluding sentence for the following *why* paragraph.

Students should spend more time reading books and less time watching television. First of all, television is a passive entertainment while reading requires mental effort and imagination. Secondly, there are many more books on many more subjects in a library than there are programs on TV. Finally, there are many things to be learned from books that will help students in college and in later life.

Extending the Lesson

Instruct students to find a newspaper editorial that states a firm opinion. Explain that, especially in an editorial of several paragraphs, the first sentence may not state the writer's opinion. Tell students to write down the editorial's first sentence and its clearest statement of opinion and then discuss the opinion with their classmates.

Objective

To check for clarity and logic in supporting facts when revising a *why* paragraph

Presenting the Lesson

1. Have students read **Here's the Idea.** Outline on the chalkboard the six main points to check for in revising an explanatory *why* paragraph. Emphasize consideration of purpose and audience. Remind students that in order to convince readers of one's point of view, a writer must state his or her opinions clearly and logically.

2. Have students read the paragraph in **Check It Out.** Discuss the questions about the paragraph, helping the class see that the writing could be improved by a stronger statement of opinion and by transitions.

3. Assign **Try Your Skill.** Have several students read their revisions aloud and discuss their improvements.

4. Read **Keep This in Mind.**

5. Assign **Now Write.** Instruct students to proofread their paragraphs for mechanical errors only after they have made the structural revisions mentioned in **Here's the Idea.**

Individualizing the Lesson

Less-Advanced Students

Lead the students through a step-by-step revision of their paragraphs. Read each question in **Here's the Idea,** pausing to allow students to check their drafts for the appropriate points.

146

A Closer Look

Revising Your Explanatory *Why* Paragraph

Here's the Idea   Whenever you express an opinion, you can be sure of one thing: some people are not going to agree with you. However, these same people can still respect your opinion. Your readers are more likely to respect your opinion if it is clearly and logically expressed. That is why it is important to revise carefully your explanatory *why* paragraph.

As you revise your paragraph, ask yourself these questions.

1. Does the topic sentence state my opinion clearly?

2. Did I state my opinion directly, avoiding phrases like "I think" or "In my opinion"?

3. Have I supported my opinion with logical reasons and accurate facts?

4. Are my reasons arranged in the order of their importance, from the least important idea to the most important idea?

5. Did I use transitional words and phrases to present my reasons and to show the order of their importance?

6. Have I ended the paragraph with a strong sentence summarizing my opinion and reasons?

After revising your paragraph, proofread it. Correct any errors in grammar, capitalization, punctuation, and spelling.

Check It Out   Read this first draft of an explanatory *why* paragraph:

If you ask me, I think television commercials are pretty bad. Nobody watches them. I always switch the channel. They interrupt the movie, and that makes people mad. Some are okay most are really hopeless and simple. Who cares about what laundry soap or cereal some athlete buys? I sure don't.

146

- Does the topic sentence express an opinion clearly and directly? Explain your answer.
- Is the opinion supported with logical reasons and accurate facts?
- Does this paragraph contain transitional words and phrases?
- Does the ending sentence sum up the opinion and reasons?

Try Your Skill Use your revising skills to rewrite the paragraph in **Check It Out.** Use the questions in this lesson to guide you. Compare your revision with those of your classmates.

Keep This in Mind

- In an explanatory *why* paragraph, state your opinion clearly and directly in your topic sentence.
- Use logical reasons and accurate facts to support your opinion.
- Use transitional words and phrases to present your reasons and facts, and to show the order of their importance.
- Write a concluding sentence that sums up your opinion and reasons.

Now Write Use the guidelines in this lesson to revise your first draft. Proofread your paragraph. Then, make a final copy. Save your paragraph in your folder.

147

Advanced Students

Have students work in pairs to revise their paragraphs. Students should especially comment on the persuasiveness of their peers' writing.

Optional Practice

Have students revise the following *why* paragraph:

I think that, in my opinion, teenagers should make an effort to get to know the senior citizens in their community. High-school students and elderly people often have more in common than they realize. Senior citizens are sometimes lonely because they may not be physically able to get out of their homes frequently. Teenagers may enrich their own lives by reaching out to an older generation. That's what I think.

Extending the Lesson

Have students send their revised paragraphs to the school newspaper or to a local newspaper as a letter to the editor.

Section **13** Objectives

1. To write a general definition and develop it with specific facts or examples

2. To organize an explanatory *what* paragraph in general-to-specific order

3. To write a first draft of an explanatory *what* paragraph that includes an effective topic sentence and an interesting ending sentence

4. To revise an explanatory *what* paragraph

Preparing the Students

Ask students to name places where they might find a paragraph that defines a word. Some possibilities are a science textbook, a newspaper article, or an encyclopedia article. Tell students that this Section will teach them how to write a third type of explanatory paragraph, a definition.

Additional Resources

Mastery Test — page 27 in the test booklet

Practice Book — pages 60–63

Duplicating Masters — pages 60–63

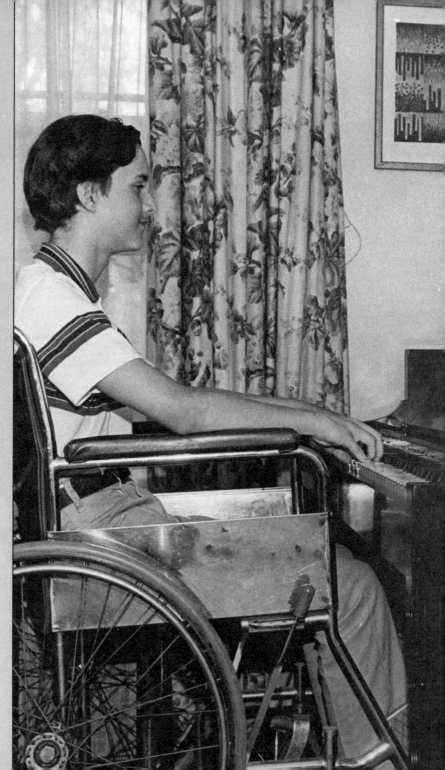

The Explanatory Paragraph

Telling *What*

Teaching Special Populations

LD See **Teaching Special Populations,** page 75.

ESL Have students discuss oral examples before beginning **Now Write.** Write several clear definitions on the chalkboard and have students discuss whether each definition is complete.

Some of the text examples may require detailed explanations for students from other cultures. Encourage students to choose simple concrete terms for their definitions. Check their work carefully. Emphasize the brief, one-sentence definitions upon which these paragraphs are based.

NSD See **Teaching Special Populations,** page 75.

Come to Terms

Pre-Writing: Learning About Definitions

Objective

To write a general definition and develop it with specific facts and examples

Presenting the Lesson

1. Read **Here's the Idea.** Pay particular attention to the sample definition, of *canoe,* so that students understand how to define a word. Have the class define the words *isosceles* and *dachshund,* and write these definitions on the chalkboard.

2. Read **Check It Out.** Help students see that the general definition of *anaconda* puts the word into its general class and adds a distinguishing detail.

3. Assign **Try Your Skill.** Help students notice the differences in specific details and organization between the two paragraphs.

4. Read **Keep This in Mind.**

5. Assign **Now Write.** Suggest general topics such as sports, school subjects, or an everyday object from which students can choose a specific term to define. Instruct students to use reference books in the classroom or the library if necessary when listing supporting details for their definitions.

Individualizing the Lesson

Less-Advanced Students

Emphasize that words to be defined should first be put into a general class. Have students name the general class for the following:

motorcycle   food processor
physical education   happiness

150

Here's the Idea   Knowing how to explain what a word means is a good skill to develop. An explanatory *what* paragraph first states a general definition. Then that definition is developed as completely as possible.

First, a good definition gives the subject, the word to be defined. Next, it puts the subject into a general class. Finally, it shows how the subject is different from all other members of its class by giving specific characteristics.

Suppose you want to define *canoe.* First, you would state that a canoe is a boat. That tells what word you are defining and to what general class it belongs. Then, you would write that a canoe is a small boat, ranging from eleven to twenty feet. That shows how a canoe is different from yachts and cabin cruisers. You might add that a canoe is moved with paddles. That distinguishes it from motorboats and sailboats. You could add that a canoe is usually an open boat. That shows how it is different from a kayak. Now you have a complete definition: A canoe is a small, open boat that is paddled through the water.

To further develop your general definition, use either facts and figures or specific examples. To develop the definition of *canoe,* you may need to look up information in an encyclopedia or other reference book. However, if you wanted to define a term or an idea, such as *success,* you would probably develop your definition by using specific examples from your own experience.

After you have chosen something to define in an explanatory *what* paragraph, write a one-sentence general definition of your subject. You can use this as the topic sentence when you write the first draft of your paragraph. Then, make a list of facts and figures or specific examples to help you develop your definition.

150

Check It Out   Read the following general definition.

Definition: An anaconda is a large, nonpoisonous snake found in tropical South America.

Notes: type of boa constrictor; born alive (up to 50 at a time); found in swamps; largest living snake; feeds on birds, fish, small mammals

- Will the general definition make a good topic sentence?
- Does the writer use facts and figures, or specific examples?

Try Your Skill   Read the following two explanatory *what* paragraphs. Which paragraph is a good definition? Which is not?

1. A German Shepherd is a big dog. Sometimes its coat color is black and tan, and sometimes it is gray or silver. These dogs used to be used to herd sheep. They can bark very loudly.

2. A breakfront is a large, wooden cabinet used to display art objects. The sides and back are made out of wood. The front consists of a series of shelves placed horizontally, from top to bottom. Enclosing the shelves are glass-paneled doors. Different pieces of art, such as fine crystal, china, and small sculptures, are placed on the shelves.

Keep This in Mind

- An explanatory *what* paragraph gives a definition.
- A good definition puts a subject in its general class. Then it gives its particular characteristics.
- You can use facts and figures or specific examples to develop the general definition in an explanatory *what* paragraph.

Now Write   Choose a topic for an explanatory *what* paragraph. Write a sentence that defines your subject generally. Then make a list of facts and figures or specific examples that will develop your general definition. Save your work.

Part 2

Objective

To organize an explanatory *what* paragraph in general-to-specific order

Presenting the Lesson

1. Read **Here's the Idea.** Ask students to name the general class that each sample word—island, road runner, and joystick—has been put in.

2. Have a volunteer read the paragraph in **Check It Out.** Call attention to the use of specific examples to define the term.

3. Assign **Try Your Skill.** You may want to do the exercise as a class discussion and have students suggest a general definition for those sentences that present only specific details.

4. Read **Keep This in Mind.**

5. Assign **Now Write.** Tell students that once they have given a general definition of their word, their supporting facts and examples should be as specific as possible.

Individualizing the Lesson

Less-Advanced Students

Help students individually to ensure that their supporting facts are as specific as possible.

Advanced Students

Discuss other possible orders for an explanatory *what* paragraph. Would any other order be effective? What kind of effect would a specific-to-general order have?

152

A Call to Order

Pre-Writing: Organizing a Definition

Here's the Idea If your geography teacher asked you to define the word *island,* what would you say? Chances are you would begin your definition with a general statement. You might say "An island is a small land mass surrounded by water." As you thought more about the word, you would probably begin adding other, more specific details. You might say that some islands are formed from coral and that others are formed from volcanic activity. You might list the names of some important islands. Your definition would move from the **general to the specific.**

Your explanatory *what* paragraph should be organized in the same way. Begin with a general definition of your subject. Examples are "A *road runner* is a bird that cannot fly," or "A *joystick* is a kind of directional control device." This general definition presents your subject in terms that are familiar to your readers.

As you continue your definition, add specific details that show the particular characteristics of your subject. Your details may be facts and figures or specific examples. Give your readers enough information so that they understand the word you are defining as well as you do.

Check It Out Read this definition of courage.

People have courage when they can remain true to their beliefs and purpose in spite of danger or opposition. Martin Luther King was a man who had courage. He remained dedicated to his cause, even when his life was threatened. Susan B. Anthony had the courage to campaign for women's rights when many powerful people were opposed to her ideas. Each of us

152

can act with courage in our daily lives. Courage sometimes means saying "no" when everyone else tells us to say "yes." It means the ability to stand up for what we believe in. It also takes courage to admit that we are wrong when we know we are wrong.

- Does this paragraph use general-to-specific order? Explain how.

Try Your Skill   Read the following sentences. In each sentence, the word being defined is in italics. On a piece of paper, write in one column the numbers of those sentences that are general definitions. In another column write down the numbers of those sentences that present specific details about the word being defined.

G 1. The *Middle Ages* was a period of European history that lasted over five hundred years.

S 2. *Parrots* have strong beaks and can crack all kinds of nuts.

G 3. Not all *oysters* contain pearls.

G 4. A *dictionary* is a book that contains definitions of words.

S 5. Oranges, lemons, and limes are examples of *citrus fruits*.

G 6. A *patriot* is a person who loves and respects his or her country.

Keep This in Mind

- Use general-to-specific order to organize your explanatory *what* paragraph.

Now Write   Use general-to-specific order to organize the pre-writing notes for your explanatory *what* paragraph. Save your organized notes in your folder.

Optional Practice

Have students arrange the following pre-writing notes defining Thanksgiving in general-to-specific order.

2 —the first Thanksgiving celebrated by the Pilgrims in 1621

1 —a holiday celebrated in the United States

3 —celebrated on the fourth Thursday in November

4 —features a traditional feast of turkey, dressing, sweet potatoes, and pumpkin pie

Extending the Lesson

Have students exchange pre-writing notes to check for effective general-to-specific order.

Part 3

Objective

To write a first draft of an explanatory *what* paragraph that includes an effective topic sentence and an interesting ending sentence

Presenting the Lesson

1. Read and discuss **Here's the Idea.** Ask students what kinds of specific details might support the sample topic sentence defining *kangaroo.*

2. Have a volunteer read the paragraph in **Check It Out.** Discuss the questions, emphasizing that the paragraph is interesting because of its specific details.

3. Assign **Try Your Skill.** After completing the assignment, students can read aloud and compare their definitions with each other and with those in a dictionary.

4. Read **Keep This in Mind** and then assign **Now Write.**

Individualizing the Lesson

Less-Advanced Students

Help students to conclude their paragraphs with a strong, interesting detail that will stick in the readers' minds.

Advanced Students

Discuss the fact that descriptive writing skills are useful in writing an explanatory *what* paragraph. Have students discuss how they could use sensory details to define the following words:

sports car	constellations
reggae music	greenhouse

What's That?

Writing the First Draft

Here's the Idea   When you begin writing the first draft of your explanatory *what* paragraph, you must pay special attention to your topic sentence. As you know, a topic sentence should tell what a paragraph is about. In an explanatory *what* paragraph, the topic sentence has other duties as well. First, it must present the word to be defined. Then, it must put the word into its general class. Finally, it must tell something about the particular characteristics of the subject. Here is an example of a good topic sentence for an explanatory *what* paragraph.

A kangaroo is a mammal that carries its young in a pouch.

word	general	particular
(subject)	class	characteristic

After you have written the topic sentence, you must expand your definition. Your topic sentence is a general statement. In the body of your paragraph, present the specific details that will develop that general definition. These details are the facts and figures or specific examples that you organized in pre-writing.

Finish your paragraph with a strong ending sentence. You may want to leave your readers with an interesting thought or detail about your subject.

Check It Out   Read the following explanatory *what* paragraph. It is based on the pre-writing notes from Part 1, **Come to Terms.**

An anaconda is a large, nonpoisonous snake found in tropical South America. It is a type of boa constrictor that crushes its prey in its coils. The female can give birth to as many as fifty living young. The anaconda is found in swamps in the northern parts of South America. It is the largest living snake. Anacondas feed chiefly on birds, fish, and mammals. It has a reputation as a man-eater, but such stories have not been proven.

- Is the topic sentence a general definition? Explain your answer.
- Does the body develop the definition with specific details?
- Does the ending sentence leave you with an interesting thought or detail about the subject?

Try Your Skill   Below is a list of possible subjects for an explanatory *what* paragraph. Choose three subjects and write a topic sentence about each one. Be sure each sentence gives the word to be defined, puts the word in its general class, and tells something about the word's particular characteristics.

guitar	novel	mobile
apple	democracy	loneliness
friend	submarine	sculptor

Keep This in Mind

- In an explanatory *what* paragraph, the topic sentence should be a general definition of the subject.
- Develop the definition with specific details in the body of the paragraph.
- Write a strong ending sentence to conclude the paragraph.

Now Write   Write the first draft of your explanatory *what* paragraph. Be sure to develop your definition clearly and completely. Save your first draft in your folder.

Have students write some details they might use in developing definitions of the following items:

horror movies
break dancing
fast food

Extending the Lesson

Give each student one volume of an encyclopedia. Have students examine the definitions given in the first paragraph of most articles. Then ask each student to find an interesting entry and to list the word defined in the entry, along with its general class and its specific characteristics. Have students exchange papers and write explanatory *what* paragraphs based on the notes.

Objective

To revise an explanatory *what* paragraph

Presenting the Lesson

1. Read and discuss **Here's the Idea.** Outline on the chalkboard the five main points to check for in revising an explanatory *what* paragraph.

2. Have students read the paragraph in **Check It Out.** Help them recognize how the paragraph has been improved with the addition of specific, sensory details.

3. Assign **Try Your Skill.** Instruct students first to check the topic sentence for clarity and then to add any necessary or specific details as in the sample paragraph in **Check It Out.**

4. Read **Keep This in Mind** and then assign **Now Write.**

Individualizing the Lesson

Less-Advanced Students

As students revise their paragraphs, encourage them to write a vivid, interesting definition as well as an informative one. Have the class refer to the Section's sample paragraphs to see how they attract the reader's attention with interesting details as well as inform.

Advanced Students

Have students read their revised paragraphs to the class, omitting the word being defined. The writers can test for clarity by seeing if their subjects are identifiable.

Definitely the Best

Revising a Definition

Here's the Idea   A definition is useful only when it is as clear as it can be. Read the first draft of your explanatory *what* paragraph. Ask yourself how you can make it easier for your readers to understand. Here are some questions to help you revise your explanatory *what* paragraph.

1. Have I fully developed my paragraph with facts and figures or specific examples, or both?

2. Have I written a topic sentence that gives the word to be defined, puts it in its general class, and tells something about the particular characteristics of the word?

3. Have I followed general-to-specific order when organizing my paragraph?

4. Have I developed my topic in the body of my paragraph?

5. Have I written a strong ending sentence?

When you have finished revising your paragraph, proofread it. Find and correct any errors in grammar and mechanics.

Check It Out   Read the following revised paragraph.

The May Apple is an ~~interesting plant~~ *american* *(that belongs to the barberry family*. It grows in the *wooded areas of* eastern part of the United States~~.~~ ~~And~~ reach*s* ~~to~~ about one foot *a height of* ~~high.~~ It has ~~large~~ *maple-like* leaf*s* and a ~~small~~ *tiny white* flower. It produces a *yellow* fruit that looks like a *small* lemon. ~~The fruit can be eaten.~~ *The may apple also* It has a *delicate,* ~~sweet~~ taste. ~~Believe it or not~~ *Oddly enough, the roots of* this plant ~~has poison roots.~~ *contain a deadly poison.*

- How has the writer improved the topic sentence?
- Did the writer proofread this paragraph? How do you know?
- Does the topic sentence state the definition of the subject?

Try Your Skill   Revise this first draft of an explanatory *what* paragraph about a gymnasium.

A gymnasium is a very big room in a school. It has a wood floor. People can play games in a gymnasium. They can also exercise there. It has basketball things that come down. Sometimes it is called "gym" for short. We have gym classes in the gym.

Keep This in Mind

- In an explanatory *what* paragraph, the topic sentence should clearly define the subject.
- Use general-to-specific order to organize an explanatory *what* paragraph.
- Write a strong ending sentence.

Now Write   Revise your explanatory *what* paragraph according to the guidelines presented in this lesson. Be sure to proofread your paragraph for errors in grammar and mechanics. Make a final copy of your paragraph and save it in your folder.

Section **14** Objectives

1. To understand the definition of a composition and to recognize the three parts of a composition

2. To choose and narrow a topic for a composition

3. To gather and organize the ideas for a composition

4. To write the first draft of a composition

5. To revise the first draft of a composition

6. To write a title for a composition

7. To write the final copy of a composition

8. To review the process of writing a composition

Preparing the Students

Draw the following diagram on the chalkboard:

word → sentence → paragraph → COMPOSITION

Explain to students that just as words make up sentences and sentences make up paragraphs, paragraphs make up compositions. Review what the students have learned about paragraphs, including these terms: topic sentence, concluding sentence, facts, examples, details, and transitions. Tell students that they are now ready to begin writing compositions.

Additional Resources

Practice Book — pages 64–70
Duplicating Masters — pages 64–70

WRITING SECTION 14

Writing a Composition

Teaching Special Populations

LD See **Teaching Special Populations,** page 75. Sustained writing is difficult for most LD students. Reinforce students' efforts each step of the way. Allow some exercises to be completed orally.

ESL Provide students with additional examples of introductions, bodies, and conclusions. Have students identify those elements in duplicated compositions.

Encourage students to let their thoughts flow while they write their first drafts. Remind them that they will revise and correct the language and organization later. Go over students' first drafts individually before they revise.

Remind ESL students to choose appropriate transitional words and phrases to connect their ideas.

Define unfamiliar words and topics presented in this Section.

NSD See **Teaching Special Populations,** page 75.

Part 1 **Working Together**
Defining a Composition

Part 2 **Getting a Head Start**
Pre-Writing: Choosing a Topic

Part 3 **Putting It All Together**
Pre-Writing: Organizing Ideas

Part 4 **A Rough Sketch**
Writing the First Draft

Part 5 **If At First**
Revising Your Composition

Part 6 **Showstoppers**
Writing a Title

Part 7 **The Final Edition**
The Final Copy of a Composition

Part 8 **Remember This**
Guidelines for Writing a Composition

Working Together

Defining a Composition

Objective

To understand the definition of a composition and to recognize the three parts of a composition

Presenting the Lesson

1. Read aloud **Here's the Idea.** Write the definition of *composition* on the board. List and define *introduction, body,* and *conclusion* on the board.

2. Read aloud and discuss the composition in **Check It Out.** Point out that the introduction is the entire first paragraph and not just one sentence. Ask how the title of the composition helps to convey its main idea.

3. Discuss the introductory paragraph in **Try Your Skill.** Have the class discuss the kinds of supporting details that should follow in a composition with this introduction.

4. Read **Keep This in Mind** and then assign **Now Write.**

Individualizing the Lesson

Less-Advanced Students

Emphasize the similarities between a paragraph and a composition. Tell the students that both have the same parts; a composition, however, allows for a broader topic. Point out that a composition always has at least three paragraphs and often more, depending on how many paragraphs develop the main idea in the body of the composition.

Advanced Students

Ask students to bring in one or two compositions that they have

Here's the Idea   A **composition** is a group of paragraphs dealing with one main idea. In a composition you can develop an idea that is too complex to be covered in just one paragraph.

In many ways a composition is like a paragraph. A composition can be narrative, descriptive, or explanatory. Like a paragraph, a composition has many details that relate to one main idea. It must have unity and coherence just as a paragraph does. A composition also has a beginning, a middle, and an end.

The beginning of a composition is called the **introduction.** The introduction states the topic in a clear and interesting way.

The middle of a composition is called the **body.** The body is made up of several paragraphs that develop the main idea. In a narrative, the body presents the events of a story. In a description, the body presents the sensory details that paint the word picture. In an explanatory composition, the body explains a process, supports an opinion, or develops a definition.

The end of a composition is called the **conclusion.** The conclusion is a paragraph that sums up the important ideas.

Check It Out   Read this composition.

I Tamed a Whirlwind

Last summer I arranged my first adoption. However, I didn't adopt a human—I adopted a horse. The United States Government Bureau of Land Management has a program called Adopt-A-Horse. This program offers wild horses to interested people who are qualified to care for the animals.

One July morning we went to pick up my horse, a mare I named Whirlwind. She was a reddish-brown color with a stringy mane and tail. Whirlwind rolled her eyes when she saw me and flattened her ears against her head. It did not seem a promising beginning.

During her first weeks with us, she either ignored me or threatened me. She was eating well but was still easily frightened. It took almost a month of attention before I could walk up close to her. When Whirlwind finally let me approach her, she also let me brush her and put on a halter and a bridle.

After a few more weeks, Whirlwind allowed me to lay a pad on her back and, after that, a light saddle. The day I mounted Whirlwind for my first ride I wondered, "Will she buck?" I had spent months working with that horse. As she calmly trotted around the corral with me on her back, I knew it had been worth all the effort. I had tamed a real whirlwind!

- Does this composition have an introduction, a body, and a conclusion? Point out each part.

Try Your Skill   In which part of a composition does this paragraph belong? Write your answer and the reasons for it.

In coastal Peru, scientists have discovered a number of fascinating drawings that cover the land. They are of animals and geometric shapes. They all are quite large. In fact, these unusual drawings cannot be seen from the ground. They can only be seen from the air. They were made centuries ago, for reasons that can only be guessed at.

Keep This in Mind

- A composition is a group of paragraphs that tells about one main idea.
- All compositions have three parts: an introduction, a body, and a conclusion.

Now Write   Write a brief paragraph that explains what a composition is. In your paragraph, define the term *composition*. Be sure to tell how many parts a composition has and what each part does. Save your paragraph in your folder.

written in other classes. They can then analyze and discuss these compositions, labeling the introduction, body, and conclusion. If any of the parts were left out, the students can decide how they could have revised the composition to include all three parts.

Optional Practice

Duplicate and distribute a well-written student composition with its paragraphs jumbled. Have students number the paragraphs in logical order and label the introduction, the paragraphs belonging to the body, and the conclusion. Discuss the effectiveness of each of the three parts.

Extending the Lesson

Ask students to clip out short articles from the features section of a newspaper or from *Reader's Digest* or *TV Guide*. Have each student select an article and label its introduction, body, and conclusion. Have students exchange articles with several classmates to check the labels.

Objective

To choose and narrow a topic for a composition

Presenting the Lesson

1. Have students read **Here's the Idea.** Discuss choosing a composition topic, emphasizing that the topic need not be personal if it is a subject that interests the writer. Also discuss the fact that although a composition offers more scope than a paragraph, its topic still must be narrow and specific.

2. Read aloud and discuss **Check It Out.** Discuss how asking the questions *who? what? where? how?* and *why?* has helped narrow the topic.

3. Assign **Try Your Skill.** Advise the students to ask *what?* first as in the example in **Check It Out.**

4. Read **Keep This in Mind.**

5. Assign **Now Write.** Reread paragraph 3 of **Here's the Idea** to remind students where to find a general topic.

Individualizing the Lesson

Less-Advanced Students

To stimulate ideas for a composition topic, write headings such as these on the chalkboard:

a humorous experience
a frightening experience
a sad experience
an interesting place
a controversial issue
a difficult problem
a fantastic idea
a complex process

Getting a Head Start

Pre-Writing: Choosing a Topic

Here's the Idea   Have you ever been in a footrace where someone has given you a "head start," a chance to get going early? Getting a "head start" gives you a better chance to win the race.

You can give yourself a head start when you write a composition, too. Do this by choosing a topic that you know something about and that interests you. Writing is easier when the subject is a familiar one. Writing is also more enjoyable when the writer is interested in the subject. Write about school, about sports you play and other activities you enjoy. Write about friends and family, about people who are special to you. Write about places you enjoy visiting, about experiences you've had. Write about subjects you are interested in and would like to learn more about.

There are many ways to find ideas for compositions. You can look for topics in your journal, where you have been writing about things that are important to you. You can also discover writing ideas through reading and by brainstorming. Class discussions and interviews with interesting people are two other sources of writing ideas.

When you have chosen a subject to write about, you will probably have to narrow it. Even though a composition is much longer than a single paragraph, you still want a topic that is specific rather than general. You can make a general subject more specific by asking the questions *who?*, *what?*, *where?*, *when?*, *how?*, and *why?* about it. To learn more about narrowing a topic, see pages 80–81.

Check It Out   Notice how the following general subject has been made more specific.

- Why is the specific topic better for a composition?

General Subject: a part-time job
  What? drug store deliveries   hospital kitchen help
        picking apples
  Where? Hill's Apple Orchard, Bristol,
         Wisconsin
  When? two weekends in a row last fall
  Who? Maria and I
  How? picked apples by hand and with long poles
  Why? To learn about working at an orchard, and to
       make some spending money
Specific Topic: Last fall, Maria and I spent two weekends
                working as apple pickers at Hill's Apple Or-
                chard in Wisconsin.

Try Your Skill   Here is a list of broad, general subjects. Choose one and ask the narrowing questions *who?*, *what?*, *where?*, *when?*, *how?*, and *why?* about it to find a specific topic. You may answer the questions with real or imaginary details. Write your specific topic.

an adventure story   a different country
a new invention   a musical concert

Keep This in Mind

- Choose a topic that interests you, and that you know something about.
- Find topics by looking in your journal, reading, brainstorming, discussing, and interviewing.
- Narrow your topic to make it specific.

Now Write   Following the guidelines in this lesson, choose and narrow a topic for a composition. Be sure to ask the questions *who?*, *what?*, *where?*, *when?*, *how?*, and *why?* as you narrow your topic. Save your narrowed topic in your folder.

163

Part 3

Objective

To gather and organize the ideas for a composition

Presenting the Lesson

1. Have students read **Here's the Idea.** Write on the chalkboard the four kinds of details that students may use in the bodies of their compositions, stressing that the kind of details chosen depends on the composition's purpose. Next write the six types of orders in which the details may be arranged.

2. After students have read the sample pre-writing notes in **Check It Out,** help the class recognize the three general facts around which the more specific details can be grouped.

3. Assign **Try Your Skill.** Ask students to consider the purpose of the sample compositon—to explain why—in determining the order of its details.

4. Read **Keep This in Mind.**

5. Assign **Now Write.** Remind the class that this is not a research report. Students may, however, want to do some light research to verify facts or add statistics to knowledge they already have.

Individualizing the Lesson

Less-Advanced Students

Give students extra time and assistance in deciding what kind of details to gather for their composition and how to organize the details. If you cannot help each student individually, let the students work in pairs to help each other.

164

Putting It All Together

Pre-Writing: Organizing Ideas

Here's the Idea   When you have narrowed your topic, you are ready to gather ideas to develop your composition. You might gather sensory details, specific examples, facts and statistics, or incidents or anecdotes. The kind of details you look for will depend on your purpose for writing. A descriptive composition would be developed with sensory details. An explanatory composition might be developed with facts and statistics. Some compositions are developed with two or more kinds of details.

You can gather ideas for a composition from your own knowledge and experience or from brainstorming. You might also gather details from books, magazines, and newspapers you have read, or from discussions and interviews you have with other people.

Before you, can begin writing about your ideas, you must organize them. First look for two or three major details among your notes. Then group the remaining pre-writing notes around these major ideas. Each group of notes can become a paragraph in the body of your composition.

When you have finished grouping your notes, decide on the order in which you want to present them. Remember, you must organize both the groups and the notes within each group. You might use **chronological order, spatial order, the order of importance, general to specific order, most familiar to least familiar order,** and **comparison and contrast.** Refer back to pages 88–89 to refresh your memory about these different methods of organization.

Check It Out   Read these pre-writing notes for a composition about bicycling.

164

bicycle riding is healthy   no energy costs
no need for expensive city garage space
stimulates heart and lungs (aerobic fitness)
bicycles are economical   don't pollute the air
need little maintenance
develops strong leg muscles   no traffic jams
bicycles can ease city problems
don't cost much (cheaper than car or motorcycle)

- What three major ideas could these notes be grouped around?

Try Your Skill   Look again at the notes in **Check It Out.** Write the three main ideas included in these notes. Then group the remaining notes around whichever main idea each note seems to belong to. Next, choose a method of organization that suits the purpose of the composition. Arrange the notes in that order.

Keep This in Mind

- Gather ideas for your composition through brainstorming, from personal experience, from literature you have read, or from discussions and interviews with other people.
- Organize your composition according to chronological order, spatial order, the order of importance, general to specific order, most familiar to least familiar order, or comparison and contrast.
- Group your notes around several main ideas.

Now Write   Make some pre-writing notes for your topic. Then group your notes around several main ideas. Finally, organize your notes in an order that suits the purpose of your composition. Save your organized notes in your folder.

Objective

To write the first draft of a composition

Presenting the Lesson

1. Read and discuss **Here's the Idea.** First, remind students that a composition contains at least three paragraphs. Discuss the fact that during pre-writing, students focus on finding supporting details for the composition's body; when writing the first draft, they must also consider an interesting introduction and a strong conclusion.

2. Have the students read the sample first draft in **Check It Out.** As the class discusses the questions following the composition, have the students analyze the sample's introduction and conclusion. Which sentence in the introduction states the composition's main idea? How does the conclusion summarize the writer's ideas?

3. Assign **Try Your Skill.** Urge students to read the composition critically to find areas for improvement.

4. Read **Keep This in Mind** and then assign **Now Write.**

Individualizing the Lesson

Less-Advanced Students

The students may find that writing a first draft is the most difficult step in the process of writing. Advise students that if they made thorough pre-writing notes and carefully considered their purpose and method of organization, the first draft will

A Rough Sketch

Writing the First Draft

Here's the Idea Before an artist begins a painting, he or she will usually draw several sketches. This gives the artist a chance to try out some ideas before actually putting paint to canvas. As a writer, you need to do some sketching, too. You need to try out your ideas before you are ready to present them to a reader. That is the purpose of writing a first draft. It gives you a chance to experiment, to discover *what* you want to say about your topic and *how* you want to say it.

When you write your first draft, keep in mind what each of the three parts of a composition is supposed to do. In the introduction, you want to capture the interest of your audience. You also want to state your topic clearly and directly so that the reader knows just what your composition is going to be about.

The body of a composition is made up of paragraphs that develop the topic. Follow your organized pre-writing notes as you write. Remember that each paragraph should have a strong topic sentence. Also, experiment with transitional words and phrases that might help the flow of ideas.

End your composition with a concluding paragraph that sums up the ideas you presented in your composition and clearly signals an end to your story, description, or explanation.

Don't forget your audience as you write. Choose language that is suitable for your readers. Include the kinds of details that the audience needs to understand and enjoy your composition. Keep your purpose in mind as well. Keep reminding yourself of what you are trying to accomplish.

Check It Out Read the following first draft and compare it with the pre-writing notes in **Check It Out** from the last lesson, **Putting It All Together.**

Lots of people in America are trying to find ways to save money and stay fit. And they want to help their cities. They should try bicycles.

Bicycles are inexpensive compared to cars. Some bikes are really cheap. There is a large, used bicycle market. Most Americans should be able to find bicycles that they can afford. And you don't have to buy gasoline for a bike which saves money too.

Bicycles are healthy. They let you exercise your body. Even on short trips you can exercise your leg muscles, heart and lungs.

Bicycles can help our cities. Every large city has its parking problem because spaces are often hard to find. And there are traffic jams during rush hour. If even one tenth of the drivers switched to bicycles, there would be some relief. Also, many cities are choking on pollution that is caused by cars. Having fewer cars would help. Cities could promote the idea of using bicycles instead of cars by providing bicycle paths and lanes.

Bicycles can play a more important role toward better health and toward relieving city problems if we only give them a try. Pedal power can be both a method of physical fitness and an inexpensive and non-polluting form of transportation.

- Has the writer made each group of ideas from the pre-writing notes into a paragraph?

Try Your Skill   Reread the first draft above. List some things you could do to improve this first draft.

Keep This in Mind

- A first draft gives the writer a chance to try out ideas, organization, and language.

Now Write   Using your organized notes, write a first draft of your composition. Be sure that your composition has an introduction, a body, and a conclusion. Save your first draft.

pose no problems. Although students should rely on their pre-writing notes, they should also feel comfortable about making any changes as they write the first draft.

Advanced Students

If students have no major difficulties in writing their first drafts, they may meet in small groups to read and critique their classmates' compositions. Remind the students to criticize constructively and to focus on general issues such as effective organization, an interesting introduction, and a strong conclusion.

Optional Practice

Hold a "writing workshop" in which students are given time to write their first drafts. You will be available to help with questions and "writer's block."

Extending the Lesson

As a preliminary exercise to writing their first drafts, have the class write a group composition. Have students choose one of the following topics and narrow it. Record pre-writing notes on the chalkboard as the students contribute supporting details. Then divide the class into groups—one to write an introduction, one a conclusion, and one to write the composition's body. After one person from each group has recorded the group's work, you can assemble and duplicate the groups' paragraphs and distribute the finished composition.

1. how high-school students of today differ from those of ten years ago
2. how high-school students can serve their community

Objective

To revise the first draft of a composition

Presenting the Lesson

1. Have students read **Here's the Idea.** Then read and discuss the revision questions. Review the use of transitional phrases, reminding the class that the kind of transitions they use depends on the way they organize their ideas. For example, a narrative composition uses transitions that indicate time (*then, first, yesterday*).

2. Have students study the revision in **Check It Out.** As the class discusses the revision, point out the improvement made in the composition's transitional phrases. Help students see how this improves the coherence of the composition.

3. Assign **Try Your Skill.** Instruct students to revise the sample composition one step at a time as they read the guidelines in this lesson.

4. Read **Keep This in Mind.**

5. Assign **Now Write.** Encourage students to make many improvements as they revise their compositions step by step.

Individualizing the Lesson

Less-Advanced Students

Lead students through a step-by-step revision of their compositions in class. Read each revision question, and then allow time for questions and discussion as the students revise their compositions.

168

If at First

Revising Your Composition

Here's the Idea   When the founding fathers of our country wrote the Constitution, they spent months revising the document. They wanted to be sure that what they wrote was exactly what they wanted to say. You will not need to spend months revising your composition. However, you will need to take your time. Be careful and attentive at this stage of the process of writing.

Here are some questions to ask yourself as you revise your composition.

1. Does the introduction tell the reader what my composition is about? Will the introduction capture the reader's attention?

2. Have I included enough details to develop my topic fully?

3. Are there any unrelated ideas I should take out?

4. Do the details in each paragraph tell about one main idea?

5. Does each paragraph have an interesting and informative topic sentence?

6. Are the paragraphs and the details within them organized logically? Does the method of organization suit the purpose of the composition?

7. Have I used good transitional phrases to lead the reader from one idea to the next? Have I used transitions both within and between paragraphs?

8. Have I used language that is direct and lively? Are my verbs specific? Are my adjectives vivid?

9. Does my conclusion sum up the ideas in my composition?

Check It Out   Notice how the first few paragraphs of the composition about bicycles have been revised.

- How have these paragraphs been improved?

How would you like to

☐ Lots of people in America are trying to find ways to save money, and stay fit. And they want to help ~~their~~ *your* cities. ~~They should try bicycles.~~ *conquer some modern urban problems?*
First of all, *Riding a bicycle is one way to achieve these goals.*
Bicycles are inexpensive compared to cars. Some bikes are *quite inexpensive.* ~~really cheap.~~ There is a large used bicycle market. *Other forms of transportation.* Most Ameri-*even market in* *s.* cans should be able to find bicycles they can afford. ~~And~~ you *In addition,* don't have to buy gasoline for a bike ~~which~~ *That* saves money, too.
Second, riding a Bicycles are healthy. ~~They let you~~ *can* exercise your *entire* body. Even *is also* on short trips, you can exercise your leg muscles, *your* heart, and *your* lungs. *Bicycling promotes strength and aerobic fitness.*

Try Your Skill Revise the last two paragraphs of the composition on bicycles on page 167. Use the guidelines presented in this lesson. Compare your revision with those of your classmates.

Keep This in Mind

- Revise a composition to improve the ideas, the organization, and the word choice.
- Proofread your composition for errors in grammar and mechanics.

Now Write Use the guidelines in this lesson to help you as you revise the first draft of your composition. Ask yourself the questions in **Here's the Idea.** Proofread your composition. Save your revised composition in your folder.

169

Part 6

Objective

To write a title for a composition

Presenting the Lesson

1. Read **Here's the Idea.** Emphasize that compositions should always be titled.

2. Read and discuss the titles in **Check It Out.** Ask students if the titles stimulate their curiosity and make them want to read the stories. Then have students use their imaginations by guessing what the stories might be about.

3. Assign **Try Your Skill.** Discuss the fact that a title for a topic such as example 3 will probably be simple and straightforward, while a title for topic number 1 might be more imaginative.

4. Read **Keep This in Mind.**

5. Assign **Now Write.** Encourage students to think of several different kinds of titles for their compositions.

Individualizing the Lesson

Less-Advanced Students

Make sure students understand that a title need not be, and usually is not, a complete sentence. Review the rule for capitalizing titles: Capitalize the first word and all important words. Instruct students not to put quotation marks around the title of their compositions unless the title is a direct quotation.

Advanced Students

After completing **Try Your Skill,** students can share their titles. Write some especially interesting and creative ones on the chalkboard.

170

Showstoppers

Writing a Title

Here's the Idea   Throughout this chapter, you have been learning about the different choices you have to make as a writer. When you write a composition, you have one more choice to make. You must choose a title.

A title should be informative and interesting. Sometimes the best title is a simple one that suggests the main idea you are writing about. Straightforward titles will probably work best for pieces of explanatory writing, particularly those about factual topics. Sometimes a good title may be unusual or surprising, such as "The Secret Life of Walter Mitty." Unusual titles often work well for narratives and descriptions, especially imaginary ones.

Check It Out   Read the following titles of stories you may have read.

"Irene, Goodnight"	"My Old Man"
"Fumble"	"A Sense of Shelter"
"The Valentine"	"A Night of Vengeance"
"I Can't Breathe"	"The Open Boat"
"Samuel"	"But Who Can Replace a Man?"

• Are these good titles? Why?

Try Your Skill   Choose four of the following possible topics for longer pieces of writing. For each topic, write two titles that might work.

1. a narrative about a childhood adventure
2. a description of a snowy morning
3. a report on careers in computers
4. an explanation of how to change a flat tire

5. an explanation of why education is important
6. an explanation of what emotions are
7. a story about a creature from outer space
8. a report on earthquakes

Keep This in Mind

- Write titles for compositions.
- A good title is interesting and informative.

Now Write Read your composition. Think of several titles that suggest the main idea of your composition. The titles should give your readers some idea of what your composition is about. They should also be interesting enough to catch your readers' attention. Write as many good titles as you can think of. Then choose the one that best suits your composition. Write it at the top of your revised composition. Save your composition in your folder.

Have students write two titles—a straightforward one that simply suggests the subject, and an imaginative one—for each of the following composition topics.

1. a definition of success
2. an explanation of aerobic exercise
3. a description of a local zoo

Extending the Lesson

1. Have students go to the library and find an interesting title for each of the following items:

1. a novel
2. a biography
3. a short story
4. an article in a newsmagazine
5. an article in a specialized magazine

2. Bring a TV guide to class. Mention the names of various television programs. Ask students to comment on especially good titles. Then have each student make up titles for three imaginary television programs.

Part 7

Objective

To write the final copy of a composition

Presenting the Lesson

1. Read and discuss **Here's the Idea.** Emphasize that presenting a neat, attractive paper is an important part of writing a composition.

2. Have students study and discuss the sample final copy in **Check It Out.** Call attention to the interesting title of the composition.

3. Assign **Try Your Skill.**

4. Read **Keep This in Mind.**

5. Assign **Now Write.** Remind students to proofread their composition after they have made the final copy to correct any errors they may have made in copying it.

Individualizing the Lesson

Less-Advanced Students

Suggest that students spend time working on neat, legible handwriting. Those students who have difficulty with their handwriting may find it worthwhile to learn to type.

Advanced Students

Students may want to share the final copies of their compositions by exchanging them or by posting them on a bulletin board.

Optional Practice

Have students produce a neat, final copy as discussed in this lesson for every assignment that is handed in.

The Final Edition

The Final Copy of a Composition

Here's the Idea   Once you have revised your composition, you must make a final copy of it. This is the only copy of your paper that your audience will see. Therefore, it is very important to present a clean and neat copy. Your ideas might be very good. However, a messy copy will make your composition unappealing to your readers.

Write your final copy on white, lined paper. Always use a pen. In the upper right-hand corner of your paper, write your name, the subject, and the date. Then, on the second line of your paper, write the title that you have decided on for your composition.

You will need to copy your composition carefully. Make sure each line is neat and readable. Leave at least one inch on the right and left sides of your paper for a margin. Leave at least one line blank at the bottom of the page. Write on only one side of the paper. If your composition runs longer than one page, be sure to number each page after the first one. Put the numeral in the center at the top.

Proofread your final copy one last time. Cross out any errors you find with a single line. If you find several mistakes, you may want to write your final copy over again. Remember, be as neat as possible.

Check It Out   Here is the beginning of the final copy of the composition on bicycles.

- Does this final copy follow the guidelines presented in this lesson?

George Santos
English
April 30, 1985

Pedal Power!

How would you like to save money, stay fit, and help your city conquer some modern urban problems? Riding a bicycle is one way to achieve these goals. First of all, bicycles are inexpensive

Extending the Lesson

Discuss the fact that a student's final copy is a finished product in the same sense that a book or a newspaper is. If your school has a printing press, the students might enjoy seeing how a piece of writing is processed from the manuscript stage to the printed page.

Try Your Skill   Answer the following questions about the final copy of a composition.

1. What kind of paper should you use for a final copy?
2. Where do you put your name, the subject, and the date?
3. Where do you put the title?
4. How much room should you leave for your right and left margins?
5. If your composition is longer than one page, where do you number the following pages?
6. How should you correct any errors you find?

Keep This in Mind

· Your final copy should be neat and free of errors. Remember, this is the only copy your readers will see.

Now Write   Follow the guidelines in this lesson as you make a final copy of your composition. Be sure it is as neat and free of errors as you can make it. Save your final copy in your folder.

Objective

To review the process of writing a composition

Presenting the Lesson

1. Have students read the chart, "Guidelines for Writing a Composition." You may want to briefly outline the steps of each stage of the process on the chalkboard, or allow students to question or discuss items on the chart.

2. Emphasize that the steps listed on the chart are used for developing each different kind of composition to be studied in subsequent lessons. Students should refer to the chart whenever they are writing a composition.

Individualizing the Lesson

Less-Advanced Students

Help students outline the chart in this lesson in a simplified form that they can keep in their folders for easy reference.

Advanced Students

Have students review their personal experiences with the process of writing. For example, did they find one step of the process much easier or harder than the others? Have they learned anything that will make writing easier in the future? Have they discovered any idiosyncrasies in their personal style of completing the writing process? What part of the writing process can they perform more effectively in the future? This review may take the form of a class discussion or of a paragraph.

174

Remember This

Guidelines for Writing a Composition

Throughout this chapter, you have learned how to plan, write, and revise a composition. Now you are ready to learn how to write different kinds of compositions. You will write stories, descriptions, and explanations. However, the way you go about developing each kind of composition will remain the same. You will always follow the process of writing.

Here is a list of the steps you should follow whenever you write a composition. Refer to these guidelines often as you write your compositions.

Guidelines for Writing a Composition

Pre-Writing

- Choose a topic that interests you and that you know something about. Narrow the topic so that you can cover it well in the assigned length of your composition.
- Identify your purpose and your audience.
- Gather details to develop your topic.
- Group similar details around two or three main ideas.
- Organize your details into an order that suits the type of composition you are writing.

Writing the First Draft

- Begin your composition with an interesting introductory paragraph. The introduction should tell your reader what your composition is about.
- After your introduction, write the body of your composition. Use your organized details to develop

your topic. Each group of details will become a paragraph in the body of your composition.

- Use transitional words and phrases to lead your readers from one idea to the next.
- Add, take out, and reorganize your ideas if you need to.
- End your first draft with a concluding paragraph that sums up your ideas.
- Add an interesting title to your composition.

Revising

- Be sure your composition has an introduction, a body, and a conclusion.
- Check to see that you have included enough details to develop your topic.
- Organize the paragraphs and the ideas within them logically.
- Be sure the topic sentence of each paragraph presents the main idea of that paragraph.
- Use effective transitional words to make your ideas flow smoothly.
- Make sure you have used vivid language. Use language that suits the audience you are writing for.
- Proofread to find and correct errors in grammar, capitalization, punctuation, and spelling.

Final Copy

- Rewrite your composition neatly in ink on white, lined paper.
- Write your name, subject, and the date in the upper right-hand corner of your paper.
- Proofread your final copy one last time. Neatly correct any errors you find.

Stimulate interest in the writing process by posting interesting newspaper articles, humorous tidbits, thought-provoking sayings, and unique cartoons on the bulletin board. For example, the comic strip "Peanuts" often has amusing comments about the process of writing.

Section **15** Objectives

1. To know the elements of a narrative composition: setting, characters, plot, and conflict

2. To plot a narrative by listing events in chronological order

3. To understand the points of view that can be used in a narrative composition

4. To write the first draft of a narrative composition

5. To know how to use dialogue in a narrative composition

6. To use effective transitions in the first draft of a narrative composition

7. To revise a narrative composition

Preparing the Students

Ask student volunteers to do the following:

1. Tell the plot of a good movie or television program they have seen recently

2. Tell something interesting that has happened to them in the last week or two

3. Tell a joke

Explain that all of the above are forms of narratives, with characters, plots, conflicts, and settings. This Section will instruct students how to put a narrative in composition form.

Additional Resources

Mastery Test — pages 28–29 in the test booklet

Practice Book — pages 71–77

Duplicating Masters — pages 71–77

The Narrative Composition

Teaching Special Populations

LD See **Teaching Special Populations,** page 75. Some of the students may have difficulty reading the sample passages. Read the examples aloud in class.

ESL When discussing character, plot, and conflict, ask students to tell folk tales from their native cultures and to identify those elements in the tales.

Ask students to identify the point of view from which they tell their tales. Then ask them to tell part of the tale from another point of view.

Assign Handbook Section 14, pages 650–652 for practice with English punctuation of dialogue. Also assign exercises in the Practice Book as necessary.

NSD Explain to these students that dialogue in narratives are often written in dialect. Discuss with them the situations when this is acceptable. Encourage NSD students to write dialogues in dialects other than their own.

Objective

To know the elements of a narrative composition: setting, characters, plot, and conflict

Presenting the Lesson

1. Have students read **Here's the Idea.** Write the terms *narrative composition, setting, characters, plot,* and *conflict* on the board as you define and discuss them. Emphasize that a narrative must have some sort of conflict in order to have a plot. Also discuss the fact that a narrative composition may tell of real or imaginary events.

2. Read the pre-writing notes in **Check It Out.** As the students discuss the study question, point out that the notes specify both time and place for "setting." Also have students note that the conflict occurs within the narrator herself.

3. Assign **Try Your Skill.** Discuss the fact that the conflict of a narrative may be as obvious as a policeman against a criminal or as subtle as a teen-ager facing problems growing up.

4. Read **Keep This in Mind.**

5. Assign **Now Write.** Remind students that writing about a personal experience often produces the most effective narrative. However, students should feel free to use their imaginations in creating a story if they wish. Emphasize that students are only to write story topics at this stage of pre-writing.

Get to the Point

Pre-Writing: Planning the Story

Here's the Idea   A narrative composition tells a story. It may tell about real events or imaginary ones. A narrative composition always does more than just entertain the reader. It also makes a point. The incidents in a narrative composition tell something about how people feel, act, react, or think in a certain situation.

All stories have some things in common. For instance, think of a half-hour TV episode. It has many of the same parts as a narrative composition. Both have a setting, characters, a plot, and a conflict.

The **setting** tells when and where the events of a story take place. A story might happen in the past, the present, or the future. A story can take place in a house, in a foreign country, or on another planet.

The **characters** are those involved in the action of the story. The characters may be real or imaginary. Although many stories are about people, animals can be the characters in a story, too.

The **plot** is the series of incidents, or happenings, that tell the story. At the center of the plot is a conflict. The **conflict** is some major problem or difficulty that a character faces. The conflict might be a struggle between two characters. It might also be a struggle between a character and some force of nature. Sometimes, the conflict is a personal problem that a character faces. The story explains how this conflict is solved.

Check It Out   Look at these pre-writing notes.

Setting:	at home, Thanksgiving Day last year
Characters:	Lauren and I, Dad, Mom, rest of family
Plot:	two inexperienced cooks fix Thanksgiving dinner
Conflict:	me struggling against time and inexperience

- Do these notes contain the necessary parts for a narrative composition?

Think of a weekly TV show that you have watched recently. Make a list of notes about the show, like the pre-writing notes in **Check It Out** above. Your notes should show the kind of planning that might have gone into that TV episode. Be especially careful about deciding what the conflict was.

Keep This in Mind

- A narrative composition tells a story that has a point. The story may be real or imaginary.
- A narrative has a plot, a conflict, at least one character, and a setting.

Now Write Think of a story you would like to tell. Have you learned something about life or about other people from a past experience? Have you heard or read about someone who has overcome an obstacle? Does the future interest you? Remember that your story may be real or imaginary. You may also begin with a real situation and then expand it with details from your imagination. Write your story ideas down on a sheet of paper. Save your ideas in your folder.

Individualizing the Lesson

Less-Advanced Students

Illustrate the elements of a narrative by discussing a fairy tale with which everyone is familiar. For example, *Cinderella* takes place in a kingdom in some bygone era; the conflict is between Cinderella and her wicked stepmother and stepsisters. Have students discuss all the elements of one or two fairy tales in this manner.

Advanced Students

Have students discuss the kind of conflict involved in each of the following plots:

1. A little boy sticks his finger in a hole in a dam to keep his town from being flooded.
2. A policeman goes undercover to catch a thief who has been robbing old people.
3. A child adjusts to having a new baby in the family.

Optional Practice

Have students list possible settings, characters, plot, and conflict for each of the following narratives:

1. a story set on the moon in the year 2085
2. a story about a Russian student in an American high school
3. a story about yourself in ten years

Extending the Lesson

Have each student find and read a short story from an anthology in the library. The students can then make notes describing the story's setting, characters, and conflict and share the story with their classmates.

The Plot Thickens

Objective

To plot a narrative by listing events in chronological order

Presenting the Lesson

1. Have students read **Here's the Idea.** Write the terms *plot* and *chronological order* on the board as you define and discuss them. Explain that a good narrative contains many specific sensory details. Also emphasize the fact that a flashback does not detract from effective chronological order.

2. Have the students read and discuss the pre-writing notes in **Check It Out.** Have the students note the point in the narrative at which the flashback is placed.

3. Assign **Try Your Skill.** Call attention to the specific details added to the narrated events in the pre-writing stage.

4. Read **Keep This in Mind.**

5. Assign **Now Write.** Tell students that they may add important events or delete any they do not need when they write the first draft of the narrative.

Individualizing the Lesson

Less-Advanced Students

Discuss the fact that pre-writing notes may be messy as the students insert events or flashbacks and add specific details. Help the students decide with which events to begin and end the story by reminding them that the story should make a point about how people feel or act in a certain situation.

180

Pre-Writing: Plotting a Story

Here's the Idea   A story is more than just an idea. It is a series of many small incidents or events. Together, these events are the **plot,** or the story line, of your narrative.

Begin developing your plot by making a list of everything that is to happen in the story. If it is an imaginary story, you can make up all of the events. If the story is a true account, try to remember all of the details and events as they happened.

As you list the events, try to add specific details to your notes. For example, suppose your main character is a girl about your age. The story is about her search for a letter. At one point in the story, she goes to an abandoned house to search for the letter. In your notes you write, "Mary enters house to look for letter." To "Mary" you could add "nervous, shivering." To "house" you might add "dark, damp, filled with cobwebs. Door creaks." Details like these can bring your story to life.

The events that tell your story should be arranged in **chronological order,** the order in which they happened. At some point, you may wish to interrupt this natural order with a flashback. A **flashback** is an incident that happened before the time when your story takes place. You can use a flashback to say something about the present conflict. For instance, one character in your story may not trust another character. To explain this mistrust, a flashback could describe an earlier incident in which the untrusting character was double-crossed by his "friend."

Check It Out   Look at these notes.

1. I had planned a perfect, relaxing day
2. Mom hurt her back
3. my sister and I cooked, cleaned
4. I was tempted to give up

5. I remember Mom's help when I broke my ankle
6. we got everything done
7. relatives liked dinner
8. Mom was proud of what we had done

- Are the events of the story in chronological order?
- What flashback has the writer included? How does it help to explain the events of the story?

Try Your Skill   Read these pre-writing notes about the first day at a new school. Arrange them in chronological order.

7 Teachers and kids were helpful and friendly

4 Taken to hospital in ambulance (wailing siren)

3 Hit by a car (screeching brakes, clang of metal)

2 Forgot to signal when turning because I was thinking about how I dreaded starting school where I knew no one

6 Couldn't sleep well, thinking how I'd stand out now, with my bandages and cast

5 Treated in the emergency room for a bruised shoulder, cuts on leg, a broken left arm (cuts stung, shoulder ached)

8 By the end of the first day, my cast was full of autographs and phone numbers

1 Riding my bike the day before school opened

Keep This in Mind

- Use chronological order to organize the events and details in your narrative composition.
- You may interrupt the natural order of events with a flashback that explains some earlier event.

Now Write   Choose a story idea from the list you made in the last lesson. Plot your narrative by making a list of all of the events that will tell your story. Add specific details to your list. Arrange the events in chronological order. Add a flashback if it will help to explain something. Save your work.

181

Advanced Students

1. Discuss descriptions of characters in a narrative composition. Tell students that they need not always describe height, hair color, etc. Instead, they should try to use details that help to characterize the person or that add to the general mood of the narrative.

2. Advise the students to add at least one specific detail to each event in their pre-writing notes. They can always delete details when they write the first draft.

Optional Practice

Have students arrange the following pre-writing notes about witnessing an accident, including the flashback, in chronological order.
Answers may vary

4 —I memorized the white car's license plate number

1 —I was mailing a letter

5 —I remembered the time a car almost hit me and I got its license plate number

3 —the man in the white car disappeared down a side street

6 —the people whose cars were hit got out of their cars

7 —I gave the policeman the man's license number

2 —a white car plowed into another car, which hit two other cars

8 —the policeman thanked me for my help

Extending the Lesson

Have students make notes listing in chronological order the events of the stories they read for **Extending the Lesson,** Part 1.

Objective

To understand the points of view that can be used in a narrative composition

Presenting the Lesson

1. Read and discuss **Here's the Idea.** Write the terms *point of view, first-person, third-person, third-person limited,* and *third-person omniscient* on the chalkboard as you define and discuss them. Point out that first-person narration is not only used in true stories but in fiction as well.

2. Read the paragraphs in **Check It Out** and discuss their points of view. Make sure students identifiy the pronoun *he* with the third-person point of view, and *I* with the first-person point of view. Also discuss the fact that the first paragraph uses the third-person omniscient point of view because it reports Russell's thoughts and feelings.

3. Assign **Try Your Skill.** Point out that there is no correct point of view for each kind of story although one point of view may be more effective than the others.

4. Read **Keep This in Mind** and then assign **Now Write.**

Individualizing the Lesson

Less-Advanced Students

Help each student determine an appropriate point of view for his or her story. Have students study the pre-writing notes they made for Part 2 to see which point of view comes naturally to the stories they are telling. Remind the students that they

Whose Story?

Pre-Writing: Choosing a Point of View

Here's the Idea Every story needs a narrator. The **narrator** is the person who tells the story. He or she may actually be one of the characters. On the other hand, the narrator may be completely outside the action, just reporting the events that occur. When you decide who will tell your story, you will also be deciding on a point of view. **Point of view** means the eyes and mind through which something is written.

Sometimes a story is told by one of the characters who is identified as *I*. Then the story is told from the **first-person point of view.** The reader sees and knows only what the character *I* sees and knows. If your narrative composition is about an experience that happened to you, you will probably want to use the first-person point of view.

If the narrator is outside the story, the story is told from the **third-person point of view.** In a story written from this point of view, the pronouns *he* and *she* are used.

If you use the third-person point of view, you have a second decision to make. You may choose to report only the actions and conversations of your characters. In this case, you will use the **third-person limited** point of view. On the other hand, you may want to show the reader what is inside the minds of your characters. Then you will use the **third-person omniscient** point of view. *Omniscient* means "knowing all things." With this point of view, the narrator sees and hears everything. The narrator also knows and reports what every character thinks and feels.

Check It Out Read these paragraphs.

1. Russell felt nervous about starting the year at a new school. As he rode his bike around the new neighborhood, Russ was

thinking about how out of place he would feel the next morning walking into Jefferson High.

2. I felt nervous about starting the year at a new school. I got on my bike for a ride around my new neighborhood, thinking about how out of place I'd feel the next morning walking into Jefferson High.

- From what point of view is each paragraph told? How do you know?

Try Your Skill   Tell what point of view you would use if you were writing each of the following kinds of stories. Explain your choices. Compare your choices with those of your classmates.

1. a suspenseful detective story
2. a rivalry between two friends for the same prize
3. a fairy tale like Cinderella
4. a story about someone lost in a blizzard

Keep This in Mind

- With the first-person point of view, the reader knows only what the narrator, *I*, sees and knows.
- With the third-person limited point of view, the reader knows only about the outward actions and conversations of the characters.
- With the third-person omniscient point of view, the reader knows about the outward actions and conversations of the characters. The reader also knows the inner thoughts and feelings of the characters.

Now Write   Select a point of view that is natural and appropriate for the story you began in Part 2. Write your choice on the paper that has your pre-writing notes. Keep your paper in your folder.

Showtime

Objective

To write the first draft of a narrative composition

Presenting the Lesson

1. Have the students read **Here's the Idea.** Advise the class that the first draft is a good time to add specific details that will make the story come alive. Also discuss the use of vivid verbs in narrating the story's events. For example, instead of writing, "Kathy walked to her friend's house," a good writer might say, "Kathy marched angrily to her friend's house."

2. Have volunteers read the introductory paragraphs in **Check It Out.** Help the class note that two paragraphs are used to include all the details necessary to set the story's scene. Also note the background information given in the first paragraph. Instruct students to give any necessary background information as early and as briefly as possible.

3. Assign **Try Your Skill.** Discuss the paragraph first, pointing out that the reader gets no feeling of suspense or tension from the paragraph as it is written.

4. Read **Keep This in Mind** and then assign **Now Write.**

Individualizing the Lesson

Less-Advanced Students

Explain the characterization difference between telling and showing by reading the following examples. Ask students which sentence in each pair *tells* the character's thoughts and actions and

Writing the First Draft

Here's the Idea When all of your pre-writing decisions have been made and you have an organized set of notes, you can begin to write your first draft. Your narrative composition should have three parts: an introduction, a body, and a conclusion.

In the introductory paragraph, let your reader know where and when the story is happening. Also tell who the characters are. Be sure to use vivid, specific details to describe both the setting and the characters. In addition, introduce the situation from which the conflict will arise. Setting the scene and suggesting the conflict will involve the reader in the action right away.

The body paragraphs develop your plot. Include all the events that tell your story. In this part of your narrative, you will introduce and develop the conflict of your story. Keep the action lively. Whenever possible, *show* rather than tell what a character is thinking or feeling.

The concluding paragraph settles the conflict and ends the story. The ending should flow naturally from the events that have come before it. Be sure to follow through with your pre-writing decisions. Don't change your point of view. Don't have a character change his or her attitudes or feelings without good reason.

Check It Out Read the beginning of this narrative.

Last Thanksgiving a family problem helped me prove that I can be a problem solver. At nine o'clock that morning I lay in bed thinking about the day I had planned. I would spend the afternoon ice skating with my friend B.J. Eating Mom's delicious dinner and talking with my visiting cousins would be the highlight of my day.

I was enjoying my pleasant daydream when a knock sounded at my door. I saw a tense look on my father's face. My glorious plans dissolved the minute I heard what Dad had to say. Mother had hurt her back and would have to stay in bed. Dad was going to take care of her and my baby brother. The person left in charge of Thanksgiving dinner was—me!

• Does the introduction set the scene and introduce the main character? Does it suggest a conflict? How?

Try Your Skill   The following paragraph is from a narrative composition. It lacks interest because the writer tells, rather than shows, the action and the thoughts of the character. Rewrite the paragraph so that it is livelier. Make changes to *show* what the character is doing and thinking.

Russell's mind was on the next day at the new school instead of on the road. At the corner of Forest and Park Streets he made a left turn. Unfortunately, he forgot to signal. He was not paying attention, so he didn't see the car. As he turned left, the car ran into him. He was thrown several feet in the air. It's a good thing he didn't land in the middle of traffic.

Keep This in Mind

• In the introduction, present the setting, the characters, and the situation that will lead to the conflict.
• In the body, develop the plot and conflict. Show what your characters are doing and feeling.
• In the conclusion, settle the conflict and end the story.

Now Write   Write the introductory paragraph of your narrative composition. Include specific details to capture your reader's interest. Keep this introduction in your folder.

which one *shows* them.

1. Marla was very angry as she went into her sister's room. tells

   Marla strode into her sister's room, her eyes flashing and her hair streaming wildly behind her. shows

2. The team was overjoyed at their victory. tells

   The girls jumped up and down, hugging and clapping, squealing and hooting with joy. shows

Advanced Students

Discuss the concept of creating suspense in writing a narrative. Tell students that good narratives often stimulate the reader's curiosity as to how the conflict will finally be resolved. Therefore, the introduction should present the conflict, which should not be totally resolved until the conclusion. Have students discuss the source of the suspense in the sample narratives in **Check It Out** and **Try Your Skill**.

Optional Practice

Have students rewrite each sentence below to show more vividly the character's thoughts and actions.

1. Jeffrey looked in disbelief as the hugh lighted object landed at his feet.
2. Mary felt sad as she watched the starving children on the news.
3. My sister was resting lazily on the living room sofa.

Extending the Lesson

Have students read a short story. Have them analyze the story's introduction, determining how it presents the story's setting, characters, and conflict.

Objective

To know how to use dialogue to reveal character

Presenting the Lesson

1. Discuss **Here's the Idea,** writing *dialogue* and *dialogue tag* on the chalkboard. Emphasize the difference between direct quotations and indirect quotations by writing the following sentences on the board:

Eric said, "I'm going home." (direct quotation)

Eric said that he's going home. (indirect quotation)

2. Have a volunteer read the dialogue in **Check It Out.** Discuss the study questions, pointing out that dialogue is a way of *showing* rather than *telling* about a character. Have the students list the various dialogue tags used in the sample dialogue.

3. Assign **Try Your Skill.** Point out that students will be changing indirect quotations to direct quotations.

4. Read **Keep This in Mind.**

5. Assign **Now Write.** Explain that the narrative's body will not consist solely of dialogue; students must decide in which parts of their narratives dialogue will be effective.

Individualizing the Lesson

Less-Advanced Students

Have students discuss what the following dialogue reveals about each of the two characters.

Talk It Out

The First Draft: Dialogue

Here's the Idea Most people are interested in what others have to say. For this reason, one of the best ways to keep a reader interested in your characters and your story is to include conversations between two or more characters. Conversation in a narrative is called **dialogue.**

Dialogue has two purposes in a story. It moves the action of a story along. It can also show what a character is like. Dialogue lets the characters reveal their thoughts and feelings. Whenever you use dialogue, keep the personalities and the ages of the characters in mind. Use words and expressions that sound natural for your characters.

When you write dialogue, always include dialogue tags. A **dialogue tag** is a short phrase such as *Rick shouted.* Dialogue tags tell who is speaking and how the words are spoken. Dialogue tags show a character's personality or feelings. Instead of *Ann said*, you might say *Ann whispered* or *Ann said nervously.*

Always put quotation marks around a speaker's exact words. Start a new paragraph whenever a different character speaks. For more information on writing dialogue correctly, look at pages 650–652 in the Handbook.

Check It Out Read the following dialogue.

I was becoming frozen with panic. Then, my younger sister Lauren called from her bed across the room, "That really sounds like fun! Can I help, too?"

"Sure," I moaned. "How good are you at magic?"

"We're having turkey, not rabbit," Lauren laughed. "Besides, I've watched Mom make the stuffing lots of times. I even learned how to make pumpkin pie and cranberry sauce at Girl Scouts."

Maybe there was hope yet, I told myself. That left only the turkey and vegetables for me to cook.

Dad said anxiously, "We are counting on you two."

"Okay, Dad," I declared, "here's where you'll find out what family spirit is all about."

- What does this dialogue reveal about these people?
- How does this dialogue move the story along?
- What do the dialogue tags reveal about the character's feelings?

Try Your Skill   Using dialogue, rewrite this part of the story about Russell's bike accident. Use correct punctuation.

Painfully, Russell picked himself up from the curb. The lady whose car had hit him got out and asked him if he was okay. He was sort of dazed and said he didn't know. Someone said he'd call an ambulance. Russell sat down on the curb, holding his left arm. The lady kept apologizing, and Russ told her not to worry.

In minutes the ambulance arrived, and Russell was helped inside. The attendant asked Russ what had happened. As a nurse checked his pulse, Russ explained as much as he remembered.

Keep This in Mind

- Dialogue makes a story more interesting. It moves the story along. It also helps reveal the feelings and personalities of the characters.
- Use dialogue tags to signal who is speaking and how the words are spoken.

Now Write   Continue writing the first draft of your narrative composition. Use dialogue to move your story along and to reveal your characters' personalities. Save your writing.

187

"Hey," said Jimmy with a sly grin, "let's go hassle that nerd, Eddie."

"No, we'd better not," said Bill, his small face wrinkling into a thoughtful frown.

"You chicken!" exclaimed Jimmy spitefully.

Advanced Students

Ask pairs of students to write a fictitious situation involving a conflict between two people, such as a son asking his father for the car keys. Then have students act out these conflicts for the other students. Ask what the dialogues reveal about each character.

Optional Practice

Have students change each indirect quotation below to a direct quotation. Encourage students to use a variety of dialogue tags. Answers will vary

1. Jay said that the Bruins had won the championship.
2. Mr. Robinson said that there would be a test on Thursday.
3. Dr. Barrett said that my arm would be in a cast for six weeks.
4. The coach told the team to give 100% in the second half.

Extending the Lesson

Hand out some comic strips to your class. After students have read and examined a comic strip, ask them to write one sentence summarizing the story and one sentence describing each character. Then have students write the dialogue in the form of direct quotations, using proper punctuation. Have them limit their dialogues to one page.

Objective

To use effective transitions in the first draft of a narrative composition

Presenting the Lesson

1. Have students read **Here's the Idea.** Have the class list additional transitional words and phrases for narratives as you list them on the chalkboard. As you discuss the importance of using transitions to identify flashbacks, ask students if they can recall any movies, television shows, or books that use flashbacks. Charles Dickens's *A Christmas Carol* is one famous example.

2. Have volunteers read the sample paragraphs in **Check It Out.** As you discuss the study questions, call attention to the point in the narrative at which the flashback was inserted and the purpose that it serves.

3. Assign **Try Your Skill.** Point out that the paragraphs as they are written lack coherence; the order in which the events occurred is unclear.

4. Read **Keep This in Mind.**

5. Assign **Now Write.** Discuss tying up any loose ends in the narrative's plot in the conclusion.

Individualizing the Lesson

Less-Advanced Students

Have students start a series of charts listing transitional words and phrases for each type of composition they write. For narratives, students should use the transitions on page 112 and in **Here's the Idea** in this lesson.

188

Once Upon a Time

The First Draft: Transitions

Here's the Idea   A narrative composition is arranged in chronological order. To help keep the order of events clear in the reader's mind, use transitions when you write your first draft.

Transitions are important to use within paragraphs, to keep the sentences flowing smoothly. Transitions can also be used between paragraphs. They help to keep the story moving and to tie the events together in a logical way.

In a narrative, transitional words and phrases express the passing of time. Examples are *then*, *after that*, and *finally*. Transitional words and phrases that can link paragraphs include *yesterday*, *the next week*, *several minutes later*, and *last year*.

Transitions are particularly important whenever you include a flashback. Without transitions, your reader would be very confused about a sudden change in time. Use transitions such as "once before," "only yesterday," or "earlier in the day" to signal the beginning of a flashback. Use a transition such as "right now" or "at this moment" to show your reader that the flashback has ended.

Check It Out   Continue reading the story about the Thanksgiving dinner.

I made the beds while Lauren made the stuffing. Lauren straightened the house while I put the turkey into the oven. I vacuumed, dusted, and set the table while she cooked her pies and cranberries. Lauren arranged a vase of snapdragons while I snapped green beans in the kitchen. I began to feel as if we were actors in one of those speeded-up silent movies.

Then it was my turn in the kitchen again. I was exhausted, and I had no idea what to do with the sweet potatoes. Fran-

188

tically, I searched for a recipe. I was ready to give up. Surely the family would understand. After all, I was only 16 years old.

Suddenly, I remembered a time Mom had worked so hard for me. Three years before, I had broken my ankle and had been stuck in bed for days. Even though she had worked all week and was tired, Mom spent the weekend making special meals for me and cheering me up. As I was remembering Mom's kindness, I found a recipe for the sweet potatoes. For some reason, I wasn't tired any more.

- What transitional words and phrases help tie the events together and show the passage of time?
- Find a flashback. What transitional phrase introduces it? ends it?

Try Your Skill Improve the following paragraph about Russell by adding good transitional words and phrases.

Russell's arm was X-rayed. It was broken. The nurse cleaned the scrapes on his legs and bandaged the cut on his knee. The doctor put a cast on Russell's left arm and put it in a sling.

Russ could hardly sleep. He had been nervous about going to a new school. Now he would be embarrassed as well. The alarm rang, and Russ felt miserable.

Keep This in Mind

- Use transitional words and phrases to show time order within paragraphs and between paragraphs.
- Signal the beginning and end of a flashback with transitions.

Now Write Finish writing the first draft of your narrative composition. Use transitional words and phrases to show chronological order. Also use them to signal a flashback if you've included one. In your ending paragraph, solve the conflict. Save your first draft in your folder.

Part 7

Objective

To revise a narrative composition

Presenting the Lesson

1. Read **Here's the Idea.** Outline the revision questions on the board as you discuss them.

2. Have students study the revised conclusion in **Check It Out.** Help the students recognize that not only are the grammar and mechanical errors corrected; the conclusion has been made more vivid, and clarity has been improved with the addition of transitions.

3. Assign **Try Your Skill.** Have students refer to the sample revision in **Check It Out** as well as to the revision guidelines.

4. Read **Keep This in Mind.**

5. Assign **Now Write.** Remind students that the purpose of a narrative composition is to show how people react in certain situations, and that a narrative is frequently entertaining.

Individualizing the Lesson

Less-Advanced Students

Lead the class through a step-by-step revision of their compositions. Give the students time to revise their writing as you read and discuss each revision question.

Advanced Students

These students may not have problems with clarity and correctness in their first drafts. Have them focus on making their narratives more vivid and interesting in the revision stage. Instruct them to replace ordinary verbs with stronger

Part 7

Take Your Time

Revising Your Narrative Composition

Here's the Idea   "Take your time and get it right" is good advice for doing any activity, including writing. As you wrote your first draft, your main concern was to put all of your ideas into paragraph form. You were trying out your pre-writing decisions to see if they worked.

The revising stage of the process gives you a chance to slow down. Take time to look at the different parts of your story. This is your opportunity to make your story as good as it can be. Use the following questions to help you revise your narrative composition.

1. What point am I trying to make with my story. Is that point clear?

2. Does the introductory paragraph set the scene and present my main characters? Does it introduce a situation from which a conflict will arise?

3. Did I include enough events and details to keep my reader interested and to tell my story well?

4. Are the events arranged in chronological order?

5. Are flashbacks used effectively?

6. Does the body of the composition develop the conflict in an interesting way?

7. Have I kept to the same point of view throughout the entire composition?

8. Did I include dialogue to help tell my story and to reveal my characters? Did I use dialogue tags well?

9. Did I use transitional words and phrases within and between paragraphs?

10. Does the conclusion solve the conflict and bring the story to a close?

190

When you are satisfied with your story, proofread it for errors in grammar and mechanics. Refer to the Handbook, pages 650–652, when you proofread your dialogue.

Check It Out   Read the following revised conclusion.

> *By late afternoon,* The house was spotless *and* the turkey smelled delicious. Lauren and *me* changed into our *good* clothes just in time to greet every one. *my aunts, uncles, and cousins.* At the dinner table *that evening* we were *showered with* praised for all our *hard* work. While the food wasn't as perfect as that of past Thanksgivings, *somehow* it was *much* more special. *The look on my mother's face* When we carried Mom's dinner into her *bedroom* it *today.* gave a whole new meaning to the word thanksgiving. *her*

- How was this paragraph improved by revision?

Try Your Skill   Using the guidelines in this lesson, revise this conclusion.

Russell was amazed at how his day went. Teachers were especially nice too him. Several students asked Do you want me to carry your books? Someone in his algibra class said Ill show you were the cafeteria is. Youll need help carrying your tray. Russell came home with his cast covered with autographs. He learned that a new school isn't so scary. What he thought would be a terrible problem was an automatic conversation-starter.

Keep This in Mind

- Revise your narrative composition so that it represents the best work that you can do.

Now Write   Using the guidelines in this lesson, revise the first draft of your narrative composition. When you have finished improving your story, proofread it. Make a final copy.

191

ones, add sensory details, and use dialogue whenever appropriate.

Optional Practice

Have students revise the following narrative paragraph, adding transitions for clarity and making it more vivid and interesting.
Answers will vary
Joe was nervous knowing a major league scout was sitting in the bleachers. He looked into the seats behind home plate. He pitched to the first three batters and they got a walk and two hits. He knew he would have to do better to have a chance at a career in baseball.

Extending the Lesson

1. Read aloud several short stories. Discuss how the conflict is resolved in the conclusion of each story. Ask which stories have surprise endings and which conclusions are most consistent with the rest of the story. Have students suggest alternate titles for the stories.

2. Divide the class into groups and ask the students to read their narratives completed in **Now Write** to each other. Have group members suggest several good titles for each composition. Ask each group to vote on a favorite composition. You might post these favorites on the bulletin board or submit them, with the authors' permission, to the school literary magazine.

191

Section 16 Objectives

1. To gather sensory details and use spatial order to organize them for a descriptive composition

2. To suggest a mood and to use appropriate transitions in writing the first draft of a descriptive composition

3. To write a strong conclusion for a descriptive composition

4. To revise a descriptive composition

Preparing the Students

Ask students to think of the kind of pizza they like best. Have them describe it, from the kind of crust to the kind of topping. Ask them to use sensory details.

Point out that the process of description that they have used to tell about pizza could also be used when writing compositions. Review the definition of a descriptive composition, and ask how it differs from a narrative composition. Tell students that Writing Section 16 will show them how to write descriptive compositions.

Additonal Resources

Practice Book — pages 78–81
Duplicating Masters — pages 78–81

The Descriptive Composition

Teaching Special Populations

LD See **Teaching Special Populations,** page 75.

ESL Have students choose an object and list at least five sensory words that describe that object. Ask other students in the class to add words to the list. Have students keep lists of useful descriptive words.

NSD See **Teaching Special Populations,** page 75.

Come to Your Senses

Pre-Writing: Using Sensory Details

Presenting the Lesson

1. Have students read **Here's the Idea.** Discuss the fact that a good descriptive composition evokes feelings in the reader. Write the term *spatial order* on the board and define it, mentioning that spatial order can take many different forms; the important thing is not to jump around in a description so that the reader cannot get a clear picture.

2. Read and discuss the pre-writing notes in **Check It Out.** Point out the spatial organization in the notes for the body. Have the students identify the sense that each detail appeals to.

3. Assign **Try Your Skill.** List the five senses (sight, hearing, taste, touch, and smell) on the chalkboard to assist students.

4. Read **Keep This in Mind.**

5. Assign **Now Write.** Help students select and narrow a topic in one of the following ways:

a. Hold a brainstorming session as a class or in small groups.

b. Have students refer to their journals.

c. Have students mention three or four general topics and then hold class discussions on them.

Individualizing the Lesson

Less-Advanced Students

Make sure students choose a topic that is broad enough for a

Here's the Idea   The goal of descriptive writing is to share with your reader what you have seen, heard, tasted, smelled, and felt. That way your reader will feel almost as if he or she were there with you.

As you think about a subject for a descriptive composition, don't overlook the people, places, and things around you. Try to see what you've never seen before.

Select a subject that appeals to several senses. For instance, a stop sign wouldn't be an interesting topic. It appeals only to the sense of sight. A busy intersection full of cars, buses, pedestrians, honking horns, and exhaust fumes would offer enough sensory details for a good descriptive composition.

Another way to gather sensory details is to search your memory. Look for details that will help you to suggest a particular feeling. Suppose you are describing the music room at school. Is it a scene of confusion before the period starts? Including details such as "open instrument cases" and "the shrill toots and screeches of instruments being tuned" will help you to give your reader this feeling.

When you finish collecting details, look through your list. Try to identify two or three main ideas about your subject. The main ideas about the music room might be *before class*, *during class*, and *after class*. They might be *the room*, *the instruments*, and *the people*. Group your pre-writing notes around the two or three main ideas you have found. Each of these idea groups will become a paragraph in your composition.

Finally, arrange your main ideas and the details grouped around them in the order in which you want your reader to notice them. This is called spatial order.

Check It Out   Read these pre-writing notes.

Topic   The Steveston Post Office and Museum

> The Building: corner of Moncton Street and First Avenue—originally, bank built in 1905—now restored and used as post office and museum
>
> Outside: rose garden, picket fence—outside painted yellow, white trim, red door
>
> First Floor: working post office—antique wooden mail-boxes—desk and filing cabinet of varnished antique oak—tall, old, black typewriter—lace curtains, fresh ocean breeze
>
> Second Floor: decorated like a 1905 house—old fishing equipment—farming tools

- To what senses do these details appeal?
- How have the idea groups been organized?

Try Your Skill   Below is an incomplete set of pre-writing notes. Complete them by adding details that appeal to different senses. Organize the notes using spatial order. Save these notes.

Topic   The school cafeteria

> Table: my friends, books and trays
> Tray: my favorite lunch—milk, apple pie
> Room: rows of tables, heads bent as people eat

Keep This in Mind

- Gather sensory details for a description.
- Group your details around several main ideas.
- Use spatial order to organize your ideas and details.

Now Write   Select a topic for your descriptive composition. Gather details that appeal to several different senses. Group your details around two or three main ideas. Then, organize your ideas and details by using spatial order. Save your work.

195

composition and that appeals to several senses. Give students the following list of topics and have them choose the ones that would be appropriate for a composition.

1. the school library or public library
2. a department store
3. a bicycle
4. their back yard
5. a grocery store
6. a flower

Advanced Students

Have students arrange the following notes for a descriptive composition in logical spatial order.

Answers will vary.

Topic: A shopping mall

A popular restaurant
  People lined up in twos and threes outside the door
  The smell of broiled hamburgers and coffee wafting outside
The mall itself
  Teenagers talking and laughing in groups
  Parents strolling babies
  Fountains sparkling and gurgling
Rows of stores
  Small shops
  Smell of perfume from department stores drifting outside

Optional Practice

Bring two or three interesting photographs to class. Have each student choose one picture to write sensory details about and then arrange the details in spatial order.

Extending the Lesson

Have students pretend they are preparing a sightseeing brochure for your town. Let groups of two or three choose a local attraction to describe. Ask them to write and organize notes for a brochure.

A Moment in Time

Writing the First Draft

To suggest a mood and to use appropriate transitions in writing the first draft of a descriptive composition

Presenting the Lesson

1. Have students read **Here's the Idea.** Discuss creating a mood in a description. Instruct students to first make sure they have a very specific topic, for example, "my back yard on a summer morning." Then the students should use at least one key word in the composition's topic sentence that expresses the mood they wish to create. For example, "My back yard on a summer morning is the picture of calm and serenity."

In discussing sensory details, refer students to the lists of descriptive words on page 122. In discussing transitional words and phrases, refer students to the list on page 124.

2. Read and discuss **Check It Out.** On the chalkboard, make five columns for the five senses, and have students list the sensory details used in this paragraph in the proper columns.

3. Assign **Try Your Skill.** Instruct the class to rewrite the paragraph completely—not just replace individual words and phrases—to create a vivid scene. Have students list some of the vague words that need to be revised, such as *best* and *excellent.*

4. Read **Keep This in Mind.**
5. Assign **Now Write.**

Here's the Idea   When you write a descriptive composition, you are trying to paint a picture with words. Your goal is to describe a specific person, place, or thing at one moment in time. For instance, your school's hall is a very different place at 8:00 in the morning than it is at 4:00 in the afternoon. For this reason, it is important to introduce your subject carefully in the introduction of your descriptive composition.

As your **introduction,** include one sentence that can serve as the topic sentence for your whole composition. This sentence should tell the reader about your subject. It should also suggest a certain mood.

The **body** of your composition contains the sensory details that develop your description. Remember that each idea group in your pre-writing notes will become a paragraph in the body of your composition.

The final paragraph is your **conclusion.** It sums up your description.

As you write your first draft, use transitional words and phrases both within your paragraphs and between them to show your reader *where* things are. Transitions such as *in the corner, on the shelf, behind the tree, to the left,* and others like them, can be especially useful.

Finally, think about the mood you are trying to create. Choose nouns, verbs, adjectives, and adverbs that will suggest a certain feeling. To learn more about mood, see pages 122–123.

Check It Out   Read this first draft of the introduction and body of a descriptive composition.

On the corner of Moncton Street and First Avenue is a little building. It was built in 1905 it was Stevestons first Bank. Now its the post office. And its also a neat museum.

Volunteers from town repaired and painted it. Now its surrounded by a new picket fence and rose bushes. It's painted light yellow with white trim and a bright red door.

Downstairs is the post office, with an oak counter and old wooden cubbyhole mailboxes. The postmaster's office is furnished with a smooth, varnished oak desk and a brass pedestal telephone. Also one of those tall old black typewriters. A breeze moves the lace curtains, and you can smell the sea.

On the second floor, two of the rooms are furnished like a 1905 home. Lots of antique furniture.

A third room has a display of antique things from farms, farmhouses, and fishing canneries in Steveston. Pitchforks, butter churns, apple peelers, fish nets. It kind of smells old.

- Does the introductory paragraph present the subject?
- Does the body contain sensory details? What are they?
- What transitions have been included?

Try Your Skill   Here is the first draft of an introduction. Rewrite it and set the scene with sensory details.

Where we go to eat after games is the best place. We get pizza or hamburgers. There's a juke box and a little area for dancing. In the booths you can fit in six or eight people.

Keep This in Mind

- The introductory paragraph of a descriptive composition presents the subject.
- The body presents the sensory details.
- The conclusion sums up the description.
- Transitional words and phrases that tell *where* help make a description clearer.

Now Write   Write the first draft of your descriptive composition. Follow your organized pre-writing notes. Write only the introduction and body. Save your work in your folder.

197

Less-Advanced Students

Discuss the use of a thesaurus in writing a sensory description. Have students use a thesaurus to find an interesting synonym for each italicized word in the sentences below.

1. The water on the lake was *smooth*.
2. The music at the party was *loud*.
3. The daffodil was *pretty*.
4. The windy March day made me feel *happy*.

Advanced Students

Write the name of your high school on the chalkboard. Ask students to think of one mood, such as excitement or pressure, that would describe the high school. Then have the students brainstorm for sensory details describing the high school. Write these details on the board.

Optional Practice

Ask students to write a topic sentence that would summarize a description of their favorite room. Then have them list twenty sensory details to describe the rooms. Encourage them to use vivid words and details that appeal to all senses.

Extending the Lesson

Divide the class into groups of five and let the groups choose one of these scenes to describe:

a beach   a football game   a kitchen

Have each group work out an introduction for a descriptive composition. Then assign each member of the group a different sense, and ask him or her to create three sensory details appealing to that sense. Ask the group to read aloud their details.

197

Objective

To write a strong conclusion for a descriptive composition

Presenting the Lesson

1. Read **Here's the Idea.** Instruct students to write a conclusion that gracefully signals the end of the composition but that does not merely repeat what has come before.

2. Have a volunteer read the sample concluding paragraph in **Check It Out.** Have students name the details in the composition that prepare the reader for the summary in the concluding paragraph.

3. Assign **Try Your Skill.** Students may find it helpful to write possible topic sentences for the two imaginary compositions before writing their concluding paragraphs.

4. Read **Keep This in Mind** and then assign **Now Write.** Urge students to use vivid sensory descriptions as they sum up their compositions.

Individualizing the Lesson

Less-Advanced Students

Read the following concluding paragraph from a descriptive composition. Have the students determine the main idea of the composition from its conclusion and write a possible topic sentence for the description.

Tie It Up

The First Draft: Ending a Description

Here's the Idea   Think of your description as a package full of interesting items. The conclusion is the string that ties them all up and holds the package together.

To write a good conclusion, look again at the main idea of each of your body paragraphs. Reread your introduction, too. Think about the mood you have created. Consider all of these factors as you wrap up your description.

The ending paragraph of your descriptive composition should leave your reader with a strong, lasting impression of your subject. How do you feel about your subject? Why is it interesting and important to you? Try to share these feelings with your reader in your conclusion.

The conclusion should follow naturally from what has come before it. If your description has created a very positive feeling about the subject, don't end with negative details. If you have described a dark and gloomy scene, keep this mood in your conclusion.

Check It Out   Reread the descriptive composition in the last lesson. Particularly notice the main idea of each paragraph. Now read the first draft of the conclusion of that description.

The Steveston Post Office-Museum takes you back in time. It reminds us of when there wasn't TV or electronic mail systems. Its nice to step back in time and see how our great-grandparents lived.

- Does the conclusion sum up the main ideas of the composition?
- Does the conclusion flow naturally from the paragraphs that have come before it?

• What mood has the writer created in the description?

Try Your Skill   Look at the pre-writing notes you made about the school cafeteria in **Try Your Skill** on page 195. Imagine you had used these notes to write a descriptive composition. Write two different ending paragraphs for such a composition. For one conclusion, imagine that lunch is the highlight of your day. For the second conclusion, imagine that the cafeteria is not your favorite place. Create any additional details that you need for either paragraph. Be sure each conclusion presents your feelings about the subject.

Keep This in Mind

- In your conclusion, sum up the ideas in your description.
- Your conclusion should tell your reader how you feel about your subject.
- Your conclusion should flow naturally from the ideas that have come before it.

Now Write   Write an ending paragraph for the first draft of your descriptive composition. Sum up your main ideas. Leave your reader with a definite impression of your feelings about the subject. Save your first draft in your folder.

All in all, the huge Smithtown shopping mall is the modern day suburban version of a big city. It has the noisy bustle and the infinite variety of people and wares of Charles Dickens's London. And it's right in our own back yard.

Advanced Students

Have students exchange only the concluding paragraphs of their descriptive compositions. Each student should then write a sentence expressing the subject and mood of the paragraph he or she has been given, to show the paragraph's writer if the conclusion's mood is consistent with the rest of the composition.

Optional Practice

Remind students that a good conclusion to a description not only sums up the body of the composition, but includes its own vivid sensory description. Have students revise the following sample conclusion to make it more vivid and interesting.

Now you see why I like Lake Algonquin. It is beautiful in all seasons of the year. It is fresh in the spring, sparkling in the summer, cool in the fall, and frigid in the winter. That's why I like it.

Extending the Lesson

Duplicate and distribute a travel brochure, deleting the conclusion of the description. Have your students write conclusions and titles for the brochures. Then have students share their writings.

Objective

To revise a descriptive composition

Presenting the Lesson

1. Read the revision checklist in **Here's the Idea,** outlining each point on the chalkboard.

2. Have students study and discuss the revised paragraph in **Check It Out.** Make sure the class recognizes how the main idea of the description—the building's link with the past—is emphasized in the revision.

3. Assign **Try Your Skill.** Remind students to organize the description around its main idea and to do a thorough revision, not merely changing individual words.

4. Read **Keep This in Mind.**

5. Assign **Now Write.** Discuss writing a title for a descriptive composition. Which of the titles in each pair below is more effective?

a. The Corner Fruit Stand/ A Cornucopia in My Neighborhood
b. A Rural Landmark/ An Old Barn
c. My Bedroom/ "Do Not Disturb"

Individualizing the Lesson

Less-Advanced Students

Lead the students through a step-by-step revision of their compositions. Provide time in class for questions and problems as you read each revision question in **Here's the Idea.** Especially emphasize suggesting a mood that is supported by vivid sensory details.

200

Part 4

Give It Your All

Revising Your Descriptive Composition

Here's the Idea   Coaches often tell their players, "I want everyone to give one hundred percent." This means that the coaches expect every player to do the best job he or she possibly can. Whenever you write, you should give one hundred percent, too. You should work to make your writing the best it can possibly be. Careful revision will help you to meet this goal.

As you revise your description, ask yourself these questions.

1. Does my introductory paragraph present the subject of my description?

2. Does each paragraph in the body have a good topic sentence?

3. Did I include enough sensory details to develop my description well?

4. Are my details arranged in clear spatial order?

5. Did I use transitional words and phrases to make the order of my details clear?

6. Does my description suggest a mood or feeling to the reader? Did I select the right nouns, verbs, adjectives, and adverbs to create this mood?

7. Does my ending paragraph sum up the main ideas of my description? Does this paragraph tell the reader how I feel about my subject?

When you have finished revising your ideas and organization, proofread your composition carefully. Check for errors in grammar and mechanics. Correct any errors that you find.

Check It Out   Read this revised introductory paragraph from the descriptive composition about the post office-museum.

·   How has revision improved the description?

200

On the corner of Moncton Street and First Avenue is a little
frame building. It ~~was built~~ in 1905, *in Steveston* it was steveston's first bank. Now
~~its~~ *the restored building is* the post office. ~~And its also~~ *as well as* a *neat* museum, *that provides a*
an interesting *charming*
glimpse of
the past.

Try Your Skill   Copy the first two body paragraphs from the
first draft about the post office-museum (see pages 196–197).
Use the guidelines in this lesson to revise them. Compare your
revisions with those of your classmates.

Keep This in Mind

- Revise your composition so that it presents a clear
  picture of your subject. Include sensory details to
  bring your description to life.
- Use spatial order to organize your details. Use transitional words and phrases to make your order
  clear.
- Present your subject in the introduction.
- In the conclusion, sum up your ideas and express
  your feelings about the subject.

Now Write   Use the guidelines in this lesson as well as your
other revising skills. Revise the first draft of your descriptive
composition. Proofread it to correct any errors in grammar and
mechanics. When you are satisfied with your composition, give
it a title. Make a final copy of your work. Proofread it one final
time. Make any corrections neatly. Save your work.

Section **17** Objectives

1. To learn to explain a process in an explanatory *how* composition

2. To arrange details in step-by-step order

3. To use appropriate transitions in writing the first draft of an explanatory *how* composition

4. To revise an explanatory *how* composition

Preparing the Students

Ask the class to imagine that they are teaching young children cursive writing. Ask each student to select a different capital letter of the alphabet and to write that letter on the chalkboard, explaining how it is written. After all the letters have been written, ask what methods students used to tell how to write the letters. Ask if children could have followed the explanations without seeing the letters written. Ask if the explanations were complete and clear.

Then review the definition of the *how* paragraph. Explain that Writing Section 17 will teach students to write an explanatory *how* composition.

Additional Resources

Practice Book — pages 82–85
Duplicating Masters — pages 82–85

The Explanatory Composition

Telling *How*

Teaching Special Populations

LD See **Teaching Special Populations,** page 75. Have students use a number of the appropriate transitional words and phrases in sentences.

ESL Encourage students to write about processes familiar to them but perhaps not well known in this country. For example, they might describe the preparation of a national dish, or explain how to celebrate a particular holiday.

Remind students that transitional words and phrases help indicate time sequence, and act as bridges between ideas. Review the list of transitional words and phrases that show time. Provide additional exercises based on these words, if necessary.

NSD See **Teaching Special Populations,** page 75.

Objective

To learn to explain a process in an explanatory *how* composition

Presenting the Lesson

1. Read aloud and discuss **Here's the Idea.** Stress the importance of selecting topics that students know well.

2. Read aloud and discuss the pre-writing notes in **Check It Out.** Students should realize that the notes have not yet been organized.

3. Assign and discuss **Try Your Skill.** Have students exchange papers with a partner and comment on the following points.

Do the notes include necessary materials, tools, or ingredients?
Are the notes complete?

4. Read **Keep This in Mind.**

5. Assign **Now Write.** Have students brainstorm for processes. Remind students that they should choose processes that they know well.

Individualizing the Lesson

Less-Advanced Students

Have the class work together to assemble pre-writing notes for a simple process such as making a sandwich. Write on the chalkboard students' suggestions for materials needed and the steps of the process.

Advanced Students

These students may want to consider telling how something works in their explanatory *how* compositions.

Do It Right

Pre-Writing: Planning an Explanation

Here's the Idea   You can explain *how* to someone else by writing an explanatory *how* composition. You can tell someone *how* to do something, or *how* something happens or works. In other words, you can explain a process.

When you are considering possible topics for an explanatory *how* composition, think about processes that you know well. Suppose your hobby is photography. You could explain how to develop and print a black-and-white photograph. Perhaps you are interested in astronomy. You might write a composition explaining how a star forms. Keep your audience in mind as you look for a topic. What kinds of subjects do you think they might be interested in?

Once you have chosen a topic, gather your details. These will include all of the major steps or stages involved in the process you are explaining. If you are explaining how to do something, be sure to list any materials, tools, or ingredients that are needed. Make sure you write each step simply and clearly.

As you develop your pre-writing notes, don't leave out any steps. Don't assume that your readers will understand certain things without being told. For instance, if you are explaining how to change a flat tire, one of the first steps to mention is "park safely away from traffic." This may seem logical to you. However, someone anxious about a flat tire may not think of it.

Check It Out   Read these pre-writing notes.

How To Change a Flat Tire

collect jack and spare tire from trunk
assemble jack, if necessary
park safely away from traffic

read any printed instructions given
will need jack and spare tire
position jack, raise car
remove hubcap
remove flat tire
loosen lug nuts
put on good tire
slide tire into place
tighten lug nuts
secure lug nuts
lower car
get flat fixed
return jack and tire to trunk

- Do these notes include all of the necessary steps in the process? Do the notes list the materials needed?

Try Your Skill   Choose one of the following general topics for an explanatory *how* composition. Gather your details. List the steps in the process. Include all necessary materials.

making a special dessert   drawing a cartoon
playing soccer   planting a garden

Keep This in Mind

- In an explanatory *how* composition, you explain how to do something or how something happens or works.
- In your pre-writing notes, list the steps in the process. Also list any tools, ingredients, or materials required.
- Explain each step simply and clearly.

Now Write   Think of a process that you know well. Develop a list of pre-writing notes. Include all of the important steps of the process as well as any necessary materials. Save your notes.

Some possible topics for this type of explanatory *how* composition follow.

1. how a car engine works
2. how a sewing machine works
3. how a camera works

Optional Practice

Demonstrate one or more processes for your class, such as: doing a magic trick, adjusting bicycle brakes, preparing a salad, playing the recorder, making a woodcut. As you demonstrate, have students take notes. Afterward, instruct them to expand their notes, making sure that they are clear and specific. Have students exchange notes to check for clarity.

Extending the Lesson

Have students find and bring to class an example of an explanatory *how* composition. This may be instructions on how to perform a process, such as a recipe or game instructions, or an article on how something works, such as an encyclopedia article on bicycles.

Step on It!

Pre-Writing: Using Step-by-Step Order

Part 2

Objective

Objective

To arrange details in step-by-step order

Presenting the Lesson

1. Have students read **Here's the Idea.** To illustrate the importance of using exact step-by-step order, ask students what would happen if a recipe directed them to put an egg into pancake batter after telling them to pour the batter on the griddle.

2. Have students read and discuss the pre-writing notes in **Check It Out.** Note especially how the tire-changing process has been divided into four main steps. Explain that the paragraphs of the composition's body will correspond to these four groups.

3. Assign and discuss **Try Your Skill.** You might have students form groups of three to organize the notes. Ask the groups to add details and a title. Have volunteers read each group's work aloud.

4. Read **Keep This in Mind.**

5. Assign **Now Write.** Students should refer to the example in **Check It Out** for help in organizing their main ideas.

Individualizing the Lesson

Less-Advanced Students

Students may need help identifying the main idea under which to group the steps of their process. Help students individually or have them work in pairs to analyze the main steps of their process.

Here's the Idea In explaining a process, it is not enough to present your steps in "just about" the right order. Your steps must be presented in the *exact* order in which they are performed or happen. This is called **step-by-step order.** Taking time now to organize your pre-writing notes in this order will make it easier for you later when you write your first draft.

Look at the details that you have listed in your pre-writing notes. As a first step, try to identify two or three main ideas within the entire process. Next, group your remaining details around these main ideas. Now you are ready to organize both your main ideas and the details grouped around them in step-by-step order.

Because the steps in the process are so important in an explanation, they are the central part of a composition. After introducing the process in the introduction, give the step-by-step explanation in the body. Each of the main idea groups from your pre-writing notes will become a separate paragraph. The conclusion should develop the final step or briefly review the entire process.

Check It Out Read these organized pre-writing notes.

How To Change a Flat Tire

1. Preparation: park safely away from traffic, collect jack and spare tire from trunk, read any printed instructions given, assemble jack, if necessary

2. Remove flat tire: loosen lug nuts, position jack, raise car, remove hubcap, remove lug nuts and bad tire

3. Put on spare tire: slide spare tire into place, tighten lug nuts and lower car, secure lug nuts

4. Clean up: return jack and flat to trunk, get flat repaired

- Are these notes organized in step-by-step order? Explain your answer.
- What information could you include in the conclusion?

Try Your Skill   Here are some jumbled notes for a composition on making a terrarium—a garden in a glass container. List the steps in the correct step-by-step order. Add any other details that seem necessary.

4 Prepare the soil.

5 Arrange plants, handling and covering roots carefully.

3 Buy enough potting soil, crushed charcoal, and gravel to fill container one-third full.

1 First find large glass container or wide-mouthed jar.

2 Buy varied selection of plants to fit container.

6 Water thoroughly and place in sunlight.

Keep This in Mind

- Use step-by-step order to organize an explanatory *how* composition.
- In the introduction present your topic. In the body, develop a separate paragraph for each main idea. In the conclusion, sum up the steps of the process or explain the final step.

Now Write   Look at your list of pre-writing details from **Do It Right.** Identify two or three main ideas in your notes. Then group your remaining details around these main ideas. Organize both your main ideas and the details under them in step-by-step order. Save your organized notes in your folder.

207

Good Connections

Writing the First Draft

To use appropriate transitions in writing the first draft of an explanatory *how* composition

Presenting the Lesson

1. Read aloud **Here's the Idea.** Have students look over the step-by-step order transitions on page 134. Tell students that they have already used transitions within paragraphs, but transitions are also used to link paragraphs together.

2. Have volunteers read the paragraphs in **Check It Out** and list the transitions within and between paragraphs. Point out that a variety of transitions are used for interest and clarity.

3. Assign and discuss **Try Your Skill.** Suggest that students refer to the transitions on page 134. Stress the need for a variety of transitions in a paragraph. Ask students to compare their paragraphs with those of other students.

4. Read **Keep This in Mind.**

5. Assign **Now Write.** Emphasize clarity as the most important quality of an explanatory *how* composition.

Individualizing the Lesson

Less-Advanced Students

Encourage the use of a variety of transitions as students write their first drafts. Tell students that they do not need to number each step in their process (*first, second, third,* etc.). Instead, they should study the sample paragraphs in **Check It Out**

Here's the Idea   Transitions are used like bridges in writing. In an explanatory *how* composition, transitions help to make the process you are explaining clear and easy to understand. They provide strong links between the different steps of the process.

In an explanatory *how* composition, use transitions that show the natural time order of the process. You may want to use such transitional words and phrases as *first, the next step, after that,* and *finally.* Sometimes you may need to use a more exact transitional phrase like *after twenty-four hours.*

You will want to use transitional words within each paragraph. They are especially important in the body of your composition where you explain the process. You will also find transitions helpful between paragraphs. You can use transitional devices to link the main ideas of the paragraphs in all three parts of your composition.

Check It Out   Here are the body paragraphs to the composition about changing the flat tire.

Before you change a tire be sure that the car is away from traffic in a safe, level spot. Put the gear shift in the "park" position with the emergency brake on. Get the jack and the spare tire from the trunk. Read any printed instructions you find given there. The jack in an older car may come in three parts and may have to be assembled.

Once your preparations have been completed, you need to raise the corner of the car that has the flat tire. Position the jack on the bumper or on the side of the car nearest the flat. Remove the hubcap that covers the wheel. Then, using the end of the jack handle as a wrench, loosen the four lug nuts that hold the tire in place. Do not remove them yet. Next, using a pumping motion with your arm, jack the car up to a height that allows you to remove the flat tire easily. Finally, remove the loosened lug nuts and slip off the flat tire.

Now you may need to jack up the car more to allow space for the spare. Slide the spare tire into place. Then replace the lug nuts, tightening them by hand. First tighten the top nut, then the bottom, then the left one, and finally the right. The next step is to jack the car down. Tighten the lug nuts securely, using the jack handle. Replace the hubcap.

- What transitional words and phrases are used to link these three paragraphs?
- What transitional words and phrases are used within each paragraph?

Try Your Skill Rewrite the following paragraph and add transitional words and phrases.

Prepare the soil. Cover the bottom of the glass container with a thin layer of gravel. Mix two parts potting soil to one part crushed charcoal. Pour in enough of the mixture to fill the bottom sixth of the container. Use your hands to pack the mixture down firmly. Pour in enough potting soil to fill another sixth of the container. Gently shake the container to level the soil. Pack the soil firmly.

Keep This in Mind

- In an explanatory *how* composition, time transitions help to make the order of the steps clear.

Now Write Write the first draft of your explanatory *how* composition. Use your organized pre-writing notes to guide you. Use transitions to link the paragraphs in all three parts of the composition. Add transitional words needed within each paragraph to show the order of the steps in the process you are explaining. Save your first draft in your folder.

to recognize how a variety of transitions have been used at crucial points in the paragraphs.

Advanced Students

When students have written their first drafts, choose one or two compositions to project on an overhead projector. Discuss whether the step-by-step order is clear and effective, and whether enough transitions have been used for coherence.

Optional Practice

Have students rewrite the following paragraph from a composition about how to plan a party by adding transitional words and phrases.

Answers will vary

Decide how many people you will invite. This depends on how much room you have and what kind of entertainment you are planning. Buy or make invitations. You can issue invitations by telephone, but people love to get invitations in the mail. Send out the invitations.

Extending the Lesson

Distribute magazines to your students and have them look for how-to articles. Remind them that some *how* explanations may be somewhat abstract, as in "How To Make Friends" or "How To Enjoy Your Summer." Once each student finds an appropriate article, have him or her list the transitions used in it.

Objective

To revise an explanatory *how* composition

Presenting the Lesson

1. Have students read **Here's the Idea.** Outline the revision checklist on the chalkboard as you discuss it.

2. Read and discuss **Check It Out.** Have students note that the sample introduction lets readers know that the composition's purpose is to explain how to do something.

3. Assign **Try Your Skill.** Then have several students read and compare their revised paragraphs.

4. Read **Keep This in Mind.**

5. Assign **Now Write.** Discuss titling an explanatory *how* composition; students may want to consider a simple, straightforward title for their compositions.

Individualizing the Lesson

Less-Advanced Students

After students have revised their compositions, have them exchange papers. The students should check their classmates' explanations for thoroughness and clarity. If students feel they would have difficulty following a composition's instructions, they should tell the writer how the explanation could be improved by rearranging steps or inserting transitions.

Advanced Students

If students have no problems with clarity in revising their explanatory *how* compositions, they should concentrate on interesting introductory

Be a Pro

Revising Your Explanation

Here's the Idea   Every activity has its pros. These are the men and women who stand out, who always do the best. In writing, the mark of a real pro is the effort he or she is willing to put into revising. Gathering ideas and writing a first draft are important steps, but they are not enough to produce a finished product. It takes patience and a stick-to-it attitude to turn a first draft into a first-class composition.

When you revise your explanatory *how* composition, keep your reader in mind. Your goal is to explain your subject well enough so that your reader can follow it easily.

Here are some questions to ask yourself as you revise.

1. Does my introduction identify the process I want to explain? Does it catch the reader's attention?

2. Does the body of the composition contain every necessary step in the process I am explaining?

3. Are my details arranged in step-by-step order?

4. Does each body paragraph contain a main idea that is supported by details that develop the explanation?

5. Did I use transitional words and phrases to show step-by-step order, both within and between paragraphs?

6. Does the conclusion summarize the steps of the process or explain the final step?

When you are satisfied that your explanation is clear and complete, proofread your composition. Correct any errors in grammar and mechanics.

Check It Out   Here is the introduction to the composition about changing a flat tire.

You need not be a garage mechanic nor a weight lifter to change a flat tire on a car. With the spare tire and the jack that you will find in the trunk, you can finish the job in a matter of minutes. You need only follow a few simple directions.

- Does the introduction identify the subject?
- How does the introduction catch the reader's attention?

Try Your Skill   Rewrite this first draft of the conclusion to the composition about changing a flat tire. Follow the guidelines in this lesson.

Remind yourself to have the flat repaired. When you are done. Return the jack and the flat tire to the trunk. That tire will become the new spare. You should be sure it is in good condition in case of any future hiway emergency.

Keep This in Mind

- Make your explanatory *how* composition complete and easy to follow.
- Arrange your details in step-by-step order.
- Use transitional words and phrases to show the order of details.

Now Write   Using the guidelines in this lesson, revise your composition. Remember to proofread it carefully. Give your composition a title. Then make a final copy. Proofread your final copy one last time. Neatly correct any remaining errors. Save your completed composition in your folder.

and concluding paragraphs. Point out that readers will not care to follow the steps in a process if their attention is not attracted to the process in the first place. Also, suggest that students write a paragraph summing up the composition's process in the conclusion instead of simply ending with the last step.

Optional Practice

Have students revise the following introduction to a composition about planning a party. The students should follow the guidelines in this lesson. Answers will vary.

Almost everbody likes ~~partys~~ parties. They may not know that giving a party can be even more fun than attending one and so this composition will explain how to plan a ~~grate~~ great party.

Extending the Lesson

Make a class "how-to" book by duplicating the students' final copies and assembling them in book form. The students will enjoy browsing through the book and perhaps learn how to do something new.

Section **18** Objectives

1. To develop and support an opinion in an explanatory *why* composition

2. To use order of importance or comparison and contrast in organizing pre-writing notes for an explanatory *why* composition

3. To use appropriate transitions in writing the first draft of an explanatory *why* composition

4. To revise an explanatory *why* composition

Preparing the Students

Ask students which of the statements below are opinions:

1. Washington is the capital of the United States. (fact)
2. Smoking can be harmful to health. (fact)
3. Current TV programs insult the intelligence. (opinion)
4. Coca-Cola is the best-selling soft drink. (fact)
5. Many rock lyrics are immoral. (opinion)
6. The legal drinking age should be raised to 25. (opinion)
7. Socialized medicine should be adopted in the United States. (opinion)
8. Shoplifting is on the increase. (fact)

Ask your students to explain the difference between fact and opinion. Emphasize that facts can be proven, but opinions may be debated. Note that statements 3, 5, 6, and 7 are opinions and that opinions must be supported before others will accept them as true. Tell students that the purpose of an explanatory *why* paragraph is to support an opinion.

Additional Resources

Practice Book — pages 86–89
Duplicating Masters — pages 86–89

The Explanatory Composition

Telling *Why*

Teaching Special Populations

LD See **Teaching Special Populations,** page 75.

ESL This will be one of the more difficult composition sections for ESL students because stating and supporting opinion requires a higher level of language than many ESL students may have achieved. Work with students slowly and thoroughly through each part of this Section.

Before students write their own opinions, choose a sample topic with which the students are familiar and elicit from the class an opinion about that topic. Then have the class discuss the opinion. List supporting evidence on the board and explain to the class which of the listed evidence would belong in an explanatory composition about that opinion.

NSD See **Teaching Special Populations,** page 75.

In Your View

Pre-Writing: Developing an Opinion

Part 1

Objective

To develop and support an opinion in an explanatory *why* composition

Presenting the Lesson

1. Have students read **Here's the Idea.** Generate some sample opinions. For example, you might ask the class what they think about the President of the U.S., prime time television soap operas, or current rock music. Any disagreement among the students will illustrate the point that people see issues differently. Next emphasize the importance of supporting opinions with facts.

2. Have students study the pre-writing notes in **Check It Out.** Discuss the study questions, pointing out the use of facts to back up the opinion.

3. Assign **Try Your Skill.** You may want to assist your students individually with their statements of opinion. Remind them to narrow their topics sufficiently.

4. Read **Keep This in Mind.**

5. Assign **Now Write.** Instruct students to refer to their journals, recent class discussions, or magazines and newspapers to discover a topic for an explanatory *why* composition.

Individualizing the Lesson

Less-Advanced Students

Emphasize the difference between fact and opinion, and make sure students use facts in their pre-writing notes to support their opinions. Have students tell whether

Here's the Idea   Two artists may start out to paint the same scene. Their finished paintings, however, may look quite different. No two people see the same scene in exactly the same way.

People see things differently in other ways, too. Suppose a roomful of people listen to a mayoral candidate speak on the issues. Many of the people will come away from the speech with different opinions about whether the candidate would be a good mayor.

When you wish to express your opinion, you can write an explanatory *why* composition. In this type of composition, you state your opinion clearly and directly. You also offer reasons to explain why you hold that opinion.

To discover a topic for an explanatory *why* composition, consider some issues that you feel strongly about. How do you feel about what happens in your school or community, or in the nation? How do you feel, for example, about job opportunities for teenagers, women's rights, or life in the city?

When you have chosen an opinion to write about, write a sentence that clearly states your opinion. Words such as *should*, *ought*, or *might* are often used to state an opinion. If your opinion involves the comparison of two subjects, your sentence might include such terms as *better*, *worse*, *safer*, *cleaner*, *more*, or *most*. This sentence can become the topic sentence of the first paragraph of your composition.

To convince your readers that your opinion is worthwhile, you must present persuasive details. These details may include specific facts or accurate statistics. You may also present a convincing example or an anecdote that supports your opinion.

Check It Out   Examine the following pre-writing notes.

Opinion: A daily newspaper is a more complete source of information than a television newscast.

Support: newspaper editorial pages—variety of opinions
coverage on newspapers can be flexible
TV—30 seconds to 2 minutes for each story
newspapers—variety of news, services
newspapers provide space as needed, maps, charts
newspapers—more in-depth coverage than TV
½ hour TV news really just 22 minutes
TV—one news commentary, 10–12 stories
newspapers provide more analysis than TV
newspapers—multiple stories on many topics

- Is this topic suitable for a *why* composition?
- Is an opinion stated clearly and directly?
- How does the writer back up the opinion?

Try Your Skill Choose three of the following general topics for explanatory *why* compositions. Narrow each topic. State your opinion about it in a clear, direct statement.

careers	sports	marriage
movies	women's rights	education

Keep This in Mind

- In an explanatory *why* composition, you present an opinion clearly and directly.
- You support your opinion with facts, statistics, reasons, examples, or an anecdote.

Now Write Think of a strong opinion that you hold. Use this as the topic for an explanatory *why* composition. Write a sentence that expresses your opinion clearly and directly. In your pre-writing notes, include reasons, facts, statistics, examples, or anecdotes. Save your pre-writing notes.

215

each statement below is a fact or an opinion.

1. The government should spend more money on education and less on defense. (opinion)
2. Seat belts help save lives. (fact)
3. Television networks worry too much about their programs' popularity and not enough about their quality. (opinion)

Advanced Students

Have students do some research to support their opinions. Advise them to go to the library and consult an almanac, the vertical file, periodicals, and/or an encyclopedia to find two or three supporting facts or statistics.

Optional Practice

For **Try Your Skill,** write several students' opinions on the chalkboard. Choose three or four of the opinions as the basis for a group discussion.

Extending the Lesson

Choose a topic for the class to debate. Divide the class into two teams. As your students debate the issue, make notes on the chalkboard of the major arguments used by each side. After the debate, discuss how both sets of notes should be organized for *why* explanations. Ask for suggestions for the introductions and conclusions.

Objective

To use order of importance or comparison and contrast in organizing pre-writing notes for an explanatory *why* composition

Presenting the Lesson

1. Have students read **Here's the Idea.** Write *order of importance* and *comparison and contrast* on the chalkboard as you define and discuss them.

2. Have students study the pre-writing notes in **Check It Out.** Discuss how the comparison and contrast organization contains three main ideas.

3. Assign **Try Your Skill.** Point out that although a comparison and contrast organization is still used, the details are organized around each point of comparison. This is a second way to organize a comparison.

4. Read **Keep This in Mind.**

5. Assign **Now Write.**

Individualizing the Lesson

Less-Advanced Students

Help students choose an appropriate order for their supporting details. Instruct students to use order of importance if they are not comparing two subjects. Then illustrate the two methods of organizing a comparison with the following outline comparing made-for-TV movies with theatrical movies.

1. Theatrical movies
   —Don't deal with current issues
   —Often use horror, violence

216

How You Say It

Pre-Writing: Organizing an Opinion

Here's the Idea   The way you organize the details that support your opinion will depend partly on your topic and partly on how you have expressed your opinion. In many cases, the most effective way to organize the supporting details of an explanatory *why* composition is in **the order of their importance.** Using this method, you arrange your details so that your strongest reason appears last. That way, the most convincing reason you have to offer will remain fresh in your reader's mind.

If your opinion expresses a preference for one of two subjects, you may want to organize your supporting details by using **comparison and contrast.** If you choose this method, you will present details about both subjects. Then you will offer some conclusions about why you prefer one subject to the other. The details you present will, of course, support your conclusion.

Whichever method you choose, your first step will be to look over your list of supporting details carefully. Try to find two or three major ideas. Group your remaining details around the main reason they help to explain. Each of these idea groups will become a paragraph in your composition.

As a final step, look at your idea groups. Arrange them in the order that you want to present them in your composition.

Check It Out   Read these organized pre-writing notes.

1. TV news coverage limited by time
   22 minutes per night for news
   10–12 stories covered
   30 seconds to 2 minutes for each story
   one news commentary

216

2. Newspaper coverage can be more flexible
multiple stories on many topics and services
provide space as needed, maps, charts
editorial pages offer a variety of opinions

3. Conclusions
newspapers provide greater variety of news, services
newspapers provide more in-depth coverage than TV
newspapers provide more analysis of events than TV

- How has the writer organized the supporting material?

Try Your Skill   The ideas and details presented about television and newspaper news in **Check It Out** can be organized in the order of their importance. Using the information from **Check It Out,** complete the pre-writing notes that have been started below. Group the details in **Check It Out** around the main idea they help to explain.

1. Newspapers provide more analysis of the news than TV does.
2. Newspapers provide more in-depth coverage than TV.
3. Newspapers provide greater variety of news, services than TV.

Keep This in Mind

- Organize the details in an explanatory *why* composition in the order of their importance or by using comparison and contrast.

Now Write   Read over the pre-writing notes that you developed in **In Your View.** Decide whether you should use the order of importance, or comparison and contrast to organize your details. Next, write the main ideas that support your opinion. Under them, list the remaining details that help to develop each main idea. Finally, organize these idea groups in the order that you want to present them in your composition. Save your notes.

2. Television movies
   —Often present current issues
   —Present a variety of movies for the whole family
3. Conclusion
   —Television movies often use themes from current issues, unlike theatrical movies
   —Television does not rely on sensationalism; presents good movies for the whole family

Show the students how a second organization would use the two points of comparison (dealing with current issues and using sensationalism) as the main ideas.

Advanced Students

Point out that a good explanatory *why* composition includes specific details and examples along with facts and statistics. Have students think of a specific example to illustrate each of the following opinions.

1. Professional athletes are overpaid.
2. Learning a foreign language expands a student's horizons.
3. TV is a valuable educational tool.

Optional Practice

Have students arrange, in order of importance, the following details supporting the opinion that people should not smoke cigarettes.
Answers will vary.
2 —bad example for younger siblings
1 —unattractive habit
4 —can eventually kill you
3 —costs too much money

Extending the Lesson

Give groups of students this assignment: choose a specific product to advertise, and list convincing reasons, in order of importance, why consumers should buy it.

Objective

To use appropriate transitions in writing the first draft of an explanatory *why* composition

Presenting the Lesson

1. Have students read **Here's the Idea.** List the transitions on the chalkboard. Discuss the purpose of the introduction and conclusion in an explanatory *why* composition.

2. Have the students read the sample paragraphs in **Check It Out.** Emphasize the importance of the transition in showing the comparison and contrast organization.

3. Assign **Try Your Skill.**

4. Read **Keep This in Mind** and then assign **Now Write.** Remind students of the purpose of an explanatory *why* composition: to convince the reader to agree with an opinion.

Individualizing the Lesson

Less-Advanced Students

Have students write their first drafts in class in three consecutive class periods. They may write the introduction one day, the body the next, and the conclusion the next. If you conduct the class in the form of a writing workshop, you can help the students individually and they can also assist each other.

Advanced Students

Share with the class a first draft that has been effectively put together by projecting it or parts of it on an overhead projector. Have students point out strong facts and examples, good organization, and

Try It

Writing the First Draft

Here's the Idea   When you have an idea, you need to try it out before you know whether or not it will work. This is as true for your writing as it is for anything else. You try out the ideas in your pre-writing notes when you write your first draft.

In the **introduction,** state your opinion clearly and directly. Let your readers know exactly what you think. You may want to use the statement of opinion that you have in your notes. In the **body** of your composition, present your supporting evidence. Each important reason or main idea from your pre-writing notes will become a separate paragraph in the body. In your **conclusion,** summarize your opinion and your reasons for holding that opinion. In other words, remind your readers *what* you believe and *why* you believe it.

When writing your first draft, you will find that transitional words and phrases help you to express your ideas clearly and logically. There are two kinds of transitions you can use. One kind helps your reader to see and follow the method of organization you have used. For example, you can use transitions to present reasons and facts in the order of their importance. These transitions include such words and phrases as *first, the first reason, more important,* and *finally.* You can also use other transitions to highlight comparison and contrast. Some examples are *on the other hand, in contrast,* and *in the same way.*

The second kind of transition helps you state reasons and facts. This kind includes such words as *because, since, thus, if, in addition, therefore, for example,* and *as a result.*

Check It Out   Read this body paragraph and the first sentence of a second body paragraph.

Time limits television's daily coverage of the news. A typical half-hour network broadcast includes only twenty-two minutes of news. During this period, there is time to cover only ten to twelve stories. Thus, the time spent on any one story varies from thirty seconds to two minutes. Most news programs do try to include some commentary on the news. A news anchor usually gives his or her opinion on an important issue. Again, however, time limits this presentation to a single opinion. Even when local stations "welcome opposing views" to their commentary, these are not aired until several days later.

In contrast, newspapers can be more flexible about space. Therefore, they can be more complete in their coverage.

- What transitional phrase links the ideas in these two paragraphs? What method of organization does this transitional phrase highlight? Explain your answer.

Try Your Skill   Reread the body paragraphs in **Check It Out.** List the transitions that you find *within* each paragraph.

Keep This in Mind

- In the introduction, state your opinion clearly and directly.
- In the body, present the ideas that support your opinion.
- In the conclusion, summarize your opinion and supporting details.
- Use transitions to present your reasons, facts, or examples and to show how they are organized.

Now Write   Using your organized pre-writing notes, write the first draft of your explanatory *why* composition. Use transitions to guide your reader from point to point. Save your first draft in your folder.

effective transitions. Also ask the class to suggest possible improvements for the revision stage.

Optional Practice

Ask your students to pretend that they are editors of the school newspaper. Have them think of someone or some people in the school who should be commended, and write the introduction to an editorial supporting that viewpoint. Remind them to lead up to their statement of opinion in the topic sentence.

Extending the Lesson

Divide the class into groups. Give each group pamphlets from a different charitable or ecological organization, such as the National Society for the Prevention of Cruelty to Animals or the National Wildlife Federation. Ask the groups to analyze these persuasive pamphlets by writing the topic sentence; labeling the introduction, body, and conclusion; underlining the main points; and writing the number of facts or reasons used to support each main point. Ask the groups to discuss the effectiveness of the supporting reasons and facts. Afterward, have each group read its pamphlet and present its conclusions.

Part 4 Your Way

Revising Your Explanation

Objective

To revise an explanatory *why* composition

Presenting the Lesson

1. Have students read **Here's the Idea.** Outline the revision questions on the chalkboard as you discuss them.

2. Have volunteers read the sample paragraphs in **Check It Out.** Help the students recognize that the first paragraph sums up the writer's reasons in a specific way, and the second paragraph does so more generally.

3. Assign **Try Your Skill.** Discuss the fact that in a composition expressing an opinion, it is especially important to write strongly positive statements. How can the last sentence of the sample introduction be improved in this respect?

4. Read **Keep This in Mind.**

5. Assign **Now Write.** Discuss writing a title for an explanatory *why* composition. Advise students to use a straightforward title that indicates the writer's opinion.

Individualizing the Lesson

Less-Advanced Students

Emphasize the importance of the conclusion of an explanatory *why* composition. The composition's body presents the facts; the conclusion must tie the facts together to show why they support the writer's opinion.

Here's the Idea Do you like to have things your own way? Almost everyone does. When you write, you have the opportunity to express your ideas just the way you want to. If you are willing to put in the time and the effort, you *can* have your own way with your own words!

Read the first draft of your explanatory *why* composition. How can you make your opinion clearer? How can you make your supporting details stronger? As you revise your first draft, ask yourself the following questions.

1. Is my opinion stated clearly in the introductory paragraph?
2. Did I support my opinion with convincing details in the body of the composition?
3. Is each of my main ideas developed with enough details?
4. Did I use good transitional words and phrases to present my opinion and the supporting details?
5. How well did I arrange my ideas, reasons, and details? Did I organize them using either the order of importance, or comparison and contrast? Did I use transitions to show this order?
6. Does the ending paragraph leave a strong impression by summing up my opinion and reasons?

When you are satisfied that you have presented your opinion as well as you can, proofread your composition. Correct any errors in grammar and mechanics.

Check It Out Read these last two paragraphs of the composition comparing daily newspapers to TV news.

As a result of these differences, newspapers can provide a greater variety, depth, and analysis of the news. Because of the variety of their news stories and services, newspapers provide many more informative and entertaining stories than television does. Because of the depth of news coverage, newspaper stories can provide more details than television or radio stories. By including a greater variety of viewpoints, newspapers can do a better job of preparing people to draw their own conclusions than television newscasts can.

Although television network news does offer a summary of major daily events, it cannot provide the same coverage that a daily newspaper can. To be informed, we need the newspaper!

- Does the first paragraph sum up the writer's reasons?
- How does the conclusion sum up the writer's opinion?
- What transitions has the writer included?

Try Your Skill   Revise this first draft of the introduction to the composition comparing daily newspapers to TV news.

I'm not saying television doesn't have a definate place in the on-the-spot news coverage of special events. Like rocket launchings or presidential inaugurals. It is just not the most complete source. I'm pretty sure newspapers are better.

Keep This in Mind

- State your opinion clearly. Support it with facts and reasons arranged in a logical order. Sum up your opinion and ideas in your conclusion.
- Use transitional words and phrases to highlight the order of your ideas and to present them clearly.

Now Write   Revise the first draft of your explanatory *why* composition. Follow the guidelines for revision in this lesson. Then make a final, neat copy of your composition. Give your composition a good title. Proofread and correct your final copy. Save your work.

Advanced Students

Have students find the names of one or two publications that publish letters to the editor expressing an opinion. The students may wish to submit a final copy of their compositions for possible publication.

Optional Practice

Have students revise the following concluding paragraph for a composition on television movies based on the pre-writing notes in **Individualizing the Lesson,** Part 2.

So you can see why I like made-for-TV movies better than movies shown in theaters. I mean, I'd rather watch *Shogun* than *Meatballs* any day. I mean, who wouldn't, right?

Extending the Lesson

Have each student find a newspaper or newsmagazine editorial and label the introduction, body, and conclusion; tell what kind of organization is used in the body; and underline transitions within and between paragraphs. Students should also carefully analyze the editorial's thesis statement (topic sentence) and its conclusion.

Section 19 Objectives

1. To plan an explanatory *what* composition, beginning with a short, one-sentence definition of a word or term

2. To organize the pre-writing notes for a definition in general to specific order

3. To write a first draft of an explanatory *what* composition

4. To revise an explanatory *what* composition

Preparing the Students

Write the following chart on the chalkboard:

General Class	Specific
cats	tiger
flowers	_____
fish	_____
bicycles	_____
movie stars	_____
emotions	_____

Ask volunteers to insert specific items for each general class. Then have each student select a specific word listed on the board and write a definition. Ask students to read their brief definitions to the class.

Point out that an explanatory *what* composition is built upon a definition. Tell students that Writing Section 19 will show them how to write explanatory *what* compositions.

Additional Resources

Practice Book — pages 90–93
Duplicating Masters — pages 90–93

The Explanatory Composition

Telling *What*

Teaching Special Populations

LD See **Teaching Special Populations,** page 75.

ESL Some words in the exercises may need to be defined for ESL students. Help students find definitions in dictionaries or encyclopedias.

Suggest that students choose topics with which they are familiar. Help students distinguish between main ideas and subordinate ideas. After students complete their first drafts, pair them, and have them read their drafts to each other.

NSD See **Teaching Special Populations,** page 75.

Part 1

What's What?

Pre-Writing: Developing a Definition

Objective

To plan an explanatory *what* composition, beginning with a short, one-sentence definition of a word or term

Presenting the Lesson

1. Have students read **Here's the Idea.** Emphasize the sample topics for a definition in paragraph 2; point out that the words or terms may be unfamiliar to some readers, so they are good topics for an explanatory *what* composition. Also discuss writing a one-sentence definition as the basis of the composition.

2. Have the class study the pre-writing notes in **Check It Out.** Emphasize the one-sentence definition that begins the pre-writing notes.

3. Assign **Try Your Skill.** Discuss the students' responses in class, pointing out that choosing a method of development is a first step in planning an explanatory *what* composition.

4. Read **Keep This in Mind.**

5. Assign **Now Write.** Have students brainstorm in order to think of suitable topics. First have students list five to ten topics that are related to jobs or hobbies. Then ask students to select only one topic. Have students pair off to discuss each other's notes and try to add more details or facts and figures.

Individualizing the Lesson

Less-Adanced Students

Ask students to select the topics below that would be appropriate for explanatory *what* compositions.

Here's the Idea Can you imagine the confusion today if everyone had his or her private meaning for the same word? Standard definitions allow us to share our knowledge, experiences, and understanding with others. Often, a dictionary entry or a short paragraph is all that is needed to explain what something is. At other times an explanatory *what* composition can be written to give an extended definition of something.

The topic for an explanatory *what* composition may be a real object, such as a *laser* or a *wolverine.* Or, it may be a term, such as *blue ribbon,* or an idea, such as *courage.* Choose a familiar topic. That will make it easier for you to write a clear definition.

Begin your pre-writing notes by writing a short, one-sentence definition of your topic. Name the word to be defined. Next, name the general class to which your subject belongs. Finally, name the particular characteristics of your subject. Here is an example:

> Friends are people who know one another well and who like one another.

To expand your short definition, gather ideas and information from either your own experience or from outside sources. For instance, you might develop the definition of a *laser* with facts and statistics from encyclopedias or other reference books. You might want to develop the definition of a term or an idea, such as *courage,* in a more personal way. If this is the case, you can use some specific examples or an anecdote from your experience.

Think about your audience as you gather your details. Keeping your audience in mind will help you to choose just the right ideas and information to develop your definition.

Check It Out Read these pre-writing notes.

Allergy is the name of a medical condition caused by substances that are harmful only to people who are sensitive to them.

allergy treatments	series of shots
questioning to find cause	scratch tests
food, skin irritants, pollen	allergy tests
sneezing, watery eyes	rashes
no complete cure	avoiding source of irritation
allergy symptoms	difficulty breathing

• What is being defined? What is the subject's general class? What are its particular characteristics?

Try Your Skill Decide whether each word below would be better developed by using facts and statistics or by using personal examples and anecdotes. Perhaps some words require a combination of both kinds of details. Write each word and then write the type of supporting details you would gather.

kindness   mammal   talent   diesel   skyscraper

Keep This in Mind

• An explanatory *what* composition defines an idea, a term, or a real thing.
• Collect specific details, personal examples, anecdotes, facts, and statistics that will define your subject clearly.

Now Write Think about some topics for an explanatory *what* composition. You may choose to define something related to a job or a hobby. You may choose to define an idea that interests you. Select a topic. Then write a short definition of your subject. Next, gather details that will expand your definition and explain it more fully. Save your pre-writing notes in your folder.

prejudice
happiness
taking good photos
a TV studio
a construction site
my first day of school
the need for daycare
pet therapy
a day I would like to forget

As a review of all types of compositions, have your students identify the type of composition that suits each topic best.

Advanced Students

Have students work together to develop a one-sentence definition of *music video*. Then have one student make notes on the chalkboard as the others volunteer information for a composition defining the term.

Optional Practice

Have students write a one-sentence definition for each of the following words or terms, following the guidelines in **Here's the Idea.**

climate	teacher
comic strip	situation comedy

Extending the Lesson

Select a filmstrip or a movie that tells about a country, a literary form, a scientific discovery, or a historical period. Make certain that the subject matter is simple. Show the film and ask students to make notes for an explanatory *what* composition on the subject. The notes should include details or facts and figures from the film. Finally, students should write definitions and introductions for the composition.

Objective

To organize the pre-writing notes for a definition in general to specific order

Presenting the Lesson

1. Read **Here's the Idea.** Write *general to specific* order on the chalkboard as you define and discuss it.

2. Have the class study the pre-writing notes in **Check It Out** and discuss the study question. Have the students imagine that they are discussing an allergy problem with a doctor. Is this the order in which a doctor would discuss allergies? Point out that this is general to specific order.

3. Assign **Try Your Skill.** Help the students pick out the three statments that are more general than the others. Instruct them to group the specific details under these general ones.

4. Read **Keep This in Mind.**

5. Assign **Now Write.** Advise students to find general ideas in their notes as they did in the sample notes in **Try Your Skill.** If their pre-writing notes consist only of specific details, students may need to create general categories that the notes can be grouped under.

Individualizing the Lesson

Less-Advanced Students

For practice in organizing definitions in general to specific order, have students pick out the general details and the specific details in the sample pre-writing notes below defining *love*. Order may vary.

Introducing . . .

Pre-Writing: Organizing a Definition

Here's the Idea   Have you ever introduced yourself to a group of strangers? In a sense, you were defining yourself. You probably began by giving your name. Then, depending upon the situation, you probably added a few more details about yourself, such as "I'm a sophomore at Central High School" or "I played defensive tackle on this year's sophomore football team." Of course, these "definitions" could be continued with additional details about the subjects you are taking in school or the important tackles you made during the season.

In introducing yourself, you began with the general and moved to the specific. In introducing a new term or idea to your readers, you would use **general to specific** order, too. You would begin by giving a general statement of definition for your subject. The rest of your composition would provide specific details to make the definition clearer and more exact.

To begin organizing your ideas, look at your pre-writing notes. Try to identify two or three main ideas within them that help to define your subject. Group your remaining details around these main ideas. Each of these idea groups will be a separate paragraph in the body of your composition.

Check It Out   Read these organized pre-writing notes.

allergy symptoms
   sneezing, watery eyes
   difficulty breathing
   rashes

allergy tests
   questioning
   scratch tests

allergy treatments
    avoiding source of irritation
    series of shots
    no complete cure

- Around what three main ideas have these pre-writing notes been grouped?

Try Your Skill

Try Your Skill Below are some pre-writing notes that define a *friend*. Identify three main ideas that help to define the topic. Then group all of the remaining details under them. Save these notes in your folder.

someone who stays with me through good and bad times
Jeff and I grew up together, next door neighbors
Jeff was a good companion during a rainy campout, kept sense of humor
someone with qualities I admire
Jeff knew my desire to make the team and supported me during baseball tryouts
dependable: Jeff took over my paper route when I was sick
someone with whom I've shared experiences, thoughts, and feelings
Jeff didn't go to the party, helped me babysit my little sister
accepting: Jeff doesn't criticize my mistakes

Keep This in Mind

- Use general to specific order in arranging the details for an explanatory *what* composition.
- Group your pre-writing notes around two or three main ideas.

Now Write

Now Write Look at the pre-writing details you gathered in **What's What?** Identify two or three main ideas that help to define your topic. Group your remaining details around these main ideas. Keep your organized pre-writing notes in your folder.

227

3a—made me send a check for starving children in Africa
1 —romantic love
2a—my sister sending me a sweater from college
2 —love for family and friends
1a—Prince of Wales giving up throne for woman he loved
3 —love for fellow man in general
1b—Rhett Butler and Scarlett O'Hara

Advanced Students

Have students continue their definition of *music video* that they started in Part 1 by organizing the class pre-writing notes in general to specific order.

Optional Practice

Have students follow the directions for **Try Your Skill** for the following notes defining *hobby*. Order may vary.

1a—tennis is a hobby that must be done with others
1 —can be done alone or with others
2 —something people do in their spare time
3 —can be quiet or active
2a—carpentry or sewing can be a hobby if it is not what the person does for a living
3a—collecting stamps or coins, building models are quiet hobbies

Extending the Lesson

Have students select a personality trait that they wish they did not have, such as stubbornness, laziness, or aggressiveness. Ask them to write a definition of that trait and to summarize three incidents when they exhibited that trait. Finally, have them think of a title for an explanatory *what* composition on the topic.

227

An Important Link

Objective

To write a first draft of an explanatory *what* composition

Presenting the Lesson

1. Read **Here's the Idea.** Emphasize the importance of thorough, detailed pre-writing notes in writing the first draft of a composition. Also discuss including a one-sentence definition of the topic in the introductory paragraph of an explanatory *what* composition.

2. Have students read the paragraphs from the sample composition in **Check It Out.** Help the class recognize that the first sentence of the composition is its topic sentence and that it is a one-sentence definition of the topic. Point out how the general to specific organization from the pre-writing notes in Part 2 has been followed in the first draft.

3. Assign **Try Your Skill.** Have a few volunteers read their conclusions to the class and have the class discuss the merits of each.

4. Read **Keep This in Mind.**

5. Assign **Now Write.** Encourage students to use specific ideas and examples to make their first drafts interesting.

Individualizing the Lesson

Less-Advanced Students

Remind students to keep their purpose and audience in mind as they write their first drafts. Since the composition's purpose is to explain a term, clarity and thoroughness are important. Students should take

Writing the First Draft

Here's the Idea   The three stages of the process of writing form a strong chain. Your first draft is the important middle link between pre-writing and revision. It is an essential step between gathering your ideas and presenting them to your reader. In your first draft, you turn your pre-writing ideas into sentences and paragraphs. You try out your ideas and your organization. As you write your first draft, remember the important role each part of it plays in developing your definition.

You should include a good, short definition of your topic as part of the introduction. This sentence will serve as the topic sentence for your first paragraph.

In the body, you will develop the definition as fully as possible. Each main idea will be a separate paragraph. Each paragraph will be developed with details from your pre-writing notes.

To finish your composition, write an interesting conclusion that sums up the main ideas of your definition.

Check It Out   Read this introduction and body of an explanatory *what* composition.

Allergy is the name of a medical condition caused by substances that are harmful only to people who are sensitive to them. Fifteen percent of Americans suffer from allergies. The substances that cause allergies are called allergens. Certain foods, such as milk, wheat, chocolate, and eggs, can cause allergic reactions. Another class of allergens includes things that come in contact with the skin, such as wool or clothing dyes. A third class of allergens is made up of things inhaled through the nose, such as house dust and plant pollen.

Allergic symptoms take many forms. Sneezing and watery eyes are typical of hay fever. Asthma causes difficulty in breathing because of the swelling of the bronchial tubes. Certain food allergies may cause rashes, hives, or stomach upsets.

Doctors can test for allergies in several ways. Questioning and observation can give clues. If a patient improves when something is removed from his or her diet or environment, that can signal an allergy. Doctors will often use a scratch test. Substances are applied to scratches made on the skin. A scratch that becomes irritated gives proof that the patient is allergic to the substance placed on that scratch.

Allergies can be treated in a number of ways. The most obvious cure is to avoid anything to which a patient is sensitive. Another treatment involves a series of shots from a doctor who specializes in allergies. The patient receives injections containing the allergic substance. Gradually his system becomes less sensitive to that substance.

- Has each main idea been developed in a separate paragraph? Explain your answer.

Try Your Skill   Look again at the paragraphs in **Check It Out.** Write a conclusion to this explanatory *what* composition. Make your conclusion interesting.

Keep This in Mind

- Include a short definition in the introduction to an explanatory *what* composition.
- Develop each body paragraph using a main idea group from your pre-writing notes.
- Summarize the main idea of your definition in the conclusion.

Now Write   Use your pre-writing notes to write a first draft of your explanatory *what* composition. Include a short definition in your introduction. Develop each main idea into a separate body paragraph. Sum up your ideas in your conclusion. Save your first draft.

229

care not to make their definitions too simple or too complicated for their intended audience. For example, how would the sample composition in **Check It Out** be changed for an audience of doctors?

Advanced Students

If students have thorough prewriting notes that make writing the first draft relatively simple, have them focus on making their compositions interesting in the first draft. Discuss the fact that although the composition's main purpose is to inform, it can still be made lively and vivid by the use of strong verbs and specific details.

Optional Practice

Have students write an introduction for a possible composition based on one of the one-sentence definitions they wrote for **Optional Practice,** Part 1.

Extending the Lesson

Ask students to "invent" a gadget of the future. Have them write definitions of these gadgets and share them with the rest of the class.

Part 4

Objective

To revise an explanatory *what* composition

Presenting the Lesson

1. Have students read **Here's the Idea.** Outline the revision questions on the chalkboard as you discuss them.

2. Have the students read the sample conclusion in **Check It Out** and discuss its revisions. Help them recognize how the conclusion has been made more specific.

3. Assign **Try Your Skill.** Instruct students to revise the conclusion's ideas and expression before considering grammar and mechanics.

4. Read **Keep This in Mind.**

5. Assign **Now Write.** Discuss titling an explanatory *what* composition. Have some students share and discuss their titles.

Individualizing the Lesson

Less-Advanced Students

Before assigning **Now Write,** ask each student to analyze his or her greatest weakness in writing—for example, writing a clear and interesting introduction, making the body clear and specific, organizing details, or correcting errors in grammar and mechanics. Have students focus on these weaknesses as they revise their explanatory *what* compositions.

Advanced Students

Have each student revise all but the concluding paragraph of his or

In Your Reader's Place

Revising Your Definition

Here's the Idea Writing can be divided into two general categories, public and private. Private writing is done by you, for you. It is the writing that you do in your diary or journal. Public writing is the type that you do for someone else to read, that is, for an audience.

An explanatory *what* composition is, of course, a form of public writing. As you revise the first draft of your explanatory *what* composition, try to imagine yourself in your reader's place. Keep in mind the age level, interests, and background of your reader. Then, reread your draft to see if everything in your definition makes sense from the reader's point of view.

As you read your first draft, ask yourself the following questions.

1. Is my topic defined in a one-sentence definition in the introduction?

2. Does my one-sentence definition name the subject, place it in a general class, and name the characteristics that make it different from others in its class?

3. Does the body of the composition extend the general definition with enough specific details, facts, statistics, or personal examples or anecdotes?

4. Does my concluding paragraph summarize the main ideas of the definition?

5. Does the development of my composition follow general to specific order?

When you are satisfied that your composition defines your subject clearly and completely for your readers, proofread it. Correct any errors in grammar and mechanics.

Check It Out Read this revised draft of the conclusion from the explanatory *what* composition about allergies.

> Millions of people ∧*are victims of all types of* have allergic reactions of one kind or another. Researchers continue to hunt for better ways to con- *from sneezing to rashes.* trol ∧ them. I hope they come up with something soon. *test for and to* ∧*allergies so that these victims can find relief.*

- How have revisions improved the writer's first draft?
- How does the conclusion sum up the main ideas?

Try Your Skill Using the guidelines in this lesson, revise this introductory paragraph for a composition defining a *friend*.

A friend is when you can really count on someone. They always come threw. You enjoy being with him or her to. There someone to talk to, and they wont laugh at what you say. Unless it's funny. You know what I mean. Like Jack he's a real example of a friend. I could mention someone else who's not.

Keep This in Mind

- In the introduction, give a short, general definition of your subject. In the body, develop your definition more fully with additional details. In the conclusion, summarize your main ideas.
- Arrange your definition from the general to the specific.

Now Write Revise your first draft. Keep your readers in mind. After you have finished your revisions and proofread your composition, give it a good title. Then make a final copy. Proofread this copy one last time. Correct any errors that you find. Save your completed composition.

231

her composition. Then the students can exchange papers and revise their classmates' conclusions. The students should carefully consider their classmates' suggestions before writing their own final copies.

Optional Practice

Have students revise the following concluding paragraph for a composition defining the word *hobby*. Answers will vary.

So anyway, a hobby is anything a person enjoys doing in their spare time. It could be reading cookbooks or skiing. Or even skydiving. Hobbys can be quiet or adventurous. I think everyone should have some kinda hobby.

Extending the Lesson

Have students assemble and analyze the final copies of the compositions they have written for Sections 15–19. Students should ask themselves the following questions as they study their writing:

Which is the most informative composition?
Which is the most entertaining composition?
Which composition did I most enjoy writing?
Which composition did I find most difficult to write?
Which composition did I do the best job on overall?

Have the class make a bulletin board or class notebook displaying each student's best composition.

Section **20** Objectives

1. To choose a topic and find sources for a report

2. To write bibliography cards and note cards correctly

3. To organize note cards by subject matter

4. To write an outline for a report

5. To write the introduction of a report

6. To write the body and conclusion of a report

7. To revise a report

8. To write footnotes and a bibliography for a report

Preparing the Students

Unfortunately, many students think of writing a report as a tiresome, long task that proves they have spent many hours working in the library. Stress that writing a report need not involve endless time in the library. Discuss writing a report as a means of discovery about a particular topic of interest to the student.

In order to motivate the class, hand out thirty to fifty copies of current maganizes from the school library. Have each student list ten to twenty topics that ·they notice as they peruse the magazines. Then spend the class period or several periods discussing some of these topics. Ask students which topics they would like to learn more about. The discussions will help students to find interesting topics and to become familiar with a few topics in depth.

Explain that the class will be writing reports and that Writing Section 20 will teach everything from how to find topics to how to write final

Writing a Report

drafts. Note that the process described in this Section can be used for reports in other classes as well.

Additional Resources

Mastery Test — page 30 in the test booklet

Practice Book — pages 94–101

Duplicating Masters — pages 94–101

Teaching Special Populations

LD See **Teaching Special Populations,** page 75. Supervise students closely as they complete each step of this process. You might keep a check list for each student of the steps completed in the process of writing. Encourage students to choose interesting topics for their reports.

If possible, provide simplified reference materials for students. When appropriate, allow students to take notes in spiral notebooks, instead of on loose note cards.

ESL Students may need extra help for most steps of this process. Offer them simplified reference materials and as much individual attention as possible.

Encourage students to write about topics in which they are interested. Remind them that they can conduct interviews with family members or friends about various cross-cultural experiences.

NSD See **Teaching Special Populations,** page 75.

A Wise Choice

Developing a Report

Objective

To choose a topic and find sources for a report

Presenting the Lesson

1. Read aloud **Here's the Idea.** Write the terms *report* and *thesis statement* on the chalkboard as you define and discuss them. Discuss the difference between a composition and a report. Note that a report is factual and requires library research. Refer students to Section 22, **Using the Library.** Review the Dewey Decimal System and the various reference works students might use to research their topics.

2. Read aloud and discuss **Check It Out.** Have students notice that there are six different kinds of sources listed. Ask where these sources are located in the library.

3. Assign **Try Your Skill.** Narrow one topic with the students to demonstrate how to narrow a topic sufficiently.

4. Read **Keep This in Mind.**

5. Assign **Now Write.** You might ask students to choose topics that appealed to them when they discussed the magazine articles. Have students work in the library during the class period. Make sure that students have narrowed their topics sufficiently.

Individualizing the Lesson

Less-Advanced Students

1. Discuss the purpose of an audience for a report. Remind students that since a report's purpose is to inform, they should be es-

Here's the Idea   A **report** is a special kind of composition that is written on a subject that you learn about from outside sources, such as books, magazines, and encyclopedias.

Often, you will be assigned a specific subject for a report. When the choice is yours, though, choose a general subject that interests you. Then go to the library and do some reading. Look for specific aspects of your subject to investigate further. One of these aspects can become the narrowed topic for your report. Choose a topic that you can cover in the assigned length of your report. When you have decided on a topic, write a few sentences that state your topic and your purpose for writing. This is called a **thesis statement.**

When you have chosen a topic, do some research in the library. Look in the card catalog for books. Check several encyclopedias. Look in the reference section, the vertical file, and the *Readers' Guide to Periodical Literature*. Write the titles of books, encyclopedias, pamphlets, and magazine articles. Also write the volume and page number of the encyclopedias and the dates of the magazines. Now you have a list of sources.

Suppose you were asked to write a five-paragraph report on any twentieth-century American organization or business. You might begin your research by looking in the subject file of the card catalog. Look under subjects in *American history*. There you would find such various possible topics as NOW (National Organization for Women), the Peace Corps, the Food and Drug Administration, and the Carnegie Hero Fund Commission).

Suppose you decided to choose the Carnegie Hero Fund as a subject. Another search of the card catalog, encyclopedia indexes, the vertical file, and the *Readers' Guide* would give you specific sources of information about this organization.

Check It Out   Look at this list of sources for a report.

1. Andrew Carnegie, a book by Joseph Frazier Wall.

2. The World Book Encyclopedia, Volume 3, pages 177-179.

3. Life magazine, March 1979 issue, pages 94-105.

4. Carnegie Hero Fund Commission Annual Report, 1977, in vertical file.

5. Famous First Facts, page 144, for first winner.

6. "A Different Kind of Hero," Pittsburgh Post-Gazette, Sept. 19, 1981, Sec. 2, p.1, col. 1.

- How would you have found the first source? the third?
- Is this a good list of sources? Explain your answer.

Try Your Skill   Choose one of the subjects listed below. First, narrow the subject to a specific topic. Then list three sources where you could get information for your report.

famous explorers   musicians or artists   dinosaurs

Keep This in Mind

- To find a topic for a report, have a general subject in mind. Search through books, magazines, and other reference works to find a specific topic.
- Gather information for a report by examining a number of different sources.

Now Write   Choose your own topic for a report. When you have chosen a topic, begin your library research. Look for books, magazines, encyclopedias, and pamphlets that may contain the information you need. Try to find at least three different kinds of sources. Note the call numbers, the book titles, the magazine issues, or the vertical file references. Save your work.

235

pecially careful not to make their facts too simple or too complicated for their intended audience.

2. Make sure students know some basic research techniques before beginning their reports. See Writing Section 22, **Using the Library.**

Advanced Students

For **Now Write,** encourage students to find at least five different kinds of sources for their report topics. Discuss the fact that it is always good to have more information than necessary when writing a report.

Optional Practice

Have students go to the library and find two specific sources of information for each of the following possible report topics.

1. NASA
2. wildebeest
3. Robert Frost

Extending the Lesson

Have each student help a partner by finding three more sources on his or her partner's topic.

Part 2

Objective

To write bibliography cards and note cards correctly

Presenting the Lesson

1. Have students read **Here's the Idea.** Discuss *bibliography cards,* emphasizing the importance of having complete bibliographical information when researching a topic and when preparing a bibliography at the end of a report. Emphasize that only one source should be placed on a card.

Ask students the purpose of note cards. Explain why each card should contain only one idea. Tell students that if they copy material directly from a source onto a card, this material should have quotation marks around it. Explain that even if the material is stated in the student's own words, it still needs the code number from the source. Lead into a discussion of plagiarism. Make sure that students understand that plagiarism is a serious form of cheating. State your school's penalty for plagiarism.

2. For **Check It Out,** have students refer to the sample cards on page 238 as you ask the study questions. Discuss the numbering systems of the bibliography cards and note cards and discuss how students will use this information when they compile their bibliographies.

3. Assign and discuss **Try Your Skill.** Have students draw two rectangles for the bibliography card and the note card. Have the class follow the form of the examples on

236

In Your Own Words

Taking Notes

Here's the Idea   Reading and gathering information are important steps in writing a report. You must write down all of the facts and ideas you want to include in your report. You must also write down all of the important information about each source that you use. Making **note cards** and **bibliography cards** are important steps in preparing a report.

For each source you use, make a bibliography card. You will need the information on these cards later. Notice that the form is different for each kind of source.

Book:	author, title, city published, publisher, date published
Magazine:	author of article (if there is one), title of article, name of magazine, date published, page number of article
Encyclopedia:	author of article (if there is one), name of encyclopedia, volume number, page number of article, date published
Newspaper:	author of article (if there is one); title of article; name of newspaper; date published; section, page, and column number of article

When you make a bibliography card, give the source a number. These numbers will help you as you write your note cards.

As you read about your topic, write down all of the important information on note cards. Follow these guidelines.

1. Use a separate 3" × 5" note card for each fact or idea.

2. At the top of each card, write a heading or a key phrase that tells the main idea of the note.

3. Label each note card with the number given to that source on its bibliography card. This way you will know where the note came from. Include the exact page reference.

236

4. Take notes in your own words. Copying another writer's work is called **plagiarism.** Plagiarism is always unacceptable. Sometimes, however, you may want to quote a source directly. When you use another writer's words, copy the words exactly as you find them. Be sure to enclose the words in quotation marks.

Check It Out   Look at the sample cards on page 238.

- Which are bibliography cards? What information does each contain?
- Which is a note card? What is its source?

Try Your Skill   Read the following information. Make a bibliography card and a note card based on it.

Ancient Egyptians considered the pharaoh a god and the son of a god. They thought he was the falcon god Horus in human form, and the son of Re, the sun god. In theory, the pharaoh owned all the land and people in Egypt. In reality, his power was limited by strong groups, including the priests and nobles.

from *The World Book Encyclopedia*, page 315,
Volume 15, 1984.

Keep This in Mind

- When you read about your topic, make note cards. Each card should contain one fact or idea.
- Take notes in your own words. Do not plagiarize.
- Use quotation marks when you quote a source.
- Make bibliography cards that contain basic information about each source of information you use.

Now Write   Take the list of sources you developed in the last lesson and a stack of 3" × 5" note cards with you to the library. Make a bibliography card for each source. As you read about your topic, make note cards about the information you find. Save the cards in your folder.

page 238. Discuss the importance of stating the main idea briefly on the note card. Check each student's card, and show accurate ones on the opaque projector. Call attention to any cards that inadvertently use the source's words without using quotation marks.

4. Read **Keep This in Mind.**

5. Assign **Now Write.** Accompany students to the library and be available to answer questions.

Individualizing the Lesson

Less-Advanced Students

Demonstrate the process of taking notes for a report. Using student examples, write the notes on the chalkboard or make transparencies of bibliography cards and note cards to show on the overhead projector. Explain how the student narrowed a subject, found sources, listed them on bibliography cards, read sources, and took notes.

Advanced Students

Discuss the use of direct quotations in reports. Tell students that they may occasionally want to quote a source directly when it states an idea in a striking way. Emphasize the use of quotation marks on their note cards to indicate direct quotations. Instruct students to use at least one direct quotation as they research their topics.

Optional Practice

Have students prepare a bibliography card for each of the following sources:

"Congress of the United States,"
Encyclopedia Americana, 1977,
p. 567, vol. 3
The Complete Book of the Olympics,
David Wallechinsky, New York,
Penguin Books, 1984
"The Greatest Soldier in Europe,"
Robert Wernick, *Smithsonian,* January 1985, pages 54–63
"Congress of the United States"
Encyclopedia Americana
Volume 3, page 567 (1977)
Wallechinsky, David
The Complete Book of the Olympics
New York: Penguin Books, 1984
Wernick, Robert
"The Greatest Soldier in Europe"
Smithsonian
January, 1985 pages 54–63

Extending the Lesson

Give students practice in note-taking by duplicating and distributing a brief encyclopedia entry, a brief magazine article, and a biographical reference book entry about the same person. Ask students to take notes and make note cards. Remind them to use their own words whenever possible, to include quotation marks where needed, and to include only one idea on each card. When students have finished, discuss which information belongs on note cards, and have students read sample cards aloud.

1.

Kane, Joseph
Famous First Facts
New York: H. H. Wilson Co., 1964

2.

Carnegie Hero Fund Commission
The World Book Encyclopedia
Volume 3, page 179 (1979)

3.

Bayer, Ann
"The Hero in Us All"
Life
March, 1979   pages 94–105

3.

origin of fund

Carnegie was impressed by bravery of two rescuers who died in a coal mine disaster in 1904. He was also worried about the widows and orphans of the rescuers.
page 94

Sort It Out

Organizing Information

Here's the Idea   If a report is planned well, it should not be difficult to write. An important step in planning a report is organizing the information. Your organized notes can become a plan for writing a first draft of your report.

First, read through your note cards. Separate them into several piles. Each pile of cards should be about one main idea. Try to group the cards into four or five main ideas. Each pile of cards can become a paragraph in the body of your report. If you find cards that do not belong with any others, you may decide not to include these ideas in your report. For now, however, save these cards. They may provide information that you can use in the introduction or conclusion of your report.

For example, if you were writing about the Carnegie Hero Fund, you might find that all your information could be grouped around four main ideas: why the fund was started, the history of the fund, eligibility requirements, and how winners are chosen.

Next, read through the cards in each pile. In what way are the cards related? In other words, what is the main idea of each pile of cards? State each main idea in a sentence. These sentences can become topic sentences when you write your first draft.

Finally, put your notes in order. First, arrange the piles of cards in the order you will write about them. Then, do the same for the note cards in each pile. Be sure that you organize your notes in a logical order. Take your time. You may want to rearrange your notes several times until you are satisfied.

Check It Out   Read these sentences that state the four main ideas about the Carnegie Hero Fund.

1. The fund was started so that brave people wouldn't suffer financially as a result of their heroism.

239

Part 3

Objective

To organize note cards by subject matter

Presenting the Lesson

1. Read aloud **Here's the Idea.** Point out that the importance of having only one idea on each note card.

2. Read and discuss **Check It Out.** Have the students notice how clear the author's main ideas are.

3. Assign **Try Your Skill.** After students have completed the exercise individually, have a student write each main idea and group names on the board.

4. Read **Keep This in Mind.**

5. Assign **Now Write.** Remind students to take their time; organizing facts may be difficult, but it is one of the most important skills involved in planning a report. Caution students that if they have more than seven piles of cards, their papers may become too long.

Individualizing the Lesson

Less-Advanced Students

1. Help students organize their notes individually or by dividing them into pairs to help each other. Tell students that organizing their facts may help them see that they need to do additional research in a particular area.

2. Give students additional practice in organizing ideas by having them group the following twentieth century inventions in three groups according to the instructions in **Try Your Skill.**

239

airplane   telephone
movie projector   radio
photocopier   word processor
automobile   helicopter
television   typewriter

Advanced Students

After students have finished **Now Write,** have them exchange their work to check for logical organization.

Optional Practice

Have students organize the following notes into two separate categories. Ask them to write sentences that summarize each group of notes. The topic of the report is the Olympic Games.

Begun in 1896
More female competitors
More sports and events
First Games in Athens
Revival of Games of ancient Greeks
Continuing improvement in performance
More athletes from more nations
Thirteen nations in first Games
Nine sports in first Games

Extending the Lesson

Hold conferences to evaluate the students' note cards. You might evaluate in two areas: the quality of the note-taking and the organization of the notes.

2. The fund began in 1904 and has awarded more than 13 million dollars.

3. Eligibility requirements are strict but fair.

4. Cases of bravery are reported and carefully studied. Winners are men and women of any age, occupation, and race.

- Is the main idea stated clearly in each sentence?
- Do you see how these sentences could become the topic sentences of paragraphs in a report?

Try Your Skill   Organize the following names into three separate groups. For each group of four names, write one sentence that expresses the main idea of the group's relationship.

George Washington, Jack Nicholson, Babe Ruth, Lucille Ball, Martina Navratilova, Brooke Shields, Clark Gable, A. J. Foyt, Cleopatra, Queen Elizabeth, Walter Payton, Julius Caesar

Keep This in Mind

- Organize note cards into separate piles. Group together cards with the same main idea. Write a sentence that states the main idea of each group of cards.
- Arrange the groups of cards and the facts within each group in a logical order.

Now Write   Take out the note cards you have written for your own report and read them. Put related cards together in four or five separate piles. Think about the main idea of each group of cards. Write a sentence that expresses the main idea of each group. Then arrange your notes in a logical order. Save your cards and sentences in your folder.

4

The Framework

Making an Outline

Here's the Idea After you have organized your note cards, the next step is to make an outline. Making an outline is a more detailed way of organizing your notes. It will show where each individual note card with its one idea fits into your paper. The outline will then become the plan for you to follow when you write the report.

The main idea of each pile of note cards you organized will become a main topic in your outline. The related facts on your note cards will become the subtopics and details of the outline. Each main idea, subtopic, and detail will be stated in a word or phrase.

All outlines follow the same form. An outline begins with a title. Below that, Roman numerals are used to indicate main ideas. Under main ideas, capital letters are used to indicate subtopics. Under subtopics, Arabic numerals are used to indicate details. If more specific details must be shown, small letters are used. In an outline, you must have no fewer than two main topics or subtopics.

Look at the outline on the next page. Notice that each part of the outline is indented from the one above. However, each symbol is in a straight line with the others like it. Notice also that each kind of symbol is followed by a period, although the words and phrases in the outline will not be followed by periods. In a completed outline, notice also that the first word will be capitalized in every line, as well as in the title.

Check It Out Examine this outline for the report about the Carnegie Hero Fund.

Part 4

Objective

To write an outline for a report

Presenting the Lesson

1. Read and discuss **Here's the Idea.** Emphasize that outlining facts is an important part of organizing a report; making an outline after the report has been written defeats the outline's purpose.

2. Have students examine the sample outline in **Check It Out.** Ask students to explain how the outline is organized. Ask if the outline follows all the guidelines explained on page 241. Point out that the outline contains only topics, not complete sentences; therefore, there are no periods except after numerals and letters.

3. Read aloud and assign **Try Your Skill.** You may want to ask the class to give you directions while you write the outline on the chalkboard, or you might have volunteers write their outlines on the board. Discuss the most logical way to write the outline.

4. Read **Keep This in Mind.**

5. Assign **Now Write.** Tell students that they may need to make at least two drafts of their outlines.

Individualizing the Lesson

Less-Advanced Students

If students have mental blocks about outlining, explain that a formal outline is simply an extension of the organizing activity they began in Part 3. If students find the numbering and lettering system of outlining difficult, tell them first to consider only grouping their ideas under headings and subheadings. Help students individually with their outlines as much as possible.

Advanced Students

After making their outlines, students may notice that they need more facts or examples. Give students one class period in the library to find additional information. Have them add the information to their outlines.

Optional Practice

Duplicate brief encyclopedia entries and ask students to outline them. Collect the outlines and reproduce especially good ones to discuss as models.

Extending the Lesson

Have students go to the library and look up one of the following topics in the *World Book Encyclopedia*. Have the students examine the outline at the end of the article and note that it only briefly describes the detailed facts in the article and that it follows the standard outline form described in this lesson. Have students discuss the purpose of these outlines in the encyclopedia.

Topics: dogs, Roman Empire, medicine

The Carnegie Hero Fund

I. Introduction
    A. Definition of hero
        1. Famous men and women
        2. Government, sports, the arts, the sciences
    B. Unknown heroes
        1. Acts of bravery
        2. Honored by Carnegie Hero Fund

II. Origin of Carnegie Hero Fund
    A. Andrew Carnegie
        1. April 15, 1904
        2. After earlier coal mine explosion, rescue
    B. Fund to award money and medals

III. Eligibility requirements
    A. "Outstanding acts of selfless heroism"
        1. Voluntary risking of life
        2. No relation to victim, no training
        3. Performed in U.S. or Canada
    B. Fairness
        1. Men and women equally eligible
        2. Past history unimportant

IV. How Hero Fund Commission works
    A. Cases reported and investigated
        1. Five or six times a year
        2. Twenty-one-member commission
    B. Winners of every age and background
        1. First winner – Louis Baumann, Jr.
        2. In 1983, aged 12 to 63
        3. Different kinds of rescues

V. History of Hero Fund
    A. Recognized many heroes
        1. Has given 13 million dollars
        2. Has honored 6,300 people
    B. Honors people fairly, democratically

- What subtopics and details explain how the Carnegie Hero Fund works?
- Point out how the form for outlining has been followed correctly.

Try Your Skill   Make an outline of the following paragraph of information taken from *The People's Almanac*.

The Invention: The Airplane (1903)
The Inventors: Orville and Wilbur Wright

The first American airplane (aeroplane) was flown by its inventors, the Wright Brothers, December 17, 1903, on a sandy beach near Kill Devil Hills, Kitty Hawk, N.C. The 16-hp, chain-driven Flyer 1, with Orville as pilot, soared 120'—at an airspeed of 30 to 35 mph and an altitude of 8" to 12'—in its 12-second maiden flight. The 4th flight that day lasted 59 seconds and spanned 852'.

Keep This in Mind

- Use your notes to write an outline of the ideas and details to be presented in your report.
- Follow the correct form for making an outline.

Now Write   Take out your organized note cards. Make an outline, using your list of main ideas and your note cards. Save your work in your folder.

First Impressions

Writing the Introduction

Objective

To write the introduction of a report

Presenting the Lesson

1. Read aloud **Here's the Idea.** Ask students the purpose of the introduction in a report. Stress that students should not use first-person (*I*) or second-person (*you*). Tell students that their introductions should not contain a dull statement such as "This report is about the poetry of Robert Frost." It should, however, contain the report's thesis statement.

2. Read and discuss the first two paragraphs of the sample report in **Check It Out.** Have students compare these paragraphs with sections I and II of the outline on page 242. Have students notice the corrections made in this sample first draft. Ask students which sentence in the introduction best sets forth the topic of the report.

3. Assign and discuss **Try Your Skill.** After students complete this assignment, ask them where they placed the main idea. Have students exchange paragraphs in order to see how others wrote the same information in paragraph form.

4. Read **Keep This in Mind.**

5. Assign **Now Write.** Check your students' outlines before they begin their introductions. If necessary, have students revise their outlines.

Here's the Idea When you have finished the outline for your report, much of what you do next will be familiar to you. Writing a report itself is much like writing any other composition. Both have three parts: an introduction, a body, and a conclusion. The function of each part is similar, too. The introduction introduces the main idea of your subject. The body develops the main idea with supporting ideas and details. The conclusion summarizes the important information presented in the paper.

However, there is one important difference between a composition and a report. Unlike other compositions, reports must never be written from the first-person point of view. Never use the words *I*, *me*, or *my*. Your personal opinion should not be included in a factual report of this kind.

When you start writing your first draft, refer to both your outline and your note cards. Use each of your outline topics as a guide to writing the topic sentence of each paragraph. The subtopics and specific facts from your note cards will provide details with which to develop each paragraph.

When you write the introduction to your report, tell the reader what the paper will be about. Some writers present some of their facts in the introduction. Other writers keep the introduction short and general. What you do will depend on your subject and on your choice.

Check It Out Here is the first draft of the introduction and first paragraph of the report on the Carnegie Hero Fund.

244

¶ A hero is a person who is known for special (acheivements) *sp?*. The names of such heroes are honored *and famous*. However, there are also ~~lesser known~~ *ordinary* people who have ~~performed acts of bravery~~ *acted bravely*. The Carnegie Hero Fund *Commission* honors ~~these heroes~~ *such as these.* Americans have *always* respected *great* men and women who have excelled in government, the arts, sports, and the sciences.

The *Carnegie Hero* Fund was started ~~in~~ 1904 *on April 15,*. Millionaire businessman Andrew Carnegie had been told of a rescue operation after a coal mine explosion in Pennsylvania *in January of that year.* Some of the rescuers *had* died in their heroic efforts to save others. In a time when there was no such thing as Social Security or Workmen's Compensation, widows and orphans *of the rescuers* were faced with poverty. Carnegie *established* ~~began~~ the fund so that brave ~~people~~ *such as these,* and their families, would not suffer financially as a result of heroic acts. The fund was to award both medals and money to specially chosen heroes.

- How does this first draft use the information shown in the outline and note cards for the report?

Individualizing the Lesson

Less-Advanced Students

Have students exchange introductory paragraphs. See if the readers can identify the main idea. If they cannot, the writer should revise the introduction so that the main idea is clearly stated.

Advanced Students

For **Now Write,** have students focus especially on writing an interesting, exciting introduction that will stimulate their readers' interest in the rest of the report.

Optional Practice

Have students write an introduction to a report on dinosaurs. Ask them to use these facts.

1. The last dinosaurs died 65 million years ago.
2. The first dinosaur bones were discovered about 200 years ago.

Extending the Lesson

Have students look up one of the following topics in an encyclopedia: ballet, Sahara Desert, Queen Elizabeth I. They should then answer the following questions about the encyclopedia article's introductory paragraph.

What is the thesis statement?
Where in the introduction is it placed?
Is the introduction detailed or general?
Does the introduction attract your interest in the subject?

- What main idea is presented in the introduction?

Try Your Skill   Here is part of an outline for a report on the life of Andrew Carnegie. Some of this information might fit nicely into the introduction to such a report. Use the information from the outline to write an introductory paragraph. Compare your introduction with those of your classmates.

I. Andrew Carnegie's contributions

    A. Made fortune in steel industry

        1. Came from Scotland as boy

        2. Founded steel-making factory in Pittsburgh

        3. Became rich through hard work

    B. Believed wealthy should help society

        1. Gave millions to schools, libraries, others

        2. Established Carnegie Hero Fund

Keep This in Mind

- Use your outline and note cards to write the first draft of a report.
- Like any composition, a report has an introduction, a body, and a conclusion.
- In the introduction, introduce the main idea of your report.

Now Write   Take out your outline and note cards. Review them, and decide whether to introduce your subject in a general or a detailed way.

Using both your outline and your note cards, write the introduction to your report. Try to present your ideas clearly, but don't worry about grammar and mechanics in this first draft. Save your work in your folder.

246

For the Most Part

Writing the Body and Conclusion

Here's the Idea   When you have written the introduction to your report, you must begin to develop and explain your main idea. Then you must sum up the ideas you have presented. You accomplish these goals in the body and conclusion of your report.

The body of a report consists of several paragraphs. Each paragraph has a topic sentence that relates to a main topic in the outline. The wording may be different, but the main idea should be the same.

As you write your first draft, refer to both your outline and your note cards. Use those facts, specific examples, and quotations that will add the most to your report. Be sure to use quotation marks when you use the words of another writer. When you prepare your final copy, you will give that writer credit in the correct way. You will learn more about this in Part 8.

A report must come to a logical ending. It should have a clear conclusion in which you tie ideas together naturally. In the conclusion you may include additional facts about the topic. However, your most important purpose is to summarize the information presented in the report.

Check It Out   On the next page is the rest of the first draft of the report on the Carnegie Hero Fund. Compare this first draft with the outline for the report.

- What specific examples or direct quotations are used to develop the body?
- Does the conclusion sum up the information presented in the report?

247

Part 6

Objective

To write the body and conclusion of a report

Presenting the Lesson

1. Read aloud **Here's the Idea.** Emphasize that one main idea is developed in each paragraph of a report. Note, too, that each paragraph should contain a beginning, a middle, and an end. Ask students the purpose of the conclusion in a report.

2. Read and discuss the sample first draft in **Check It Out.** Discuss the use of the interesting, specific examples in the report's body, which prevent the report from being merely a list of dry facts and statistics.

3. Assign **Try Your Skill.** When students have completed the assignment, have them list the details orally. Emphasize that the notes and outline must both be consulted when students write the body and conclusion of their reports.

4. Read **Keep This in Mind.**

5. Assign **Now Write.** Stress that sentences should be clear and that plagiarism must be avoided. You will probably want to assist your students individually with this assignment. You might schedule conferences to discuss the body and the conclusion of each student's report. The Handbook section of the textbook will be helpful at this time. You can refer students with specific usage problems to the corresponding Handbook sections.

247

Individualizing the Lesson

Less-Advanced Students

If students have difficulty writing the first draft of their report's body and conclusion, help them pinpoint and correct one or more of the following weaknesses in their preceding work.

—unclear understanding of audience and purpose
—weak thesis statement
—insufficient notes of facts and details
—poorly organized outline

Advanced Students

Jumble the paragraphs of a student report and show it on the opaque projector or on ditto copies. Ask students to put the paragraphs in the proper order and to evaluate the effectiveness of the conclusion.

Optional Practice

Write two sentence fragments on the chalkboard: "What I like most about your report is . . ." and "I want to know more about . . ." Pair students to read each other's first drafts. Then ask each student to complete these partial statements with constructive comments about the other person's report.

Extending the Lesson

Read aloud the concluding paragraphs of several chapters in a history textbook. Discuss how effectively each summarizes a main idea.

The Fund tries to recognize what it terms "outstanding acts of selfless heroism." To be eligible for an award, a person must voluntarily risk or give his or her life to try to save the life of an unrelated person. The hero may not be a person trained for the rescue work involved and must be old enough to recognize the risks. Carnegie said that the fund should reward both men and women, and that their past histories could not be considered. "Heroes deserve pardon and a fresh start," he wrote. The only other requirement was that the heroic act be performed in the United States or Canada. Five or six times every year, a twenty-one-member committee (commission) in Pittsburgh, Pennsylvania, reviews the cases that have come to its attention. Investigators (sp?) are sent to interview those rescued, as well as any eyewitnesses. The degree of risk involved in a rescue is studied to judge whether a person (winner) receives a gold, silver, or bronze medal. There has certainly been no such thing as a typical winner. The first winner in 1905 was a seventeen-year-old boy named Louis Baumann, Jr., a laborer who saved another teenaged laborer from drowning. Recently, the 1983 winners ranged in age from twelve-year-old Janet De Kett to sixty-three-year-old Leroy Panzer. Both males and females have won awards. There have been people from different most races and from many different occupations. The acts of heroism have also been varied, although many heroes have saved someone from drowning or from a fire.

#Today,

The carnegie Hero Fund is more than seventy-five years old. During its *existance* lifetime it has considered more than 50,000 heroic acts. It has awarded more than thirteen million dollars, to more than 6,300 winners. It is *visable* evidence that there is a deep admiration for, *people who help others* heroes. In this Democratic spirit, brave human beings — Whatever their sex, race, age, or background — become honored heroes.

Try Your Skill   Look back at the outline for the Hero Fund report in Part 4, **The Framework.** Compare Part V of the outline with the conclusion in the first draft above. On a sheet of paper, list details that the writer added while writing the first draft.

Keep This in Mind

- Use your outline and note cards to write the first draft of the body and conclusion of a report.
- Use facts, specific examples, and direct quotations to develop the body.
- Write a conclusion that summarizes the information presented in the report.

Now Write   Review your outline and your notes, and write the body and conclusion of your report. Keep your writing lively, clear, and direct. Make sure you use quotation marks if you use other writers' words. Sum up the main ideas in your conclusion. Save your first draft in your folder.

Objective

To revise a report

Presenting the Lesson

1. Have students read **Here's the Idea.** Outline the revision questions on the chalkboard as you discuss them.

2. Have students examine the revised paragraph in **Check It Out.** Help the class recognize that the paragraph's overall organization has been revised to more effectively introduce the topic.

3. Assign **Try Your Skill.**

4. Read **Keep This in Mind.**

5. Assign **Now Write.** Point out that first drafts tend to be messy when they are revised, as in the sample in **Check It Out.** Students should not worry about neatness at this point as long as their revisions are legible.

Individualizing the Lesson

Less-Advanced Students

After students have made major revisions in their reports, devote one class period to proofreading for errors in grammar and mechanics. Note on the chalkboard any points of punctuation, grammar, capitalization, and spelling that the class has found troublesome. Urge students to keep an eye out for errors that they have made in the past. Instruct them to look up questionable items in the dictionary or Handbook. Finally, have students exchange papers near the end of the period and help their classmates proofread.

250

Check Up

Revising a Report

Here's the Idea   Now that you have a first draft, you're almost finished. However, you have a few more steps to complete. Revising your report is the first of these steps.

As you revise your work, remember that a report depends on an accurate presentation of facts. Check the accuracy of dates and figures. Make sure that special words and names are spelled correctly. You may have to go back and check your sources.

Try reading your report aloud to yourself. Sometimes your ears will catch mistakes that your eyes have missed. As you read your report, ask yourself these questions.

1. Does my introduction tell the reader what my report will be about? Is the introduction interesting and informative?

2. Does the report follow my outline?

3. Are all of the facts and dates accurate? Do they develop my topic thoroughly?

4. Have I used quotation marks when copying a writer's work word for word?

5. Is each paragraph about one main idea? Does each fact in a paragraph develop that main idea?

6. Have I used effective transitions between sentences and paragraphs?

7. Does my conclusion summarize the main ideas?

Proofreading is the last step in revising. Read your paper carefully. Look for and correct any errors in grammar, capitalization, punctuation, and spelling. Once again, check dates, figures, and the spelling of special words and names.

Check It Out   Read this revised introductory paragraph.

250

A hero is a person who is known for special (acheivements). [sp?] The names of such heroes are honored and famous. However, there are also *ordinary* lesser known people who have ~~performed acts of bravery~~ *acted bravely*. The Carnegie Hero Fund *Commission* honors *such* these heroes *as these*. Americans have *always* respected *great* men and women who have excelled in government, (the arts,) sports, and the sciences.

- What has the writer done to improve the paragraph?

Try Your Skill   This concluding paragraph has been revised, but it has not been proofread. The paragraph has five errors in grammar and mechanics. Find and correct these errors.

Today, the carnegie Hero Fund is more than seventy-five years old. During its existance, it has considered more than 50,000 heroic acts. It has awarded more than thirteen million dollars, to more than 6,300 winners. It is visable evidence that there is a deep admiration of people who help others. In this Democratic spirit, brave human beings—Whatever their sex, race, age, or background—become honored heroes.

Keep This in Mind

- Revise your report for accuracy of facts and ideas, for organization, and for word choice.
- Proofread your report to correct errors in grammar, capitalization, punctuation, and spelling.

Now Write   Using the guidelines in this lesson, revise your report. Then proofread it. Save your revised work.

251

Part 8

Credit Lines

Footnotes and Bibliography

Objective

To write footnotes and a bibliography for a report

Presenting the Lesson

1. Read aloud **Here's the Idea.** It may take more than one reading for the class to understand these concepts. Ask students why footnotes and a bibliography are used in a report. Write more examples of footnotes and bibliography entries on the chalkboard. Explain that the sample footnotes show the correct form for a book, an encyclopedia article, a magazine article, and a newspaper article respectively. Ask students what kind of source each bibliography entry is for. Emphasize that punctuation and indentation for footnote and bibliography entries must be done exactly as shown.

2. Have the class study and discuss the sample entries in **Check It Out.**

3. Assign **Try Your Skill.** Have one volunteer go to the chalkboard and write the footnote entry. Then have another volunteer write the bibliography entry. Ask if any corrections are needed.

4. Read **Keep This in Mind.**

5. Assign **Now Write.** Discuss titling a report. Have students read the final copy of the sample report beginning on page 255 and comment on the report's title.

Individualizing the Lesson

Less-Advanced Students

Students may not have included any direct quotations needing foot-

Here's the Idea You are now ready to complete your footnotes and a bibliography.

A **footnote** gives credit to a writer whose words or ideas you used. A direct quotation must be footnoted. When you include a direct quotation, place a number right after the quotation, slightly above the line. The first quotation will be numbered *1*, the second quotation *2*, and so on.

"I came on this trip to learn something of America."[1]

Then, on a separate page at the end of your paper, make a list of your footnotes. List them in the same order that the quotes appeared in your paper. Use the forms shown below.

[1] John Steinbeck, *America and Americans* (New York: Bantam Books, 1968), p. 33.

[2] Abraham Lincoln, *The World Book Encyclopedia*, 1984 ed.

[3] Roger Rosenblatt, "The Man in the Water," *Time*, 25 Jan., 1982, p. 76.

[4] "A Different Kind of Hero," *Pittsburgh Post Gazette*, 19 Sept. 1981, Sec. 2, p. 1, col. 1.

You also have to prepare a bibliography. A **bibliography** is a complete list of the sources you used. It appears on a separate, final page. Each entry contains the information from your bibliography cards. Each type of source has its own special form.

A bibliography is arranged alphabetically by the last name of the author. Every line after the first line of an entry is indented. If no author is given, use the first main word of the title to determine the order. Here are the correct forms to use.

"A Different Kind of Hero." *Pittsburgh Post Gazette*, 19 Sept. 1981, Sec. 2, p. 1, col. 1.

"Abraham Lincoln." *The World Book Encyclopedia*.

Rosenblatt, Roger. "The Man in the Water." *Time*, 25 Jan. 1982, p. 76.

Steinbeck, John. *America and Americans*. New York: Bantam Books, 1968.

Check It Out Study the form of the footnote entry and one of the bibliography entries from the report on the Carnegie Fund.

Footnote
[1] Andrew Carnegie, as quoted in Carnegie Hero Fund Commission, *Carnegie Hero Fund Commission Annual Report* (Pittsburgh: Carnegie Hero Fund Commission, 1977, p. 5.

Bibliography
Bayer, Ann. "The Hero in Us All." *Life*, March, 1979, pp. 94–105.

• Do the entries follow the proper form?

1. Have groups of students make posters illustrating the forms for footnotes and bibliographies. Allow the class to use humorous titles and authors' names. Display the posters in the classroom.

2. Encourage students to make any appropriate illustrations, charts, or graphs to accompany their reports.

Try Your Skill Read the following quotation. Assume it is the third quotation you have used. Write a footnote for it. Then write a bibliography entry for the source. Follow the correct form. Answers below.

> "The person with solid virtues who can be admired for something more substantial than his fame often proves to be the unsung hero: the teacher, the nurse, the mother, the honest cop, the hard worker at lonely, underpaid, unglamorous, unpublicized jobs."

from a book called *The Image*, by Daniel J. Boorstin, Atheneum Publishers, New York, 1962, on page 76.

Keep This in Mind

- Use footnotes to give credit to writers whose words or ideas you use in a report.
- Prepare a bibliography to show the sources of information you used in writing a report.

Now Write Write the footnotes for any direct quotes in your report. Follow the correct form. Remember to number each quote in your report. Then, prepare a bibliography.

Neatly copy your report. Use a separate page for footnotes and the bibliography. The bibliography should be the last page of your report. Write a title. Save your completed report.

For help in preparing a final copy, see Handbook Section 16, **The Correct Form for Writing.** Also, examine the final copy of the report shown on the following pages.

[3]Daniel J. Boorstin, The Image (New York: Atheneum Publishers, 1962), p. 76.

Boorstin, Daniel J. The Image New York: Atheneum Publishers, 1962.

Susan Mishikawa

English

April 20, 1985

A Special Kind of Hero

A hero is a person who is known for special achievements. Americans have always respected great men and women who have excelled in government, sports, the arts, and the sciences. The names of such heroes are honored and famous. However, there are also ordinary people who have acted bravely. The Carnegie Hero Fund Commission honors such heroes as these.

The Carnegie Hero Fund was started on April 15, 1904. Millionaire businessman Andrew Carnegie had been told of a rescue operation after a coal mine explosion in Pennsylvania in January of that year. Some of the rescuers had died in their heroic efforts to save others. In a time when there was no such thing as Social Security or Workmen's Compensation, widows and orphans of the rescuers were faced with poverty. Carnegie established the fund so that brave people such as these, and their families, would not suffer financially as a result of heroic acts. The fund was to award both medals and money to specially chosen heroes.

Throughout its history, the Carnegie Hero Fund has tried to recognize what it terms "outstanding acts of selfless heroism." To be eligible for an award, a person must voluntarily risk or give his or her life to try to save the life of an unrelated person. The hero may

255

not be a person trained for the rescue work involved, and must be old enough to recognize the risks. Carnegie said that the fund should award both men and women, and that their past histories could not be considered. "Heroes deserve pardon and a fresh start," he wrote.[1] The only other requirement was that the heroic act be performed in the United States or Canada.

Five or six times every year, a twenty-one-member commission in Pittsburgh, Pennsylvania, reviews the cases that have come to its attention. Investigators are sent to interview those rescued, as well as any eyewitnesses. The degree of risk involved in a rescue is studied to judge whether a winner receives a gold, silver, or bronze medal. There has certainly been no such thing as a typical winner. The very first winner in 1905 was a seventeen-year-old boy named Louis Baumann, Jr., a laborer who saved another teenaged laborer from drowning. Recently, the 1983 winners ranged in age from twelve-year-old Janet De Kett to sixty-three-year-old Leroy Panzer. Both males and females have won awards. There have been people from different races and from many different occupations. The acts of heroism have also been varied, although many heroes have saved someone from drowning or from a fire.

Today, the Carnegie Hero Fund is more than seventy-five years old. During its existence, it has considered more than 50,000 heroic acts. It has awarded more than thirteen million dollars to more than 6,300 winners. It is visible evidence that there is a deep admiration of people who help others. In this democratic spirit, brave human beings—whatever their sex, race, age, or background—become hon-

ored heroes.

Footnote

¹ Andrew Carnegie, as quoted in Carnegie Hero Fund Commission, Carnegie Hero Fund Commission Annual Report (Pittsburgh:
Carnegie Hero Fund Commission, 1977), p. 5.

Bibliography

Bayer, Ann. "The Hero in Us All." Life, March 1979, pp. 94–105.

"Carnegie Hero Fund Commission." World Book Encyclopedia. 1979 ed.

"A Different Kind of Hero." Pittsburgh Post Gazette, 19 Sept. 1981,
    Sec. 2, p. 1, col. 1.

Carnegie Hero Fund Commission. Carnegie Hero Fund Commission
    Annual Report. Pittsburgh: Carnegie Hero Fund Commission, 1977.

Kane, Joseph. Famous First Facts. New York: H. H. Wilson Company,
    1964.

Section 21 Objectives

1. To check statements of fact by using fair, up-to-date, reliable sources

2. To recognize opinions and support them with facts

3. To recognize and avoid generalizations and stereotypes

4. To recognize and avoid circular reasoning

5. To recognize and avoid loaded language

Preparing the Students

State one or more of the following opinions to the class:

Everyone should read at least one book a week.

Adults never listen to teenagers.

Football is the most exciting sport because it is very thrilling.

Ask the class if they agree with these statements. If there is disagreement, have students discuss why they disagree. Point out that it is fine to state opinions in speaking or in writing; however, the opinons must be stated fairly and be supported with facts. Section 21 will teach students how to state opinions like those above fairly and reasonably.

Additional Resources

Mastery Test — page 31 in the test booklet

Practice Book — pages 102–106

Duplicating Masters — pages 102–106

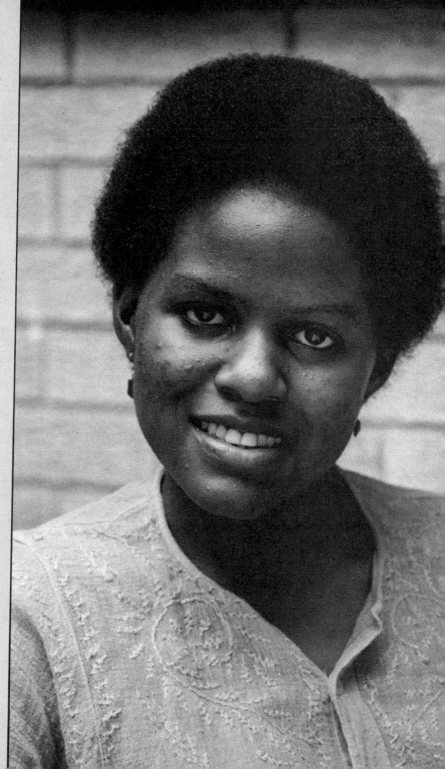

Critical Thinking

Teaching Special Populations

ESL To many of these students, the difference between a statement of fact and a statement of opinion is subtle. Provide students with additional examples of facts and opinions. Suggest that students look for opinions in magazines or newspapers, and discuss their findings in class.

Discuss stereotypes in the United States and in the students' native cultures.

Objective

To check statements of fact by using fair, up-to-date, reliable sources

Presenting the Lesson

1. Have students read **Here's the Idea.** Write *fact, definition,* and *observation* on the chalkboard as you define and discuss them. Discuss the guidelines for evaluating sources. Ask students to contribute additional examples of poor sources in each category. For example, a person who dropped out of law school might be an unreliable source for a legal question.

2. Ask a volunteer to read the situations in **Check It Out.** Have the class discuss why the sources are poor and suggest better ones.

3. Assign **Try Your Skill.** Tell students to be as specific as possible in naming sources to check the statements.

4. Read **Keep This in Mind.**

5. Assign **Now Write.** Urge students to choose a topic that interests them and to use a variety of reference works to find facts. After completing the assignment, students may share their facts.

Individualizing the Lesson

Less-Advanced Students

Emphasize the use of fair, up-to-date, reliable sources in checking statements of fact. Have students discuss whether the sources in the following situations are good ones; if not, why?

What Do You Know?

Checking Statements of Fact

Here's the Idea   Sometimes in school you have to gather facts for use in a composition, a report, or a talk. Whenever you do this, check your facts to make sure they are accurate.

A **fact** is a statement that can be proved true. There are two kinds of facts, definitions and observations. A **definition** tells what a word means. An **observation** tells about something that can be seen, tasted, touched, heard, or smelled.

Definition: A linguist is a person who studies language.
Observation: Roses come in many different colors.

To check a definition, look up the word in a dictionary. To check an observation, you can make the observation yourself. You can also ask an expert or look in a reference work. Whatever source you use when checking a fact, make sure that the source is a good one. The following guidelines will help you.

1. **Make sure that your source is reliable.** A reliable source is one that you can trust to give you the truth. Such sources include encyclopedias, dictionaries, almanacs, and atlases. Other good sources are people with special training, knowledge, or experience. Books or magazine articles written by these people are also good sources.

2. **Make sure that your source is up-to-date.** If your source is a book, check the copyright date. Make sure that the book contains recent information. A science text written in 1940 would not be an up-to-date source. Much of its information would be outdated. Some of it, because of recent discoveries, might even be wrong.

3. **Make sure that your source is fair.** A fair source is one that does not take sides. For example, a doctor would be a good source on the effects of cigarette smoking. A cigarette advertisement might not be. The ad might be slanted because of the desire of the cigarette company to sell its products.

Check It Out Study the following situations.

1. Marge wanted to find out the world record for the 100-yard dash. She checked the 1978 edition of the *Guinness Book of World Records*.

2. Yolanda wanted to find out whether Judge Martin would make a good congressman. She called the Martin-for-Congress campaign headquarters.

- Which source is unfair? Which is outdated?

Try Your Skill Tell whether the following statements are definitions or observations. Then, name a source that you could use to check each statement. Sources will vary.

D 1. A warren is a group of rabbits.
O 2. Surface temperatures on Venus are greater than on Earth.
O 3. The moon has four phases.
D 4. One of the meanings of *hound* is "to chase or follow."

Keep This in Mind

- A fact is a statement that can be proved true. It can be a definition or an observation.
- To check facts, you can make an observation. You can also ask an expert or consult a reference work.
- Always make sure your sources are reliable, up-to-date, and fair.

Now Write Choose one of the following topics. Look up your topic in several reference works. Make a list of five facts having to do with your topic. Remember, a fact is a statement that can be proved true. Tell the source of each fact. Label your paper **What Do You Know?** Save it in your folder.

astronomy	holidays
first aid	Japan
football	whales

1. Checking a 1982 almanac to find out which U.S. city has the second largest population
2. Reading a report by a senator from a farming state to find out if the administration is doing enough to help farmers

Advanced Students

Have students name a fair, reliable source for checking each of the following facts. Answers will vary.

1. The Get-Thin-Quick Diet is easy and effective.
2. Jogging can harm your feet and legs.
3. Congressman Smith is interested in helping needy people.

Optional Practice

Add the following statements to **Try Your Skill.** Sources will vary.

O 1. A parallelogram has four sides.
O 2. The country of Belgium borders France.
D 3. Linen is cloth made from flax.
O 4. In 1981, there were 581,000 people employed as lawyers and judges in the U.S.

Extending the Lesson

Have students check each of the following facts in the library and write down the name of the source they use. Answers will vary.

1. The temperature in London, England rarely goes below 35 degrees in the winter.
2. A pediatrician is a doctor who treats infants and children.
3. Lyndon Johnson became Senate majority leader in 1955.
4. The Mandarin Chinese language is spoken by more people than any other language in the world.

Part 2

What Do You Think?

Checking Statements of Opinion

Objective

To recognize opinions and support them with facts

Presenting the Lesson

1. Read and discuss **Here's the Idea.** Write *opinion, judgment words, command words, sound opinion,* and *unsound opinion* on the chalkboard as you define and discuss them. Make sure students understand the difference between facts and opinions. Have the class study the list of judgment words and command words. Emphasize that an opinion is sound only if it can be supported by facts.

2. Ask a volunteer to read the statements in **Check It Out.** Have the class discuss whether the statements are facts or opinions and which words signal the opinions.

3. Assign **Try Your Skill.** Students should be able to think of supporting facts without consulting reference books.

4. Read **Keep This in Mind.**

5. Assign **Now Write.** Remind students that their opinions should contain a judgment word or a command word. Have students share their opinions and supporting facts when they have completed the assignment.

Individualizing the Lesson

Less-Advanced Students

Give students additional practice in distinguishing between facts and opinions. Have them tell which statements below are facts and which are opinions.

Here's the Idea A fact, as you know, is a statement that can be proved true. An **opinion,** on the other hand, is a statement that cannot be proved true.

Fact: Rainbows are caused by sunlight shining through raindrops.

Opinion: Rainbows are the most beautiful sight in all of nature.

Opinions sometimes contain **judgment words.** These are words that tell how someone feels about something.

Judgment Words		
awful	fine	magnificent
bad	good	terrible
beautiful	interesting	terrific
clever	intelligent	wonderful
excellent	likable	valuable

Some opinions also contain **command words.** These are words that tell what should be done about something.

Command Words		
should	ought to	must

Whenever you state an opinion while speaking or writing, make sure that the opinion is sound. A **sound opinion** is one that can be supported by facts. An **unsound opinion** is one that cannot be supported by facts. Whenever you state an opinion, make sure you can back it up with facts.

262

Check It Out   Read the following statements.

1. Pakistan is a country in Asia.
2. Pakistan is an interesting country.
3. American tourists should consider visiting Pakistan.

- Which of these statements is a fact?
- Which of these statements are opinions? What judgment or command words are used in these opinions?

Try Your Skill   Write two facts to support each of the following opinions.

1. Drivers should obey traffic signs.
2. People ought to be quiet in movie theaters.
3. Smoking is a terrible habit.
4. Kangaroos are unusual animals.

Keep This in Mind

- Opinions are statements that cannot be proved true.
- Opinions often contain judgment words or command words.
- A sound opinion is one that can be supported by facts.
- An unsound opinion cannot be supported by facts.

Now Write   Choose one of the following topics and write an opinion about it.

a school policy or rule   movies
poetry   fashions in clothing

Use your opinion as the topic sentence of a paragraph. In the body of the paragraph, give several facts to support your opinion. Label your paper **What Do You Think?** Save it in your folder.

263

263

Objective

To recognize and avoid generalizations and stereotypes

Presenting the Lesson

1. Have students read **Here's the Idea.** Write *generalization, unfair generalization, absolute words, qualifiers,* and *stereotype* on the chalkboard as you define and discuss them. Emphasize that a generalization is fair only if there are sufficient specific facts to support it. Ask students to mention some unfair generalizations that they have heard about teenagers; then have them mention some made by teenagers about adults. Explain that a stereotype is a kind of generalization.

2. Have a volunteer read the pairs of statements in **Check It Out.** Help students recognize that each unfair generalization has been corrected by replacing an absolute word with a qualifier.

3. Assign **Try Your Skill.**

4. Read **Keep This in Mind** and then assign **Now Write.** Then have students discuss the stereotypes they wrote about. The students may want to express their feelings about being the victims of stereotyping.

Individualizing the Lesson

Less-Advanced Students

Emphasize the difference between a valid generalization and an unfair generalization with the following examples.

Big Talk

Generalizations and Stereotypes

Here's the Idea   Suppose you read the following facts.

Chimpanzees do not have tails.
Gorillas do not have tails.
Orangutans do not have tails.

Based on these facts, you might make the following observation.

Apes do not have tails.

This kind of observation is called a generalization. A **generalization** is a broad statement based on several specific facts.

Sometimes a generalization is made without enough facts to back it up. Suppose that you page through a newspaper and find a few spelling errors. You might make the following generalization.

This newspaper always contains spelling errors.

This generalization is unfair. You do not have enough facts to support the statement. Therefore, it is an **unfair generalization.**

There are two ways to keep from making unfair generalizations. One way is to avoid statements that say something about whole groups of people or things. Think about the statement "Teenagers want to rebel." This is an unfair generalization. Some teenagers may want to rebel. Many others do not. A better generalization would be "Some teenagers want to rebel."

Another way to keep from making unfair generalizations is to avoid **absolute words.** These are words that refer to every thing or event of a kind:

all	everyone	none	nobody
each	everywhere	no	never

These words should usually be replaced with qualifiers. **Qualifiers** are words that limit the statement being made:

at times	many	often	sometimes	much
few	most	rarely	frequently	

One of the most harmful types of generalization is the stereotype. A **stereotype** is an unfair generalization about people of a particular race, nationality, religion, or social group. The statement *All city dwellers are unfriendly* is a stereotype. Avoid stereotypes in your speech and writing.

Check It Out   Read the following pairs of statements.

All politicians are dishonest.

A *few* politicians are dishonest.

It *never* rains in Death Valley.

It *hardly ever* rains in Death Valley.

- Which of these statements are unfair generalizations?
- How were these unfair generalizations corrected?

Try Your Skill   Add qualifiers to correct these statements.

1. No one enjoys listening to disco anymore.
2. Teachers always give homework assignments.
3. Advertisements are misleading.

Keep This in Mind

- A generalization is a broad statement. It summarizes many specific facts.
- An unfair generalization is a statement that is too broad. It is not supported by facts.
- A stereotype is an unfair generalization about a particular group of people.
- Avoid unfair generalizations and stereotypes.

Now Write   Teenagers are often victims of stereotyping. In a brief composition, list several stereotypes of teenagers that you have heard. Explain why each stereotype is wrong. Label your paper **Big Talk.** Save it in your folder.

265

Objective

To recognize and avoid circular reasoning

Presenting the Lesson

1. Read and discuss **Here's the Idea.** Write *circular reasoning* on the chalkboard as you define and discuss it.

2. Have a volunteer read each statement in **Check It Out.** Ask the class to contribute facts to support each opinion.

3. Assign **Try Your Skill.**

4. Read **Keep This in Mind** and then assign **Now Write.** Inform students that choosing specific supporting facts will help them avoid circular reasoning.

Individualizing the Lesson

Less-Advanced Students

Have students complete the following statements. Instruct them to use specific facts to support the statements and not to carelessly restate the premise in different words. Answers will vary.

1. It is important to read poetry in school because _____

2. Watching television is a worthwhile pastime because _____

3. It is important for high school students to think of their future careers because _____

Advanced Students

For **Try Your Skill,** have students rewrite each example of circular reasoning. They may have to do some brief research to find supporting facts for some of the statements.

266

Round and Round

Avoiding Circular Reasoning

Here's the Idea   In Part 3 you learned about two common errors in reasoning, unfair generalizations and stereotypes. Another common error is **circular reasoning.** Circular reasoning occurs when someone tries to support an opinion by simply restating it in different words. The following statement is an example of circular reasoning.

> Joggers should not run on concrete surfaces because concrete surfaces are not good for jogging.

Notice that no facts are given to support the opinion "Joggers should not run on concrete surfaces." Instead, the opinion is simply restated in the words "concrete surfaces are not good for jogging."

To avoid the error of circular reasoning, support your opinions with facts. The opinion above can be supported like this:

> Joggers should not run on concrete surfaces because running on hard surfaces can cause stress fractures.

Notice that this argument does not repeat itself. Instead, a fact is given to support the opinion.

Check It Out   Read the following statements.

1. Fishing is a relaxing sport because, when a person goes fishing, he or she can relax.

2. Videotape recorders are expensive because they cost a lot of money.

3. To be successful, people must study hard. Studying hard, after all, is a key to success.

- What is wrong with the reasoning in these statements?
- How could this reasoning be improved?

266

Try Your Skill   Read the following statements. Tell which are examples of circular reasoning. Explain your answers.

1. Reggae is the best music because it is better than other types of music.
2. Computers are useful tools because they can do calculations very quickly.
3. Salvador Dali's paintings are odd because they are so peculiar.
4. Auto racing is dangerous because there is so much danger involved.

Keep This in Mind

- Circular reasoning occurs when someone tries to support an opinion by simply restating it in different words.
- Circular reasoning can be avoided by supporting opinions with facts.

Now Write   The following statements are examples of circular reasoning. Rewrite these statements, supporting each opinion with a fact. Label your paper **Round and Round.** Save it in your folder.

1. Space exploration is beneficial because we get many benefits from it.
2. Knowing how to read well is important because it's good to know how to read well.
3. Swimming is excellent exercise because people who swim get lots of good exercise.

Optional Practice

Add the following statements to **Now Write.** Answers will vary.

1. People should not worry about the clothes they wear because clothes are not worth worrying about.
2. Movies are a great form of entertainment because they are so amusing.
3. Charlie Chaplin was the best comedian ever because he was hilarious.

Extending the Lesson

Have students write a paragraph supporting an opinion about one of the following topics. Then students can exchange papers to check the logic of their classmates' arguments, watching especially for circular reasoning.

1. the American public school system
2. women choosing to be full-time homemakers
3. the role of advertising in American society

Stick to the Facts

Avoiding Loaded Language

Objective

To recognize and avoid loaded langauge

Presenting the Lesson

1. Read and discuss **Here's the Idea**. Write the terms *persuasion*, *loaded language, snarl word,* and *purr word* on the chalkboard as you define and discuss them. Ask students for examples of the use of snarl words and purr words.

2. Ask two volunteers to read the selections in **Check It Out**. In discussing the selections, have students compare two or three specific words or phrases that are given different slants through the use of snarl words and purr words.

3. Assign **Try Your Skill**. This may be done as an oral exercise.

4. Read **Keep This in Mind**.

5. Assign **Now Write**. Encourage students to find examples of both snarl words and purr words.

Individualizing the Lesson

Less-Advanced Students

Discuss the fact that loaded language is based on an emotional rather than a logical response. Ask students what emotions are evoked by each selection in **Check It Out**. Urge students to question any writing or speaking that is meant to appeal to the audience's emotions. Give the following additional examples of snarl words and purr words.

The film is sad and moving.
The film is a tear-jerker.

The furniture is a real bargain.
The furniture is cheap.

Here's the Idea Has a salesperson ever tried to convince you to buy a certain product? Have you ever heard a politician try to convince people to support his or her opinions? Have you ever tried to convince your friends or relatives that something is true? These are all examples of persuasion. **Persuasion** is the art of convincing other people to see things the way you do.

Successful persuasive speaking and writing is built on sound opinions. Sound opinions are ones that are supported by facts. Sometimes, however, people do not support their opinions with facts. Instead, they simply state their opinions forcefully, using loaded language.

Loaded language is language that appeals to a person's emotions. Often, such language is used in place of facts to sway the opinions of readers and listeners. There are two kinds of loaded language, snarl words and purr words. A **snarl word** is one that creates a negative feeling. A **purr word** is one that creates a positive feeling. Read the following examples.

Snarl Words: Ms. Smith is a *cheapskate*.
Jack is *pig-headed*.

Purr Words: Ms. Smith is a *careful spender*.
Jack is *strong-willed*.

Notice that these sentences do not give any real facts about Jack or Ms. Smith. They simply express the feelings of the speaker or writer. Learn to recognize the loaded language around you. Remember that such language is no substitute for sound opinions based on facts.

Check It Out Read the following selections from political speeches.

The *brilliant leaders* of the labor unions have once again *enlightened* the members of Congress. Let it be known that we *support* such *patriotic* efforts to *free* our nation's workers.

The *ignorant bosses* of the labor unions have once again *brainwashed* the members of Congress. Let it be known that we *reject* such *un-American* efforts to *enslave* our nation's workers.

- Which selection contains purr words? Which contains snarl words?
- What differences of opinion are expressed in the two selections?
- Are any facts given to support these opinions?

Try Your Skill   Find the snarl words and purr words in the following sentences.

1. William is <u>outspoken</u> and <u>independent</u>. purr
2. William is a <u>self-centered loudmouth</u>. snarl
3. The movie is <u>action-packed</u> and <u>spectacular</u>. purr
4. The movie is <u>violent</u> and <u>full of cheap thrills</u>. snarl

Keep This in Mind

- Loaded language is made of snarl words and purr words.
- Snarl words create negative feelings.
- Purr words create positive feelings.
- Loaded language is often used in place of sound opinions.

Now Write   Gather some examples of loaded language in advertisements and television commercials. Write a brief explanation of each example you find. Tell what unsupported opinion is being expressed. Tell whether snarl words or purr words are used. Label your paper **Stick to the Facts.** Save it in your folder.

Discuss the fact that names of products are often purr words. Some examples are Spic 'n' Span, Ultra Brite toothpaste, and Silkience shampoo. Have students collect additional examples of product names that use loaded language.

Optional Practice

The following sentences contain snarl words. Have students use purr words to change the meaning of each sentence as in the sentence pairs in **Try Your Skill.** Answers will vary.

1. Mr. Johnson is rude and pushy.
2. Janet is irresponsible.
3. Ms. Simpson's new novel is full of mushy love scenes.
4. The band's music is tuneless and ear-splitting.

Extending the Lesson

Have students create an imaginary product and make up an advertisement using purr words for it. Encourage students to be creative both in language and in art work for their advertisements.

Section **22** Objectives

1. To understand the library system for arranging and shelving fiction and nonfiction books

2. To use the library's card catalog to locate books

3. To understand the organization and content of encyclopedias

4. To know how to use specific types of reference books

Preparing the Students

Ask each student to draw a map of the school library. Students should label the check-out desk, fiction shelves, nonfiction shelves, magazine section, reference area, recording section, and any other parts they know.

After students have completed this assignment, have them compare their maps. See if any two are alike. Ask if your class can tell you where to find the novels, the reference books, the vertical (pamphlet) file, the copier (if there is one), and the card catalog. If the class is familiar with the layout of the library, ask them where specific kinds of books are located.

Ask the student who drew the most accurate map to copy it onto a ditto master. Distribute copies for students to keep. Explain that Writing Section 22 will help students to use their library more efficiently.

Additional Resources

Mastery Test — pages 32–33 in the test booklet

Practice Book — pages 107–110

Duplicating Masters — pages 107–110

Using the Library

Teaching Special Populations

LD Use actual library materials as you discuss this Section, or take the class to the library for practice. Do the exercises in class with your students. Encourage students to use the library for work and for pleasure.

ESL Teach this Section in the library itself, or provide as much library practice as possible. Have students find books relating to their native cultures in the library, and encourage them to borrow books on topics of interest to them. Explain that many aspects of their new country are explained in library books.

271

Objective

To understand the library system for arranging and shelving fiction and nonfiction books

Presenting the Lesson

1. Before you begin **Here's the Idea,** ask students to define *fiction* and *nonfiction* and give examples. Then read aloud **Here's the Idea.** Emphasize that fiction and nonfiction books are always shelved separately. Discuss the Dewey Decimal System, pointing out the ten categories listed on page 272. After explaining call numbers, have the class look at the model of a book. Show the spine of a real book, and ask students to explain its call number.

2. Discuss the two questions in **Check It Out.** Ask students why the nonfiction books were assigned those Dewey Decimal categories.

3. Assign and discuss **Try Your Skill.**

4. Read **Keep This in Mind.**

5. Assign **Now Write** after your class tours the school library. Then have students add more specific information to their library maps.

Individualizing the Lesson

Less-Advanced Students

1. Explain that although it is helpful to be familiar with the Dewey Decimal classifications, it is not necessary to memorize them. Most libraries post a chart illustrating the Dewey Decimal system.

Know It All

How To Find What You Need

Here's the Idea The library is the best place to find books or magazines to read for pleasure. It is also the best place to go when you have work to do—to begin research for a report, for example. You have to know about a subject to be able to write well about it. A library has the information you will need.

You will find that library books are classified into two general groups, fiction and nonfiction. **Fiction** books are placed on a separate section of shelves. The books are arranged alphabetically according to the author's last name. The novel *Of Mice and Men,* by John Steinbeck, would be filed under **S.**

Nonfiction books are arranged on shelves according to their subjects. Many libraries use a system called the **Dewey Decimal System.** This system groups nonfiction books into ten numbered categories.

000–099	**General Works**	(encyclopedias, almanacs)
100–199	**Philosophy**	(ethics, psychology, occult)
200–299	**Religion**	(the Bible, mythology)
300–399	**Social Science**	(economics, law, education, government)
400–499	**Language**	(languages, grammars, dictionaries)
500–599	**Science**	(math, biology, astronomy)
600–699	**Useful Arts**	(cooking, farming, carpentry, television, business)
700–799	**Fine Arts**	(music, sports, painting, dance)
800–899	**Literature**	(poetry, plays)
900–999	**History**	(biography, travel, geography)

On the spine of every nonfiction book is its **call number.** This number includes the Dewey Decimal number and other helpful information. Some libraries also add the letter *B* to the spine of a biography or the letter *R* to the spine of a reference work. Look at this model of a nonfiction book.

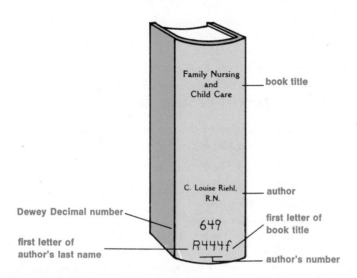

book title — Family Nursing and Child Care

author — C. Louise Riehl, R.N.

Dewey Decimal number — 649

first letter of author's last name — R444f — first letter of book title — author's number

Check It Out   Look at the spines of these books.

- How can you tell which books are fiction and which are nonfiction?
- How can you tell what the general category of each nonfiction book is?

2. If possible, take the students on a guided tour of the school library. Show them where to find fiction, nonfiction, reference books, and magazines. Point out the card catalog and show how to find the Dewey Decimal number on a nonfiction book.

Advanced Students

Add the following items to Exercise 2, **Try Your Skill.**

the paintings of Claude Monet 700–799
some recipes from New Orleans 600–699
Roman mythology 200–299
child psychology 100–199
the life of Albert Einstein 900–999

Optional Practice

At the library, have each student select one book for each Dewey Decimal category and write its title, author, and call number. In class, have students read some of their titles. Ask the rest of the class to guess the Dewey Decimal category.

Extending the Lesson

If you have a public library in your community, contact the library director and ask if your class might visit for an afternoon. Arrange for a brief tour, showing where materials are located and how to obtain a library card.

Using Books Effectively

Explain to your students that knowing how to use books effectively can help them to get more out of their studying and research. Then introduce them to these important parts of books.

The Table of Contents The table of contents is a list of all of the chapters or sections of a book along with the page numbers on which these chapters or sections can be found. Urge students to consult the table of contents whenever they want a broad overview of the material a book contains.

The Index The index is a detailed, alphabetical list of all of the important subjects a book contains along with appropriate page references. Tell students that the index will help them to discover whether or not a book contains information on a specific topic or person.

The Appendix Some books may contain an appendix. An appendix is a special section of a book, often placed toward the end, that gives important information that supplements or supports the material presented in the book. An appendix may contain graphs, charts, or statistics.

The Bibliography A book may contain a bibliography. A bibliography is a list of books the writer used to prepare his or her book or that the writer feels will be helpful to any one who wants more information about the subject of the book. Tell your students that whenever they want or need more information about the subject of a book, they should check to see if the author has provided a bibliography.

Special Reference Books Many reference books have a special section in the front of the book called "How to Use This Book." This section explains how the book is organized, and the easiest and fastest way to find information in the book. Encourage your students to look for this section whenever they use reference books.

Try Your Skill   Write the answers to the following questions.

1. Under what letter on the library shelves would you find the following books of fiction?

Julie of the Wolves by Jean Craighead George
Rumble-Fish by S. E. Hinton
Where the Lilies Bloom by Vera and Bill Cleaver
Bless the Beasts and Children by Glendon Swarthout
Listen for the Fig Tree by Sharon Bell Mathis

2. In which categories of the Dewey Decimal System would you find information on the following subjects?

the poetry of Emily Dickinson 800-899
practical uses of geometry 500-599
how Congress works   300-399
the Spanish language 400-499
what to visit in New York City 900-999

Keep This in Mind

· In the library, fiction books are filed alphabetically by the author's last name.
· Nonfiction books may be classified in ten major categories of the Dewey Decimal System.

Now Write   As your teacher directs, become familiar with your school or public library. Learn how to use the library to find what you want. Find out where fiction and nonfiction books are. Find out where magazines, reference books, and special collections are.

On your visit to the library, find at least three fiction books and three nonfiction books that you might like to read. Write the titles and authors of the books you choose. Also copy the call number or special marking that is written on the spine of one of the books. Label your paper **Know It All** and put it into your folder.

Find It Fast

How To Use the Card Catalog

Here's the Idea   The card catalog is the place to start looking for books in a library. Every book in the library is listed in this file at least three times—by author, by title, and by subject.

Each card—author card, title card, and subject card—contains the same information. The information is simply arranged under different headings for easy reference. Each card gives the call number of a nonfiction book in the upper left corner. This number also appears on the spine of the book and determines where the book is located in the library.

Each card lists the author, the title, the publisher, the date of publication, and the number of pages in the book. Each card tells whether the book has illustrations or maps. A card may also describe the book or list related books.

On an **author card,** the author's name is given at the top, last name first. Author cards are filed alphabetically by the author's last name. If there is more than one author, the card is filed by the name of the author whose name is shown first in the book.

author card	650.1 LOU	Loughary, John William
		Career & life planning guide/by John W. Loughary, Theresa M. Ripley. —Chicago: Follett Publishing Co., c1976.
		180 p.: ill; 24 cm.
		Includes bibliographical references.
		○

275

Part 2

Objective

To use the library's card catalog to locate books

Presenting the Lesson

1. Read aloud **Here's the Idea.** Ask students why three kinds of cards are needed. On the chalkboard, write the three types of cards: author, title, and subject. Below each, diagram the contents of the card. Point out that on the author card, the title is found underneath the author's name, and it is sometimes printed in lower case letters. Also review the purpose of cross reference cards and guide cards.

2. Read and discuss **Check It Out.** First have students identify the book's call number, author, title, publishing company, copyright date, and number of pages. Mention that *ill* means that the book is illustrated, and *24cm* is the height of the book.

3. Assign **Try Your Skill.** Suggest that students refer to the three models on pages 275–276. Ask that they create additional details, such as the publishing company, copyright date, and number of pages. You might point out that *651.26* and *En35c* are both parts of the call number. Have students exchange papers and see if they can identify all three types of cards.

4. Read **Keep This in Mind.**

5. Assign **Now Write.** You might assign this exercise as homework so that students will use the career sections of the card catalog at different times.

Individualizing the Lesson

Less-Advanced Students

Show sample cards on the opaque projector. Ask the class to identify whether each card is an author, title, or subject card. Also quiz students on other information contained on the card.

Advanced Students

Have students do the following activities using the card catalog in the library. Answers will vary.

1. Find the title of an illustrated book about World War II.
2. Find the title of a book of poems by Ogden Nash.
3. Find the call number of the book *Cosmos* by Carl Sagan.
4. Find the title of a biography of Eleanor Roosevelt.
5. Find the title and call number of a book about karate.

Optional Practice

Have students use the card catalog to find three books that pertain to each of these categories.

books by James Michener
books with titles beginning
    with the word *Light*
books about Bermuda
books about radio
novels with titles starting
    with *Around*

Extending the Lesson

Have groups of two or three students make posters illustrating the kinds of cards in the card catalog. You might allow students to use humorous book titles and authors' names on the posters. Display them in class or in the library.

On a **title card,** the title appears on the top line, with only the first word of the title capitalized. Title cards are filed alphabetically by the first word of the title. However, if *A, An,* or *The* appears as the first word in a title, look for the card under the first letter of the second word in the title.

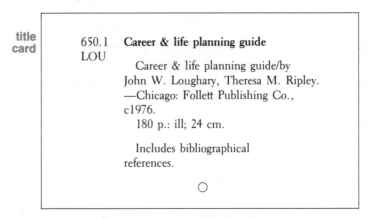

title
card

650.1
LOU

Career & life planning guide

Career & life planning guide/by John W. Loughary, Theresa M. Ripley. —Chicago: Follett Publishing Co., c1976.
180 p.: ill; 24 cm.

Includes bibliographical references.

On a **subject card,** the subject appears on the top line. The subject may be written in capital letters or in red. Subject cards are filed alphabetically by the first letter of the subject.

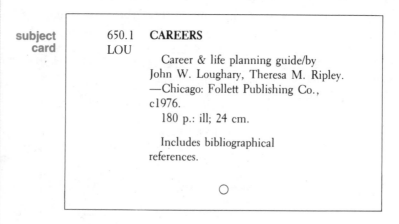

subject
card

650.1
LOU

CAREERS

Career & life planning guide/by John W. Loughary, Theresa M. Ripley. —Chicago: Follett Publishing Co., c1976.
180 p.: ill; 24 cm.

Includes bibliographical references.

Sometimes you will find a card that states *See* or *See also*. This **cross reference card** refers you to another subject heading that is related to the one you want.

Your search for cards in the card catalog will be easier because of **guide cards.** These blank cards have tabs on which are written general subject headings. These headings will help you to follow the alphabetical arrangement of the card catalog.

Check It Out   Look at the three sample cards shown.

- Under what letter would each card be filed? Where would you look for more books by John William Loughary or Theresa M. Ripley? Where would you find more books on careers?

Try Your Skill   Here are the author, title, and call number for a career book. Draw three rectangles to represent file cards. Use the information below to make an author card, a title card, and a subject card. Make up other details for the cards.

> *Careers in Data Processing*, by Stanley L. Englebardt, 651.26   En35c

Keep This in Mind

- In a library, every book is listed in the card catalog on three different cards—author, title, and subject. Each card gives the author, title, publisher, number of pages, and other important information. The card for a nonfiction book includes the call number.

Now Write   Think of a career that interests you, and that you can research in your school or public library. Using the card catalog, find a subject card, title card, and author card related to your possible career. Draw three rectangles to represent the file cards and copy the information from the actual cards. Label your paper **Find It Fast** and put it into your folder.

277

Objective

To understand the organization and content of encyclopedias

Presenting the Lesson

1. Read aloud **Here's the Idea.** As you read the text you might wish to use the C volume of an encyclopedia. Turn to "Careers" and point out the guide words and the parts of the article.

Discuss the best way to use encyclopedias. Note that students sometimes rely on encyclopedias only, without referring to other books and magazines in the library. Tell students that even though encyclopedias are useful, they often are condensed, and should be used as a starting point. Have students pay special attention to the discussion of plagiarism in the last paragraph of **Here's the Idea.**

2. Take your students to the school library and assign **Check It Out.** Explain that recognizing key words is important when looking for a subject in an encyclopedia.

3. Assign and discuss **Try Your Skill.** You may want to have students check their answers in the encyclopedia.

4. Read **Keep This in Mind** and then assign **Now Write.** This may be an out-of-class assignment unless your class can visit the library.

Individualizing the Lesson

Less-Advanced Students

Encourage students to learn to use more than one encyclopedia.

278

The Sourcebook

How To Use an Encyclopedia

Here's the Idea   When you are searching for general information about a topic, you might want to begin by checking an encyclopedia. An encyclopedia is a reference work that contains articles on a great many subjects. The subjects are arranged in alphabetical order according to their subjects from the first volume through the last. On the spine of each volume is a single letter or guide letters that tell you what subjects are included. Look at the set of encyclopedias arranged below.

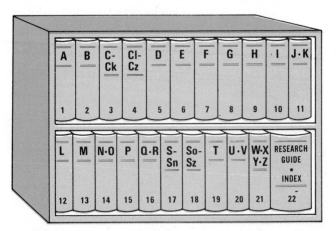

Suppose that you were writing a report on careers related to office work. You might check the *World Book Encyclopedia*, *Collier's Encyclopedia*, or the *Britannica Junior Encyclopaedia*. Find the appropriate volume and look up "Careers." Notice that there are guide words at the top of the pages that can help you to find your subject easily.

An encyclopedia article on an important subject is usually presented in several parts with subtitles. An article on "Careers" may include such parts as "Choosing and Planning a Career,"

278

"Getting a Job," and "The World of Work." Depending on your purpose, you may want to read only parts of an article or all of it.

At the end of a major article you may find other helpful information. You may find a list of related articles in the encyclopedia or a list of books for further reading. In addition, some encyclopedias provide a guide or outline to help you organize your study of a particular subject.

Most encyclopedias also include an index, which may be the first or last volume of the set. Use the index to find information included under several related subjects in different articles. Some encyclopedias also publish yearbooks, which contain up-to-date information about certain subjects.

In addition to general encyclopedias, others provide information on specific subjects. For instance, some of these specialized encyclopedias might cover sports, animals, cooking, or health. Others might cover music, art, or careers. You will probably find such encyclopedias in the reference room or reference area of the library.

You will find several sets of encyclopedias in any large library. You will notice that different encyclopedias will have different reading levels. To find one that will best help you, skim through several or ask a librarian for help.

Whenever you research a subject, always use more than one source of information. Check other encyclopedias or other kinds of reference books. If different sources give different information, use the most recent or most reliable source.

Whenever you use any encyclopedia or reference source, remember two important guidelines. First, you must name the original source of your information. Second, if you use the exact words of the source, you must use quotation marks. Quotation marks show that you have copied exactly a meaningful statement of fact or opinion.

Check It Out   Examine the encyclopedias in your school or public library. Choose one set and answer these questions. You may want to check the index of the encyclopedia.

Have them look up a topic that interests them in three different encyclopedias and write down one interesting fact about their topic from each encyclopedia. They should note the title of the encyclopedia after each fact. Some possible topics are interesting animals such as wildebeest or jaguars; or a natural phenomenon such as Niagara Falls or the Grand Canyon.

Advanced Students

Give each student a volume of an encyclopedia. Ask students to make up five questions about information in their volume. Collect these questions, as well as all encyclopedias, and distribute the questions to different students. Then have students locate the answers in the encyclopedia. Ask them to list the encyclopedia, the number and guide letter of the volume, the page number, and the entry title they used to answer each question.

Optional Practice

Have students use an encyclopedia to answer the questions in **Try Your Skill.**

Extending the Lesson

Use the opaque projector to show your class the entries from three different encyclopedias on a topic such as *bowling*. Ask them to compare and contrast the encyclopedias in the areas of entry length, amount of information, type of information, extent of illustration, and simplicity of style.

- In what volume will you find information about Edgar Allan Poe? modern architecture? heredity? chess? the telescope? Hawaiian volcanoes? North Dakota?

Try Your Skill In each of the following questions write the key word that you would look up first in an encyclopedia.

1. What is the population of <u>Nevada</u>?
2. Name three specialized uses of <u>television.</u>
3. Who was the President of the <u>Confederate States of America</u>?
4. What is the principal language spoken in <u>Brazil</u>?
5. Through what countries does the <u>Danube River</u> flow?
6. Why is <u>Samuel Johnson</u> ^{or} important to the history of the <u>dictionary</u>?
7. What <u>Indian tribes</u> are native to Kansas?
8. What is the difference between latex and oil-based <u>paint</u>?
9. Which states are the leading growers of <u>peanuts</u>?
10. Name two important twentieth-century <u>painters.</u>

Keep This in Mind

- An encyclopedia is a general reference work that contains information on many different subjects. Articles are arranged alphabetically in numbered volumes. Examine a variety of encyclopedias, and select one that you can read easily.

Now Write Write the name of the career that you researched in the card catalog in the last lesson. Look up that career in at least two encyclopedias. Write a few of the most interesting facts you find in each, and compare the information. List the name of the encyclopedias that you use, the numbers and guide letters of the volumes, the page numbers of the articles, and the titles of other related articles or books on the subject. Label your paper **The Sourcebook,** and put it into your folder.

As a Matter of Fact

How To Use Reference Works

Here's the Idea The reference section of your library has many useful books. In addition to dictionaries and encyclopedias, there are reference works that provide information on particular areas of interest. Each kind of specialized reference explains how its information is arranged, explains what symbols and abbreviations are used, and shows a sample entry. Whenever you use a reference book for the first time, examine these introductory explanations. You will then be able to use the reference easily. There are several kinds of references.

Atlases are books of maps. Some atlases contain information about population, weather, and places throughout the world. The *National Geographic Atlas of the World*, the *Universal World Atlas*, and the *Atlas of World History* are among the most widely used atlases.

Almanacs and **yearbooks** are published every year. They are the most useful sources of up-to-date facts and statistics. In these references you will find current information about world events, governments, population, sports, and annual awards. You may want to use the *Guinness Book of World Records*, the *World Almanac and Book of Facts*, the *Information Please Almanac, Atlas, and Yearbook*, or the *Stateman's Yearbook*.

Biographical references are books that contain information about the lives of important people. *The Book of Presidents*, *Current Biography*, *Who's Who*, *Twentieth Century Authors*, and the *Dictionary of American Biography* are among these useful reference works.

A **vertical file** is a collection of pamphlets, handbooks, catalogs, and clippings kept in a file cabinet. This collection is different in every library. However, it may include information about local events, travel, and careers.

281

Objective

To know how to use specific types of reference books

Presenting the Lesson

1. As you read **Here's the Idea,** list on the chalkboard the special types of reference books. You might bring examples of each to class. Ask students if they have ever used these reference works and where the books are located in your school or public library. Discuss how and when to use each type.

2. Have students study the portion of the *Readers' Guide* listed in **Check It Out.** Point out that the title of the article is always printed first, following the boldly printed guide words. The magazine title is always abbreviated. You might borrow a volume of the *Readers' Guide* from your school library to show students the magazine abbreviations listed in the front. Explain that the issue date is always listed last. Write the abbreviations for the months on the chalkboard. Finally, tell students that the page numbers are listed to the right of the colon, and the number to the left of the colon is the volume number.

3. Assign and discuss **Try Your Skill.**

4. Read **Keep This in Mind** and then assign **Now Write.**

Individualizing the Lesson

Less-Advanced Students

Give students additional practice in using the *Readers' Guide*. For **Now Write,** have students look up

281

the person or place they choose in the *Readers' Guide*. If possible, take them to the library to show them where the *Readers' Guide* is located. Point out that the library may not subscribe to all the magazines referred to in the *Readers' Guide*. Students should find out which magazines are available and where they are kept.

Also discuss the kinds of subjects that are best researched in the *Readers' Guide*. For example, a contemporary athlete might have several listings in this index, whereas a nineteenth-century novelist would be best researched in other reference books.

Advanced Students

Have students answer questions 1–6 in **Try Your Skill**. They should list the source of each answer: its title, call number, volume number, and page number.

Optional Practice

Have students use the *Readers' Guide* to find three magazine articles on each of these topics.

soccer · art
Australia plants

Ask students to list the titles of the articles (in quotation marks), the magazines (underlined), the issue dates, and the page numbers.

Extending the Lesson

Hold a reference work treasure hunt. Divide the class into groups and have each group write eight questions on these subjects:

Magazines are important sources of information about a wide range of subjects. A library may subscribe to many of the leading magazines published in the United States. To find specific information in magazine articles, learn to use the *Readers' Guide to Periodical Literature*. The *Readers' Guide* contains the titles of articles, stories, and poems published in more than a hundred leading magazines. One hardcover volume of the *Readers' Guide* covers material published during the entire year. Several smaller, paperback volumes cover material over shorter time periods. You will find the *Readers' Guide* useful in researching any subject, once you learn to use the specially abbreviated format.

Check It Out   Look at this portion of a page from the *Readers' Guide to Periodical Literature*.

Wetlands

cross reference _____ |*See also*|
Everglades
Marshes
Discovering America's exotic wetlands, G. S. Bush. il

name of magazine _____ |*Better Homes Gard*| 61:159-60 + S '83
Strengthening wetlands protection [Clean water act] J. Elder. *Sierra* 68:41 S/O '83
Wiping out the wetlands [West Tennessee Tributaries

author _____ Project|| L. Williamson.| il *Outdoor Life* 172:12-14 Ag '83
Wetzsteon, Ross

title of article _____ |Are men too macho to be friends?| *Mademoiselle* 89:216-17 + Jl '83
Beauty junkies: men who are hooked on looks.

volume number _____ *Mademoiselle* 89:190-1 + Ag '83
La Cage aux Folles comes to Broadway. il pors *N Y*

page reference _____ 16|30-7| Ag 22 '83
Why fathers get the new-baby blues. *Redbook* 161:19 + Jl '83
(jt. auth) See Larson, Kay, and Wetzsteon, Ross
Weusi-Puryear, Omonike
A train trip through history. il por *Essence* 14:41-2 + Ag '83
Wexler, Anne
                                          about
Good intentions: the relentless rise of Anne Wexler. D.

date of magazine _____ Owen. il por *Harpers* 267:26-8 +| Ag '83|
Wexler, Mark
The fish that spawns on land. il *Natl Wild!* 21:33-6 Je/Jl '83
Wexler, Reynolds, Harrison & Schule, Inc.
Good inentions: the relentless rise of Anne Wexler. D. Owen. il por *Harpers* 267:26-8 + Ag '83

- Read through one listing for an article on "Wetlands" in this sample, and explain all the information given. Where is the *Readers' Guide* located in your school or public library? What other kinds of references are in the reference section of your library?

Try Your Skill   What reference works would you be most likely to use to answer each of these questions? Write your answers, mentioning a specific reference wherever possible. If magazines would be the best reference, write *Readers' Guide*.

1. Which states of the United States have towns named London?
2. Which of the current United States track and field stars are most likely to win Olympic medals?
3. What jobs are currently available in public service?
4. What present-day countries were part of the Roman Empire at its height?
5. Who are today's most important Russian leaders?
6. About which products has the Food and Drug Administration issued warnings recently?

Keep This in Mind

- There are several major kinds of specific reference works. Learn to use the ones available in your library.

Now Write   Think of a person or a place that interests you. Look up information on your topic in several specific reference books. List the references that contain the most useful information. Also list their call numbers, and the volumes and page numbers where the information is given. Label your paper **As a Matter of Fact** and put your work into your folder.

two world events that happened last year
two famous people
two places in other countries
two events in local history

Have groups exchange lists of questions and find the answers in special reference works in the library. Ask groups to list their sources along with their answers. See which group finishes first.

Section 23 Objectives

1. To understand and accurately record assignments
2. To carefully follow spoken and written directions
3. To organize study time and a study area
4. To learn and use the SQ3R study method
5. To take notes efficiently on readings, lectures, and class discussions
6. To use different types of reading for different purposes
7. To recognize and use five kinds of graphic aids
8. To know how to read some common types of graphs
9. To know how to prepare for and take tests
10. To know how to take objective tests
11. To know how to take written tests

Preparing the Students

Ask students to consider or write down answers to the following questions:

1. Do you keep an assignment notebook? How is it organized?
2. What is generally the most difficult kind of assignment for you?
3. What steps do you take in reading a new chapter in a textbook?
4. What steps do you take in studying for a test?
5. What is the most difficult assignment you have had in school this year?

Discuss the class's responses. Tell students they will learn to improve their study and research skills in Section 23.

Study and Research Skills

285

Additional Resources

Practice Book — pages 111–121
Duplicating Masters — pages 111–121

Teaching Special Populations

LD This Section is especially important for LD students. Stress the exercises on following verbal and written directions.

Give students assignment sheets with enough blanks for several weeks. Then require students to prepare their assignment pages.

Help students to understand what is meant by key assignment words such as *compare, explain, list, locate,* and *illustrate.* Have them explain what kinds of assignments would require these steps, and what actions such instructions require.

Provide supervised practice in outlining and reading comprehension skills.

Give students practice in understanding and answering test questions.

ESL Tell students that the skills presented in this Section can help them succeed in all of their classes, not just in English. Place extra emphasis on this Section, and provide extra time and practice.

Tell students that libraries usually provide quiet reading rooms for study.

NSD Tell students that assignments and test questions are always presented in standard English. Explain to them that these questions should always be answered in standard English as well.

285

Objective

To understand and accurately record assignments

Presenting the Lesson

1. Have students read **Here's the Idea.** Emphasize that an assignment must be clearly understood in order to be completed properly. Ask the class to discuss any problems they may have generally in understanding their assignments. Encourage students to always ask teachers specific questions about any unclear aspects of an assignment.

2. Have students examine the sample assignment notebook excerpt in **Check It Out.** They should check it against the list of necessary information in **Here's the Idea** to see if it is complete.

3. Assign **Try Your Skill.** Then have students share and discuss their answers.

4. Read **Keep This in Mind.**

5. Assign **Now Write.** If students already keep an assignment notebook, tell them to reorganize it according to the model in **Check It Out.**

Individualizing the Lesson

Less-Advanced Students

For **Now Write,** have students record their assignments for two or three days and then bring their notebooks to class. Check each student's notebook or have students pair off and check one another's. Make sure everyone is following the format in **Check It Out** and recording

286

Things To Do

Understanding Your Assignments

Here's the Idea   Being a high school student can sometimes be hard work. You must study for tests and write papers. You must give talks and do reading assignments. You must answer exercise questions and complete special projects. In other words, you often have a great deal to do in very little time. Learning good study and research skills can help you to use your time wisely. It can also help you to improve your grades on assignments and tests.

One of the most important study skills you can learn is how to understand your assignments. Whenever you are given an assignment, listen closely to all the details. Then, write the assignment carefully in an assignment notebook. Each entry in this notebook should contain the following information:

1. The subject or class
2. Specific directions for the assignment
3. The date the assignment is given
4. The date the assignment is due

Make sure to record all the details you are given. These details may include page numbers, the materials or supplies you will need, and the form of your final product. If you have any questions about an assignment, ask your teacher.

Check It Out   Read the following entry from an assignment notebook.

• Does this entry contain all the necessary information?

286

Subject	Assignment	Date Given	Date Due
Math	Read pp. 21-28. Do problems 1-7 on p. 29.	Oct. 6	Oct. 7

Try Your Skill

Read the sample health assignment below. Then, answer the questions that follow the assignment.

For the next seven days, keep a list of everything you eat and drink each day. At the end of the week, compare your list with the nutrition chart on page 121 of your textbook. Write a paragraph telling whether you think you are eating properly. Your list and your paragraph will be due on Thursday, two days after you finish your list.

1. What things does this assignment ask you to do?
2. What will your final product be?
3. What supplies will you need?
4. When is the assignment due?

Keep This in Mind

- Listen carefully when assignments are given.
- Record assignments in an assignment notebook.
- Include the subject or class, any specific directions, the date the assignment is given, and the due date.
- Know what supplies you will need and what your final product will be.

Now Write

Begin your own assignment notebook. Follow the model given in **Check It Out.** Use this notebook to record the assignments for all of your classes.

all necessary information. Invite students to ask any specific questions or make comments about their assignments.

Advanced Students

Have students answer the questions in **Try Your Skill** for the sample speech assignment below.

Prepare a speech explaining how to do something related to your hobby or job. Hand in the written speech one week from today. Be prepared to give the speech, using necessary props, the day after that.

Optional Practice

Give students the following sample assignments, all given on Tuesday, March 10. Students should record the necessary information for an assignment notebook following the format in **Check It Out.**

History: For tomorrow, read Chapter 10 and write the answers to the study questions on page 210.

Spanish: Start learning the nouns listed on page 140 for a test on March 13.

English: Write a first draft of a descriptive paragraph by March 12.

Science: Read Chapter 6 for tomorrow. Start planning a project due April 10.

Extending the Lesson

Students may wish to discuss their assignment notebooks with their other teachers. They can show the instructors the notebook format and discuss any specific ways in which the students can better understand and record each class's assignments.

Objective

To carefully follow spoken and written directions

Presenting the Lesson

1. Read **Here's the Idea.** Outline on the chalkboard the guidelines for following spoken directions and written directions. Discuss examples of important times to follow directions, such as when performing a chemistry experiment or when following the recipe for a complicated dish.

2. Have students read the sample directions in **Check It Out.** Have the class answer questions.

3. Assign **Try Your Skill.** Then have students discuss their steps, making sure they have not omitted the first step, choosing a novel.

4. Read **Keep This in Mind.**

5. Assign **Now Write.** Encourage students to think of wide-ranging activities such as listening to a tape in a language laboratory or learning a new song in music class.

Individualizing the Lesson

Less-Advanced Students

Have students point out the key word or words that explain what to do in each assignment below. Then have students write or discuss exactly what each activity entails.

1. Study the graph on page 40 and explain what it shows about the earth's climate.
2. Copy the list of French verbs on page 120 and memorize the spelling of each one.

288

A Recipe for Success

Following Directions

Here's the Idea   The directions that you follow in school are much like recipes. They tell you what to do and in what order. By following these directions carefully, you can achieve excellent results on your assignments.

Directions may be either spoken or written. These guidelines will help you when following spoken directions:

Following Spoken Directions
1. Listen carefully to the entire assignment. Write down the directions as you hear them.
2. Note the steps involved in the assignment. Also make sure you know the order of these steps.
3. Listen for key words that tell you what to do. Such words include *read, write, answer, explain, describe, draw, memorize,* and *study.*
4. If you have questions about the directions, ask your teacher to explain them.

These guidelines will help you when following written directions:

Following Written Directions
1. Read the directions completely before beginning the assignment.
2. Divide the assignment into steps. Put these steps in a logical order.
3. Ask your teacher to explain any steps that you don't understand.
4. Before you begin to work, gather materials you will need to complete the assignment.

Check It Out   Read the following sample directions.

The following English words all come from other languages.

kayak	catsup	almanac
canyon	trombone	petite
squash	vampire	pretzel

Find each word in a dictionary. Tell what language each word was borrowed from. Then, use each word in a sentence.

- What steps are included in this assignment?
- What materials will you need?
- What do the directions ask you to hand in?
- What could you ask to make the assignment clearer?

Try Your Skill   Break the following assignment into smaller steps. Tell everything that you must do to complete the assignment. List the steps in the proper order.

Write a two-page book report on any novel from the school library. Your report will be due in two weeks.

Keep This in Mind

- Before you begin an assignment, listen to or read all directions carefully.
- Break assignments into steps. Put these steps in a logical order.
- If you don't understand some part of the directions, ask your teacher to explain that part.

Now Write   Choose a simple activity from one of your classes. It may be an experiment from a science class. It may also be a project from a class such as home economics or woodshop. Write step-by-step instructions for carrying out this activity. Include all the necessary steps. Place these steps in a logical order. Label your paper **A Recipe for Success.** Save it in your folder.

289

3. Imagine that you have just landed on Mars. Draw a picture of the landscape that you see.

Advanced Students

Divide students into pairs. Have each student explain how to perform a simple activity while the other student takes notes on the directions. The students may ask questions and revise their notes. Then they can exchange papers to check the clarity and thoroughness of the directions.

Optional Practice

Have students follow the instructions in **Try Your Skill** for the following sample assignments. Answers will vary.

1. Write a report about one battle of the American Revolution. Use information from at least three sources.
2. With a partner, memorize a dialogue from your French textbook and perform it for the class.

Extending the Lesson

Have each student write down step-by-step instructions for preparing a simple dish such as a sandwich or scrambled eggs. After exchanging recipes, each student should follow the instructions at home. The next day students can compare notes on their results and evaluate their direction writing and direction following skills.

Planning Ahead

Objective

To organize study time and a study area

Presenting the Lesson

1. Have students read **Here's the Idea.** Emphasize that place and time are both important considerations when students are making a study plan. Outline on the chalkboard the requirements for a study area as you discuss them. Students may enjoy discussing their own study areas, both those that work well and those that need improvement.

Write on the chalkboard *short-term assignments, long-term assignments,* and *study plan* as you define and discuss them.

2. Have students examine the sample study plan in **Check It Out** and discuss the study questions. Have students note that the study plan includes extracurricular activities that will affect study time.

Assign **Try Your Skill.** This may be done orally in class.

Record **Keep This in Mind** and the assign **Now Write.**

Individualizing the Lesson

Advanced Students

Discuss the importance of dividing long-term assignments into smaller steps. For example, knowing that a science report is not due for two weeks can give a student a false sense of security if he or she forgets that writing the report entails finding sources, taking notes, organizing material, writing a first draft, and writing a final copy. Have stu-

A Time and a Place for Study

Here's the Idea To study effectively, you must organize your study area and your study time. Your study area can be a desk or a table at school, at a library, or at home. Make sure that your study area meets the following requirements:

1. **A study area must be quiet.** Conversation, television, or loud music can hurt your concentration.
2. **A study area must have good lighting.** Poor lighting can cause eyestrain and headaches.
3. **A study area must be organized and neat.** A messy study area can cause you to waste time searching for materials.
4. **A study area must be properly equipped.** A dictionary, paper, pens, and pencils should be kept close at hand.
5. **A study area must be available at a regular time.** Make sure your study area is available at a specific time each day.

To complete your assignments by their due dates, you must also organize your time. Each day, look over your homework assignments. Those due the next day are **short-term assignments.** Those that require more than one day are **long-term assignments.** If an assignment is short-term, set a time to complete it before the next day. If an assignment is long-term, divide it into smaller steps. Then, set times for completing each step.

All of these assignments should be recorded on a **study plan.** Make seven columns on a sheet of paper. Label these with the days of the week. Record your activities on this plan. Also record the times when you can complete your assignments.

Check It Out Look at the following study plan.

- What short-term assignment is listed on this study plan?
- What long-term assignment is listed on the plan? Into what steps is it divided?

Mon.	Tues.	Wed.	Thurs.	Fri.	Sat.	Sun.
Decide on topic for report	Speech Club meeting	Dr. Haver 4:45	Vocab quiz	Finish first draft of report	Speech Meet	Dinner at Aunt Rosario's
	Gather information for report	Gather information for report	Organize notes for report and begin writing first draft		Revise report for Monday	
		Study for vocab quiz				

Try Your Skill Label each of the following assignments as short-term or long-term.

1. Learn these ten words for a spelling test tomorrow.
2. Keep a journal for one month.
3. Over the next few weeks, collect five advertisements that are misleading. These may come from newspapers or magazines. Place these in a scrapbook. Tell why each is misleading.
4. Take notes on tonight's social studies reading.

Keep This in Mind

- Your study area should be quiet, well lit, and well organized. It should also be properly equipped and available at a regular time.
- Break all long-term assignments into smaller steps.
- Enter all assignments on a study plan.

Now Write Make a study plan like the one shown in **Check It Out.** Record your major activities and assignments for one week. Follow the plan. Make such a study plan each week.

dents break the following long-term assignments into smaller steps.

1. Read a book about a historical event and give an oral report on it.
2. Write a narrative composition.
3. Keep a spring nature journal in which you record day-to-day changes of the season for two weeks.

Advanced Students

Have students organize a one-week study plan with the following assignments. Answers will vary.

short-term: math problems on Monday and Wednesday; grammar exercises on Tuesday

long-term: History exam on four chapters on Friday; Spanish paragraph on Friday; persuasive speech on Thursday

Optional Practice

Have students write a description of their study areas and decide whether they meet the requirements outlined in **Here's the Idea.** Then have them outline ways to improve the study areas.

Extending the Lesson

After students have kept their study plans for two or three weeks, have them analyze the plans' effectiveness by asking these questions:

1. Were long-term assignments divided into manageable segments?
2. Were they scheduled to allow sufficient time for completion?
3. Did I take into account all extracurricular activities that affected my study time?
4. Was my study plan effective in helping me organize my time? How can it be improved?

Part 4

Objective

To learn and use the SQ3R study method

Presenting the Lesson

1. Read **Here's the Idea.** Discuss the SQ3R study method, asking students when this method would be useful. Help them recognize that it is helpful both when reading material for the first time and when reviewing it for a test.

2. Have the class study the sample study questions in **Check It Out.** Point out that the answers to each chapter's questions would give a general overview of the chapter.

3. Assign **Try Your Skill.** Instruct students to read each step of the SQ3R method on page 292 and then perform the step on the selection. Have students exchange their lists of study questions and notes to check for an understanding of the selection's main points.

4. Read **Keep This in Mind.**

5. Assign **Now Write.** Urge students to choose a chapter assigned for either a first reading or for review that is difficult or complex.

Individualizing the Lesson

Less-Advanced Students

Give students additional practice in using the SQ3R method with the following selection.

Figurative Language in Poetry

Poetry uses colorful language to bring the poet's experiences alive. *Figurative language* compares two unlike things in an nonliteral way.

Try To Remember

The SQ3R Study Method

Here's the Idea   Success in school often depends on remembering what you read. You can do this most easily if you use an organized method of study. One such method is called SQ3R. It is made up of five steps: **S**urvey, **Q**uestion, **R**ead, **R**ecite, and **R**eview. These steps are explained in the following chart:

The SQ3R Study Method	
Survey	Look over the material to get a general idea of what it is about. Read the titles and subtitles. Notice the illustrations. Read the introduction and summary.
Question	Make a list of questions that you should be able to answer after your reading. Use any study questions presented at the end of the chapter or provided by your teacher. You can also make up your own questions by turning chapter titles and headings into questions. Any illustrations, maps, tables, or graphs can also be used as a basis for questions.
Read	Read the selection to find the answers to your questions. Look for main ideas and supporting details. Pay particular attention to definitions, topic sentences, and chapter headings.
Recite	After reading, recite the answers to your questions. Make brief notes to help you remember the answers. Also make notes on other important points from the material.
Review	Try to answer each of your original questions without consulting your notes. If necessary, review the selection to find the answers. Then look over your notes to impress the material on your mind. This will help you to remember it later on.

Check It Out   Look at these headings from a chapter in a social studies textbook. Read the questions that can be made from these chapter headings.

Chapter Heading	Questions
1. A Changing Society	a. What society is changing?
	b. How is this society changing?
	c. Why is it changing?
2. Water and Air Pollution	a. What causes this pollution?
	b. How large is the problem?
	c. What can be done to correct it?

- How would asking such questions help you to study the material under each heading?

Try Your Skill   Study the following selection. Use the SQ3R study method.

Dangers Confronting Wildlife

Since the early 1600's, more than two hundred species of animals have become extinct. **Extinction** occurs when the last animal of a particular kind dies. This has been the fate of the passenger pigeon, the dodo, and the California grizzly.

Causes of Extinction. Most animals that become extinct do so as a result of human actions. Some animal species die out due to hunting or trapping. Some die out because of pesticides and other forms of pollution. Others die out because their **habitats**— the places where they live—are destroyed by mining, lumbering, or construction.

Keep This in Mind

- The five steps of the SQ3R method are *Survey, Question, Read, Recite,* and *Review.*
- Apply the SQ3R method to all of your reading assignments.

Now Write   Use the SQ3R method to study a chapter in one of your textbooks. Write your questions, answers, and notes on a sheet of paper. Label this paper **Try To Remember.** Save your work.

293

Similes. One figure of speech is the simile. It compares two unlike things using the words *like* or *as.* For example, a writer might say that a classroom before the period starts is like a carnival.

Advanced Students

Bring several newsmagazines to class and have each student choose one article to study by the SQ3R method.

Optional Practice

Have the class study Part 5 of this Section using the SQ3R method. Discuss Part 5 by having students share their study questions and notes on important points.

Extending the Lesson

Have each student bring to class a short magazine article of interest. Students can exchange articles and use them to practice the SQ3R method. Students can exchange study questions and notes to check one another's grasp of the material.

Part 5

Objective

To take notes efficiently on readings, lectures, and class discusstions

Presenting the Lesson

1. Have students read **Here's the Idea.** Read the guidelines for note-taking, discussing the fact that effective note-taking requires practice. Emphasize listening for verbal clues to important points when taking notes of a lecture instead of trying to write down every word. Also point out that in class discussions, fellow students may make statements worth writing down. Ideas that occur to oneself during a class discussion may also be worth noting in writing.

2. Have the class study the sample notes in **Check It Out.** Point out that no two students' notes of the same material will be the same; the main thing is to write down the important points in a logical, readable way.

3. Assign **Try Your Skill.** Have students discuss the selection's main points and any abbreviations they have used.

4. Read **Keep This in Mind.**

5. Assign **Now Write.** Point out that taking notes in their classes will help students now and give them valuable practice for high school and college classes in the future.

Individualizing the Lesson

Less-Advanced Students

Students may need additional help in determining material's main

294

Got the Idea?

Taking Notes

Here's the Idea   In Part 4 you learned how to use a valuable study tool: the SQ3R study method. Another valuable study tool is your notes. Notes are important because you can use them to review for tests and quizzes. Always take notes on the reading you do for your classes. You will also want to take notes on information presented in class by your teachers or other students. Follow these guidelines when taking notes:

1. Keep your notes in a notebook. Divide your notebook into sections. Label each section for a specific subject. Write the date and the subject at the top of each page of notes. Make notes about the main ideas presented in class or in your reading.

2. Take notes as you read. Take notes on key words, definitions, and main ideas. Include any questions and answers that you come up with when using the SQ3R study method.

3. Take notes as you listen. Listen for clues that tell you what information is important. These clues include such phrases as *most importantly, the cause was,* and *to review.*

4. Write neatly. Make sure you will be able to read your notes.

5. Use phrases, abbreviations, and symbols. Write in short phrases. Use abbreviations and symbols such as the following:

w/	with	info.	information
w/o	without	Eng.	English
+	and	tho	though
*	important information	def:	definition
		=	equals
M	memorize this	ex.	example

You can also create your own abbreviations. Be sure they are clear enough so that you will understand them later.

6. If you wish, use a rough outline form. Write main ideas at the left margin. Under these main ideas, jot down supporting details.

Check It Out Read the following notes.

Science April 3

Types of Rock

Igneous rock
—def: rock formed by heat
—ex: granite
Sedimentary rock
—def: rock made from material
deposited by water or wind
—ex: sandstone

• What do the abbreviations in these notes mean?
• Do you see how the rough outline form was used?

Try Your Skill Using the guidelines in this lesson, take notes on the selection on endangered wildlife given in Part 4. Compare your notes with those of your classmates.

Keep This in Mind
• Record your notes in a notebook.
• Use phrases, abbreviations, and symbols.

Now Write Begin a notebook for use in your classes. Divide the notebook into separate sections for each class. Take notes on what you read for your classes. Also take notes as you listen.

ideas and taking efficient notes on them. For **Try Your Skill**, have two or three students write their notes on the chalkboard and discuss them. You may do this with additional note-taking exercises as well.

Advanced Students

Students may already have developed good note-taking techniques. Have each student list some of his or her frequently used abbreviations and helpful techniques and exchange them with the rest of the class. These can be assembled onto one page to be duplicated and distributed to the entire class.

Optional Practice

Have students go to the library and read and take notes on one interesting magazine article. Then the students can use their notes to report on their articles to the class.

Extending the Lesson

Have students watch a specific documentary, presidential speech, or news conference on television and take notes on it. Students can use their notes as they discuss the program in class the next day. (If the above programs are not scheduled, students can take notes on the evening news.)

Part 6

Objective

To use different types of reading for different purposes

Presenting the Lesson

1. Read **Here's the Idea.** Write *in-depth reading, fast reading, skimming,* and *scanning* on the chalkboard as you define and discuss them. Help students understand the difference between skimming and scanning. Explain that students might skim an article that they are using as a source for a report; however, they might scan it first to make sure it has relevant information.

2. Read aloud the examples in **Check It Out.** Have students tell why skimming would be better in one situation and scanning in the other.

3. Assign **Try Your Skill.**

4. Read **Keep This in Mind** and then assign **Now Write.** Encourage students to be imaginative in thinking up questions about the country they choose.

Individualizing the Lesson

Less-Advanced Students

Have students discuss the most effective reading method(s) in each of the following situations.

1. reading a front-page newspaper story skimming
2. rereading a textbook chapter for a class discussion scanning
3. reading a biography for a book report in-depth
4. checking to see if the writer of a movie review likes the movie

   scanning

Adjusting Your Reading Rate

Here's the Idea   When a carpenter builds a house, he or she uses many tools. Some are for measuring, some for sawing, and some for hammering. Similarly, when you study written material, you can use several types of reading. Like the carpenter's tools, these types of reading have different purposes.

In-depth reading is used to study new or difficult material. When reading in this way, use the SQ3R method. Survey the material. Make a list of questions. Then, move your eyes slowly, reading every word. As you read, pay close attention to definitions, topic sentences, key words, and titles or headings. Once you find a main idea, look for any supporting details.

Fast reading serves many different purposes. It is particularly useful for surveying or reviewing material. Two types of fast reading are skimming and scanning.

1. Skimming is used to get a general idea of the content of a selection. It is also used to survey material as the first step in the SQ3R study method. When you skim a selection, move your eyes quickly over the material. Do not read every word. Glance at titles, subtitles, headings, pictures, and graphic aids. Also look at the first and last sentences of paragraphs. In this way, you can find out what a selection is about without reading it closely.

2. Scanning is used to locate specific information. Again, do not read very word. Move your eyes quickly across each line or down each page. Look for words or phrases that are related to the information that you need. When you spot such a key word or phrase, stop scanning and read more slowly.

Check It Out   Read the following reading tasks.

1. Kyle's teacher gave him study questions about Chapter 6 in his science text. He needed to find answers for these questions.

2. Marsha was preparing a talk on home computers. She found a book called *The Computer: Yesterday and Today*. She wanted to find out if it contained information she could use.

- Which situation calls for skimming? Which calls for scanning?

Try Your Skill   Follow these directions one at a time. Do not read all the directions first.

1. Skim the following passage to find out what it is about.
2. Scan the passage to answer the following questions:
   a. Why do scientists send radio messages into space?
   b. Aside from the earth, where else might intelligent life exist?

Most scientists believe that the Earth is the only planet in the solar system with intelligent life. However, intelligent life may exist on planets outside the solar system. To communicate with other intelligent life forms, scientists are now sending radio messages into space. They are also using radio telescopes to listen for any messages that are being sent from other planets. One day we may hear a "hello" from across the universe.

Keep This in Mind

- Use different types of reading for different purposes.
- To learn new or difficult material, use in-depth reading.
- Skim to survey material.
- Scan to locate specific information.

Now Write   Choose a foreign country that you would like to know more about. Write four questions about this country that you would like to know the answers to. Then, find an entry on the country in an encyclopedia. Scan the article to find the answers. Write the answers. Save your work.

Objective

To recognize and use five kinds of graphic aids

Presenting the Lesson

1. Read **Here's the Idea.** List each kind of graphic aid on the chalkboard as you define and discuss it. Have students discuss materials in which they are likely to find graphic aids; textbooks, encyclopedias, and newsmagazine articles are some examples.

2. Have students examine the graphic aids in **Check It Out.** Then have the class identify each kind of graphic aid.

3. Assign **Try Your Skill.** Then have volunteers give their answers and explain how they arrived at them.

4. Read **Keep This in Mind.**

5. Assign **Now Write.** Have three or four students put their charts on the chalkboard; discuss the different ways in which they may be done.

Individualizing the Lesson

Less-Advanced Students

Emphasize the fact that graphic aids present important information that supplements written material or makes it clearer. Have students keep a chart for one week on which they list the number of diagrams, maps, tables and charts, and graphs they come across in their reading. The chart should indicate where each graphic aid was found.

Advanced Students

Have students research some information about the class and make

---

See Here!

Using Graphic Aids

Here's the Idea   Not all of the materials you have to study are written. Some information is presented to you in the form of **graphic aids.** A graphic aid is used to present material simply and clearly. The following kinds of graphic aids are commonly found in textbooks:

Pictures and illustrations are used to show how things look. They are also used to create a mood or feeling. Always read any captions or labels given with a picture.

Diagrams are drawings that show the parts of a thing. They allow you to identify each part and to see how the parts are related. Always read any captions or labels given with a diagram.

Maps show locations of cities, countries, mountains, rivers, and other parts of the earth. They can also show such information as the population or climate of a particular region. Always look for the **legend** that is included on most maps. The legend will help you to figure out distances or directions on the map.

Tables and **charts** are used to list or compare information. The information is usually presented in labeled columns. Always read any captions or titles given with tables or charts.

Graphs show relationships between facts. Sometimes they show how facts change over time. (See Part 8 for more information on graphs.) Always read any captions, titles, or labels given with graphs.

Check It Out   Study these graphic aids.

- Which graphic aid is an illustration? a diagram? a map? a chart? a graph?

MARMOSETS

Animals and Their Young	
ANIMALS	**YOUNG**
cow	calf
deer	fawn
goose	gosling
swan	cygnet
turkey	poult

BARBADOS
NORTH POINT

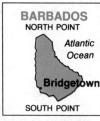

Atlantic Ocean

Bridgetown

SOUTH POINT

Parts of an Arrow

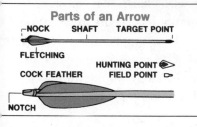

NOCK   SHAFT   TARGET POINT

FLETCHING

HUNTING POINT
COCK FEATHER   FIELD POINT

NOTCH

Production of Goods in Georgia

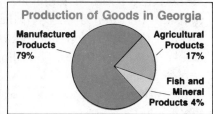

Manufactured Products 79%

Agricultural Products 17%

Fish and Mineral Products 4%

Try Your Skill   Complete the following sentences, using information from the preceding graphic aids.

1. Seventeen percent of all goods produced in Georgia are agricultural products.
2. A young swan is a cygnet.
3. The capital city of Barbados is Bridgetown.
4. Two kinds of arrow points are the hunting and the field.

Keep This in Mind

- Information is often presented as graphic aids.
- Graphic aids include photographs, illustrations, diagrams, maps, tables, charts, and graphs.

Now Write   Make a chart to present the information contained in the following passage. Label your paper **See Here!** Save it.

Evergreens are trees that do not lose their leaves in the fall. Such trees include pines, spruces, cedars, live oaks, and firs. Deciduous trees do lose their leaves in the fall. Such trees include maples, birches, elms, tulips, and redbuds.

299

a graphic aid to illustrate the information. For instance, they may find out the states in which the class members were born, the languages they speak, or their birthdates.

Optional Practice

Have students look up the encyclopedia article on a country that they found for **Now Write,** Part 6. Have them make a chart showing how many of each kind of graphic aid discussed in this lesson are included in the article.

Extending the Lesson

Have each student find a recent magazine or newspaper article that includes a diagram, map, table, chart, or graph. Instruct students to read the article, cut out the graphic aid and tell what kind it is, and write a sentence or two explaining why the graphic aid is helpful or important to the article.

Part 8

Objective

To know how to read some common types of graphs

Presenting the Lesson

1. Read **Here's the Idea.** Write the name of each kind of graph on the chalkboard as you define and discuss it.

2. Have the class study the graphs in **Check It Out** and then identify their types.

3. Assign **Try Your Skill.** Have volunteers give their answers and tell how they arrived at them. Discuss the importance of reading the graphs' titles when interpreting the graphs.

4. Read **Keep This in Mind** and then assign **Now Write.** Ask two or three students to put their graphs on the chalkboard for the class to discuss.

Individualizing the Lesson

Less-Advanced Students

For **Now Write,** the students may want to make large individual or group graphs using poster board and construction paper.

Advanced Students

Have students make a circle graph illustrating the world use of different types of fossil fuels according to the following statistics:

petroleum—50%
coal—30%
natural gas—20%

Special Relationships

Reading Graphs

Here's the Idea   Graphs are special charts that show relationships between facts. To read a graph, look at the information given at the sides, top, and bottom of the graph. Also read any labels, captions, or titles. The following are some common graphs:

A **circle graph** uses a circle to show the parts of something. The circle is divided into sections. Each section represents a part of the whole.

A **bar graph** shows how two sets of facts are related. One set of facts is given in words. Bars are used to show the number amounts.

A **picture graph** is like a bar graph. However, it uses pictures instead of bars.

A **line graph** uses a line to show how something has changed or will change over a period of time.

Check It Out   Study the following graphs.

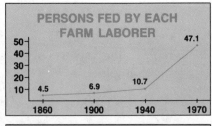

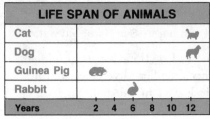

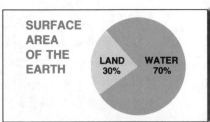

- Which of these is a circle graph? a bar graph? a picture graph? a line graph?

Try Your Skill Using information from the preceding graphs, answer the following questions.

1. Which lives longer, a <u>rabbit</u> or a guinea pig?
2. How many of the world's rivers are longer than the Mississippi? three
3. What percentage of the Earth's surface is covered by water? 70%
4. How many persons were fed by each farm laborer in 1940? 10.7

Keep This in Mind

- Graphs are used to show relationships between facts.
- Common graphs include circle graphs, bar graphs, picture graphs, and line graphs.
- When reading a graph, pay particular attention to titles, captions, or labels.

Now Write Make a bar or a picture graph to show the following information:

World Speed Records
Bicycle: 59 miles per hour
Motorcycle: 318 miles per hour
Airplane: 2,193 miles per hour
Automobile: 739 miles per hour

Label your paper **Special Relationships.** Save it in your folder.

Have each student look up the necessary facts in an almanac and then make a line graph showing one of the following sets of facts:

1. The number of students enrolled in four-year colleges in 1978, 1980, and 1982
2. The number of women employed as lawyers in the U.S. in 1978, 1980, and 1982

Extending the Lesson

Have each student find and bring to class one graph of each type studied in this lesson. Some good sources are encyclopedia, newspaper, and newsmagazine articles.

Objective

To know how to prepare for and take tests

Presenting the Lesson

1. Have students read **Here's the Idea.** Outline the guidelines for taking tests on the chalkboard as you discuss them. Point out the roles that the SQ3R method and skimming play in preparing for and taking tests. Emphasize that preparing for a test is an ongoing process and requires careful planning and organization; cramming is an ineffective way to prepare for a test, especially if it leaves a student tired on the day of the test. Students may want to discuss positive and negative testing experiences they have had.

2. Have a student read aloud the passage in **Check It Out.** Lead the class in discussing how Carolyn should have read the directions for the entire test in the beginning and planned her time more wisely.

3. Assign **Try Your Skill.** Have students discuss their study techniques and take notes on helpful hints from their classmates.

4. Read **Keep This in Mind.**

5. Assign **Now Write.** Urge students to write about a kind of test they must frequently take or which has been troublesome for them in the past.

Individualizing the Lesson

Less-Advanced Students

Students may experience nervousness in taking tests. Explain

What's the Question?

Preparing for and Taking Tests

Here's the Idea   Have you ever done poorly on a test? Nearly everyone has at one time or another. One way to avoid this experience is to learn how to prepare for and take tests.

Guidelines for Taking Tests

BEFORE THE TEST

1. Know what you will be tested on. What chapters will the test cover? Will class discussions be included? If you have any questions, ask your teacher.

2. Make a study plan. Allow plenty of time for review. (See Part 3, **Planning Ahead.**)

3. Make a list of study questions. Include any questions that you wrote while using the SQ3R study method. Also include any study questions given in class or in your textbooks.

4. Review the materials covered by the test. Skim your notes, textbook chapters, and other reading materials. Find the answers to your study questions.

5. Make a list of important names, dates, definitions, or events. Ask a friend or family member to quiz you on these.

6. Review your materials several times.

7. Eat and sleep properly before the test.

DURING THE TEST

1. Begin by skimming the test. Look to see what types of questions the test includes.

2. Read all directions and test questions carefully. Make sure you understand the directions before answering questions.

3. Budget your time. Decide on the order in which you will answer the questions. Answer the easiest questions first. Save the most difficult questions for last. Do not spend too much time on any single part of the test. Allow extra time for answering long or complicated questions.

4. Review the test when you are finished. Read over the test. Make sure you have not left out any answers. Try to answer any questions that you have not already answered. Check any answers that you are not certain about.

Check It Out   Read the following passage.

Carolyn took a test on William Gibson's play, *The Miracle Worker*. She had thirty minutes to take the test. She spent twenty minutes on the first part. This part contained twenty-five true/false questions. Each was worth one point. Then, she read the directions for the second part of the test. The second part was an essay question worth seventy-five points.

· What did Carolyn do wrong? Why?

Try Your Skill   Make a list of different things that you have done to prepare for tests. Possibilities include such activities as highlighting your notes and making flashcards. Compare your list with those of your classmates.

Keep This in Mind

· Always prepare well before taking a test.
· When taking a test, read all the directions and budget your time well. Remember to save time to check your answers.

Now Write   Explain in a brief paragraph how you would go about preparing for one of the following tests.

1. a spelling test on twenty words
2. an essay test on two poems discussed in your class
3. a quiz on one chapter of a history textbook

Label your paper **What's the Question?** Save it in your folder.

303

that nervousness may affect test performance; students should make sure they have prepared thoroughly according to the guidelines in this lesson and then relax as much as possible when they take the test. Have students bring in a test from any class. They can discuss their preparation and test taking and ask questions about any problems they had.

Advanced Students

Discuss forming study groups for test preparation. Three to six students can meet outside of class to exchange notes and study questions. They can also practice drilling each other on material as in guideline 5 on page 302.

Optional Practice

Have students write paragraphs for one or two additional tests described in **Now Write.**

Extending the Lesson

Have students write paragraphs describing their most recent test-taking experience. They should discuss their preparation and performance and then tell how they would change these after having studied the guidelines in this lesson.

Part 10

Objective

To know how to take objective tests

Presenting the Lesson

1. Have students read **Here's the Idea.** Discuss the techniques for answering objective test questions, emphasizing that learning these techniques can greatly improve students' test performance.

2. Have the class read the test questions in **Check It Out.** Have students identify the type of each test question and tell how they would go about answering it. For example, the word *always* in the first question is a clue that the statement may be false.

3. Assign **Try Your Skill.** This may be done as an oral classroom exercise.

4. Read **Keep This in Mind.**

5. Assign **Now Write.** Instruct students to choose an article that should interest their classmates and to review the guidelines on objective test questions as they write their tests.

Individualizing the Lesson

Less-Advanced Students

Have students bring in an objective test. Ask them to study each question they answered incorrectly and see whether they could have answered it correctly by following the guidelines in this lesson. Point out that students must first know the material covered in a test; then they can use these test-taking tech-

What's the Answer?

Taking Objective Tests

Here's the Idea   **Objective tests** have simple right or wrong answers. The chart below describes the types of questions usually found on objective tests.

Types of Test Questions—Objective Tests

1. **True/false questions** give you a statement and ask you to tell if the statement is true or false. Keep in mind the following guidelines.

    a. Remember that if any part of a statement is false, all of it is false.

    b. Remember that words like *all, always, only, never,* and *everyone* often appear in false statements.

    c. Remember that words like *some, often, a few, most,* and *usually* often appear in true statements.

2. **Matching questions** ask you to match items in one column with items in another column. The following guidelines can be used to answer matching questions.

    a. Check the directions. See if each item is used only once. Also check to see if some are not used at all.

    b. Read all items in both columns before starting.

    c. Match those you know first.

    d. Cross out items as you use them.

3. **Multiple choice questions** ask you to choose the best answer to a question from a group of answers given on the test. The following guidelines will help you to answer these questions.

    a. Read *all* of the choices before answering.

    b. Eliminate any obviously incorrect answers first.

    c. Choose the answer that is most complete or accurate.

    d. Pay particular attention to choices such as *none of the above* or *all of the above.*

Check It Out   Read the following test questions.

1. True or False: Twins always have eyes of the same color.

    F

2. Tass is the official news agency of which of the following
    countries?
    A. Wyoming   B. England   (C.) The Soviet Union
    D. China

3. Match the musicians in the first column with the categories
    of music in the second column.
    1. Charlie Parker ___*d*___   a. Classical
    2. Beethoven ___*a*___   b. Country
    3. Dolly Parton ___*b*___   c. Rock and Roll
    4. The Rolling Stones ___*c*___   d. Jazz

    • What kind of answer is required by each question?

Try Your Skill   Match the types of test questions with their
guidelines. Write your answers.

    c 1. True/false   *a* 2. Matching   *b* 3. Multiple Choice
a. Read all items in both columns before starting.
b. Pay particular attention to choices such as *none of the above*.
c. Words like *some* and *a few* often appear in true statements.

Keep This in Mind

- Objective tests have right or wrong answers.
- *True/false, matching,* and *multiple choice* are common types of objective test questions.

Now Write   Write an objective test covering the information
in a newspaper or magazine article. Include two true/false questions and two multiple choice questions. Also include a matching question. Exchange your article with a classmate. Read your
classmate's article. Then take the test on it.

305

niques to improve their performance.

Advanced Students

Have students create an objective test based on a hobby, personal
interest, or job. The test should contain two questions of each type discussed in this lesson.

Optional Practice

Have students write one of each
type of objective test question on
one or more of the following topics.
Students can then exchange papers and answer the questions.

1. people in the news recently
2. local points of interest
3. a front-page news story of the past
   month
4. the history of your state

Extending the Lesson

Have the class create a "trivia
test." Have each student write an
objective test question on each of
the following categories: television
and movies, sports, current events,
and school news. Assemble the
questions and duplicate the test for
the class to take. The class may
want to present a token award to the
student who answers the most
questions correctly.

Part 11

Objective

To know how to take written tests

Taking Written Tests

Presenting the Lesson

1. Have students read **Here's the Idea.** Discuss the guidelines for answering written test questions, emphasizing that the writing skills learned in English class should be used in answering completion, short answer, and essay questions.

2. Have volunteers read aloud the sample test questions in **Check It Out.** Have the class identify the type of each question and give answers in the correct form for questions 1 and 3. Ask students to name the action word in question 2 that tells how to answer the question.

3. Assign **Try Your Skill.** After students have completed the exercise individually, ask volunteers to read their answers.

4. Read **Keep This in Mind.**

5. Assign **Now Write.** Instruct students to use a specific action word in their essay question. After completing the assignment, students may compare their essay questions.

Individualizing the Lesson

Less-Advanced Students

Give students practice in answering essay questions. Time them for fifteen or twenty minutes as they write a paragraph on one of the following questions.

1. Explain the SQ3R study method.
2. Describe the ideal study area.
3. Compare two kinds of reading: skimming and scanning.

Here's the Idea   Some tests require written answers. The most common of these are completion, short answer, and essay tests. Answers to questions on these tests should follow the rules of good writing.

Types of Test Questions—Written Tests

1. **Completion questions** require that you add a word or a phrase to an incomplete sentence. Use these guidelines:

   a. If several words are required, write all of them.
   b. Write neatly. Use good spelling, grammar, punctuation, and capitalization.

2. **Short answer questions** require that you write one or two sentences to answer the question. Bear in mind the following guidelines when answering questions of this kind:

   a. Use complete sentences.
   b. Answer the question completely.
   c. Use correct spelling, grammar, punctuation, and capitalization.

3. **Essay questions** require you to write one or more paragraphs to answer the question. Follow these guidelines:

   a. Look for action words like *explain* and *compare*. These are words that tell you what to do when you answer a question.
   b. Make a list of the details you will need to answer the question.
   c. Make a rough outline of your essay on a separate sheet of paper.
   d. Make sure each paragraph contains a topic sentence. Proofread your completed essay.

Check It Out   Read the following sample test questions.

1. Who was the inventor of the steam engine? (Answer in a complete sentence.)

2. In a short paragraph, describe the differences between mammals and reptiles.

3. _____ is the largest planet in the solar system.

- Which of these is a completion question? Which is a short answer question? Which is an essay question?

Try Your Skill   Review Part 10, **What's the Answer?** Then, answer the following questions.

1. What is a true/false question? (Answer in a complete sentence.)

2. What guidelines should you follow when answering a matching question? (Answer in a complete paragraph.)

3. A _____ question is followed by a list of answers, only one of which is correct.

Keep This in Mind

- Answer completion questions with a word or a phrase.
- Answer short answer questions with one or two complete sentences.
- Answer essay questions with complete paragraphs.

Now Write   Write an essay question that could be asked on a test about the material in this chapter. Then, write the answer to your question. Follow the guidelines given in this lesson. Label your paper **Spell It Out.** Save it in your folder.

Section **24** Objectives

1. To know how to write friendly letters

2. To properly prepare letters for the mail

3. To write business letters correctly

4. To know how to write letters of request

5. To fill out forms properly

Preparing the Students

Ask students to raise their hands if they have ever written notes to friends, written thank-you notes for gifts, or written letters requesting information or products. Then ask students to raise their hands if they think they will ever again need to write one of these kinds of letters.

Point out the importance of writing letters. Ask students what kind of impression a well-written letter makes on a friend or a business person. Tell them that Writing Section 24 will explain how to write both friendly letters and business letters.

Additional Resources

Mastery Test — pages 34–36 in the test booklet

Practice Book — pages 122–126

Duplicating Masters — pages 122–126

Letters and Forms

Teaching Special Populations

LD Demonstrate each step listed for the preparation of a letter. Help individual students write and prepare their letters for mailing.

ESL Some ESL students come from cultures where American letter-writing conventions are considered rude or ignorant. Many cultures are not familiar with the block form of American business letters, for example. Some also space addresses and write dates differently. Ask students what letter-writing conventions exist in their native cultures. Discuss these differences in class.

NSD Assign many practice letters. Remind students that slang and other nonstandard language is always inappropriate in business letters. Have students identify the audience for which each of their letters is written.

A Better Letter

How To Write Friendly Letters

Presenting the Lesson

1. Read aloud **Here's the Idea.** On the chalkboard, diagram and label the five main parts of a friendly letter. Tell students that because a friendly letter is sent to someone they know well, the language can be lively and informal. However, because it is a standard way to communicate with other people, it should follow the specific form detailed in this lesson.

2. Read and discuss the friendly letter in **Check It Out.** Have students notice the placement of the heading, salutation, body, closing, and signature. Point out that there are no abbreviations in the heading, that the salutation is followed by a comma, that each paragraph is indented, that the first letter of the closing is capitalized, and that only the first name is used for the signature.

3. After students complete **Try Your Skill,** have five volunteers go to the chalkboard. Assign each volunteer one of the five parts of a friendly letter. Have them write their parts on the chalkboard in consecutive order, beginning with the heading. Then have the class compare their letters with the one written on the chalkboard and make any necessary corrections.

4. Read **Keep This in Mind.**

5. Assign **Now Write.** Have the students brainstorm for ideas. First,

Here's the Idea A **friendly letter** is a letter that you write to someone you know. It should be conversational, detailed, and neat. Every friendly letter has five main parts.

The **heading** consists of three lines: two for your address and one for the date. It appears at the top right corner of your letter. Do not use any abbreviations in the heading.

The **salutation** is the greeting. Usually beginning with *Dear*, it is written on the next line below the heading. It starts at the left margin of the page and is followed by a comma.

In the **body,** the main part of the letter, you say what you'd like to say. The body begins on the line following the salutation. The first word of the body and each new paragraph should be indented.

The **closing** is your way of saying "goodbye." You might use such closings as *Your friend, Fondly*, or *Love*. The closing is written on the line below the last word of the body and is followed by a comma. The first word of the closing should line up with the first words of the heading.

Your **signature** is the last part of your letter. Skip a line after the closing and sign your name in line with the first word of the closing. Usually, only your first name is needed.

Some forms of friendly letters are written only for special occasions. These social notes, which include invitations and thank-you notes, also have five main parts. However, the heading may be shortened to the date only.

If you send an **invitation,** include specific information about the time and place. If you receive an invitation, reply immediately.

You may also send **thank-you** notes. One kind of thank-you note is written after you have received a gift. A second kind of thank-you note thanks someone for his or her hospitality. If you stayed overnight as a guest in someone's house, you would write this kind of note. Whenever you write either of these kinds of notes, be sure to express your appreciation to the other person.

Check It Out   Read the following letter.

7113 Prospect Street
New York, New York 10019
August 1, 1985

Dear Mr. Ortega,

Thank you so much for taking me with you and Ramón on the canoe trip to Lake Champlain, in Vermont. Even though I was a beginner, I learned so much about canoeing — the hard way! Also, it really was nice to get out of the city for a week.

I hope you both will get a chance to come to New York to visit.

Sincerely,
Frank

- Identify the five parts of this form of friendly letter.
- What kind of social note is this?

311

Individualizing the Lesson

Less-Advanced Students

have them think of the names of five out-of-town friends or relatives. Then ask them to select one of the names and think of what they would like to say to this person.

Have students bring in a friendly letter received by them or by someone in their family and label each main part. If a part is missing, they should write the name of that part in the proper area.

Advanced Students

Help students make their letters for **Now Write** lively and interesting. First of all, tell them to keep their audience in mind and write as if they were having a conversation. Secondly, remind them to use specific details and sensory description where appropriate. Finally, have students analyze how the writer in **Check It Out** made his letter conversational and interesting.

Optional Practice

For **Now Write,** have students write both a friendly letter about their recent activities and a social note that is either an invitation or a thank-you note. For the social note, students may write about an imaginary event or gift.

Extending the Lesson

One week before your school's open house or parent-teacher conferences, assign this exercise. Have students write letters to their parents, inviting them to the school

311

function. List necessary information, such as the date, time, place, and agenda, on the chalkboard. You may also want to write sample body paragraphs on the board. Remind students to position, punctuate, and capitalize each part of the letter correctly.

Try Your Skill   Arrange the following information into the correct form for a friendly letter. Add capital letters and the correct punctuation wherever necessary.

4296 mcAtee street, linden California 95236, September 28, 1984. dear alice I've found the snapshots of you and your family that you had asked about. I'm having extra copies made and will send you a set when they are ready. Good luck with the school yearbook. I hope you can use the pictures in it. your friend sally

Keep This in Mind

- Write friendly letters that are conversational, detailed, and neat. They should follow the correct form. The heading, salutation, body, closing, and signature should each be written correctly.
- Social notes are short forms of friendly letters. Write invitations that are specific. Write thank-you notes that express your appreciation.

Now Write   Write a friendly letter to a friend or relative. You may choose to write a social note. Write about what you've been doing recently. Use your home address and today's date in the heading. Be sure that the five parts of your letter follow the correct form. Label your paper **A Better Letter** and put it into your folder. Make a copy of the letter that you could send. Save the copy too.

A Mailing List

How To Prepare Letters for the Mail

Here's the Idea   After you have finished writing a letter, fold it neatly. Select an envelope that matches the width of your stationery. Insert the folded letter and seal the envelope.

Prepare the envelope carefully by following these steps:

1. Address the envelope. Add your return address.
2. Double-check all numbers to make sure they are correct.
3. Include the correct ZIP code.
4. Put a stamp on the envelope.

Always check addresses on envelopes and packages for accuracy. If you need any information, call your local post office.

Check It Out   Look at the envelope below.

Ellen Hawes
3552 Ramona Road
Flushing, MI 48433

Donna Mayberry
67 Hillsborough Street
Salt Lake City, UT 84102

- Who wrote the letter? Who will receive it? What state abbreviations are used? How could you check all the information?

313

Part 2

Objective

To properly prepare letters for the mail

Presenting the Lesson

1. Read aloud and discuss **Here's the Idea.** Use a piece of typing paper to demonstrate how to fold a letter and insert it into an envelope.

2. Discuss the questions at the end of **Check It Out.** Point out the placement of the two addresses. Note that state names are now abbreviated with two capital letters and no periods.

3. Assign **Try Your Skill.** Have students divide a piece of notebook paper into thirds with two horizontal lines. On the back of the paper, they should do the same. Tell students to pretend that they have six envelopes. After the students unscramble the addresses and write them correctly on their "envelopes," have volunteers write the correct forms for the envelopes on the chalkboard.

4. Read **Keep This in Mind** and then assign **Now Write.**

Individualizing the Lesson

Less-Advanced Students

Invite a post-office employee to class to discuss the delivery of mail and to emphasize the importance of addressing letters neatly and correctly.

Advanced Students

Have students bring to class five names and addresses of friends

314

and relatives and address one envelope to each. Students may draw envelopes on paper instead of using real ones.

Optional Practice

1. Have students find and copy a list of the correct two-letter state abbreviations.

2. Have students locate the ZIP code directory at their local post office. Have them practice using the directory by finding ZIP codes for the following addresses:

1. 101 Humboldt Street
   Denver, Colorado 80218
2. 600 15th Street
   Santa Monica, California 90402
3. Georgetown University
   Washington, D. C. 20057

Extending the Lesson

Ask students to take out their letters written for the preceding **Extending the Lesson.** Give each student an envelope or ask each student to bring an envelope to class. Have students address the envelopes to their parents and use the school address as the return address. If you can obtain permission, have the letters mailed to the parents at the school's expense.

Try Your Skill   Write each of the jumbled addresses below as it should appear on an envelope. Also write a return address.

1. Susan Nash, 14 Bayview Road, Cordova, New Mexico 87523

2. 1444 Sullivan Street, Winnetka, Illinois 60093, Paul McGeary

3. Riesel, Texas 77682, Maria Chavez, 2132 Pilson Boulevard

4. Dr. David Linehan, 4518 West End Avenue, Albany, New York 12207

5. 29 Columbia Place, Mark S. Fischman, Bar Harbor, Maine 04609

6. San Francisco, California 94101, 7930 Union Street, Kim Yee Wong

Keep This in Mind

- Prepare a letter for the mail carefully. Fold the letter neatly. Check all information for accuracy.

Now Write   Take out the friendly letter you wrote for the last lesson, **A Better Letter.** On a clean sheet of paper, write the title of this lesson, **A Mailing List.** Draw a rectangle to represent an envelope. Address it as if you were going to mail it to your friend or relative. Keep this paper in your folder.

Copy your work onto a real envelope. Fold the copy of the letter that you will mail and put it into the envelope. Put a stamp on your letter and mail it.

Business Is Business

How To Write Business Letters

Here's the Idea   At times you may want to order a product by mail, complain about something you ordered, or request information about something. At each of these times, you would write or type a **business letter.** In most businesses, letters and reports are typed. However, it is not required that you type any of your business letters.

A business letter may use one of two forms. One form is the **block** form, which should be used only if you type a letter. In the block form, begin every part of the letter at the left margin. Leave two lines of space between paragraphs, and do not indent them. A **modified block** form may be used either for handwritten or typewritten letters. In this form, put the heading, closing, and signature at the right side of the page, as you do in a friendly letter. Indent the paragraphs and leave no space between them.

A business letter has six parts. It has the five parts of a friendly letter, plus the inside address. The **inside address** is the name and address of the company to which you are writing. If possible, the inside address should include the name of a department or employee in the company. Place the inside address below the heading and above the salutation. Begin at the left margin.

If you are writing to a specific person, use *Dear Mr., Mrs., Miss,* or *Ms.* before the person's name. At other times, use a general greeting like, *Dear Sir or Madam.* Place the salutation two lines below the inside address and place a colon(:) after it.

For the more formal closing, write *Sincerely, Yours truly,* or *Very truly yours,* followed by a comma. If you do type your letter, leave four lines of space between the closing and your typed signature. Then, write your signature in the space.

Whether you write or type a business letter, use the correct form. Make your letter as polite, specific, and neat as you can. It

Part 3

Objective

To write correct business letters

Presenting the Lesson

1. Read **Here's the Idea.** Discuss the purpose of a business letter and how a business letter differs from a friendly letter. On the chalkboard, diagram the two forms for a business letter. Ask students to define *inside address* and discuss the differences between a heading and an inside address.

2. Read and discuss the business letter in **Check It Out.** Point out the clear, direct language of the letter.

3. Assign and discuss **Try Your Skill.** Have students identify the purpose of the letter. Point out that the letter contains many errors. Discuss the correct form.

4. Read **Keep This in Mind.**

5. Assign **Now Write.** Have students think of some information they would be interested in receiving and find the name and address of a company that has the information. Or students may want to order a product or complain about a defective product they have bought.

Individualizing the Lesson

Less-Advanced Students

Have students bring to class a business letter received by them or by someone in their family. Have them label each main part of the letter and tell whether it uses the block or modified block form.

315

Advanced Students

Emphasize that a business letter should always be polite, even if it is written to register a complaint. Have students revise the following body of a business letter to make it more courteous. Answers will vary.

I'm really upset because you sent me the wrong color sweater! I was all set to wear the sweater to a party until I saw that it was this ugly gray color. I distinctly wrote "peach" on the order form. I'm surprised that such a reputable company would make such a stupid mistake. Either send me my peach sweater immediately or give me my money back!

Optional Practice

Have students think of a city or state they would like to visit. Instruct them to write letters to the chamber of commerce or department of tourism for that city or state to ask for travel information.

Extending the Lesson

Ask students to think of a TV program that they find either especially good or especially objectionable. Have them write letters to the network station, requesting either that the show be continued or that it be cancelled. List the addresses of the four network stations on the chalkboard.

form. Make your letter as polite, specific, and neat as you can. It is a good idea to make a copy, for your records, of business letters that you write.

Check It Out Read this business letter carefully, and then answer the questions that follow.

44 Wheeler Street
Newark, New Jersey 07124
February 23, 1985

Appalachian Mountain Club
5 Joy Street
Boston, Massachusetts 02106

Dear Sir or Madam:

I am planning to hike along part of the Appalachian Trail this summer. Could you please tell me how to get maps of the trail in the New Jersey and Pennsylvania areas? I would appreciate any information you have on that part of the trail.

Very truly yours,

Daniel Casey

Daniel Casey

- What is the purpose of this business letter?
- In what form is this letter?
- Identify the six parts of the letter.

Try Your Skill Rewrite the following letter so that it reads and looks like a correct business letter. Check for errors in spelling, punctuation and capitalization. Remember to use the block form.

```
                        1001 Jordan St.
                    Miami, Fla.


Tape-Tronics, Inc.
2194 Warren Ave.

Denver, Col. 80246

        Hello!

I saw your ad for tape cas ettes in some issue
o
of Stereo World.  I ordered a cassett tape of
the soundtrack from Star Wars.  I paid $5.95 for
it.  When it came I discovered that it was broken.
        What a disappointment!  i've enclosed
the tape and I think you really ought to send me
another one, don't you?

        May    the Force be   wi th you,

    Michael

    Michael
```

Now Write   Write or type a business letter to a real organization. Draw an envelope and address it. Label your paper **Business Is Business.** Keep your letter in your folder.

Part 4

Objective

To know how to write letters of request

Presenting the Lesson

1. Read **Here's the Idea.** Ask students to tell about any letters of request they have written and the responses they received. Discuss the points to remember when writing a letter of request.

2. Have the class read the letter in **Check It Out** and discuss the questions about it. Have students point out specific examples of polite language.

3. After students complete **Try Your Skill,** have six volunteers go to the chalkboard. Assign each volunteer one of the six parts of a business letter. Have them write their parts on the chalkboard in consecutive order. Then have the class discuss any revisions they would make in the letter's body to make it more specific, brief, or polite.

4. Read **Keep This in Mind** and then assign **Now Write.**

Individualizing the Lesson

Less-Advanced Students

Discuss keeping the audience in mind when writing a business letter. Have students characterize the probable recipient of a letter like those assigned in this lesson. Point out that a business person is not interested in detailed background information and is likely to respond positively to a polite request.

What Do You Need?

How To Write Letters of Request

Here's the Idea One common type of business letter is the **letter of request.** Such letters are used to get information about specific jobs, schools, products, and services. They can also be used to gather facts for reports.

Suppose you are planning a trip to a distant city. By writing to the Chamber of Commerce in that city, you can get information that will help you to plan your trip. The Chamber of Commerce can tell you about restaurants, places to stay, and points of interest. Gathering this information beforehand will help to make your trip a success.

Letters of request are business letters. Therefore, they should contain the six parts of a business letter, and they should follow either the *block* or *modified block* form. However, there are three additional points that you need to keep in mind when you write or type a letter of request.

1. **Be specific.** Tell exactly *what* you need and *why* you need it. Provide all the information that the other person needs in order to fill your request. If you are placing an order, be sure that you state exactly what you want and where it is to be sent. Also include any necessary details about the size, color, cost, or identification number of the product. Most businesses and organizations can fill your request promptly if it is precise and complete.

2. **Be brief.** Do not waste your reader's time by including unnecessary information.

3. **Be polite.** Remember that you are asking someone else to do you a favor. Therefore, be sure that your letter is courteous, clear, and to the point. Remember, too, that a polite letter is a neat letter.

Check It Out Read the following letter of request.

- Is this letter specific, brief, and polite?
- Is it in block or modified block form?

---

55 Sunnydale Road
Phoenix, Arizona 85026
January 5, 1985

United States Track and Field Hall of Fame
P.O. Box 297
Angola, Indiana 46703

Dear Sir or Madam:

I am writing a report on Track and Field records held by
United States athletes. According to my track coach, the
fastest speed ever recorded for a human runner is twenty-
seven miles per hour. This was the record set by Robert Lee
Hayes in 1963. Has anyone ever broken this record? If so,
what is the current record, and who holds it? Please send me
whatever information you have.

Thank you for your help.

Sincerely,

Caroline Hardin

Caroline Hardin

Try Your Skill   Write a sample letter to CBS Television, 630 McClurg Court, Chicago, Illinois 60611. Find out whether any CBS daytime programs are filmed in Chicago. Then, request information about becoming a member of the audience of one of these programs. Use your home address. Write the letter in block form. Compare your letter with those of your classmates.

Keep This in Mind

- A letter of request should be specific, brief, and polite.
- Use block or modified block form when writing this kind of business letter.

Now Write   Write a letter to a travel agency requesting information about a place that you would like to visit. Find the correct address in a telephone book. Use modified block form. Draw an envelope and address it. Save your letter and envelope in your folder.

Sign Here, Please

How To Fill Out Forms

Here's the Idea   Schools, businesses, and agencies use forms to record various information. This information ranges from locker combinations to employment applications. Perhaps you will have to complete forms for purposes such as these:

1. Getting a job
2. Buying a house or car
3. Starting a bank account
4. Ordering a product
5. Changing your address
6. Filing your income taxes
7. Applying to schools

Because forms are so widely used, you should learn how to fill them out properly. These guidelines will help you:

Filling Out Forms

1. **Read the directions carefully.** Notice any special directions such as "Print" or "Please type."
2. **Gather the information you need to complete the form.** This information will vary from form to form. Many forms require your name and address, the date, and your social security number. Some forms require special information, such as the occupations of your parents.
3. **Have the proper tools.** You may need a pen, a pencil, or a typewriter. Do not use a pencil unless told to do so.
4. **Complete the form.** Reread each direction carefully. Then, give the information requested. If a question on the form does not apply to you, write *Does not apply.*
5. **Make sure that the form is neat and readable.**
6. **Check the form when you are done.** Make sure that you have followed directions. See that you have answered all questions completely. Check for spelling errors.

Objective

To fill out forms properly

Presenting the Lesson

1. Read **Here's the Idea.** Have students name some occasions for which they have had to fill out forms. Discuss the chart, "Filling Out Forms," outlining the guidelines on the chalkboard.

2. Have the class study the form in **Check It Out.** Discuss the study questions, helping students recognize that the form should be printed in ink. Also call attention to the important statement directly above the applicant's signature.

3. Assign **Try Your Skill.** Have students exchange papers to check the accuracy of their classmates' forms.

4. Read **Keep This in Mind.**

5. Assign **Now Write.** You may have students copy the application first as for **Try Your Skill.**

Individualizing the Lesson

Less-Advanced Students

Give students additional practice in filling out forms. Duplicate a form of any kind that has many blanks to be filled out and have students fill them out in the classroom.

Advanced Students

Have students imagine that they are running an agency to match high school students who need part-time work to people who need students for part-time jobs. Have the students create one form for students to fill out and one form for the employers to fill out.

Optional Practice

Have each student bring a mail-order catalog containing an order form to class. Have the students pretend that they are ordering at least five items from the catalog and fill out the form correctly. Then have students exchange forms and determine whether they have been filled out properly.

Extending the Lesson

Have students obtain an application form for one of the following items that they are interested in applying for. They should then bring the forms to class to fill out, asking any questions and exchanging forms with classmates to check each other's work.

1. social security card
2. learner's permit
3. bank account
4. school admission

Check It Out   Read the following form.

APPLICATION FOR LEARNER'S PERMIT

(Please print all information in ink)

FULL NAME
Patricia Guerrero

RESIDENCE ADDRESS
5203 N. Glenwood

CITY OR TOWN
Chicago

COUNTY	SOCIAL SECURITY NUMBER	HEIGHT	WEIGHT	COLOR HAIR	COLOR EYES	SEX	DATE OF BIRTH
Cook	324-83-2329	FT. 5 IN. 5	120	brown	brown	F	MO. 8 DAY 3 YEAR 70

DO NOT COMPLETE SECTION. FOR OFFICE USE ONLY.

TYPE APPLICATION		1 2 3 4 5 6 7 8 9 A B C E
TYPE LIC.	LIC. CLASS A B C D L M	TYPES OF IDENTIFICATION
RESTRICTION None ☐ 1 2 3 4 5	IF NO 6, EXPLAIN 6 BELOW	DRIVER ED. CERT. NO. SCHOOL CODE
RESTRICTED TO		

I HEREBY AFFIRM THAT THE INFORMATION I HAVE FURNISHED IN THIS APPLICATION FOR LEARNER'S PERMIT IS TRUE TO THE BEST OF MY KNOWLEDGE AND BELIEF.

WRITTEN SIGNATURE
OF APPLICANT   *Patricia Guerrero*

- What information is requested by this form?
- What special directions are given on the form?

Copy onto your own paper the application for a learner's permit given in **Check It Out**. Use a pencil. Then, using a pen, complete this form. Make sure that the information you include is accurate.

- Read all the directions before completing a form.
- Gather the information and tools you need.
- Make sure the form is neat, accurate, and complete.

Now Write Imagine that you wish to order the following items:

Two red spiral notebooks at $2.00 each, catalog number 19433

One Sharpy Brand pencil sharpener at $8.00, catalog number 00215

On your own paper write the information you would use to complete this form. Use your own name, address, and telephone number. Label your paper **Sign Here, Please.** Save it in your folder.

208116

Office Products, Inc.
TO PURCHASE MERCHANDISE FROM OUR CATALOG, COMPLETE THIS
FORM AND PRESENT IT TO THE CATALOG DEPARTMENT. **PLEASE PRINT.**

ORDER FORM

NAME Jeanne Vonich
ADDRESS 233 S.W. Gaines
CITY Portland, Oregon   STATE   ZIP 9 7 3 0 2
PHONE 555-2837   ORDER TO BE PAID FOR BY: ☐ CHECK ☐ BANKCARD ☑ CASH

CUSTOMER

CATALOG NUMBER	OFFICE USE ONLY		PRODUCT DESCRIPTION	YOUR COST EACH
3 2 4 7 B	1		3-ring notebook	1 99
3 2 8 8 A	2		pkg. notebook paper	79
2 1 1 3 A	1		bottle correction fluid	1 25
8 2 2 7 A	3		legal pads	75
7 6 9 0 B	3		tape	1 40

Section 25 Objectives

1. To make an activities schedule
2. To assess job skills
3. To know how to write a résumé
4. To know how to read help-wanted ads
5. To know how to write a letter of inquiry about employment
6. To know how to complete a job application
7. To know how to fill out three kinds of work-related forms
8. To know how to write a letter of inquiry to a school

Preparing the Students

Ask the class how many students presently have part-time jobs. Next ask how many would like to get jobs for the summer or at some time during their high-school years. Finally ask how many plan to get a job at some time in their lives. Point out that almost everyone must work for a living sooner or later and that some specific knowledge and skills are required to obtain a job. This Section will give students practice in those skills that will come in handy as they enter the working world.

Additional Resources

Mastery Test — page 36 in the test booklet

Practice Book — pages 128–137

Duplicating Masters — pages 128–137

WRITING SECTION 25

Skills for Your Future

325

Teaching Special Populations

LD Discuss with students their skills and interests that might lead to future jobs. If students respond unrealistically, discuss their actual skills that could lead to employment.

On a one-on-one basis, help students fill out forms. Suggest that students with poor penmanship type (or have typed) employment applications.

ESL Spend extra time deciphering help wanted ads with ESL students. Have students bring ads to class, and list the abbreviations found in those ads on the chalkboard.

Discuss with students how their bilingual background can work to their advantage when they apply for jobs or to schools. Have them list jobs that would be appropriate for individuals with their current language skills.

Work carefully with ESL students to help them understand cultural differences they need to know when applying for a job (for example, Americans usually stand an arm length or more away when conversing, and may back away when someone comes closer).

Objective

To make an activities schedule

Presenting the Lesson

1. Read **Here's the Idea.** Have students discuss any part-time jobs that they now have, asking those who do work how they manage their study and work schedules. Write *activities schedule* on the chalkboard as you define and discuss it.

2. Have the class study the activities schedule in **Check It Out.** Discuss the study questions, asking if there are any activities the student could rearrange if he or she did get a part-time job.

3. Assign **Try Your Skill.** Tell students to be realistic in their assessments, remembering that everyone needs some free time.

4. Read **Keep This in Mind** and then assign **Now Write.**

Individualizing the Lesson

Less-Advanced Students

Emphasize that an activities schedule is a one-time report and not an on-going project like a study plan. It is for the student's own use to clearly show how his or her time is used. Instruct students to allow time on their schedules for any monthly activities such as dentist appointments or monthly club meetings.

Advanced Students

Hold a discussion about the pros and cons of working part time while attending high school. Make sure you hear from those students who hold part-time jobs. People who

326

What's the Time?

Making an Activities Schedule

Here's the Idea   Many of the skills that you learn in school can benefit you outside of school as well. For example, you can use your language skills to help you to find a part-time job. Remember, though, that you already have one full-time job— your schoolwork. Do not take on a part-time job unless you have enough time to work *and* to meet your other commitments.* To find out whether you have enough time for a part-time job, make an activities schedule. An **activities schedule** is a chart that shows how much time you give each week to schoolwork and to other activities.

Check It Out   Study the following activities schedule.

Time	Mon.	Tues.	Wed.	Thurs.	Fri.	Sat.	Sun.
3-4 p.m.	Track Practice		Track Practice			library research	
4-5 p.m.		Piano Lessons			Dentist	↓	
5-6 p.m.	Practice Piano		Practice Piano			Practice Piano	Home-work
6-7 p.m.					Home-work		↓
7-8 p.m.	Home-work	Home-work	Home-work	Home-work		Roller Skating	Youth Group
8-9 p.m.	↓	↓	↓	↓	Movie		
9-10 p.m.						↓	↓

*Federal and state laws protect teens from overwork and dangerous working conditions. Under Federal law, if you are fourteen or fifteen years old, you may work only up to three hours on a school day and up to eighteen hours per week. (Hours are extended during the summer.) State laws vary. Check with your guidance counselor about your state's child labor laws.

326

- How much free time does this person have in the evening?
- How much time can this person give to a part-time job?

Try Your Skill   Study the activities schedule given in **Check It Out.** Write a paragraph giving advice to the person who has this schedule. Explain whether you think this person should take a part-time job. If you think there is enough time for a job, tell how many hours you think this person should work every week. Give reasons to support your suggestions.

Keep This in Mind

- Your language skills can help you to get a part-time job.
- School is your full-time job.
- Do not take on a part-time job unless you have enough time to work and to meet your other commitments.
- Check the amount of time you have for work by making an activities schedule.

Now Write   Make an activities schedule for yourself. On this schedule, include all of your activities and hours of study for one week. At the bottom of the paper, tell how many hours of free time you have. Label your paper **What's the Time?** Save it in your folder.

have definitely decided not to work while in high school will also probably want to state their viewpoints.

Optional Practice

Have each student interview two students who have part-time jobs. Have them find out how many hours are devoted to the job each week and how many to homework. Have them find out how the students have done in school since starting to work part time.

Extending the Lesson

Invite the guidance counselor or a state official to class to explain the state's child labor laws mentioned in the footnote on page 326. The speaker can clarify your state's law and explain the reasons behind it.

Part 2

Objective

To assess job skills

Presenting the Lesson

1. Read **Here's the Idea.** Emphasize the fact that everybody is not suited for the same type of job.

2. Have the class study the questions in **Check It Out.** Discuss the study questions, asking students what kind of job the person might be suited for.

3. Assign **Try Your Skill.** Encourage students to be honest and thoughtful in considering their talents.

4. Read **Keep This in Mind.**

5. Assign **Now Write.** Remind students to be realistic in identifying jobs that are available to high school students.

Individualizing the Lesson

Less-Advanced Students

Students may need extra encouragement in recognizing their strengths and talents. For **Try Your Skill,** they may find it easier to first list jobs they have done and situations in which they have been successful and then choose the corresponding skills from the list. For example, if a student is good at babysitting, he or she may choose skills such as "entertaining" and "managing."

Advanced Students

Have students think of two jobs that a person with each of the following sets of skills might be good at:

Answers will vary.

328

You Can Do It!

Assessing Your Skills

Here's the Idea   Once you have decided to take a part-time job, you must then decide what kinds of jobs are right for you. To do this, make a list of your interests and skills. Then, think of jobs that match the interests and skills on your list. If you enjoy working with animals, you might look for a job in an animal shelter. If you like working outdoors, you might consider doing yard work, painting houses, or working for a delivery service. The type of job that you choose should be suited to you.

Check It Out   The following questions will help you to measure your job-related interests. Notice how one person has answered these questions.

1. Do you prefer working with people or with machines?

   a. People   (b. Machines)

2. Do you prefer working indoors or outside?

   a. Indoors   (b. Outside)

3. Do you prefer working by yourself or with others?

   (a. By myself)   b. With others

4. Do you prefer working with numbers or with words?

   a. Numbers   (b. Words)

- Would this person be happy working as a cashier in a busy restaurant? Why or why not?

328

Try Your Skill Read the following list of skills. Choose four skills that you are particularly good at. Tell where and when you have used each skill. Then, name one job in which each skill is particularly valuable.

Acting	Driving	Playing
Building	Entertaining	Proving
Calculating	Leading	Questioning
Classifying	Listening	Reading
Computing	Managing	Remembering
Counseling	Measuring	Repairing
Dancing	Organizing	Researching
Decorating	Operating	Speaking
Designing	Painting	Teaching
Drawing	Persuading	Writing

Keep This in Mind

- Before you look for a job, make a list of your interests and skills.
- Look for jobs that suit your interests and skills.

Now Write Answer the questions given in **Check It Out.** Then, based on your answers to these questions, identify one or two jobs that fit your interests. Write a paragraph describing the type of job that is right for you. Label your paper **Can You Do It?** Save the paper in your folder.

1. decorating, designing, organizing, painting
2. classifying, managing, remembering, writing
3. counseling, listening, persuading, speaking

Optional Practice

Have students choose two skills from the list in **Try Your Skill** that are important in each of the following jobs:

1. delivery person for a florist
2. mail clerk for an office
3. sales clerk in a small shop

Extending the Lesson

Have students interview two adults about their jobs by using the list in **Try Your Skill.** Students should write down the person's job and then have the person choose four skills that he or she is particularly good at. Are these skills utilized in the person's present job? If not, what kind of job might they be used for?

What Have You Done?

Writing a Résumé

Part **3**

Objective

To know how to write a résumé

Presenting the Lesson

1. Read aloud **Here's the Idea.** Ask students to define *résumé* (a French word meaning "summary") and explain the difference between an application for employment and a résumé. Remind students to ask permission before writing their references' names on the résumé. Discuss the fact that a résumé is often an employer's first introduction to a prospective employee, so it is important for the résumé to make a good impression.

2. Read and discuss **Check It Out.** Ask why an employer would find this résumé helpful.

3. Assign **Try Your Skill.** Have your class rewrite the entire résumé, adding the additional information to it. Ask students to exchange papers and to check for proper placement and clear wording.

4. Read **Keep This in Mind** and then assign **Now Write.**

Individualizing the Lesson

Less-Advanced Students

In writing a résumé, students should refer to the list of skills they compiled for **Try Your Skill,** Part 2. Encourage students to think positively about their skills, referring to the varied talents listed on the résumé on page 332.

Advanced Students

Have students find the names and addresses of five companies,

Here's the Idea   Once you have decided what kind of job you would like, you are ready to begin presenting yourself to employers. One way to do this is by writing a résumé.

A **résumé** (rez′•oo•mā′) is a list that summarizes your life in relation to work. A résumé contains basic information about you, your education, work experience, and skills.

Many employers and schools ask you to submit a résumé in addition to an application form or letter. Sometimes you are asked for a résumé before you'll be given an interview. A résumé is valuable to schools and employers for several reasons. Your résumé shows how well you are able to organize factual information. Your résumé shows who you are in a simple, easy-to-read form. Using résumés is one way that employers and schools narrow a large number of applicants to a selected few.

No two résumés are exactly alike, but most are one page long and typewritten. To create your own résumé, follow these directions.

1. State your name, address, and telephone number, including the area code.

2. State your job objective. What kind of position or general type of work are you seeking?

3. Summarize your education. List your high school, its address, your expected date of graduation, and any subjects relevant to the job. If you have attended more than one school, list the most recent first.

4. Summarize your job experience. State the beginning and ending dates of your employment, the name and address of your

employer, the position you held, and your duties. Include any volunteer experience. Again, list your most recent jobs first.

5. Mention any meaningful personal achievements. Include skills, such as computer language, foreign language, office skills, or community work. Also include awards, societies, or clubs, any offices held at school, hobbies, and related interests.

6. Name at least two references. You may list several adults—teachers or employers, for example—who can give you good character or employment references. You may also say that you will supply references on request.

As your life and work experiences change, so should your résumé. Revise your résumé so that it is up-to-date.

Check It Out   Examine the résumé on page 332.

- Is this résumé clear and well organized? Does it include all the necessary information?

Try Your Skill   Update the résumé shown in this lesson by correctly adding the following information to it.

1. worked as camp counselor, Camp Hillcrest, Medling, New York
2. earned Water Safety Instructor certificate
3. elected co-captain of basketball team
4. experienced in running video camera

Keep This in Mind

- A résumé summarizes basic information about your life in relation to work.
- Make sure your résumé is clear, well organized, and up-to-date.
- Include all necessary information that shows you and your skills.

stores, or restaurants at which they might be interested in working. Instruct the students to save these addresses as they discuss help-wanted ads and letters about employment in the next two lessons.

Optional Practice

Have pairs of students take turns playing the role of employer and interviewing each other, using the résumés they wrote. In preparation for the interview, ask students to study their classmates' résumés, and to write a few questions to ask during the interview.

Extending the Lesson

Invite a personnel representative from a local company to class to discuss writing a résumé. He or she may also discuss employment opportunities for young people and how to interview for a job.

Now Write   Now you are ready to write your own résumé. First take notes, organizing them in a way that shows your talents best. Don't worry if your résumé is brief. Organize what information you do have well. Print or type a neat final copy. Label it **What Have You Done?** Keep it in your folder.

John Michael Baker

17 Allen Road
Bloomington, Indiana
(603) 555-3476

OBJECTIVE | A summer job with a community theater group.

EDUCATION | Bloomington North High School
Bloomington, Indiana
Member of Junior class graduating June, 1985, with courses in theater and history of film.

WORK EXPERIENCE
1982-1983 | Projectionist
Bloomington North High School
Bloomington, Indiana
Helped audio-visual department run the 35 mm projector, on voluntary basis.
Built sets for drama club

Summer, 1983 | Usher
College Street Cinema
Bloomington, Indiana
Duties included taking tickets and seating patrons.

PERSONAL | Able to operate a film projector.
Won English award, 1982.
Member of drama club, basketball team, and student council.
Appeared in student productions of As You Like It, South Pacific, and Arsenic and Old Lace.

REFERENCES | Available upon request.

Wanted!

Reading Help-Wanted Ads

Here's the Idea An important step in looking for a job is finding out what jobs are available. You can do this by checking the help-wanted ads in your local newspaper. These ads are organized alphabetically by job title. Ads for full-time jobs are usually listed separately from ads for part-time jobs. A help-wanted ad may contain any or all of the following information:

1. Job title
2. Job description
3. Skills or experience required
4. Days or shifts to be worked
5. Number of hours per week
6. Salary or wages to be paid
7. How to contact the employer

Read the help-wanted ads carefully. Note details such as those listed above. Decide whether your skills and experience match those required for the job. Also decide whether you are available at the times given in the ad.

Check It Out Read the following help-wanted ads.

OFFICE—Filing Clerk. Full-time days, M-F. Filing for busy medical office. Some scheduling of appts. Exper. preferred. Start at $5.20 hr. Call Dr. Plessas, 555-1263.

RETAIL SALES, bakery. Christmas holiday only. Full-time, evenings. Weekends included. Mature, experienced person pref. Call Sandi, 555-2800.

STOCK & CLEAN UP work. 15 hrs./wk., after school and wknds. Apply in person. Melinke Auto Supply, 253 Warrington Rd.

Part 4

Objective

To know how to read help-wanted ads

Presenting the Lesson

1. Read **Here's the Idea.** As you discuss the information contained in a help-wanted ad, point out each item in one of the sample ads in **Check It Out.**

2. Have students read the ads in **Check It Out.** Discuss the study questions, helping students recognize that only one of the advertised jobs is appropriate for a high school student.

3. Assign **Try Your Skill.** Help students with any abbreviations or notations in the ads that they do not understand.

4. Read **Keep This in Mind.**

5. Assign **Now Write.** If you live in an area with more than one newspaper, students may want to consult more than one. Advise students who live in or near a large city to consult neighborhood or suburban papers as well as the main city newspapers. Also point out that the Sunday edition of most papers usually contains the most help-wanted ads.

Individualizing the Lesson

Less-Advanced Students

Bring the help-wanted section of a local newspaper to class. Show students how the part-time jobs and full-time jobs are arranged. Pass around the sheets of help-wanted ads for the students to look over.

Have them ask questions about any information listed on the ads that is unclear to them.

Have students find ads for two or three jobs that they would like to be qualified for in the future. Have them discuss either in class or in a paragraph why the jobs are appealing.

Optional Practice

Have each student bring in an interesting help-wanted ad, not necessarily for a part-time job. Have students exchange ads and answer the questions in **Try Your Skill.**

Extending the Lesson

Have students analyze the employment situation in their area by answering the following questions about the newspaper's help-wanted section.

What job classification has the most ads?

What is the proportion (approximately) of part-time jobs to full-time jobs?

What is the approximate average starting salary for the following jobs?

data processor
auto mechanic
engineer
receptionist
sales clerk

• Which of these jobs is most appropriate for a high school student? Which of these jobs are not appropriate? Why?

Try Your Skill   Reread the want ads in **Check It Out.** For each ad, answer the following questions.

1. Is the job full-time or part-time?
2. What kind of work is this?
3. Does the ad specify "experience preferred"?
4. Is the job a daytime job or an evening job?
5. Does the job include weekend hours?
6. How are you asked to contact the employer?

Keep This in Mind

• Help-wanted ads list jobs alphabetically, according to job type.
• Full-time and part-time jobs are usually listed separately.
• Read help-wanted ads carefully to learn specific information about jobs.

Now Write   Read the help-wanted ads in your local paper. Find an ad for a part-time job that suits your interests and skills. Attach the ad to a sheet of paper. Read the ad carefully. Write a paragraph telling why you think this job is suited to you. Label your paper **Wanted!** Save it in your folder.

Here I Am!

Writing Letters About Employment

Here's the Idea   In Part 4 you learned how to use the help-wanted ads to find out what jobs are available. Another way to find out about possible job openings is to write letters to employers. When you write a letter to an employer, you must present yourself in the best possible way. If your letter is sloppy, full of mistakes, or vague and unclear, the employer will assume that you are sloppy, careless, and confused. If you were an employer, would you hire as a secretary someone who made typing errors in an employment letter? Would you hire a painter who wrote sloppily? You can see how important it is to create a good impression through your letter.

You will be in competition with other teenagers for the few jobs available. Your letter seeking employment must show how you are specially suited for a particular job. Address your letter to the manager or personnel director of an organization. Be sure that your letter includes the following information.

1. the kind of job you are looking for: full time? part time? temporary (as for summer only)?

2. the name of the job you are seeking

3. a brief description of yourself: age? grade level in school?

4. a brief description of any credentials you might have: previous experience? related courses in school?

5. your availability: what days? if part-time, what hours? starting when?

6. a request for an interview, if the job is in your area

Make sure that your letter follows the correct form for business letters. (See Section 24.) It should be informative, polite, and neat. Proofread your letter carefully. A job offer may depend on your attention to detail.

335

Objective

To know how to write a letter of inquiry about employment

Presenting the Lesson

1. Read aloud **Here's the Idea.** Stress the importance of accuracy in spelling and mechanics, precision in penmanship, and clarity in sentence structure. Point out that writing this type of business letter is an important first step toward finding a job.

2. Read and discuss **Check It Out.** Ask students if the letter includes all six items listed on page 335. Ask how the information is organized. Point out the clear, direct style of the letter, as well as the block form.

3. Assign **Try Your Skill.** Have students pair off and take turns pretending to be the employer. Have them comment on each other's letters and check for the six items listed on page 335.

4. Read **Keep This in Mind.**

5. Assign **Now Write.** Suggest that students first list answers to the questions on page 335. Then students may write their first drafts and compare them with drafts composed by other students. After all corrections have been made, students may write their final drafts.

Individualizing the Lesson

Less-Advanced Students

Review the correct form for business letters in Section 24, including the six main parts of a business letter. Have students point out the six main parts of the sample letter on page 336.

Advanced Students

For **Now Write,** have students use the list they made for Part 3, **Advanced Students,** to find a prospective employer to write. Students should also refer to the help-wanted ads they found in Part 4.

Optional Practice

In choosing an employer to address a letter to for **Now Write,** have students research methods of finding out about available jobs in addition to help-wanted ads. Some high schools have a bulletin board posting job opportunities; or the guidance counselors may know about job openings. Remind students to keep in touch with friends and relatives about job possibilities.

Extending the Lesson

If you have a vocational counselor at your school, ask him or her to speak to your class about the first steps in applying for a job. The presentation might explain how many letters to send to different companies, how to keep files of letters sent to companies, and tips for writing successful letters.

Check It Out   Read this letter.

```
17 Allen Road
Bloomington, Indiana
May 15, 1984


Manager
Bloomington Community Theater
729 Lincoln Drive
Bloomington, Indiana 47401


Dear Sir or Madam:


I would like very much to become a part of the Bloomington
Community Theater's summer season. Please consider me an
applicant for a position in your box office or on your set
crew. I plan to major in theater in junior college and
have had two years' experience as a member of the drama
club at Bloomington North High School. During my second
year in the drama club, I supervised the building of sets
for three major productions. I have also worked as a
ticket taker at the College Street Cinema.

I will be available from June 26 through Labor Day. I am
seventeen years old and a junior in high school.

Enclosed is a copy of my résumé. I will call you next week
about arranging an interview.


Yours truly,

John Baker

John Baker
```

- Does this letter include all the necessary information? Is it polite, informative, and neat?

Try Your Skill Write an employment letter for yourself. Imagine that you are inquiring about one of the following jobs. For the purpose of this exercise, make up related work experience.

1. Wanted: Experienced waiter at Mountain View Inn, Main Street, Aspen, Colorado 81611, for part-time, year-round job.

2. Wanted: Summer camp counselor and swimming instructor for Camp Hillcrest, Paradise Lane, Medling, New York 12354.

3. Wanted: sales clerk during Christmas vacation, Kimball's Department Store, 2206 Jackson Street, Miami Beach, Florida 33140.

Keep This in Mind

- Make sure that a letter about employment makes a good impression. It should be polite, informative, and neat. Include specific information about yourself and the job you want.

Now Write Choose a business, restaurant, or store in your area and think of a job that you might like to have there. Write a letter asking to be considered for the job. Be sure to include all necessary information. Proofread your letter carefully. Label it **Here I Am!** and put it into your folder. You may want to copy your letter and send it.

Speak for Yourself

Completing a Job Application

Presenting the Lesson

1. Read aloud and discuss **Here's the Idea.**

2. Read and discuss **Check It Out.** Point out that the answers are printed, not written. Discuss the fact that employers usually verify information by contacting schools and previous employers.

3. Before you assign **Try Your Skill,** duplicate the sample application on page 340. (The publisher grants permission to the classroom teacher to reproduce this page.) Have students complete the application. They should refer to the four guidelines listed on pages 338–339. Remind students that the people whom they intend to use as references should be consulted before their names are written on applications. When students finish the exercise, have them exchange applications to proofread and note confusing answers.

4. Read **Keep This in Mind.**

5. For the **Now Write** exercise, ask the manager of a local department store for applications. Assign **Now Write.** Pair students to proofread each other's applications.

Individualizing the Lesson

Less-Advanced Students

For **Try Your Skill** or **Now Write,** lead the students through a step-by-step completion of a job application.

Here's the Idea   Learning to complete a job application is a practical skill. Throughout your lifetime you are likely to hold several different jobs. You may work full time, part time, or for temporary periods of time. Each time you apply for a job you will probably be asked to fill out one of the company's application forms. The forms themselves will vary from one business to another. However, there are certain guidelines that you should always follow.

1. Be prepared to answer several basic questions. You will be asked to state your address, telephone number, date of birth, social security number, and your citizenship. You will be asked about your education, and any past work experience. You will also be asked to name references. That is, you will be asked to name two or three people not related to you who have known you a long time and who would be willing to discuss your strengths and abilities. A reference may be a former employer, a teacher, or a clergyman, for example.

2. Be neat. Print your answers carefully. You will be judged on your ability to follow directions and to work neatly. Use a good pen with blue or black ink. Because there is rarely enough space for the information requested, plan your answers before you print them. If you do make an error, cross it out neatly with a single line. Read all instructions carefully, especially those in fine print. For instance, you may be asked to give your last name first and your first name last.

3. Complete every item. There may be questions that you cannot answer, such as a question about military service or home ownership. However, you should never leave any space

blank on an application. Leaving a blank space is confusing. If an item does not apply to you, write "does not apply" in that space.

4. Be honest. You will be asked to sign your name to a statement that all information is accurate.

Check It Out   Examine the completed job application on page 340.

- Have all the items on the form been answered completely? How might an employer check to be sure that answers are accurate and honest?
- Has the application been filled in carefully and neatly? Have all of the instructions been followed?

Try Your Skill   Suppose that you were applying for a part-time job as a checker in a local supermarket. On a separate sheet of paper, copy the application form as it is shown on page 340. Then fill out the application form as you would actually complete it. Your teacher may give you a copy of the form to complete.

> ### Keep This in Mind
> - Answer all items on an application form honestly, accurately, and completely.
> - Fill in the items on an application form by printing in ink as neatly as possible. Work carefully and read all instructions.

Now Write   Complete a real application for employment. Use a form given to you by your teacher or one from a business in your community. Complete the form honestly and neatly following the guidelines you have learned. Label the form **Speak for Yourself,** and keep it in your folder.

Discuss each item as students fill it out. Emphasize neatness and thoroughness. Have students note that the student's references in the sample application on page 340 are people who are likely to be familiar with those skills related to the job the student is applying for.

Advanced Students

For **Now Write,** have students obtain their own employment applications. Discuss the fact that even when students are merely requesting a job application, courteous behavior and a pleasant appearance are important.

Optional Practice

For **Now Write,** have students obtain at least two different applications for employment and fill them both out. Discuss the fact that if students are looking for employment, it may be wise to submit more than one application.

Extending the Lesson

If students are interested in finding jobs in the community, have them write and send letters to potential employers requesting job applications. In preparation for filling out the applications, have students list the information noted on page 338. When students receive their applications, have them fill in their answers. You might check over the applications before students deliver them to the businesses.

Application for Employment

Personal Information   Date 5/23/84   Social Security Number 986-78-4121

Name Baker (Last)   John (First)   Michael (Middle)

Present Address 17 Allen Road (Street)   Bloomington, (City)   Ind. (State)   47401 (Zip)

Phone Number 555-3476   Date of Birth 10/21/68   U.S. Citizen (Yes) No

Employment Desired

Position Set Crew Member / Box Office Worker   Date You Can Start June 26   Salary Desired Open

Are You Employed Now? No   Where? Does not apply   Duties Does not a

Education	Name and Location of School	Years Attended	Date Graduated	Course of Study
Grammar School	Platt Grammar School Bloomington, Ind.	1973-1981	1981	Does not ap
High School	Bloomington North H.S. Bloomington, Ind.	1981-present	Does not apply	Gene
College or Trade School	Does not apply			
Military Service	Does not apply			

Former Employers   *(List your last two employers, starting with the more recent one)*

Dates	Name and Address of Employer	Salary	Position	Reason for Lea
From To Summer, 1983	College Street Cinema Bloomington, Ind.	3.35/hour	Ticket Taker/Usher	to return to school
From 9/82 To 6/83	Bloomington North H.S. Bloomington, Ind.	Does not apply	Drama Club Member	Does not app

References   *Name two persons, not related to you, who have known you at least one year.*

Name	Address	Business
Roberta Benson	Bloomington North H.S. Bloomington, Ind. 47401	Drama Coac
Carlo Mancini	1100 Walker St. Bloomington, Ind.	Owner, Colle Street Cinema

In Case of Emergency Notify Mark and Donna Baker (Name)   17 Allen Road Bloomington, Ind. (Address)   555-34 (Phone N)

I authorize investigation of all statements contained in this application. I understand that misre
sentation or omission of facts called for is cause for dismissal.

May 23, 1984
Date

John Michael Bake
Signature of Applicant

Working Papers

Completing Other Job-Related Forms

Here's the Idea Once you have accepted a job, you will have to complete several work-related forms. The following are the most common:

1. Social Security Application Form. In order to be paid, you must have a social security number. To get a number, you must fill out a form. The form asks for information about when you were born. It also asks whether you are a United States citizen. Social security forms are available from the social security office.

2. Application for a Work Permit. Most states require workers under 16 years old to obtain a work permit. The application for a work permit asks for your birthdate, the location of your job, the kind of job you have, and the number of hours you will work. The application also asks about your health and your school record. To get one of these forms, see your high school guidance counselor.

3. W-4 Form. The federal government requires that all workers fill out a W-4 form. This form provides information that is used to figure the taxes that will be taken from your pay. The form asks you how many people you will support with your salary.

There is one place on this form that is especially important. In this place you can indicate that you do not support yourself and that you earn a minimum amount of money. That way, any taxes you have to pay will be refunded to you at the end of the year.

In addition to this form, you may have to fill out a form for state income taxes. Your employer will give you the tax forms that you need.

Check It Out Examine the work permit application on the next page.

Part 7

Objective

To know how to fill out three kinds of work-related forms

Presenting the Lesson

1. Read **Here's the Idea,** discussing the three kinds of work-related forms. Emphasize that all three forms are required by law.

2. Have the class study the work permit application in **Check It Out.** Discuss the study questions, pointing out that the students need only fill out the top part of the form.

3. Assign **Try Your Skill.** Remind students to read the form's directions carefully so that they only fill in the blanks intended for the student.

4. Read **Keep This in Mind.**

5. Assign **Now Write.** Have students bring to class the address of their local social security office. This is a good opportunity for those students who don't yet have a social security number to obtain one.

Individualizing the Lesson

Less-Advanced Students

For **Try Your Skill** or **Now Write,** lead the class step by step in filling out one of the forms. Instruct students to read all directions and statements such as the one at the bottom of the work permit form on page 342 before signing a form.

Advanced Students

Have a student who has recently gotten a job tell the class about the various forms he or she was required to fill out.

Optional Practice

Obtain some W-4 forms or have the students do so. Have students examine the form and ask about any parts they do not understand. Guide the students in filling out the forms for practice if you have enough forms or can make copies of one.

Extending the Lesson

Have students make a bulletin board illustrating the forms discussed in this lesson and the correct way to fill them out.

Date _9/24/85_

Year in school _10_

Application for Work Permit

Name of student _Theresa Lima_

Address _203 Spring St._ _Newport,_ _RI._ _028_
Street   City   State   Zip

Date of Birth _5-19-69_

Newport, _Rhode Island_ _Newpo_
City of Birth   State of Birth   County of Birth

Parent/Guardian's Name _Edward Lima_

Employer's Statement

Name of Company or Agency _Colonial Food Shoppe_

Address of Company _327 Main Ave._ _Newport, RI_
Street   State

Phone No. _555-5435_ Nature of Industry _Restaurant_

Name of Student's Supervisor _Mrs. Iola Reed_

Student's Job Title and a description of the work that the student will do:
Waitress: Serving food to customers and keeping tables clean.

Student will work _3_ school days per week, _3_ hours per school day. He/she will work _6_ hours Saturday or _0_ hours on Sunday.

Are alcoholic beverages sold or served? Yes _____ No _✓_

Is this summer work only? Yes _____ No _✓_

Iola Reed, Manager
Signature of Company official & title

GIVING INCORRECT OR IMPROPER INFORMATION ON THIS FORM SHALL CONSTITUTE A CLA "C" MISDEMEANOR PURSUANT TO THE LAWS OF THE STATE.

- What information is requested on this form?
- What questions must be answered by the student?
- What questions must be answered by the employer?

Try Your Skill On a separate sheet of paper, copy the sample work permit application given in **Check It Out.** Complete your part of this form.

Keep This in Mind

- Your employer may ask you to fill out several job-related forms.
- The most common job-related forms are the social security application form, the application for a work permit, and the W-4 form.

Now Write Visit or write your local social security office. Obtain an application for a social security number. Complete this form. If you do not as yet have a social security number, mail this form to the appropriate office. Otherwise, save the completed form in your folder.

School Days

Writing Letters to Schools

Objective

To know how to write a letter of inquiry to a school

Presenting the Lesson

1. Read aloud and discuss **Here's the Idea.** Point out that ideally a letter to a school should be typed.

2. Read and discuss **Check It Out.** Ask students if the letter follows the four guidelines on the preceding page. Ask the class whether the letter uses the block or the modified block form.

3. Assign **Try Your Skill.** When students have completed the assignment, have six students go to the chalkboard and each write one main part of their letter. Have the class discuss any necessary revisions, especially to the body of the letter.

4. Read **Keep This in Mind.**

5. Assign **Now Write.** Tell students to find names and addresses of schools in such reference books as *Lovejoy's Career and Vocational School Guide* and *Barron's Profiles of American Colleges.*

Individualizing the Lesson

Less-Advanced Students

Read aloud and discuss the sample letter on page 345. Point out that the letter is brief, polite, and includes important information. Have students point out each item of information the student gives about herself and each item she requests from the college.

Here's the Idea You may be considering going to a vocational school or college. When you write to schools or colleges, write a business letter. Address the letter to the Admissions Office. Keep the letter brief, but include the following specific information.

1. Include information about yourself, the name of your school, your grade level, and the date of your graduation.

2. Include information about your planned major field or area of interest, if you have one.

3. Include a request for information about the school's entrance requirements, tuition costs, courses offered, scholarships, financial aid, and anything else you may want to know.

4. Include a request for a catalog.

Check It Out Read the letter on page 345.

- What specific information does this business letter include?
- What specific information does it request?

Try Your Skill You're a high school junior, interested in acting and performing. You are considering applying to State College, 687 Center Street, Billings, Montana 49101. You want to know if they offer a degree in theater and what the course requirements are. Write to the college. Ask for their catalog and any other information you need.

Keep This in Mind

- When you write to vocational schools and colleges, use correct business letter form. Include specific information about yourself and request specific information from the school.

Now Write Write a letter to a vocational school or college that you might be interested in attending. Use either of the forms for business letters. Request a catalog. If you have a field of interest, mention it. Ask for information about the aspects of the program that interest you.

Proofread the letter carefully. Label it **School Days,** and put it into your folder. If you wish, make a copy of your letter and mail it.

```
Old Shirley Road
Anchorage, Kentucky  40223
April 8, 1985

Admissions Office
Jefferson Junior College of Business
1000 Omaha Avenue
Louisville, Kentucky  40212

Dear Sir or Madam:

I am currently a junior at O'Brien High School in Anchorage.
I am interested in enrolling in Jefferson Junior College of
Business in the fall of 1986, after my graduation.

I plan to major in business administration. Please send me
all the information on the requirements for such a degree, as
well as entrance requirements, and tuition costs.

I would also appreciate receiving a copy of your catalog.


Sincerely,

Kate Sherman
Kate Sherman
```

Advanced Students

Discuss the fact that students who are interested in attending college should gather information about a variety of colleges throughout their high school years. Have students find the names and addresses of five colleges that interest them in one of the reference books listed in **Presenting the Lesson** or another reference book at the library.

Optional Practice

Discuss obtaining loan and scholarship information. Advise students who are interested in financial aid to write an additional letter, to the Office of Financial Aid of the school or college they write to in **Now Write.** Have students make sure they include in the letter the year they plan to enter the school or college.

Extending the Lesson

Have students mail their letters for **Now Write** and bring in the school and college catalogs they receive to share with their classmates.

345

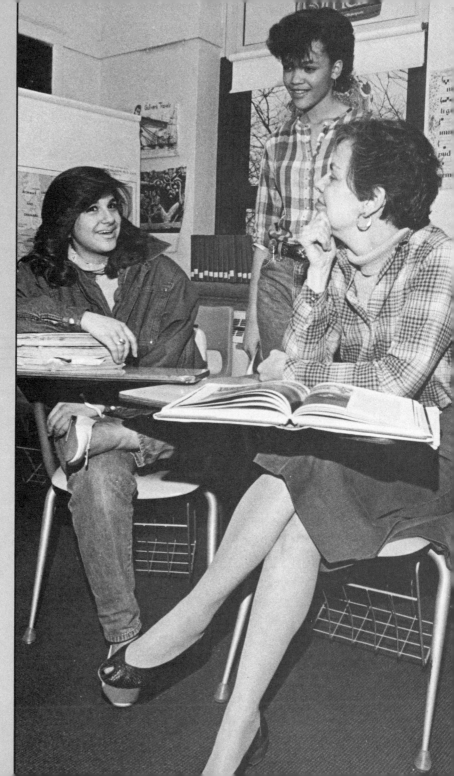

Section **26** Objectives

1. To know the difference between an informal talk and a formal speech

2. To prepare an informal talk

3. To narrow a topic and determine the purpose and audience for a formal speech

4. To gather and organize information for a formal speech

5. To write a formal speech

6. To know how to present oneself when speaking before an audience

7. To practice the presentation of a speech

8. To listen to and judge talks considerately

Preparing the Students

Ask students if they have ever seen tapes of speeches by the following figures on television: John Kennedy, Martin Luther King, Jr., Jimmy Carter, Walter Mondale, Geraldine Ferrarro, Jesse Jackson, or Ronald Reagan. Have students discuss their impressions of any of the speakers they have seen. Point out the important part public speaking played in the careers of these people. Then explain that even though students may never be in the public limelight, there will be times when they must speak to a group of people. This Section will tell them how to write and present both formal and informal speeches.

Additional Resources

Mastery Test — page 37 in the test booklet

Practice Book — pages 138–145

Duplicating Masters — pages 138–145

Speaking and Listening

Teaching Special Populations

LD Tailor this Section to your students' abilities. Those with emotional problems, speech problems, or behavioral problems should not be expected to participate in the exercises. Some students may be better able to present speeches to a tape recorder than to a live audience.

ESL Stress good listening skills as your classes listen to ESL students' speeches. Discuss differences in body language from culture to culture. Explain that certain gestures are considered rude in some cultures, for example, direct eye contact.

Drill ESL students by having them memorize and deliver a short passage from a work of literature or a magazine article.

Suggest that students talk about an interesting topic with which they are comfortable. Remind them that it is the topic that should command attention, not the speaker.

Help students work on the syntax, vocabulary, and organization of their talks.

NSD Remind students to practice their speeches in standard English. Help them individually with their pronunciation, and ask them to avoid the use of contractions.

Encourage each student to speak in class or read aloud daily.

Speak Your Mind

Formal and Informal Speaking

Objective

To know the difference between an informal talk and a formal speech

Presenting the Lesson

1. Read **Here's the Idea,** writing *informal talk* and *formal speech* on the chalkboard as you define and discuss them. Discuss the fact that students will often have to give talks, especially informal ones, throughout high school and as an adult. Point out that practice and experience will help students overcome stage fright. Have the class study the chart, "Informal Talks." Then discuss it, asking students for additional examples of each kind of talk.

2. Have volunteers read aloud the examples in **Check It Out.** Discuss the study questions, having students identify the kinds of informal talks.

3. Discuss **Try Your Skill** in class. Have volunteers read aloud each situation and tell whether it requires a formal speech or an informal talk.

4. Read **Keep This in Mind.**

5. Assign **Now Write.** Remind students that this is an informal talk, and their language can be conversational.

Individualizing the Lesson

Less-Advanced Students

Give students practice in delivering informal talks by having them present the introductions they wrote for **Now Write.** You may want to divide the class into small groups and have the students take turns introducing themselves to their groups.

Here's the Idea Talking is a natural activity, like eating or sleeping. It is something you do every day, often without a second's thought. However, talking in front of an audience is another matter. When asked to give a talk, you may suddenly feel nervous. You may find it hard to organize your ideas.

One way to get over nervousness is to be prepared. If you prepare well before a talk, you will feel more confident. The kind of preparation you do depends on the type of talk you will give.

There are two major types of talks, formal and informal. An **informal talk** is a short presentation of specific information. It requires little preparation. It can usually be delivered in two minutes or less. Here are some common types of informal talks:

Informal Talks

Type of Talk	Purpose	Examples
1. Announcements	to tell about some past or future event	telling when and where your team's next football game will be
2. Demonstrations	to show how something is done	showing how to operate a camera
3. Directions	to tell people how to do something or how to get somewhere	explaining how to get to a nearby school
4. Introductions	to present people to audiences	presenting a visiting speaker at school

A **formal speech** is usually longer than an informal talk. A formal speech presents a subject in detail. It requires more preparation. An oral report on health care in Brazil would be a formal speech.

Check It Out   Read the following talks.

1. LuAnne stood up and said, "All members of the varsity swimming team please come to Room 254 after school. Coach Allen will assign practice times and distribute this season's schedule."

2. "The class picnic will be held in Burnam Woods," said Lee. "Take the number 21 bus to the River depot. Transfer to the number 12 bus going east. It will take you to the edge of the woods."

- Are these informal or formal talks? How do you know?

Try Your Skill   Which of these situations require formal speeches? Which require informal talks?

F 1. Mr. Lorne gave a presentation about job opportunities.
F 2. Steve gave an oral report about exploring caves in Georgia.
I 3. Rosa told the new students how to get to the library.

Keep This in Mind

- There are two types of talks, formal and informal.
- An informal talk is short. It requires little preparation. It is used to present information quickly.
- A formal speech presents a subject in detail. It is longer than an informal talk and requires more preparation.

Now Write   Imagine that you are working as a counselor at a summer camp. On the first day, the camp director asks all the counselors to introduce themselves to the campers. Write a brief introduction. Tell your age, hobbies, activities at school, and anything else you think is interesting about yourself. Label your paper **Speak Your Mind.** Save it in your folder.

Advanced Students

Add the following situations to **Try Your Skill.**

1. Betsy told her homeroom when yearbooks would be available and where they should be picked up. I
2. Elliott showed the other art students how to use oil paints on canvas. I
3. Joe spoke to the service club about volunteer opportunities in the community. F

Optional Practice

Give students five minutes to make notes on directions from the school to their homes. Then divide students into groups of four or five and have each student give an informal talk explaining his or her directions.

Extending the Lesson

Give students a week to look for and report on an example of an informal talk and of a formal speech. They may find their examples in school, in extracurricular activities, or on television. Have them write a paragraph describing each talk.

Objective

To prepare an informal talk

Presenting the Lesson

1. Have students read **Here's the Idea.** Write the four types of informal talks on the chalkboard. Discuss each type, mentioning the necessary information for each and the best way to organize it. Ask students to describe any talks of each type that they have given.

2. Have volunteers read the informal talks in **Check It Out.** Discuss the study questions, having students review the information in **Here's the Idea** to make sure the sample talks are thorough.

3. Assign **Try Your Skill.** Remind students that an announcement should be brief and to the point.

4. Read **Keep This in Mind.**

5. Assign **Now Write.** Instruct students to write down any props necessary to the demonstration. Have them exchange papers to check the organization and thoroughness of the steps.

Individualizing the Lesson

Less-Advanced Students

Suggest the following activities as topics for a demonstration for **Now Write:**

loading a camera
pitching a baseball
serving a tennis ball
sewing a button on a garment
performing a dance step

Get the Facts

Preparing an Informal Talk

Here's the Idea   Every informal talk presents a group of related facts. To prepare such a talk, you must decide what facts you need to present. Then, you must gather these facts and put them in a sensible order. The facts you need to include in your talk will depend on the kind of talk you are planning.

1. **Announcements** should answer the questions *who? what? when? where?* and *why?* When making an announcement, keep it short and simple. Do not include unnecessary details.

2. **Demonstrations** should break down the activity to be demonstrated into separate steps. Each step should be performed for the audience and explained as it is performed. Suppose you wanted to demonstrate *origami*, the Japanese art of making paper sculptures. To do this, you would actually make such a sculpture. You would explain each step as you created the sculpture. If you wish to use any objects or props in a demonstration, practice with these beforehand. During the talk, keep your props close at hand. Make sure the audience can see them.

3. **Directions** should include all necessary or helpful details. Arrange your details in step-by-step order. Don't leave out any steps. If steps are left out or presented in the wrong order, the listener may become confused.

4. **Introductions** should give information about the person being introduced. This information should make your audience interested in the person. To gather information for an introduction, you may have to interview your subject. Be sure that your completed introduction is both enthusiastic and polite.

Check It Out   Read the following informal talks.

1. The Russell County Civic Club is sponsoring a soapbox derby to be held at the Andretti Speedway on July 16. The entry fee will be $25.00. Proceeds will be used to build wheelchair ramps for the Columbia Community Center. Interested students should contact Mr. Margolis before April 15.

2. To get to the planetarium, go east on Arlington Avenue to Ridge Road. Turn left onto Ridge and continue north for two blocks. The planetarium is on the southeast corner of the intersection of Ridge and Vine.

- What type of informal talk is each of these examples?
- Does each of these informal talks include all of the necessary information? Explain your answer.

Try Your Skill   Choose an upcoming event at your school. Write an announcement telling about this event. Be sure your announcement answers the questions *who? what? when? where?* and *why?*

Keep This in Mind

- Before you give an informal talk, decide what facts you need to present.
- Gather these facts and put them in a sensible order.
- Do not leave out any necessary information.

Now Write   Choose a simple activity that you know how to do well. Write a demonstration to show others how to perform this activity. Make two columns on a piece of paper. In one column, write what you will *say* during each step of your demonstration. In the other column, write what you will *do* during each step. Make sure to include all the necessary steps. Arrange them in the order in which they are to be performed. Label your paper **Get the Facts.** Save it in your folder.

Objective

To narrow a topic and determine the purpose and audience for a formal speech

Presenting the Lesson

1. Read aloud **Here's the Idea.** Have the class study the chart, "Preparing the Talk." Ask students if there are any differences between preparing a speech and preparing a composition in the pre-writing stage. Emphasize awareness of purpose and audience.

2. Have volunteers read aloud the descriptions in **Check It Out.** Help students see why the speech in example 1 is inappropriate; ask the class to think of a better speech reflecting Ramon's interest to present to his English class.

3. Assign **Try Your Skill.** Encourage students to choose topics that they know something about or are particularly interested in.

4. Read **Keep This in Mind.**

5. Assign **Now Write.** Students may find that their chosen topic may not interest their classmates; if so, they should change their topic or narrow the general one they have chosen.

Individualizing the Lesson

Less-Advanced Students

Have students identify the purpose (to inform, to persuade, or to entertain) of each of the following speeches:

1. an after-dinner speech entitled "Confessions of an Old Movie Addict" entertain

Form-Fitting

Preparing a Formal Speech

Here's the Idea You have probably heard many formal speeches both in and out of school. A book report presented orally in class is a formal speech. So is a sermon, a campaign speech, or a keynote address made at an awards banquet.

Formal speeches cover specific subjects in depth. Therefore, they are longer than informal talks. They also require more preparation. When preparing a formal speech, follow the same pre-writing steps that you follow when writing a composition.

Preparing a Talk

1. Choose your topic. If you are allowed to choose your own topic, make it one that will interest both you and your audience. Choose a topic that is fresh or unusual. Be sure to choose a topic that you know something about.

2. Narrow your topic. Limit your topic so that it fits the available time. If you have only ten minutes for your talk, you cannot discuss the entire Civil War. You might, however, be able to talk about one battle.

3. Determine your purpose. Decide whether you wish to inform, to persuade, or to entertain. This will help you decide what kinds of ideas to include and to stress in your talk.

4. Identify your audience. Ask yourself the following questions. How old are my audience members? What are their interests and backgrounds? How much do they already know about my subject? Avoid subjects that your audience will not understand or will not find interesting.

Check It Out   Read these descriptions of formal speeches.

1. Ramon is really interested in auto mechanics. He gave a speech in his English class. He chose the following topic: "A Comparison of Fuel Injection Systems on Foreign and Domestic Cars."

2. Marsha is president of the Spanish Club. She gave a speech to a group of foreign exchange students. They had just arrived in the United States from South America. She chose the topic "Why Governments Should Sponsor Student-Exchange Programs."

• What is the purpose of each talk?
• Which talk is appropriate to its audience? Which one is probably not? Why?

Try Your Skill   Here are some topics for formal speeches:

1. ancient Egypt   4. dinosaurs
2. horror films   5. advertisements
3. musical instruments 6. Africa

Choose four topics from this list. Narrow each one so that it is suitable for a five-minute speech. You may want to refer to an encyclopedia. Write each narrowed topic. Then, tell whether the topic is for a speech that informs, persuades, or entertains.

> ## Keep This in Mind
>
> • Choose an interesting topic and narrow it.
> • Determine your purpose. The purpose may be to inform, to persuade, or to entertain.
> • Make sure that your speech suits your audience.

Now Write   Choose one of the topics you narrowed in **Try Your Skill.** Write it on a piece of paper. Under this topic, write the purpose of your speech. Then write the average age of the people in your class. Write why you think these people will be interested in your topic. Label your paper **Form-Fitting.** Save it.

353

2. a speech to the political science club called "Why Students Should Keep Informed" persuade
3. a speech to the drama club called "The Plays on Broadway This Season" inform

Advanced Students

For **Now Write,** have students write a narrowed topic for each of the three purposes discussed in this lesson. For example, "horror films" might be narrowed to "Why I Will Never See Another Horror Movie" to entertain; "The Many Film Versions of *Frankenstein*" to inform; and "Young Children Should Not See Horror Films" to persuade.

Optional Practice

Have students choose and narrow a speech topic for each of the following formal speech situations:

1. an informative speech to a group of 12-year-old Girl Scouts
2. an entertaining speech for the school sports awards banquet
3. an informative speech to a group of parents of high-school students

Extending the Lesson

Have students listen to one of the following types of formal speeches and then write a paragraph discussing the speech's topic, purpose, and audience.

1. sermon
2. presidential address
3. class lecture
4. campaign speech
5. informative or entertaining speech for a school club

(See **Extending the Lesson,** Parts 4 and 6, for additional work with this exercise.)

Part 4

Objective

To gather and organize information for a formal speech

Presenting the Lesson

1. Read and discuss **Here's the Idea.** Have students review Section 20, **Writing a Report,** and Section 22, **Using the Library,** before gathering and organizing the information for their speeches.

2. Have a student read the situation in **Check It Out.** Write on the board the class's suggestion for a main idea and have students revise it until it is satisfactory. Have students refer to the list of sources in **Here's the Idea** to decide where to find information on the topic.

3. Assign **Try Your Skill.** After students have completed the assignment, discuss whether chronological order, order of importance, or spatial order is most appropriate for the notes.

4. Read **Keep This in Mind** and then assign **Now Write.**

Individualizing the Lesson

Less-Advanced Students

Work with students individually as much as possible in stating a main idea and organizing their information. Help students write a statement of their main idea that indicates the purpose and topic of their speech as specifically as possible.

Advanced Students

Have students keep the time constraints of a speech in mind as they research their topic. Remind them

Back to the Source

Gathering and Organizing Information

Here's the Idea To write a formal speech, you must narrow your topic, decide on your purpose, and identify your audience. Then you should write a sentence that states the main idea of your speech. Use this sentence as a guide when you gather information for your speech.

Here are some sources that you can use when gathering information.

Sources of Information

personal experience	encyclopedias	atlases
interviews	books	newspapers
magazines	dictionaries	pamphlets

Always gather information from more than one source. Take notes on information about your main idea. Write this information on note cards. Write one piece of information on each card.

Once you have enough information, organize your note cards. Divide them into groups of related ideas. If a note is not related to your main idea, leave it out. Place your groups of note cards in the order that you will talk about them. You can use chronological order, order of importance, or spatial order.

Look for gaps in the information you have gathered. If necessary, do more research to fill in these gaps.

Check It Out In February, Sarah prepared a talk for her social studies class. Because February was Black History Month, she decided to give a talk about Hiram Rhodes Revels. Mr. Revels was a minister, a soldier, and the president of a university. He was also the first black senator in the United States.

- How could Sarah state her main idea?
- What sources could she check for information?

Try Your Skill   Read the following notes for a speech on the life and work of Hiram Rhodes Revels. Organize these notes in a logical way. Leave out any that are not related to the main idea.

1 Mr. Revels was born in Fayetteville, North Carolina, in 1827.

8 After he served in the United States Senate, Mr. Revels was named president of Alcorn University.

5 Mr. Revels was the first black member of the United States Senate.

4 During the Civil War (1861–1865), Mr. Revels recruited soldiers for the Union Army.

6 Mr. Revels served in the United States Senate from 1870 to 1871.

2 Mr. Revels became a minister of the African Methodist Episcopal Church in 1845.

~~The Civil War was long and bloody.~~

3 Between 1845 and 1861, Mr. Revels helped to start black churches and schools in the Midwest and South.

7 While in the Senate, Mr. Revels campaigned for civil rights.

Keep This in Mind

- State the main idea of your talk in a single sentence.
- Gather information about your main idea.
- Possible sources of information include written materials, personal experience, and other people.
- Write information on note cards. Arrange these cards in a logical order.

Now Write   Write a sentence that states the main idea of the topic you chose in **Form-Fitting.** Do some research for a speech on this topic. Take notes for your speech. Put these notes in a logical order. Save your notes in your folder.

355

Objective

To write a formal speech

Presenting the Lesson

1. Read **Here's the Idea.** Emphasize the importance of getting the audience's interest in the introductory part of the speech and of clearly summarizing the main points in the conclusion.

2. Ask a student to read the conclusion in **Check It Out.** Discuss the study questions, pointing out how clearly and concisely the speech's main ideas are summarized.

3. Assign **Try Your Skill,** first discussing the kinds of introductions these sentences call for. Remind students that the main idea should be in the last sentence of the introduction.

4. Read **Keep This in Mind.**

5. Assign **Now Write.** Have students review Section 14, Part 5, "Revising Your Composition," before they revise their speeches.

Individualizing the Lesson

Less-Advanced Students

Helps students individually as they write their speeches. Make sure they have a clear idea of their audience and purpose and that they have gathered enough information. After students have written their introductions, have them exchange papers and comment on how well their classmates have captured the audience's interest.

All Together Now

Writing a Formal Speech

Here's the Idea   Once you have organized your note cards, you are ready to write your speech. The speech should have three parts: an introduction, a body, and a conclusion.

The **introduction** prepares your audience. Do this in one of the following ways:

State an interesting fact.
Ask an interesting question.
Make an interesting comparison.
Tell an interesting story.
Show an interesting object.

End your introduction with a single sentence that states the main idea of your talk.

The **body** supports or develops your main idea. Include in the body the information from your note cards. Make sure that all of this information is related to your main idea. Also, be sure the information is presented in a logical order.

The **conclusion** wraps up your talk. If the purpose of your talk is to entertain, end on a note of amusement or interest. If your talk is to inform or persuade, end it in one of these ways:

1. Repeat the main idea in different words. Then, summarize the major points made in the body of the talk.

2. Draw a lesson or moral from the ideas presented in the body of the talk.

Check It Out   Read the following conclusion to a talk.

So you can see that there are three good reasons for not using robot workers in factories. First, robots take jobs away from human workers. Second, only human workers can recognize unexpected problems and correct them. Third, robots cost a great deal of money. These are, I believe, excellent reasons for relying on people instead of machines.

- What sentence restates the main idea?
- What major points are summarized in this conclusion?

Try Your Skill The following sentences each state the main idea of a talk. Using these sentences, write two introductions for talks.

1. However, the most far-fetched stories of all are the ones on the evening news.
2. As you can see, motorcycles can be extremely dangerous unless proper safety rules are observed.

Keep This in Mind

- The introduction of a speech should capture the attention of your audience. It should also state your main idea.
- The body should develop your main idea. It should present information taken from your note cards.
- The conclusion may restate your main idea and summarize major points. It may state a lesson or moral. It may also be a high point of entertainment.

Now Write Using the notes you gathered in Part 4, write a formal speech. Include an introduction, a body, and a conclusion. Then, revise your first draft. Label your first and final drafts **All Together Now.** Save them in your folder.

Advanced Students

Have students add examples, questions, facts, or stories to the following introduction to an informative talk to make it more interesting. Answers will vary.
I want to tell you about how I've traveled around the world just by reading books. Books can be the ship that carries you to different lands, to meet all kinds of people, to enjoy a variety of experiences.

Optional Practice

Have students exchange the first drafts of their speeches and suggest improvements based on the following questions:

1. Does the introduction capture the audience's attention? Is the main idea stated in the last sentence of the introduction?
2. Is the body organized logically? Does it include transitions to help the audience move from one idea to the next?
3. Does the body include specific details and examples to hold the audience's interest?
4. Does the conclusion clearly summarize the speech's main points if the speech is informative or persuasive? Does the speech have a "big finish" if it is entertaining?

Extending the Lesson

Have students write alternate introductions for their speeches, using a second method listed on page 356. They can then decide which introduction best attracts the audience's interest.

Part 6

Objective

To know how to present oneself when speaking before an audience

Presenting the Lesson

1. Read **Here's the Idea.** Outline the guidelines for making a good impression when giving a speech, pointing out that each element plays an important part in the speaker's total impression.

2. Have volunteers read each set of sentences in **Check It Out.** Make sure the readers follow the punctuation clues to read each sentence in the set differently. Have the class answer the study questions, discussing how the vocal differences in the readings signaled differences in meaning.

3. Have students divide into small groups to practice reading aloud the sentences in **Try Your Skill.** Then ask volunteers to read the sentences for the class. Emphasize clear enunciation.

4. Read **Keep This in Mind.**

5. Assign **Now Write.** Suggest that students read their speeches aloud to themselves to determine what gestures, facial expressions, and vocal expressions will add emphasis to their speeches in a natural way.

Individualizing the Lesson

Less-Advanced Students

Invite a speech or drama instructor to class to demonstrate the importance of gestures, voice, and facial expressions in delivering a speech.

Public Appearances

Presenting Yourself to an Audience

Here's the Idea   Politicians have to be very careful about how they look, act, and speak in public. They must appear relaxed and confident. They must choose clothes, gestures, and facial expressions that will impress voters. They must speak clearly and make sure they are heard. These same matters are important whenever you give a talk. To make a good impression, you must plan how you are going to present yourself. The following guidelines will help you:

1. Appearance. Wear clothes that suit the occasion. Try to appear relaxed and confident. Stand up straight, but do not stand rigidly.

2. Eye Contact. To keep the attention of your audience, look directly at audience members. If you find this hard to do, look just above the heads of audience members. Do not read to your audience. Do not stare at any one thing, including your props or notes.

3. Voice. Speak so that everyone can hear you. Make sure that your voice is neither too loud nor too quiet. Pronounce your words clearly. Do not rush or speak too slowly. Do not speak in a monotone. Make sure your tone of voice fits what you are saying. Vary your volume, pitch, and pace. Pause for emphasis, especially before important points.

4. Gestures and Facial Expressions. Use natural gestures and facial expressions. These will help you to appear more relaxed and confident. They will also help to show how you feel about what you are saying. For example, if you are talking about something amusing, you can look amused. If you are making an important point, you can stress its importance with a gesture of your hand.

Check It Out   Read aloud the following pairs of statements.

1. Who? Are you kidding?
   Who are you kidding?

2. He didn't say. I'm going home.
   He didn't say "I'm going home!"

3. Let everyone in. Accept that fellow!
   Let everyone in except that fellow!

- Do pauses change the meaning of these statements?
- What other differences do you notice between these pairs of statements?

Try Your Skill   Read the following sentences aloud. Practice pronouncing each word clearly.

1. Sperry speaks especially well.
2. The guest started to taste the stew.
3. He wouldn't do it, would he?
4. Susan sings these three things.
5. "He fumbled it," Martin mumbled.

Keep This in Mind

- Look and sound your best whenever you speak.
- Stand up straight and look at your audience. Speak loudly enough to be heard. Vary your volume, pitch, and pace. Pause at appropriate places.
- Communicate your feelings through natural gestures and facial expressions.

Now Write   Study the talk you wrote for Part 5. In the margins, make notes about gestures and facial expressions you can use. Also note what tone of voice you should use at the beginning of the talk. If there are points in the talk where your tone should change, note these, too. Mark any point in the talk where you want to pause for emphasis. Save your paper.

359

Objective

To practice the presentation of a speech

Presenting the Lesson

1. Have students read **Here's the Idea.** Discuss the use of notes when speaking. Tell students to write their notes on 3 x 5 index cards and to hold them steadily and inconspicuously. Discuss memorization and practice techniques, emphasizing that ample practice is the best cure for stage fright.

2. Read the situation in **Check It Out.** Discuss the study questions, helping students recognize that practicing gestures and facial expressions in front of a mirror and listening to himself on a tape could also be effective techniques for David.

3. Assign **Try Your Skill.** Students may work in pairs and take turns practicing the talks.

4. Read **Keep This in Mind.**

5. Assign **Now Write.** Pair off students to practice their talks after they have practiced at home by themselves.

Individualizing the Lesson

Less-Advanced Students

Give students these suggestions for conquering stage fright.

1. Practice as much and in as many different ways as possible: by yourself, in front of a mirror, into a tape recorder, and for friends and relatives.

2. Take a deep breath and relax as you prepare to deliver your speech.

Getting It Right

Practicing a Talk

Here's the Idea Practice is as important to giving a talk as it is to presenting a play. As you practice, you improve your delivery until you feel good about it. In this way, you become confident about what you are going to say.

Before you begin to practice, you must decide how much of the talk you wish to memorize. Some people choose to memorize the entire talk. Other people prefer to memorize just the introduction and the conclusion. They can then refer to notes or to an outline for the body of the talk. If you do choose to use notes or an outline, practice with these. While speaking, try not to look at your notes or outline too often.

The following guidelines can be used when memorizing all or part of a talk.

1. Read one line.
2. Recite the line several times without looking at it.
3. Read the next line.
4. Recite both lines without looking.
5. Go through all the material in this manner. When you miss a line, start all over again.

Practice the talk by saying it aloud several times. If a tape recorder is available, record your talk. Play back the tape to check your voice. It is also a good idea to practice before a mirror. In this way you can check your posture, facial expressions, and gestures. When practicing, follow the guidelines for giving a talk explained in Part 6, **Public Appearances.** Ask friends or relatives to listen to your talk. They may be able to suggest possible improvements.

Check It Out   David is captain of the football team. He was asked to give a talk at the school awards assembly. He wrote a talk called "How Not To Win a State Championship." He memorized the introduction and conclusion of this talk. He made an outline of the body. He gave his talk to a friend several times.

- What did David do right when preparing his talk?
- What else could David have done?

Try Your Skill   Practice giving one of the sample talks included in Part 2, **Get the Facts.** As you practice, make a list of problems that you notice in your delivery. Also list any improvements that you make, including any gestures or facial expressions that you add.

> ## Keep This in Mind
>
> - You may memorize the entire talk. You may also memorize just the introduction and conclusion. You can then refer to notes or to an outline for the body of your talk.
> - Practice your talk aloud several times. Use a mirror as you practice. Also, use a tape recorder if possible.
> - When you practice, follow the guidelines for good speaking given in Part 6, **Public Appearances.**
> - Ask a friend or relative to listen to your talk. Ask for suggestions for improvement.

Now Write   Practice the talk you wrote in Part 5, **All Together Now.** Memorize the introduction and conclusion. Use note cards or an outline for the body. Practice your talk by yourself. Then, practice it in front of a relative or friend. List any improvements you make on a sheet of paper. Label the paper **Getting It Right.** Save it in your folder. If your teacher tells you to do so, give your talk to your class.

361

3. Be confident, or pretend that you feel confident. Remember that you have a friendly audience and that you are as good a speaker as your classmates are.

Advanced Students

Bring a tape recorder or video recorder to class and record two versions of each student's speech: a practice version and a final one. Ask students to evaluate their own performances, especially checking for improvements made in practice.

Optional Practice

Have students give their talks to the class.

Extending the Lesson

Encourage students to continue using their public speaking skills by volunteering to speak on a special interest to a class or club, or by signing up for a speech or drama class.

Objective

To listen to and judge talks considerately

Presenting the Lesson

1. Read **Here's the Idea.** List on the board the headings of the guidelines for judging talks. Point out that students should be the kind of audience for other speakers that they would like to have when they speak. In discussing the guidelines for judging talks, have students remember the points they learned when preparing their own speeches. Emphasize a polite and constructive attitude in judging other people's talks.

2. Read the situation in **Check It Out** and have the class discuss the study questions.

3. Assign **Try Your Skill.** Tell students to be specific in their critiques.

4. Read **Keep This in Mind.**

5. Assign **Now Write.** You may divide students into pairs and have them judge one another's talk. Each student can write an evaluation immediately after his or her partner speaks; the pairs can meet after all the students have presented their talks to discuss their evaluations.

Individualizing the Lesson

Less-Advanced Students

Discuss the best way to offer constructive criticism. For example, have students suppose that Ed's speech included many interesting facts about the Egyptian pyramids,

The Critics Rave

Listening to and Judging Talks

Here's the Idea   Knowing how to listen to a talk is as important as knowing how to give a talk. The following guidelines will help you to become a good listener.

1. Sit where you can hear the speaker clearly.
2. Give the speaker your full attention.
3. Do not make distracting noises or movements.
4. Let your eyes and your expression show interest.
5. Think about what you are hearing. Listen for main ideas and supporting details. You may wish to take notes.
6. Do not judge the speaker's ideas before you hear how they are supported. Be open-minded.

If your teacher asks you to judge another student's talk, be polite. Refer to the following guidelines for judging talks.

CONTENT

Topic:	Was the main point of the talk clear?
Purpose:	Was the purpose of the talk clear? Did the speaker accomplish this purpose?
Audience:	Did the talk suit its audience?
Development:	Did the speaker present enough information? Was any of it unnecessary?
Introduction:	Did the introduction capture your interest? Did it state the main idea?
Body:	Did the body offer details to support the main idea? Were the important points clear?
Organization:	Were the speaker's ideas presented in a logical order?
Conclusion:	Was the conclusion of the talk satisfactory, or did the talk end abruptly?

PRESENTATION

Eye Contact: Did the speaker look at the audience? Did the speaker look at his or her notes too often?

Posture: Did the speaker appear confident and relaxed?

Voice: Was the speaker easy to hear and understand? Did the speaker vary volume and tone of voice?

Gestures: Were the speaker's gestures natural?

Expressions: Were the speaker's facial expressions natural?

Preparation: Was the talk practiced thoroughly?

Check It Out Phillip got up to talk. He waited until the class was quiet. Then, he began to speak. Halfway through Phillip's talk, someone entered the room. Everyone turned to see who had come in.

- How could the audience have been more considerate?

Try Your Skill Copy the main headings of the checklist for judging talks. Then, listen to a speaker on a television news show. Judge the quality of the speaker's performance. Write your comments under the correct headings on your checklist.

Keep This in Mind

- When listening to a talk, show interest. Do not distract the speaker. Think about what you are hearing.
- If you are asked to judge a talk, be polite and specific. Judge the talk, not the speaker.

Now Listen Copy the major headings of the checklist for judging talks. Use this checklist to judge a talk in your class. Compare your comments with those of your classmates. Tell the speaker how his or her talk could be improved. Label your paper **The Critics Rave.** Save it in your folder.

but his delivery was mumbled. Explain that Ed would find positively worded criticism easy to accept. For example, "Your story about how the pyramids were built was really interesting. If you speak more clearly, everyone can enjoy the results of your research."

Advanced Students

Have students suppose that they made the following notes as part of their evaluation of a classmate's speech. Have them discuss how they would orally offer some constructive criticism to the speaker.

Introduction: interesting story, made me curious about how dinosaur fossils were discovered
Audience: archaeological details difficult for audience to follow
Body: many interesting details
Voice: talked too fast

Optional Practice

Have students use the checklist in this lesson to evaluate their own taped or videotaped speech presentation.

Extending the Lesson

Obtain a film or videotape of a speech by one of the political figures listed in the introduction to this Section. Have students evaluate the person's speech using the guidelines in this lesson.

Handbook

A detailed Table of Contents for the Handbook appears in the front of this book.

Section Objectives

1. To distinguish between sentence fragments and complete sentences

2. To identify the four kinds of sentences and to use the proper punctuation for each

3. To identify the subject and the predicate in a sentence

4. To identify the verb and its subject

5. To identify main verbs, helping verbs, and separated parts of a verb

6. To identify subjects in unusual positions

7. To identify direct objects and indirect objects, and to understand their functions in sentences

8. To distinguish between action verbs and linking verbs, and between predicate words and direct objects

9. To recognize compound sentence parts

Preparing the Students

Before reading the introduction, discuss how writing a sentence is like building a building. Stress planning, proper materials, craftsmanship, and the completion of one's work.

Read the introduction on page 367 with the students.

Additional Resources

Diagnostic Test — page 1 in the test booklet

Mastery Test — pages 38–41 in the test booklet

Additional Exercises — pages 392–399 in the student text

Practice Book — pages 149–161

Duplicating Masters — pages 149–161

Special Populations — See special section at the back of this Teacher's Edition.

The Sentence and Its Parts

To build any structure, you need a solid foundation. To build good writing, too, you need a solid foundation. That base is the sentence, made up of several main parts.

In speaking, sometimes just one or two words are enough to express meaning. For example, you might answer a question with "No" or "Later." Your listener can always ask you to explain.

In writing, however, you must use complete sentences. Without well-built sentences, your writing would fall apart. Your reader would not understand your meaning.

In this section, you will study the different parts of sentences. You will also learn how to put these parts together to give your writing a solid base.

Part 1

Objective

To distinguish between sentence fragments and complete sentences

Presenting the Lesson

1. Read the definition of a sentence on page 368. Discuss the concept of a complete thought. Point out that in order to be a complete thought, a group of words must tell both *who* or *what* and *what happened.*

2. Place the following groups of words on the board. Explain that each is a fragment because each expresses only the *who* or *what* element or the *what happened* element, but not both. Have students tell whether each fragment expresses *who* or *what* or *what happened.*

            what happened
Won a bronze medal in the Olympics.
Eleanor and Franklin Roosevelt. who
Is teaching driver-training. what
An after-school job. what

3. Assign and discuss the Exercises on pages 368–369.

Individualizing the Lesson

Less-Advanced Students

Work with students to complete the sentence fragments in the word groups on the board. Then do the Exercises orally with the class.

Advanced Students

Have students complete the sentence fragments from the word groups written on the board. Then assign the Exercises.

The surest way to get your meaning across is to use complete sentences.

A sentence is a group of words that expresses a complete thought. In other words, a sentence tells a whole idea. A sentence does not make the reader ask, "Who or what did something?" or "What happened?"

The following groups of words are sentences.

> Terry plays jazz piano.
> This new car runs on special fuel.
> Where does Samantha work?

If a writer leaves out part of the idea, the result is usually a sentence fragment. **A sentence fragment** is a group of words that does not express a complete thought. For example, these are sentence fragments:

> Plays jazz piano. (Who plays jazz piano?)
> This new car. (What happened to this new car?)

Exercise A Number your paper from 1 to 10. For each group of words that is a sentence, write **S.** For each sentence fragment, write **F.**

S 1. A reporter interviewed the President.

S 2. Where is the counselor's office?

F 3. Forgot her homework.

S 4. Eric entered the contest.

S 5. An airplane was hijacked.

F 6. The sport of basketball.

F 7. Was behind the tall fence.

F 8. The most popular kind of shoes.

S 9. The center recycles newspapers.

S 10. Beth speaks two languages.

Exercise B   Follow the directions for Exercise A.

F   1. Heavy machinery at the site.

F   2. Exploded in the dark sky.

F   3. Crossed the wide lake.

S   4. Chris found a bargain.

S   5. Who will fix that faucet?

F   6. A ten-speed bicycle.

S   7. This jet has three engines.

S   8. Fireworks ended the celebration.

S   9. Has the plane arrived?

S   10. Tara finished the job.

Part 2   Kinds of Sentences

You put words together into sentences for different purposes. Sometimes your purpose is to explain. At other times your purpose is to ask something or to give an order. At still other times, you may want to show strong feeling.

For each of these purposes there is a different kind of sentence.

A **declarative sentence** makes a statement.

> This plant is delicate.   Kara left on the bus.

An **interrogative sentence** asks a question.

> Has Vicky called?   What is the starting lineup?

An **imperative sentence** tells someone to do something.

> Sit in the front row.   Wait for a reply.

An **exclamatory sentence** expresses strong emotions.

> What a game that was!   Don't jump!

369

Less-Advanced Students

Have students find one photo illustrating each kind of sentence, and then have them write a sentence for each photo. Remind them to be sure to use the proper punctuation.

Advanced Students

Divide students into pairs. Have them write a story or carry on a conversation without talking by passing a sheet of paper back and forth between them. Tell them to take turns writing sentences.

Have students use each of the four kinds of sentences. Tell them to identify each type of sentence as it is used. Have students check each other's writing to see that the sentence type agrees with the sentence label, and that proper punctuation is used.

Optional Practice

Have students identify the type of sentence for each of the following and add proper end punctuation.

Int 1. Have you ever gone deep sea fishing?

Imp 2. You must never go near the water.

D 3. The sermon was about charity.

E 4. What fun we had at the beach!

Int 5. What will we eat for lunch?

Imp 6. Watch me on the Channel 5 news tonight.

D 7. My family went camping last weekend.

Int 8. Is that smog or smoke?

Imp 9. Fans, get your scorecards ready.

E 10. Help!

Punctuating Sentences

Each kind of sentence has an end mark. The purpose of a sentence determines the punctuation.

A declarative sentence ends with a period.

An interrogative sentence ends with a question mark.

An imperative sentence ends with a period.

An exclamatory sentence ends with an exclamation mark.

Sometimes a sentence is imperative in one situation but exclamatory in another situation.

> Find the security guard. (*imperative*)
> Find the security guard! (*exclamatory*)

Exercise A Number your paper from 1 to 10. For each of the following sentences, write *Declarative, Interrogative, Imperative,* or *Exclamatory* to show what kind it is. Also write the proper punctuation marks.

D 1. The rear fender is dented.

E 2. Watch out!

Imp 3. Please deposit the exact change.

E 4. How strong you are!

E 5. Wow! We're here at last!

D 6. Carrie found a summer job.

Int 7. Has the pizza been delivered?

Int 8. Do you know shorthand?

Imp 9. Ask the manager.

D 10. Jamie asked for the car.

Exercise B Follow the directions for Exercise A.

Int 1. Who is the best candidate?

D 2. Ms. Allen is a police dispatcher.

Int 3. What is the chef's specialty?

E 4. How lucky you are!

Int 5. Have you traveled in the West?

D 6. I am dieting.

E 7. What a terrific idea that is!

E 8. Don't touch that live wire!

Int 9. Does Molly sing in the choir?

Imp 10. Apply at the main office.

Part 3 Subjects and Predicates

Every sentence is made up of two basic parts: the subject and the predicate. The **subject** tells whom or what the sentence is about. The **predicate** tells what the subject did or what happens.

Subject (Who or What)	Predicate (What the subject did or what happens)
The playful cat	chased the ball of yarn.
A cold rain	fell all through the night.
My brother	laughed at his own mistake.

Each of these sentences expresses a complete thought. Each of them tells something about a person, place, or thing.

An easy way to understand the parts of a sentence is to think of the sentence as telling who did something, or what happened. The subject tells *who* or *what*. The predicate tells *did* or *happened*.

Who or What	Did or Happened
The runner	crossed the finish line.
My parents	left for Chicago.
The bike	needs air in its tires.

The subject of the sentence tells who or what did something or whom or what the sentence is about.

371

Extending the Lesson

Have students write sentences of the type indicated, using the subjects and verbs given.

Answers will vary.

1. declarative — subject—spaghetti
2. interrogative — subject—puppies
3. exclamatory — verb—crashed
4. imperative — verb—stop
5. imperative — verb—listen

Part 3

Objective

To identify the subject and the predicate in a sentence

Presenting the Lesson

1. Review with students the elements necessary to make a complete sentence. Explain that the two elements of a sentence (*who* or *what* and *what happened*) are referred to as the subject and the predicate.

2. Read and discuss pages 371–372.

3. Write *subject* and *predicate* on the chalkboard to head two columns. Ask students to define both terms.

4. Read the following sentences aloud. For each sentence, ask students to tell you which part of the sentence tells *who* or *what* did something. Write that part under *subject* on the chalkboard. Ask students to tell you which part tells *what is done* or *what happened*. Write that part under *predicate*.

1. Larry made scrambled eggs.

2. The boxing <u>match</u> <u>lasted</u> eight rounds.
3. <u>I</u> <u>want</u> a stereo for my birthday.
4. <u>Betsy</u> <u>babysits</u> for the Kellers.
5. <u>Barbara Walters</u> <u>interviewed</u> Margaret Thatcher.

5. It is suggested that Exercise A on page 372 be done orally with the class. Assign Exercise B.

Individualizing the Lesson

Less-Advanced Students

Provide students with copies of the day's school announcements or newspaper articles. Have them find subjects and predicates in simple sentences.

Advanced Students

Have students write five new sentences by substituting different subjects in five of the sentences in Exercise A. Have them do the same with predicates in five sentences in Exercise B.

Optional Practice

Write the following groups of words on the board. Students should match an appropriate subject and predicate to make a sensible sentence.

a is helping Anne find a book
b the puppy
c the small private plane
c could seat only four people
d our garage
d needs a new roof
a a librarian
b chewed up my gym shoe

Extending the Lesson

Small groups of students may play this game. Each student writes five complete sentences on a sheet

The predicate of the sentence tells what is done, what happens, or what is.

Exercise A   Head two columns on your paper *Subject* and *Predicate*. Write the proper words from each sentence in the columns.

Example: My sister | fixed her bicycle.

Subject	Predicate
My sister	fixed her bicycle.

1. Heavy white smoke | came out of the chimney.
2. Dracula | is probably the most famous vampire.
3. Beth | walked home with Jenny.
4. My parents | fished from the bridge.
5. Gayle | made spaghetti with meatballs.
6. The Packers | played the Bears on Sunday.
7. I | enjoy science fiction.
8. Rebecca | learned self-defense last summer.
9. The sport of rugby | is very rugged.
10. Rugby | is a British sport similar to our football.

Exercise B   Follow the directions for Exercise A.

1. My friend Tim | built a lamp with scrap wood.
2. Photography | is Elizabeth's main interest.
3. North Dakota | produces barley, wheat, and flaxseed.
4. Kathy | ate all the pizza.
5. The bike-a-thon | raised money for muscular dystrophy.
6. Our homeroom | played intramural hockey yesterday.
7. Tennis | is my favorite sport.
8. Monarch butterflies | migrate every year.
9. Sugar cane | is the chief product of Hawaii.
10. Our 4-H Club | showed black angus cattle at the State Fair.

Part 4 Simple Subjects and Predicates

In every sentence there are a few words that are more important than the rest. These key words make the basic framework of the sentence. Study these examples.

Subject	Predicate
The playful **cat**	**chased** the ball of yarn.
A cold **rain**	**fell** throughout the night.
My **brother**	**laughed** at his own mistake.

The **complete subject** of a sentence is all the words that tell *who* or *what*.

The complete subject of the first sentence is *the playful cat.* The key word is *cat.* It is the **simple subject.** You could simply say *cat chased the ball of yarn.*

The **complete predicate** is all the words that tell what was done or what happened. The complete predicate in the first sentence is *chased the ball of yarn.* The key word is *chased.* Without this word you would not have a sentence. *Chased* is the **simple predicate.**

The key word in the subject of a sentence is called the simple subject.

The key word in the predicate is the simple predicate.

The simple predicate is the **verb.**

Finding the Verb and Its Subject

The verb and its subject are the basic framework of every sentence. All the rest of the sentence is built around it. To find this framework, first find the verb.

A verb shows action or state of being. After you have found the verb, ask *who* or *what* before it. This answer will give you the subject of the verb.

373

of paper, and then rips another sheet of paper into ten strips, or uses ten index cards. On each strip of paper or card, each student writes one subject or one predicate from his or her sentences. All subject cards are collected, shuffled, and placed in one pile. All predicate cards are handled in the same way. The game begins as one student at a time draws one card from the subject pile and one card from the predicate pile. They should make a sentence from this combination. The resulting humorous sentence should be read aloud.

Part 4

Objective

To identify the verb and its subject

Presenting the Lesson

1. Read and discuss pages 373–374. Remind students that until now, they have been dealing with complete subjects and complete predicates. Now they will study the *simple subject* and the *simple predicate,* or *verb.*

2. Write the following sentences on the board. Leave a space between each subject and predicate.

1. The early <u>bird</u>   catches the worm.
2. A wild and crazy <u>guy</u>   told some jokes.
3. A small green <u>book</u>   fell off the shelf.
4. Many working <u>people</u>   take this bus.

5. The school treated my
   nurse   brother.

Ask students to identify the simple subject and simple predicate in each sentence. Underline the subject and verb as they are identified.

3. Do Exercise A, pages 374–375 orally with the class. Begin each item by asking "What is the verb?" Then, ask *who* or *what* before the verb.

4. Assign and discuss Exercise B on page 375.

Individualizing the Lesson

Less-Advanced Students

Have each student copy five sentences from a book or magazine article. Then have them underline the verb and its simple subject in each sentence.

Advanced Students

Have students write five sentences. Then have them exchange their papers with another student. The second student should underline the verb and its simple subject.

Optional Practice

Place the following sentences on a worksheet. In each sentence have students underline the verb twice and the subject once.

1. Our new neighbors moved in yesterday.
2. My sister attended the concert downtown.
3. Craig's family bought a snowblower.
4. The workers planted trees and flowers in the park.
5. Jack took the shortcut through the alley.

My brother's apartment is downtown.
   Verb: is
   What is? apartment
   The subject is *apartment.*

The coat in the closet belongs to me.
   Verb: belongs
   What belongs? coat
   The subject is *coat.*

Diagraming Sentences

A sentence diagram is a drawing of the way the parts of a sentence fit together. It helps you to see how the sentence works.

A diagram highlights the key parts of the sentence, the subject and verb. These key parts appear on the main horizontal line. The subject comes first and then the verb. They are separated by a vertical line that crosses the main line.

Other parts of the sentence have their own specific places. One rule of diagraming is that only words capitalized in the sentence are capitalized in the diagram. No punctuation is used.

Jimmy Connors won.

My Uncle Bob cooked dinner.

Exercise A Label two columns *Verb* and *Subject.* Number your paper from 1 to 10. For each sentence, write the verb and its subject.

1. The bike in the garage has a flat tire.
2. The computer printed our class schedules.
3. A hot-air balloon rocked in the breeze.

4. Oranges <u>arrived</u> from Florida.

5. The lively <u>crowd</u> <u>rose</u> to its feet to greet the team.

6. The tall <u>center</u> <u>sank</u> the final basket.

7. The <u>locker</u> next to the library <u>belongs</u> to Mandy.

8. My <u>sister</u> Laura <u>won</u> an award at the art fair.

9. The <u>woman</u> in the pin-striped suit <u>is</u> my math teacher.

10. The <u>pirate</u> Ann Bonny <u>fought</u> fiercely.

Exercise B   Follow the directions for Exercise A.

1. A tiny <u>spark</u> <u>started</u> the huge forest fire.

2. The slide <u>show</u> <u>explained</u> energy.

3. The <u>corridor</u> outside the cafeteria <u>leads</u> to the music room.

4. A stray <u>cat</u> <u>wandered</u> aimlessly into the garage.

5. The <u>booklet</u> on employment <u>suggests</u> possible jobs.

6. The chestnut-brown <u>horse</u> <u>trotted</u> around the track.

7. A lone <u>sailboat</u> <u>drifted</u> into the harbor.

8. The friendly <u>driver</u> <u>assisted</u> the passenger off the bus.

9. A continuous, heavy <u>snow</u> <u>paralyzed</u> Baltimore.

10. The <u>drought</u> <u>reduced</u> the waterfall to a trickle.

Part 5   The Parts of a Verb

A verb may consist of one word or of several words. It may be made up of a **main verb** and one or more **helping verbs.**

In naming the verb of any sentence, be sure to name all the words that it is made of.

Helping Verbs	+ Main Verb	= Verb
might have	gone	might have gone
will	see	will see
are	driving	are driving
could	go	could go

6. The <u>boat</u> in the harbor <u>needs</u> a new sail.

7. My favorite <u>author</u> just <u>wrote</u> a new mystery.

8. This wooden <u>chair</u> always <u>hurts</u> my back.

Extending the Lesson

Place the following sentences on the blackboard or a worksheet. Have students diagram the subject and verb of each sentence, referring to the models on page 374.

1. A flock of geese flew over the parking lot.

2. Barbara found some old photographs in the attic.

3. Some football players wear elbow pads.

4. Our car gets thirty miles per gallon of gasoline.

5. Curious fish circled the sunken treasure chest.

Part 5

Objective

To identify main verbs, helping verbs, and separated parts of a verb

Presenting the Lesson

1. Remind students that the simple predicate (verb) is the key word in the predicate part of the sentence. Tell students that the verb may consist of one word or of several words.

2. Read page 375 and the top of page 376.

3. Put the following pairs of sentences on the board. Have students identify the verbs in each sentence. Point out that some words may be used either as a main verb or as a helping verb.

1. Kerry <u>was</u> our team captain.
2. Gregg <u>was wearing</u> your jacket.
3. This shampoo <u>has</u> lemon in it.
4. Heavy snow <u>has been falling</u> all day.

4. Read and discuss "Separated Parts of a Verb" on page 376.

5. Assign and discuss Exercises A and B on pages 376–377.

Individualizing the Lesson

Less-Advanced Students

Tell students to first divide the sentences in the Exercises into subjects and predicates, then to look for simple subjects and verbs. Do Exercise A as a class. Then have students complete Exercise B independently. Sentences will vary.

Advanced Students

Have students suggest alternative verbs or helping verbs for each sentence in the Exercises.

Optional Practice

Put the following verbs on the board. Have students write a sentence using each.

has been fixing	wasn't trying
doesn't know	will be
am	hasn't written
am reading	has
could have been eating	couldn't be seen
	was thinking

Extending the Lesson

Have students complete one of the following exercises, depending upon their writing abilities and/or

376

Some verbs may be used both as main verbs and as helping verbs:

Kevin *has* a part in the play.
The government *has banned* some drugs.

Pam *is* our representative.
Cal *is waiting* by the car.

These are the most commonly used helping verbs:

am	are	have	will	may
is	be	do	would	might
was	has	does	can	shall
were	had	did	could	should

Separated Parts of a Verb

Sometimes the parts of a verb are separated from each other by words that are not part of the verb. In each of the following sentences, the verb is in bold print. The words in between are not part of the verb.

I **have** never **been** to Daytona Beach.
We **did** not **see** the accident.
The bus **has** often **been** late.

Some verbs are joined with other words to make contractions. Some examples are *wouldn't*, *you're*, and *haven't*. In naming verbs that appear in contractions, name only the verb itself. The word *not* is an adverb. It is never part of a verb.

Terry **does**'nt **have** a watch. (*Does have* is the verb.)
I've **made** arrangements for the picnic. (*I've* is a contraction for *I have. Have made* is the verb.)
The speed limit **was**n't **enforced.** (*Was enforced* is the verb.)

Exercise A List the <u>verbs</u> in the following sentences.

1. We <u>have</u> not <u>gone</u> to the lake once this summer.
2. The package <u>may have been delivered</u> to the wrong house.

376

3. The planet Venus was <u>passing</u> between the Earth and the sun.
4. I <u>have</u> never <u>been</u> to Martha's Vineyard, an island off the coast of Massachusetts.
5. Cheryl <u>did</u> not <u>see</u> the eclipse.
6. The 747 <u>will arrive</u> at midnight.
7. Tim <u>has mastered</u> that video game.
8. Our class <u>is going</u> on a field trip next week.
9. This report <u>has</u> not <u>been completed</u>.
10. The buses <u>don't</u> often <u>arrive</u> late.

Exercise B Follow the directions for Exercise A.

1. Our play rehearsal <u>wasn't</u> very successful.
2. Raul <u>was</u> carefully <u>walking</u> around the quarry.
3. The ambulance <u>was</u> cautiously <u>approaching</u> every intersection.
4. Jim and I <u>will finish</u> this job later.
5. It <u>hasn't</u> <u>rained</u> for a month.
6. We <u>aren't</u> <u>giving</u> our panel discussion today.
7. I <u>don't</u> really <u>like</u> Barry Manilow or Linda Ronstadt.
8. We <u>haven't</u> <u>planted</u> a flower garden this year.
9. My sister and I <u>made</u> a terrarium, however.
10. The counselors <u>had</u> quickly <u>collected</u> the test booklets.

Part 6 Subjects in Unusual Positions

Usually, you expect to find the subject of a sentence before the verb. Sometimes, though, part or all of the verb comes before the subject.

How can you find the subject when it is in an unusual position? First find the verb. Then ask *who* or *what*. The answer will be the subject.

the accessibility of newspapers and magazines.

1. Students should write a one-page summary of the plot of a favorite TV show or movie. After the page is written neatly, students should use a red pen to underline all verbs. In sentences in which both helping verbs and main verbs appear, the main verb should be circled as well as underlined.

2. Students should clip out a news story or magazine column. Using a red pen, they should underline all verbs. In sentences in which both helping verbs and main verbs appear, the main verb should be circled as well as underlined.

Part 6

Objective

To identify subjects in unusual positions

Presenting the Lesson

1. Read and discuss page 377. Stress that even when the subject does not come before the verb, the subject is located by first finding the verb and then asking *who* or *what* before the verb.

2. Place the following sentence pairs on the board.

No <u>driver</u> is on the bus.
There is no <u>driver</u> on the bus.

The <u>books</u> you need are there.
There are the <u>books</u> you need.

A printed <u>answer</u> isn't there.
There isn't a printed <u>answer.</u>

Have students find the subject in the first sentence in each pair. Point out

378

that the second sentence of each pair has exactly the same meaning. The subject and verb are identical—but have been reversed in order. Have students find the subject in the second sentence of each pair.

3. Read and discuss page 378.

4. Do Exercise A on pages 378–379 orally with the class.

5. Assign and discuss Exercise B on page 379.

6. Read and discuss pages 379–380.

7. Assign and discuss Exercises A and B on page 381.

Individualizing the Lesson

Less-Advanced Students

1. Have each student find at least one published example of a sentence with unusual word order. Then have students identify the verb and its subject in the sentence.

2. Compile a list of the sentences found by the students, then have them identify the verb and its subject in each sentence.

Advanced Students

Have students write one sentence for each type of unusual word order discussed in this part.

Optional Practice

Have students rewrite the following sentences with the subject in a different position. After sentences are rewritten, students should underline the verb twice and the subject once. Answers will vary.

1. A swarm of bees flew through the field.

2. Here are the books for your sister.

3. Slowly came the final tally.

Sentences Beginning with *There*

Sentences beginning with *there* often reverse the order of subject and verb. Sometimes *there* is used to explain the verb. It tells where something is or happens.

> There stood the boy. (*Boy* is the subject; *stood* is the verb.)
> There is our bus. (*Bus* is the subject; *is* is the verb.)

In other sentences, *there* is only an introductory word to help get the sentence started.

> There is no candy in the machine. (*Candy* is the subject; *is* is the verb.)
> There are some mistakes here. (*Mistakes* is the subject; *are* is the verb.)

In diagraming sentences that begin with *there*, you must decide whether *there* tells *where* or whether it is simply an introductory word. When *there* tells *where*, place it on a slanted line below the verb. When *there* is an introductory word, place it on a separate line above the subject.

The director stood there.

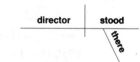

There came a loud bang.

Exercise A Write the subject and the verb in each sentence.

1. There they are.
2. There will be basketball practice tomorrow.
3. There he goes.
4. There stood the trophy.

5. There go the runners.
6. There I sat.
7. There I waited in line for over an hour.
8. There will be a picnic tomorrow.
9. There was a sudden pause.
10. There will be horse races.

Exercise B Follow the directions for Exercise A.

1. There might be a thunderstorm later tonight.
2. There is a rehearsal on Friday.
3. There will be no school on Monday.
4. There is the lock for your bicycle.
5. There are several exits.
6. There goes the runner.
7. There is pie for dessert.
8. There came a chilly wind.
9. There will be an assembly at noon.
10. There are several students in line.

Other Sentences with Unusual Word Order

In most sentences beginning with *there*, the verb comes before the subject. There are other kinds of sentences with unusual word order. Here are some.

1. Sentences beginning with *here*

Here is your hat. (*Hat* is the subject; *is* is the verb.)
Here are the keys. (*Keys* is the subject; *are* is the verb.)

Unlike *there*, the word *here* always tell *where* about the verb.

2. Questions

Are you leaving? (*You* is the subject; *are leaving* is the verb.)
Has the mail come? (*Mail* is the subject; *has come* is the verb.)

4. The army's defeat was here.
5. The deer ran into the forest.
6. There is the theater.

Extending the Lesson

Have students diagram the following sentences. Instruct students to review examples of diagrams on pages 377–380.

1. Does David know about our plans?
2. Put your boots by the door.
3. Around my neck hung the medal.
4. Here are the notes from class.
5. There must be an escape hatch.
6. Answer the phone.

3. Sentences beginning with phrases or other words.

Onto the field dashed the team. (*Team* is the subject; *dashed* is the verb.)

Finally came the signal. (*Signal* is the subject; *came* is the verb.)

To find the subject in a sentence with unusual word order, first find the verb. Then ask *who* or *what*.

Into the pool dived the lifeguard.
Verb: dived
Who or what dived? lifeguard
Subject: lifeguard

Unusual word order does not affect a sentence diagram. To diagram sentences with unusual word order, find the verb and its subject. Place them on the main line.

Did the roof collapse?

roof	Did collapse

Sentences Giving Commands

In sentences that give commands or make requests, the subject is usually not given. Since commands and requests are always given to the person spoken to, the subject is *you*. Since the *you* is not stated directly, it is said to be *understood*.

Bring me the newspaper. (*You* is the subject of *bring*.)
Wipe your feet. (*You* is the subject of *wipe*.)

In the diagram of a command, write the subject *you* in parentheses.

Listen to this song.

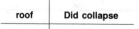

(you)	Listen

Exercise A Label two columns *Subject* and *Verb*. Number your paper from 1 to 10 and write the subject and verb for each sentence.

1. Down the path raced Angela.
2. Down came the rain.
3. Did you read the article about Canada?
4. Economy is one advantage of the bicycle.

(You)5. Hang on!
6. Are there two minutes left?
7. Is our team in the play-offs?
8. There goes the bus.
9. On the porch hung several plants.
10. Have you seen that movie?

Exercise B Follow the directions for Exercise A.

1. Over the phone came the reply.

(You)2. Don't just stand there.
3. Here are the T-shirts for the basketball team.
4. Have you heard the new Pat Benatar album?
5. All along the shoreline swimmers basked in the sun.
6. After the storm people emerged from the building.
7. Are these books due today?
8. Out came the sun.
9. Here comes the mail.
10. Do you enjoy biographies?

Part 7   Objects of Verbs

Some verbs complete the meaning of a sentence without the help of other words. The action that they describe is complete.

The taxi *arrived.*   Snow *has fallen.*
We *are going.*   The lawn mower *broke.*

381

1. Read pages 381–383.

2. Stress that a direct object completes the meaning of the sentence by telling *what* or *whom* after the verb.

3. Place the following sentences on the board. Ask students which are complete and which need objects to complete the action of their verbs.

C 1. The stop sign blew down.

2. Mr. Miller <u>wants</u>.

C 3. Gloria is <u>waiting</u>.

4. The children <u>are bringing</u>.

5. The old Buick <u>needs</u>.

As students identify sentences 2, 4, and 5 as needing objects, guide them to locate the verb and then to ask *what* or *whom*. Ask students for suggestions to complete these sentences.

4. Point out the differrence between direct objects and words which tell *how, where, when,* or *to what extent.*

5. Assign and discuss the Exercise on page 383.

6. Read pages 383–384. Emphasize these points:

1. Indirect objects appear only in sentences with direct objects.

2. The indirect object always appears before the direct object.

3. Indirect objects answer the questions *to whom* or *for whom* or *to what* or *for what* after the verb.

4. Indirect objects are not found after the words *to* or *for.*

7. Place these sentences on the board. Have students make three columns on their papers headed *Verb, Direct Object,* and *Indirect Object.* Have students fill in the col-

Some verbs, however, do not express a complete meaning by themselves. They need other words to complete the meaning of a sentence.

Jim raised _____. (Raised what?)
Sue met _____. (Met whom?)

Direct Objects

The word that completes the action of a verb is called the **direct object** of the verb.

Jim raised *vegetables.*
Sue met *Chris.*

In the sentences above, *vegetables* completes the action of *raised. Chris* completes the action of *met.*

To find the direct object, first find the verb. Then ask *what* or *whom* after it.

Anne painted a picture.
Verb: painted
Painted what? picture
Direct object: picture

Carlos saw the President.
Verb: saw
Saw whom? President
Direct object: President

Many verbs used without objects are followed by words that tell *how, where, when,* or *to what extent.* Do not confuse these words with direct objects. The direct object only tells *what* or *whom.*

These sentences do not have direct objects:

Don worked *quickly. (Quickly* tells *how.)*
Leslie arrived *yesterday. (Yesterday* tells *when.)*

These sentences do have direct objects:

Sue raised the *issue.* (*Issue* tells *what.*)
We found the *manager.* (*Manager* tells *whom.*)

In a diagram, place the direct object on the main line after the verb. A vertical line above the main line separates the verb from the direct object.

Chuck gives guitar lessons.

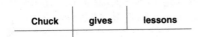

Exercise   Number your paper from 1 to 10. Some of the italicized words are direct objects. Others are not. Write *Direct Object* beside the number of each sentence with a direct object.

1. Please return *soon.*
DO 2. Please return my *camera.*
3. The band plays *well.*
DO 4. The band plays good *music.*
5. Karen wrote the letter *quickly.*
DO 6. Karen wrote a *poem.*
7. Several guests left *early.*
DO 8. Someone left a red *sweater.*
9. Michele tried *again.*
DO 10. Mark called the *operator* again.

Indirect Objects

Some words tell *to whom* or *for whom* something is done. Other words tell *to what* or *for what* something is done. These words are called the **indirect objects** of the verb.

Indirect objects appear only in sentences with direct objects. They are found between the verb and the direct object.

We gave **Mary** some *money.* (We gave *to* Mary.)
Anne knitted **Kim** a *sweater.* (Anne knitted *for* Kim.)

383

umns with the correct words in each sentence. Not every sentence will contain all three parts.

1. Sandy told me her good news.
   V   IO   DO
2. You can deliver the papers tomorrow.
   V   V   DO
3. Paul asked Ms. Riggs a question.
   V   V   IO   DO
4. She answered it quickly.
   V   DO
5. I gave my cat some cheese.
   V   IO   DO

8. Assign and discuss Exercises A, B, and C on pages 384–385.

Individualizing the Lesson

Less-Advanced Students

Have each student find, in a newspaper or magazine, one sentence with an indirect object and one sentence with a direct object. Have them circle the direct object and underline the indirect object. Finally, have them explain what question the indirect or direct object answers.

Advanced Students

Have students write five sentences: two with direct objects, two with indirect objects, and one with neither. Have them exchange papers. They should circle the direct object and underline the indirect object in each sentence. Have them draw a box around the sentence that contains neither.

Optional Practice

Using Exercises A and B on pages 384–385, have students explain which question—*for whom, to whom, for what, to what, what,* or *whom*—each direct or indirect object answers. Have them also indicate which sentences answer none of the questions.

Extending the Lesson

For students who understand the function of objects, assign the following exercise.

Expand the sentences below by making the additions indicated. Write a new sentence for each addition. Answers will vary.

1. Tina Turner sang.
   a. add a direct object
   b. add an indirect object and a direct object
2. Artie is driving.
   a. add a direct object
3. Maria was reading.
   a. add a direct object
   b. add an indirect object and a direct object
4. Julia Child cooked.
   a. add a direct object
5. Janice wrote.
   a. add a direct object
   b. add an indirect object and a direct object

We gave the **boat** a *coat* of paint. (We gave *to* the boat.)
Jeff made his **dog** a *collar*. (Jeff made *for* the dog.)

In the sentences above, the words in bold type are the indirect objects. The words in italics are the direct objects. The words *to* or *for* are never used with the indirect object.

They baked *me* a cake. (*Me* is the indirect object of *baked*.)
They baked a cake for *me*. (*Me* is not the indirect object.)

Jan told Bill the news. (*Bill* is the indirect object of *told*.)
Jan told the news to Bill. (*Bill* is not the indirect object.)

In a diagram, place the indirect object below the verb. Write it on a line that is parallel to the main line.

Russell gave Maggie her cue.

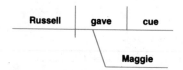

Exercise A   Number your paper from 1 to 10. Label three columns *Verb*, *Indirect Object*, and *Direct Object*. For each sentence below, write those parts. Not all sentences will have all three parts.

Example: Todd drew us a very rough map.

Verb	Indirect Object	Direct Object
drew	us	map

1. I hooked Mom a rug for her birthday.
2. The official gave the co-captains the trophy.
3. Maria made us a Mexican dinner.
4. Paul gave the chili a stir.
5. I brought Cindy a book from the library.
6. We gave our parents a scare.
7. Will you bring me some ice?

8. The sun sparkled on the waves.
   $\overset{v}{}$

9. Nathan must have ironed my shirt.
   $\overset{v}{}\,\overset{v}{}\,\overset{v}{}\,\overset{DO}{}$

10. Pat got a digital watch for Christmas.
    $\overset{v}{}\qquad\overset{DO}{}$

Exercise B Follow the directions for Exercise A.

1. Did you buy me some more film?

2. Liz shouted down the stairs.

3. Steve warned Paula about the tickets.

4. Judy and Donna were whistling an old Beach Boys' song.

5. Uncle Don gave the cactus to me.

6. Our class cleaned the courtyard.

7. Jill lent me her thesaurus.

8. Did you align the wheels?

9. Please get me some stamps.

10. Joy painted the steps to our porch.

Exercise C: Writing Look at the verbs in the following sentences. If the verb has no direct object, write another sentence using the same verb with a direct object. If the verb has a direct object, rewrite the sentence including an indirect object. Answers will vary.

Example: The monkey climbed high.
          (no direct object)
          The monkey climbed the tree.
          Liz made a card.
          (direct object)
          Liz made Dad a card.

1. The choir sang beautifully.

DO 2. Randy made some vegetable <u>soup</u>.

3. I have already packed.

DO 4. Jennifer bought a <u>present</u>.

5. All afternoon, Dennis read.

Objective

To distinguish between action verbs and linking verbs, and between predicate words and direct objects

Presenting the Lesson

1. Remind the class that direct and indirect objects help complete the action of the verb. All of the verbs dealt with in Part 6 were action verbs. Their action was received or complemented by a direct object or by an indirect object and a direct object. Now, inform students that they will learn about different kinds of verbs, called *linking verbs*. Explain that linking verbs do not express action. Rather, they tell of a state of being.

2. Read and discuss pages 386–387. Make certain that students are familiar with all of the forms of *be* on page 386, including those used with helping verbs. Make certain that students are familiar with all of the other common linking verbs on page 387.

3. Stress that the "link" in linking verbs is between the subject and the predicate word. Point out that the predicate word tells something about the subject. Assign the Exercise on page 387.

4. Place the following sentences on the chalkboard:

1. Marla is the (co-captain.)
2. Dr. Nold was a fine (dentist.)
3. That bicycle is a (ten-speed.)
4. The photographs look (beautiful.)
5. Dad sounded (worried) on the phone.

386

Part 8 Linking Verbs and Predicate Words

Some verbs do not express action. They tell of a state of being. These verbs often link the subject of a sentence with a word or group of words in the predicate. When they link the subject with some other word or words, they are often called **linking verbs.**

She *is* a doctor.   Jill *is* artistic.
They *are* good swimmers.   We *are* hungry.

The most common linking verb is the verb *be*. This verb can have many forms. Study these forms of *be* so that you will recognize them.

be	been	is	was
being	am	are	were

The verbs *be, being,* and *been* are always used with other helping verbs. Here are some examples:

might be	is being	have been
could be	are being	might have been
will be	was being	would have been

The words linked to the subject by a linking verb like *be* are called **predicate words.** There are **predicate nouns, predicate pronouns,** and **predicate adjectives.** All of them tell something about the subject.

Renee is a *swimmer*. (predicate noun)

This is *she*. (predicate pronoun)

Bill was *happy*. (predicate adjective)

Notice how the subjects and the predicate words in the above sentences are linked by the verb *is* or *was*.

Here are some other common linking verbs:

seem   feel   become   look
appear   taste   grow   sound

Like *be*, these verbs can have various forms (*seems, appears, felt*). They can be used with helping verbs (*will appear, could feel, might have become*).

The music *sounded* beautiful.

The plants *grew* taller.

I *have become* an expert.

In diagrams, place the predicate word on the main line with the subject and verb. Place a slanted line between the verb and the predicate word. That line, like the predicate word, points back to the subject.

High Noon is a classic film.

Exercise   As your teacher directs, point out the subject, linking verb, and predicate word in each sentence.

1. The driver was angry.^{PW}
2. The house seemed empty.^{PW}
3. This is he.^{PW}
4. The flowers looked dry.^{PW}
5. Has Kathy been sick?^{PW}
6. Snakes are reptiles.^{PW}
7. The song sounded good.^{PW}
8. Karen felt lonesome.^{PW}
9. Was it she?^{PW}
10. Sue became chairperson.^{PW}

Using one sentence at a time, ask students to identify the verb. Underline the verb on the chalkboard as it is identified. Ask students to identify the subject. Draw a circle around the subject. Ask students to identify a word which tells about the subject. Circle the (predicate word.) Draw an arrow from the predicate word to the subject. Stress that the link is between the predicate word and the subject. In sentences 1–3, the predicate word renames the subject. In sentences 4 and 5, the predicate word describes the subject.

5. Read page 388. Use the following sentences to reinforce understanding of the difference between predicate words and direct objects.

The waiter dropped the food.
The waiter was clumsy.

Bette Midler won a Grammy award.
Bette Midler is a singer.

Dracula bit the victim's neck.
Dracula is my favorite movie.

In each pair of sentences, point out that the first sentence contains an action verb which has its action completed by a direct object. Remind students that the direct objects answers *what* or *whom* after the verb. Point out that the second sentence in each pair contains a linking verb. Ask students what words are linked in each sentence.

6. Assign and discuss the Exercise on pages 388–389.

Individualizing the Lesson

Less-Advanced Students

Have students label three columns *Subject*, *Linking Verb*, and *Predicate Word*. Have them write the appropraite parts of each sentence in the columns for the Exercise on page 387.

the appropraite parts of each sentence in the columns for the Exercise on page 387.

Advanced Students

Have each student write five sentences using linking verbs and predicate words. Then have them identify the verb, subject, and predicate word in each sentence.

Optional Practice

Have students write sentences using each of the following linking verbs. In their completed sentences, students should underline the verb once, underline the subject twice, circle the predicate word, and draw an arrow from the predicate word to the subject.

Answers will vary.

are becoming	will be
is	would have been
tasted	appears
are	felt
seemed	has been

Extending the Lesson

Place these sentences on a worksheet, leaving plenty of space between sentences. Have students do the following for each sentence.

a. Locate the verb and underline it twice.

b. Mark **AV** over each action verb. Mark **LV** over each linking verb.

c. Circle all objects and predicate words.

d. Mark **DO** over each direct object. Mark **PW** over each predicate word.

1. Eric wore a Superman costume for Halloween.
(AV over wore, DO over costume)

2. The bread seemed stale.
(LV over seemed, PW over stale)

3. The Johnsons bought the ranch in Texas.
(AV over bought, DO over ranch)

388

Direct Object or Predicate Word?

There are two ways to complete a verb. One way is with a direct object. Another way is with a predicate word. How can you tell the difference between predicate words and direct objects?

The verb will tell you. Is the verb an action verb? If so, the word following it that tells *what* or *whom* is a direct object.

> Ronald wore a T-shirt. (*Wore* is an action verb. *T-shirt* is a direct object.)
>
> Dara helped Steve. (*Helped* is an action verb. *Steve* is a direct object.)

Is the verb a linking verb? Is it followed by a word that tells about the subject? If so, the word is a predicate word.

> The meat is tender. (*Is* is a linking verb. *Tender* is a predicate word.)
>
> Lobsters are shellfish. (*Are* is a linking verb. *Shellfish* is a predicate word.)

Compare these sentences:

> Ms. Alvarez is a *teacher*.
> Ms. Alvarez called the *teacher*.

In the first sentence, *teacher* is a predicate word. It follows a linking verb, *is*, and tells about the subject, *Ms. Alvarez*. In the next sentence, *teacher* is a direct object. It tells *whom* about the action verb, *called*.

Exercise Make four columns on your paper. Head the columns *Subject, Verb, Direct Object,* and *Predicate Word.* Find these parts in the sentences below and place them in the correct columns.

1. Tracey Miles is a designer for a magazine. (PW over designer)

2. Tracey is skillful at her work. (PW over skillful)

3. She plans the design of the magazine. (DO over design)

4. The cover is her idea. (PW over idea)

388

5. She also <u>illustrates</u> <u>articles</u>. [DO]
6. <u>Tracey</u> <u>coordinates</u> her <u>work</u> with the editors. [DO over work]
7. <u>Photographs</u> <u>are used</u> frequently.
8. <u>Ken Lyle</u> <u>is</u> the <u>photographer</u>. [PW]
9. <u>Tracey</u> <u>gives</u> him <u>assignments</u>. [DO]
10. The <u>magazine</u> <u>is</u> <u>slick</u> in appearance. [PW]

Part 9 Compound Sentence Parts

The word *compound* means "having two or more parts."

Every sentence part that you have studied in this chapter can be compound—subjects, verbs, direct objects, indirect objects, and predicate words.

If the compound form has only two parts, there is usually a conjunction (*and, or, but*) between them. If there are three or more parts, the conjunction usually comes between the last two.

Diagraming Compound Subjects

To diagram the parts of a compound subject, split the subject line. Put the conjunction on a dotted line that connects the subjects.

Soap, butter, and potatoes spilled from the bag.

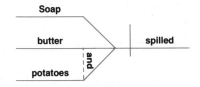

Diagraming Compound Verbs

To diagram compound verbs, split the verb line in the same way.

4. Manuella Ortega <u>is</u> president of her class. [LV PW]
5. The car windows <u>are</u> <u>dirty</u>. [LV PW]
6. Jason <u>seems</u> <u>restless</u> today. [LV PW]
7. A cotton shirt <u>feels</u> <u>cool</u> on a warm day. [LV PW]
8. Claude <u>tuned</u> his <u>guitar</u>. [AV DO]
9. That horse <u>will be</u> a <u>winner</u>. [LV PW]
10. The pilot <u>should have been</u> more careful. [LV PW]

Part 9

Objective

To recognize compound sentence parts

Presenting the Lesson

1. Review the sentence parts covered thus far: subject, verb, direct object, indirect object, and predicate word.

2. Place the following sentences on the board. Ask students to identify the part indicated in parentheses.

1. <u>Gilda</u> and <u>Jane</u> read the news report. (subject)
2. Jerry <u>cut</u> and <u>sanded</u> the wood. (verb)
3. Lindsay plays both <u>piano</u> and <u>violin</u>. (direct object)
4. The dean gave <u>Fran</u> and <u>me</u> a lecture. (indirect object)
5. Today has been <u>cold</u> and <u>rainy</u>. (predicate word)

Point out how each sentence element identified consists of two parts.

3. Read and discuss pages 389–390.

4. Do Exercise A on page 391 orally with the class.

5. For students who need more practice in identifying compound sentence parts, assign the exercise in **Optional Practice.**

6. Assign and discuss Exercise B on page 391.

Individualizing the Lesson

Less-Advanced Students

1. Have students work in pairs to complete Exercise A.

2. Work with students as a group to develop a story based on one of the sentences in Exercise A. Have students choose sentences to tell the story. When a sentence does not include a compound part, help them turn it into a sentence with a compound part. Then have them do Exercise B on page 391.

Advanced Students

Have each student write a letter to another student in class. Tell students to include as many compound sentence parts as they can. "Deliver" each letter to the appropriate student and have that student identify the compound part in each sentence. If students can change sentences without compound parts to include compounds, have them do so before returning the letter to its writer.

Optional Practice

Place the following exercise on a worksheet. Ask students to find the compound parts in the following sentences. Students should tell whether the compound parts are compound subjects, compound

Dr. Rosen called and asked for you.

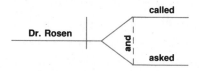

Diagraming Compound Direct Objects

To diagram compound direct objects, split the object line.

Diamonds cut metal and stone.

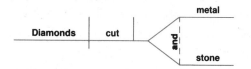

Diagraming Compound Indirect Objects

To diagram compound indirect objects, split the indirect object line.

The man handed Curt and Sue leaflets.

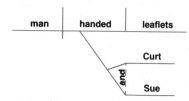

Diagraming Compound Predicate Words

To diagram compound predicate words, split the line.

The players were Connors and McEnroe.

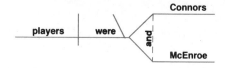

Exercise A   Find the compound parts in the following sentences. Tell whether they are compound subjects, verbs, direct objects, indirect objects, or predicate words.

IO 1. Did you give Cindy and Steve the posters?

S 2. Marla and Jeff made hanging planters in shop class.

V 3. The engine hesitated and then purred.

S 4. Tara and Charlene painted the scenery.

S, V 5. Daisy and I washed and waxed the car.

O 6. We brought Fritos and popcorn to the picnic.

P 7. The water was cool and clear.

V 8. Last weekend we skated and swam.

O 9. We suspended the balloons, the decorations, and the prizes from the ceiling.

O 10. The gymnasts on our team showed discipline, skill, and control.

Exercise B: Writing   In each of the following sentences, make the part noted in parentheses compound. Write the new sentence.

Answers will vary.

Example: We unpacked the crates. (*direct object*)
   We unpacked the crates and the cartons.

1. Ms. Lopez gave Jerry a tie.   (*direct object*)

2. Next came the President's car.   (*subject*)

3. Did you remember the Kleenex?   (*direct object*)

4. There are pickles over here.   (*subject*)

5. The hypnotist's performance was phony.   (*predicate word*)

6. Jon carried the groceries into the house. (*direct object*)

7. The pizza was spicy!   (*predicate word*)

8. Linda fixed the handlebars. (*direct object*)

9. Mr. and Mrs. Karnatz gave Meredith a job at the store. (*indirect object*)

10. There are ten divers competing.   (*subject*)

391

verbs, compound objects, or compound predicate words.

S 1. Lisa and Louis are twins.

PW 2. Mr. Haines has become rich and famous.

DO 3. We picked some corn and tomatoes from our garden.

V 4. Red Cross helpers fed and clothed the victims.

PW 5. The elm tree grew tall and stately over the years.

S 6. Tennis and basketball are good exercise.

DO 7. Everyone should bring suits, towels, and lunch to the beach.

DO 8. Betsy likes sports and music.

V 9. Barry stacked the logs and built a fire.

IO 10. The director gave Emily and Adam their cues.

Extending the Lesson

Place the following partial sentences on the board or on a worksheet. Have students complete the sentences with the compound parts indicated. Answers will vary.

1. _____ were destroyed in the fire. (compound subject)

2. John _____ the door. (compound verb)

3. Terry opened _____. (compound direct object)

4. The workers _____ the house. (compound verb)

5. _____ are delicious foods. (compound subject)

Additional Exercises

These Additional Exercises may be used for additional practice of the concepts presented in this Section. Each exercise focuses on a single concept, and should be used after the page number indicated in parentheses.

Review

If you have not assigned these Additional Exercises before this time, you can also use them as an excellent Section Review.

ADDITIONAL EXERCISES

The Sentence and Its Parts

A. Sentences and Fragments   Number your paper from 1 to 10. For each group of words that is a sentence, write *Sentence.* Write *Fragment* for each group of words that is not a sentence.

S   1. Sandra opened her book.

F   2. The photographs in the album.

F   3. A pencil without an eraser.

S   4. Alex put on the catcher's mitt.

S   5. Lightning struck.

F   6. Ran in the marathon.

S   7. Several classrooms were empty.

F   8. A tall, thin boy in a red T-shirt.

S   9. Your backpack is unzipped.

F 10. Wiped up the splinters of glass with a wet paper towel.

B. Kinds of Sentences   Number your paper from 1 to 10. For each of the following sentences, write *Declarative, Interrogative, Imperative,* or *Exclamatory* to show what kind it is. Add the correct punctuation mark at the end of each sentence.

Int 1. Where is the tallest roller coaster ?

D 2. Don sells magazine subscriptions.

E 3. Stop at the library after school !

E 4. What a great skater she is !

Imp 5. Check the batteries.

Int 6. What happened to the window ?

E 7. How happy he looks !

Int 8. How did the movie end ?

Int 9. Don't you want any milk ?

Imp 10. Don't skate in the street.

C. Subjects and Predicates Copy these sentences. Draw a vertical line between the subject and the predicate in each sentence.

1. The cattle | stampeded.
2. The jury | returned to the courtroom.
3. The players | signed their contracts.
4. Jason | returned that album.
5. Stacy | operates a computer.
6. The sky | looks gray and cloudy.
7. Ms. Sanders | sponsors the French club.
8. Cornfields | lined the road.
9. The telephone | rang in the middle of the night.
10. Johnny | buckled the child's seat belt.

D. Verbs and Their Subjects Number your paper from 1 to 10. For each sentence write the verb and then its subject.

1. Garrett owes me a dollar.
2. Several buses passed.
3. An old sled was propped against the wall.
4. The door at the end of the hall is the exit.
5. My brother finally found a job.
6. Ruthie probably left early.
7. The sun in his eyes blinded him for a minute.
8. The rain on the roof sounds cozy.
9. The fans in the bleachers were shouting happily.
10. A red car with Ohio license plates stopped.

E. Main Verbs and Helping Verbs Number your paper from 1 to 10. Label two columns HV (helping verb) and MV (main verb). Write the helping verbs and main verbs from the sentences in the proper columns.

1. Spring has finally arrived.
2. The class is studying the Civil War.

3. Darlene doesn't usually say much.
4. You should try again.
5. The Richard Pryor movie is still playing at the Varsity.
6. Sara had actually forgotten the incident.
7. Marc did not swing at the next ball.
8. Our team's strategy has never failed yet.
9. Conley has entered the math competition.
10. The whistle of a train can sound lonesome.

F. Sentences with Unusual Order   Number your paper from 1 to 10. Label two columns *Subject* and *Verb*. Write the subject and verb for each sentence.

1. There are not enough forks.
2. Did you bring your mitt?
3. Down the street came the snowplow.
(You) 4. Take a brochure.
5. There she is.
6. There goes the championship.
7. Here comes Sheila.
(You) 8. Wait a minute.
9. Onto the table leaped the cat.
10. Are the mosquitoes bothering you?

G. Direct Objects and Indirect Objects   Number your paper from 1 to 10. Decide what the italicized word is in each sentence. Write *Direct Object* or *Indirect Object* beside each number.

DO 1. The rains caused a *flood*.
DO 2. Natalie molded the *clay*.
DO 3. I will leave a *note* for you.
IO 4. Jake prepared his *guests* some lunch.
DO 5. The children played *hopscotch*.
IO 6. The tailor gave the *coat* a new lining.

_{DO} 7. I wrote an *outline* of the chapter.

_{IO} 8. Laura sent *Chris* a get-well card.

_{DO} 9. Put another *plate* on the table.

_{IO}10. Give the *plants* some water.

H. Sentence Parts Number your paper from 1 to 10. Label three columns *Verb*, *Indirect Object*, and *Direct Object*. For each sentence below fill in those parts that you find. Not every sentence will have an indirect object.

1. Harry will shell some walnuts.
     _V   _{DO}

2. Kate has gotten Fred a chair.
    _V _V   _{IO}   _{DO}

3. You owe Mary an explanation.
      _V _{IO}   _{DO}

4. The coach gave Brian another chance.
          _V   _{IO}   _{DO}

5. I put the button in my pocket.
   _V   _{DO}

6. Tara's hit won us the game.
         _V _{IO}   _{DO}

7. That basket has won the game for us.
          _V _V   _{DO}

8. Janet had sent the pictures to her grandfather.
      _V _V   _{DO}

9. Please pass the salad to Margie.
       _V   _{DO}

10. Please pass Hank the potatoes.
       _V   _{IO}   _{DO}

I. Predicate Words, Linking Verbs, and Objects Number your paper from 1 to 10. Label four columns *Subject*, *Verb*, *Direct Object*, and *Predicate Word*. Fill in the parts that you find for each sentence. You will find either a direct object or a predicate word in each sentence.

1. Sunflowers grow tall. _{PW}

2. The tennis players were amateurs. _{PW}

3. James sketched the scene. _{DO}

4. The old skates had metal wheels. _{DO}

5. The wheels were metal. _{PW}

6. Juanita became a dentist. _{PW}

7. Ocean water tastes salty. _{PW}

8. Is Lindsay upset? [PW]

9. Is Dwight bringing a radio? [DO]

10. The paint looks wet to me. [PW]

J. Compound Parts As your teacher directs, show the compound parts in the following sentences. Tell whether they are compound subjects, verbs, objects, or predicate words.

S 1. Rachel and Jodie are outfielders.

P 2. Woody Allen is an actor, a director, and a writer.

V 3. We fished, swam, and boated in the lake.

V 4. The engine started but then stopped.

V 5. The travelers sat and waited in the station.

O 6. Jeff read his horoscope and the editorials.

P 7. The river was wide but shallow.

S 8. Last season Clarence and Derek looked less promising.

O 9. Did you put cinnamon or nutmeg in the cocoa?

S 10. Maps, posters, and cartoons covered the wall.

MIXED REVIEW

The Sentence and Its Parts

A. Finding subjects and predicates and identifying fragments Decide whether the following groups of words are sentences or fragments. Copy each sentence and draw a vertical line between the subject and predicate. Then write *Declarative, Interrogative, Imperative,* or *Exclamatory* to show what kind of sentence it is. If a group of words is not a sentence, write *Fragment.*

D 1. The sand burned my feet
F 2. Have built a cage for the rabbits
Int 3. Has the paint dried yet
Imp 4. Use a bigger shovel (You)
F 5. A thick blue notebook with pockets
D 6. Tracy took her radio
Imp 7. Give us a chance (You)
Int 8. Can Johnny swim that far
E 9. How slow this bus is
Int 10. How do you play this game

B. Finding helping verbs, main verbs, and simple subjects Number your paper from 1 to 10. Label three columns *Helping Verbs,* HV *Main Verbs,* MV and *Simple Subjects.* S For each sentence, write the parts in the proper columns.

1. The wind was slowly rising.
2. Maria has not answered my letter.
3. Leslie had never used a camera.
4. From the roof Vicky was watching the parade.
5. There might be another exit.
6. Hungry deer were venturing out of the woods.
7. Near the back was standing Michael.

Mixed Review

These exercises provide review of the concepts presented in this Section. Each exercise challenges the students to apply several of the skills they have acquired during previous study. Because the "mixed" feature of these activities makes them more difficult, the teacher may wish to have less-advanced students do them orally or in small groups.

$\overset{S}{\underset{(You)}{}}$8. $\overset{HV}{\text{Don't}}$ $\overset{MV}{\text{shut}}$ the suitcase yet.

9. $\overset{HV}{\text{Don't}}$ these $\overset{S}{\text{games}}$ $\overset{MV}{\text{need}}$ batteries?

10. $\overset{HV}{\text{Can}}$ the $\overset{S}{\text{parrot}}$ really $\overset{MV}{\text{answer}}$ questions?

C. Finding sentence parts   Number your paper from 1 to 10. Label five columns on your paper *Subject*, *Verb*, *Predicate* $\overset{PW}{\text{Word}}$, $\overset{IO}{\text{Indirect Object}}$, and $\overset{DO}{\text{Direct Object}}$. Fill in the parts that you find in each sentence. No sentence will have every part.

1. Nick tamed the $\overset{DO}{\text{chipmunk}}$.
2. Rita got $\overset{IO}{\text{Lee}}$ a $\overset{DO}{\text{chair}}$.
3. The tenants left the $\overset{DO}{\text{building}}$.
4. Doug Williams is a $\overset{PW}{\text{quarterback}}$.
5. Chrissy was watching the $\overset{DO}{\text{clock}}$.
6. The wrestler seemed $\overset{PW}{\text{angry}}$.
7. The motorboat made $\overset{DO}{\text{waves}}$.
8. The fumes spread slowly.
9. A woman handed $\overset{IO}{\text{Joey}}$ a $\overset{DO}{\text{flyer}}$.
10. The music is too $\overset{PW}{\text{slow}}$.

D. Finding compound sentence parts   Number your paper from 1 to 10. Write the compound parts for the following sentences. Write the kind of compound part each is.

v 1. The cat hissed and pounced.
o 2. I sent Sean a card and a package for his birthday.
IO 3. You should tell Brooke or Hannah the reason.
s 4. Canoes, rowboats, and rafts are for rent.
o 5. A grizzly bear inspires fear and awe.
P 6. The snow was light but wet.
v 7. The gymnast fell but landed safely.
P 8. The shadows were long, dark, and thin.
s 9. Sam, Rachel, or Kelly can run errands for Mr. Cruz.
o 10. The clerks speak English, Spanish, and French.

USING GRAMMAR IN WRITING
The Sentence and Its Parts

A. Below are some subjects and predicates. They could be part of a movie review. Make up a title for this movie. Then add a predicate to each subject and add a subject to each predicate. Finally, arrange the complete sentences in a logical order and write them in paragraph form. You may add some complete sentences of your own, if you wish.

> the movie
> the surprise ending
> was screaming in terror
> the thin, shadowy figure on the screen
> didn't watch the scary parts
> suddenly lurched forward
> its stars

B. Choose an elected official in your city or state. It could be a mayor, a governor, a representative, or a senator. Think about what you would like to ask and tell this person. Write three declarative sentences stating things that you think this person should know. Then write three questions you would like to ask. Finally, write two imperative sentences that tell this official what you would like him or her to do. Write your ideas in the form of a letter. If you would like to, mail the letter.

Examples:

Declarative Statement:	Many young people are worried about getting jobs.
Question:	When did you enter public life?
Imperative Statement:	Don't approve cuts in the school budget.

C. Last night you had a strange dream. Describe your dream, using several sentences that have the subject in an unusual position.

These challenging and enjoyable activities allow the students to see how the concepts of grammar, usage, and mechanics may be applied in actual writing situations. Each exercise is designed to allow students practice in several of the skills they have acquired in this Section. The activities also provide opportunities for students to write creatively about a wide variety of interesting and unusual subjects.

Section Objectives

1. To avoid and correct sentence fragments

2. To avoid and correct run-on sentences

Preparing the Students

Ask students if they have ever had the experience of listening to someone who is very excited tell a story. The person rushes his or her ideas together and leaves out important details. The ideas are not easy to follow.

Explain that this is also a frequent problem in writing; if the writer is not careful in creating sentences, a reader may not be able to understand his or her ideas.

Tell students that this Section will point out two common problems in writing.

Read the introduction on page 400. Remind students that sentences are the foundation on which good writing rests. Avoiding fragments and run-ons will help students make their writing foundation solid.

Additional Resources

Diagnostic Test — page 1 in the test booklet

Mastery Test — pages 42–43 in the test booklet

Additional Exercises — pages 405–408 in the student text

Practice Book — pages 162–164

Duplicating Masters — pages 162–164

Special Populations — See special section at the back of this Teacher's Edition.

Using Complete Sentences

You use language to communicate thoughts and feelings. Certainly, you want to communicate accurately and clearly whenever you write.

Sentences are the building blocks of your writing. To be clear, these sentences should be complete.

Sometimes you omit part of an idea from a sentence. This results in a **sentence fragment**. Sentence fragments are confusing.

Sometimes you join two or more sentences as one. The resulting **run-on sentence** is also confusing.

This section will help you to avoid these two errors in your writing.

Part 1   Avoiding Sentence Fragments

A sentence fragment is an incomplete sentence. It does not express a complete thought. Avoid sentence fragments in your writing.

In a fragment, either the subject or the verb is missing. The reader may wonder *who* or *what*? Or the reader may wonder *what happened*? or *what about it*?

> Fragment: Neil and his friend Ray.
> (What happened? What about them? The verb is missing.)
>
> Sentence: Neil and his friend Ray joined the team.
>
> Fragment: Sings country music. (Who sings? The subject is missing.)
>
> Sentence: Crystal Gayle sings country music.

Fragments Resulting from Incomplete Thoughts

Sentence fragments usually result from carelessness. The writer writes a piece of an idea without finishing it. Then he or she races on to the next idea. Maybe the writer's pen isn't keeping up with the stream of ideas. Fragments result.

Here is an example of a series of fragments:

> The leaders of the two nations. A summit conference in Paris. Discussing nuclear weapons.

The writer intended these complete thoughts:

> The leaders of the two nations met yesterday.
> They held a summit conference in Paris.
> They discussed nuclear weapons.

You can see that the group of fragments is confusing. The group of complete thoughts is much clearer.

Objective

To avoid and correct sentence fragments

Presenting the Lesson

1. Ask students to define a fragment as used in these examples.

> Only a fragment of the picture could be seen
> Fragments of cloth were scattered on the floor.
> The child could recall only fragments of his dream.

Lead the class to understand that fragments are bits and pieces. They belong to a larger whole and are incomplete by themselves. Fragments don't convey a whole picture or a whole story.

Explain that sometimes, even though a writer has a complete idea in mind, he or she may write in fragments because the ideas are not expressed completely. To communicate effectively, a good writer must avoid fragments.

2. Read and discuss page 401, paying careful attention to examples of fragments and their corrections.

3. Put these fragments on the board. Ask students whether the *subject* or the *verb* is missing. Have students supply missing elements to make complete sentences.

V 1. The doctor and nurse.

S 2. Fell down from its nest.

S 3. Danced all night at the party.

V 4. Leah, the main character in the book.

S 5. Hired Yvette Simms for the job.

4. Read and discuss page 402. Point out that sometimes the writer has written all of the parts needed to express a complete thought, but he or she has punctuated these parts incorrectly and thus created fragments.

5. Put these sentences and fragments on the board. Analyze each with the class, determining which part is a fragment and correcting the error in punctuation to eliminate the fragment.

1. It was noisy in the library. With all the students there.
2. We enjoyed the movie. Especially the special effects.
3. Try to lift the cartons. Of heavy books. Without straining your back.
4. By New Year's, I must lose five pounds.
5. After the election. The mayor left town.

6. Assign and discuss Exercises A and B on pages 402–403.

Individualizing the Lesson

Less-Advanced Students

Do Exercise A as a class. Then assign Exercise B.

Advanced Students

Have students write as many different completions for the fragments in Exercises A and B as they can. Encourage them to be original but logical.

Optional Practice

Put the following sentences and fragments on a worksheet or on the chalkboard. Have students identify which are fragments and rewrite them as complete sentences.
Answers will vary.

Fragments Resulting from Incorrect Punctuation

A sentence ends with a punctuation mark: a period, a question mark, or an exclamation mark. A new sentence begins with a capital letter. Sometimes a writer uses an end mark and a capital letter too soon. The result is a sentence fragment.

Fragment: Ushers at each show. Handed out programs.
Sentence: Ushers at each show handed out programs.

Fragment: By the final quarter of the game. Talbot had recovered from his injury.
Sentence: By the final quarter of the game, Talbot had recovered from his injury.

Fragment: The dance floor was crowded. With young couples.
Sentence: The dance floor was crowded with young couples.

Exercise A   For each group of words that is a sentence, write *S* on your paper. For each sentence fragment, write *F*. Be ready to add words to change the fragments into sentences.

S 1. I saw a TV show last Sunday afternoon
S 2. The show was about dolphins
F 3. Actually a kind of small whale
S 4. Dolphins are very intelligent
F 5. Playful animals
F 6. Under the water in the big tank
S 7. It is very entertaining to watch the dolphins
F 8. Just for fun
S 9. Dolphins can hear very well
F 10. Because dolphins breathe air

Exercise B   Follow the directions for Exercise A.

S 1. Tracy Austin is one of the best tennis players today
F 2. A very high wind and then some flashes of lightning

F 3. During the relay race

F 4. A report about car fumes in the city

F 5. Mr. Troy, owner of Troy and Brown Sports Shop

F 6. Whose work on the blackboard

F 7. Andrew Wyeth, the artist

S 8. Martha Jane Canary was better known as "Calamity Jane"

S 9. The fire engines rushed down the street

S 10. No one else gave a report on solar energy

Part 2 Avoiding Run-on Sentences

A **run-on sentence** is two or more sentences written as one.

A run-on joins two ideas that should be separate. The resulting sentence is confusing because the reader needs a signal at the end of each complete thought.

You can correct a run-on by using a period at the end of each sentence.

Here are examples of run-on sentences.

Run-on: The dune buggy bumped over the sand it headed south.

Correct: The dune buggy bumped over the sand. It headed south.

Run-on: Seth opened the garage door inside was a motorcycle.

Correct: Seth opened the garage door. Inside was a motorcycle.

Often a run-on sentence results from using a comma instead of a period.

Run-on: We can't find Marcy's phone number, it is unlisted.

Correct: We can't find Marcy's phone number. It is unlisted.

Run-on: The man was arrested, he was held without bail.

Correct: The man was arrested. He was held without bail.

403

F 1. I left your gloves. Inside your locker.

F 2. A six-car pileup on the expressway.

F 3. Most clothing goes on sale. After Christmas and after the Fourth of July.

S 4. Laura had her braces taken off. She looks wonderful.

F 5. Blanca, our white poodle puppy.

Extending the Lesson

Have students find sentence fragments in plays or in conversations in novels. Have them explain what is missing from each fragment, then have them complete each one.

Part 2

Objective

To avoid and correct run-on sentences

Presenting the Lesson

1. Read and discuss page 403. Stress that the problem in run-on sentences is that the writer runs together two separate, complete thoughts. Run-ons cause confusion because they don't allow the reader to form ideas in a logical way. When proper punctuation is missing, the reader doesn't have the necessary guides for making sense of the words.

2. Do Exercise A on page 404 orally with the class. After breaking each run-on into two sentences, determine whether each resulting sentence is complete.

3. Assign and discuss Exercise B.

403

Individualizing the Lesson

Less Advanced Students

Have students identify the subject and the verb in each sentence in Exercise A as a class. Then have them correct the run-ons.

Advanced Students

Rewrite a paragraph from one of the students' textbooks, including fragments and run-ons. Have students rewrite this paragraph, correcting fragments and run-ons.

Optional Practice

Put the following sentences on the board. Have students determine which are run-ons. Have students correct and rewrite run-on sentences. Answers will vary.

R 1. The days are getting shorter, we rode home in the dark.

R 2. Sesame Street is still on television, it was on when I was a little kid.

R 3. Nancy brought grapes and peaches don't they look delicious?

C 4. Before painting the posters, Carl put on a smock.

Extending the Lesson

Discuss alternate ways of correcting run-ons. Have students correct the following run-ons in ways other than by creating two separate sentences. Answers will vary.

1. I read the whole story, I didn't understand all of it.

2. Larry bought a tape deck for his car now he listens to music when he drives.

3. A police officer stopped the van, one of its headlights was out.

4. You didn't water the plant enough it died.

404

Exercise A   Correct the following run-on sentences.

1. Our state has a lottery. the grand prize is one million dollars.

2. Cable television is becoming popular, it offers varied programing.

3. Kristen trains Seeing Eye dogs she enjoys her work.

4. Todd replaced the wiring, now the doorbell works.

5. Lopez stole third base, later he scored a home run.

6. Karen ran the 100-meter dash she placed second.

7. The pilots waited in the cockpit, they studied the flight plan.

8. Frank's dog was lost, we searched the neighborhood for it.

9. Fuel was scarce, there was talk of gas rationing.

10. Julie studied the math problem. she figured out the right answer.

Exercise B   Follow the directions for Exercise A.

1. Charla breeds Siamese cats. she has eight of them.

2. The committee held a hearing, the topic was new energy sources.

3. The burglar alarm sounded. no one heard it.

4. The hikers followed mountain trails, they finally reached the peak.

5. Films about outer space use special effects, the results are striking.

6. Julie runs every day. she usually runs three miles.

7. Insulation is important for houses, it keeps heat inside during the winter.

8. One scientist made a man-powered plane, it flies short distances.

9. Reggie put her books into her locker. then she went to the cafeteria.

10. A drawbridge spans the river. it is raised for tall ships.

404

ADDITIONAL EXERCISES

Using Complete Sentences

A. Sentences and Sentence Fragments Number your paper from 1 to 10. Write *Fragment* or *Sentence* for each of the following groups of words to show what each group is.

F 1. Plans the diet for the patients at the hospital.

S 2. Antique car owners hold a parade each year at the county fairgrounds.

F 3. Many careers in the medical field.

S 4. This year's spring play has not been selected.

S 5. Eggs, meat, and nuts are high in protein.

F 6. Waited in line at the movie theater.

S 7. Farmers plow their fields.

S 8. Red, white, and green are the colors of their flag.

F 9. Only twenty-eight days in February.

F 10. Forgot to bring a can opener.

B. Sentences and Run-on Sentences Number your paper from 1 to 10. Write *Run-on* or *Sentence* for each of the following groups of words to show what each group is.

R 1. The dessert is refreshing it's raspberry sherbet.

S 2. The car needs two quarts of oil.

R 3. Many students volunteered two were chosen.

R 4. The stage crew made the sets, they are elaborate.

S 5. Jane will return your books to the library for you.

R 6. Francis entered the speech contest, he won second prize.

S 7. Mom hung the photographs in the hallway.

R 8. Jim is on a diet, he has lost four pounds.

S 9. The Richardsons are traveling in Canada this summer.

S 10. Tulips and daffodils bloomed near the fountain in the square.

C. Sentences, Sentence Fragments, and Run-on Sentences Number your paper from 1 to 10. Write *Fragment*, *Sentence*, or *Run-on* for each of the following groups of words to show what each group is.

S 1. The rock group held a recording session.

F 2. A comedy about city life.

S 3. A reporter approached the Senator.

R 4. Townhouses line the street they are elegant.

F 5. The tennis tournament at Wimbledon.

F 6. Horse-drawn carriages driving through the park.

R 7. The Woolworth Building is a skyscraper, it was built in 1913.

S 8. Olga carried her hockey stick in a special case.

F 9. A tour of the main floor of the White House.

R 10. Two movies are playing at the drive-in they are horror films.

MIXED REVIEW

Using Complete Sentences

A. Identifying sentences, fragments, and run-ons Write *Fragment*, *Sentence*, or *Run-on* for each of the following groups of words to show what each one is. Then correct fragments by adding words to make complete sentences. Correct run-ons by using the correct capitalization and punctuation to show where each complete thought begins and ends. Answers will vary for Numbers 1, 7, and 8.

F 1. Nothing but news programs on that station.

R 2. Sara swam to the pier; /she practiced her diving there.

S 3. A thorn on the rosebush scratched my knee.

S 4. There was a rip in the softball.

R 5. Sawdust spilled out of the box; /some got in Ted's eyes.

S 6. Run into the water.

F 7. Ran more hot water into the tub.

F 8. One strap of the helmet.

S 9. Nina, Martin, and I dug the barbecue pit.

R 10. The rain started; /Monty closed the flaps of the tent.

B. Correcting fragments and run-ons The following paragraph contains fragments and run-on sentences. Rewrite the paragraph, correcting the fragments and run-ons.

There are many stories about mean or weak people. With a secret streak of good inside. Big Bad John, for example, Held up the roof of a mine during a cave-in. The other miners escaped, Big Bad John sacrificed his life for them. Another example is the nervous coward Clark Kent, He was really Superman. He was the champion of all in need, Especially the underdog. There are also folksongs about good outlaws, these Robin Hoods paid off mortgages for poor farmers. Maybe we would rather believe the best. About everybody.

407

Mixed Review

  These exercises provide review of the concepts presented in this Section. Each exercise challenges the students to apply several of the skills they have acquired during previous study. Because the "mixed" feature of these activities makes them more difficult, the teacher may wish to have less-advanced students do them orally or in small groups.

These challenging and enjoyable activities allow the students to see how the concepts of grammar, usage, and mechanics may be applied in actual writing situations. Each exercise is designed to allow students practice in several of the skills they have acquired in this Section. The activities also provide opportunities for students to write creatively about a wide variety of interesting and unusual subjects.

USING GRAMMAR IN WRITING
Using Complete Sentences

A. Your history teacher asked the class to take notes on an in-class movie about women of the Revolutionary War. You took notes quickly, trying to catch everything. Now you need to rewrite the notes. Correct all fragments and run-on sentences.

Women of the American Revolution

American women played an active role. In the Revolution. They pushed plows and gathered crops. As the men went to war.

"Old Mom" Rinker of Philadelphia made daily reports on the British army to Washington she hid messages in balls of yarn she rolled balls over a cliff.

Lydia Darragh was a Philadelphia housewife her home faced British Headquarters. She watched the British she then sewed important information into jacket buttons. Which her son wore on frequent visits to General Washington.

Deborah Sampson disguised herself. As a man. She fought in the Continental Army for four years.

Another Revolutionary heroine, Margaret Corbin, took over her husband's cannon when he was wounded.

B. You have offered to do a few chores for your neighbors while they are away. Rewrite the instructions that were left for you. Correct fragments and run-on sentences.

Water the plants. Twice a week the can is under the kitchen sink. Feed the fish every day watch for baby guppies if you see any put them in the smaller tank. Feed the gerbils. And clean their cage once a week. Mow the lawn. While we're gone if you don't mind. Bring in the mail. And the newspapers and leave them on the dining room table. Thanks so much you are a super neighbor I'll return the favor just say when.

Using Nouns

Section Objectives

1. To understand the concept of a noun and to identify nouns in sentences

2. To distinguish between common nouns and proper nouns

3. To identify nouns used as subjects, direct objects, indirect objects, and predicate nouns

4. To form the plural of nouns correctly

5. To form and use possessive nouns correctly

Preparing the Students

Ask students if any of them have young brothers or sisters, or know any very small children. Ask what the first words the youngsters said were. Most words will relate to people (DaDa, Mama), things (milk, doll), and possibly places (bed, park). Ask students what all of these words have in common.

Explain that one of the most basic elements of language is the noun, which names people, places, and things.

Additional Resources

Diagnostic Test — page 2 in the test booklet

Mastery Test — pages 44–45 in the test booklet

Additional Exercises — pages 422–426 in the student text

Practice Book — pages 165–170

Duplicating Masters — pages 165–170

Special Populations — See special section at the back of this Teacher's Edition.

Experts have studied the various parts of language. They have found that all the words used in sentences fall into certain groups or classes.

Many people use language without knowing very much about these groups. Skillful writers and speakers, however, have a good understanding of these groups of words.

In this section you will study in detail one very important group of words: **nouns.**

Objectives

1. To understand the concept of a noun and to identify nouns in sentences

2. To distinguish between common nouns and proper nouns

Presenting the Lesson

1. Read the top of page 410. Pay special attention to examples of persons, places, and things.

2. Place the three headings *Persons*, *Places*, and *Things* on the chalkboard to form three columns. Ask students to volunteer names of persons, places, and things to be listed under each heading. Try to elicit examples of abstract nouns, such as *loyalty* and *love*.

3. Assign and discuss the Exercise on page 410.

4. Read "Proper Nouns and Common Nouns" on pages 410–411. Point out capitalization of proper nouns in examples.

5. Place the following common nouns on the board. Ask students to give at least five examples of proper nouns for each.

city	automobile
street	athlete
actor	novel

6. Assign and discuss Exercises A and B on page 411.

Individualizing the Lesson

Less-Advanced Students

Have the students circle ten proper nouns and ten common nouns in a newspaper or magazine article.

Part 1　What Are Nouns?

One important use of language is to name the people, places, and things around you. Words used to name are called **nouns.**

A noun is a word used to name a person, place, or thing.

Nouns name all sorts of things. They name things you can see, such as horses, boats, and footballs. They name things you cannot see, such as feelings, beliefs, and ideas.

Persons:　doctor, girl, Kim, Willie Mays
Places:　home, park, Chicago, Spain
Things:　book, building, loyalty, love

Exercise　Make three columns on a sheet of paper. Use these headings: (1) *Names of Persons*, (2) *Names of Places*, (3) *Names of Things*. Under the proper heading, list each noun in the following paragraph.

An unusually strong earthquake occurred in China in 1976. Tremors from the quake were felt hundreds of miles away. In the severely damaged city of Tientsin, thousands of Chinese fled from collapsing buildings. The industrial city of Tangshan was destroyed, and its nearby mines were also damaged. An estimated 655,000 people lost their lives.

Proper Nouns and Common Nouns

How do these two nouns differ?

country　　Sweden

They represent the two kinds of nouns. A **common noun** is a general name of a person, place, or thing. *Country* is a common noun. There are many countries. But names such as *Sweden, Canada, Brazil,* and *China* are names of particular countries. They are **proper nouns.**

A common noun is a general name for a person, place, or thing.

A common noun begins with a small letter.

A proper noun is the name of a particular person, place, or thing. A proper noun is always capitalized.

Below are more examples of common nouns and proper nouns. Notice that a noun may consist of more than one word.

Common Nouns	Proper Nouns
waterfall	Victoria Falls
teacher	Rebecca Woods
state	West Virginia
theater	Rialto
game	Probe
month	July

Exercise A Make two columns on your paper. Head one column *Common Nouns* and the other *Proper Nouns*. Decide whether the nouns below are common or proper. Place each in the correct column. Capitalize the proper nouns.

1. crater lake, gulf of mexico, lake champlain
2. continent, africa, europe, peninsula, korea, italy
3. book, *reader's digest*, magazine, *sports illustrated*, seventeen
4. montana, kansas, state, indiana, region
5. salt lake city, las vegas, town, atlanta, city
6. dancer, maria tallchief, opera, joan sutherland
7. track meet, olympic games, cincinnati reds, hockey, world series
8. mountain, andes, old smoky, hills
9. artist, georgia o'keeffe, sculptor, alexander calder
10. monument, mount rushmore, statue of liberty, building, empire state building

Exercise B: Writing Write five sentences of your own, using at least one proper noun in each sentence. Answers may vary.

Part 2 How Are Nouns Used?

Nouns are used in many different ways within sentences. Nouns are often the subjects of sentences. They can also be direct objects, indirect objects, and predicate nouns.

Nouns Used as Subjects

Nouns are frequently used as the **subjects** of sentences. You have already learned that the subject tells *who* or *what* is being talked about.

> The *trainer* taped my knee. (The noun *trainer* is the subject of the verb *taped*.)
> Before the game the *team* reviewed plays. (The noun *team* is the subject of the verb *reviewed*.)
> *Maria* and *Tyrone* dove into the pool. (Both the nouns *Maria* and *Tyrone* are subjects of the verb *dove*.)
> The *winner* of the tournament got a prize. (The noun *winner* is the subject of the verb *got*. Notice that in this sentence the subject is not next to the verb.)

Exercise A Number your paper from 1 to 10. Write the nouns used as the subjects of these sentences.

1. Thick <u>vines</u> covered the windows.
2. The <u>cafeteria</u> at school has a salad bar.
3. The <u>natives</u> chew sugar cane.
4. <u>Brenda</u> caught two trout.
5. <u>Dana</u> wore new cowboy boots.
6. <u>Connie</u> prefers stick shift.
7. <u>Dale</u> and <u>Lee</u> failed the driver's test.
8. The <u>soldiers</u> marched along.
9. <u>Pineapples</u> grow in Hawaii.
10. Some <u>snakes</u> play dead convincingly.

1. The cost of fuel has risen.
2. Kathleen and Amy rode on mopeds.
3. Sally and Shawn found a ten-dollar bill.
4. Carpenters nailed the beams.
5. Poisonous plants grow in that garden.
6. Chief Joseph led his tribe toward Canada.
7. A cloud of smoke rose from the explosion.
8. Penny got a bus transfer.
9. The librarians buy new books.
10. Fruits and vegetables filled the baskets.

Nouns Used as Direct Objects

Nouns may be used as **direct objects.** The direct object completes the action of the verb. It tells *what* or *whom* about the verb.

> Rachel mowed the *lawn.* (The noun *lawn* tells *what* about the verb *mowed.*)
>
> A detective questioned *Mr. Ryan.* (The noun *Mr. Ryan* tells *whom* about the verb *questioned.*)
>
> A mob surrounded the *singer.* (The noun *singer* tells *whom* about the verb *surrounded.*)
>
> We bought *pens* and *paper.* (Both the nouns *pens* and *paper* are direct objects. They tell *what* about the verb *bought.*)

Exercise A   Write the nouns used as direct objects in the following sentences.

1. Suzy cooks Chinese food.
2. Hornets built a nest in the garage.
3. Carmen joined the gymnastics club.
4. Sal operates a crane.
5. The store has a neon sign.
6. A cashier bagged the groceries.

proper nouns. Point out the compound subject in number 7.

3. Assign and discuss Exercise B on page 413.

4. Read and discuss page 413. Remind students that in order to find the direct object, they should locate the verb first and then ask *what* or *whom* immediately after the verb.

5. Do Exercise A on page 413–414 orally with the class.

6. Assign and discuss Exercise B on page 414.

7. Read and discuss page 414. Point out that when the words *to* or *for* appear in the sentence, the word which follows them is not an indirect object. Example: Eduardo gave a lottery ticket *to* me.

8. Do Exercise A on page 415 orally with the class. If time permits, identify subject, verb, direct object, and indirect object for each sentence.

9. Assign and discuss Exercise B.

10. Read pages 415–416. Stress that a predicate noun renames the subject.

11. Do Exercise A on page 416 orally with the class.

12. Assign and discuss Exercise B.

Individualizing the Lesson

Less-Advanced Students

Have students work in pairs on each Exercise A under each section of noun usage. Assign all the B Exercises for independent work.

Advanced Students

Have students write two sentences using nouns in each way discussed in the lesson: subject, direct object, indirect object, predicate noun.

Optional Practice

Place the following sentences on the board or on a worksheet. Have students underline all nouns. Above each noun, have students write *S* (subject), *DO* (direct object), *IO* (indirect object), or *PN* (predicate noun) to indicate the way each noun is used in the sentences.

1. *60 Minutes* ^S is my favorite television ^{PN} program.
2. Batman ^S gave Robin ^{IO} a special assignment. ^{DO}
3. Honda ^S and Kawasaki ^S make fine motorcycles. DO
4. The cups ^S and saucers ^S are dirty.
5. This car ^S needs new plugs ^{DO} and points. ^{DO}
6. Tardiness ^S and absence ^S have been major problems. ^{PN}
7. The farmer ^S planted corn, ^{DO} peas, ^{DO} and beans. DO
8. Both the House ^S and the Senate ^S approved the bill. DO
9. Cindy ^S sent many friends ^{IO} and relatives ^{IO} her pictures. ^{DO}
10. Patience ^S is a virtue. PN

Extending the Lesson

For students who can successfully identify nouns and their function, some practice in diagraming would be appropriate. For diagraming practice, five sentences each may be drawn from the following Exercises: Exercise B, page 414, Exercise B, page 415, Exercise B, page 416.

---

7. The beach has fine <u>sand</u>.
8. Bulldozers wrecked the <u>building</u>.
9. Jenny clipped the <u>bushes</u> and <u>hedges</u>.
10. Our house needs a new <u>roof</u> and new <u>gutters</u>.

Exercise B Follow the directions for Exercise A.

1. All drivers should have <u>insurance</u>.
2. Leslie got <u>blisters</u> from her new shoes.
3. Dennis gathers <u>shells</u> on the beach.
4. Kate wrote a <u>story</u> for the newspaper.
5. We tossed a <u>Frisbee</u>.
6. Window washers use a <u>scaffold</u>.
7. We used two <u>coats</u> of paint on the garage.
8. That farmer plants <u>corn</u> and <u>soybeans</u>.
9. Mice invaded the <u>attic</u> and the <u>basement</u>.
10. The Lyles own several <u>acres</u> of farmland.

Nouns Used as Indirect Objects

Nouns may be used as subjects and direct objects. They may also be used as **indirect objects.** The indirect object of the verb tells *to whom* or *for whom,* or *to what* or *for what* about the verb. However, you do not use the word *to* or *for* with an indirect object.

> The agency found *Monica* a job. (The noun *Monica* is the indirect object. It tells *for whom* the job was found.)
>
> Stephanie gave the *library* her old books. (The noun *library* is the indirect object. It tells *to what* the books were given.)
>
> We gave the *tourists* directions. (The noun *tourists* is the indirect object. It tells *to whom* the directions were given.)

Indirect objects are used with direct objects. The indirect object appears between the verb and the direct object.

Exercise A   Write the nouns used as indirect objects in the following sentences.

1. Bill served his family a vegetarian meal.
2. Casey gave his grandmother a card.
3. Maria tossed Ellen her hat.
4. I sent Brad a postcard.
5. Tracey taught Mel ping-pong.
6. The day-care center gives children lunch.
7. Eliza brought Judy a gift.
8. Someone sent the police a message.
9. Lena made Beth and Alana their costumes.
10. Karen told only her best friends the truth.

Exercise B   Follow the directions for Exercise A.

1. We showed Kara the new rink.
2. The trainer gave the dogs a long rest.
3. The bank gave Natalie a loan.
4. Aunt Audrey brought Deedee jewelry from Mexico.
5. Carlos told the committee his idea.
6. The coach showed Jean a curve ball.
7. The babysitter read Melissa and Don a story.
8. Mom found Grandma a new apartment.
9. Ms. Sanchez offered Valerie a job.
10. Liz brought Mom and Dad an anniversary present.

Nouns Used as Predicate Nouns

Nouns are often used as predicate words. A **predicate noun** is a noun in the predicate linked to the subject. A predicate noun follows a linking verb. The predicate noun usually means the same as the subject. The linking verb acts almost as an equal sign between the subject and the predicate noun.

415

Greg is a left-handed *pitcher*.

The maple is a fast-growing *tree*.

Ms. Husak became a *partner* in the firm.

Primary colors are *red*, *blue*, and *yellow*.

Exercise A Write the nouns used as predicate nouns in the following sentences.

1. A mango is a fruit.
2. Studio One is a local disco.
3. My brother became a taxi driver.
4. Curt's home is a trailer.
5. Dessert tonight will be sherbet.
6. Ms. Wells is an actress in commercials.
7. Fire drills are routine practices here.
8. The new office aides are Steve and Lindsay.
9. The attic is a good place for storage.
10. The only refreshments were pretzels and lemonade.

Exercise B Follow the directions for Exercise A.

1. The bleachers are the least expensive seats.
2. Tony's specialties are pizza and lasagna.
3. The nearest expressway is the North Freeway.
4. Conroy became coach of the Eagles.
5. Gasohol is a new fuel.
6. Judy Blume is a popular writer.
7. Cuba is a narrow island.
8. The Armada was a Spanish fleet.
9. The guests were diplomats and Senators.
10. Madge's Kitchen is a neighborhood restaurant.

416

Part 3   Plural Forms of Nouns

A noun that stands for one thing is **singular**. *Store*, *pipe*, *manager*, and *bowl* are singular. A noun that stands for more than one thing is **plural**. *Stores*, *pipes*, *managers*, and *bowls* are plural.

Most of the time, you don't even stop to think about making a noun plural. Sometimes, though, you may have to recall the rules for forming plurals of nouns.

1. **To most singular nouns, add -*s* to form the plural:**

    books   desks   ropes   boots

2. **When a singular noun ends in *s*, *sh*, *ch*, *x*, or *z*, add -*es*:**

    coaches   boxes   buzzes   glasses   bushes

3. **When a singular noun ends in *o*, add -*s* to make it plural:**

    solos   pianos   studios   rodeos   photos

For a few nouns ending in *o*, preceded by a consonant, add -*es*:

    tomatoes   heroes   echoes   potatoes   cargoes

4. **When the singular noun ends in *y* with a consonant before it, change the *y* to *i* and add -*es*:**

    city—cities   lady—ladies   country—countries

If the *y* is preceded by a vowel (*a, e, i, o, u*) do not change the *y* to *i*. Simply add -*s*:

    toy—toys   play—plays   day—days

5. **Some nouns ending in *f* simply add -*s*:**

    beliefs   chiefs   dwarfs   handkerchiefs

Many words ending in *f* or *fe* change the *f* to *v* and add -*es* or -*s*. Since there is no rule to follow, these words have to be

417

417

1. The (paintbrush) *paintbrushes* were too stiff to use.
2. After he broke his leg, Dan used (crutch) *crutches* for one month.
3. The (piano) *pianos* and (cello) *cellos* stood ready for the orchestra.
4. Helen put (mango) *mangoes* in the fruit salad.
5. War (hero) *heroes* are given medals.
6. Yellow (daisy) *daisies* grow outside our windows.
7. The lawyer typed her own (brief) *briefs*.
8. The (fish) *fish* were biting; Meg caught several (trout) *trout*.
9. The dentist wants to pull my wisdom (tooth) *teeth*.
10. A flock of (goose) *geese* flew high overhead.

Extending the Lesson

Compile a list of nouns to be used to develop a story orally. Start the first sentence of the story yourself. Give each student one of the nouns from the list. Have the student change the noun into its plural form. Then have the student use the plural noun in a sentence that builds on the preceeding sentence and advances the story.

memorized. Here are some examples of such words:

leaf—leaves   thief—thieves   life—lives
half—halves   shelf—shelves   knife—knives

6. Some nouns have the same form for both the singular and plural. These, too, must be memorized.

deer   tuna   trout   sheep   moose

7. Some nouns form their plurals in special ways:

child—children   goose—geese   man—men
mouse—mice   ox—oxen   woman—women

The dictionary will help you to form plurals. Here is a dictionary entry for the word *shelf*. Notice that the entry shows the plural, *shelves*. Most dictionaries show the plurals if they are formed in an irregular way. When you are in doubt about plurals, check a dictionary.

shelf (shelf) *n., pl.* **shelves** [prob. < MLowG. *schelf:* for IE. base see CUTLASS] **1.** a thin, flat length of wood, metal, etc. fixed horizontally to a wall or built into a frame, as in a bookcase, and used for holding things **2.** the contents of a shelf, or the amount it will hold **3.** something like a shelf; specif., *a)* a flat ledge of rock *b)* a sand bar or reef —**on the shelf** not active, in use, etc. —**shelf'like'** *adj.*

Exercise A   Write the plural of each of these nouns. Then use your dictionary to see if you are right.

1. bookshelf *bookshelves*
2. chimney *chimneys*
3. elf *elves*
4. wish *wishes*
5. tomato *tomatoes*
6. dish *dishes*
7. wife *wives*
8. sheep *sheep*
9. fox *foxes*
10. goose *geese*
11. treaty *treaties*
12. watch *watches*
13. church *churches*
14. brush *brushes*
15. orderly *orderlies*
16. jelly *jellies*
17. county *counties*
18. mouse *mice*
19. witch *witches*
20. piano *pianos*

Exercise B   Write each sentence, correcting the errors in the plural forms of nouns.

1. Several <u>companys</u> sell frozen mashed <u>potatos</u>. *companies, potatoes*
2. First, cut the <u>loafs</u> into thin slices. *loaves*

3. The <u>thiefs</u> took several loaves of bread. _{thieves}
4. The <u>babys</u> were getting new <u>tooths</u>. _{babies, teeth}
5. We placed all of the <u>dishes</u> on the <u>benchs</u> in the hallway. _{dishes, benches}
6. Several different <u>companys</u> make CB <u>radioes</u>. _{companies, radios}
7. The <u>deers</u> were eating the green shoots on the <u>bushs</u>. _{deer, bushes}
8. Use these <u>brushs</u> to stain the <u>bookshelfs</u>. _{brushes, bookshelves}
9. The larger boxes had <u>scratchs</u> on them. _{scratches}
10. My blue jeans are covered with <u>patchs</u>. _{patches}

Part 4 Possessive Forms of Nouns

People own or possess things. There is a shorthand way to note ownership. You would say:

Carol's coat   the *doctor's* bag   our *neighbor's* house

To show that something belongs to or is part of a person, you would use the same form:

Jill's face   *Ann's* tooth   *Bill's* worries

In either case, the *'s* makes the nouns show ownership. Nouns like *Carol's, doctor's,* and *Ann's* are called **possessive nouns.**

Most often, people and animals possess things. Occasionally, however, things are also used in the possessive. You might say *a city's problems, the day's end,* or *a stone's throw.*

Forming Possessives

There are three rules for making nouns possessive:

1. If the noun is singular, add an apostrophe and s:

Singular Noun	Possessive Noun
Bess	Bess's
Mother	Mother's
theater	theater's

419

Part 4

Objective

To form and use possessive nouns correctly

Presenting the Lesson

Read and discuss pages 419–420. Go over the rules for forming possessives carefully, especially noting examples. Ask students for additional examples for each rule.

2. Do Exercise A on page 420 with the class.

3. Assign and discuss Exercise B on pages 420–421.

4. Assign and discuss Exercise C on page 421.

Individualizing the Lesson

Less-Advanced Students

Have students indicate the rule that applies to each word in Exercise A. Have students use each possessive form in Exercise B in a sentence.

Advanced Students

Have students create the possessive form of ten nouns not included in any of the Exercises. Then

419

have them use each of the new nouns in a sentence.

Optional Practice

Have students divide their papers into four columns, labeled *Singular*, *Plural*, *Singular Possessive*, and *Plural Possessive*. Students should copy the following nouns in the column labeled *Singular*. They should then fill in the other three columns for each word. Answers below.

1. officer   6. girl
2. city   7. winner
3. day   8. monkey
4. citizen   9. baby
5. lady   10. dancer

1. officers, officer's, officers'
2. cities, city's, cities'
3. days, day's, days'
4. citizens, citizen's, citizens'
5. ladies, lady's, ladies'
6. girls, girl's, girls'
7. winners, winner's, winners'
8. monkeys, monkey's, monkeys'
9. babies, baby's, babies'
10. dancers, dancer's, dancers'

Extending the Lesson

Have students use each of the following nouns in sentences. Students should be able to identify the nouns they use as either singular, plural, singular possessive, or plural possessive. Sentences will vary.

SP 1. Melanie's   PP 6. women's
 P 2. Mondays   SP 7. New York's
SP 3. Friday's   SP 8. soprano's
PP 4. The Grays' PP 9. heroes'
 S 5. dress   SP 10. Betty's

2. If the noun is plural and ends in *s*, add just the apostrophe:

Plural Noun	Possessive Noun
Hoffmans	Hoffmans'
students	students'
committees	committees'

3. If the noun is plural but does not end in *s*, add both the apostrophe and *s*:

Plural Noun	Possessive Noun
children	children's
men	men's
women	women's

Exercise A   Write the possessive form of these nouns.

1. Andrea's   11. Thomas's
2. watchman's   12. Les's
3. carpenter's   13. mirror's
4. child's   14. conductor's
5. Marsha's   15. Tricia's
6. princess's   16. winner's
7. mouse's   17. Tracy's
8. bee's   18. singer's
9. Mary's   19. lake's
10. waitress's   20. Vince's

Exercise B   Follow the directions for Exercise A.

1. dentists'   7. countries'
2. churches'   8. dogs'
3. women's   9. watchmen's
4. children's   10. teachers'
5. people's   11. dresses'
6. birds'   12. stereos'

420

13. sheep's   17. foxes'
14. schools'   18. ducks'
15. boys'   19. engineers'
16. ladies'   20. statues'

Exercise C   Write the possessive form for each italicized word.

1. My *brother* short story won first prize in the contest. _{brother's}

2. *Maurita* and *Amy* paintings were on display in the art room. ^{Maurita's, Amy's}

3. *Ms. Thomas* car was parked in the driveway. ^{Thomas's}

4. Our *class* assignment sheets were sitting on the *teacher* desk. ^{class's, teacher's}

5. The Student *Council* decision was supported by the *teachers* committee and the *principal* office. ^{Council's, teachers'} ^{principal's}

6. The *farmer* newly planted field was washed out by the heavy rain. _{farmer's}

7. The *painter* ladders stood on our front porch. _{painter's}

8. *Jonathan* motorcycle needs new brakes. _{Jonathan's}

9. Our *neighbor* stereo is one of the best I've ever seen. ^{neighbor's}

10. *Janine* time broke the school record for the 100-yard dash. _{Janine's}

Additional Exercises

These Additional Exercises may be used for additional practice of the concepts presented in this Section. Each exercise focuses on a single concept, and should be used after the page number indicated in parentheses.

Review

If you have not assigned these Additional Exercises before this time, you can also use them as an excellent Section Review.

ADDITIONAL EXERCISES

Using Nouns

A. Common Nouns and Proper Nouns Label two columns *Common Nouns* and *Proper Nouns*. Decide whether the following nouns are common or proper. Write each in the correct column. Capitalize the proper nouns.

1. leaders, harriet tubman, abraham lincoln, queen victoria, geronimo
2. garfield, animal, cat, snoopy, pets
3. wednesday, april, birthday, month, weekend
4. mountains, blue sisters mountain, foothills, mount whitney
5. comedy, television, comedian, movie, chevy chase
6. general motors, nabisco, automobile, cookie, cadillac
7. althea gibson, champions, annie oakley, sports, team
8. creeks, rivers, oceans, great salt lake, willow creek
9. science fiction, ray bradbury, luke skywalker, wizards, princess leia
10. mexico, country, pen pal, state, north dakota

B. Nouns as Subjects Number your paper from 1 to 10. Write the nouns used as subjects in each of the following sentences.

1. George has a small part in the play.
2. Melissa has a watch from Switzerland.
3. Pirate's Alley is in New Orleans.
4. China, Nepal, and India have the world's tallest mountains.
5. *Sports Illustrated* uses excellent photographs.
6. Some snails live in water.
7. The sink in the kitchen is made of stainless steel.
8. The fearless ladybug landed on my hand.

9. Four <u>employers</u> in that building hire part-time workers.
10. The <u>orchard</u> and <u>garden</u> were bare.

C. Nouns as Direct Objects   Number your paper from 1 to 10. Write the <u>nouns used as direct objects</u> in each of the following sentences.

1. The coach drew a <u>diagram</u> on the chalkboard.
2. Sandy was driving the <u>tractor</u>.
3. The mail carrier rang the <u>doorbell</u> again.
4. Gwen can do perfect <u>cartwheels</u>.
5. Bart took a <u>course</u> in photography.
6. Crosby held the <u>racquet</u> with both hands.
7. Nancy paddled the <u>canoe</u> to the riverbank.
8. Phyllis greeted <u>Denny</u> and <u>Karen</u> at the door.
9. All of the stores had slashed their <u>prices</u>.
10. Mr. Cole held the big dog's <u>leash</u> tightly.

D. Nouns as Indirect Objects   Number your paper from 1 to 10. Write the <u>indirect objects</u> in the following sentences.

1. The suspect told the <u>police</u> his story.
2. The editor gave the <u>reporter</u> a new assignment.
3. Roberta read <u>Jeff</u> her report.
4. Pete bought his <u>brother</u> a football helmet.
5. Dee made <u>Katie</u> a *piñata* for the party.
6. The driver flashed <u>Mr. Owens</u> a big smile.
7. The leader gave her <u>troops</u> the signal.
8. Rosa showed the <u>inspector</u> the basement.
9. Hattie kicked <u>Joanne</u> the ball.
10. The animal shelter found the <u>dog</u> a new home.

E. Predicate Nouns   Number your paper from 1 to 10. List the <u>predicate nouns</u> in these sentences.

1. Whales are the largest <u>mammals</u>.
2. Two towns on Cape Cod are <u>Hyannis</u> and <u>Orleans</u>.

3. Josett and Charles are <u>members</u> of the track team.
4. The piranha is a small, deadly <u>fish</u>.
5. The ghost town became an <u>attraction</u> for tourists.
6. Her lunch is always <u>cheese, rolls</u>, and an <u>apple</u>.
7. The gift was certainly a <u>surprise</u>.
8. Johnny's hat was an old <u>beret</u>.
9. Angela could be a <u>writer</u> someday.
10. Our next stop will be <u>Mount Vernon</u>.

F. Plurals of Nouns   Number your paper from 1 to 30. Write the plural form of each word. Some forms may already be correct.

1. bunch — bunches	11. potato — potatoes	21. handkerchief — handkerchiefs
2. tomato — tomatoes	12. bay — bays	22. inch — inches
3. pony — ponies	13. guppy — guppies	23. loss — losses
4. shelf — shelves	14. ditch — ditches	24. candy — candies
5. foot — feet	15. sneeze — sneezes	25. ax — axes
6. belief — beliefs	16. hero — heroes	26. ox — oxen
7. knife — knives	17. beauty — beauties	27. card — cards
8. teeth	18. photo — photos	28. guitar — guitars
9. children	19. woman — women	29. half — halves
10. motorcade — motorcades	20. deer	30. laugh — laughs

G. Possessive of Nouns   Write the following phrases, adding the possessive forms asked for in the parentheses.

1. (singular possessive of *Jenny*) suitcase — Jenny's
2. (singular possessive of *Elvis*) records — Elvis's
3. (plural possessive of *lady*) gloves — ladies'
4. the (singular possessive of *wax*) color — wax's
5. (plural possessive of *woman*) rights — women's
6. the (plural possessive of *Williams*) yard — Williams's
7. the (singular possessive of *glass*) rim — glass's
8. the (singular possessive of *dictionary*) cover — dictionary's
9. the (plural possessive of *child*) playground — children's
10. the (plural possessive of *coach*) conference — coaches'

MIXED REVIEW

Using Nouns

A. Identifying nouns and their uses Copy the nouns from these sentences. After each, write *Subject, Direct Object, Indirect Object,* or *Predicate Noun* to show how it is used.

1. Ice^S covers the Arctic Ocean.^{DO}

    Ice [S] covers the Arctic Ocean [DO].

2. Our hottest month [S] was July [PN].

3. A footlocker [S] is a large trunk [PN].

4. Amanda picked Kevin [IO] an apple [DO].

5. The man [S] picked a card [DO].

6. Unfortunately, the last bus [S] had left.

7. The dog [S] has broken two collars [DO], a leash [DO], and a chain [DO].

8. Fred [S] soon became captain [PN].

9. Pam [S] bought her little nephew [IO] a turtle [DO].

10. Sometimes Chet [S] likes a hearty breakfast [DO].

B. Using plural and possessive forms correctly Rewrite these sentences, correcting the errors in the plural and possessive forms of nouns. If a sentence is correct, write *Correct*.

1. A cats eyes were glowing in Ms. Jones's dark backyard. cat's

2. The two boy's radios were playing different songs. boys'

3. One waitress' tips came to twenty dollars. waitress's

4. The trains wheels clattered along the railroad track's. train's, tracks

5. Jo's plans for the holidays include several parties. C

6. A vampire bat's teeth are like razors. C

7. Rons' glasses kept sliding down his nose. Ron's

8. The yellow Ford is Mr. Coley car. Mr. Coley's

9. Four house on the street have red porches. houses

10. Men's handkerchiefs are usually large. C

425

Using Grammar in Writing

These challenging and enjoyable activities allow the students to see how the concepts of grammar, usage, and mechanics may be applied in actual writing situations. Each exercise is designed to allow students practice in several of the skills they have acquired in this Section. The activities also provide opportunities for students to write creatively about a wide variety of interesting and unusual subjects.

USING GRAMMAR IN WRITING
Using Nouns

A. You have signed up for a winter survival course. As part of the course, you will have to spend a week alone in a log cabin in the mountains. There is no running water or electricity in the cabin. There is only an ax to chop wood. You must take along whatever else you will need to survive. Whatever you take you must carry on your back or on a small sled. Make a list of what you think you will have to take along. Then turn the list into a paragraph. Underline each common noun once and each proper noun twice.

B. Imagine that you could own and operate any kind of specialty store. What kind of store would you choose? Where would it be located? Write a paragraph about your store. Tell about the items you would stock and the customers you would attract. Underline all nouns. Label them singular (s), plural (pl.), or possessive (p). Form plurals and possessives correctly.

C. Write each of the following words on a separate piece of paper:

skateboard	hamster
kitchen	pizza
stereo	

Fold the paper in two, so that you cannot see what is written inside. Then, on the outside, write one of each of the following categories.

subject	predicate noun
direct object	possessive
indirect object	

Each of the nouns is now matched with a different category. Write five sentences, using each noun in the way described on the outside of the paper.

426

HANDBOOK SECTION 4

Using Pronouns

Your speech and writing would be very awkward if you had only nouns to refer to persons, places, or things. You would have to say this:

> Beth found Beth's book in Beth's locker.
> Beth took Beth's book back to the library.

Fortunately, there are words that can be used in place of nouns. These are called **pronouns.** With pronouns you can say this:

> Beth found *her* book in *her* locker. *She* took *it* back to the library.

The words *her* and *she* are pronouns that stand for the noun *Beth* and are used in place of it. The word *it* is a pronoun that stands for the word *book* and is used in its place.

427

Section Objectives

1. To understand the concept of the pronoun and to recognize singular and plural personal pronouns
2. To recognize and use personal pronouns in the subject form, object form, and possessive form
3. To use the correct pronoun in compound sentence parts
4. To use pronouns that agree with their antecedents in number
5. To form compound personal pronouns and to use them correctly
6. To use demonstrative pronouns correctly
7. To recognize and use interrogative pronouns correctly
8. To distinguish between singular and plural indefinite pronouns
9. To check for agreement in number between indefinite pronouns and their verbs and other possessive pronouns that refer to them
10. To use pronouns correctly in situations that often cause problems

Preparing the Students

Explain that pronouns are a useful part of speech because they help avoid repetition by taking the place of nouns.

Read and discuss the introduction on page 427.

Additional Resources

Diagnostic Test — page 2 in the test booklet
Mastery Test — pages 46–47 in the test booklet
Additional Exercises — pages 448–454 in the student text
Practice Book — pages 171–179

427

Duplicating Masters — pages 171–179

Special Populations — See special section at the back of this Teacher's Edition.

Part 1

Objective

To understand the concept of the pronoun and to recognize singular and plural personal pronouns

Presenting the Lesson

1. Read page 428. Carefully study examples of pronouns used in the three situations illustrated. Go over the list of singular and plural personal pronouns on page 428.

2. Using the list of pronouns at the bottom of page 428, go around the class and have each student use one pronoun in a sentence.

3. Assign and discuss Exercises A and B on page 429.

Individualizing the Lesson

Less-Advanced Students

Have students divide their paper into columns headed *Singular* and *Plural*. Have them write the pronouns in Exercises A and B in the appropriate column.

Encourage students to refer to the chart on page 428 whenever they have a question about pronoun usage.

Advanced Students

Have students write five sentences using singular pronouns and

428

Part 1 Personal Pronouns

A **pronoun** is a word used in place of a noun. Pronouns are valuable words. They may be used in three situations:

1. They may refer to the person speaking.

   I raised *my* hand.
   We will go.
   That flashlight is *mine*.

2. They may refer to someone spoken to.

   Have *you* forgotten *your* gloves?
   Are the notebooks *yours*?

3. They may refer to other persons, places, and things.

   Jill reached for the paddle, but *it* floated away.
   The boys are looking for *him*.
   Nancy says that the book is *hers*.
   He spoke to *her* yesterday.
   They brought *their* cameras with *them*.

From these examples you can see that a pronoun often refers to a person. For this reason, the largest group of pronouns is called **personal pronouns.**

Personal pronouns have many variations. One way of grouping them is according to whether they are singular or plural.

Singular:	I	me	my, mine
	you	you	your, yours
	he	him	his
	she	her	her, hers
	it	it	its
Plural:	we	us	our, ours
	you	you	your, yours
	they	them	their, theirs

428

Exercise A Number your paper from 1 to 10. Write the pronouns you find in the following sentences. After each pronoun, write the noun or nouns it stands for.

1. Dorinda rolled up her sleeves. Dorinda
2. The radio station has changed its format. station
3. John and Ginny visited their cousins in Texas. John and Ginny
4. Ken came by and picked up his class notes. Ken
5. The alderman said he would sponsor our proposal. alderman, the speaker
6. The Sierra Nevadas are mountains in California. They include Mount Whitney. Sierra Nevadas
7. Sue left her math book in her locker. Sue, Sue
8. Snow covered the ball park this morning, but it melted quickly. snow
9. Linda and her best friend are going to New York, and they will compete in a contest there. Linda, Linda and friend
10. Jay opened the envelope, but it was empty. envelope

Exercise B Follow the directions for Exercise A.

1. Bill looked for his books but couldn't find them. Bill, books
2. The sun had sun dogs, a circle of bright rainbow spots, around it. They are formed from ice particles. sun, sun dogs
3. Last summer, our neighbors painted their house, and my mom and I built window boxes. the speaker, neighbors, the speaker, the speaker
4. Joel and Jim Hertz raised tomatoes. They sold them to their neighbors and made money. Joel and Jim, tomatoes, Joel & Jim
5. Anita wore her jeans to the picnic because she felt comfortable in them. Anita, Anita, jeans
6. My parents and I are going to the jazz concert tonight. the speaker, the speaker
7. Mary, have you sharpened your skates yet? Mary, Mary
8. Would you and Jeff like to team up with Carol and me? person spoken to, the speaker
9. A seismograph records earthquakes. It indicates their intensity. seismograph, earthquakes
10. Did you give Pam and him the packages we had wrapped? person spoken to, person spoken of, the speaker and person spoken to

429

five sentences using plural pronouns. After each pronoun, students should write the noun or nouns it stands for.

Optional Practice

Have students fill the blanks in the following sentences with pronouns. Students should identify the noun to which each pronoun refers.

1. The seniors are making plans for ___their___ prom. ___They___ are having ___it___ at a hotel downtown.
2. Geri told ___her___ boss that ___she___ had to leave early.
3. Scott and Ralph took ___their___ brothers with ___them___ to the park.
4. All teenagers want to be treated like adults; give ___them___ a chance so ___they___ can show ___their___ best sides.

Extending the Lesson

Refer students to a paragraph in their literature textbook or to a paragraph in a magazine article. Have them circle the pronouns they find, write *S* or *P* to indicate whether the pronoun is singular or plural, and then write the antecedent(s) of the pronoun.

Objective

To recognize and use personal pronouns in the subject form, object form, and possessive form

Presenting the Lesson

1. Ask students to supply pronouns in the following sentence:

The teacher asked Sharon if (she) would put (her) diagram on the board, since (hers) was the best in the class.

After writing *she*, *her*, and *hers* on the board, ask students to what noun all three pronouns refer. Stress that although all three refer to *Sharon*, they are in different forms. Explain that pronouns change form according to the ways in which they are used.

2. Read page 430.

3. Do the exercise on pages 430–431. Analyze each pronoun to determine if it is in the subject, object, or possessive form. Students should try to make this determination in terms of the pronoun's function in the sentence, and then check with the chart on page 430.

4. Read page 431 and the top of 432. Remind students that pronouns can be used anywhere a noun can be used. Two common uses of nouns are as subjects and as predicate nouns. Emphasize that pronouns used as subjects and pronouns used as predicate pronouns have the same form.

5. Read page 432 and the top of 433. Review direct objects and indirect objects with students.

Part 2 The Forms of Pronouns

Unlike nouns, pronouns change forms when they are used in different ways. Personal pronouns have three forms. They are **subject form, object form,** and **possessive form.** All three forms of a pronoun refer to the same person. However, the pronoun changes form as its use in a sentence changes. Read these examples:

I waited. (*I* is the subject.)
Tom watched *me*. (*Me* is the direct object.)
My glasses broke. (*My* shows possession.)

Study this list of the three forms of personal pronouns.

Subject	Object	Possessive
I	me	my, mine
you	you	your, yours
he, she, it	her, him, it	her, hers, his, its
we	us	our, ours
you	you	your, yours
they	them	their, theirs

Exercise   The following sentences use pronouns correctly in different ways. Read each sentence aloud.

1. Donna and *she* sold *their* bikes.
2. The nurse is *he*.
3. The root beer lost *its* fizz.
4. Alana told *us* the bad news.
5. Have *you* learned *your* lines?
6. The blue suitcase is *hers*.
7. Scott broke *his* glasses.
8. The counselor gave *him* and *me* advice.
9. *We* waited for *our* cues.
10. *He* and Cindy plunged into the river.

11. Bad weather halted *them*.

12. Mr. Jonas asked *her my* name.

13. The green jacket is *mine*. *It* is warm.

14. The last students were *he* and *I*.

15. *They* will give a signal to *you*.

The Subject Form of Pronouns

Subject Pronouns

I	we
you	you
he, she it	they

The **subject form** of personal pronouns is used at two times. The subject form is used for subjects of sentences. In addition, the subject form is used for **predicate pronouns.**

Like a predicate noun, a predicate pronoun follows a linking verb. Like a predicate noun, a predicate pronoun refers to the same thing as the subject. The two seem equal.

These sentences may help you to recognize predicate pronouns:

> The linebacker is *he*. (The predicate pronoun *he* is used after the linking verb *is*.)

> My stand-in was *she*. (The predicate pronoun *she* is used with the linking verb *was*.)

In these examples the subject form of pronouns is used for the subjects of sentences:

> *I* carry identification.
> *We* know the code.
> *She* often complains.
> Yesterday *they* left town.

In the following sentences the subject form of pronouns is used for predicate pronouns. Predicate pronouns are often misused. As a result, they may sound strange to you.

431

6. Read page 433. Carefully study examples. Point out that possessive pronouns can be used in the five ways nouns can be used.

7. Have students supply the correct possessive pronouns in these sentences. Have students tell whether the possessive pronoun used tells about a noun, or is used by itself as subject, direct object, object of the preposition, indirect object, or predicate pronoun. Pronouns may vary.

1. We gave our dog ___its___ bath. DO

2. The winners received cash. I spent ___it___ right away. PN

3. Fran entered the art show; the best entry was ___hers___. OP

4. Your turn will come after ___mine___. IO

5. Come on, give ___me___ a break. S.DO

6. Joyce lost her favorite scarf. ___She___ found ___it___ in the yard.

8. Do Exercise A on pages 433–434 orally with the class.

9. Assign and discuss Exercises B and C on page 434.

Individualizing the Lesson

Less-Advanced Students

In Exercise A, help students decide how each pronoun is used. Have them determine by themselves how the correct pronouns are used in Exercise B.

Advanced Students

Have students determine how each pronoun is used in the sentences in Exercises A, B, and C.

Optional Practice

Have students rewrite the following sentences, substituting pronouns for the italicized words.

1. The students wrote the students' [their] assignment just as the students' [their] teacher had told the students [them] to do.

2. The voters re-elected the Senator. The voters [They] liked the Senator [him] better than the Senator's [his] opponents. The voters [They] felt that the best candidate was the Senator [he].

3. The group performed a folk song as the group's [their] final number. The fans cheered for the group [them] so loudly that the group [they] sang an encore for the fans [them].

Extending the Lesson

Have students divide their paper into three columns marked *Subject Form, Object Form,* and *Possessive Form.* Then refer students to one page of a short story. Have them examine all the pronouns on the page and write them in the appropriate category. Discuss how each pronoun is used in its sentence.

Our guests were the Bakers and *they.*
My favorite actors are Richard Pryor and *he.*
The only fan still cheering was *I.*
Two good neighbors are *you* and Ben.
The best runner is certainly *she.*

The Object Form of Pronouns

Object Pronouns

me	us
you	you
him, her, it	them

Personal pronouns are often used as objects. If a pronoun is not a subject or a predicate pronoun, it is an object. Then you use the object form of the pronoun.

There are three kinds of objects: direct objects, indirect objects, and objects of prepositions. Prepositions are short connecting words like *to, from, by, of,* and *for.* Often pronouns are used after such words. See **Handbook Section 7** for more explanation of prepositions.

These examples show the object form of pronouns as direct objects:

The security guard knew *her.*
Two trucks towed *them.*
The newscaster reported *it.*
Commercials bore *me.*
The long grass tickled *us.*

In the following sentences, the object form of pronouns is used for indirect objects:

Al tossed *us* some money.
Mom gave *me* the answer.
His boss sends *him* his check.
I told *you* the address.

These sentences also use the object form of pronouns as objects of prepositions:

My dog swam to *me*.   A coupon came with *it*.
Tim babysits for *them*.   You caught a cold from *us*.

The Possessive Form of Pronouns

Possessive Pronouns

my, mine	our, ours
your, yours	your, yours
his, her, hers, its	their, theirs

Personal pronouns have another form to show possession. This possessive form indicates ownership or belonging.

The possessive form may be used in two ways. Sometimes you use it to tell about nouns.

Josh counted *his* change.   We enjoy *your* visits.
Did Marla react to *their* remarks? *Our* old car stalls.

At other times you use the possessive pronoun by itself. Like a noun, the possessive form may be a subject of a verb, a predicate word, or an object.

Those paintings are *his*. (predicate word)
Mine are more colorful. (subject)
Have you finished *yours*? (direct object)
She gave *hers* a final glaze. (indirect object)
Derek's house is next to *ours*. (object of preposition)

Exercise A   Write the correct pronoun from the parentheses. Read the complete sentence to yourself.

1. Ms. Walsh gave the job to (I, me).
2. That was (she, her).
3. Does this copy belong to (he, him)?
4. Donna and I helped (they, them) with the yard work.
5. Hasn't anybody seen (he, him)?
6. It was (she, her) who answered the call.

7. Was it (<u>they</u>, them) who called?
8. Are any of these letters (your, <u>yours</u>)?
9. This is (<u>he</u>, him).
10. Will you give these books to (she, <u>her</u>)?

Exercise B   Follow the directions for Exercise A.

1. Each of (we, <u>us</u>) had a look at it.
2. I'm sure it was (<u>he</u>, him) on the telephone.
3. I have both of (their, <u>theirs</u>).
4. That looks more like (I, <u>me</u>).
5. Mother asked (I, <u>me</u>) to be home by ten o'clock.
6. The award was given to (she, <u>her</u>) for outstanding achievement.
7. The reporter wanted to talk to Kelly and (I, <u>me</u>).
8. Could it have been (<u>they</u>, them)?
9. The block party was organized by Rosie and (they, <u>them</u>).
10. (<u>I</u>, Me) am going to the weight room.

Exercise C   The personal pronouns in the following sentences are in italics. Write each one. After it, write *Subject Form* (SF) or *Object Form* (OF).

OF 1. The manager sold *us* the T-shirts at a discount.
OF 2. Carl couldn't hear *me*.
OF 3. I gave *you* the schedule.
SF, OF 4. *They* were taking *her* to dinner.
SF, OF 5. *He* gave the gifts to *them*.
SF, OF 6. *We* have been waiting for *him*.
OF 7. The car just missed *him*.
OF 8. Ms. Anderson gave *us* several problems for homework.
OF 9. Did Aunt Ellen get a good picture of *us*?
SF 10. The third person in the front row is *she*.

Part 3 Pronouns in Compound Sentence Parts

You seldom make mistakes when you use one personal pronoun by itself. You would never say "Give *I* the pencil."

Trouble arises when a pronoun is used with another pronoun or with a noun. Would you say "Brian and me built a radio" or "Brian and I built a radio"?

Have you heard people say "between you and I"? Does this sound right? Should it be "between you and me"? How can you tell?

Two or more words joined by *and, or,* or *nor* are compound parts. Look at these sentences with pronouns correctly used in compound parts.

> *Terry* and *she* went to the rink. (*Terry* and *she* are both subjects. The subject form *she* is used.)
>
> We visited the *Browns* and *them.* (*Browns* and *them* are direct objects. The object form is used.)
>
> The package was for *Jack* and *me.* (*Jack* and *me* are objects of *for.* The object form is used.)

Now read the sentences above a second time. This time drop out the noun in each compound part. For example, read "*She* went to the rink." Each sentence will sound right and sensible to you.

Whenever you are in doubt about which form of a pronoun to use in a compound sentence part, drop the noun. Read the sentence with just the pronoun, and you will usually choose the right one.

If there are two pronouns in the compound part, read the sentence for each pronoun separately.

> Ms. Huber will call for you and (she, her).
> Ms. Huber will call for you.
> Ms. Huber will call for *her.*

435

Part 3

Objective

To use the correct pronoun form in compound sentence parts

Presenting the Lesson

1. Read page 435. Remind students that they have already dealt with compound parts of sentences (Section 1, Part 9). Tell them that there are two ways to check to make sure that the correct form of a pronoun is used in a compound sentence part. One way, as suggested on page 435, is to read the sentence with just the pronoun in question, eliminating the other noun or pronoun. Another way to decide which form of the pronoun to use is to determine whether the pronoun in question is used as a subject or as an object. If it is used as a subject, the subject form should be used (refer students to the list on page 431). If the pronoun is used as an object, the object form should be used (refer students to the list on page 432).

2. Assign and discuss Exercises A and B on page 436.

Individualizing the Lesson

Less-Advanced Students

Remind students to test the pronoun choice in each sentence by dropping the noun from the compound sentence part. Do Exercise A as a class; assign Exercise B.

Advanced Students

Have students tell how each pronoun is used in each sentence in Exercises A and B.

435

Have students complete the following exercise, choosing the right pronoun from the parentheses in each sentence.

1. The twins and (I, me) are training for the relay race.
2. An invitation to Eric and (he, him) arrived today.
3. The priest blessed (they, them) and (we, us).
4. The secret must be kept between you and (I, me).
5. The monitors were freshmen and (we, us).
6. Gregory and (he, him) are the best guards.
7. Call your parents and (they, them) when you get to Cleveland.
8. Ryan and (I, me) went to camp together.

Extending the Lesson

Have students return to Exercise A, Exercise B, or the **Optional Practice** and state in what form the correct pronoun appears. If it is in subject form, students should tell if it functions as a subject or a predicate pronoun. If it is object form, students should tell if it is used as a direct object, an indirect object, or an object of the preposition.

Exercise A   Write the correct pronoun from the parentheses in each sentence. Read the complete sentence to yourself.

1. Wait for Lori and (I, me) after school.
2. Jeff lives between (they and I, them and me).
3. Gayle and (she, her) are trying out for the cheerleading team.
4. The manager gave Al and (I, me) a pass.
5. There is no difference in weight between (he and I, him and me).
6. Dawn and (she, her) will bring the road maps.
7. Can you give Sandy and (we, us) a ride to school in the morning?
8. (She, Her) and I are the newspaper editors.
9. The ushers were Marla and (she, her).
10. Just between you and (I, me), that movie wasn't very good.

Exercise B: Writing   All but one of the following sentences contain a pronoun error. Write the sentences, correcting the errors.

1. Judy and ~~her~~ [she] just went out the back door.
2. Ms. McGowan made Meg and ~~I~~ [me] a sandwich for dinner.
3. The telephone must be for either you or ~~she.~~ [her]
4. Everyone except Janet and ~~she~~ [her] had enough money.
5. The packages were divided evenly between Tanya and ~~I.~~ [me]
6. My parents and ~~me~~ [I] are going to the family reunion tonight.
7. Larry and ~~them~~ [they] have gone to Detroit for the summer vacation.
8. The bus driver gave Mary Beth and ~~I~~ [me] directions.
9. Peggy and Linda sat next to Lauri and ~~I~~ [me] at the concert.
10. The helicopter kept circling around Pam and me. C

Part 4   Pronouns and Antecedents

You have learned that a pronoun is used in place of a noun. This noun is the word to which the pronoun refers. The noun usually comes first, either in the same sentence or in the preceding sentence. The noun for which a pronoun stands is its **antecedent.**

> The men had taken off *their* coats.
> (*Their* stands for *men. Men* is the antecedent.)
>
> We waited for Kay. She was making a phone call.
> (*She* stands for *Kay. Kay* is the antecedent.)

Pronouns themselves may be the antecedents of other pronouns:

> Do you have *your* music lesson today?
> (*You* is the antecedent of *your*.)

A pronoun must agree with its antecedent in number.

Here the word *agree* means that the pronoun must be the same in number as its antecedent. The word *number* here means singular or plural. The pronoun must be singular if the word it stands for is singular. It must be plural if the word it stands for is plural.

> The runners took *their* places.
> (*Runners* is *plural*; *their* is plural.)
>
> The scientist spoke about *her* early research.
> (*Scientist* is singular; *her* is singular.)
>
> Scott brought *his* own records.
> (*Scott* is singular; *his* is singular.)
>
> The girls left *their* projects in the shop.
> (*Girls* is plural; *their* is plural.)
>
> The dog left its bone on the porch.
> (*Dog* is singular; *its* is singular.)

437

Objective

To use pronouns that agree with their antecedents in number

Presenting the Lesson

1. Read page 437. Make certain that students understand the definitions of *antecedent, number,* and *agree.*

2. Some analysis of the word *antecedent* may help students understand this concept. Explain the Latin derivation: *ante-* = before, *cede* = go or yield. An antecedent is that which goes before. Related words which will help illustrate the meaning of antecedent are: *antedate* (dated before), *anteroom* (room before, hallway), *anterior* (front), *precede* (go before), and *recede* (go back).

3. Assign and discuss Exercises A and B on page 438. Assign and discuss Exercise C.

Individualizing the Lesson

Less-Advanced Students

Have students circle the personal pronouns in a section from a short story or novel. Then have them underline the antecedent of each pronoun.

Advanced Students

Tell students to write five sentences using pronouns. They should then identify the antecedent of each pronoun. Have students decide how each pronoun is used.

Have students identify the ante-cedents in the sentences in **Extending the Lesson.**

Extending the Lesson

Have students choose a pronoun that will agree in number with its antecedent from those given in parentheses.

1. Both birds in the nest called for (his, their) mother.
2. Tie the ribbons on each box, but don't cut (it, them).
3. A nurse must keep (his or her, their) uniform clean.
4. Russell and Scott have (their, his) own skis.
5. Dad's shirt sleeves are too long, so he rolls (it, them) up.
6. Three doctors from the hospital offered (his, their) help.
7. The drapes burst into flames after the candle touched (it, them).
8. The mechanics used (his or her, their) own tools.
9. The needles on the tree are falling from (its, their) branches.
10. Every student should do (his or her, their) best.

Exercise A   The personal pronouns in these sentences are italicized. Find the antecedent of each pronoun. Write it.

1. The executive sent *her* secretary to the meeting. executive
2. Everyone thinks *you* can do the job, Sarah. Sarah
3. The box isn't pretty, but the paper around *it* is. box
4. Many people in the audience had tears in *their* eyes. people
5. The boy with the skateboard had a cast on *his* arm. boy
6. *You* don't usually bring *your* sister to the pool, Kathy. Kathy, Kathy
7. The glass had a crack in *it*. glass
8. *Brad* bought *his* own materials. Brad
9. The members of the cast took *their* places. members
10. The storm shelter had *its* entrance boarded up. shelter

Exercise B   Follow the directions for Exercise A.

1. Susie brought *her* radio. Susie
2. The photographer used different lenses when *he* photographer needed *them*. lenses
3. Phil fixed *his* crooked necktie. Phil
4. The ballpark has a fence around *it*. ballpark
5. Mrs. Kohl was knitting a sweater for *her* baby. Mrs. Kohl
6. Bring *your* gym clothes for the intramural game. person spoken to
7. Curt looked in *his* wallet and panicked. Curt
8. Lara and Pete told *their* friends about the time trials. Lara and Pete
9. The paramedics carried all of *their* equipment. paramedics
10. Chris's coat had a tear in *it*. coat

Exercise C: Writing   Below is a fragment of a simple sentence. Write six different sentences from this fragment by adding a pronoun in the second space, and its antecedent in the first space. Some of the nouns must be plural. Answers will vary.

Example: _____ left _____ luggage on the bus.

The businessmen left *their* luggage on the bus.

Part 5 Compound Personal Pronouns

A **compound personal pronoun** is formed by adding *-self* or *-selves* to certain personal pronouns:

myself	ourselves
yourself	yourselves
himself	
herself	themselves
itself	

You use compound personal pronouns for emphasis:

Aaron *himself* read the announcement.
The hostages freed *themselves* from the bonds.
I'll find the solution *myself*.
We *ourselves* choose a president.

Exercise A Beside each number write the correct compound personal pronoun for each of the following sentences. After it, write the noun or pronoun to which it refers.

1. Ms. Adel suggested we do the painting (pronoun). *ourselves*
2. Nancy, Carrie, and Sue made the dinner (pronoun). *themselves*
3. Bret let (pronoun) down by the rope. *himself*
4. The fans shouted (pronoun) hoarse. *themselves*
5. The fire burned (pronoun) out. *itself*
6. I will finish washing the car by (pronoun). *myself*
7. We will solve our problems (pronoun). *ourselves*
8. Cut (pronoun) a slice of watermelon. *yourself, (you)*
9. We don't weigh (pronoun) very often. *ourselves*
10. I built and stained these bookcases by (pronoun). *myself*

Exercise B Follow the directions for Exercise A.

1. Will you two be able to finish the job (pronoun)? *yourselves*
2. Bridget organized the presentation by (pronoun). *herself*

439

Part 5

Objective

To form compound personal pronouns and to use them correctly

Presenting the Lesson

1. Read page 439, studying the list of compound personal pronouns and examples of their use.
2. Assign and discuss Exercises A and B on pages 439–440.

Individualizing the Lesson

Less-Advanced Students

Before they begin the Exercises, make sure students realize that compound personal pronouns must agree in both number and gender with the words they refer to. Do Exercise A orally with the class.

Advanced Students

Have students write ten sentences of their own using compound personal pronouns. Have them underline the nouns or pronouns to which each compound personal pronoun refers.

Optional Practice

Have students revise each sentence in Exercise A so that it uses a different compound personal pronoun.

Extending the Lesson

Have students write sentences using each of the eight pronouns on page 439. Have students underline each compound personal pronoun and circle the noun or pronoun to which it refers.

439

3. Jamie, don't rush (pronoun). yourself
4. We set up the equipment (pronoun). ourselves
5. The door just locked (pronoun). itself
6. Diane must not have enjoyed (pronoun) at the rally last week. herself
7. Read the article (pronoun); I think you'll both enjoy it very much. yourselves
8. We just bought (pronoun) a new tape deck. ourselves
9. The store more than pays for (pronoun). itself
10. He wasn't sure of (pronoun) on the high ladder. himself

Part 6 Demonstrative Pronouns

The pronouns *this*, *that*, *these*, and *those* are used to point out persons or things. They are called **demonstrative pronouns.**

This and *these* point to persons or things that are near. *That* and *those* point to persons or things farther away.

This is the right road.   *These* belong to Jim.
That is my camera.   *Those* are my boots.

Exercise   Number your paper from 1 to 10. Write the correct demonstrative pronoun for the blank space in each sentence.

1. _____ are the tools you wanted to borrow. These, Those
2. _____ was my brother who gave the speech. That
3. _____ were the books I was telling you about. These, Those
4. _____ is my sister in the front row. That
5. _____ are my boots over there. Those
6. _____ was Kate on the telephone. That
7. _____ are the chapters I read last night. These, Those
8. _____ are probably better than those. These
9. _____ is my bike parked over there. That
10. _____ was Ryan in the doorway. That

Part 6

Objective

To use demonstrative pronouns correctly

Presenting the Lesson

Read page 440. Assign and discuss the Exercise.

Individualizing the Lesson

Less-Advanced Students

Review how to recognize singular and plural verbs.

Advanced Students

Have students write ten sentences requiring demonstrative pronouns.

Optional Practice

Have students rewrite the sentences in the exercise, keeping the demonstrative pronoun the same but changing the rest of the sentence.

Extending the Lesson

Have students take turns pointing to and identifying things in the classroom using the correct demonstrative pronoun.

Part 7 Interrogative Pronouns

The pronouns *who*, *whom*, *whose*, *which*, and *what* are used to ask questions. They are called **interrogative pronouns.**

Who rang the bell?   *Which* is your paper?
Whom do you mean?   *What* did you say?
Whose are those shoes?

Exercise Write all the pronouns in these sentences. After each pronoun, write *Demonstrative* or *Interrogative* to show which it is.

Example: Are these for Trish?
These—Demonstrative

D 1. Those are the best skates to buy.
I 2. Which of the new TV shows is most enjoyable?
D 3. This is Jay's cassette player.
   4. The doctor knew the answer to that question.
I 5. What are Judith and Phil waiting for?
I 6. Which is the new fuse?
   7. The girls can solve this problem.
I 8. Who recorded that song?
I 9. Which of the motorcycles is most powerful?
D 10. These are the finalists.

Part 8 Indefinite Pronouns

Pronouns like *anyone* and *nobody* do not refer to any definite person or thing. They are called **indefinite pronouns.**

Most indefinite pronouns are singular in number. They refer to only one person or thing. Here they are:

another	each	everything	one
anybody	either	neither	somebody
anyone	everybody	nobody	someone
anything	everyone	no one	

441

Part 7

Objective

To recognize and use interrogative pronouns correctly

Presenting the Lesson

Read page 441. Point out that interrogative pronouns usually appear as the first word in a sentence but that they may also follow the prepositions *to*, *for*, or *from*. Assign and discuss the exercise on page 441.

Individualizing the Lesson

Less-Advanced Students

Review with students how to identify interrogative pronouns.

Advanced Students

Have students write five questions using interrogative pronouns.

Optional Practice

Have students supply demonstrative or interrogative pronouns in the following sentences.

1. __Who__ came in the back door?
2. __This__ can't be happening to me!
3. To __whom__ should I deliver __this__?
4. Is __this/that__ the horse you usually ride?

Part 8

Objectives

1. To distinguish between singular and plural indefinite pronouns

441

Presenting the Lesson

1. Read pages 441–442. Stress that all of the indefinite pronouns in the first list are always singular. Only the four indefinite pronouns in the second list are always plural. To determine if *all, some,* or *none* are singular or plural, students must decide whether they are meant to be singular or plural in individual sentences. Point out that in all of the examples on pages 441–442, not only do indefinite pronouns agree in number with possessive pronouns, but they also agree with their verbs: everyone *has,* not everyone *have.* Stress that *his or her* is the acceptable reference to both sexes. *Their* should only be used to indicate a plural.

2. Assign Exercise A on pages 442–443. Go over answers and have students locate other possessive pronouns in each sentence and check for agreement in number.

3. Assign and discuss Exercise B on page 443.

Individualizing the Lesson

Less-Advanced Students

1. Have students divide their papers into two columns labeled *Singular* and *Plural.* Then tell them to write the pronouns in each sentence in Exercises A and B in the appropriate column.

2. Have students write six sentences using six different indefinite

442

Use the singular possessive pronouns *his, her,* and *its* with the above pronouns.

> Everyone has *his* invitation.
> Everyone has *his* or *her* invitation.

Notice that in the second example, the phrase *his* or *her* is used. You may use this phrase when a singular pronoun refers to either males or females.

A few indefinite pronouns are plural. They refer to more than one person or thing. These plural indefinite pronouns are used with the plural possessive *their.* Read these examples.

> both   many   few   several
>
> *Both* explained *their* stories.
> *Few* of the students had *their* own calculators.
> *Many* of the plants dropped *their* leaves.
> *Several* in the class expressed *their* opinions.

The following pronouns may be singular or plural, depending upon their meaning in the sentence. Read these examples.

> all   some   none
>
> *All* the pie *is* gone. (singular)
> *All* of the members *are* here. (plural)
>
> *Some* of the milk *is* sour. (singular)
> *Some* of the apples *are* ripe. (plural)
>
> *None* of the time *was* wasted. (singular)
> *None* of the flowers *were* left. (plural)

Exercise A   Number your paper from 1 to 10. For each sentence write the <u>indefinite pronoun</u> or pronouns.

1. <u>Either</u> of the counselors will help you with your schedule.
2. In the spring, almost <u>everyone</u> sunbathes in the courtyard.
3. <u>All</u> of the photographs for the yearbook were too dark.
4. <u>Somebody</u> has left his or her jacket on the bus.

442

5. Is <u>anything</u> the matter?
6. <u>Both</u> of the games last week were postponed because of rain.
7. During the noon hour, <u>anyone</u> can leave campus to eat lunch.
8. <u>One</u> of the student productions will be *The Wiz*.
9. <u>Each</u> of the students filled out his or her registration cards.
10. <u>Everyone</u> was choosing classes for the fall semester.

Exercise B Choose the right <u>pronoun</u> from the parentheses.

1. Most of the cans had lost (its, <u>their</u>) labels.
2. Somebody has left (<u>his or her</u>, their) wallet on my desk.
3. Few were able to finish (his or her, <u>their</u>) work.
4. Has everyone taken (<u>his or her</u>, their) turn?
5. If anyone wants to go, tell (<u>him or her</u>, them) to see Paul.
6. Everyone had an opportunity to state (<u>his or her</u>, their) opinion.
7. None of the magazines had increased (its, <u>their</u>) circulation.
8. Nobody expected to hear (<u>his or her</u>, their) own name over the loudspeaker.
9. At the first rehearsal, none of the actors could remember (his or her, <u>their</u>) lines.
10. Each of the students explained (<u>his or her</u>, their) design to the class.

Part 9 Special Pronoun Problems

Sometimes you may have trouble using pronouns correctly. You can avoid making mistakes if you are aware of some special problems involving pronouns.

444

Possessive Pronouns and Contractions

Some contractions are formed by joining a pronoun and a verb, omitting one or more letters. The apostrophe shows where letters are left out.

it's = it + is   they're = they + are

you're = you + are   who's = who + is

The possessive forms of the pronouns *its, your, their,* and *whose* sound the same as these contractions: *it's, you're, they're,* and *who's.* Because they sound alike, the contractions and possessives are sometimes confused.

Wrong: The groundhog saw it's shadow.
Right: The groundhog saw its shadow.

Right: You're (You are) late for your appointment.
Right: They're (They are) planning to show their slides.
Right: Who's (Who is) favored to win?

Exercise A   Write the correct word from the two in parentheses.

1. (They're, Their) going to pick up the uniforms.
2. Have you made up (you're, your) mind?
3. (You're, Your) idea might work.
4. Are you sure that (they're, their) coming?
5. (Who's, Whose) going to the Eagles concert?
6. (They're, Their) glad (its, it's) Friday.
7. (Who's, Whose) going to remove the spider?
8. The amusement park gave free passes to (it's, its) first 500 entrants.
9. (Who's, Whose) bike is chained to the tree?
10. (Who's, Whose) got a dime that I can borrow?

Exercise B   Write the words for which the contractions in these sentences stand.

1. It's twenty miles from this town to Omaha. It is
2. The book is called *Who's Who*. Who is

444

3. When's the pizza being delivered? When is
4. Who'd have thought it would snow in May? Who would
5. They've come to repair the water main. They have
6. Who's been in my locker? Who has
7. You've got a good sense of humor. You have
8. It's your turn now. It is
9. Who's next? Who is
10. We've walked the whole way. We have

Who and Whom

The pronouns *who* and *whom* often cause problems. To use *who* and *whom* correctly, keep these points in mind: *Who* is used as the subject of a verb.

> *Who* told you that story? (*Who* is the subject of *told*.)
> *Who* is wearing the yellow sweater? (*Who* is the subject of *is wearing*.)

Whom is used as an object.

> *Whom* did you meet? (*Whom* is object of *did meet*.)
> To *whom* did you go? (*Whom* is object of the preposition *to*.)

Exercise A Choose the right interrogative pronoun from the two given in parentheses.

1. (Who, Whom) watched that show?
2. (Who, Whom) will you choose?
3. (Who, Whom) are these people?
4. Of (who, whom) were you thinking?
5. To (who, whom) do these gym shoes belong?
6. (Who, Whom) swam ten lengths?
7. (Who, Whom) has the time?
8. (Who, Whom) owns these binoculars?
9. (Who, Whom) did Steve forget?
10. For (who, whom) was the phone call?

4. ___Who___ plans to enter the contest?
5. Do you like ___those___ pomegranates?
6. ___Who's___ making all that noise?
7. ___Who___ will be the winner?
8. Mr. Gibbs gave ___us boys___ quite a workout.
9. To ___whom___ is the check made payable?
10. ___You're___ playing our song on ___your___ record player.

Extending the Lesson

Have students write five sentences describing the characteristics of their class. Tell them to use *we* and *us* with *students*. Have them include the words *them* and *those* and *who's* and *whose* in their description, also.

Exercise B   Follow the directions for Exercise A.

1. (Who, Whom) has these initials?
2. From (who, whom) is this letter?
3. (Who, Whom) painted this picture?
4. (Who, Whom) do you know in Alaska?
5. To (who, whom) is Randy talking?
6. To (who, whom) did you give the library books?
7. To (who, whom) should I give these letters?
8. For (who, whom) shall I ask?
9. For (who, whom) did you ask?
10. (Who, Whom) will get the MVP award in hockey?

We Boys—Us Boys; We Girls—Us Girls

When you use phrases like *we girls* and *us boys*, you must be sure that you are using the right form of the pronoun. You can tell which pronoun to use by dropping the noun and saying the sentence without it.

Problem: (We, Us) girls will be at Jan's house.
Correct: *We* will be at Jan's house.
Correct: *We* girls will be at Jan's house.

Problem: Will you pay for (we, us) boys?
Correct: Will you pay for *us*?
Correct: Will you pay for *us* boys?

Them and Those

Them and *those* are two more words that are sometimes confused. The word *them* is always a pronoun. It is always used as an object. It is not used to tell about a noun.

We found *them* here. (object of verb)
We have heard from *them*. (object of preposition *from*)

446

Those is sometimes used to tell about a noun.

> *Those* birds are vultures. (adjective modifying *birds*)
> We will order *those* tools. (adjective modifying *tools*)

Exercise A Write the correct words from the two in parentheses.

1. Who piled all (them, those) boards up?
2. Would you like to sit with (we, us) girls at the play?
3. (Them, Those) portraits look very old.
4. (We, Us) players are going to the Knicks-Bulls basketball game.
5. Will you call for (we, us) boys on the way to the stadium?
6. Many people drive (them, those) vans.
7. Will you drive (we, us) girls to the shopping center?
8. Most of (we, us) boys will help paint the bleachers.
9. You won't need all of (them, those) pencils.
10. (We, Us) students held a pep rally yesterday.

Exercise B Follow the directions for Exercise A.

1. Many commercials are made for (we, us) teenagers.
2. May I borrow (them, those) sunglasses?
3. I called one of (them, those) hotlines.
4. The coach gave (we, us) players a pep talk.
5. (Them, Those) shops at the mall are open late.
6. (We, Us) fans cheered the team.
7. (We, Us) sophomores sponsored a charity drive.
8. No one looks at (them, those) posters.
9. (We, Us) consumers must shop wisely.
10. Our advisers gave (we, us) students our schedules.

Additional Exercises

These Additional Exercises may be used for additional practice of the concepts presented in this Section. Each exercise focuses on a single concept, and should be used after the page number indicated in parentheses.

Review

If you have not assigned these Additional Exercises before this time, you can also use them as an excellent Section Review.

ADDITIONAL EXERCISES

Using Pronouns

A. Personal Pronouns Write each pronoun you find in the following sentences and the noun or nouns it stands for.

1. Heidi tried out her new skates. Heidi
2. Did you set the clock back, Phil? Phil
3. Betty felt sick last night, but now she is better. Betty
4. Jim mailed Brooke a card, but it never arrived. card
5. Mountain laurel is pretty, but its leaves are poisonous. laurel
6. The twins are identical. People often confuse them. twins
7. Tom was washing his hair while Mike talked to him. Tom, Tom
8. Mr. Devi removed his glasses and put them in a case. Mr. Devi, glasses
9. Maria, you can take your turn now. Maria, Maria
10. The horses were in their stalls when Kim locked up. horses

B. Forms of Pronouns Choose the correct pronoun from the two pronouns given in parentheses.

1. The referee shook his fist at (I, me).
2. The best dancer was (she, her).
3. A detour sent (we, us) down a side street.
4. Cal's driving examiner gave (he, him) another chance.
5. (They, Them) are leather seats.
6. Is this book (your, yours)?
7. The fault is certainly not (our, ours).
8. The woman in the wide-brimmed hat is (her, she).
9. The man leaning against the car is (he, him).
10. Does anybody know (he, him)?

C. Pronouns in Compound Sentence Parts Choose the correct pronoun from the two given in parentheses.

1. Gordon and (I, me) were digging for clams.
2. Watch Wendy and (I, me) closely.

3. I saved seats for you and (he, <u>him</u>).
4. The clerk sent Chris and (she, <u>her</u>) instructions.
5. The article mentioned the juniors and (<u>us</u>, we).
6. Holly and (her, <u>she</u>) were playing Clue.
7. (Them and us, <u>They and we</u>) share the yard.
8. There is no difference in age between you and (I, <u>me</u>).
9. Ms. Haddad gave Martin and (<u>me</u>, I) new test booklets.
10. The 4-H Club float came after the band and (he, <u>him</u>).

D. Pronouns and Antecedents The personal pronouns in these sentences are italicized. Write the <u>antecedent</u> of each pronoun.

1. Rugby <u>shirts</u> have stripes on *them*.
2. <u>Latasha</u> expects *her* aunt for dinner.
3. <u>Carin and Lisa</u> celebrated *their* birthdays together.
4. *You* reversed the numbers, <u>Toby</u>.
5. The <u>dog</u> worked hard to remove *its* collar.
6. The <u>buckle</u> had Jon's initials on *it*.
7. <u>Rachel</u> put on *her* jacket and gloves.
8. The <u>scouts</u> practiced pitching *their* tents.
9. <u>Dwayne</u> gets nervous when *he* sees lightning.
10. The <u>painters</u> brought *their* own ladders and brushes.

E. Compound Personal Pronouns On your paper write a correct compound personal pronoun for each of the following sentences. Write the <u>noun</u> or <u>pronoun</u> to which it refers.

1. <u>Nick</u> made (pronoun) do another push-up. himself
2. <u>Inez</u> lowered (pronoun) from the window with a rope. herself
3. The <u>swimmers</u> were drying (pronoun) off. themselves
4. <u>Nina, Ben,</u> and <u>I</u> heard (pronoun) on tape. ourselves
5. <u>I</u> could not force (pronoun) to eat snails. myself
6. <u>We</u> watched (pronoun) on TV. ourselves
7. Make (pronoun) a sandwich, <u>Marco</u>. yourself
8. The <u>city</u> (pronoun) was almost bankrupt. itself

449

9. Apples fall from the trees by (pronoun). themselves
10. Paul believes in improving (pronoun). himself

F. Different Kinds of Pronouns Write all the pronouns in each sentence. After each pronoun, write *Indefinite*, *Demonstrative*, or *Interrogative* to show what kind it is.

D 1. <u>These</u> are the albums on sale.

I 2. <u>Which</u> of the hats belongs to Sally?

D 3. Is <u>this</u> what confused Roger?

D 4. <u>That</u> is the squid's ink sac.

Ind. 5. Aaron handed <u>each</u> of the pedestrians an ad.

Ind. 6. Has <u>anybody</u> seen Charley?

Ind. 7. Georgia knew <u>everyone</u> at the party.

I 8. <u>Who</u> would like these strawberries?

D 9. Well, <u>those</u> are the rules.

Ind. Ind. 10. <u>None</u> of the guests noticed <u>anything</u>.

G. Possessive Pronouns with Indefinite Choose the correct <u>pronoun</u> from those in parentheses.

1. Everyone must wear (<u>his or her</u>, their) ID badge.

2. Each of the boys had (<u>his</u>, their) swimsuit.

3. None of the music had lost (<u>its</u>, their) appeal.

4. None of the dancers wore (her or his, <u>their</u>) shoes.

5. Has everybody brought (<u>his or her</u>, their) track shoes?

6. Neither of the girls has (<u>her</u>, their) driver's license.

7. Either of the plans has (<u>its</u>, their) good points.

8. Both of the women know (her, <u>their</u>) jobs.

9. I put everything back in (<u>its</u>, their) place.

10. Nobody wanted to give (<u>his or her</u>, their) report first.

H. Possessive Pronouns and Contractions Choose the correct word from the two given in parentheses.

1. It's (<u>your</u>, you're) turn to cook.

2. (<u>They're</u>, Their) putting in a new street light.

3. (Whose, Who's) on second base?
4. (Its, It's) engine is new.
5. (Its, It's) a new engine.
6. Are you wearing (you're, your) new boots?
7. (Whose, Who's) the winner?
8. Those ranchers sold (they're, their) cattle at a loss.
9. (Whose, Who's) are these skates?
10. I wonder if (your, you're) right.

I. **Who and Whom**   Choose the correct interrogative pronoun.

1. (Who, Whom) was the note meant for?
2. (Who, Whom) pilots the plane?
3. (Who, Whom) will second the motion?
4. With (who, whom) were you talking?
5. (Who, Whom) made these tapes?
6. At (who, whom) is she staring?
7. (Who, Whom) should I ask?
8. (Who, Whom) asked you?
9. By (who, whom) did you sit?
10. With (who, whom) is Veronica dancing?

J. **Special Pronoun Problems**   Choose the correct word
from the two words given in parentheses.

1. (We, Us) passengers had a bumpy flight.
2. (Them, Those) running shoes have good support.
3. Who watches (them, those) soap operas?
4. A retired actor coached (we, us) students.
5. (We, Us) Spanish students volunteered as interpreters.
6. I enjoyed doing (them, those) yoga exercises.
7. Mr. Zoback shelled (them, those) shrimp.
8. The waiter ignored (we, us) teenagers.
9. The hardest workers were (we, us) students.
10. The photographer took a picture of (we, us) winners.

MIXED REVIEW

Using Pronouns

A. Using personal pronouns Write the correct pronoun for each of the following sentences. After each one write its antecedent.

1. An animal can lose half (its, <u>its</u>) weight during hibernation. animal
2. The goalie is (her, <u>she</u>). goalie
3. Is the baseball cap (your, <u>yours</u>), Neal? Neal
4. Mel dived under the waves when (it, <u>they</u>) seemed too big to ride. waves
5. Please don't interrupt Kate. (Her, <u>She</u>) is studying. Kate
6. The bumpers are made of rubber. (Them, <u>They</u>) absorb shocks. bumpers
7. My name is Terry Lesak. Were you paging (I, <u>me</u>)? Terry Lesak
8. Nan pointed out the stars and told me (they, <u>their</u>) names. stars
9. The snake is shedding (it, <u>its</u>) skin. snake
10. Bob slapped Ralph on the back and congratulated (he, <u>him</u>). Ralph

B. Using compound pronouns and pronouns in compound parts correctly Eight of the following sentences use pronouns incorrectly. Rewrite correctly any sentences that do. If a sentence is correct, write *Correct*.

1. Can you and ~~him~~ see the movie screen? he
2. Juanita and ~~her~~ fixed the bike themselves. she
3. Did Art and you make dinner for ~~yourself~~? yourselves
4. I myself sold subscriptions to the Meads and them. c
5. I am going to buy ~~me~~ a new calculator. myself
6. The guests with the best disguises were Althea and ~~him~~. he

452

7. Between you and I, Brenda doesn't know the answer herself. me

8. The Ortiz family and they have the same zip code. c

9. Ms. Franyo hired Emily and I. me

10. The basketball team and us use the gym on different days. we

C. Using the correct form of pronouns   Write the correct word from those given in parentheses.

1. (Who, Whose) name is on the paper?
2. (This, That) is my locker at the end of the corridor.
3. (This, These) will be the legs of the table I'm making.
4. Neither of the actors knew (his, their) lines.
5. One of the classes postponed (its, their) field trip.
6. Several of the classes canceled (its, their) field trips.
7. Each of the pottery glazes has lead in (it, them).
8. (These, Those) are my new earrings right here.
9. Someone has left (her, their) leg warmers on the bench.
10. Many of our neighbors have planted (his or her, their) own gardens.

D. Using pronouns correctly   Write the correct pronoun from those given in parentheses.

1. (Who's, Whose) in your band?
2. (Its, It's) great news.
3. (Its, It's) shell is cracked.
4. (Who, Whom) tacked this notice to the tree?
5. To (who, whom) do I report a stray dog?
6. (Your, You're) next, Corky.
7. (Your, You're) hair looks good that way.
8. (We, Us) lifeguards must pass several tests.
9. Betsy is proud of (them, those) trophies.
10. (Their, They're) wearing orange vests.

Using Grammar in Writing

These challenging and enjoyable activities allow the students to see how the concepts of grammar, usage, and mechanics may be applied in actual writing situations. Each exercise is designed to allow students practice in several of the skills they have acquired in this Section. The activities also provide opportunities for students to write creatively about a wide variety of interesting and unusual subjects.

USING GRAMMAR IN WRITING
Using Pronouns

A. Think of a character from a short story or novel that you have read recently. The character might be the hero or heroine of the story. He or she might even be the villain. Write a paragraph about that character. What about this person is memorable? Tell about any interesting personality traits as well as what the character actually did in the story. Use several pronouns in your description. Also try to use all three pronoun forms: subject, object, and possessive.

B. A famous Italian painting has disappeared from a local art museum. It is obvious that the thief is inexperienced, because a number of clues have been left behind. You are the detective trying to crack the case. Write a brief description of the case, as well as the clues you have found so far. Use at least five of the following indefinite pronouns in your report.

> somebody everything neither one either anything
> each everybody another few many several

> Example: *Somebody* dropped his or her gray kid glove near the scene of the crime.

C. Think of a famous person or group of people from the past or present. You may decide on an actor, a scientist, a team, or a band, for example. Write a paragraph telling about your subject, using pronouns in place of names. Underline the pronouns and label them subject, object, or possessive.

Share the paragraphs in class. See if your classmates can guess the identities of the famous people.

Using Verbs

Of all the parts of speech, the verb is the most important. It is the moving power, the motor, of a sentence. Without it, there is no sentence.

Verbs also help you to say exactly what you mean. One verb can convey a variety of meanings. These are forms of one verb:

I *go*.   I *went*.
I *am going*.   I *have gone*.
I *am going to go*.   I *had gone*.
She *goes*.   She *should have gone*.

In **Handbook Section 1** you learned to identify verbs. In this section you will study verbs in greater detail.

Duplicating Masters — pages 180–192

Special Populations — See special section at the back of this Teacher's Edition.

Part 1

Objectives

1. To identify verbs as either action verbs or linking verbs

2. To differentiate between transitive and intransitive verbs

Presenting the Lesson

1. Read page 456. Stress the definitions of action verbs and linking verbs. Use the examples on page 456 to illustrate how one verb can be used either as an action verb or as a linking verb.

2. Read page 457. Stress that the words *transitive* and *intransitive* only apply to action verbs. Explain that *transitive* is derived from the Latin word meaning "to pass over to." A transitive verb passes its action over to a stated direct object. An intransitive verb's action is complete in itself, rather than passed on to a direct object. Remind students that *in-* is a negative prefix, making *intransitive* mean "not carrying its action over to an object."

3. Assign and discuss Exercise A on pages 457–458. For additional practice, have students tell whether each action verb is transitive or intransitive.

4. Assign and discuss Exercise B on page 458. For all transitive verbs, have students identify the direct object.

456

Part 1   What Are Verbs?

A verb is a word that tells of an action or a state of being.

Action Verbs

Some verbs tell of an action:

> Mom *started* the car.   The rain *drenched* us.

Sometimes the action is one you cannot see:

> Dennis *needed* help.   Kate *had* a good idea.

Whether you can see the action or not, an **action verb** tells that something is happening, has happened, or will happen.

Linking Verbs

Some verbs do not tell of an action. They merely tell that something is. They express a **state of being:**

> The clock *is* slow.   The sky *looks* gloomy.
> This house *seems* empty.   The gloves *feel* soft.

These verbs are called **linking verbs** because they connect, or link, the subject with some other word or words in the sentence.

Here are the most common linking verbs:

be (am, are, is, was,	look	smell
were, been, being)	appear	taste
become	feel	grow
seem	sound	

Many linking verbs can also be used as action verbs.

Linking Verb	Action Verb
The melon *looked* ripe.	Ann *looked* at the melon.
The melon *feels* ripe.	Ann *felt* the melon.
The night *grew* cold.	Tom *grows* tomatoes.

Transitive and Intransitive Verbs

Some action verbs have direct objects. They are called **transitive verbs.**

> Carl *read* the newspaper. (*Newspaper* is the direct object of *read*.)
>
> An orderly *took* the patient to his room. (*Patient* is the direct object of *took*.)

Some action verbs do not have direct objects. They are called **intransitive verbs.**

> They *eat* by candlelight. (*Eat* has no object.)
> Our group *traveled* on a bus. (*Traveled* has no object.)

There are some verbs that are always transitive or always intransitive. However, many verbs can be either. The same verb may be transitive in one sentence and intransitive in another.

Transitive Verb	Intransitive Verb
I *read* paperbacks.	I *read* at night.
Marlene *changed* her opinion.	Her ideas *changed* tremendously.
The player *kicked* the ball.	She *kicked* and fought.

Exercise A Find the verb in each sentence. Write it. After the verb write *Action* or *Linking* to show what kind it is.

A 1. Many visitors waited in line for tickets.

A 2. The horses raced toward the finish line.

A 3. The florist appeared at the door with flowers for my sister.

A 4. Sherry looked for her name in the article.

L 5. That sauce smells delicious.

L 6. These plums taste sour.

L 7. Those bananas look overripe.

457

Less-Advanced Students

Give students extra practice in differentiating action verbs from linking verbs and transitive verbs from intransitive verbs. Do Exercises A and B orally in class.

Advanced Students

Have students write ten sentences using only intransitive verbs. Then have them write ten sentences using only transitive verbs.

Optional Practice

Have students identify the verb in each of the following sentences. Students should label each verb as *Action* or *Linking*. For each action verb, students should indicate whether the verb is transitive or intransitive.

1. Canvas covered the playing field. (A,T)
2. Holidays seem more festive in small towns. (L)
3. Six books fell from the shelf. (A,I)
4. My winter parka feels so warm! (L)
5. Janet looked ill this morning. (L)
6. Hector writes with either hand. (A,I)
7. Diana Ross signed her name on the picture. (A,T)
8. The United States sells much grain to foreign countries. (A,T)
9. This book is very interesting so far. (L)
10. The warning lights flashed. (A,I)

457

The sun <u>broke</u> through the smog at noon.

L 9. The sky <u>looks</u> golden.

L10. The record <u>sounds</u> scratchy.

Exercise B Find the <u>verb</u> in each sentence. Label it *Transitive* or *Intransitive*.

T 1. The ball <u>missed</u> the basket by a foot.

T 2. Washington <u>produces</u> a large apple crop.

T 3. Has Sonia <u>quit</u> her job?

I 4. Moviegoers <u>lined</u> up in front of the theater.

I 5. Ms. Gondolfo <u>paid</u> for the meal.

T 6. The driver <u>stopped</u> her van.

I 7. Many workers <u>went</u> on strike.

T 8. Don <u>owns</u> a valuable coin.

I 9. Demonstrators <u>protested</u> in the streets.

T10. That mirror <u>distorts</u> your image.

Part 2 Helping Verbs and Main Verbs

You have learned that a great many verbs consist of more than one word. Verbs can be made up of a **main verb** and one or more **helping verbs.**

Helping Verbs	+ Main Verb	= Verb
had	gone	had gone
was	seen	was seen
can	go	can go
might have	gone	might have gone
must have been	caught	must have been caught
is	standing	is standing
will be	judging	will be judging
should have been	working	should have been working

Have students write sentences using the following verbs in the ways indicated. Answers will vary.

1. taste (action—transitive)
2. taste (linking)
3. run (action—intransitive)
4. sound (action—transitive)
5. sound (linking)

Part 2

Objective

To identify main verbs, helping verbs, and separated verb parts

Presenting the Lesson

1. Read pages 458–459. Go over the list of commonly used helping verbs. Emphasize that some verbs may be used either as helping verbs or as main verbs.

2. Assign and discuss Exercises A and B on pages 459–460.

Individualizing the Lesson

Less-Advanced Students

Have students read aloud a brief conversation from a novel or a scene from a play. Have them identify main verbs and helping verbs as they are reading.

Advanced Students

Have students work in pairs to write a brief dialogue. Each student should play one role in the dialogue and write only that part of the conversation. Tell the students to be sure to use helping verbs from the list on page 458.

The most common helping verbs are *be, have,* and *do.* They can also be used as main verbs. Here are their forms.

be—be, been, am, is, are, was, were
have—has, have, had
do—does, do, did

Used as Main Verb	Used as Helping Verb
Can you *do* this job?	I *do know* your sister.
Lea *has* my key.	Sue *has gone* home.
Where *were* you?	The boys *were working.*

Here is a list of words frequently used as helping verbs.

can	shall	will	may	must
could	should	would	might	

Sometimes the parts of a verb are separated from each other. The words between them are not part of the verb.

I *did* not *ask* the right question.
Mac *was* certainly *trying* hard.

The parts of the verb are often separated in questions.

Will the band *play*?
When *did* the party *end*?

Exercise A Find the parts of the verb in each sentence. Put them in two columns labeled *Helping Verbs* and *Main Verbs*.

Example: They will deliver the packages tomorrow.

Helping Verbs	Main Verbs
will	deliver

1. Everyone has gone home.
   ^{HV} ^{MV}
2. Will Manny and Liz go to the baseball game with us?
   ^{HV} ^{MV}
3. We are going to the aquarium tomorrow.
   ^{HV} ^{MV}
4. We have completed our study of the digestive system.
   ^{HV} ^{MV}
5. It must have snowed all night.
   ^{HV} ^{HV} ^{MV}
6. After the concert, we are going to the pizzeria.
   ^{HV} ^{MV}

459

Have students identify the main verbs and the helping verbs in these sentences.

1. Is everyone going to the pep rally?
2. Someone is knocking on our back door.
3. Can you imagine such a surprise?
4. Your briefcase is open.
5. Lisa is opening her gifts now.
6. The plant should be turned toward the sun.
7. The room should never be too warm.
8. Snow was already falling this afternoon.
9. The book has a blue and green cover.
10. Josh has been working hard this year.

Extending the Lesson

Have students write sentences using the following verbs as indicated. Answers will vary.

1. *crying* plus two helping verbs
2. *might have been* plus a main verb
3. *was* as a main verb
4. *was* as a helping verb
5. *could be* plus a main verb
6. *could* plus a main verb in a question
7. *been* plus a helping verb
8. *should be* plus a main verb
9. *enjoyed* plus a helping verb
10. *did* plus a main verb in a question

Part 3

Objectives

1. To understand the concept of verb tense

2. To use verbs in the simple tenses and the perfect tenses

Presenting the Lesson

1. Read pages 460–461. Go over definitions of *tense, present tense, past tense,* and *future tense.* Use the following structure to help students see the changes in meaning and form. Write the headings *Today, Yesterday,* and *Tomorrow* on the board.

Ask students to fill in sentences using the appropriate forms of these verbs: *work, eat, go, jump,* and *clean.* Students should note the addition of *-ed* and the changes in spelling to form the past tense, and the use of *shall* or *will* with present tense to form the future tense.

2. Read "The Perfect Tenses" on pages 461–462. Explain that the three perfect tenses are used to compare actions occurring at two times.

The present perfect tense is used to refer to some indefinite time in the past or to show action that began in the past and continues into the present. For example:

Eric has already begun his homework.
Julie has studied piano for eight years.

The past perfect tense tells of an action completed in the past before some other past action. For example:

Mike had never seen a skyscraper before he visited New York.

7. I was writing my essay during study hall.
8. My sister is running in the marathon race.
9. Colleen and I have skated at the new roller rink.
10. Did the hot-air balloons land in the stadium?

Exercise B Follow the directions for Exercise A.

1. Consumers are concerned about the price of fuel.
2. Energy conservation has become everyone's responsibility.
3. Mopeds have been designed for economical transportation.
4. No licenses are required for moped drivers in many states.
5. It is considered a bicycle with a motor.
6. A moped can go up to thirty miles per hour.
7. Car pools and public transportation do conserve energy.
8. Will we always make the effort to save energy?
9. Solar energy can help us in the years ahead.
10. Someday we may heat our homes with solar energy.

Part 3   The Tenses of Verbs

Verbs are time-telling words. They not only tell of an action or a state of being. They also tell *when* the action takes place. They tell whether the action or state of being is past, present, or future.

Verbs tell time in two ways:

1. By changing their spelling:

   walk → walked   sleep → slept

2. By using helping verbs:

   will creep   has crept   had crept

Verbs express six different times. Each verb has a form to express each of these six different times. The forms of a verb used to indicate time are called the **tenses** of a verb.

The Simple Tenses

The **present tense** of the verb shows present time. Usually the present form is the same as the name of the verb: *run, go, walk, like* (I *run*, you *go*, they *walk*, we *like*). Add *-s* or *-es* to the verb when it is used with a singular noun or *he, she,* or *it* (Tim *runs,* Ellen *goes,* he *walks,* she *likes*).

The **past tense** shows past time. Regular verbs form the past tense by adding *-d* or *-ed* to the present tense:

walk + -ed = walked   like + -d = liked

Irregular verbs show the past tense by a change of spelling:

shine → shone   swing → swung   go → went

The **future tense** indicates future time. It is formed by using *shall* or *will* with the present tense:

shall go   will run   shall forget   will want

The three tenses described above are called the **simple tenses.**

1. The present tense tells what is happening now: I *think*, I *am*.
2. The past tense tells what happened before: I *thought*, I *was*.
3. The future tense tells what will happen later: I *will think*, I *will be*.

The Perfect Tenses

Sometimes you want to speak of two different times, one earlier than the other. To make these times clear, you use the **perfect tenses.** The perfect tenses are formed by using the helping verbs *has, have,* and *had.*

461

The future perfect tense tells of an action that will be completed before some other time in the future. For example:

By the time we arrive in Seattle, we will have traveled through five towns.

Have students form the perfect tenses of these verbs: *talk, paint, close, live,* and *write.*

3. Assign and discuss Exercises A and B on page 462.

Individualizing the Lesson

Less-Advanced Students

Work with the students to complete the first five sentences in each Exercise. Then have them complete the Exercises independently.

Advanced Students

Have students rewrite each sentence in the Exercises, changing the tense of the verb.

Optional Practice

Have students identify the verbs in each sentence and name their tenses.

1. What was your motive? past
2. Dan will have finished painting the shelves by tonight. future perfect
3. Shall I leave with you? future
4. His car has run out of gas. present perfect
5. Their family goes to church every week. present
6. That librarian always helps me. present
7. Mary folded her paycheck carefully. past
8. Have you recorded your answers? present perfect

Extending the Lesson

Do this as an oral exercise. Give each student, one at a time, a verb. Vary the tenses. Have the student

461

identify the tense of the verb, then change the tense to the tense you indicate, and use the new verb in a sentence.

Part 4

Objective

To identify and form the principal parts of regular verbs

Presenting the Lesson

1. Read pages 462–463. Explain that the verbs dealt with in this part are called regular verbs because the past and the past participle are the same and are formed by adding *-d* or *-ed* to the present. Students must be reminded that spelling changes such as in *try—tried* or *knit—knitted* do not affect the status of a verb as a regular verb.

2. Assign and discuss the Exercise on page 463.

Individualizing the Lesson

Less-Advanced Students

Do the Exercise orally with the class.

Advanced Students

Have students write one sentence using each verb form listed on the top of page 463.

Optional Practice

Have students list principal parts of these verbs. Answers above on page 463.

plan	walk	blend
scrub	play	place
slap	marry	scream

462

Present Perfect: has run, have run
Past Perfect: had run
Future Perfect: will have run, shall have run

Exercise A Write the tense of each <u>verb</u> in these sentences.

1. My parents and I <u>have traveled</u> to Mexico. present perfect
2. We <u>will have heard</u> the results by tomorrow. future perfect
3. My brother and I <u>walk</u> to school. present
4. <u>Will</u> you <u>come</u> to the party tonight? future
5. <u>Have</u> you ever <u>refereed</u> a volleyball game? present perfect
6. The new record store <u>will open</u> in June. future
7. Where <u>are</u> the scissors? present
8. We <u>have</u> always <u>enjoyed</u> Paul McCartney's music. present perfect
9. When <u>will</u> the bank <u>open</u>? future
10. Lynn <u>has opened</u> a savings account. present perfect

Exercise B: Writing Write a sentence for each of the verbs below. Use the verb in the tense indicated. Sentences will vary.

1. fill (past tense) filled
2. drop (past perfect tense) had dropped
3. stay (future tense) will, shall stay
4. glisten (past tense) glistened
5. close (future perfect tense) will, shall have closed
6. splash (present tense) splash, splashes
7. flash (past tense) flashed
8. cause (present tense) cause, causes
9. attach (past perfect tense) had attached
10. touch (future tense) will, shall touch

Part 4   The Principal Parts of Verbs

Every verb has certain basic forms. Nearly all other forms of the verb are based on them. These essential forms of a verb are called the **principal parts** of the verb.

The principal parts of a verb are the **present tense,** the **past tense,** and the **past participle.**

462

Present	Past	Past Participle
talk	talked	talked
knit	knitted	knitted
add	added	added
divide	divided	divided

The present tense and past tense are used without helping verbs. The past participle is used with helping verbs. Here are some examples.

has added   was added
had added   should have added

As you can see, the past and the past participle forms of *talk, knit, add,* and *divide* are the same. These are **regular verbs.** In all regular verbs the past and past participle are formed by adding *-d (divided)* or *-ed (talked)* to the present form.

Many regular verbs change their spelling when *-d* or *-ed* is added to them.

knit + -ed = knitted   hurry + -ed = hurried
fit + -ed = fitted   try + -ed = tried

Exercise The verbs below are regular verbs. Make three columns on your paper. Head them *Present, Past,* and *Past Participle.* Place the principal parts of the verbs in the correct columns.

Past tense and past participle are the same for these regular verbs.

1. worry worried
2. sob sobbed
3. pay paid
4. grab grabbed
5. help helped
6. pass passed
7. slip slipped
8. use used
9. rob robbed
10. rap rapped
11. hurry hurried
12. rub rubbed

Part 5 Irregular Verbs

There are hundreds of verbs in our language that follow the regular pattern. They add *-d* or *-ed* to the present to form the past and past participle.

Verbs that do not follow this pattern are called **irregular verbs.** There are only about sixty irregular verbs that are often used. Many have only one change. They present few problems.

463

(Past and Past Participle Are the Same)

planned	walked	blended
scrubbed	played	placed
slapped	married	screamed

Extending the Lesson

Have students write sentences using each of the principal parts of five of the verbs in the Exercise on page 463.

Part 5

Objective

To use the principal parts of irregular verbs correctly

Presenting the Lesson

1. Review with students what is meant by principal parts of verbs. Ask students to recall why the verbs dealt with in Part 4 were called regular verbs. Stress that those verbs are regular because their past and past participle are the same. Both parts are formed by adding *-d* or *-ed* to the present.

Ask students if it is acceptable English to say "I eat, I eated, I have eated" or "he thinks, he thinked, he had thinked." Explain that many commonly used verbs are irregular in the way their past and past participle are formed.

2. Read pages 463–464. Go over the dictionary entry on page 464.

3. Read page 465 and the top of page 466. Read aloud the principal parts of all verbs listed. For added practice, have students use principal parts from the list of irregular verbs in sentences.

4. Assign and discuss Exercises A and B on page 466. Have students tell whether the correct form is the past or the past participle.

5. Read Group 3 on page 467, again reading principal parts aloud, and again having students use various parts in sentences.

6. Assign and discuss Exercises A and B on pages 467–468.

7. Read page 468, following the same procedure with verbs in Group 4 as done for previous groups.

8. Assign and discuss Exercises A and B on pages 468–469.

9. Read pages 469–470, handling verbs in Group 5 as done with previous groups.

10. Assign and discuss Exercises A and B on page 470.

Individualizing the Lesson

Less-Advanced Students

Have students work each Exercise A in pairs or groups. Assign each Exercise B for independent work.

Advanced Students

Have students write three original sentences using the principal parts of one verb from each group they have studied.

Optional Practice

Have students fill the blank in each of the following sentences with the correct form of the verb in parentheses. Students should tell whether the form used is the past or the past participle.

known, past part.
1. I should have (know) _____ better.

2. Have the lawyers (choose) _____ the jury members? chosen, past part.

464

buy	bought	(have) bought
make	made	(have) made
feel	felt	(have) felt

A few irregular verbs do not change at all from one principal part to another. They offer no problems in usage.

hit   let   set   shut

Most verb problems come from the irregular verbs that have three different forms:

| throw | threw | (have) thrown |
| ring | rang | (have) rung |

If you are not sure about a verb form, look it up in a dictionary. If the verb is regular, only one form will usually be listed.

If the verb is irregular, the dictionary will give the irregular forms. It will give two forms if the past and past participle are the same: *say, said*. It will give all three principal parts if they are all different: *sing, sang, sung*.

Dictionary Entry for *Begin*

present

be•gin (bi gin′), v. to start being, doing, acting, etc.; get under way [Work *begins* at 8:00 A.M. His cold **began** with a sore throat.] be•gan′, *p.*; be•gun′, *p.p.*

past participle

past

There are two general rules for using irregular verbs:

1. With the past participle, use a helping verb, such as *has, have,* or *had*.

have ridden   has swum
has broken   had thrown

464

2. With the past tense, use no helping verb.

The show *began* early.
The books *lay* on the table.

The Past Forms

Two principal parts of the verb are the past form and the past participle form. The difficulty in using irregular verbs is usually in deciding between these two past forms.

Principal parts are usually presented in this order: present, past, past participle. Learning them in that order may avoid confusion.

Irregular verbs fall into five groups.

Group 1 The easiest irregular verbs to remember are the ones that keep the same form for all three principal parts.

Present	Past	Past Participle
burst	burst	(have) burst
cost	cost	(have) cost
put	put	(have) put
set	set	(have) set

Here are some sentences using verbs from Group 1:

Please *put* ice in the lemonade.
The pipes *burst* in the cold.
I *have* already *set* the books on his desk.

Group 2 These irregular verbs are fairly easy to remember. They are the same in both past and past participle forms.

Present	Past	Past Participle
bring	brought	(have) brought
catch	caught	(have) caught
lead	led	(have) led
lend	lent	(have) lent
lose	lost	(have) lost
say	said	(have) said
sit	sat	(have) sat

3. The alarm (ring) _____ to warn the guards. rang, past

4. The Beatles (begin) _____ to be famous in 1963. began, past

5. The thieves were (catch) _____ making their getaway. caught, past

6. Our neighbor has (lend) _____ us his lawnmower. lent, past part.

7. The knees on my jeans (wear) _____ out, so I put patches on them. wore, past

8. Who could have (drink) _____ all the milk? drunk, past part.

9. The poem was (write) _____ especially for you. written, past

10. Leaves (fall) _____ from the wind-blown trees. fell, past

Extending the Lesson

Distribute pages from a newspaper. Have students search for and underline the irregular verbs. Then have them write each verb's principal parts on a sheet of paper. Tell students to use the dictionary to see that they have spelled all principal parts correctly.

Finally, have students use each verb in an original sentence.

465

These sentences use verbs from Group 2:

> I *say* exactly what I think.
> We *caught* the dripping water in a bucket.
> Some of us *have brought* friends along.

Exercise A Choose the correct form of the verb from the forms given.

1. The child had been (losed, lost) for hours.
2. Our art supplies were (put, putted) away.
3. We (sat, sitted) in the rumble seat of the Model T.
4. Have you (sayed, said) anything about your plans?
5. The group had (led, leaded) off the set with a Barry Manilow song.
6. That album (cost, costed) less on sale.
7. Wendy (catched, caught) her addition error.
8. David (setted, set) his sculpture on its base.
9. A dam in the Southwest (bursted, burst).
10. The advertisement (brought, brang, bringed) many customers.

Exercise B Follow the directions for Exercise A.

1. The wolf (lost, losed) the scent of its prey.
2. I should never have (lent, lended) Walt my calculator.
3. A nurse (set, setted) the breakfast tray on a table.
4. As usual, Barbara (leaded, led) the team in RBI's.
5. Supplies were (bringed, brung, brought) from the mainland.
6. Barry (catched, caught) the salmon before dawn broke.
7. Renting the formal wear had (costed, cost) much less than buying it.
8. Money has been (putted, put) aside for emergencies.
9. Sondra (catched, caught) a hint of bitterness in Dan's tone.
10. The dean (sayed, said) vandals had broken into the school.

Group 3 This group of irregular verbs makes the past participle by adding *-n* or *-en* to the past form.

Present	Past	Past Participle
break	broke	(have) broken
choose	chose	(have) chosen
freeze	froze	(have) frozen
speak	spoke	(have) spoken
steal	stole	(have) stolen
tear	tore	(have) torn
wear	wore	(have) worn

These sentences use verbs from Group 3:

Mike *wears* a hat all the time.
The mayor *spoke* at the meeting.
The radio knob *has broken* off.

Exercise A   Choose the correct form of the verb from the forms given.

1. Carlos has (broke, broken) his appointment with the dentist.
2. The cat usually (wore, worn) a flea collar.
3. Nick's little brother (stole, stolen) the show.
4. Monday was (chose, chosen) as the meeting date.
5. Nearly the entire lake has (froze, frozen).
6. A shredding machine (tore, torn) the paper to bits.
7. The President has (spoke, spoken) with his aides about the economy.
8. The knees of my jeans are (wore, worn) out.
9. All winter the ground was (froze, frozen) solid.
10. Britt (chose, chosen) a different math class.

Exercise B   Follow the directions for Exercise A.

1. A wrecking ball had (tore, torn) the building apart.
2. Salvador (broke, broken) three eggs for an omelette

467

3. My car's hubcaps have been (stole, <u>stolen</u>).
4. Mr. Sanchez (<u>spoke</u>, spoken) about the services of the community aid center.
5. Cash and bonds were (stole, <u>stolen</u>) from the Brink's truck.
6. Have you (spoke, <u>spoken</u>) with your counselor?
7. Gary has (tore, <u>torn</u>) his pants on the barbed wire.
8. Someone else had (chose, <u>chosen</u>) this radio station.
9. The stereo needle is (wore, <u>worn</u>) out.
10. The jet (<u>broke</u>, broken) the sound barrier.

Group 4 One group of irregular verbs changes only its last vowel. The vowel is *i* in the present form, *a* in the past form, and *u* in the past participle form.

Present	Past	Past Participle
begin	began	begun
drink	drank	drunk
ring	rang	rung
sing	sang	sung
swim	swam	swum

These sentences use verbs from Group 4:

I *swim* only the backstroke.
The concert *began* with a jazz number.
The lunch bell *has* already *rung*.

Exercise A Choose the correct past form of the <u>verb</u> from the forms given.

1. The blood drive (<u>began</u>, begun) last Wednesday.
2. The boxer did not realize the bell had (rang, <u>rung</u>).
3. The city has (began, <u>begun</u>) its summer festival.
4. Bells (<u>rang</u>, rung) in the new year.
5. Goldfish (<u>swam</u>, swum) in the garden pool.
6. We (<u>drank</u>, drunk) homemade root beer.
7. Our choir has (sang, <u>sung</u>) in three states.

8. Gretchen has (swam, <u>swum</u>) in two relays.
9. Bill (<u>sang</u>, sung) and played the drums.
10. Kit has never (drank, <u>drunk</u>) pineapple juice.

Exercise B   Follow the directions for Exercise A.

1. Someone (<u>rang</u>, rung) our doorbell and asked for directions.
2. Insects (<u>swam</u>, swum) on the stagnant water.
3. Have you ever (swam, <u>swum</u>) in saltwater?
4. My brother had (drank, <u>drunk</u>) all of the milk.
5. Finally, the plans (<u>began</u>, begun) to take shape.
6. The group should have (sang, <u>sung</u>) more songs.
7. The school chorus (<u>sang</u>, sung) at the benefit.
8. The phone has (rang, <u>rung</u>) many times tonight.
9. Workers have (began, <u>begun</u>) the construction.
10. Accidentally, the child (<u>drank</u>, drunk) soapy water.

Group 5 Another group of irregular verbs forms the past participle from the present form rather than the past form. The present and the past participle are either the same or similar.

Present	Past	Past Participle
come	came	come
do	did	done
eat	ate	eaten
fall	fell	fallen
give	gave	given
go	went	gone
grow	grew	grown
know	knew	known
ride	rode	ridden
run	ran	run
see	saw	seen
take	took	taken
throw	threw	thrown
write	wrote	written

Here are some sentences using verbs from Group 5:

Karen *rides* the subway to her job.
Monica *ran* the movie projector.
The Dolphins *have taken* second place in their division.

Exercise A Choose the correct past form of the <u>verb</u> from the forms given.

1. Potatoes are (grew, <u>grown</u>) in Idaho.
2. *Shane* was (wrote, <u>written</u>) by Jack Schaefer.
3. The gymnasts have (did, <u>done</u>) their routines dozens of times.
4. Gleason (<u>threw</u>, thrown) the ball to third base.
5. Organizing the meet has (took, <u>taken</u>) a long time.
6. From the airplane we (<u>saw</u>, seen) fireworks.
7. The fleeing prisoner (<u>came</u>, come) to a roadblock.
8. Several of the most beautiful trees (<u>fell</u>, fallen) during the storm.
9. Vanessa had already (went, <u>gone</u>) to the library.
10. Many of them have (ran, <u>run</u>) in marathons.

Exercise B Follow the directions for Exercise A.

1. Jess's car had (ran, <u>run</u>) out of gas.
2. Photos are (took, <u>taken</u>) at each dance.
3. Have you ever (ate, <u>eaten</u>) corn dogs?
4. Both leaders have (went, <u>gone</u>) to the peace talks.
5. The volunteers have (gave, <u>given</u>) away most of the food.
6. The cavalry (<u>rode</u>, ridden) across the wide plain.
7. Jerryl should have (knew, <u>known</u>) the facts.
8. Screeching, an ambulance (<u>came</u>, come) down the street.
9. Lee has (saw, <u>seen</u>) every Clint Eastwood movie.
10. Jill (<u>did</u>, done) a somersault in the water.

Part 6 Troublesome Pairs of Verbs

There are certain pairs of verbs that cause trouble because they are similar in meaning. They are similar, but they are not the same. You cannot substitute one of the pair for the other. Learn the differences so that you can use these words correctly.

Learn and Teach

Learn means "to gain knowledge or skill." Example: Did you *learn to dive?*

Teach means "to help someone learn." Example: That photographer *teaches* beginners.

The principal parts of these verbs are

learn, learned, learned   **teach, taught, taught**

Learn

Present: Learn to swim well.
Past: Janet learned quickly.
Past Participle: We have learned our lesson.

Teach

Present: Please teach me the system.
Past: My mother taught music.
Past Participle: Pam has taught us the jackknife dive and the butterfly stroke.

Let and Leave

Let means "to allow or permit." Example: *Let* the children stay.

Leave means "to go away from" or "to allow something to remain where it is." Example: *Leave* your car on the street and come inside.

Objective

To use the principal parts of troublesome pairs of verbs correctly: *learn* and *teach*, *let* and *leave*, *lie* and *lay*, *may* and *can*, *rise* and *raise*, *sit* and *set*

Presenting the Lesson

1. Read and discuss pages 471–474. Stress the difference in meaning and use between the verbs in each pair.

2. Assign and discuss Exercises A and B on page 474. Have students state why each sentence requires the one correct verb. Have them tell the meaning of the verb used.

Individualizing the Lesson

Less-Advanced Students

Have students memorize the definition of each troublesome verb. Assign the Exercises.

After they have completed the Exercises, have students go through them again, this time writing the definition of the word they chose in the margin. Tell students that if a definition does not fit the sentence they should refer to pages 471–474 to determine the correct answer.

Advanced Students

Have students write an original sentence for each troublesome verb. Have them check their use of the verb with the definition and examples given.

Optional Practice

Have students write the indicated forms of each of the following verbs and then use each in a sentence.

1. past participle of *sit*   have sat
2. present of *raise*   raise
3. past of *raise*   raised
4. past participle of *rise*   has risen
5. past of *set*   set
6. past of *lie*   lay
7. past of *lay*   laid
8. past participle of *lie*   has lain
9. past of *let*   let
10. past of *teach*   taught

Extending the Lesson

Have each student find, in another textbook, two examples of sentences using two of the troublesome verbs correctly.

The principal parts of those verbs are

let, let, let   leave, left, left

Let

Present: Let me help you.
Past: Bill let us stay.
Past Participle: We have let the weeds grow.

Leave

Present: Leave your coats here.
Past: The girls left early.
Past Participle: Sue has left for the day.

Lie and *Lay*

Lie means "to rest in a horizontal position" or "to be situated." Example: The soldiers *lie* on cots.

Lay means "to place." Example: *Lay* down your cards.
The principal parts of these verbs are

lie, lay, lain   lay, laid, laid

Lie

Present: Lie down and relax.
Past: The mare lay on the grass.
Past Participle: Dad has lain down.

Lay

Present: Lay the blankets here.
Past: We laid our towels on the sand.
Past Participle: Tom has laid his books on the chair.

May and *Can*

May refers to permission or to something that is possible. *Might* is another form of the word. There are no principal parts. *May* and *might* are used only as helping verbs.

May we go swimming?   You *might* catch cold.

Can refers to ability. *Could* is another form of the verb. There are no principal parts. *Can* and *could* are used as helping verbs.

Janet *can* play the flute.   We *could* see a light.

Rise and Raise

Rise means "to get up or to go higher." Example: Hot air *rises*.

Raise means "to lift or cause to go higher." It also means "to cause to grow." Example: *Raise* the ladder to the roof. Mr. Jenkins *raises* vegetables.

The principal parts of these verbs are

rise, rose, risen   raise, raised, raised

Rise

Present:	The balloon rises fast.
Past:	The curtain rose quickly.
Past Participle:	The moon has risen.

Raise

Present:	Please raise the window.
Past:	Jeff raised his voice.
Past Participle:	The recruits have raised the flag.

Sit and Set

Sit means "to rest in or occupy a seat." Example: *Sit* down.

Set means "to put or place." Example: *Set* your backpacks on the ground.

The principal parts of these verbs are

sit, sat, sat   set, set, set

Sit

Present:	Sit on the steps.
Past:	We sat in the car.
Past Participle:	We have sat for an hour.

473

Set

Present: Set the plant here.
Past: Beth set the box down.
Past Participle: We have set the plates on the table.

Exercise A   Number your paper from 1 to 10. Choose the correct verb.

1. A soft, cool mist had been (rising, raising) from the lagoon.
2. The dog won't (lie, lay) down.
3. (Let, Leave) your books in your locker.
4. (Let, Leave) your assignment on the desk.
5. The audience (rose, raised) and applauded the orchestra.
6. (Lie, Lay) still and listen.
7. You must have (lain, laid) your package down by the fountain.
8. The geyser (rose, raised) at least a hundred feet up in the air.
9. The sun (rises, raises) over those hills at 6:00 A.M.
10. They (lay, laid) wall-to-wall carpeting in the living room.

Exercise B   Follow the directions for Exercise A.

1. We usually (sit, set) on the porch steps and talk.
2. The moon (sat, set) well before midnight.
3. (May, Can) I use your telephone?
4. (May, Can) I go to the movie tonight?
5. I (set, sat) the box on the big chair.
6. (Learn, Teach) Ryan not to bellyflop, will you?
7. (May, Can) we borrow your tape recorder?
8. They were (sitting, setting) up waiting for Roger.
9. That's a snap. I (might, could) do that easily.
10. Marcia (learned, taught) the speech by heart.

ADDITIONAL EXERCISES

Using Verbs

A. Verbs Number your paper from 1 to 10. Write the <u>verb</u> in each sentence. After the verb write *Action* or *Linking* to show what kind it is.

A 1. Many patients <u>waited</u> for the doctor.

A 2. The players on the bench <u>traded</u> jokes.

L 3. Our nearest neighbors <u>are</u> the Ogdens.

A 4. Rafael Septien <u>won</u> the game with a last-second field goal.

L 5. One tire on the car <u>looked</u> flat.

A 6. Connie <u>drew</u> doodles on the phone pad.

A 7. Coach Jansen <u>reviewed</u> strategy for the game.

A 8. Susan <u>looked</u> through the telescope.

L 9. Several students from our school <u>were</u> contestants.

L 10. The sand <u>felt</u> hot to our bare feet.

B. Helping Verbs and Main Verbs Label two columns *Helping Verbs* and *Main Verbs*. Find all the parts of the verbs. Write them in the proper columns.

1. Many people are [HV] buying [MV] subcompact cars.

2. The teacher was [HV] patiently explaining [MV] the directions.

3. Jessica did [HV] not understand [MV] the puzzle.

4. A photo will [HV] decide [MV] the winner of the race.

5. "Doonesbury" was [HV] created [MV] by Gary Trudeau.

6. The thresher had [HV] harvested [MV] the wheat.

7. Dad has [HV] always watched [MV] "The CBS News."

8. Something must [HV] be [HV] nibbling [MV] the bait.

9. Barney will [HV] probably join [MV] the Marines.

10. Angela would [HV] certainly have [HV] been [HV] picked [MV] first.

475

Additional Exercises

These Additional Exercises may be used for additional practice of the concepts presented in this Section. Each exercise focuses on a single concept, and should be used after the page number indicated in parentheses.

Review

If you have not assigned these Additional Exercises before this time, you can also use them as an excellent Section Review.

475

C. Verb Tenses Name the verb tense in each sentence.

1. Jon's leg was in a cast. past
2. The construction crew had arrived before dawn. past perfect
3. By next week I will have lost three pounds. future perfect
4. We will not forget. future
5. The beach has eroded over the winter. present perfect
6. Margie took the package to the post office. past
7. Warren uses a mask and flippers. present
8. Cotton and silk are good fabrics for hot climates. present
9. Ants crawled around on the picnic table. past
10. Will you have finished dinner by then? future perfect

D. Principal Parts of Verbs Change the italicized verb in each sentence into the form stated in the parentheses.

Example: Judy *braid* her hair. (past)
Judy braided her hair.

1. The state trooper *help* the motorist. (past) helped
2. This room *need* a fresh coat of paint. (present) needs
3. The class has *finish* the physical fitness tests. (past participle) finished
4. Tracy *tie* a slipknot. (past) tied
5. Joyce *fish* the toy boat out of the pond. (past) fished
6. Franklin had just *turn* around. (past participle) turned
7. A cow *graze* by the fence. (past) grazed
8. Jerry *dust* the shelves with a damp cloth. (past) dusted
9. Military families *move* frequently. (present) correct
10. Carrie had *look* for a job in Denver. (past participle) looked

E. Irregular Verbs: Groups 1 and 2 Choose the correct form of the verb from those given.

1. Corinne (set, setted) her alarm for 5:00 A.M.
2. In one month my sister has (losed, lost) two umbrellas.
3. We have (brung, brought) firewood to the campsite.

4. Nobody (catched, caught) the bride's bouquet.
5. The mob (burst, bursted) through the barriers.
6. The Pied Piper (leaded, led) the children away.
7. The jacket (cost, costed) less than the shirt.
8. The soldier (sayed, said) the password.
9. Some people (sat, sitted) in the aisles.
10. I have already (lended, lent) you my allowance.

F. Irregular Verbs: Group 3 Choose the correct form of the verb from those given.

1. The disc jockey (spoke, spoken) with a rough voice.
2. The heavy pendant had (broke, broken) the delicate chain.
3. The sleet has (froze, frozen) on the windshield.
4. The car was (stole, stolen, stealed).
5. By whom is the state flower (chose, chosen, choosed)?
6. Anita (wore, worn) her baseball cap.
7. Several pages had been (tore, torn, teared) from the magazine.
8. Michael has never (wore, worn, weared) clogs before.
9. The tomatoes (froze, frozen) on the vines.
10. The fire inspector has (spoke, spoken) with the tenants.

G. Irregular Verbs: Group 4 Choose the correct form of the verb from the forms given.

1. No performance has ever (began, begun) on time.
2. Amanda (drank, drunk) from the tall glass.
3. Sandy has (sang, sung) in several musicals.
4. Jerome (rang, rung) the doorbell and waited.
5. Marisa (swam, swum) in the meet.
6. Gordon (began, begun) the hike cheerfully.
7. Lou Rawls (sang, sung) the national anthem before the game.

8. The tadpoles had (swam, swum) into the net.
9. Jan had (drank, drunk) all the water in the canteen.
10. The camp cook has already (rang, rung) the dinner gong.

H. Irregular Verbs: Group 5 Choose the correct form of the verb from the forms given.

1. Every weekend Ward has (went, gone) hiking.
2. Noah (saw, seen) a movie studio in Hollywood.
3. The lawyer has (took, taken) notes on our answers.
4. After Joe's basket, time (ran, run) out.
5. Your prediction (came, come) true.
6. Mrs. Lee has (gave, given) Erin an aspirin.
7. Have you already (ate, eaten)?
8. The judge (did, done) her best to be fair.
9. Early astrologers had not (knew, known) about the planet Pluto.
10. By mistake, Toni had (wrote, writ, written) her old address.

I. Troublesome Pairs of Verbs Choose the correct verb from the verbs given.

1. Danny (learned, taught) judo from a teacher with a Black Belt.
2. Heather has (learned, taught) me handball.
3. Kyle (let, left) his dog at a kennel.
4. Sunbathers (lay, laid) on the pool deck.
5. Steve (lay, laid) his money on the counter.
6. (May, Can) I please borrow that album?
7. Ms. Gonzalez never (rose, raised) her voice.
8. Our heating bills (rose, raised) sharply.
9. Gene (sat, set) in the tourist section.
10. Ginger (sat, set) her trophies on a shelf.

MIXED REVIEW

Using Verbs

A.   Finding action verbs and linking verbs   Write the verbs
from each sentence. Next, write whether they are *Action* or *Linking
Verbs*. If a verb is an action verb, write whether it is *Transitive* or
Intransitive.

A   1. The machine gives change for a dollar bill. T

A   2. These tires need air. T

L   3. Claire looks taller.

A   4. Jamie looked under the log. I

L   5. Sugar Ray Leonard was a boxer.

A   6. I pressed the button for the fifth floor. T

A   7. The explorers pressed on. I

L   8. Lauren soon felt more cheerful.

A   9. Ron felt the smooth stone. T

A 10. A neon sign shone from the window of the store. I

B.   Identifying verbs and main verbs   Label two columns on
your paper *Helping Verbs* and *Main Verbs*. Fill in the parts from
each of the following sentences.

1. The canoe should have a spare paddle.
2. I could hear a car on the gravel road.
3. How much time do you have between classes?
4. Nate would have preferred a job on Saturdays.
5. A woman with a cane was slowly walking along the
   beach.
6. Is Tara still wearing a retainer?
7. Billie was braiding her little sister's hair.
8. Frank might not have heard you.
9. A camel does not really carry extra water in its hump.
10. The climbers had accidentally loosened some rocks of
    the canyon wall.

479

C. Using verb forms correctly Write each of the following sentences, using the verb and the verb form given in parentheses.

Example: You (*say*, present perfect) that before.
You have said that before.

1. Some fat from the hamburger (*drip*, past) into the fire. dripped
2. Brady (*want*, present) a room of his own. wants
3. Shauna (*arrange*, present perfect) everything. has arranged
4. The kitten (*burst*, past) the soap bubbles. burst
5. The little bells on her bracelet (*ring*, past). rang
6. Donna (*hose*, future) down the dusty street. will hose
7. The boy (*catch*, past perfect) a firefly. had caught
8. You (*give*, past) the emphasis to the wrong syllable. gave
9. I (*lose*, present perfect) my train of thought. have lost
10. Keith (*write*, future perfect) the term paper by then.
    will have written

D. Using the correct verb Write the correct verb form from those given in parentheses.

1. Tammy (learned, taught) Mel some chess strategy.
2. The dead pine tree had finally (fell, fallen).
3. The cows have (ate, eaten) all the corn in the barn.
4. Cable television (costed, cost) less last year.
5. The guinea pig (lay, laid) down under the tiger lilies.
6. Junior had (lain, laid) a paper cloth over the picnic table.
7. (Leave, Let) Justine figure it out for herself.
8. Marcia (sets, sits) on the fire escape and reads.
9. The water level was rapidly (raising, rising).
10. Dan (raised, rose) corn and beans in his garden.

USING GRAMMAR IN WRITING
Using Verbs

A.   Everyone has had experiences in life that have taught important lessons. Even bad experiences and mistakes can result in something positive. That is where we get the saying "I'm sadder but wiser now."

Think of a bad experience you have gone through or a mistake you have made. Consider what you have learned from the experience. Write a paragraph about what happened. Use verbs in the past, present, and future tenses. To do that, remember that the mistake was in the past, that what you now know is in the present, and that the knowledge you gained will affect you in the future.

B.   Your room is a mess. You have rented Tora, a cleaning robot, for the afternoon. Tora will do a magnificent job if programmed with detailed instructions. Write several sets of instructions for Tora. Since Tora is also learning grammar right now, underline each verb and label it as transitive (T) or intransitive (I).

   Example: Direction 1: Pick up the shirts. Move to the closet.
      Lift a hanger. Hang the shirt on the hanger.

C.   You were on location as a movie was being filmed. You were most fascinated by the filming of a stunt actor at work. Describe what he or she was doing. Use several of the following verbs in their past tense and past participal forms. Use several linking verbs in your paragraph, too.

do	fall	ride	run	throw	take
break	catch	lose	have	swim	wear

Using Grammar in Writing

These challenging and enjoyable activities allow the students to see how the concepts of grammar, usage, and mechanics may be applied in actual writing situations. Each exercise is designed to allow students practice in several of the skills they have acquired in this Section. The activities also provide opportunities for students to write creatively about a wide variety of interesting and unusual subjects.

Section Objectives

1. To recognize adjectives and understand their function

2. To form and use the comparative and superlative forms of adjectives correctly

3. To recognize adverbs and understand their function in modifying verbs, adjectives, or other adverbs

4. To form and use the comparative and superlative forms of adverbs correctly

5. To differentiate between adverbs and adjectives and to use the correct modifier in sentences

6. To avoid special problems with modifiers: *them* and *those*, the extra *here* and *there*, *kind* and *sort*, *good* and *well*, and the double negative

Preparing the Students

Explain to students that while a sentence may be complete when it consists of a subject and verb *(The swimmer dived.)*, it will be much more vivid and specific if modifiers are used to describe it. *(The inexperienced swimmer dived awkwardly. The terrified swimmer dived recklessly. The professional swimmer dived faultlessly.)* Modifiers— adjectives and adverbs—are necessary for adding detail and precision to writing.

Read the introduction on page 482 with the students.

Additional Resources

Diagnostic Test — page 4 in the test booklet

Mastery Test — pages 52–55 in the test booklet

Additional Exercises — pages 504– 509 in the student text

482

Using Modifiers

Nouns and pronouns help you name and identify people, places, and things in the world around you. Verbs help you make statements and ask questions about them.

Modifiers help you describe what you have seen and heard.

> There was a *brilliant* flash.
> We heard the jet *faintly* in the distance.

In addition, modifiers help you state what you think and see about people, places, and things.

> The room was *messy*.
> Our co-captains were *extremely* energetic.

You have already studied nouns, pronouns, and verbs in detail. In this section you will study modifiers closely.

482

Part 1 Adjectives

What is the difference between these sentences?

Rain fell.
A cold, hard rain fell.

The difference is in the descriptive words that tell what kind of rain fell. These words are **adjectives.** They are one kind of modifier. A **modifier** is a word that *modifies*, or changes, the meaning of another word.

An adjective is a word that modifies a noun or pronoun.

Some adjectives tell *what kind* about the words they modify:

Look at the *colorful* balloons.   Sal likes *old* cars.
That is a *sad* ballad.   Vi wears *wild* clothes.

Some adjectives tell *how many* or *how much* about the words they modify:

Jim found *twenty* dollars.   Gene has *many* friends.
We have had *little* rain.   The jeep has *more* power.

Some adjectives tell *which one* or *which ones* about the words they modify:

That door sticks.   *This* wheel squeaks.
These pens work better.   Hand me *those* nails.

Proper Adjectives

Proper adjectives are adjectives formed from proper nouns. They are always capitalized. Here are some examples of proper adjectives:

an *American* dollar   the *French* flag
a *Chinese* restaurant   an *English* custom
the *Spanish* language   an *Oriental* rug

483

Practice Book — pages 193–201

Duplicating Masters — pages 193–201

Special Populations — See special section at the back of this Teacher's Edition.

Part 1

Objective

To recognize adjectives and understand their function

Presenting the Lesson

1. Read page 483. Make certain that students understand the meaning of *modify* and the definition of *adjective.* Study the examples of how adjectives function in three ways. Using the following additional examples, ask students to identify the adjectives and say whether they tell *what kind, how many,* or *which one.*

Good things come in small packages.
The security guard will search these bags.
Alice spilled three cups of steaming coffee.
This weather reminds me of our splendid vacation in sunny Florida.

2. Read "Proper Adjectives" on page 483. Remind students that while the proper adjective is capitalized, the noun that it modifies is not capitalized.

3. Read page 484 dealing with predicate adjectives, articles, and pronouns.

4. Read pages 485–486 dealing with diagraming adjectives. Study

483

examples showing the placement of adjectives, articles, predicate adjectives, and compound predicate adjectives.

5. Assign and discuss Exercise A on page 486. In going over the Exercise, have students explain what each adjective tells about the noun or pronoun it modifies.

6. Assign and discuss Exercise B on pages 486–487.

Individualizing the Lesson

Less-Advanced Students

1. Remind students that adjectives tell *what kind, how many,* or *which one.*

2. Have students number their paper from 1–20. Tell them to write what each adjective in Exercises A and B tells about the noun or pronoun in the sentence.

Advanced Students

Have students write five original sentences using adjectives and five using predicate adjectives. You may want to introduce the use of a thesaurus at this time.

Tell students to underline the adjectives and predicate adjectives and then to indicate whether the adjectives tell *what kind, how many,* or *which one* about the noun or pronoun.

Optional Practice

Reproduce these sentences on a worksheet or the board. Have students fill in the blanks with vivid adjectives. Answers will vary.

Predicate Adjectives

Sometimes an adjective is separated from the word it modifies by a linking verb:

Everyone was *quiet.* (*Quiet* modifies *Everyone.*)

Phil seemed *bitter.* (*Bitter* modifies *Phil.*)

An adjective that follows a linking verb and that modifies the subject is called a **predicate adjective.** It is an adjective in the predicate part of the sentence that modifies the subject. You can see that *quiet* and *bitter* are predicate adjectives.

Articles

The adjectives *a, an,* and *the* are called **articles.**

The is the **definite article.** It refers to a particular person or thing.

Please buy me *the* book. (a particular book)

A and *an* are **indefinite articles.**

Please bring me *a* book. (any book)
Please give me *an* apple. (any apple)

Note that you use *a* before a consonant sound (*a* book, *a* cap, *a* dog). You use *an* before a vowel sound (*an* apple, *an* egg, *an* olive).

The sound, not the spelling, makes the differences. Do you say *a honest man* or *an honest man?* *a house* or *an house?*

Pronouns Used as Adjectives

The words *this, that, these,* and *those* can be used as adjectives.

I enjoyed *this* movie, but Gerry preferred *that* one.
These eggs are fresh, but *those* eggs are not.

When used as modifiers, these words are called **demonstrative adjectives.** They tell *which one* or *which ones* about the words they modify. When these words are used alone instead of as modifiers, they are **demonstrative pronouns.**

I made *this* belt. (adjective modifying *belt*)
I made *this*. (demonstrative pronoun)
Those chairs are new. (adjective modifying *chairs*)
Those are new. (demonstrative pronoun)

The words *my, your, his, her, its, our,* and *their* are possessive pronouns that are used as adjectives. They are modifiers that tell *which one* or *which ones.*

my friend	*our* house
your sandals	*your* awards
his pencil, *her* pen, *its* name	*their* church

Diagraming Adjectives

In a diagram, an adjective is placed on a slanted line. The line extends down from the noun or pronoun that the adjective modifies.

The Yankees are wearing blue uniforms.

You diagram predicate adjectives just like predicate nouns and predicate pronouns. They appear on the main line after a slanted line.

That water looks slimy.

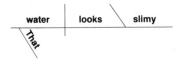

A compound predicate adjective, like a compound predicate noun or pronoun, is placed on a branched line.

485

1. A _____ plane circled the _____ city.
2. _____ children ran _____ through the _____ park.
3. The _____ waitress served the _____ _____ soup.
4. The _____, _____ dinosaur made a _____ sound.

Extending the Lesson

Have students diagram the following sentences. Answers will vary.

1. That tall pine tree looks perfect.
2. A noisy, enthusiastic crowd met the popular Japanese baseball team.
3. Kevin wore a navy wool suit.
4. The British film was interesting and funny.
5. This new travel guide is informative and colorful.

The child looked lonely and afraid.

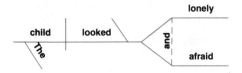

Exercise A Number your paper from 1 to 10. Write the adjectives you find in each sentence. After each adjective, write the word it modifies. Do not write articles.

1. Two sleek, silver cars were parked in the circular driveway.
2. I feel comfortable in my plaid flannel shirt, corduroy jeans, and brown suede boots.
3. That jockey in the blue satin shirt mounted the black racehorse.
4. Happy teammates carried the goalie off the muddy field.
5. James bought a Mexican belt and an African shirt at that new shop.
6. The red, orange, yellow, and brown leaves on acres of forest land painted a beautiful scene.
7. A tall, wiry player stood at the free-throw line and sank the winning basket.
8. Wicker baskets filled with white daisies and yellow roses decorated the tables.
9. I have worn these jeans for two years.
10. The coach drew a complex formation on a grimy old envelope.

Exercise B Number your paper from 1 to 10. Find the predicate adjectives in these sentences. Write them.

1. The cat was gray and white.
2. The woods smelled fresh and clean in the sunlight.
3. Gradually the air grew warm.

4. The other campers around us were <u>busy</u> and <u>noisy</u>.
5. The evening sun was <u>red</u>.
6. Over the town, the fog looked <u>steamy</u> and <u>strange</u>.
7. Everyone appeared <u>happy</u>.
8. The program seemed <u>long</u>.
9. Ahead of us the path was <u>smooth</u> and <u>easy</u>.
10. The thermos felt <u>full</u>.

Exercise C: Writing Write ten sentences of your own using as many vivid adjectives as you can. Try to include each of the different kinds of adjectives. Underline the adjectives you use.

Part 2 Adjectives in Comparisons

You compare people and things in order to learn about the world. You compare new things to things you already know. You say, "This new plane is *bigger* than a jumbo jet. It is *noisier* too." Or you say, "My friends are *older* than I am."

Adjectives are very useful in comparing things and people. In comparisons, adjectives have special forms or spellings.

The Comparative

If you compare one thing or person with another, you use the comparative form of the adjective. The comparative form is made in two ways:

1. For short adjectives like *sweet* and *happy*, add *-er*.

   sweet + -er = sweeter   quick + -er = quicker
   happy + -er = happier   wise + -er = wiser

2. For longer adjectives like *beautiful*, use *more*.

   more beautiful   more capable

Most adjectives ending in *-ful* and *-ous* form the comparative with *more*.

   more healthful   more ambitious

487

Objective

To form and use the comparative and superlative forms of adjectives correctly

Presenting the Lesson

1. Read pages 487–489. Go over the rules for using comparatives on page 488 carefully. Read the list of irregular comparisons on page 489.
2. Assign and discuss Exercises A and B on pages 489–490. In correcting errors, have students tell why the correction is necessary.

Individualizing the Lesson

Less-Advanced Students

As you do Exercise A with students, have them explain why the comparisons in the sentences are wrong. Encourage students to use the rules on page 480. Assign Exercise B.

487

The Superlative

When you compare a thing or a person with two or more others, you use the **superlative** form of the adjective. Moreover, when you compare a thing or person with all others like it, you use the superlative.

> June is the *tallest* of the three girls.
> Pat is the *smartest* person I know.
> This is the *most* interesting book I have ever read.

The superlative form of adjectives is formed by adding *-est* or by using *most*. For adjectives that add *-er* to form the comparative, add *-est* for the superlative. For those that use *more* to form the comparative, use *most* for the superlative.

Adjective	Comparative	Superlative
high	higher	highest
strong	stronger	strongest
agreeable	more agreeable	most agreeable
careful	more careful	most careful

There are three things to remember when using adjectives for comparison:

1. Use the comparative to compare two persons or things. Use the superlative to compare more than two.

> This car is *wider* than that one.
> Paul is the *thinnest* of the three boys.

2. Do not leave out the word *other* when you are comparing something with everything else of its kind.

Incorrect:	New York is larger than any American city.
	(This says that New York is not an American city.)
Correct:	New York is larger than any other American city.
Incorrect:	Claire runs faster than any girl in her class.
	(Is Claire a girl?)
Correct:	Claire runs faster than any *other* girl in her class.

3. Do not use both -*er* and *more*, or -*est* and *most* at the same time.

Incorrect: Diamonds are more harder than jade.

Correct: Diamonds are *harder* than jade.

Incorrect: Diamonds are the most hardest of all materials.

Correct: Diamonds are the *hardest* of all materials.

Irregular Comparisons

You form the comparative and superlative of some adjectives by changing the words completely:

Adjective	Comparative	Superlative
good	better	best
well	better	best
bad	worse	worst
little	less *or* lesser	least
much	more	most
many	more	most
far	farther	farthest

Exercise A   Two of the comparisons in the following sentences are correct, but the others are wrong. If a sentence is correct, write *Correct*. If there is an error, write the sentence correctly.

1. Our new dog is much more ~~friendlier~~ than the old one. friendly
2. Of the two plants, the fern is the healthier. c
3. The dictionary was more helpful than the almanac. c
4. It was the ~~awfulest~~ storm I had ever seen. most awful
5. These shelves are ~~more high~~ than those over there. higher
6. The Honda is the ~~smaller~~ of these three motorcycles. smallest
7. It was the ~~most~~ warmest day of the summer.
8. Biology is harder than any ‿ subject in school. other
9. What happened was even ~~surprisinger~~. more surprising
10. The ~~most~~ funniest thing happened yesterday.

Exercise B   Follow the directions for Exercise A.

1. He chose the lesser of the two penalties. c
2. She had ~~littler~~ time than usual. less

3. Marcy felt worse than she had felt in a long time. c
4. That was the ~~worser~~ of the two jokes. worse
5. Her joke was the ~~goodest~~ of all. best
6. My painting was bad, but Janet's was the ~~worstest~~. worst
7. This is the ~~most~~ best I can do.
8. That was a ~~more~~ better game than the one last week.
9. At the ~~leastest~~ noise Annie jumped. least
10. Between reggae and disco, reggae is the ~~hardest~~ for me to dance to. harder

Part 3

Objective

To recognize adverbs and understand their function in modifying verbs, adjectives, or other adverbs

Presenting the Lesson

1. Read pages 490–491, "Adverbs Used with Verbs." Stress the four ways in which adverbs modify verbs. Study the examples of adverbs which fit into each category. Have students add adverbs to the following sentence as they were added to the example: *The quarterback threw the ball.* Students should add several different adverbs to tell *how, when, where,* and *to what extent.*

2. Read page 491 regarding use of adverbs with adjectives or other adverbs. Have students add several different adverbs to modify the adjective or adverb in these sentences: *Jan walked slowly. The baby was fussy.*

3. Read pages 491–492 dealing with the formation of adverbs. Tell students that in order to determine

Part 3 Adverbs

In order to make your meaning clear, vivid, and complete, you usually have to tell *how, when, where,* or *to what extent* something is true. **Adverbs** are modifiers used for this purpose.

Adverbs Used with Verbs

Adverbs are used to modify verbs. Adverbs tell *how, when, where,* or *to what extent* an active happened.

Study the following list of adverbs:

How?	When?	Where?	To What Extent?
secretly	then	nearby	too
quickly	later	underground	very
sorrowfully	afterwards	here	extremely
hurriedly	finally	there	quite

Now try using some of the above adverbs in this sentence:

The pirates buried their gold.

The pirates *secretly* buried their gold.

Finally, the pirates buried their gold.

The pirates buried their gold *here.*

The pirates buried their gold, *very carefully.*

You can see what a great difference the adverbs make in the above sentences. They make the meaning of the verb *buried* more precise, and they add vividness and completeness to the whole sentence.

Adverbs Used with Adjectives or Other Adverbs

Besides being used to modify verbs, adverbs are also used to modify adjectives and other adverbs. Notice the italicized adverbs in the following sentences:

> Niki was happy.

> Niki was *extremely* happy. (*Extremely* tells to *what extent* Niki was happy. It is an adverb modifying an adjective, *happy*.)

> Rick spoke slowly.

> Rick spoke *too* slowly. (*Too* tells *to what extent* Rick spoke slowly. It is an adverb modifying another adverb, *slowly*.)

Here are some more adverbs that are often used to modify adjectives or other adverbs:

very	quite	somewhat	so	most
just	nearly	rather	more	

These adverbs all tell *to what extent* something is true.

You can see how useful adverbs are in making the adjectives or other adverbs that you use clearer and more complete.

Adverbs are words that modify verbs, adjectives, and other adverbs.

Forming Adverbs

Many adverbs are made by adding *-ly* to an adjective:

> secret + -ly = secretly   bright + -ly = brightly

Sometimes the addition of *-ly* involves a spelling change in the adjective.

whether a word such as *early* or *fast* is an adjective or adverb, they should decide what word it modifies. If it modifies a noun or pronoun, it is an adjective. If it modifies a verb, adjective or adverb, it is an adverb.

4. Read page 492 on diagraming adverbs. Go over examples.

5. Assign and discuss Exercises A and B on page 493.

6. Assign and discuss Exercise C on pages 493–494.

Individualizing the Lesson

Less-Advanced Students

Work with students to help them complete the first five sentences of Exercise A. Assign the remainder of Exercise A and all of Exercise B as independent work.

Advanced Students

Have students write original sentences using each of the adverbs they create in Exercise C. Have them circle each adverb in the sentences they write and then underline each word the adverb modifies.

Optional Practice

Have students supply adverbs to fill in blanks in the following sentences. Answers will vary.

1. The time passed _____ during the exam.
2. Bob _____ forgets to wash the dishes.
3. Gretchen laughed _____ at the joke.
4. The team rowed the boat _____.
5. Some _____ spicy pizza made my stomach feel jumpy.

6. The bus traveled _____ along the highway.
7. Joel's handwriting is _____ impossible to read.
8. Come _____ to help with the project.
9. The bells chimed _____ and _____.
10. We searched _____ for something to eat.

Extending the Lesson

Have students underline all the adverbs in a newspaper sports story. Tell them to write the adverb and the word it modifies on their paper. Then have students use each adverb in an original sentence.

easy + -ly = easily (*y* changed to *i*)
capable + -ly = capably (final *le* dropped)
full + -ly = fully (*ll* changed to *l*)

Many words, like *quite* or *so*, can be used only as adverbs:

This footprint is *quite* recent.

Sue never looked *so* happy before.

Some other words, like *early* or *fast*, can be used either as adverbs or as adjectives:

Bill arrived *early*. (adverb, modifying the verb *arrived*)
He ate an *early* breakfast. (adjective, modifying the noun *breakfast*)

Dana can run *fast*. (adverb, modifying the verb *run*)
She is a *fast* runner. (adjective, modifying the noun *runner*)

Diagraming Adverbs

To diagram an adverb, place it on a slanted line under the word it modifies.

Ben watches TV regularly.

Besides modifying verbs, adverbs may modify adjectives or other adverbs. Here is how these adverbs appear in a diagram:

Very rough waves hit us quite hard.

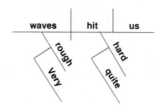

492

492

Exercise A Number your paper from 1 to 10. Write the <u>adverb</u> in each sentence. After each adverb write the <u>word it modifies</u>. Be ready to explain what the adverb tells about the word it modifies.

Example: The actors usually stay here.

usually modifies *stay*, tells *when*

here modifies *stay*, tells *where*

1. That movie was quite informative.
2. We have never studied about Greenland.
3. The runners raced vigorously around the track.
4. The doctor left hurriedly.
5. The newspaper was rather careful about its editorials.
6. The quarterback limped painfully off the field.
7. The runway lights shone brightly at the airport.
8. Our canoe drifted lazily down the river.
9. The summer rain fell heavily.
10. The pounding stopped immediately.

Exercise B Follow the directions for Exercise A.

1. That pounding has started again.
2. That pitcher seemed somewhat unsure of himself.
3. Alicia smiled weakly.
4. Those two dogs wander aimlessly through the streets.
5. Rescuers arrived too late. *(too modifies late)*
6. The visiting football teams usually stay at the Hilton.
7. Because the train was ahead of schedule, we arrived early.
8. The play went quite smoothly until the last act. *(quite modifies smoothly)*
9. Mexico City's climate is usually ideal.
10. It is extremely important that you relay the message.

Exercise C Change the following adjectives into adverbs by adding *-ly*. Use a dictionary to check your spelling.

493

easily   surely   beautifully   peacefully   carefully
easy   sure   beautiful   peaceful   careful
cruelly   icily   smoothly   dizzily   happily
cruel   icy   smooth   dizzy   happy
heavily   fully   terribly   crazily   coolly
heavy   full   terrible   crazy   cool
sadly   loudly   impatiently   grimly   hopefully
sad   loud   impatient   grim   hopeful

Part 4

Objective

To form and use the comparative and superlative forms of adverbs correctly

Presenting the Lesson

1. Remind students of the major points studied regarding adjectives in comparisons. Review the use of comparative adjectives to compare two things, and superlative adjectives to compare more than two things. Review also the formation of comparative and superlative by the addition of *-er*, *-est*, or *more* and *most*.

2. Read pages 494–495. Stress the four rules to keep in mind for using adverbs in comparisons. Go over examples of adverbs which have complete word changes to form their comparatives and superlatives.

3. Assign and discuss Exercises A and B on pages 495–496.

Individualizing the Lesson

Less-Advanced Students

Do Exercise A with the class. As you review Exercise B with students, have them explain why the comparisons are wrong (or right). Encourage them to use the rules on page 495.

Part 4   Adverbs in Comparisons

Adverbs can compare one action with another. You say, "This party ended early, but Selina's ended *earlier*." Or you say, "This team plays *more roughly* than any other team." Adverbs have special forms for use in making comparisons, just as adjectives do.

The Comparative

When you compare one action with another, you use the comparative form of the adverb. The comparative form is made in two ways:

1. For short adverbs like *soon* and *fast*, add *-er*.

    We arrived *sooner* than you did.
    Kim can run *faster* than Peg.

2. For most adverbs ending in *-ly*, use *more* to make the comparative.

    Bill acted *more quickly* than Jeff.
    The water flowed *more rapidly* than before.

The Superlative

When one action is compared with two or more others of the same kind, you use the superlative form of the adverb.

    Peg and Bill ran fast, but Kim runs *fastest*.
    Of the three boys, Scott speaks Spanish the *most fluently*.

The superlative form of adverbs is formed by adding *-est* or by using *most*. Adverbs that form the comparative with *-er* form the superlative with *-est*. Those that use *more* for the comparative use *most* for the superlative.

Adverb	Comparative	Superlative
soon	sooner	soonest
rapidly	more rapidly	most rapidly
clearly	more clearly	most clearly

In using the comparative and superlative forms of adverbs, keep in mind the following four rules:

1. Use the comparative to compare two actions and the superlative to compare more than two.

It rained *harder* today than yesterday.
Of all the players, Terry tries the *hardest*.

2. Do not leave out the word *other* when you are comparing one action with every other action of the same kind.

Incorrect: Tara runs faster than any student in our school.
Correct: Tara runs faster than any *other* student in our school.

3. Do not use both *-er* and *more*, or *-est* and *most* at the same time.

Incorrect: Tara runs more faster than Eve.
Correct: Tara runs *faster* than Eve.

4. Some adverbs make their comparative and superlative forms by complete word changes.

Adverb	Comparative	Superlative
well	better	best
much	more	most
little	less	least
badly	worse	worst

Exercise A Write the comparative and superlative forms.

faster, fastest
1. fast
more, most happily
3. happily
more, most bravely
5. bravely
more, most recently
7. recently
more, most wildly
2. wildly
more, most closely
4. closely
more, most slowly
6. slowly
harder, hardest
8. hard

495

1. Have students use the comparatives and superlatives formed in Exercise A to write original sentences.

2. Have students use Exercise B to write new sentences. If the sentence includes a comparative, students should rewrite the sentence using a superlative. If the sentence includes a superlative, students should rewrite the sentence using a comparative.

Optional Practice

Have students write the comparative and superlative forms of each of the following adverbs and use each comparative and superlative form in a sentence. Answers below. Sentences will vary.

1. easily	6. well
2. eagerly	7. hurriedly
3. long	8. wisely
4. carefully	9. early
5. seriously	10. quickly

1. more, most
2. more, most
3. longer, longest
4. more, most
5. more, most
6. better, best
7. more, most
8. more, most
9. earlier, earliest
10. more, most

Extending the Lesson

Have students supply comparative or superlative adverbs to complete the following sentences.

1. The young pitcher threw _____ than the pitching coach.

2. Linda did her work _____ than her sister.

3. Of all the animals in the game pre-serve, the jaguar moves _____ .

4. Lauren seems to skate the _____ of all the members on the hockey team.

5. This typewriter works _____ than that one.

Part 5

Objective

To differentiate between adverbs and adjectives and to use the correct modifier in sentences

Presenting the Lesson

1. Read pages 496–497. Go over the distinctions between adjectives and adverbs, stressing what each modifier tells about the word it modifies.

2. Do Exercise A together with the class. As each modifier is identified, have students tell whether it is an adverb or an adjective. Besides telling what word it modifies, students should tell the part of speech of the word modified, and what the modifier tells about the word modified. Refer to the chart on page 497.

3. Assign and discuss Exercise B on pages 497–498.

4. Read pages 498–499 regarding adverbs and predicate adjectives. Remind students that when a predicate adjective follows a linking verb, it describes the subject. When an adverb follows an action verb, it describes the action of the verb.

5. Assign and discuss the Exercise on page 499. In addition to choosing the right modifier, have

Exercise B If a sentence is correct, write *Correct*. If there is an error in the comparison of adverbs, write the sentence correctly.

1. These photographs were trimmed ~~more~~ better than those.
2. That fish jumped ~~more~~ higher than any other.
3. Write the directions out more ~~completer~~. completely
4. We drove more carefully after seeing the collision. c
5. Vacation ended ~~more soon~~ than we had expected. sooner
6. This recipe is the ~~more~~ consistently successful of all. most
7. Can't you walk ~~more fast~~ than that? faster
8. You could see the view more clearly from here. c
9. He tried ~~more~~ harder than Wayne.
10. Will you read that paragraph again more ~~slower~~, please? slowly

Part 5 Adjective or Adverb?

Study these sentences. Which sentence sounds right to you?

The crew worked *quick*.   The crew worked *quickly*.

The second sentence is the correct one. An adverb (*quickly*) should be used, not an adjective (*quick*) to modify the verb *worked*.

Sometimes it is hard to decide whether to use an adjective or an adverb. At those times, ask yourself these questions:

1. Which word does the modifier go with? If it goes with an action verb (like *worked* in the sentence above), it is an adverb. It is also an adverb if it goes with an adjective or another adverb. If it goes with a noun or pronoun, it is an adjective.

2. What does the modifier tell about the word it goes with? If the modifier tells *how, when, where,* or *to what extent,* it is an adverb. If it tells *which one, what kind,* or *how many,* it is an adjective. In the sentences above, the modifier tells *how* the crew worked. Therefore, *quickly* is an adverb.

An Adverb Tells	An Adjective Tells
How	Which One
When	What Kind
Where	How Many
To What Extent	
About a Verb, Adjective, or Adverb.	**About a Noun or Pronoun.**

Exercise A List each <u>adjective</u> and <u>adverb</u>, together with the (words they modify.) (Do not list articles.)

Example: The tall runner in the red shirt won easily.

tall modifies *runner*

red modifies *shirt*

easily modifies *won*

1. Dancers (moved) gracefully across the tiny (stage.)
2. The American (ambassador) (spoke) openly and honestly about our foreign (policy.)
3. He (paid) the bill quite (promptly.)
4. The suspect (answered) the questions rather (cautiously.)
5. The young (swimmers) (dove) eagerly into the large (pool.)
6. The small (child) (cried) loudly in the dentist's office.
7. The two angry (men) soon (exchanged) insults.
8. Red, white, and blue (bunting) (was) decoratively (hung.)
9. Commuters (walked) briskly toward the long, yellow (train.)
10. That (restaurant) is famous for its strawberry (pies.)

Choose the correct <u>modifier</u> from the two in parentheses. Tell what (word it modifies,) and whether it is an adjective or adverb.

1. Ted (appeared) at the door (prompt, <u>promptly</u>) at eight. Adv.
2. Everything (fitted) in place just (beautiful, <u>beautifully</u>). Adv.

497

students tell whether the modifier is an adverb or an adjective. Students should double check their choices by identifying the sentence's verb as action or linking.

Individualizing the Lesson

Less-Advanced Students

Do the first half of the Exercises on pages 497–499 with students. Assign the remainder.

Advanced Students

Have students suggest alternatives for each of the modifiers in Exercise A on page 497 and the Exercise on page 499. Encourage students to use a thesaurus or dictionary to find the most vivid and precise modifiers.

Optional Practice

Have students identify modifiers in the following sentences and tell whether each is an adjective or adverb.

1. The unhappy [Adj.] children complained bitterly. [Adv.]
2. Our [Adj.] long [Adj.] hike in the national [Adj.] park was enjoyable. [Adj.]
3. Roberta spread mayonnaise thickly [Adv.] on the fresh [Adj.] bread.
4. The spectators shouted angrily, [Adv.] and the players became furious. [Adj.]

Extending the Lesson

Sentence Bee. Have students list ten linking verbs on the board. Then, in spelling bee fashion, have them make up a sentence for each, using the proper predicate adjective. If they use the verb as an action verb or use an adverb, they lose their turn.

497

3. Debbie's drawings were (real, <u>really</u>)(good.) Adv.
4. The medics (reacted) very (quick, <u>quickly</u>). Adv.
5. Ms. Watson (explained) the assignment (clear, <u>clearly</u>). Adv.
6. A patrolman (peered) (cautious, <u>cautiously</u>) around the corner. Adv.
7. We (walked) home very (slow, <u>slowly</u>). Adv.
8. My brother (drives) (careful, <u>carefully</u>). Adv.
9. Please (work) (quiet, <u>quietly</u>) during the test. Adv.
10. Becky (spoke) (firm, <u>firmly</u>) to the clerk. Adv.

Adverbs and Predicate Adjectives

You will remember that a predicate adjective appears after a linking verb and modifies the subject.

The rose is red. (*red* modifies *rose*)

The sky became cloudy. (*cloudy* modifies *sky*)

The pizza tastes good. (*good* modifies *pizza*)

You also remember that in addition to the forms of *be*, the following can be used as linking verbs: *become, seem, appear, look, sound, feel, taste, grow,* and *smell*.

Sometimes these verbs are action verbs. When they are action verbs, they are followed by adverbs, not adjectives. The adverbs modify the verbs and tell *how, when, where,* or *to what extent*.

Look at the following sentences to see when adjectives are used and when adverbs are used:

Action Verbs with Adverbs	**Linking Verbs with Adjectives**
Bob *felt* his way *slowly*.	The *cloth* felt *smooth*.
We *tasted* the fudge *early*.	The *fudge* tasted *good*.
A stranger *appeared suddenly*.	The *dog* appears *sick*.

Erin *looked up.* The *water* looks *green.*

The plant *grew fast.* The *horse* grew *tired.*

We *smelled* smoke *suddenly.* The *flower* smells *good.*

If you are uncertain about whether to use an adverb or adjective after verbs like *sound*, *smell*, and *look*, try these tests:

1. Does the modifier tell *how, when, where,* or *to what extent*? If it does, the modifier is probably an adverb.

2. Can you substitute *is* or *was* for the verb? If you can, the modifier is probably an adjective.

Exercise Choose the right modifier for each of the following sentences.

1. Carol's idea sounded (reasonable, reasonably).
2. Press (firm, firmly) on the button.
3. The director spoke (calm, calmly).
4. At the start of the game we played (bad, badly).
5. Someone in the audience was laughing (hysterical, hysterically).
6. The ice looked (thick, thickly).
7. This aspirin tastes (bitter, bitterly).
8. The tape stopped (abrupt, abruptly).
9. That house looks (empty, emptily).
10. The music sounded (strange, strangely).

Part 6 Special Problems with Modifiers

Them and *Those*

Them is always a pronoun. It is used only as an object.

Those is an adjective if it is followed by a noun. It is a pronoun if it is used alone.

Part 6

Objective

To avoid special problems with modifiers: *them* and *those*, the extra *here* and *there*, *kind* and *sort*, *good* and *well*, and the double negative

1. Read pages 499–502 and discuss each possible problem situation. Stress the examples and their explanations.

2. Assign and discuss Exercise A on page 502. Ask students why the correct choice is needed.

3. Assign and discuss Exercise B on pages 502–503. Ask students to tell whether the correct modifier is an adjective or an adverb, and to tell why that particular part of speech is needed.

4. Assign and discuss Exercise C on page 503.

Individualizing the Lesson

Less-Advanced Students

1. Do Exercise A orally with students.

2. For Exercise B, tell students to indicate whether the correct word is used as an adverb or as an adjective. Have students underline the word or words modified.

Advanced Students

Have students write one original sentence using each problem modifier correctly.

Optional Practice

Have students correct errors in the following sentences. If the sentence has no errors, it should be labeled *Correct*. Students should be able to explain why the correction is needed.

1. Does that ~~there~~ salad look ~~rightly~~ ^{right} to you?
2. Everyone likes ~~them~~ ^{those} jogging shoes.
3. Those kind~~s~~ of crackers become stale quick~~.~~ly.

500

We heard *them* in the night. (pronoun)

Those bikes are too heavy. (adjective modifying *bikes*)
Those are our gifts. (pronoun)

The Extra *Here* and *There*

How often have you heard someone say, "this here book" or "that there window"? The word *this* includes the meaning of *here*. The word *that* includes the meaning of *there*.

Saying *this here* is like saying, "This book is my mine," or like repeating your name every time you say *I* or *me*: "Please pass me John Jones the milk."

Kind and *Sort*

Kind and *sort* are singular. Use *this* or *that* with *kind* and *sort*. *Kinds* and *sorts* are plural. Use *these* or *those* with *kinds* and *sorts*.

We like *this kind* of dessert. (singular)
Those kinds of food give you energy. (plural)

Good and *Well*

The meanings of *good* and *well* are very much alike, but they are not exactly the same. You cannot substitute one for the other in all sentences. Study the following sentences. Can you see the difference between *good* and *well*?

I feel *good*.   His health is *good*.
I feel *well*.   Betty plays *well*.

Good is always an adjective.
Well is sometimes an adjective and sometimes an adverb.

500

Well is an adjective when it means "in good health."

Well is an adverb when it modifies an action verb, telling that something was done properly or skillfully.

> This patient is *well*. (adjective modifying *patient*)
> Marsha writes *well*. (adverb modifying *writes*)

Bad and Badly

Bad is an adjective. It is always used after linking verbs.

> I felt *bad*. (*not* I felt badly)
> The team looked *bad*.

Badly is an adverb.

> The team played *badly*.
> They were beaten *badly*.

The Double Negative

A **double negative** is the use of two negative words together when only one is needed. Good speakers and writers take care to avoid the double negative.

Incorrect:	We haven't no more tape.
Correct:	We have*n't* *any* more tape.
Incorrect:	Jack didn't win nothing in the tournament.
Correct:	Jack did*n't* win *anything* in the tournament.
Incorrect:	She hasn't never gone there.
Correct:	She has*n't* *ever* gone there.

You can see in the sentences above that the first negative word is *not*. When you use contractions like *haven't* and *didn't*, do not use negative words after them.

The most common negative words are *no*, *none*, *not*, *nothing*, and *never*.

After contractions like *haven't* and *didn't*, use words such as

501

any, anything, and *ever.* Do not use *no, nothing, never,* or any other negative words after such contractions.

> The club *hasn't any* president.
> We *couldn't* hear *anything.*
> We *haven't ever* seen an eclipse.
> The band *can't* play *any* popular *songs.*

Hardly, barely, and *scarcely* are often used as negative words. Do not use them after contractions like *haven't* and *didn't.*

Incorrect: The cars haven't scarcely moved.
Correct: The cars *have scarcely* moved.

Incorrect: They can't barely hear the pilot.
Correct: They *can barely* hear the pilot.

Incorrect: The scuba divers couldn't hardly breathe.
Correct: The scuba divers *could hardly* breathe.

Exercise A Choose the right word in these sentences:

1. (This, This here) TV show is my favorite.
2. My family won't eat (them, those) foods.
3. (Them, Those) gloves are too small.
4. We chose (those, those there) designs for our posters.
5. Carlotta always uses (that, that there) kind of notebook.
6. (This, This here) watch needs a new band.
7. (Them, Those) are deer tracks.
8. These (kind, kinds) of auditions take a long time.
9. These (sort, sorts) of arguments are pointless.
10. Do you like (them, those) cowboy boots?

Exercise B Write the correct word.

1. Both teams played (bad, badly) in the second half.
2. John was sick, but now he's (good, well) again.

3. Some of the gymnasts performed (bad, <u>badly</u>) in the meet.
4. That photo looks (<u>good</u>, well) enough to frame!
5. Shake the bottle (good, <u>well</u>).
6. That swim felt (<u>good</u>, well).
7. The plans for the new store have worked out (bad, <u>badly</u>).
8. The meat tasted (<u>bad</u>, badly).
9. Mr. Marks looks (<u>good</u>, well) in his new jacket.
10. Most of the performers did quite (good, <u>well</u>) in last night's production.

Exercise C: Writing Correct the double negatives in these sentences. If a sentence contains no double negative, write <u>Correct</u>.

1. We couldn't tune in that channel. C
2. Nobody could have had more fun. C
3. Rhoda hasn't ~~never~~ been sick. ever
4. The movers ~~couldn't~~ hardly lift the heavy box. could
5. There ~~isn't~~ no time for games. is
6. Marguerita couldn't find the map. C
7. Ms. Ryan won't let ~~nobody~~ use the power tools. anybody
8. The girls ~~couldn't~~ scarcely believe their ears. could
9. Bryan hasn't had ~~no~~ driving lesson this week. a
10. We had plenty of food, but Ellen didn't want ~~none.~~ any

These Additional Exercises may be used for additional practice of the concepts presented in this Section. Each exercise focuses on a single concept, and should be used after the page number indicated in parentheses.

Review

If you have not assigned these Additional Exercises before this time, you can also use them as an excellent Section Review.

ADDITIONAL EXERCISES

Using Modifiers

A. Adjectives Write the adjectives in each sentence. After each adjective, write the word it modifies. Do not include articles.

1. Polly told a hilarious joke.
2. An iron gate blocked the entrance.
3. Tiny white lights glittered on the trees.
4. A rusty green truck clattered down the alley.
5. Only one engine on the old plane was working.
6. In that bookrack are current magazines.
7. That garage holds three cars.
8. Most students wanted a formal prom.
9. Dad prepared a delicious Chinese dinner.
10. The French singer sang a lovely melody.

B. Predicate Adjectives Label three columns *Subject, Linking Verb,* and *Predicate Adjective.* For each sentence write the words under the appropriate columns.

1. The Cohens are happy in their new townhouse.
2. The humidity seems high today.
3. The surf is rough along the rocky coast.
4. Asbestos in the air is dangerous.
5. That large dog seems unfriendly.
6. Our best basketball player is unusually short.
7. Brendan's excuse was certainly unusual.
8. Daisies grew wild along the highway.
9. Jennifer seems sure of herself.
10. Elliot felt miserable after the quarrel.

C. Adjectives in Comparisons Write the correct form of each adjective.

1. The dunes are (taller, more tall) along the south coast.

2. No one could be (jealouser, <u>more jealous</u>) than Toby.
3. Rebecca has a (<u>better</u>, more gooder) tan than I do.
4. Of the two cars, this one is (<u>rustier</u>, rustiest).
5. This course seems the (more difficult, <u>most difficult</u>) of all.
6. That dog has a (<u>worse</u>, worst) temper than the collie.
7. Liz threw the javelin the (most far, <u>farthest</u>) of anyone.
8. Be (<u>more careful</u>, carefuller) next time.
9. Chuck did his (goodest, <u>best</u>, bestest) work at night.
10. Of the four cities, Detroit got the (more, <u>most</u>) snow.

D. Adverbs Write the <u>adverbs</u> in the following sentences. After each adverb, write the <u>word it modifies</u>.

1. Our group <u>walked</u> slowly through the museum.
2. Gloria patiently <u>fastened</u> each bolt.
3. The naval officers <u>saluted</u> crisply.
4. The satellite generally <u>broadcasts</u> everywhere.
5. We <u>listened</u> sympathetically to Anna's very sad story.
6. Fortunately, the painters <u>were</u> quite neat. (*quite* modifies *neat*)
7. My friends <u>sat</u> <u>down</u> and <u>chatted</u> happily.
8. Near the fireplace, we felt <u>much</u> cozier.
9. Tony <u>talks</u> too much during study period. (*too* modifies *much*)
10. Yesterday Ted <u>got</u> a very <u>bad</u> sunburn.

E. Adverbs in Comparisons Two of the comparisons in the following sentences are correct. If a sentence is correct, write *Correct*. If there is an error, write the sentence correctly.

1. Borg is pitching ~~badder~~ than usual. worse
2. This movie ended ~~sadder~~ than the sequel. more sadly
3. Of all the shirts, this one fits ~~better.~~ best
4. Reginald shakes hands more firmly than Bill. c
5. Cathy jumped highest on her third try. c
6. Isn't Houston, Texas, growing faster than any ∧city? other

505

7. Heather played more ~~recklesslier~~ toward the end of the game. recklessly

8. Michelle has practiced ~~leastest~~ often of the four girls. least

9. A horse is more intelligent than any ∧ mammal. other

10. A burn usually hurts ~~worst~~ than a cut. worse

F. Adjective or Adverb? Write the correct modifier for each sentence.

1. The sulfur gas smells (terrible, terribly).
2. Yvonne spoke (polite, politely) to the police officer.
3. The band didn't sound (bad, badly).
4. The band didn't play (bad, badly).
5. Leonard will defeat him (easy, easily).
6. The team felt (wonderful, wonderfully) about the victory.
7. (Sudden, Suddenly) the coach ordered a two-minute drill.
8. The ice at the rink felt (smooth, smoothly).
9. The confidence man spoke (smooth, smoothly).
10. The alarm could be heard (clear, clearly) in every room.

G. Special Problems with Modifiers If a sentence is correct, write Correct. If there is an error, write the sentence correctly.

1. The jazz pianist won't play ~~no~~ ragtime. any
2. Josh swam ~~good~~ in the semifinals. well
3. ~~Them~~ changes in Britt's plans seem sudden. Those
4. Dogs can barely tolerate those ~~kind~~ of noises. kinds
5. I ~~couldn't~~ hardly see them through the snow. could
6. These sorts of fruits taste ~~well~~ with cheese. good
7. Where did you buy ~~them~~ shoelaces? those
8. Please put those overdue books on the table. C
9. Those ~~there~~ steel guitars sound good.
10. Esther handled ~~them~~ hurdles ~~good,~~ but Jill didn't clear ~~none~~ of them. those. well any

MIXED REVIEW

Using Modifiers

A. Find adjectives and adverbs Copy the following sentences. Underline each adjective once and each adverb twice. Then draw an arrow from each modifier to the word it modifies. Do not include articles.

1. Fat raindrops plopped onto the dusty leaves.
2. A white cat walked carefully across the top of the yellow fence.
3. Rinse the shirt immediately in cold water.
4. Celia has probably left already.
5. These peppercorns crack fairly easily.
6. That door opens with a magnetic card.
7. The old boots look too scruffy.
8. Five people squeezed into the tiny booth.
9. Bess walked up and later rode the elevator down.
10. Walk carefully down those steep stairs.

B. Use modifiers correctly All of these sentences contain errors in the use of modifiers. Rewrite each sentence correctly.

1. The miniature horse is more smaller than a pony.
2. That is certainly the leastest of Jeff's concerns. least
3. Blair High School did better than any school on the tests. other
4. Emily spent the mostest time on the tiniest drawing. most
5. Of the four boys, Stan is easier to talk with. easiest
6. Oak is the hardest of the two woods. harder
7. The sun is four billion years more older than the star Vega.
8. Keith did badlier than Ryan at the meet. worse

Mixed Review

These exercises provide review of the concepts presented in this Section. Each exercise challenges the students to apply several of the skills they have acquired during previous study. Because the "mixed" feature of these activities makes them more difficult, the teacher may wish to have less-advanced students do them orally or in small groups.

9. He most definitely did his ~~bestest.~~ best

10. The flu is usually ~~worst~~ than a cold. worse

C. Choose the correct modifier Write the correct word from the words in parentheses.

1. The bridge looks too (weak, weakly) for traffic.
2. Rachel looked (close, closely) at the directions.
3. The speech students soon became more (confident, confidently).
4. Television reception is (real, really) poor here.
5. Shauna doesn't like (them, those) wraparound sunglasses.
6. I (would, wouldn't) never have thought of that.
7. Jackson didn't meet (anybody, nobody) at the dance.
8. Heidi does (good, well) in math.
9. Mr. Wilder played the organ (beautiful, beautifully).
10. Have you ever used (this, this here, these) kind of computer?

USING GRAMMAR IN WRITING
Using Modifiers

A. Your local newspaper is accepting nominations for the Young Athlete of the Year. Write a paragraph about a real or imaginary athlete at your school. Use modifiers to describe the candidate and the specific way he or she demonstrates skill in a sport. Compare this person to other athletes, too. Underline all modifiers and label them *adjective* or *adverb*.

                                       adj.
     Example: Myrna Greenfield is a superb gymnast.
                           adv.
     She performs expertly on the bar and the rings.

B. Think of something you own that you would like to get rid of. It could be something old, or something you no longer need. Write a classified ad to sell the item. Use good adjectives and adverbs to make your ad persuasive. Include predicate adjectives and some modifiers in the comparative and superlative forms.

C. You are a set designer working on a new science-fiction movie. The director has had to fly out of town. He has left you a brief outline of the set he wants for a particular scene. You have to write a full description of the set for the design crew. Using original and striking modifiers, complete the director's instructions.

     Here are my ideas for the Scene 1 set. It is dark. There are two moons in the sky. One is above the space capsule. (What size and color?) There is a group of strange plants in the left-hand corner. (What kind?) The aliens' temple is in the background. Could you suggest a design for this? Do you have any other ideas? See you Thursday!
                                  Thompson

Using Grammar in Writing

These challenging and enjoyable activities allow the students to see how the concepts of grammar, usage, and mechanics may be applied in actual writing situations. Each exercise is designed to allow students practice in several of the skills they have acquired in this Section. The activities also provide opportunities for students to write creatively about a wide variety of interesting and unusual subjects.

Using Prepositions and Conjunctions

Often you can say what you mean by using short sentences like these:

> The grocer weighed the meat.
> Last night I found a dollar bill.

Frequently, however, what you have to say is more complicated. Perhaps you want to say not merely that you found a dollar bill last night but also that you found it in the driveway.

You may want to tell someone that the grocer weighed not only the meat but also the pears and the potatoes. To express more complicated ideas like these, you use **connectives,** such as *and* and *in*.

> The grocer weighed the meat, the pears, *and* the potatoes.
> Last night I found a dollar bill *in* the driveway.

This chapter will help you learn to use two important kinds of connectives: **prepositions** and **conjunctions.**

Part 1 Prepositions

Connectives are words that are used to join two or more other words or groups of words. **Prepositions** are one important kind of connective.

Notice the prepositions in the following sentences:

> The plane flew *into the storm.*
> The plane flew *around the storm.*
> The plane flew *through the storm.*

In the first sentence, *into* connects *storm*, its object, with the verb *flew*. It points out the relationship between the words *flew* and *storm*.

In the next two sentences, *around* and *through* connect *storm* with the verb *flew*. They show the relationship between *flew* and *storm*.

You can see that *into*, *around*, and *through* join parts of each sentence. Like all prepositions, they make clear a certain relationship between the words that they connect.

In all cases, too, the prepositions are used in **phrases,** groups of words without subjects or verbs. The prepositional phrases above are *into the storm, around the storm*, and *through the storm*. Prepositions begin phrases that relate to the rest of the sentence.

A preposition is a word used with a noun or pronoun, called its *object*, to show the relationship between the noun or pronoun and some other word in the sentence.

A prepositional phrase consists of a preposition, its object, and modifiers of the object.

On the next page is a list of words often used as prepositions. Most of these prepositions tell *where*. Others show a relationship of *time*. Some show other special relationships. Study these prepositions and see if you can tell the relationship that each of them can show between words.

511

Objectives

1. To recognize prepositions and prepositional phrases and to understand their function

2. To distinguish between prepositions and adverbs

Presenting the Lesson

1. Read page 511. Stress that prepositions are connectives; they serve to connect a noun or pronoun to another part of the sentence. If students look at the word *preposition*, they should see in it the word *position*. Prepositions tell the position of their objects in terms of time, location, or other special relationships.

2. Go over the list of words often used as prepositions on page 512. Go around the classroom and have students use each preposition in a sentence. Have students describe the relationship indicated by the preposition.

3. Assign and discuss Exercises A and B on page 512–513.

4. Read "Preposition or Adverb?" on page 513. Remind students that both prepositions and adverbs can tell *where* or *when* or *how*, but that prepositions always occur in phrases rather than by themselves.

5. Assign and discuss Exercises A and B on pages 513–514.

Individualizing the Lesson

Less-Advanced Students

For Exercises A and B on pages 512–513, tell students to test for an object by asking *what?* after each word that could be a preposition. Do Exercise A on pages 513–514 with the class. Assign Exercise B on page 514.

Advanced Students

Have students write ten original sentences using the prepositions on page 512.

Optional Practice

Have students identify prepositional phrases in the following sentences.

1. After the game the team rushed to the locker room.
2. Over the weekend the ink in my pen ran dry.
3. The car turned down this street and into the alley.
4. Gwen told us about the trip she took with her family to Nashville.
5. Between the stream and the forest, we pitched our tents in a circle around the campfire.

Extending the Lesson

Have students complete each of the following sentences in three different ways using three different prepositional phrases.
Sentences will vary.
1. The nuclear energy plant is located _____.
2. The airplane flew _____.
3. Our city needs improvement _____.
4. Everyone _____ feels better when the sun shines.
5. The animals can be kept _____.

Words Often Used as Prepositions

about	behind	during	off	to
above	below	except	on	toward
across	beneath	for	onto	under
after	beside	from	out	until
against	between	in	outside	up
along	beyond	inside	over	upon
among	but (except)	into	past	with
around	by	like	since	within
at	concerning	near	through	without
before	down	of	throughout	

Exercise A Number your paper from 1 to 10. Write the prepositional phrases in the following sentences.

Example: On Saturday, Bret and Julie went to the beach.
On Saturday, to the beach

1. During the night we were awakened by thunder.
2. After the play, we're going to Mike's house.
3. A prop plane with several passengers made an emergency landing in a cornfield.
4. The library will hold the book until tomorrow.
5. I hurried up the stairs and into the room.
6. The residents of Franklin Park are concerned about the noise pollution.
7. The football squad huddled around the coach for last-minute instructions.
8. Stack these cartons against the wall, and put these books on the shelf.
9. The city was without power for several hours.
10. In the library there are several aquariums and plants on various bookshelves.

512

Exercise B Follow the directions for Exercise A.

1. <u>On the island</u> <u>of Oahu</u> we visited the Polynesian Cultural Center.
2. <u>With a hat</u> <u>in her hand</u>, Lou strolled <u>down the ramp</u>.
3. Two sky-writing planes flew <u>over the stadium</u> <u>during the baseball game</u>.
4. The bicycle shop is located <u>on Green Bay Road</u>.
5. <u>In July</u> we are going <u>to Florida</u> <u>for a visit</u> <u>with my aunt</u>.
6. Student Council will meet <u>before school</u> <u>on Friday</u>.
7. Tony Dorsett dazzled the crowd <u>in the Coliseum</u> <u>with a 93-yard run</u>.
8. We rode the elevator <u>to the top</u> <u>of the John Hancock Building</u>.
9. Carrie rowed the boat <u>across the lagoon</u> <u>without help</u>.
10. The pancake house <u>near the expressway</u> is open <u>around the clock</u>.

Preposition or Adverb?

Many words used as prepositions may also be used as adverbs. There is an easy way to tell the difference. A preposition never appears alone. It is always followed by its object—a noun or pronoun. If the word appears in a phrase, it is probably a preposition. If it is not in a phrase, it is probably an adverb.

I drew a line *across the paper*. (preposition)
He dared me to jump *across*. (adverb)

Ted put his books *down*. (adverb)
He ran *down the street*. (preposition)

Exercise A Decide whether the italicized words in these sentences are adverbs or prepositions. Write *Adverb* or *Preposition* for each sentence.

A 1. All local traffic was allowed *through*.
A 2. Pete threw his old track shoes *out*.

A   3. The committee turned our request *down*.

A   4. The light bulb burned *out*.

P   5. The stock cars raced *around* the track.

A   6. Janice turned *around*.

P   7. There is a new shopping center *near* our house.

P   8. The Frisbee flew *across* the picnic table.

A   9. The doctor is *in*.

A 10. We all went *inside*.

Exercise B   Follow the directions for Exercise A.

P   1. Marsha and Jory biked *along* the lake shore.

A   2. We heard a noise *below*.

A   3. The chain came *off*.

P   4. The chain came *off* the bicycle.

A   5. My sister rolled *over* sleepily.

P   6. The tunnel collapsed *around* them.

P   7. We waited *outside* the theater.

P   8. John, Vince, and I sat *inside* the tent.

P   9. That dog always stays *within* its own yard.

P 10. Lew and Niki talked *about* their jobs.

Part 2

Objective

To determine whether a prepositional phrase functions as an adjective phrase or an adverb phrase

Presenting the lesson

1. Read pages 514–515. Study examples carefully, noting explanations telling what each phrase tells about the word it modifies. Pay special attention to examples of two successive prepositional phrases.

Part 2   Prepositional Phrases as Modifiers

A modifier may be a group of words as well as a single word. Frequently a prepositional phrase is a modifier. A **prepositional phrase** is a group of words including a preposition and its object. All the words modifying the object are also part of the phrase.

An adjective phrase is a prepositional phrase modifying a noun or a pronoun.

The player *in the blue jersey* scored.
    (*In the blue jersey* is an adjective phrase modifying the noun *player*. It tells *which one*.)

The mayor had a conference *with her aides.*
   (*With her aides* is an adjective phrase telling *what kind* of
   conference.)

Somebody *with red hair* entered the bank.
   (*With red hair* is an adjective phrase. It modifies the
   pronoun *somebody.*)

Like adjectives, adjective phrases tell *what kind* or *which one.*

An adverb phrase is a prepositional phrase modifying a verb.

The fields were attacked *by grasshoppers.*
   (*By grasshoppers* is an adverb phrase. It tells *how* about
   the verb *were attacked.*)

After a rest, we jogged on.
   (*After a rest* tells *when* about the verb *jogged.*)

The motorcycle skidded *around the corner.*
   (*Around the corner* tells *where* about the verb *skidded.*)

Like adverbs, adverb phrases tell *how, when, where,* and *to
what extent* about verbs.
   You will often find two prepositional phrases in a row. Sometimes the second phrase is an adjective phrase modifying the
object of the first phrase.

We piled *into the back of the van.*
   (*Into the back* is an adverb phrase telling *where* about the
   verb *piled.*)
   (*Of the van* is an adjective phrase modifying the noun
   back.)

The ship sailed *with a crew of twelve.*
   (*With a crew* is an adverb phrase telling *how* about the
   verb *sailed.*)
   (*Of twelve* is an adjective phrase. It tells *what kind* of
   crew.)

515

2. Study diagrams of prepositional phrases on page 516.
3. Assign and discuss Exercises
A and B on pages 516–517.

Individualizing the Lesson

Less-Advanced Students

Tell students to refer to the chart
of prepositions on page 512 as they
are doing the Exercises.

Have students do Exercise A on
pages 516–517 in two steps. First
they should just circle the prepositional phrases. Then work with the
class to identify the words modified
by the prepositional phrases. Have
the students explain why the phrase
is an adjective or adverb phrase.

Assign Exercise B as independent work.

Advanced Students

Have students identify prepositional phrases in a magazine or
newspaper article or in their social
studies text. Then have them identify the word modified by each
phrase. Finally, have students determine whether the prepositional
phrase is an adjective or adverb
phrase.

Optional Practice

Ask students questions such as
"When do you leave for school in the
morning?," "Where do you live?,"
and "How do you get to your next
class?" Tell them to write their answers to your questions, using prepositional phrases in their answers.

Have students underline the
prepositional phrases in their answers. Then have them draw an arrow to the word the phrase modifies

and then determine whether the phrase is an adjective phrase or an adverb phrase.

Extending the Lesson

Have students write the following sentences, placing the prepositional phrases in the correct places. Answers will vary.

1. Jack was looking for a notebook. (at the stationery store) (without lines)

2. Chris has been studying piano. (with the same teacher) (for three years)

3. The sailboat glided out. (with four passengers) (of the harbor)

4. There was a family of cats. (under the porch) (with long hair)

5. One team will meet. (in the park) (after dinner) (for basketball practice)

6. There was a horse. (on the other side) (with a long silky tail)

7. We planted a garden. (with flower and vegetable seeds) (between the house and the driveway)

8. I ran. (after school) (to Terry's house) (through the open field)

9. Judy painted the bookcase. (in the backyard) (before lunch) (with white paint)

10. Ted and I hurried. (at five o'clock) (of the hospital volunteer group) (to the meeting)

Diagraming Prepositional Phrases

In diagrams, a prepositional phrase is placed below the word it modifies. Place the object on a horizontal line and the preposition on a slanted line.

That boy with the blue jacket lives on our street.

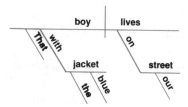

Sometimes two or more nouns or pronouns may be used as objects in a prepositional phrase. You then split the object line.

Put ice in the cooler and the thermos.

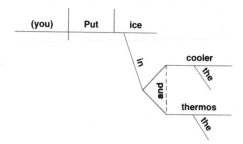

Exercise A Copy these sentences. Circle each prepositional phrase. Draw an arrow from the phrase to the word it modifies. Tell whether the phrase is an adjective phrase or an adverb phrase.

Example: He took the book (with the pictures) of Ireland.

with the pictures: adjective phrase
of Ireland: adjective phrase

1. The sign over the top of the door says "No Exit." Adj., Adj.

2. The window on the east side of the garage needs repair. Adj., Adj.

3. We peered through the windows of the mansion. Adv., Adj.

4. Pattie added some pepper to her soup. Adv.
5. The woman in the white suit is my social studies Adj. teacher.
6. The man in the navy sport coat plays for the Celtics. Adj., Adv.
7. A fierce watchdog sat at the bottom of the staircase. Adv., Adj.
8. The performer near the back of the stage is Eartha Kitt. Adv., Adj.
9. The rowboat in the water near the dock has a leak. Adj., Adj.
10. The nails are in the box under the workbench. Adv., Adj.

Exercise B   Follow the directions for Exercise A.

1. The movie on television features Billy Dee Williams. Adj.
2. Jane Addams is well known for her contributions in social work. Adv., Adj.
3. Are you going to the shop down the street? Adv., Adj.
4. The photographer took these pictures with a wide-angle lens. Adv.
5. The sign on the door in the office said that school will end at 1:30 P.M. today. Adj., Adj. Adv.
6. The newspaper article about astrology is informative. Adj.
7. The passengers on the jet were served a special dinner.
8. The Wright Brothers' plane hangs above space modules in the museum. Adv., Adj. Adj.
9. I wrote an essay about my visit to New York. Adj., Adj.
10. Ron enjoyed his work with small children last summer. Adj.

Part 3   Conjunctions

A second kind of word used to connect parts of a sentence is the conjunction.

A **conjunction** is a word that joins words or groups of words. Notice the conjunctions in the following sentences.

Lucy *and* Linda look alike. (connects nouns)
Todd will call his father *or* mother. (connects nouns)
Mr. Morley hemmed *and* hawed. (connects verbs)

Objective

To recognize coordinating and correlative conjunctions and to understand their functions

Presenting the Lesson

1. Read the introduction to Part 3 on pages 517–518, emphasizing the definition of *conjunction* and the examples of sentences containing conjunctions.

2. Analyze the word *conjunction* with students to help them understand what conjunctions are. Ask students to tell you what a *junction* is. They should relate the word to the coming together of two streets or roads. Explain that a junction is a point of joining. The word part *con* means *with*. Thus, a conjunction serves to join two words or groups of words with one another.

3. Read page 518, explaining coordinating conjunctions. Go over examples carefully, making certain students understand which sentence parts are made compound by the use of conjunctions.

4. Read about correlative conjunctions on page 519.

5. Assign and discuss Exercises A, B, and C on pages 519–520.

Individualizing the Lesson

Less-Advanced Students

Have students copy the sentences in Exercises A and B. Then have them circle the conjunction and underline the word or groups of words joined by the conjunction. Have them work on Exercise C in pairs.

Advanced Students

Have students write five sentences containing coordinating conjunctions and five sentences containing correlative conjunctions. Have them circle the conjunctions.

Optional Practice

Have students write the kind of compound constructions they find in each of the following sentences. Students should write the constructions with their conjunctions.

The cannister smelled spicy *but* damp. (connects adjectives)
The guide book is *either* in the closet *or* on the desk. (connects prepositional phrases)

Conjunctions are unlike prepositions in that they do not have objects. They are like prepositions in that they do show a certain relationship between the words they connect.

Coordinating Conjunctions

To connect single words or parts of a sentence that are of the same kind, you use **coordinating conjunctions.** The most common coordinating conjunctions are *and*, *but*, and *or*.

When coordinating conjunctions link words, they usually form a compound construction. This may be a compound subject, compound verb, or compound direct object, for example.

Mandy *and* Tom went to a rock concert.
  (*And* connects *Mandy* and *Tom*, making them a compound subject of the verb *went*.)
The pitcher spun *and* threw to second base.
  (*And* connects *spun* and *threw*, forming a compound verb.)
Gary picked up the crate *and* lowered it onto a cart.
  (*And* connects the two predicates, *picked up the crate* and *lowered it onto a cart*.)
Carrie felt dizzy *but* happy.
  (*But* connects predicate adjectives, *dizzy* and *happy*.)
Dan polished the chrome quickly *but* well.
  (*But* connects the adverbs *quickly* and *well*.)
Terry plays clarinet *and* piano.
  (*And* connects *clarinet* and *piano*, the compound direct object of *plays*.)
Ask your teacher *or* advisor that question.
  (*Or* connects *teacher* and *advisor*, making them a compound indirect object of the verb *ask*.)
Without food *or* drink, the sailors barely survived.
  (*Or* connects *food* and *drink*, compound objects of the preposition *without*.)

Correlative Conjunctions

A few conjunctions are used in pairs:

both . . . and   not only . . . but (also)
either . . . or   whether . . . or
neither . . . nor

Such conjunctions are called **correlative conjunctions.**

Both the benches *and* the tables had been painted.
Either you *or* I have made an error.
Neither football *nor* baseball can be played on the field.
We need *not only* nails *but also* a hammer.
Shall I call *whether* it rains *or* snows?

Exercise A   Find the conjunctions in the following sentences. Write the words or word groups connected by the conjunction.

Example: Marni and Bret designed the ads.

Conjunction: and
Connected Words: Marni, Bret

1. Farmers and miners now use machines for much of their work.
2. Freezing rain and poor visibility delayed most flights.
3. Either the yearbook staff or the newspaper staff will sell refreshments at the home football games.
4. We must sew slowly and methodically in home economics.
5. Pennsylvania is both an industrial and a rural state.
6. We had corn on the cob and barbecued chicken.
7. Are you going to the movies or to the roller rink?
8. Marcia and I are going either to the water polo game or to the indoor tennis meet.
9. Tom and I couldn't get tickets for the match.
10. The slight breeze, pleasant temperatures, and overcast skies were assets to the marathon runners.

519

S1. Both the lights and the telephones were cut off by the hail storm.
DO2. Please turn off the radio and the record player.
DO3. The wind blew our garbage cans and patio furniture into the street.
V4. The weight lifter strained and struggled with the heaviest weights.
V5. I tried but couldn't open the jar of peanut butter.
PN6. My favorite movies were *The Outsiders* and *Return of the Jedi.*
DO7. Did the detective find any clues or fingerprints?
S8. Neither Mary nor Glenda was on time for the bus.
PA9. The weather will be warm and sunny for the picnic!
10. Gabriel felt ill but went to class anyway. Predicate

Extending the Lesson

Have the students write a brief story about what they did over the weekend. Tell them to be sure to use as many conjunctions—both coordinating and correlative—as possible. Have students circle the conjunctions in their sentences.

Exercise B Write the kind of compound construction you find in each sentence. Write the <u>construction</u> with its <u>conjunction</u>.

1. She <u>stared</u>, then <u>glared</u>, <u>and</u> finally <u>grinned</u>. verb
2. The <u>roadblock</u> <u>and</u> the <u>detour</u> have delayed our trip. subject
3. <u>Either</u> <u>John Riggins</u> <u>or</u> <u>Walter Payton</u> would have used that line's blocking to better advantage. subject
4. You can see <u>an opera with Leontyne Price</u> <u>or</u> <u>the Grand Kabuki by the National Theatre of Japan</u>. direct object
5. My sister has studied <u>long</u> <u>and</u> <u>hard</u> for her medical exams. adverb
6. <u>Neither</u> the <u>newspaper</u> <u>nor</u> the <u>radio</u> reported the correct score. subject
7. Canoeing is a <u>strenuous</u> <u>but</u> <u>enjoyable</u> sport. adjective
8. <u>Skateboards</u>, <u>painter's pants</u>, <u>Bubble Yum</u>, <u>and</u> <u>Frisbees</u> were fads of the mid-1970's. subject
9. I like <u>neither</u> <u>avocados</u> <u>nor</u> <u>asparagus</u>. direct object
10. We <u>not only</u> <u>raised enough money for the class trip</u> <u>but also</u> <u>made a donation to the children's hospital</u>. predicate

Exercise C: Writing Write two sentences using *and*, two sentences using *or*, and two sentences using *but*. After each sentence write the words or groups of words that are joined by the conjunctions.

ADDITIONAL EXERCISES

Using Prepositions and Conjunctions

Additional Exercises

These Additional Exercises may be used for additional practice of the concepts presented in this Section. Each exercise focuses on a single concept, and should be used after the page number indicated in parentheses.

Review

If you have not assigned these Additional Exercises before this time, you can also use them as an excellent Section Review.

A. Prepositions Number your paper from 1 to 10. Write the prepositions in the following sentences. Write the object of each preposition.

1. The police found fingerprints on the safe.
2. Hernandez pitched two no-hitters during this season.
3. Sally met Joel near the stadium.
4. Tacos are often served with hot sauce.
5. The waiter took the four of us to our table.
6. We can't make ice cream without a bag of rock salt.
7. Subtitles are at the bottom of the movie screen.
8. An account of the race will appear in the newspaper.
9. The photos in the display case were taken by Lindsay.
10. At the sound of the gun, the swimmers plunged into the pool.

B. Preposition or Adverb? Decide whether the italicized words in these sentences are prepositions or adverbs. Write *Preposition* or *Adverb* for each sentence.

A 1. Several full buses went *past*.
P 2. Celia ran *past* the finish line.
A 3. Arthur held a welcome sign *up*.
A 4. You've met Lucy *before*, haven't you?
P 5. The ball soared *across* the field.
P 6. Birds chirp nervously *before* rain.
P 7. The wasp finally landed *on* the light fixture.
A 8. Climb *on*, Steve.
A 9. Jackie turned the burner *off* quickly.
P 10. Don't go *off* the path.

521

C. Prepositional Phrases as Modifiers Copy these sentences. Circle each prepositional phrase. Draw an arrow from the phrase to the word it modifies.

1. Lee takes those kinds of vitamins.
2. Craig prepared for the job interview.
3. Many trees are destroyed by Dutch elm disease.
4. The subway trains run on electric rails.
5. We'll put the top of the convertible down.
6. Gene and Todd exchange presents on their birthdays.
7. Kate used the recipe on the back of the cereal box.
8. One team from the Big Ten plays in the Rose Bowl game.
9. That game is usually played on New Year's Day.
10. The girls in the hallway heard the singing.

D. Conjunctions Copy these sentences. Underline the conjunctions. Circle the words connected by the conjunctions.

1. Do you prefer Rod Stewart or Jackson Browne?
2. Neither Kim nor Rebecca went to the concert.
3. That apartment is bright and spacious.
4. Robots are useful for routine but dangerous jobs.
5. The survival kit included neither a radio nor a blanket.
6. Nathan is both a wrestler and a boxer.
7. On holidays and weekends the store is closed.
8. The chief spoke loudly but calmly.
9. Keith sanded and varnished the door.
10. Give Ms. Dean or her assistant your time sheets.

MIXED REVIEW

Using Prepositions and Conjunctions

A. Recognizing prepositional phrases Copy these sentences. Circle the prepositional phrases. Draw arrows from each prepositional phrase to the word it modifies. Write whether it is an adjective or an adverb phrase.

1. Two fat raccoons stared at us. Adv.
2. Windsurfers with red sails skimmed across the water. Adj., Adv.
3. Without a thought for her safety, Karen jumped in. Adv., Adj.
4. At dusk the streetlamps go on. Adv.
5. Every gym student except Wes shinnied up the rope. Adj., Adv.
6. Beneath the porch is a storage shed. Adv.
7. Once there were many billboards along our highways. Adv.
8. At the top of the stairs loomed a figure in a long cape. Adv., Adj., Adj.
9. With the ball under his arm, John ran up the field. Adj., Adj., Adv.
10. Betsy left the key on a ledge above the door. Adv., Adj.

B. Recognizing prepositions, conjunctions, and adverbs
Write the italicized words in the following sentences. After each, write *Adverb, Preposition,* or *Conjunction* to show how it is used in the sentence.

C 1. Ty added a snail *and* some shells to the goldfish bowl.
P 2. Nancy peeled the price tag *off* the gift.
A 3. One of the swimmer's flippers came *off.*
P 4. Everybody *but* Vivian has signed the birthday card.
C 5. This material is thin *but* warm.
C 6. *Either* the telephone *or* the doorbell is ringing.
C 7. Mary Wilson *and* Florence Ballard were two of the Supremes.
P 8. These hoof prints were made *by* a deer.
A 9. The rescue crew is standing *by.*
A 10. Josh came *over* and talked for a while.

523

Mixed Review

These exercises provide review of the concepts presented in this Section. Each exercise challenges the students to apply several of the skills they have acquired during previous study. Because the "mixed" feature of these activities makes them more difficult, the teacher may wish to have less-advanced students do them orally or in small groups.

523

Using Grammar in Writing

These challenging and enjoyable activities allow the students to see how the concepts of grammar, usage, and mechanics may be applied in actual writing situations. Each exercise is designed to allow students practice in several of the skills they have acquired in this Section. The activities also provide opportunities for students to write creatively about a wide variety of interesting and unusual subjects.

USING GRAMMAR IN WRITING
Using Prepositions and Conjunctions

A. Find the prepositional phrases in Eleanor Farjeon's poem "Cats." Study her format and use it to write a poem of your own. Change the phrase "Cats sleep anywhere" to something else: for example, "Trains go everywhere." Use lively prepositional phrases and details.

Cats

Cats sleep
Anywhere,
Any table,
Any chair,
Top of piano,
Window-ledge,
In the middle,
On the edge,
Open drawer,
Empty shoe,
Anybody's
Lap will do,
Fitted in a
Cardboard box,
In the cupboard
With your frocks—
Anywhere!
They don't care!
Cats sleep
Anywhere.

—ELEANOR FARJEON

B. Your friend is to speak to a drama group at another school. She is blind. She asks you to accompany her to the room where she will be speaking. Describe the room so that your friend can almost "see" it. Underline all prepositional phrases.

Review of Parts of Speech

Section Objectives

1. To recognize and use interjections

2. To review the eight parts of speech

3. To recognize the use of a single word as different parts of speech

Preparing the Students

Ask students to name the seven parts of speech studied thus far. Ask for several examples of each part of speech. Ask students why each part of speech is important in helping to communicate. Explain that Section 8 will present a review of the seven parts of speech, and it will also present the eighth part of speech.

Additional Resources

Mastery Test — pages 58–59 in the test booklet

Additional Exercises — pages 529–531 in the student text

Practice Book — pages 207–209

Duplicating Masters — pages 207–209

Special Populations — See special section at the back of this Teacher's Edition.

Part 1 The Parts of Speech

In earlier sections you have studied verbs, nouns, pronouns, adjectives, adverbs, prepositions, and conjunctions. There is one other word group, **interjections.** Interjections will be explained in this section.

All of these eight word groups are called the **parts of speech.** A word becomes a particular part of speech because of the way it is used in a sentence.

525

Part 1

Objectives

1. To recognize and use interjections

2. To review the eight parts of speech

Presenting the Lesson

1. Read pages 525–526. Ask students to suggest more words or phrases commonly used as interjections.

2. Review the eight parts of speech listed in the box on page 526. Review definitions, functions, and examples of each part of speech.

3. Do Exercise A on page 526 orally with the class. As students identify parts of speech, have them tell how they function in each sentence.

4. Assign and discuss Exercise B on page 527.

Individualizing the Lesson

Less-Advanced Students

Work on Exercise A as a class. Assign Exercise B.

Advanced Students

Have students write a brief report from memory of a recent movie they have seen. Tell them to write only on every other line of their paper. Then have them write above each word what part of speech that word is.

Optional Practice

Have students write five sentences using interjections.

Extending the Lesson

Have students identify the parts of speech of each word in the following sentences.

1. Your new brown purse is beautiful.
   (Pro Adj Adj N V Adv)
2. Can Seymour play first base?
   (V N V Adj N)
3. Heavens! The leaves are falling from the trees already.
   (Int Adj N V V Prep Adj N Adv)

526

What Are Interjections?

An interjection is a word or group of words used to express strong feelings.

Sometimes an interjection is a sound rather than an actual word. It may convey anger, surprise, disgust, joy, or sorrow. In any case, an interjection shows strong feeling. As a result, it is often followed by an **exclamation mark** (!).

These are examples of interjections:

Phew! We made it.
Never! I won't ever do that.
Terrific!
Yipes! I'm late again.
Great! You made the squad.

Now you are familiar with all eight parts of speech:

The Parts of Speech			
nouns	verbs	adverbs	conjunctions
pronouns	adjectives	prepositions	interjections

Exercise A   Write each italicized word. Next to it, write what part of speech it is.

1. Americans *now* have more leisure time.   adverb
2. *Many* of us enjoy hobbies and sports.   pronoun
3. Some of us relax with *vigorous* exercise.   adjective
4. Spectator sports are *quite* popular, too.   adverb
5. Television watching occupies a great deal of *time*.   noun
6. The average family watches for *six* hours a day.   adjective
7. Some people *use* their leisure time wisely.   verb
8. Others waste time *and* feel bored.   conjunction
9. *In* America the work week is shrinking.   preposition
10. *Wow!* We have more time for fun.   interjection

526

Conj   N   Conj N   V
4. Neither breakfast nor lunch ap-
      Prep Pro
   pealed to me.
   Pro V   Prep N   Prep N
5. We traveled to Boston by bus.

Exercise B   Follow the directions for Exercise A.

1. The hospital *staff* has three shifts. noun
2. *Somebody* has erased my favorite tape. pronoun
3. *Yuck!* Who left gum on the rug? interjection
4. Margo is prepared *for* emergencies. preposition
5. Dawn is *too* early for a bike ride. adverb
6. Chili may be very spicy *or* very mild. conjunction
7. A new *Greek* restaurant opened uptown. adjective
8. The receptionist *answered* all inquiries. verb
9. *She* recommended a specialist in allergies. pronoun
10. The gas tank exploded *in* flames. preposition

Part 2   Words Used as Different Parts of Speech

In order to tell what part of speech a word is, you must see how it is used in a sentence. Many times the same word can be used as different parts of speech.

Here are some examples:

Windmills *stand* near the farm. (*Stand* is used as a verb.)
Bob built a *stand* for his shell collection. (*Stand* is used as a noun.)
Pete drank a *bottle* of Tab. (*Bottle* is used as a noun, the direct object of *drank.*)
Tara stepped on a *bottle* cap. (*Bottle* is used as an adjective modifying *cap.*)
That dart came *close* to the bull's-eye. (*Close* is used as an adverb modifying *came.*)
Only a close friend would understand. (*Close* is used as an adjective modifying *friend.*)
The plan fell *through.* (*Through* is used as an adverb modifying *fell.*)
Justin pushed his way *through* the crowd. (*Through* is used as a preposition.)

527

Part 2

Objective

To recognize the use of a single word as various parts of speech

Presenting the Lesson

1. Read pages 527–528, studying examples of words used as two different parts of speech. Remind students that they have already studied some words that may be used as two different parts of speech: pronouns and adjectives (pages 484–485), prepositions and adverbs (page 513), adjectives and adverbs (page 496).

2. Assign and discuss Exercises A and B on page 528.

Individualizing the Lesson

Less-Advanced Students

Before students do the Exercises, have them underline the subject and verb in each sentence. Work on Exercise A together. Assign Exercise B.

Advanced Students

Write this sentence on the chalkboard:

            N   V   Adj   N
Did the coach time that race?

Have students identify the part of speech of each underlined word. Then have students use each underlined word in a different sentence as a different part of speech.

527

Encourage the students to use a dictionary to find out what other parts of speech each word can be.

Optional Practice

Have students identify the part of speech of the italicized word or words in each sentence.

1. *Clo̱se* the door. (V)
2. *Bo̱y!* was that a *clo̱se* *ca̱ll*. (Int) (Adj) (N)
3. That *bo̱y* should *ca̱ll* his father. (N) (V)
4. The magician will *pla̱ce* the card *u̱nder* the pile. (V) (Prep)
5. Our puppy found a *pla̱ce* on the fence where he could crawl *u̱nder*. (N) (Adv)
6. *The̱se* *fli̱es* are driving me crazy. (Adj) (N)
7. *The̱se* are the jets the pilot *fli̱es* to Miami. (Pro) (V)
8. After you *lo̱ck* the car, come *o̱ver* to the office. (V) (Adv)
9. Jon put a *lo̱ck* *o̱n* his locker. (N) (Prep)
10. The dog rolled *o̱ver*. (Adv)

Extending the Lesson

Have students look up the following words in the dictionary and list all possible parts of speech for each. Students should write original sentences using each word as the parts of speech listed. Answers below.

1. run   2. pass   3. thin
4. score 5. slide

1. V, N, Adj
2. V, N
3. Adj, Adv, V
4. N, V
5. V, N

Those are your choices. (*Those* is used as a pronoun, the subject of the sentence.)

I cannot accept *those* excuses. (*Those* is used as an adjective modifying the noun *excuses.*)

Lauren has a stylish *tan* jacket. (*Tan* is used as an adjective modifying the noun *jacket.*)

Workers *tan* leather with special care. (*Tan* is used as a verb.)

Exercise A   Write the italicized word. Next to it, write what part of speech it is in that sentence.

1. We took a long *drive* in the country.   noun
2. You *drive* past my house every day.   verb
3. Janie won that gigantic pillow at the county *fair*.   noun
4. The dealer offered a *fair* price.   adjective
5. Each debater studied *note* cards.   adjective
6. I *note* a touch of bitterness in your voice.   verb
7. *Which* traits do you admire most?   adjective
8. *Which* of these comedians is funniest?   pronoun
9. A snake slithered *by* our blanket.   preposition
10. Two old friends from grade school stopped *by*.   adverb

Exercise B   Follow the directions for Exercise A.

1. We forgot *paper* plates for the picnic.   adjective
2. Expensive *paper* usually has a watermark.   noun
3. Because of the fog, the plane flew *low*.   adverb
4. My *low* grades will improve this semester.   adjective
5. *That* face has been haunting me.   adjective
6. *That* was a terrifying experience!   pronoun
7. Many companies *fire* new employees first.   verb
8. A terrible *fire* left many families homeless.   noun
9. Nell's finances *narrow* her choices.   verb
10. The *narrow* stairway is barely passable.   adjective

. Then copy the italicized
is in that sentence.

ion

uggage. adjective

rtain countries. noun

rted cars. adjective

talled. adverb

adjective

tooth decay. adjective

he entire game. preposition

ol. adjective

correct. interjection

14. Movers *efficiently* loaded our furniture into the van. adverb
15. *Signs* in Death Valley warn drivers to conserve water. noun
16. *Very* few motels have vacancies tonight. adverb
17. The hotel is *on* the outskirts of Cleveland. preposition
18. A medical *technician* took the X-rays. noun
19. Did you see that movie *or* its sequel? conjunction
20. *Which* of the stars got top billing? pronoun
21. *Nobody* expected such a close game. pronoun
22. An agent handles *those* singers' bookings. adjective
23. The *park* is patrolled by mounted police. noun
24. Neither Sandy *nor* Vic acts very friendly. conjunction
25. All of the bowling trophies are *hers*. pronoun

Additional Exercises

These Additional Exercises may be used for additional practice of the concepts presented in this Section. Each exercise focuses on a single concept, and should be used after the page number indicated in parentheses.

Review

If you have not assigned these Additional Exercises before this time, you can also use them as an excellent Section Review.

These exercises provide re-view of the concepts pre-sented in this Section. Each exercise challenges the stu-dents to apply several of the skills they have acquired dur-ing previous study. Because the "mixed" feature of these activities makes them more difficult, the teacher may wish to have less-advanced stu-dents do them orally or in small groups.

MIXED REVIEW

Review of Parts of Speech

Recognizing the parts of speech   Copy the italicized words from this paragraph. Write _Noun_, _Verb_, _Pronoun_, _Adjective_, _Adverb_, _Preposition_, _Conjunction_, or _Interjection_, to show what part of speech each is used as.

1 = N
2 = N
3 = Adj
4 = Pro
5 = Adv
6 = P
7 = Adj
8 = Pro
9 = V
10 = N
11 = Adj
12 = C
13 = Adj
14 = V
15 = Pro
16 = N
17 = Pro

Once my *Saturdays* were a *time* for relaxation. *Those* peaceful days are gone, however. Now *I* get *up* at seven *in* the morning for a jazz *dance* class. After *that*, I *walk* my sister to her music *lesson*. I eat a *quick* lunch *and* then spend *two* hours at the library. I *time myself* because I must be at *work by* four. There the hours *whiz by*. Finally the *Saturday rush* is over. I get back home and can *barely* stagger in. *Gee! Sometimes* I *long* for the good old days.

18 = V
19 = Adv
20 = Adj
21 = N
22 = Adv
23 = I
24 = Adv
25 = V

Identifying the parts of speech   Write what part of speech each of the following italicized words is.

1. _Whew!_ That game was a close one. I
2. We _always_ travel at night because it is cooler. Adv
3. My _dad's_ car is rusty. Adj
4. I ran all the way _to_ the store in five minutes. P
5. Please give the finished report to Dan _or_ me. C
6. Even when Ed is late _he_ cannot hurry. Pro
7. He rushed, _but_ he was still late. C
8. The _study_ of history is important. N
9. We were all amused by her _entertaining_ story. Adj
10. The thunderstorm last night _surprised_ us. V

USING GRAMMAR IN WRITING
Review of the Parts of Speech

Using Grammar in Writing

These challenging and enjoyable activities allow the students to see how the concepts of grammar, usage, and mechanics may be applied in actual writing situations. Each exercise is designed to allow students practice in several of the skills they have acquired in this Section. The activities also provide opportunities for students to write creatively about a wide variety of interesting and unusual subjects.

A. Complete the following story. Add words used as the parts of speech called for in each blank. Add other modifiers if you need them. Remember that the verb can be made up of two or more words.

interjection = interj.   conjunction = conj.   noun = n.
adjective = adj.   pronoun = pro.   adverb = adv.
verb = v.   preposition = prep.

_____interj._____! That _____n._____ was _____adj._____. I
_____v._____ for a chance to explore a real _____n._____,
_____conj._____ I got the chance. Will anyone _____adv._____
believe my _____adj._____ story? If _____pro._____ told me
they saw a _____n._____ _____prep._____ a _____n._____,
I'd say _____pro._____ was _____adj._____ _____conj._____
_____adj._____. Fortunately, I do have _____n._____.
_____pro._____ will be convinced when they _____v._____
the _____n._____.

B. Identify the part of speech of each italicized word in the following paragraph. Then choose six of the words and write a new sentence for each one. Use each word as a different part of speech than it was used as in the original paragraph.

The next *time* discouragement *strikes*, remember this young man. He met *defeat* the first time he ran for *public* office. When he tried to become a storekeeper, the *store* went bankrupt. He sought a job with the United States *land* office and failed. He ran for the United States Senate and was beaten. He also *lost* the nomination for the United States Vice-Presidency. Yet he always *stuck* to his ideals and *dreams*. Finally he was elected to the *top* office in the land. Who was he? If your *guess* is Abraham Lincoln, you're *right*.

531

Section Objectives

1. To understand how word order affects meaning

2. To recognize the NV sentence pattern

3. To recognize the NVN sentence pattern

4. To recognize the NVNN sentence pattern

5. To recognize the N LV N sentence pattern

6. To recognize the N LV Adj sentence pattern

Preparing the Students

Write a variety of sentences on the chalkboard, then point out the various parts of speech in each sentence. Also point out the word pattern of each sentence. Show students how similar parts of speech occupy similar positions in sentences.

Additional Resources

Additional Exercises — pages 539–541 in the student text

Special Populations — See special section at the back of this Teacher's Edition.

Sentence Patterns

In general, meaning is expressed in English by groups of words acting together. The most important of these groups is the sentence. A sentence is made up of words that are arranged in a certain order. One word follows another from the beginning to the end of the sentence. The order is not simply haphazard. There are fixed patterns into which words are placed to express meaning. In this section you will study five **sentence patterns.**

Part 1 Word Order and Meaning

To make sense, words must be put together in order according to certain patterns. Not just any order will do. Look at the groups of words below. Which groups make sense?

Lightning struck nearby.   Noise filled the arcade.
Struck nearby lightning.   Noise the arcade filled.

The first group in each pair makes sense because the words are in the right order for one of the patterns of an English sentence. The second group in each pair does not make sense because the words are not in the right order. Our experience with sentences has taught us what the right order is, so we can see at once when the order is wrong.

Sometimes there is more than one right order for the words in a sentence. Each order makes sense and expresses an idea, but when the order is different, the ideas expressed may be different too. Read the following pairs of sentences.

The audience watched the mime.
The mime watched the audience.

The suitcase filled the box.
The box filled the suitcase.

The words are the same in each sentence, but the word order is not. The difference in word order makes an important difference in meaning.

Exercise   Read the sentence. Then change the order of the words to change the meaning. Write each new sentence on your paper.

1. Most runners passed Tony.   Tony passed most runners.
2. Mondays are weekdays.   Weekdays are Mondays.
3. Lisa is the winner.   The winner is Lisa.
4. Autumn follows summer.   Summer follows autumn.
5. Sarah teased Eli.   Eli teased Sarah.
6. Some people are athletes.   Some athletes are people.

533

Part 2

Objective

To recognize the NV sentence pattern

Presenting the Lesson

1. Read page 534 and study the examples of the NV pattern. Explain that the pattern of NV is not altered by the addition of modifiers (adjectives, adverbs, prepositional phrases) or articles. Explain that even a compound subject or verb can be included in a NV pattern.

2. Assign and discuss Exercises A, B, and C on page 534.

Individualizing the Lesson

Less-Advanced Students

Work with the students to complete Exercise C.

Advanced Students

Have students expand the sentences in Exercises B and C by adding modifiers to the subject and the verb.

Optional Practice

Have students place N and V over the appropriate words in the following NV sentences.

1. My gold shirt ripped during the dance practice.
2. The exhausted fireman collapsed.
3. The tires of the jeep spun around.
4. A cold draft blew on us.

Extending the Lesson

Have the students identify the NV pattern in the sentences from a short story.

Part 2   The N V Pattern

One simple pattern for English sentences is called the **N V pattern.** In this chart, *N* stands for the noun (or pronoun) in the complete subject, and *V* stands for the verb in the complete predicate.

N	V
Night	approached.
The moon	rose.
The stars	were twinkling.
The skyline	glittered brightly.

The word order in these sentences follows the pattern noun-verb, or N V. This pattern is call the N V pattern.

Exercise A   Make a chart for the N V pattern. Label one column N and the other V. Write these sentences on the chart.

1. Old wounds|heal slowly.
2. Jesse|swam furiously.
3. Vacation|flew by.
4. The glass|broke.
5. New boots|hurt.
6. A shipment|arrived today.

Exercise B   Copy this chart. Complete each N V pattern.
Answers will vary.

N	V
1. _____	collapsed.
2. Two pigeons	_____.
3. _____	sped away.
4. Lucille	_____.
5. _____	squealed.

Exercise C: Writing   Make a chart of your own for the N V pattern. Write five sentences in the N V pattern. Answers will vary.

Part 3 The N V N Pattern

A sentence in the **N V N pattern** has three parts. The first *N* stands for the subject noun. The *V* stands for the verb. The second *N* stands for the direct object noun. Read the sentences in the following chart. They are in the N V N pattern.

N	V	N
Roselyn	made	the team.
Gwen and Bob	played	their guitars.
Bright lights	dotted	the skyline.
My helmet	protects	my head.
No one	claimed	the bracelet.

Exercise A Make a chart for the N V N pattern. Label the three columns, *N*, *V*, and *N*. Write these sentences on the chart.

1. Tony | bought | a record.
2. Dan | polished | the car.
3. My sister | trains | horses.
4. We | expected | fireworks.
5. I | finished | the yogurt.
6. Marilyn | plays | basketball.
7. David | helped | the nurse.
8. Rodney | prepared | lunch.

Exercise B Copy this chart. Complete each N V N pattern.

N	V	N
1. _____	missed	the point.
2. Karen	told	_____.
3. _____	suggested	_____.
4. Mrs. Ford	_____	her car.
5. _____	wrote	that song.
6. The store	sells	_____.

Exercise C: Writing Make a chart of your own for the N V N pattern. Write five sentences in the N V N pattern. Answers will vary.

535

Objective

To recognize the NVN sentence pattern

Presenting the Lesson

Read page 535 and study the examples of the NVN pattern. Remind students that the V in this pattern will always be a transitive action verb.

Individualizing the Lesson

Less-Advanced Students

Work with the students to complete Exercise C.

Advanced Students

Have students add modifiers to the sentence in Exercises A and B.

Optional Practice

Have students create NVN sentences using the words below in the designated positions. Answers will vary.

1. predicted   (verb)
2. reporter   (subject)
3. visited   (verb)
4. chop suey   (direct object)
5. government   (subject)

Extending the Lesson

Have students suggest alternate objects for the sentences in Exercise A.

Objective

To recognize the NVNN sentence pattern

Presenting the Lesson

1. Read page 536 and study the examples of the NVNN pattern.

2. Assign and discuss Exercises A, B, and C.

Individualizing the Lesson

Less-Advanced Students

Work with students to complete Exercise C.

Advanced Students

Have students add modifiers to the sentences they write for Exercises B and C.

Optional Practice

Have students mark N, V, N, and N over the subject, verb, indirect object, and direct object in these sentences.

1. My aunt's rose garden gives Tony an asthma attack.
2. Mr. Drummond read students the newspaper article.
3. You can send your boss a bill for your transportation.
4. Snoopy brings Woodstock his birdseed.
5. Nancy is knitting Jerry a scarf.

Extending the Lesson

Have students use each verb below in a NVN and a NVNN sentence. Answers will vary.

bring   sell   write

Part 4   The N V N N Pattern

A sentence in the **N V N N pattern** has four parts. The first *N* stands for the subject noun or pronoun. The *V* stands for the verb. The second *N* stands for the indirect object noun, and the third *N* stands for the direct object noun. Read the sentences in the following chart. They are in the N V N N pattern.

N	V	N	N
Mindy	sold	Brian	her skateboard.
Chris	told	us	the score.
Your parents	gave	me	your old bike.

Exercise A   Make a chart for the N V N N pattern. Label the four columns *N*, *V*, *N*, and *N*. Write these sentences on the chart.

1. Jean |told |Suzanne |the rumor.
2. We |sent |our cousins |a telegram.
3. Your T-shirt |gives |the world |your message.
4. Stamp collecting |made |me |money.
5. A portable radio |brought |us |the news.
6. Our team |gave |the winners |a cheer.

Exercise B   Make a chart like the one below. Complete each sentence in the N V N N pattern. Answers will vary.

N	V	N	N
1. _____	brought	Jerome	_____.
2. Carla	offered	_____	_____.
3. Everyone	_____	_____	support.
4. _____	_____	Kevin	four dollars.
5. I	sent	_____	_____.

Exercise C: Writing   Make a chart of your own for the N V N N pattern. Write five sentences in the N V N N pattern. Answers will vary.

Part 5   The N LV N Pattern

A sentence in the **N LV N pattern** has three parts. The first *N* stands for the subject noun. *LV* stands for a linking or state-of-being verb. The second *N* stands for the predicate noun that follows the linking verb. The sentences in this chart are in the N LV N pattern.

N	LV	N
Dill	is	an herb.
Loretta	was	the fastest runner.
The highway	was	a maze.
Scallops	are	shellfish.

Exercise A   Make a chart for the N LV N pattern. Label the three columns *N*, *LV*, and *N*. Write these sentences on the chart.

1. The sidewalk is a mess.
2. Sneakers are shoes.
3. This restaurant is a hit.
4. The capital is Katmandu.
5. Alicia is an artist.
6. Lenny was the cook.
7. Fruit was the dessert.
8. A pheasant is a bird.

Exercise B   Make a chart like the one below. Complete each sentence in the N LV N pattern. Answers will vary.

N	LV	N
1. _____	is	my lucky day.
2. Frank	was	_____.
3. _____	are	liquids.
4. Julia	_____	a bicycle racer.
5. _____	were	_____.

Exercise C: Writing   Make a chart of your own. Label the columns *N*, *LV*, and *N*. Write five sentences in the N LV N pattern. Answers will vary.

537

Part 6

Objective

To recognize the N LV Adj sentence pattern

Presenting the Lesson

1. Read and discuss page 538. Point out that while the N LV Adj sentence is similar to the N LV N in its use of a linking verb, the difference is in the use of a predicate adjective to describe the subject.

2. Assign and discuss Exercises A, B, and C on page 538.

Individualizing the Lesson

Less-Advanced Students

Work with students to complete Exercise C.

Advanced Students

Have students add modifiers to the subjects, verbs, and predicate objects in Exercise C.

Optional Practice

Have students label each of the following N LV N or N LV Adj.

1. De Paul University was the winner of today's game.
2. Their basketball team is great.
3. Basketball has always been my favorite sport.

Extending the Lesson

Have students label each sentence NV, NVN, NVNN, N LV N or N LV Adj.

1. Many states have ratified the Equal Rights Amendment.
2. Carnations always smell so fresh!
3. Julia Child is a superb cook.

538

Sentences in the **N LV Adj pattern** have three parts. The *N* stands for the subject noun. *LV* stands for a linking verb. *Adj* stands for the predicate adjective. The sentences in the following chart are in the N LV Adj pattern.

N	LV	Adj
Your car	looks	new.
Sunflowers	are	tall.
Renee	seems	satisfied.
My decision	is	final.
The lemonade	tastes	refreshing.

Exercise A   Make a chart for the N LV Adj pattern. Label the three columns *N, LV,* and *Adj.* Write these sentences on the chart.

1. The view was spectacular.
2. His ideas were excellent.
3. The tomatoes were juicy.
4. The horses sound nervous.
5. Robin felt weary.
6. The room was dark.
7. Charlie seems patient.
8. These peppers are hot.

Exercise B   Make a chart like the one below. Complete each sentence in the N LV Adj pattern.   Answers will vary.

N	LV	Adj
1. Foster	looked	_____.
2. My pack	seems	_____.
3. _____	is	alone.
4. City Hall	_____	open.
5. _____	sounded	_____.

Exercise C: Writing   Make a chart of your own. Label the columns *N, LV,* and *Adj.* Write five sentences in the N LV Adj pattern.
Answers will vary.

538

ADDITIONAL EXERCISES

Sentence Patterns

Sentence Patterns   Write the pattern for each of the following sentences. Each sentence will fit one of these patterns: NV, N V N, N V N N, N LV N, N LV Adj.

1. Henry enjoyed the concert. N-V-N
2. Everybody lent Milton a hand. N-V-N-N
3. That strip of land is a runway. N-LV-N
4. Pizza Hut is my favorite restaurant. N-LV-N
5. The drum solo was too long. N-LV-Adj.
6. The Confederate Army surrendered. N-V
7. Their bus left without them. N-V
8. Alison wrote her cousin the news. N-V-N-N
9. The humidity felt miserable. N-LV-Adj.
10. Rhonda seemed quite sincere. N-LV-Adj.
11. That hammer was a good tool. N-LV-N
12. Everyone ate the shrimp curry. N-V-N
13. Shawn swims powerfully. N-V
14. Richard gave his brother the old bat. N-V-N-N
15. Nobody remembered Mr. Allard's birthday. N-V-N
16. Cobwebs hung from the ceiling. N-V
17. The bumpersticker gave us a laugh. N-V-N-N
18. We searched for shells at low tide. N-V
19. Christine works at the hospital on Saturdays. N-V
20. Somebody sent Johnny an odd Valentine. N-V-N-N
21. Ms. Fellman adjusted the rearview mirror. N-V-N
22. Argentina is a big country. N-LV-N
23. Carrie became thin over the summer. N-LV-Adj.
24. In its early days, the United States was an agricultural country. N-LV-N
25. Colts frisked happily around the pasture. N-V

Additional Exercises

These Additional Exercises may be used for additional practice of the concepts presented in this Section. Each exercise focuses on a single concept, and should be used after the page number indicated in parentheses.

Review

If you have not assigned these Additional Exercises before this time, you can also use them as an excellent Section Review.

These exercises provide review of the concepts presented in this Section. Each exercise challenges the students to apply several of the skills they have acquired during previous study. Because the "mixed" feature of these activities makes them more difficult, the teacher may wish to have less-advanced students do them orally or in small groups.

MIXED REVIEW

Sentence Patterns

A. Finding sentence patterns Write the pattern for each of the following sentences.

1. Darryl typed his report. N-V-N
2. This window always sticks. N-V
3. The class gave Marcy a farewell party. N-V-N-N
4. The cartoon was very funny. N-LV-Adj.
5. New South Wales is in Australia. N-V
6. The sandwiches were soggy. N-LV-Adj.
7. Missy pedaled faster. N-V
8. He tells everyone the same story. N-V-N-N
9. My favorite comedian is Robin Williams. N-LV-N
10. Noah wearily rubbed his forehead. N-V-N

B. Using sentence patterns Write two original sentences for each of the following sentence patterns. Sentences will vary.

1. N V
2. N V N
3. N V N N
4. N LV N
5. N LV Adj.

USING GRAMMAR IN WRITING
Sentence Patterns

A. Newspaper headlines must be short and attention-getting. Most often, they are written in a simple NV or NVN pattern. Make up six headlines about events around your neighborhood and school. Write NV and NVN sentences that will make people want to read the story that follows the headlines.

> **Examples:** Schools Reopen (NV)
> Mavericks Defeat the Pirates (NVN)

B. Choose one of the headlines that you wrote for Exercise A. Make up a story that fits the headline. Include all five kinds of sentence patterns in your story. Label each pattern.

C. A greeting card company is looking for new writers of verses for its cards. Choose at least three occasions for sending cards: Valentine's Day, Mother's Day, Christmas, birthdays, and anniversaries, for example. Write a humorous or serious verse to go on each of five different cards. The verses do not have to rhyme, but the lines in each one should follow the same sentence pattern. Use a different pattern for each card. If you like, you can include illustrations with the cards.

> **Example:** N LV N pattern
> I am the sea,
> You are the shore.
> I am the moon,
> You are the sun.
> We are friends.

Using Grammar in Writing

These challenging and enjoyable activities allow the students to see how the concepts of grammar, usage, and mechanics may be applied in actual writing situations. Each exercise is designed to allow students practice in several of the skills they have acquired in this Section. The activities also provide opportunities for students to write creatively about a wide variety of interesting and unusual subjects.

Using Verbals

You have learned that there are eight parts of speech. The eight parts of speech are these:

nouns   verbs   adjectives   conjunctions
pronouns   adverbs   prepositions   interjections

In addition to the eight parts of speech, the English language contains three other kinds of words. These are **gerunds, participles,** and **infinitives.** These words are called verbals. A **verbal** is a word that is formed from a verb but acts as another part of speech.

In this section you will study the three kinds of verbals, and learn how they are used in the sentence.

Part 1   Gerunds

A gerund is a verb form that is used as a noun. A gerund is formed by adding *-ing* to the present form of the verb: *run—running, laugh—laughing, sleep—sleeping.* A gerund may be used in any way that a noun is used.

Like nouns, gerunds may be used as subjects.

> *Skating* requires precise form.
> (*Skating* is a gerund, the subject of the verb *requires.*)

Like nouns, gerunds may be used as objects.

> Karen enjoys *singing.*
> (*Singing* is a gerund, the direct object of the verb *enjoys.*)

Like nouns, gerunds may be used as objects of prepositions.

> There is no space for *dancing.*
> (*Dancing* is a gerund, the object of the preposition *for.*)

The Gerund Phrase

Gerunds may have modifiers and objects.

The gerund and its modifiers and objects form a **gerund phrase.** Then the entire phrase functions as a noun.

Since gerunds come from verbs, they can have objects.

> *Roping a steer* intrigues Kitt.
> (*Roping* is a gerund; *steer* is the object of *roping.* The phrase *roping a steer* is the subject of the verb *intrigues.*)

Since gerunds come from verbs, they can be modified by adverbs.

> We use this car for *running around.*
> (*Running* is a gerund; *around* is an adverb modifying *running.* The phrase *running around* is the object of the preposition *for.*)

Special Populations — See special section at the back of this Teacher's Edition.

Part 1

Objective

To recognize gerunds and gerund phrases, and to understand the ways in which they are formed and used

Presenting the Lesson

1. Read the definition of a gerund on page 543. Point out that gerunds are always the *-ing* form of a verb. Study the examples showing gerunds in typical uses.

2. Read pages 543–544 which discuss gerund phrases. Go over examples carefully. Students may find it confusing that gerunds can be modified by both adverbs and adjectives. Stress that gerunds come from verbs but are used as nouns.

3. Read how to diagram gerunds and gerund phrases on pages 544–545. Study sample diagrams which show the special nature of these words.

4. Assign and discuss Exercises A and B on pages 545–546. Students should notice how frequently gerunds are used as subjects of sentences.

Do Exercise A on pages 545–546 orally with students. Assign and discuss Exercise B.

Advanced Students

Have the students write five sentences that include gerund phrases. Tell them to identify the objects and modifiers of the gerund phrases in the sentences.

Optional Practice

Have students list 10 action verbs on their papers. Then have them add -ing to each word. Next, ask them to expand each word into a phrase. Finally, ask them to expand each phrase into a sentence.

Extending the Lesson

Have students create sentences using the following gerunds or gerund phrases in the positions indicated. Answers will vary.

1. eating too much (object of preposition)
2. voting for class officers (subject)
3. playing my guitar (direct object)
4. tumbling and vaulting (direct object)
5. landing the aircraft smoothly (subject)

Since gerunds are used as nouns, they can be modified by adjectives.

> *Careful reading* requires concentration.
> (*Reading* is a gerund; *careful* is an adjective modifying *reading*. The phrase *careful reading* is the subject of the verb *requires*.)

Gerunds can also be modified by prepositional phrases.

> *Cycling in city traffic* is frustrating.
> (*Cycling* is a gerund; *in city traffic* is a prepositional phrase modifying *cycling*. The entire phrase is the subject of *is*.)

As you can tell from the above examples, gerunds look like verbs but are not used as verbs. *Skating, singing, dancing, roping, running, reading,* and *cycling* all appear to be verbs but are used as nouns. That usage makes them gerunds.

Diagraming Gerunds

A gerund or gerund phrase that is used as the subject or direct object of a verb is diagramed on a bridge above the line. Place the gerund itself on a line drawn as a step. If the gerund has modifiers, show them on lines slanted down from the gerund. If the gerund has an object, show it on a horizontal line following the gerund.

Understanding dreams takes practice.

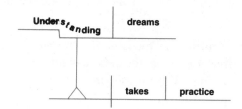

These ethnic festivals encourage understanding other cultures.

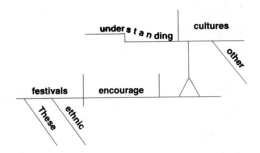

A gerund or gerund phrase that is used as the object of a preposition is diagramed below the base line. Place the preposition on a slanted line below the word modified. Place the gerund on a line drawn as a step. (The gerund may also have modifiers or an object.)

Jenny is paid for giving tours.

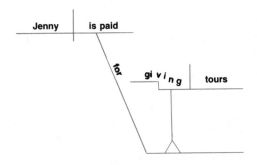

Exercise A   Find the <u>gerunds</u> or <u>gerund phrases</u>. As your teacher directs, show how the gerund is used.

Example: Planning the sports meet was fun.
Planning the sports meet: gerund phrase, subject of *was*

1. <u>Running</u> has become a popular activity. subject
2. <u>Putting on a play</u> takes teamwork. subject

3. <u>Cleaning the attic</u> was not my idea of fun. <small>subject</small>
4. <u>Washing that wall</u> took all afternoon. <small>subject</small>
5. <u>Painting the scenery</u> took six hours. <small>subject</small>
6. <u>Skydiving</u> takes nerve. <small>subject</small>
7. <u>Rushing</u> can waste time. <small>subject</small>
8. Ken started <u>paneling the basement.</u> <small>direct object</small>
9. A ceramics class teaches skills in <u>pottery making.</u> <small>object of preposition</small>
10. Paramedical work requires <u>quick thinking.</u> <small>direct object</small>

Follow the directions for Exercise A.

1. Joe learned <u>fencing</u> last summer. <small>direct object</small>
2. Students who study Russian begin by <u>learning a new alphabet.</u> <small>object of preposition</small>
3. <u>Waiting on tables</u> is Serena's summer job. <small>subject</small>
4. <u>Visiting Dallas</u> was interesting. <small>subject</small>
5. Jack has always liked <u>biking.</u> <small>direct object</small>
6. <u>Wearing sunglasses</u> rests her eyes. <small>subject</small>
7. They got sick from <u>overeating.</u> <small>object of preposition</small>
8. Clare likes <u>walking in the rain.</u> <small>direct object</small>
9. <u>Eating outside</u> was a pleasant change. <small>subject</small>
10. <u>Driving to Alaska</u> would be expensive. <small>subject</small>

Part 2 Participles

A participle is a verb form that is used as an adjective.

There are two kinds of participles, past and present. You probably remember the **past participle,** one of the principal parts of the verb. It is formed by adding -*d* or -*ed* to the present tense: *talk—talked.* The past participles of irregular verbs are exceptions and must be learned separately: *sing—sung, know—known.*

The other kind of participle is the **present participle.** All present participles are formed by adding -*ing* to the present form of the verb: *talk—talking, sing—singing, know—knowing.*

Part 2

Objectives

1. To recognize participles and participial phrases, and to understand the ways in which they are formed and used

2. To distinguish between gerunds and participles

Presenting the Lesson

1. Read the definition of participles on pages 546–547. Some review of past participles might be beneficial. Look at pages 462–470,

546

These are additional examples:

Verb	Past Participle	Present Participle
join	joined	joining
take	taken	taking
try	tried	trying
grow	grown	growing

Participles are always used as adjectives. They can modify nouns or pronouns.

Smiling, Jan accepted the award.
    (*Smiling* is a present participle modifying the noun *Jan*.)
Lunging, he hit the fence.
    (*Lunging* is a participle modifying the pronoun *he*.)
That Nova has a *rebuilt* engine.
    (*Rebuilt* is a past participle modifying the noun *engine*.)

The Participial Phrase

Participles may have modifiers or objects. The participle and its modifiers or objects then form a **participial phrase.** The entire participial phrase is used as an adjective.

Since participles come from verbs, they may have objects.

Turning the pages, Barb found an old letter.
    (*Turning the pages* is a participial phrase modifying *Barb*. *Pages* is the object of the participle *turning*.)

Since participles come from verbs, they may also be modified by adverbs.

Jena, *turning suddenly*, collided with Mr. Gans.
    (*Turning suddenly* is a participial phrase modifying *Jena*. *Suddenly* is an adverb modifying the participle *turning*.)

Participles may also be modified by prepositional phrases.

Exhausted from the race, the last swimmer crawled out.
    (*Exhuasted from the race* is a participial phrase modifying *swimmer*. *From the race* is a prepositional phrase modifying the participle *exhausted*.)

paying particular attention to past participle forms of irregular verbs. Explain to students that when used as a verbal, a participle has no helping verbs and functions as an adjective. Ask students to supply the past participle form for the following irregular verbs: *feel, throw, cost, lead, freeze, begin.* Note that all present participles are formed by adding *-ing* to the present tense. Then have students form the present participle for these verbs: *do, grow.*

2. Read pages 547–548. Stress that participles are verb forms used as another part of speech (adjectives). Thus, they can exhibit properties of verbs (have direct objects, be modified by adverbs, etc.) while they function as adjectives (modifying nouns or pronouns).

3. Read page 548. Study the sample diagrams which illustrate the special nature of participles.

4. Assign and discuss Exercises A and B on pages 548–549. Students should note the position of participial phrases in sentences in which the participial phrase modifies the subject.

5. Read page 549 which should help students distinguish between gerunds and participles. Point out that when a participle or a participial phrase begins a sentence (as a modifier of the subject), it is usually followed by a comma. A gerund or gerund phrase which begins a sentence (as the subject) is never followed by a comma.

6. Do the exercise on page 550 orally. Have students tell how the gerund or participle is used (as the subject, as a modifier of the subject, etc.).

Work through the first few sentences in Exercise A with students. Remind them to look for -ed and -ing words that act as adjectives. Assign the remainder of the Exercises to be done independently.

Advanced Students

Have the students write five original sentences that include participles. Tell the student to identify the word the participle modifies.

Optional Practice

Have students write sentences using the gerunds or participles in the manner indicated. Answers will vary.

1. intercepting the pass (participle modifying subject)
2. broken (participle modifying subject)
3. losing his patience (participle modifying subject)
4. brushing your teeth (gerund as subject)

Extending the Lesson

Discuss the idea of parallel construction in writing. Tell students that a series beginning with nouns must continue with nouns; one that begins with adjectives must continue with adjectives. Similarly the tense of participles should not shift in the middle of a series. Ask students how they would revise the following sentences.

After the relay race the team was panting hard, sweating profusely, and looking exhausted.

The old woman made the basket with braided twigs, twisted rope, and kneaded clay she kneaded.

As you can see from the above examples, participles may look like verbs, but are not used as verbs. *Smiling, turning, lunging, rebuilt,* and *exhausted* appear to be verbs but are used as adjectives. That usage makes them participles.

Diagraming Participles

A participle is diagramed below the noun or pronoun it modifies. Place the participle itself on an angled line. If the participle has modifiers, show them on lines slanted down from the participle. If the participle has an object, place it on a horizontal line following the participle.

Wildly signaling the ref, Marty called timeout.

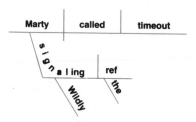

Exercise A Write the participles or participial phrases in these sentences. Show which word the participle modifies.

Example: Moving slowly, Ron crept close to the deer.
Moving slowly (participial phrase, modifying *Ron*)

1. Tested in our laboratories, the parts are guaranteed.
2. Spread thin, the glue dries in an hour.
3. Jumping clear, Nan opened her parachute.
4. Crossing the old bridge, she passed the general store.
5. Frozen, the pie tastes even better.
6. The exhausted marathon runners crossed the finish line.
7. Moving effortlessly, the skaters danced across the ice.
8. Looking through binoculars, Jim could see the skyline.

9. <u>Concentrating deeply</u>, the <u>center</u> sank the free throw.

10. <u>Moving quickly</u>, the <u>goalie</u> blocked the kick.

Exercise B Follow the directions for Exercise A.

1. <u>Driving hard</u>, the running <u>back</u> dove over the goal line.
2. Lisa showed us the leg <u>band</u> <u>worn by rare birds</u>.
3. The <u>ball</u> ricocheted, <u>hitting the taillight</u>.
4. <u>Waiting patiently</u>, the <u>passengers</u> stood in line at the gate.
5. <u>Seeing the rain</u>, <u>Mr. Mill</u> waited.
6. <u>Clutching the phone tightly</u>, <u>she</u> listened.
7. Watch for gravel <u>trucks</u> <u>leaving the quarry</u>.
8. <u>Fascinated by the talk</u>, <u>we</u> listened without a sound.
9. He forgot that <u>paperback</u> <u>lying on the table</u>.
10. <u>Breathing hard</u>, <u>Nancy</u> crossed the finish line.

Distinguishing Between Gerunds and Participles

The two kinds of verbals you have studied, gerunds and participles, sometimes look similar.

The gerund, like the present participle, is formed by adding -*ing* to the present form of the verb. How can you tell whether a word is a gerund or a participle? It depends upon how the word is used. If it is used as a modifier, it is a participle. If it is used as a noun, it is a gerund. Look at the verbals in these two sentences:

> *Walking swiftly* is good exercise.
> (*Walking* is a gerund, the subject of the verb *is*. *Swiftly* is an adverb modifying *walking*.)
> Walking swiftly, we caught up with Nicole.
> (*Walking* is a present participle modifying *we*. *Swiftly* again modifies *walking*.)

549

Part 3

Objectives

1. To recognize infinitives and infinitive phrases and to understand the ways in which they are formed and used
2. To avoid split infinitives

Presenting the Lesson

1. Read pages 550–551. Make certain that students understand the difference between the sign of the infinitive *to* and the preposition *to*. Have students identify the infinitives in the following sentences.

1. Mark said to follow him to school.
2. To educate yourself you must learn to ask questions.
3. I hope to go to your graduation.
4. Plan to arrive early; come to the back door.
5. Joan has gone to bed already because she wants to sleep ten hours tonight.

550

Exercise For each sentence, write the gerund or participle and say which it is.

1. Cleaning is done every Saturday.
2. Cleaning the car, Pat found her notebook.
3. Fixing engines was Mr. Buswell's specialty.
4. Fixing a sandwich, Gerry listened to the sportscast.
5. Watching television bothers his eyes.
6. Watching television, Jo forgot the oven was on.
7. Removing the tree was difficult.
8. Panning for gold, the old man waded into the stream.
9. Moving quickly, the paramedics aided several victims.
10. Swimming is good for most people's health.

Part 3 Infinitives

The third kind of verbal is the **infinitive.**

The infinitive is the verbal form that usually appears with the word *to* before it. *To* is called the sign of the infinitive.

to take	to give	to teach	to look
to build	to sing	to bring	to answer

Note: You have already studied the word *to* as a preposition. *To* is a preposition if it is followed by a noun or pronoun as its object. *To* is the sign of the infinitive if it is followed by a verb. These examples show the difference:

Prepositional Phrases	**Infinitives**
We went to the arcade.	We wanted to skydive.
Jeremy stayed to the end.	Lowell plans to diet.

The Infinitive Phrase

Like other verbals, the infinitive can have modifiers and objects. The infinitive with its objects and modifiers is called an **infinitive phrase.**

550

Since the infinitive comes from a verb, it is like a verb in several ways. For example, an infinitive may have an object.

> Chris learned *to run a lathe.*
> (*Lathe* is the direct object of the infinitive *to run.*)
> Ann-Marie wants *to show her friends her new skates.*
> (*Friends* is the indirect object and *skates* is the direct object of the infinitive *to show.*)

Since the infinitive comes from a verb, it may be modified by adverbs.

> You will need *to work fast.*
> (*Fast* is an adverb modifying the infinitive *to work.*)
> Beth arranged to *leave school early.*
> (*Early* is an adverb modifying the infinitive *to leave.*)

Infinitives may also be modified by prepositional phrases.

> Linda wanted *to drive to the station.*
> (*To the station* is a prepositional phrase modifying the infinitive *to drive.*)
> The candidates promised *to debate on TV.*
> (*On TV* is a prepositional phrase modifying the infinitive *to debate.*)

Uses of the Infinitive Phrase

Unlike the other verbals, infinitives and infinitive phrases can be used as more than one part of speech. Infinitives can be used as (1) nouns, (2) adjectives, or (3) adverbs.

You have studied the use of nouns as subjects and direct objects of verbs. Infinitives and infinitive phrases, too, can be used as subjects, direct objects, or other noun usages.

> Subject: *To ask for a raise* sometimes pays off.
> (*To ask for a raise* is the subject of *pays.*)
>
> Direct Object: Sue wanted *to leave the theater.*
> (*To leave the theater* is the direct object of *wanted.*)

Go over the examples showing infinitives with objects and infinitives modified by adverbs and prepositional phrases.

2. Read pages 551–552 concerning uses of the infinitive phrase. Again stress to students that an infinitive is classified as a verbal because it is formed from a verb but used as another part of speech. Go over all examples of infinitives used as nouns, adjectives, and adverbs.

3. Read page 552 and discuss avoiding the split infinitive.

4. Read pages 552–553 which show how to diagram infinitives and infinitive phrases. Study the sample diagrams of infinitives. These will help to illustrate the special nature of these words. Have students note how the infinitive can be used as a noun and as a modifier.

5. Assign and discuss Exercise A on pages 553–554. In going over items, have students tell whether the infinitive functions as a noun, an adjective, or an adverb.

6. Assign and discuss Exercise B on page 554. Again, have students identify the function of each infinitive.

Individualizing the Lesson
Less-Advanced Students

Before students begin the Exercises, remind them to look for *to +
verb* and to include all modifiers in the phrase. Have the students underline the infinitive in each phrase. Work on Exercise A together; assign Exercise B.

Advanced Students

Have students explain how each infinitive phrase in the Exercises is used in its sentence. Then have students analyze each infinitive phrase, identifying any objects or modifiers.

Optional Practice

Have students complete each of the following sentences with infinitives. Then have them indicate how the resulting infinitive phrases are used. Answers will vary.

1. Eva wanted _____ to the concert.
2. David was too young _____ in the game.
3. _____ is my favorite hobby.
4. Would you like _____ your bicycle?

Extending the Lesson

Have students write sentences using the following infinitives and infinitive phrases in the ways indicated. Answers will vary.

1. to win the gold medal (noun as direct object)
2. to earn extra money (adverb)
3. to grow vegetables (noun as direct object)
4. to play hockey (noun as subject)
5. to take photographs (adjective)

Infinitives and infinitive phrases can also be used as modifiers. If the infinitive or infinitive phrase modifies a noun or pronoun, it is used as an adjective. If it modifies a verb, adjective, or adverb, it is used as an adverb.

Adjective: An advisor is the one *to counsel you.*
                   (*To counsel you* modifies the pronoun *one.*)

Adjective: The catcher is the player *to watch.*
                   (*To watch* modifies the noun *player.*)

Adverb: Tickets for the spring concert are hard *to get.*
                   (*To get* modifies the adjective *hard.*)

Adverb: The army retreated *to avoid defeat.*
                   (*To avoid defeat* modifies the verb *retreated.*)

Adverb: The stereo played too softly *to hear.*
                   (*To hear* modifies the adverb *softly.*)

As you can see from the examples above, infinitives look like verbs but are not used as verbs. Infinitives are used as nouns, adjectives, or adverbs.

The Split Infinitive

At times a modifier is placed between the word *to* and the verb in an infinitive. That placement of a modifier is said to split the infinitive. A split infinitive usually sounds awkward and should be avoided.

Awkward: Anna expects to *easily* win.
Better: Anna expects to win *easily.*

Diagraming Infinitives

An infinitive or infinitive phrase used as a noun is diagramed on a bridge above the line. *To*, the sign of the infinitive, is placed on a slanted line. Place the infinitive on a horizontal line. If the infinitive has modifiers, show them on lines slanted down from the infinitive. If the infinitive has an object, show it on a horizontal line following the infinitive.

My sister wants to go to the store now.

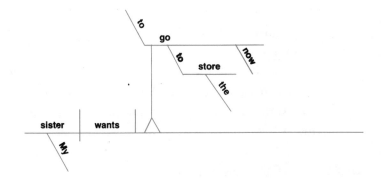

An infinitive or infinitive phrase used as an adjective or adverb is diagramed below the word modified by the infinitive. (The infinitive may also have modifiers or an object.)

Gwendolyn Brooks was first to read her poems.

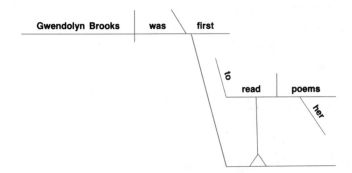

Exercise A Write each infinitive or infinitive phrase. Be prepared to tell how it is used in the sentence.

Example: They were ready to drop the whole thing.
To drop the whole thing: infinitive phrase

1. This is the best book to use. modifies *book*
2. Bill ran to get a flashlight. modifies *ran*

3. To finish this project by Monday is my goal. subject
4. We tried to remember the address. object
5. We were too late to see the Mets' game. modifies *late*
6. Judy and I were told to bring our registration cards to orientation. object
7. Tom Landry tried to encourage the Cowboys. object
8. Mary and I plan to watch *Saturday Night Live.* object
9. Mr. Anderson wants to explain the new procedures. object
10. Sue still has homework to do. modifies *homework*

Exercise B Follow the directions for Exercise A.

1. This slope is too steep to climb. modifies *steep*
2. The best thing to do is to wait. modifies *thing*, predicate noun
3. Would you like to eat breakfast at the pancake house? object
4. Remind me to fill the tank with unleaded gas. object
5. Do you want to play hockey after school? object
6. Andrea is too young to get a driver's permit. modifies *young*
7. He wanted to get a job in Alaska. object
8. Did you remember to buy film? object
9. To read the first two chapters of this book is our assignment. subject
10. Amy has someone to help her with the job. modifies *someone*

Part 4   A Review of Verbals

In this section, you have been introduced to the three kinds of verbals. These special words are verb forms, but are never used as verbs. Verbals are used as other parts of speech.

Gerunds, participles, and infinitives are the three kinds of verbals. All three may be used by themselves. They may also be used in phrases. These phrases are called gerund phrases, participial phrases, and infinitive phrases. Because they are like verbs, all three kinds of verbals may have objects or modifiers.

Part 4

Objective

To review the formation and use of gerunds, participles, and infinitives

Presenting the Lesson

1. Read pages 554–555. Go over the definitions of verbals, gerunds, participles, and infinitives. Study the

554

A **gerund** is a verb form used as a noun. (Gerunds end in *-ing*.) A gerund may be used in all the ways a noun may be used.

> *Running* tones muscles. (subject)
> Dad enjoys *running daily*. (direct object)
> Try *long-distance running*. (direct object)
> By *running* I keep in shape. (object of preposition)

A **participle** is a verb form used as an adjective. (Past participles of regular verbs end in *-d* or *-ed*. Present participles end in *-ing*.) Participles, like adjectives, modify nouns or pronouns.

> *Breaking formation*, the majorette ran from the field.
> I see someone *breaking into our car*.
> The inmates *breaking out of jail* were spotted.
> *Breaking a tradition*, we canceled the rally.

An **infinitive** is a verbal that usually appears with the word *to* before it. Infinitives may be used as several parts of speech. Infinitives may be used as nouns, as adjectives, or as adverbs.

> We all want *to live like kings*. (noun)
> *To win the contest* is Cal's aim. (noun)
> Jess has a reputation *to maintain*. (adjective)
> It is hard *to live on these wages*. (adverb)
> Barb went *to live in the mountains*. (adverb)

Exercise A   Write the verbal or verbal phrase in each sentence. Tell whether the verbal is a gerund, participle, or infinitive.

G 1. These blackberries are perfect for <u>picking</u>.

I 2. Bo dared us <u>to race him</u>.

I 3. Leroy likes <u>to finish furniture</u>.

P 4. <u>Using bottles and crayons</u>, Tammy made candles.

I 5. We waited <u>to catch a glimpse of</u> John Travolta.

G 6. <u>Accepting praise</u> takes poise.

G 7. <u>Waking up</u> is hard for many people.

I 8. The problem was difficult <u>to understand</u>.

P 9. A <u>broken</u> vial was the first clue.

P 10. <u>Resigning her job</u>, Margo walked out.

examples of the three types of verbals.

2. Do Exercise A on page 555 orally. Have students also tell how each verbal is used (as subject, adjective, etc.).

3. Assign and discuss Exercises B and C on page 556.

Individualizing the Lesson

Less-Advanced Students

1. Remind students that a gerund is formed by adding *-ing*, a participle by adding *-ed* or *-ing*, and an infinitive by adding *to* in front of a verb.

2. Work with students to determine how each verbal or verbal phrase is used in each sentence in Exercises A and B.

Advanced Students

Have students follow directions for Exercise C with four verbals of their own choice.

Optional Practice

Have students write sentences using the following verbals. For each sentence, students should tell whether the verbal is a gerund, participle, or infinitive and tell how it is used in the sentence. Answers will vary.

1. zipping his jacket
2. to forget my lunch
3. going to college
4. frightened by the siren
5. jogging along the lake
6. to score a touchdown
7. reading novels
8. riding a roller coaster
9. to lose ten pounds
10. shaking her head

Have students find examples of each type of verbal in the lyrics to a popular song (or songs). Tell them to copy the verbals they find, then explain how each is used.

Exercise B   Follow the directions for Exercise A.

P   1. <u>Grinning widely</u>, Wes threw a water balloon.

P   2. The people <u>judging the contest</u> are fair.

I   3. The Senator wants <u>to create a new image</u>.

P   4. Our <u>badly beaten</u> team hobbled off the field.

P   5. The local <u>learning</u> center offers many courses.

G   6. <u>Falling asleep in class</u> is Tim's problem.

G   7. Use the darkroom for <u>developing film</u>.

I   8. The race was too close <u>to call</u>.

G   9. Sarah practiced <u>passing the ball</u> accurately.

I   10. My brother went <u>to see that exhibit</u>.

Exercise C: Writing   Write four sentences using the following verbals as gerunds. Then write four new sentences using them as participles. Sentences will vary.

talking	smoking
running	flying

ADDITIONAL EXERCISES

Using Verbals

A. Gerunds and Gerund Phrases Find the gerunds and gerund phrases in these sentences.

1. <u>Kidnapping</u> is a federal offense.
2. The audience responded by <u>applauding loudly</u>.
3. Some people oppose <u>advertising</u> on children's TV.
4. <u>Replacing the muffler</u> will make your car quieter.
5. The group has strange ways of <u>persuading people</u>.
6. The cookbook recommended <u>soaking the beans</u>.
7. <u>Taking the largest piece</u> is bad manners.
8. Try <u>getting more sleep</u>.
9. Dan has a habit of <u>repeating himself</u>.
10. Discourage the dog from <u>barking</u> for no reason.

B. Participles and Participial Phrases Find the participles and participial phrases in these sentences.

1. My <u>broken</u> arm was wrapped in a flexible cast.
2. <u>Lying in a hammock</u>, Julia read *People* magazine.
3. <u>Sighting the strange lights</u>, Lloyd thought of UFO's.
4. <u>Dressed for a ballgame</u>, Val felt foolish at the banquet.
5. The hikers, <u>using a compass</u>, found their way back.
6. The restaurant's specialty is <u>fried</u> mushrooms.
7. The dentist saw the patient with the <u>chipped</u> tooth.
8. <u>Waving her cane</u>, the woman chased the thief.
9. The <u>prosecuting</u> attorney questioned the witness.
10. The family has no recent photos of the <u>missing</u> child.

C. Gerund or Participle? Write the gerund or participle for each sentence, and write which it is.

G 1. <u>Using</u> two Rubik's cubes was Ian's idea. subject
P 2. <u>Using</u> Dr. Cruz as a reference, Mae applied for the job. modifies *Mae*

557

Additional Exercises

These Additional Exercises may be used for additional practice of the concepts presented in this Section. Each exercise focuses on a single concept, and should be used after the page number indicated in parentheses.

Review

If you have not assigned these Additional Exercises before this time, you can also use them as an excellent Section Review.

P 3. Tinted with natural dyes, the Indian rug was beautiful.
modifies *Indian*

P 4. Tinted glass was used for the windows. modifies *glass*

P 5. Frosting the trees, the snow transformed the street.
modifies *snow*

G 6. I prefer drying my hair in the sun. object

P 7. Rearing suddenly, the pony threw Dennis. modifies *pony*

G 8. Raising vegetables can be a profitable hobby. subject

P 9. Moving at 500 miles per hour, the tidal wave advanced.
modifies *wave*

G 10. Janeen considered moving her project to the basement. object

D. Infinitives and Infinitive Phrases Find the infinitives and infinitive phrases in these sentences.

1. Howard Cosell's style is easy to mimic.
2. Michelle likes to tape her favorite albums.
3. Linda is the toughest player to beat.
4. Marnie wants to drive a stick shift.
5. Lou tried to remove the gum from her shoe.
6. Ralph had managed to get the singer's autograph.
7. I want to give this sketch to Lucinda.
8. To outwit Francine takes too much effort.
9. Harriet expects to get here by two o'clock.
10. The program failed to find a new sponsor.

E. Kinds of Verbals Write the verbal or verbal phrase in each sentence. Label it *Gerund, Participle,* or *Infinitive.*

P 1. The state has special programs for returning veterans.

G 2. Are there paths for biking around the lake?

P 3. Donna, enjoying the conversation, lost track of time.

G 4. Rona believes in winning friends with gifts.

I 5. Paco wants to study Brazil and its culture.

I 6. Peter remembered to signal the turn.

P 7. Even a stopped clock is right twice a day.

P 8. Roger served cheddar cheese and smoked ham.

I 9. The crew was asked to construct the rig quickly.

G 10. Roz has been thinking of looking for a new job.

MIXED REVIEW

Using Verbals

A. Recognizing verbals Write the verbals and verbal phrases from the following sentences. Then write whether the verbal or verbal phrase is a gerund, a gerund phrase, a participle, a participial phrase, an infinitive, or an infinitive phrase.

G   1. Pioneers avoided crossing the Rockies in winter.

G   2. Using a dirty eraser was a mistake.

P   3. Using a lighter ball, Jean bowled a strike.

P   4. The other bowling ball was too heavy.

I   5. Claude wants to change his schedule.

I   6. The middle seats in the third row are the ones to get.

I   7. I have two minutes to get to my next class.

G   8. Finding a good job may take time.

P   9. The stolen car was finally found.

I 10. Don't forget to take your gym suit home today.

B. Identifying verbals and their uses Write the verbals and verbal phrases from the following sentences. If a verbal is used as a noun, write whether it is a subject, object, or predicate word. If the verbal is used as a modifier, write whether it is an adjective or adverb.

1. I didn't mean to interrupt you. object

2. Adam made the scrambled eggs in an iron skillet. adjective

3. The handlebars need some adjusting. object

4. Staying up late before a test is a bad practice. subject

5. The marching band practices on the football field. adjective

6. Dion needs some time to think. adjective

7. Using a sharp stone, the child drew on the sidewalk. adjective

8. We could hear something rustling in the woods. adjective

9. Squinting is one sign of poor vision. subject

10. Rachel left to look for a pay phone. adverb

Mixed Review

These exercises provide review of the concepts presented in this Section. Each exercise challenges the students to apply several of the skills they have acquired during previous study. Because the "mixed" feature of these activities makes them more difficult, the teacher may wish to have less-advanced students do them orally or in small groups.

These challenging and enjoyable activities allow the students to see how the concepts of grammar, usage, and mechanics may be applied in actual writing situations. Each exercise is designed to allow students practice in several of the skills they have acquired in this Section. The activities also provide opportunities for students to write creatively about a wide variety of interesting and unusual subjects.

USING GRAMMAR IN WRITING
Using Verbals

A. Each section of our country experiences some kind of severe weather condition, such as hurricanes, blizzards, tornadoes, and floods. Write about a time when your area was affected. Use as many verbals as you can. Label them as gerunds, participles, or infinitives. These examples may be helpful.

Gerunds	Participles	Infinitives
flooding	blowing winds	to prepare
rescuing	stranded cars	to restore power
driving	drifting snow	to clear roads

B. The following sentence contains a participial phrase, a gerund, and an infinitive phrase. Think of a character in a movie that you would like to play. Finish the paragraph. Use each type of verbal at least once more. Underline and label them.

Sitting in the theater, I couldn't help wondering what it would be like to play the part of _____ in _____.

C. You are directing a play. The stage directions for the final scene are given below. At the first rehearsal, you realize that the actions are too slow. In order to increase the tension, you combine each pair of stage directions. The actors can then perform a number of actions at the same time. At the next rehearsal, the scene is quick and dramatic.

Below are the stage directions. Join each pair of sentences by using a participial phrase.

> Example: Tom pours a glass of water. He undoes his tie.
> Pouring a glass of water, Tom undoes his tie.

(1) Tom lifts the glass to his mouth. He hears a knock at the door.
(2) Ann enters the room. She takes a letter from her purse.
(3) She stares at Tom. She flings the letter to the floor.
(4) Tom looks offended. He picks up the letter.

CUMULATIVE REVIEW

The Parts of Speech

A. Identifying parts of speech Write what part of speech each underlined word is used as.

The Norwegian [Adj.] Birkebeiner, which is a famous cross-country ski [Adj.] race, began in 1932. It [Pro.] commemorates the rescue of [Prep.] a child prince by the Birkebeiner, a Viking tribe. The tribe had to travel 55 kilometers to rescue the prince, who later became the king [N] of Norway. In 1972 an [Adj.] American Birkebeiner was started. Cross-country skiing [N] had started [V] to become popular by then, and [Conj.] skiers wanted a challenge [N]. They [Pro.] got it in the Birke-beiner. The course is [V] 55 kilometers long, which is 34.2 miles. It runs through the hilly woods between [Prep.] the town of Hayward and the Telemark Lodge in northern Wisconsin. The race has become really [Adv.] popular [Adj.]. There were only fifty-four racers in the 1972 Birkebeiner, but [Conj.] ten thousand are expected [V] in 1984.

B. Recognizing how words are used Decide how each underlined word is used. Write *Subject*, *Verb*, *Direct Object*, *Indirect Object*, *Object of the Preposition*, *Predicate Noun*, or *Predicate Adjective* for each word.

1. The Hawaiian dish poi is made from the taro plant [OP].
2. Peas and beans are legumes [PN].
3. Richard seems surprised [PA] by the news.
4. Pass me [IO] the sports section, please.
5. Uncle Frank carved [V] the wooden figures.
6. Have the guests [S] arrived yet?
7. Kent ordered a double cheeseburger [DO] for lunch.
8. Marcia prefers painting [DO] with acrylics.
9. The toddler's nose was freckled [PA].
10. Cooking with a microwave oven requires practice [DO].

Cumulative Review

These exercises are designed to cover broad areas of grammar, usage, and mechanics. They require the application of skills taught thus far in the text. The exercises may be used for testing purposes, or as an excellent resource for review.

Section Objectives

1. To make verbs agree in number with their subjects

2. To use a verb that agrees in number with compound subjects

3. To use a verb that agrees in number with an indefinite pronoun that is its subject

4. To avoid errors in agreement between subjects and verbs in sentences using *don't* and *doesn't* and in sentences beginning with *here, there,* and *where*

Preparing the Students

Explain to students that sometimes while getting dressed you might glance in the mirror and say, "These pants just don't go with this shirt." In language, too, some combinations just don't agree with one another. Section 11 will help students match verbs and subjects which do agree. Read the introduction on page 562.

Additional Resources

Mastery Test — pages 62–63 in the test booklet

Additional Exercises — pages 570–574 in the student text

Practice Book — pages 217–221

Duplicating Masters — 217–221

Special Populations — See special section at the back of this Teacher's Edition.

Making Subjects and Verbs Agree

When your ideas are like those of a friend, you agree. When verbs and subjects are alike in certain ways, they also agree. In this section, you will learn how to make subjects and verbs agree.

562

562

Part 1 Making Subjects and Verbs Agree in Number

When a word refers to one thing, it is **singular.** When it refers to more than one thing, it is **plural.** The **number** of a word refers to whether the word is singular or plural.

A verb must agree in number with its subject.

If the subject is singular, the verb must be singular. If the subject is plural, the verb must be plural.

Singular	Plural
He *sings.*	They *sing.*
She *listens.*	They *listen.*
It *whistles.*	They *whistle.*
The baby *babbles.*	Babies *babble.*
The engine *hums.*	Engines *hum.*
An editorial *persuades.*	Advertisers *persuade.*

In these examples, you can see that the singular of a verb ends in *s.* The *s* disappears in the plural.

You will have problems in agreement of subject and verb when you are not sure what the subject is. To find the subject, first find the verb. Then ask *who?* or *what?* before it.

> One of the players is sick.
> *Verb:* is
> *Who is?* one
> The subject is *one.*

The subject of the verb is never found in a prepositional phrase.

Watch out for phrases that come between the verb and the subject.

> *One* of the eggs *broke.*
> The *coins* on the desk *were* valuable.
> The *auction* of antiques *begins* today.
> All *competitors* in the meet *expect* victory.

563

Part 1

Objective

To make verbs agree in number with their subjects

Presenting the Lesson

1. Read pages 563–564. Make certain that students understand the meaning of *singular, plural,* and *number.* Write these verbs on the board: *walk, sit, drink, cry, laugh.* Have students supply an appropriate singular or plural form of one of the verbs to go with each of the following subjects. Ask students to tell whether these matched subjects and verbs are singular or plural.

Answers will vary.

1. birds	5. three men
2. children	6. we
3. a baby	7. she
4. people	8. David

2. Assign and discuss Exercises A and B on pages 564–565. Have students identify each subject and tell whether it is singular or plural.

Individualizing the Lesson

Less-Advanced Students

Have students underline the subjects in the following sentences.

1. One of your shoelaces is untied.
2. My keys, as well as my wallet, are at home.
3. Gloria, together wih Archie and Edith, is coming.
4. The geese in the pond need to be fed.
5. All of the books on the shelf are dusty.

Work on Exercise A with the class. Assign Exercise B.

563

Advanced Students

Have students write sentences using the verb that was *not* selected as correct in Exercises A and B. Tell students to make sure the verb agrees in number with the subject.

Optional Practice

Present the following sentences to students on a worksheet. Two of the sentences are correct while the others contain errors in agreement between subject and verb. For each sentence, have students identify the subject, tell whether it is singular or plural, and determine if the verb agrees in number. If the sentence is correct, have students write C. If the verb does not agree with the subject, have students correct the verb.

S1. My sweater, together with a down vest, keep me warm.keeps

P2. The sheets of paper left on the pad is not enough.are

C3. The sentences in the exercise are easy.

P4. Refills for my favorite pen keeps going up in price.keep

S5. Crime, as well as poverty, are a problem in our city. is

C6. Each child, together with his or her parents, has a conference with the teacher.

S7. One of the straps on my ski boots are broken. is

S8. A ticket, including door prizes, cost five dollars. costs

Extending the Lesson

Have students tell whether the subjects and verbs in a paragraph from a magazine are singular or plural. Ask them to explain how they can tell.

Phrases beginning with the words *with, together with, including, as well as,* and *in addition to* are not part of the subject.

The *pilot*, in addition to the crew, *is* here.
Mr. *Bard*, together with his children, *has* arrived.
Energy, as well as inflation, *is* a national problem.
The class *fee*, including supplies, *is* ten dollars.

Exercise A Choose the verb that agrees with the subject.

1. The choice of the judges (was, were) not very popular.
2. All the billboards along the road (has, have) been taken down.
3. Several pages in the book (is, are) missing.
4. The drawings on display (was, were) done by Helen.
5. The bus with all the players (arrives, arrive) at three.
6. The schedule for all the sports events (is, are) in the program.
7. One of my front teeth (is, are) loose.
8. The captain, together with his crew, (looks, look) after the ship.
9. The pop machines in the lobby (was, were) broken.
10. The new schedule for the weekends (has, have) more buses and subway trains.

Exercise B Follow the directions for Exercise A.

1. A request for money and supplies (was, were) granted.
2. The members of the swim team (reports, report) to the pool every morning.
3. The moon, as well as the stars, (is, are) hidden.
4. My homeroom (contributes, contribute) to the Toys-for-Tots campaign.
5. Those rusty cars in the driveway (belongs, belong) to the Hadleys.
6. The doctor, together with her staff, (is, are) often here.
7. The edges of the playing field (was, were) still wet.

8. Two of my teachers (coaches, <u>coach</u>) the volleyball team.

9. The girls on the hockey team (likes, <u>like</u>) the new coach.

10. The attendants at the airport (requires, <u>require</u>) passengers to check their luggage.

Part 2   Compound Subjects

Compound subjects joined by *and* require a plural verb.

The *truck* and the *trailer* **were** badly damaged.
The *walls* and the *ceiling* **are** soundproofed.

When the parts of a compound subject are joined by *or* or *nor*, the verb agrees with the subject nearer to the verb.

Either Mom or the *boys* **have** come home.

Neither the boys nor *Mom* **has been** home yet.

Either the musicians or their *leader* **has** your music.

Choose the verb that agrees with the subject.

1. Corrine and her family (is, <u>are</u>) arriving tomorrow.
2. Neither my gym shoes nor my uniform (<u>needs</u>, need) to be washed.
3. Both winter and summer (is, <u>are</u>) mild here.
4. Either a raccoon or some dogs (has, <u>have</u>) gotten into the garbage.
5. The evening news and the late newspaper (reports, <u>report</u>) the sports results of the day.
6. Neither the tent nor the sleeping bags (arrives, <u>arrive</u>) until tomorrow.
7. Both the tugs and the Loganville ferry (docks, <u>dock</u>) here.
8. Al and Ken (hasn't, <u>haven't</u>) finished repairing their old car.

Objective

To use verbs that agree in number with compound subjects

Presenting the Lesson

1. Read page 565. Point out the difference between compound subjects joined by *and* (always requiring a plural verb) and those joined by *or* or *nor* (requiring a verb which agrees with the nearer subject).

2. Do Exercise A on pages 565–566 orally with the class. Have students tell why the verb chosen is correct.

3. Assign and discuss Exercise B on page 566.

Individualizing the Lesson

Less-Advanced Students

1. Review the definitions of *compound subject* and *conjunction* with the students. Remind them to look for the use of *and,* which requires a plural verb, and *or,* or *nor,* which make a verb compatible with the nearest subject.

2. Have students copy the sentences in Exercises A and B. Then tell them to underline the subject and circle the conjunction before choosing the correct verb to use.

Advanced Students

Have students write five sentences that contain a compound subject. Tell them to make sure the verb agrees in number with the subject.

Optional Practice

Have students complete the following sentences using verbs that agree with the compound subjects given. Answers will vary.

1. The boss and her secretary _____.
2. The carpet and drapes _____.
3. Either the doctor or the nurses _____.
4. Neither my cousins nor my aunt _____.
5. Either sandwiches or a salad _____.

Extending the Lesson

Have students copy five sentences with compound subjects from their textbooks. Tell them to underline the subject, circle the conjunction, and note the subject-verb agreement.

Part 3

Objective

To use a verb that agrees in number with an indefinite pronoun that is its subject

Presenting the Lesson

1. Read pages 566–567. Go over the list of pronouns that are always singular. Have students practice using each of these singular indefinite pronouns as the subject of a sentence. Do the same with the indefinite pronouns that are always plural. Carefully study the examples of indefinite pronouns which can be either singular or plural. Remind students that phrases that appear be-

9. Either the coach or the co-captains (calls, <u>call</u>) the time-outs.
10. The players and the referee (is, <u>are</u>) arguing about the call.

Exercise B Follow the directions for Exercise A.

1. Either Phil or his sister (<u>is</u>, are) bringing us home.
2. Neither alarms nor music (<u>wakens</u>, waken) me.
3. Either our local newspaper or our local radio stations (publicizes, <u>publicize</u>) our school's sporting events.
4. Neither complaints nor threats (has, <u>have</u>) any effect on the umpire.
5. Buildings or billboards often (obscures, <u>obscure</u>) the horizon.
6. Neither fishing nor hunting (<u>is</u>, are) permitted.
7. Both the Business Club and the Spanish Club (helps, <u>help</u>) decorate the lobby for Christmas.
8. Both the ordinary frogs and the bullfrog (tunes, <u>tune</u>) up at sundown.
9. Neither the cookies nor the cake (<u>tastes</u>, taste) burnt to me.
10. The water and the beach (looks, <u>look</u>) inviting.

Part 3   Indefinite Pronouns

Sometimes you will have to make a verb agree with an indefinite pronoun. Then you will have to know if the pronoun is singular or plural. You will remember that some indefinite pronouns are singular, some are plural, and some may be either. The indefinite pronouns in the list below are **singular:**

another	each	everything	one
anybody	either	neither	somebody
anyone	everybody	nobody	someone
anything	everyone	no one	something

Each of the race cars *was* given a number.
Everybody has a job to do.
Neither of us *has* a qualifying time.

The indefinite pronouns below are *plural*:

both   few   many   several

Few of the riders *wear* crash helmets.
Many of us *like* soft rock.

These indefinite pronouns are **singular** if they refer to one thing. They are **plural** if they refer to several things.

all   any   most   none   some

All of the estate *is* for sale.
All of my relatives *are* here.

Some of the film *is* still usable.
Some of my friends *are* older.

Most of the food *is* delicious.
Most of the cables *are* underground.

Exercise A   Choose the verb that agrees with the subject.

1. No one (expects, expect) the legislation to pass.
2. Another of the feature stories (compares, compare) the prices of sporting goods.
3. Most of the school (needs, need) painting.
4. Either Michelle or Ted (is, are) ushering.
5. Some of the students (earns, earn) extra money as ushers.
6. Another of those talk shows (comes, come) on tonight at 10:00 o'clock.
7. Many of Debbie's friends (was, were) away.
8. Everyone in Rock Hill (was, were) here.
9. All of the books (has, have) been shelved in alphabetical order.
10. Each of the ensemble members (plays, play) at least two instruments.

567

tween the subject and verb do not affect the number of the verb.

2. Assign and discuss Exercises A and B on pages 567–568.

Individualizing the Lesson

Less-Advanced Students

Have students copy the sentences in Exercises A and B, then have them circle the indefinite pronouns. Have them indicate whether each pronoun is singular or plural, then choose the correct verb.

Advanced Students

Have students write ten sentences with indefinite pronouns as subjects. Read sentences aloud in class to check for correct subject-verb agreement.

Optional Practice

Have students complete the following sentences using verbs that agree in number with their subjects.
Answers will vary.
1. Each   of   your   grandparents
   _____.
2. Several of these grammar exercises _____.
3. Most of the marbles _____.
4. Most of the milk _____.
5. Many of the drivers _____.
6. Everything in the top drawers
   _____.
7. All of my muscles _____.
8. Some of the thread _____.
9. Few of the speakers _____.
10. Each of the guests _____.

Part 4

Objective

To avoid errors in agreement between subjects and verbs in sentences using *don't* and *doesn't* and in sentences beginning with *here*, *there*, and *where*

Presenting the Lesson

1. Read page 568. Study examples of the correct use of *don't* and *doesn't*. Study examples of sentences beginning with *here*, *where*, and *there*. Be sure students identify the subject in each example.

2. Assign and discuss Exercises A and B on page 569.

Individualizing the Lesson

Less-Advanced Students

In Exercises A and B have students underline the subject of each sentence before choosing the correct verb.

Advanced Students

Have students take turns asking each other to complete the sentences correctly in the Exercises.

568

Exercise B Follow the directions for Exercise A.

1. Neither of us (is, are) ready to give our speech.
2. Most of the hay (dries, dry) in a week.
3. Neither of the maps (shows, show) Rainbow Springs.
4. All of these newspapers (goes, go) to the recycling plants.
5. Nobody in the art class (uses, use) oil paints.
6. One of my brothers (is, are) in the navy.
7. Everyone in the audience (was, were) captivated by the performances.
8. All of the telephones (is, are) busy right now.
9. Most of the players (practices, practice) in the morning and the afternoon.
10. Somebody (is, are) responsible for writing up the club's minutes.

Part 4   Other Problems of Agreement

Sometimes *don't* is used where *doesn't* is correct.

The pronouns it, he, and she are used with doesn't. All other personal pronouns are used with *don't*.

It *doesn't* look like rain now.	I *don't* dance.
She *doesn't* need more money.	You *don't* sing.
He *doesn't* swim well enough.	They *don't* know.

In sentences beginning with here, there, and where, the subject comes after the verb.

You must think ahead to determine whether the subject is singular or plural. Then make the verb agree with the subject.

Here *is* your ticket.
There *are* the keys for the cottage.
Where *is* the projector?

Exercise A Choose the verb that agrees with the subject.

1. That idea (<u>doesn't</u>, don't) make any sense.
2. Where (is, <u>are</u>) the boxes for these ornaments?
3. Here (is, <u>are</u>) the tube socks and T-shirts the team ordered.
4. There (<u>goes</u>, go) the siren.
5. It (<u>doesn't</u>, don't) look as if the sky will clear before noon.
6. Where (<u>is</u>, are) the emergency room?
7. Here (<u>is</u>, are) all the sheet metal that I could find.
8. Beth (<u>doesn't</u>, don't) want to go apple picking with us.
9. There (is, <u>are</u>) several deer on the front lawn.
10. There (is, <u>are</u>) the new batteries for the flashlight.

Exercise B Choose the verb that agrees with the subject.

1. Where (does, <u>do</u>) these cartons go?
2. There (is, <u>are</u>) the judge and the two lawyers.
3. There (<u>is</u>, are) the float we built for the homecoming parade.
4. Erica (<u>doesn't</u>, don't) agree with us.
5. Here (is, <u>are</u>) the magazines you wanted.
6. There (was, <u>were</u>) few skiers on the chairlift.
7. There (<u>goes</u>, go) the other team onto the ice.
8. (<u>Doesn't</u>, Don't) Jennie want to ride with us?
9. Where (<u>is</u>, are) my tennis racket?
10. Here (is, <u>are</u>) some of the pictures we took last winter.

Additional Exercises

These Additional Exercises may be used for additional practice of the concepts presented in this Section. Each exercise focuses on a single concept, and should be used after the page number indicated in parentheses.

Review

If you have not assigned these Additional Exercises before this time, you can also use them as an excellent Section Review.

ADDITIONAL EXERCISES

Making Subjects and Verbs Agree

A. Agreement of Subjects and Verbs   Choose the verb that agrees with the subject.

1. Some sections of the city (has, have) no bus service.
2. Smog (is, are) a form of pollution.
3. Sandbars in this river (causes, cause) accidents.
4. The camera angles (changes, change) for each shot.
5. A path for joggers (circles, circle) the campus.
6. The evidence on these films (looks, look) convincing.
7. Three neighbors, together with my sister, (runs, run) a summer camp.
8. Lunch, including tax and tip, (costs, cost) four dollars.
9. A deli, in addition to two shops, (has, have) opened.
10. The terrorists, as well as the hostage, (was, were) scared.

B. Compound Subjects   Choose the correct verb.

1. Neither music nor noise (keeps, keep) Caroline awake.
2. Either the spark plugs or the carburetor (is, are) faulty.
3. Neither the coach nor the captains (has, have) a strategy.
4. Both McDonald's and Burger King (employs, employ) high school students.
5. A floodlight and a lantern (illuminates, illuminate) the yard.
6. The violet and the dandelion (blooms, bloom) together.
7. Neither Efram Herrera nor the other players (was, were) interviewed.
8. Either bleach or baking soda (works, work) on stains.
9. Both Claudette and Molly (is, are) sopranos.
10. Either the janitor or Ms. Lurie (has, have) the keys.

MIXED REVIEW

Making Subjects and Verbs Agree

A. Choosing the correct verb   In each of the following sentences, write the verb that agrees with the subject.

1. The legs of the table (is, <u>are</u>) uneven.
2. A basket of apples (<u>makes</u>, make) an attractive decoration.
3. School photographs, including the class picture, (is, <u>are</u>) in color.
4. Rusty's outline, as well as his notes, (<u>shows</u>, show) much work.
5. The hamsters in the window of the pet store (looks, <u>look</u>) playful.
6. The dirt bikes, in addition to the scooter, (needs, <u>need</u>) some work.
7. Mimi and Dee (teaches, <u>teach</u>) a baton twirling class.
8. Either Bobby or Julie (<u>does</u>, do) the grocery shopping.
9. Neither your jacket nor your boots (is, <u>are</u>) dry yet.
10. Either the wheels or the engine (<u>is</u>, are) squeaking.

B. Using the correct verb   Some of the following sentences contain errors in subject-verb agreement. If a sentence contains an error, rewrite the sentence correctly. If a sentence is already correct, write *Correct*.

1. Everything always takes time. c
2. Neither of the televisions ~~work~~. works
3. One of the hamburgers ~~are~~ rare. is
4. Everybody in the bleachers ~~seem~~ too excited. seems
5. Something ~~sound~~ wrong to me. sounds
6. All of the gym T-shirts ~~has~~ the students' names on them. have
7. All of a softshell crab ~~are~~ edible. is

Mixed Review

These exercises provide review of the concepts presented in this Section. Each exercise challenges the students to apply several of the skills they have acquired during previous study. Because the "mixed" feature of these activities makes them more difficult, the teacher may wish to have less-advanced students do them orally or in small groups.

571

8. The town ~~don't~~ have a public library. _{doesn't}

9. Many of the schools ~~doesn't~~ have computers. _{don't}

10. Where ~~is~~ the showers? _{are}

C. Using indefinite pronouns Choose the correct verb for each sentence.

1. Everyone on TV (<u>wears</u>, wear) special makeup.
2. Everything at the garage sale (<u>has</u>, have) a price tag.
3. Neither of the cars (<u>is</u>, are) working.
4. Most of the actors (reads, <u>read</u>) from a teleprompter.
5. Both of the pools (has, <u>have</u>) diving areas.
6. All of the cards (is, <u>are</u>) on the table.
7. All of the paste (<u>has</u>, have) dried up.
8. None of the tents (<u>has</u>, have) mosquito netting.
9. Each of those baseball players (<u>is</u>, are) a free agent.
10. Either of your topics (<u>is</u>, are) suitable.

D. Understanding problems of agreement Choose the correct verb for each sentence.

1. He (<u>doesn't</u>, don't) know all the details of the project.
2. It (<u>doesn't</u>, don't) seem right to leave all this work.
3. She (<u>doesn't</u>, don't) plan to go to business school.
4. Here (is, <u>are</u>) the photographs for the art fair.
5. Where (<u>is</u>, are) our lane for the relay race?
6. There (is, <u>are</u>) several barbells in the weight room.
7. (<u>Doesn't</u>, Don't) the school have a picnic every year?
8. (Doesn't, <u>Don't</u>) spiders scare you?
9. There (is, <u>are</u>) Christmas trees for sale at that lot.
10. Where (was, <u>were</u>) the guards during the burglary?

USING GRAMMAR IN WRITING
Making Subjects and Verbs Agree

A. A news team has just arrived on the scene of a volcano that is erupting. The newscaster is reporting what she sees, but there is noise and confusion. Only about half of her words can be heard. Here they are.

> At four o'clock this afternoon, one of the . . . . The top of the volcano . . . . Fire and ashes . . . . Gases from the lava . . . . The State Police force, as well as forest rangers, ... Estimated damage, according to several sources, ... The governor, who had been out sailing with family members, ... Everyone in the area . . . in a state of shock. Many cabins, including one owned by a movie star, ... Someone who lives in the mountains . . . .

Rewrite the newscast, completing each incomplete thought. Be sure all verbs agree with their subjects. The entire newscast should be in the present tense.

B. Choose two members of your family. You can be one of them, if you wish. Write about the similarities and differences between them. Think about their talents, their personalities and their physical characteristics. As you compare and contrast, use some of the following words. Be sure all subjects and verbs agree.

do	does	both	either	neither
doesn't	don't	few	many	several

Using Grammar in Writing

These challenging and enjoyable activities allow the students to see how the concepts of grammar, usage, and mechanics may be applied in actual writing situations. Each exercise is designed to allow students practice in several of the skills they have acquired in this Section. The activities also provide opportunities for students to write creatively about a wide variety of interesting and unusual subjects.

These exercises are designed to cover broad areas of grammar, usage, and mechanics. They require the application of skills taught thus far in the text. The exercises may be used for testing purposes, or as an excellent resource for review.

CUMULATIVE REVIEW

Usage

A. Choosing the correct word   Write the correct word.

1. (Who, <u>Whom</u>) can you ask to help you?
2. (Lie, <u>Lay</u>) the puppy in (<u>its</u>, it's) box.
3. (May, <u>Can</u>) Ellen play soccer (good, <u>well</u>)?
4. Does Jason wear (<u>this</u>, these) kind of jacket?
5. Mindy hasn't (never, <u>ever</u>) heard (them, <u>those</u>) tapes.
6. Avi, you (<u>can</u>, may) (<u>sit</u>, set) in the front seat.
7. (Its, <u>It's</u>) Kevin's cat (laying, <u>lying</u>) in the basket.
8. (<u>Their</u>, They're) costumes look (<u>good</u>, well) in that light.
9. Coach Martin will (learn, <u>teach</u>) us (that, <u>those</u>) plays.
10. (<u>Sit</u>, Set) and tell me why you feel so (<u>bad</u>, badly).

B. Using words correctly   Ten of the underlined words contain errors in the use of verbs, nouns, pronouns, adverbs, and adjectives. Ten are correct. Proofread the paragraph. Correct the errors.

My <u>most</u> vivid memory of my trip to Manhattan <u>was</u> my first taxi ride. I stepped up to the curb <u>and</u> waved <u>timidly</u> at a cab, but it sped right by me. "<u>Them</u> cab-bies <u>won't</u> ~~never~~ stop if you do that," said my cousin Max. Then <u>him</u> showed <u>me</u> his technique. He stepped boldly into the street, waved briskly, and whistled <u>loud</u>. <u>Two</u> cabs screeched <u>to a halt</u> in front of <u>him</u>. Each of the drivers honked <u>their</u> horn. We climbed in the <u>nearest</u> one, and Max said, "The World Trade Center, please." With a slight nod, the cabby accelerated <u>quick</u> and zoomed through a yellow <u>lights</u>. He traveled at breakneck speeds, careened around corners, and tail-gated other cars until they <u>moved out of his</u> way. When we arrived, my knees were shaking <u>bad</u>, and my heart was pounding. "He <u>don't</u> <u>know</u> how to drive!" I exclaimed. "From now on, we'll take the subway."

(handwritten corrections) Those; he; loudly; his/her; nearer; quickly; badly; doesn't

Using Compound and Complex Sentences

Section Objectives

1. To review the parts of the simple sentence

2. To recognize and form compound sentences and to differentiate between compound sentences and simple sentences with compound predicates

3. To recognize and form complex sentences

4. To recognize main clauses and subordinate clauses and to distingish clauses from phrases

5. To recognize subordinating conjunctions and understand their function

6. To recognize adverb clauses and to understand how they are used in sentences

7. To recognize adjective clauses and to understand how they are used in sentences

8. To recognize noun clauses and understand how they are used in sentences

9. To be able to identify noun, adverb, and adjective subordinate clauses

10. To be able to recognize and correct subordinate clause sentence fragments

11. To review simple, compound, and complex sentences

Preparing the Students

Explain to students that good writing, like good cooking or good music, depends upon variety. Section 12 will introduce the students to three types of sentences, each of which contributes to good, interesting writing. Read the introduction on page 575.

You have already learned about the parts of a sentence. Now you will look closely at the different kinds of sentences. In this section you will see the three kinds of sentences that you use. They are simple sentences, compound sentences, and complex sentences.

Part 1

Objective

To review the parts of the simple sentence

Presenting the Lesson

1. Read pages 576–577. Review definitions of *simple subject, simple predicate, subject, predicate,* and *compound.* Look carefully at examples of compound sentence parts. Make sure that students understand the definition of a simple sentence.

2. Assign Exercise A on page 577.

3. Assign and discuss Exercise B on page 578.

Individualizing the Lesson

Less-Advanced Students

Do Exercise A orally. Then have students copy the sentences in Exercise B, underlining the subject once and the predicate twice. Then have them circle the compound.

576

Part 1   Review of the Sentence

From your study of the sentence, you have learned that the sentence has two basic parts. They are the subject and the predicate.

Subject	Predicate
Nobody	remembered.
Missy	blinked.
Opinions	change.
Counselors	understood.
Counselors	understood my problem.
Several counselors at the clinic	understood my problem.

The **subject** of a sentence names the person or thing about which something is said. The **predicate** tells what the subject did or what happened.

The **simple predicate** is the verb. The subject of the verb is called the **simple subject.**

In the subject of the sentence, you will find the simple subject and any words that modify it. In the predicate of the sentence, you will find verbs, objects, predicate words, and their modifiers.

Compound Parts of the Sentence

All of the parts of the sentence may be **compound.** In other words, each may have more than one part.

Compound subject:	Florida and Hawaii are resort areas.
Compound verb:	The TV screen flashed and flickered.
Compound predicate:	The campers built a fire and toasted marshmallows.
Compound object:	Police tailed the taxi and the van.
Compound predicate word:	That commercial is clever and catchy.

Definition of the Sentence

Each of the above sentences, even if it has compound parts, expresses one main idea. These sentences, like all of those you have worked with in previous sections, are called **simple sentences.**

Now you are ready for a definition of the simple sentence.

A simple sentence is a sentence that contains only one subject and one predicate. The subject and the predicate, or any part of the subject or predicate, may be compound.

Exercise A Copy each of the following simple sentences. Then draw a line between the subject and the predicate.

Example: Tom Mix and William S. Hart | were famous
actors in old Western movies.

1. Movie-goers in the 1920's | admired such greats as Greta Garbo, Rudolph Valentino, and Douglas Fairbanks.
2. Slapstick comedy | was performed by Charlie Chaplin, Harold Lloyd, and Buster Keaton.
3. "Talkies," or movies with sound, | became popular in the late 1920's.
4. The movies in the 1930's | started such people as Shirley Temple, Mae West, and Clark Gable.
5. The city of Hollywood | was known as "the celluloid paradise."
6. One of the greatest movies | was released in 1939.
7. This particular movie | was discussed in hundreds of magazines and newspapers.
8. *Gone with the Wind* | swept movie-goers off their feet.
9. The stars, Vivien Leigh and Clark Gable, | were recognized by everyone.
10. Their movie | became a film classic.

Advanced Students

Have students write ten original sentences using various compound parts in each sentence.

Optional Practice

Have students write sentences containing the following parts.

1. compound subject
2. compound predicate
3. compound subject and compound predicate
4. compound direct object
5. compound subject and compound predicate words

Extending the Lesson

Have students find examples of simple sentences in a short story or magazine article written for young adults or adults. Then have them look for simple sentences in a book written for children. Discuss the fact that more mature writing is characterized by more involved sentence structure.

Exercise B Number your paper from 1 to 10. Write the compound subjects, verbs, and objects you find in these simple sentences.

s 1. Yesterday's <u>teens</u> and today's <u>youth</u> have had a variety of interests.

s 2. <u>Mini-skirts</u>, long <u>hair</u>, <u>Afros</u>, and <u>Beatlemania</u> were accepted by most young people in the '60's.

v 3. Young people <u>have danced</u> and <u>have listened</u> to all different kinds of music.

s, o 4. Big <u>bands</u> and rock-and-roll <u>music</u> characterized the <u>1940's</u> and <u>1950's</u>.

o 5. Some fads of the '70's included <u>skateboards</u>, <u>platform shoes</u>, <u>Levis</u>, and <u>T-shirts</u>.

o 6. Today's youth buys <u>albums</u> and <u>tapes</u> of many different musicians.

s 7. Popular <u>music</u> and <u>fashion</u> often dictate fads.

s 8. The <u>Beatles</u> and the <u>Rolling Stones</u> introduced a new kind of music.

s,op 9. Since then, <u>radios</u> and <u>stereos</u> have played the music of <u>Michael Jackson</u>, <u>Linda Ronstadt</u>, <u>Diana Ross</u>, the <u>Eagles</u>, and many <u>others</u>.

s10. In ten years, what will <u>you</u> and your <u>friends</u> be interested in?

Part 2 The Compound Sentence

When two simple sentences are very closely related, they are often joined to form one sentence. This sentence has more than one subject and more than one predicate. Such a sentence is called a **compound sentence.**

A compound sentence consists of two or more simple sentences joined together.

The parts of a compound sentence may be joined by a coordi-

Part 2

Objective

To recognize and form compound sentences and to differentiate between compound sentences and simple sentences with compound predicates

Presenting the Lesson

1. Read pages 578–579. Be sure students understand the definition

nating conjunction (*and, or, but*) or by a semicolon (;). These are examples:

> The movie was long, **but** it was exciting.
> Riviera won the first match, **and** Johnson won the second.
> The dentist might begin to drill, **or** he might take X-rays first.
> Protestors are gathering near the plant; they oppose nuclear power.

Why are compound sentences useful? You may realize why as you read this passage.

> The school has a special industrial arts class. The class has a yearly project. It teaches skills. It also makes money. The project is the actual construction of a house. Some schools teach carpentry or electricity. This project includes masonry, plumbing, and plastering. The completed house brings a profit. Students profit too.

You can see that using short sentences in a row sounds monotonous.

Notice how much better the paragraph sounds with compound sentences.

> The school has a special industrial arts class, *and* the class has a yearly project. It teaches skills, *and* it also makes money. The project is the actual construction of a house. Some schools teach carpentry or electricity, *but* this class includes masonry, plumbing, and plastering. The completed house brings a profit, *and* students profit too.

Diagraming Compound Sentences

The diagram of a compound sentence shows that it is two or more simple sentences joined together. First diagram each simple sentence. Then join the two sentences by a dotted line with a "step" for the coordinating conjunction.

of a compound sentence and the usefulness of compound sentences. Study the examples on page 579 showing the use of the three coordinating conjunctions and the semicolon to join compound sentences.

2. Read pages 579–580 which show the way to diagram a compound sentence. Point out the use of the dotted line with a step for the coordinating conjunction.

3. Do Exercises A and B on pages 580–581 as a class activity. Volunteers may put their answers on the board. Ask students in which sentences the coordinating conjunction could be replaced with a semicolon.

4. Read pages 581–582. Stress that in a compound sentence there will be two stated subjects as well as two stated verbs.

5. Do Exercise A on pages 582–583 as a class activity. In addition to determining whether the sentences are compound or simple with a compound predicate, have students tell what the subject and verb of each sentence are.

6. Assign and discuss Exercise B on page 583.

7. Read pages 583–584 discussing how to punctuate compound sentences. Make sure students understand why a comma is used before the coordinating conjunction. Point out that a semicolon may replace a coordinating conjunction, but may not be used with a coordinating conjunction. Study examples carefully.

8. Assign and discuss Exercises A and B on pages 584–585.

1. Work with students to complete Exercise A of each set of exercises.

2. Have students copy the sentences from the B Exercises on pages 583 and 585. Then have them circle the verbs and underline the subjects in each sentence before they follow the directions.

Advanced Students

1. Have students form compound sentences from all of the simple sentences in Exercises A and B on pages 582–583.

2. Have students write five original compound sentences. Remind them to use either conjunctions or semicolons.

Optional Practice

Have students form compound sentences from the following simple sentences by combining closely related ideas. Students should add conjunctions and punctuation as necessary.

1. Joanna broke her leg/,but
ᵗThe doctor put a cast on and gave her crutches.

2. Did anyone call while I was out?,or
ʷ Were there any deliveries?

3. The movie begins at 8:00/,but
I have to work until 9:00.

4. Our family is sports-minded/,but Dad doesn't know the first thing about soccer.

5. Fred worked last summer/,and
ʰ He used the money to buy a bicycle.

Marla advertised her bike, but she got no response.

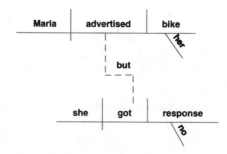

Exercise A   Number your paper from 1 to 10. Label three columns *Subject/Verb, Conjunction,* and *Subject/Verb.* For each sentence, fill in the columns.

Example: The car was full, but they made room for me.

Subject/Verb	Conjunction	Subject/Verb
car was	but	they made

1. After dinner we all played horseshoes, and then we had a quick swim.
2. Amanda spoke into the microphone, but no one could hear her.
3. Sandy wanted a vacation, but her boss wouldn't allow it.
4. I will ride in the bike-a-thon, but I need at least ten sponsors.
5. It rained all night, and the baseball game was canceled.
6. You must follow the map carefully, or you will miss the turn.
7. Craig dislikes most sportscasters, but he does like Brent Mussberger.
8. The unemployment rate had risen, but the cost of living had gone down.
9. Will you sell your old car, or will you trade it in?
10. The missile disintegrated, and parts landed in the ocean.

Exercise B Follow the directions for Exercise A.

1. Amelia Earhart was a schoolteacher, but she later
   became the first woman to fly the Atlantic.
2. Tanya and I were playing checkers, but I like chess
   better.
3. Do you like modern dance, or do you prefer classical
   ballet?
4. The football game was scheduled for TV tonight, but
   the President's speech pre-empted all programming.
5. Lucinda and I went cycling, and my brothers did the
   yardwork.
6. Babe Ruth was a leading contributor to the game of
   baseball, but Babe Didrikson contributed to women's
   participation in all sports.
7. I enjoy all the books of Paul Zindel, but *My Darling,*
   My Hamburger is my favorite.
8. The lake froze over, and the ice fishers set up their
   equipment.
9. Ted entered the room, and the guests yelled "surprise!"
10. Some women change their names after marrying, but
    others keep their maiden names.

Compound Predicate or Compound Sentence?

A **compound predicate** is two predicates within one sentence.
Each predicate contains a verb. At least one verb is completed
by an object or predicate word.

> Sally *went to the restaurant* and *met Ann.* (The two parts of
> this compound predicate are joined by *and.*)

You will want to be able to see the difference between a
compound sentence and a simple sentence with a compound
predicate. Both use coordinating conjunctions but in different
ways. To tell the difference, look for the verbs. If both verbs

Have students find published examples of compound sentences,
then have them underline each simple sentence and circle the conjunction or punctuation that joins them. Discuss how the ideas in each simple sentence are related, and whether the conjunction or semicolon that joins them is the most effective one for connecting those ideas.

have the same subject, the sentence is a simple sentence. If each verb has a different subject, the sentence is compound.

Look at these examples:

> s.　v.　　　　　v.
> *Allan repaired* the set and *watched* TV. (This simple sentence has a compound predicate. Both verbs, *repaired* and *watched*, have the same subject, *Allan*.)

> s.　　v.　　　　　　s.　　v.
> A *handyman repaired* the set and *Allan watched* TV. (This is a compound sentence. The verb *repaired* has its own subject, *handyman*. The verb *watched* has its own subject, *Allan*.)

> s.　v.　　　　　　　v.　　v.
> *Frieda plays* billiards often and *has* just *learned* tennis. (This is a simple sentence. Both verbs have the same subject *Frieda*. The conjunction *and* joins two parts of a compound predicate.)

> s.　v.　　　　　　　s.　v.　　　v.
> *Frieda plays* billiards often, and *Emily has* just *learned* tennis. (Here are two simple sentences, each with a subject and verb. They are joined by *and* into a compound sentence.)

Exercise A Copy the following sentences. Underline each subject once and each verb twice. After each sentence write *Simple* or *Compound* to show what kind of sentence it is.

s　1. The lifeguard jumped down and dashed into the water.
s　2. For an hour we sat by the telephone and just waited.
s　3. Marietta waved happily and ran toward her brother.
s　4. The dogs snarled and barked at the mail carrier.
c　5. The jet lost altitude, but no one was hurt.
c　6. The early bird gets the worm, but who wants worms?
c　7. Has Don arrived, or has he been delayed?
c　8. I finished my homework, and then I cleaned my room.
c　9. I like all science fiction movies, but I really enjoy the old *Star Trek* programs.

s 10. A <u>plane</u> <u>takes off</u> or <u>lands</u> at O'Hare Airport every 45 seconds.

Exercise B Write *Simple* or *Compound* for each sentence to show what kind it is.

s 1. The Wright Brothers flew their plane in Kitty Hawk, North Carolina, on December 17, 1903.

c 2. A four-cylinder engine and two propellers gave power to their plane, and their glider flew a hundred feet.

s 3. We saw the Mardi Gras celebration in New Orleans.

s 4. The Chinese exhibit was a gesture of good will to the people of the United States from the Chinese.

s 5. Queen Elizabeth II became the monarch of Britain and the Commonwealth at the age of twenty-five.

c 6. Paper currency is printed at the Bureau of Engraving and Printing in Washington, D.C., but some coins are made at the U.S. Mint in Denver.

s 7. Elfreth's Alley is the oldest continuously occupied residential street in America.

s 8. It dates back to the 1690's and is one of the historic landmarks of Philadelphia.

s 9. Jamestown, Virginia, was the first permanent English colony in the New World.

c 10. The original Fort James was built in 1607, and today's visitors to the fort may see a full-scale reconstruction.

Punctuating Compound Sentences

In compound sentences, a **comma** should be used before the coordinating conjunction.

There are good reasons for the comma. Without it, a compound sentence can be quite confusing. The comma shows you where to pause. It also keeps main ideas together. Place the comma before the conjunction.

<pre>
s.   v.   s.   v.
</pre>
Pretzels are my favorite party food, **and** 7-Up is my favorite soft drink.

<pre>
s.   v.   s.   v.
</pre>
Clams are found on the beach, **and** low tide is the best time for digging.

Instead of a conjunction and a comma, a **semicolon (;)** is sometimes used to separate the main ideas in a compound sentence.

Pretzels are my favorite party food; 7-Up is my favorite soft drink.

Clams are found on the beach; low tide is the best time for digging.

Remember that a comma is used with a conjunction in a compound sentence. However, a comma is not used with compound subjects, predicates, or other compound parts.

<pre>
s.   v.   v.
</pre>
Waves pounded the small sailboats and lashed against the weatherbeaten dock.

<pre>
s.   v.   v.
</pre>
Everyone at the Oscar awards ceremony rose and applauded.

Finally, the comma is not necessary in very short compound sentences.

We danced and Allan watched.
Either you know or you don't.

Exercise A   In the following sentences, commas have been omitted from all the compound constructions. If a sentence is correct, write *Correct*. If it needs a comma, write the two words between which the comma belongs, and put in the comma.

Example: We called for Vic but he was not ready.
Vic, but

1. A flight attendant must serve meals and keep airline passengers comfortable. c
2. My favorite actress is Cicely Tyson, and I have met her.

3. A tree fell during the storm and blocked our street. c
4. Sam and Andrea arrived and distributed the passes. c
5. Is your job mental work, or is it physical labor?
6. The new television season has started, but I don't like any of the new shows.
7. The blizzard started on New Year's Eve, and it raged for two days.
8. Anna climbed up the rope, and her P.E. instructor watched.
9. I must begin or I'll be late. c
10. Rick Burns is a popular disc jockey, but he has been fired.

Exercise B Follow the directions for Exercise A.

1. The front page of a newspaper reports the major happenings, and the features section provides entertainment.
2. Melanie, David, and Orlando attended the concert and went out for pizza afterwards. c
3. Some people vote and others don't. c
4. At Acadia National Park our family and friends backpacked and rode horses. c
5. Our hockey team won in the semifinals but lost in the championship game. c
6. Pennsylvania has several Amish villages, and the people there follow very old customs.
7. Many people complain about homework, but most of them do it.
8. In the 1800's immigrants flocked to the United States and registered at Ellis Island. c
9. Do you like your name, or would you like to choose a different one?
10. The subway station provided route maps, but we first had to figure out the fare machine.

Objectives

1. To recognize and form complex sentences

2. To recognize main clauses and subordinate clauses and to distingish clauses from phrases

3. To recognize subordinating conjunctions and understand their function

Presenting the Lesson

1. Read page 586. Study examples of clauses, and stress that while a clause may be a complete sentence, it should be thought of as a group of words within a sentence.

2. Read page 587, studying examples of phrases and clauses. Ask students to identify the following groups of words as either phrases or clauses.

P in a big hurry
C as I waited for the bus
C before anyone arrived
P during the intermission
C since it was warm outside

3. Read page 587 and the top of page 588. Study the examples of subordinate clauses. Be sure students understand the definitions of *subordinate* and *dependent*. Carefully study the list of words often used as subordinating conjunctions. Ask students to offer examples of sentences containing subordinate clauses introduced by subordinating conjunctions on the list. Go over the list of other words which often introduce subordinate clauses on page 588. Again, have students offer examples of sen-

Part 3   Complex Sentences

You have learned about simple sentences and compound sentences. There is another kind of sentence that will help you to express ideas: the **complex sentence.**

In order to understand the structure of a complex sentence, you must first know about clauses.

A clause is a group of words that contains a verb and its subject.

According to this definition, a simple sentence is a clause. It has both a verb and a subject.

> s.   v.
> Kim asked for some privacy.

> s.   v.
> Many arguments start that way.

However, it will be easier to understand sentence structures if you think of a clause as part of a sentence. Think of a clause as a group of words within a sentence.

What about compound sentences? Do they contain clauses? Yes, they do contain two or more groups of words with a subject and a verb. These are examples:

> s.   v.   s.   v.
> Janet whacked the ball, and it flew into the bleachers.

> s.   v.   s.   v.
> My friends live far away, but we write often.

Any compound sentence can be broken down into its main parts.

> Janet whacked the ball. It flew into the bleachers.
> My friends live far away. We write often.

Each of the clauses in a compound sentence can be a sentence by itself.

Phrases and Clauses

Can you tell the difference between a phrase and a clause?

Phrases: across the field

           in the opening scene

                    s.   v.

Clauses: after the game began

                    s.   v.

           where you live

A clause has a subject and a verb. A phrase does not.

Subordinate Clauses

Subordinate clauses are different from main clauses. Read these clauses:

          s.   v.

When the door opened

   s.   v.

If you disagree

Neither group of words above expresses a complete thought. Neither can stand by itself. Each leaves the reader wondering *then what*?

What happens if you omit the first word in each group of words? Each becomes a complete sentence. You can see then that the words *when* and *if* have an important function.

Words like *when* and *if* are called **subordinating conjunctions.** They **subordinate** the groups of words they introduce. This means that they make the clause *dependent* on the main clause to complete its meaning. The clauses are called dependent or **subordinate clauses.** Not every subordinate clause begins with a subordinating conjunction, but many do.

The words in the following list are often used as subordinating conjunctions.

Note: Some of the words in the list can be used in other ways. They are subordinating conjunctions only when they introduce clauses.

tences using these words to introduce subordinate clauses.

4. Assign the exercise on page 588. In going over the exercise, have one student read his or her subordinate clause and another student add a main clause to complete the thought.

5. Read the definition of a complex sentence on page 588.

6. Assign and discuss Exercises A and B on page 589.

Individualizing the Lesson

Less-Advanced Students

1. Work with students to create subordinate clauses out of the first five sentences of the Exercise on page 588. Have them complete the Exercise independently.

2. Have students underline the subjects and verbs in each sentence in Exercise A, page 589. Then have students refer to the chart of subordinate conjunctions on page 588 to help them locate the subordinate clause.

Advanced Students

1. Have students use the subordinate clauses they created in the Exercise on page 588 in a sentence.

2. Have students write a brief description of themselves. Tell them to use simple, compound, and complex sentences. Have them identify each type of sentence.

Optional Practice

Have students identify the italicized group of words in each sentence as a phrase, a main clause, or a subordinate clause.

P1. The quiet room *in the library* is always empty.

S 2. *Since I have so much homework, I* will go there.

S 3. *While I am studying,* please fix dinner.

M 4. *Let's eat early tonight* because there is a good program on TV.

S 5. *If I finish all my work,* I can even watch the late movie.

Extending the Lesson

Have students make complex sentences out of these pairs of related sentences. Answers will vary.

1. This is the sculpture. The city is going to replace it.
2. You cannot park here. You have a special permit.
3. The wind blows off the lake. The temperature drops.
4. Elsie took the lower bunk. She is afraid of heights.
5. Bob didn't wear his glasses. He can't see the screen.

Words Often Used as Subordinating Conjunctions			
after	because	so that	whatever
although	before	than	when
as	if	though	whenever
as if	in order that	till	where
as long as	provided	unless	wherever
as though	since	until	while

Not all subordinate clauses begin with subordinating conjunctions. Subordinate clauses are sometimes introduced by other words. These are some:

that	who, whom, whose	which	why
what	whoever, whomever	how	

Exercise Using *if, because, when, after,* and *since,* make subordinate clauses out of these sentences.

1. The party ended.
2. The crowd had left.
3. The car stopped.
4. The dog howled.
5. The power went off.
6. You can go.
7. Our packages are ready.
8. It was very foggy.
9. The window is broken.
10. It rained on Saturday.

Definition of the Complex Sentence

Now that you know about main clauses and subordinate clauses, you can understand complex sentences.

A complex sentence is a sentence that contains one main clause and one or more subordinate clauses.

Main Clause	Subordinate Clause
Neighbors complained	because the party was noisy.
We ate Doritos	while we waited.
Oakland is the team	that leads the league.

588

Exercise A Find the (subordinate clause) in each sentence. Copy it. Underline the subject once and the verb twice.

1. I put the library books in my backpack (so that I wouldn't forget them.)
2. Where were you (when I called for you?)
3. Stop and see us (when you come back.)
4. A stuffed pizza is one (that has double layers of ingredients.)
5. Nobody knows (why Sarah seems unhappy.)
6. The water was colder (than I thought.)
7. Karen never speaks up, (although she usually knows the answers.)
8. (While we were in Philadelphia,) we saw Independence Hall and Betsy Ross's home.
9. (Although the land around Denver is flat,) it is almost a mile high.
10. We can't start the game (until the field is drier.)

Exercise B Follow the directions for Exercise A.

1. This is the place (where the astronauts train.)
2. Kate snapped a photo (as we fell into the pool.)
3. Dad insists (that Teresa drives too fast.)
4. Steve felt better (after he had talked to his girlfriend.)
5. The manager asked Donna (if she would work on Tuesday.)
6. Kevin sleeps during the day (because he works at night.)
7. (When business slows down,) the factory lays off workers.
8. We conserved water (because a drought had cut the supply.)
9. Chicago is the place (where deep-dish pizza was developed.)
10. Adrienne admits (that she is not a good loser.)

589

Objective

To recognize adverb clauses and to understand how they are used in sentences

Presenting the Lesson

1. Read page 590. Go over the definition of an adverb clause, studying examples to differentiate between an adverb clause and an adverb phrase.

2. Go over the diagraming of a sentence containing an adverb clause on pages 590–591.

3. Do Exercise A on page 591 as a class activity. After students locate adverb clauses and identify their subjects and verbs, have them also tell what word the clause modifies and what the clause tells about the word. Students should also identify the subordinate conjunction.

4. Assign and discuss Exercise B on pages 591–592.

Individualizing the Lesson

Less-Advanced Students

Do Exercise A as a class. For Exercise B, have students tell if the adverb clause tells *how, when, where* or *to what extent.*

Advanced Students

Have students diagram the first four sentences in each Exercise.

Optional Practice

Have students complete the following complex sentences by adding words to each to form an adverb clause. Have them tell what

Part 4   Adverb Clauses

You know that each complex sentence contains a subordinate clause. There are three kinds of subordinate clauses. One kind is the **adverb clause.**

An **adverb** is a word that modifies a verb, an adjective, or another adverb.

Adverb: Pam sat *down.*

An **adverb phrase** is a prepositional phrase used as an adverb. Adverb phrases usually modify verbs.

Adverb phrase: Pam sat *in the rocking chair.*

An adverb clause is a subordinate clause used as an adverb.

Adverb clause: The gymnast smiled *as she finished her routine.*

Pam sat *where she would be comfortable.*

Greg ran *as fast as he could.*

Adverbs and adverb phrases or clauses tell *how, when, where,* or *to what extent* about the word they modify.

Remember that a *clause* contains a subject and a verb. A *phrase* has neither a subject nor a verb.

Diagraming Adverb Clauses

The adverb clause is placed on its own line below the main clause. A dotted line is drawn from the adverb clause to the word it modifies in the main clause. The subordinating conjunction is placed on the dotted line.

The game ended when the Reds made a double play.

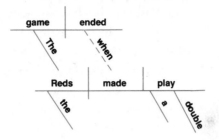

Exercise A Copy the (adverb clause) from each sentence. Underline its subject once and its verb twice.

Example: Until I was five, I lived in New Mexico.
Until <u>I</u> <u>was</u> five

1. There were plenty of boxes (because <u>we</u> <u>had saved</u> many of them from Christmas.)
2. (Before <u>we</u> <u>could visit</u> the small villages,) we had to learn Japanese.
3. (When <u>we</u> <u>arrived</u> in Seattle,) it was very cold.
4. (Although <u>he</u> <u>had lived</u> all his life in England,) Rick adjusted quickly to his new American lifestyle.
5. Two partridges rose and flew away (as <u>I</u> <u>approached.</u>)
6. (As the <u>mist</u> <u>cleared</u>,) Pike's Peak came into view.
7. (If South American mail <u>planes</u> <u>are</u> late,) search planes are alerted.
8. The geyser erupted again (before <u>we</u> <u>left.</u>)
9. (Since <u>it</u> <u>began</u> to rain,) we went home.
10. (If <u>you</u> <u>had been</u> there on Saturday,) you would have seen the precision marching.

Exercise B Follow the directions for Exercise A.

1. We slept in the car (because <u>all</u> of the motels <u>were</u> full.)
2. (Although <u>he</u> <u>consulted</u> with advisers,) the President didn't listen to them.

591

word their clause modifies and what the clause tells about that word. Answers will vary.
1. Jana can attend the movie if _____.
2. Since _____, you will have to do fifty push-ups.
3. My baby sister cries as soon as _____.
4. If _____, keep trying.
5. The official dropped his penalty flag when _____.

Extending the Lesson

Have students rewrite the following compound sentences as complex sentences, changing the italicized clause into a subordinate clause. Have them refer to the list of subordinating conjunctions on page 588. Answers will vary.

1. *Pablo Picasso died*, and his paintings are even more valuable.
2. *We were so hungry* and we stopped at Choy's Restaurant.
3. The janitor swept the floor and *we waited in the hall*.
4. *The car was going too fast* and it almost missed the turn.
5. *Our team played its best* but we did not win the tournament.

3. (If negotiations succeed,) the strike will end.
4. You will stay in shape (as long as you exercise.)
5. (If you want to stop,) angle your skates inward.
6. (When the light goes on,) the show is on the air.
7. The girl was placed in a foster home (when she was six.)
8. (Whenever the actor went to New York,) he ate at Mama Leone's.
9. Many motorists speed (unless patrol cars are nearby.)
10. The party doesn't begin (until Roberto arrives.)

1. To recognize adjective clauses and to understand how they are used in sentences
2. To recognize relative pronouns and to understand their function in introducing clauses

Presenting the Lesson

1. Read pages 592–593. Go over the definition of an adjective clause. Study the examples of adjective clauses noting the word each adjective clause modifies and what the clause tells about that word.
2. Read pages 593–594. Make sure students understand the three functions listed.
3. Study the diagrams of sentences containing adjective clauses. Have students note how the subordinate adjective clause is placed below the main clause and connected by a dotted line to the noun or pronoun it modifies.

Part 5   Adjective Clauses

Another kind of subordinate clause is the adjective clause.
An **adjective** is a word that modifies a noun or pronoun.

   Adjective: Barry makes *juicy* hamburgers.

An adjective phrase is a phrase that modifies a noun or pronoun.

   Adjective phrase: The dog ate that section *of the paper.*

Adjective clauses modify nouns and pronouns:

   Someone *who speaks Japanese* will translate.

   We'll eat at the first restaurant *that we see.*

   The Depression was a time *when the economy collapsed.*

   Diet drinks are for people *who want to cut calories.*

   An adjective clause is a subordinate clause used as an adjective to modify a noun or pronoun.

Usually, the adjective clause comes immediately after the word it modifies.

Adjectives and adjective phrases or clauses tell *what kind* or *which one*. Remember that only clauses have subjects and verbs.

Several words are used to introduce adjective clauses. Two of them are *where* and *when*.

This is the power plant *where the accident occurred*.

The time *when most concerts start* is 8:00 P.M.

Who and *Whom* in Clauses

Three other words which often begin adjective clauses are *who*, *whom*, and *whose*. They relate the clause to the noun or pronoun it modifies. When used in this way, *who*, *whom*, and *whose* are called **relative pronouns.** The name is appropriate since the words relate a clause, called a **relative clause,** to a word in the sentence. *That* and *which* may also be relative pronouns.

These are the relative pronouns:

who	whom	whose	that	which

Relative pronouns have three functions:

1. They introduce adjective clauses.

2. They relate the adjective clause to a word in the main clause.

3. Within the adjective clause, they act as subject, object, or predicate pronoun of the verb. They may also be the object of a preposition in the clause.

Adelman is the aide *whom the mayor trusts most*.
(*Whom* is the direct object of *trusts*.)

The Dahls are the family *with whom I stayed*.
(*Whom* is the object of the preposition *with*.)

Is Peterson the journalist *who wrote this article?*
(*Who* is the subject of *wrote*.)

593

4. Do Exercise A on pages 594–595 as a class activity.

5. Assign and discuss Exercise B on page 595.

Individualizing the Lesson

Less-Advanced Students

1. Have students do the Exercises in class, writing some of the sentences on the board.

2. Have students use the relative pronouns listed on page 593 in sentences.

Advanced Students

1. Have students write a letter telling a friend about a new record or book they like. Encourage them to use adjective clauses throughout their letter. Tell them to circle each adjective clause, underline its subject once, and underline its verb twice.

2. Have students diagram three sentences from each Exercise.

Optional Practice

Have students complete the following complex sentences by adding words to form adjective clauses. Answer will vary.

1. This is the room where _____.
2. The people who _____ called my home today.
3. One reason that _____ was the awful weather.
4. Peter is the person who _____.
5. That is the automobile that _____.

Extending the Lesson

Have students rewrite each pair of sentences as a complex sentence, using the underlined sentence as the subordinate clause.

593

1. Where is the pen? <u>I just had it</u>. (that)
2. The new coach gave us some excellent advice. <u>He had played on a championship team</u>. (who)
3. The trees on our street had beautiful flowers this spring. <u>They were planted two years ago</u>. (that)
4. I want to see the movie. <u>It is playing at our local theater</u>. (that)
5. Linda won first prize. <u>She is a fine swimmer</u>. (who)

Where is the pen that I just had?

The new coach, who had played on a championship team, gave us some excellent advice.

The trees that were planted two years ago had beautiful flowers this spring.

I want to see the movie that is playing at our local theater.

Linda, who is a fine swimmer, won first prize.

If you have trouble deciding whether to use *who* or *whom*, check to see how the word is used within the clause. The subject form is *who*. The object form is *whom*.

Diagraming Adjective Clauses

In a diagram of a sentence containing an adjective clause, the main clause and the adjective clause are written on separate main lines. Draw a dotted line from the relative pronoun to the word in the main clause that the adjective clause modifies.

The people who painted this mural are local artists.

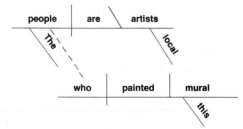

The guide to whom we spoke directed us to Pike's Peak.

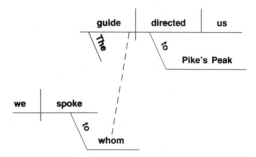

Exercise A   Copy the (adjective clause) from each sentence. Underline the subject once and the verb twice. Before the clause, write the word it modifies.

1. It was one of those days (when <u>everything</u> <u>went</u> wrong.) days
2. Is this the coat (that <u>you</u> <u>want</u>?) coat

594

3. The mayor is a woman(who teaches at the college.) woman
4. The team(that wins this game)will be champions. team
5. We couldn't find anyone(who had seen the accident.) anyone
6. A woman(who was carrying many packages)sat down beside me. woman
7. We lost the picture(that you gave us.) picture
8. The family(who owns the grocery)lives next door. family
9. Burt,(who was still awake,)smelled the smoke. Burt
10. The doctor(with whom we consulted)advised surgery. doctor

Exercise B   Follow the directions for Exercise A.

1. The games(that are most popular)are electronic.   games
2. The President discussed issues(that concerned the people.) issues
3. Montreal is the team(that has won the Stanley Cup.) team
4. The only time(when I was afraid)was during the hurricane.   time
5. The relatives(whom Ernie visited)run a cafe.   relatives
6. We went to the Kentucky Derby,(which is held at Churchill Downs.) Kentucky Derby
7. One place(where we can talk)is the coffee shop.   place
8. The factory(where candy is made)is open for tours.   factory
9. Summerfest,(which is held in August,)features many stars.   Summerfest
10. This is the book(that I was telling you about.) book

Part 6   Noun Clauses

The third kind of subordinate clause is the noun clause.

A noun clause is a clause used as a noun in a sentence.

The noun clause can be used in any way that a noun is used. Like nouns, noun clauses can be used as subjects, as objects of

Part 6

Objective

To recognize noun clauses and understand how they are used in sentences

Presenting the Lesson

1. Read the definition of a noun clause and study the examples of noun clauses on pages 595–596. Go over the words on page 596 which commonly introduce noun clauses.

2. Study the examples of diagrams of noun clauses on page 597. Point out that the noun clause is placed on a bridge above the main clause. Remind students that adjective and adverb clauses were diagramed on a line below the words they modified.

3. Assign and discuss Exercises A and B on page 598.

Individualizing the Lesson

Less-Advanced Students

Work with students to complete the sentences in Exercise A. Then assign Exercise B.

Advanced Students

1. Have students write a brief account of a recent event in which they were involved. Tell them to be sure to include noun clauses in most of the sentences. Have them indicate how each clause is used.

2. Have students diagram five sentences from the Exercises.

Optional Practice

Have students complete the following complex sentences by adding words to form noun clauses.

1. Do you know why _____ Answers will vary.
2. Whoever _____ is welcome.
3. I have never understood how _____.
4. The volunteers did whatever _____.
5. The surprise is that _____.

Extending the Lesson

Have students find an example of a noun clause in a textbook. Then have them explain how the clause is used. This activity can be done at the chalkboard.

verbs, as predicate words after linking verbs, and as objects of prepositions. Noun clauses do not modify anything because nouns are not modifiers.

Uses of Noun Clauses

Subject:	*What the hypnotist did* astonished us.
	What Sandra wanted was good food.
Direct object:	An X-ray shows *when a patient has a fracture.*
	We know *whom you mean.*
Object of preposition:	Give the clothes to *whoever can use them.*
	(The clause is the object of the preposition *to.*)
	Jack works hard for *what he gets.*
	(The clause is the object of the preposition *for.*)
Predicate noun:	The problem is *that no one speaks Spanish.*
	Meigs Field is *where Air Force 1 landed.*

You can see that many noun clauses are introduced by *that* and *what*. Some are introduced by *whatever*, *whoever*, and *whomever*. Other noun clauses are introduced by *who*, *whose*, and *whom*. Still others are introduced by *where*, *when*, *why*, and *how*.

Diagraming Noun Clauses

A noun clause is diagramed on a bridge at the place where the clause is used in a sentence. The word that introduces the clause is placed on a horizontal line above the clause.

1. **Noun clause used as subject**

   Where the millionaire went is a mystery.

   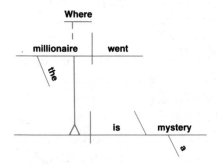

2. **Noun clause used as object of the verb**

   We saw that you were in a hurry.

   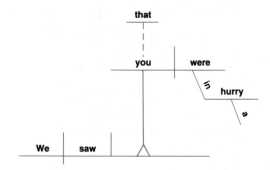

3. **Noun clause used as object of the preposition**

   The pilot was unaware of what he was doing.

   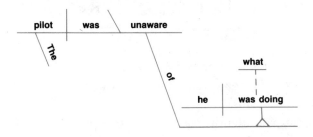

Exercise A Copy the noun clauses in these sentences. Underline the subject once and the verb twice. Tell how the clause is used.

S 1. (Whoever appeared) was put to work.

OP 2. I was just thinking about (what you said.)

DO 3. Do you remember (who told you that?)

DO 4. I don't know (where the Marcuses live.)

DO 5. I will do (whatever you decide.)

S 6. (Whoever wins) gets this trophy.

OP 7. Show this card to (whoever is at the door.)

DO 8. Paula didn't know (where Kevin was going.)

DO 9. Our class will support (whatever candidate is chosen.)

S 10. (How the project will be funded) hasn't been decided.

Exercise B Follow the directions for Exercise A.

DO 1. Timmy imitated (whatever Rob did.)

DO 2. The mechanic said (that our car was fine.)

DO 3. Amity wondered (where she had left her books.)

PN 4. Our first meeting was (what I had expected.)

S 5. (Whoever sees a fire) should report it.

S 6. (Whatever Jerry cooks) is delicious.

DO 7. Madame Ruba showed us (how she reads palms.)

OP 8. We pay for (what we get.)

DO 9. I didn't know (what happened.)

DO 10. Russell found (that the day went quickly.)

Part 7 A Review of Subordinate Clauses

You have now been introduced to the three kinds of subordinate clauses. They are the adverb clause, the adjective clause, and the noun clause.

How can you identify these clauses? You can tell the kind of clause only from its use in the sentence. If a clause is used as a

Part 7

Objective

To be able to identify noun, adverb, and adjective subordinate clauses

Presenting the Lesson

1. Read pages 598–599. Remind students that noun, adverb, and adjective clauses are all subordinate clauses. When they occur with a main clause, they form a complex sentence. Review the uses of each kind of clause.

2. Do Exercise A on page 599 orally with the class.

3. Assign and discuss Exercise B.

Individualizing the Lesson

Less-Advanced Students

Review with students the words which commonly introduce the three

noun, it is a noun clause. If the clause is a modifier, it is an adverb or adjective clause.

Exercise A Write the (subordinate clause) as you find it in each sentence. If the clause is a noun clause, tell how it is used in the sentence. If the clause is used as an adjective or adverb clause, tell what it modifies.

1. I don't believe (that the experiment is possible.) N, Object
2. Someone said (that we would have a holiday tomorrow.) N, Object
3. Can you study (while the TV is on?) Adv.
4. We did not know (who the man was.) N, Object
5. Jeff ducked (before the snowball hit him.) Adv.
6. The plane (that leaves at 7:00 P.M.) has a feature movie. Adj.
7. We arrived (when Dr. Jordan was speaking.) Adv.
8. What is the time (that we agreed on?) Adj.
9. Dad lived in Colorado (when he was growing up.) Adv.
10. (How the engine works) is a mystery to me. N, Subject

Exercise B Follow the directions for Exercise A.

1. Superstitions are beliefs (that are not rational.) Adj.
2. Superstitions often begin (when people fear the unknown.) Adv.
3. Many superstitions still exist (even though they started long ago.) Adv.
4. People sometimes wonder (how certain superstitions began.) N. Object
5. The superstition (that black cats bring bad luck) began with the Egyptians. Adj.
6. They thought (that a cat was a witch in disguise.) N. Object
7. Another practice (that is based on superstition) involves sneezing. Adj.
8. (When people sneeze,) we often say "bless you." Adv.
9. Ancient people believed (that breath was life.) N. Object
10. Sneezing was feared (because breath was lost.) Adv.

599

kinds of clauses. Have them circle the words in each sentence in Exercises A and B.

Advanced Students

Have students write three sentences using each kind of subordinate clause. Have them indicate how the noun clauses are used and what word the adverb and or adjective clauses modify.

Optional Practice

Have students add main clauses to each of the following subordinate clauses to make a complex sentence. Then have students tell how each of the subordinate clauses is used (noun, adverb, or adjective clause). Sentences will vary.

1. whoever spilled the tea
2. that I found in the basement
3. what Jeff would like
4. when the cheering died down
5. that I don't have enough money
6. since the price of gasoline went up
7. where the car keys are
8. whatever she wants

Extending the Lesson

Compile a list of ten words that generally introduce adverb, adjective, or noun clauses. Remind students that some words can introduce more than one kind of subordinate clause. Read a word to the class and have each student write the word on his or her paper. Then have students write a complex sentence using each word as a subordinative conjunction or relative pronoun. Have students indicate whether the word they used introduces an adverb, an adjective, or a noun clause.

599

Objective

To be able to recognize and correct subordinate clause sentence fragments

Presenting the Lesson

1. Read page 600. Stress that a subordinate clause is dependent upon the main clause to complete its meaning. A subordinate clause is always incomplete unless it is attached to a main clause. Study the examples of subordinate clauses written as fragments.

2. Do Exercise A on pages 600–601 as a class activity.

3. Assign and discuss Exercise B on page 601.

Individualizing the Lesson

Less-Advanced Students

Have students find two examples of sentence fragments in magazine or newspaper advertisements. Have them complete each fragment they find.

Advanced Students

Have each student write ten subordinate clauses; then have students exchange papers. Once papers have been exchanged, tell students to make each clause into a sentence.

Optional Practice

Have students complete the following sentence fragments:
Answers will vary.
If the game ends in a tie
Until I can find a job
Because of the exam we have on Monday day

600

Part 8 More About Sentence Fragments

Now you will learn about a different kind of sentence fragment, the subordinate clause.

You have already studied sentence fragments. Those sentence fragments lacked either a subject or a verb:

Ran to the store   Jason and his friends

The subordinate clause can also be a sentence fragment if it is not part of a sentence. A subordinate clause is not meant to stand alone. Even though it has a subject and a verb, it is a sentence fragment because it does not express a complete thought. It leaves the reader confused.

Look at the word groups below. Which is a sentence, and which is a subordinate clause?

It is time to leave
If it is time to leave

A subordinate clause must not be written as a complete sentence. It must always be joined to a main clause.

Fragment: If it is time to leave
Sentence: If it is time to leave, we will hunt for our jackets.
Fragment: When the boxer swung
Sentence: When the boxer swung, he injured his shoulder.

By recognizing subordinate clauses, you can better avoid writing sentence fragments.

Exercise A   Number your paper from 1 to 10. Decide whether the groups of words below are sentences or fragments. Write *S* for *Sentence* or *F* for *Fragment*. Add words to make each fragment a complete sentence. Punctuate and capitalize where necessary.
Sentences will vary.

F   1. because of the storm our lights went off

F   2. because the doctor advised plenty of rest

F   3. where the school always has its football games

600

S 4. ~~W~~ where is the box of candy?

S 5. since yesterday morning the air has been clear.

F 6. since we have no food left

S 7. after the argument we shook hands.

F 8. after the show had ended

S 9. when are you leaving for Dallas?

F 10. when the old mine was closed down

Exercise B Follow the directions for Exercise A.

F 1. where the car went off the road

S 2. when the wind is from the south, we get rain.

S 3. where is the box for this puzzle?

F 4. until the manager came out and stopped the noise

S 5. down the mountain rolled a boulder.

F 6. since the beginning of school

S 7. since you agree, we can go ahead with the plans.

F 8. before the lifeguard could reach the boat

F 9. while we waited for our ride

S 10. although the movie was canceled, we had a group discussion

Part 9   A Review of Sentences

In this section you have learned about the three basic kinds of sentences.

You know that a **simple sentence** contains one subject and one predicate. A simple sentence expresses one main idea. You will remember, however, that parts of the simple sentence may be compound.

s.   v.   v.
The plane did a barrel roll and lost altitude.

s.   v.   v.   v.
Our movie projector was not working well and scratched the film.

Extending the Lesson

Have students rewrite the following paragraph, correcting the fragments. Students should be able to explain how fragments were corrected.

Paul Zindel is an author of teen fiction. Whom I really admire. I always read his novels. As soon as the library gets them. Because Zindel has a good sense of humor, His characters are always enjoyable to read about. My parents laugh. When I tell them the names of some of Zindel's books. My favorites are *Pardon Me, You're Stepping On My Eyeball* and *The Undertaker's Gone Bananas.* Which I highly recommend.

Part 9

Objective

To review simple, compound, and complex sentences

Presenting the Lesson

1. Read pages 601–602, reviewing definitions and examples of simple, compound, and complex sentences. Remind students of certain identifying traits of compound sentences (comma plus coordinating conjunction, or semicolon) and complex sentences (subordinate conjunctions, relative pronouns, certain words such as *that, where, whoever*).

2. Do Exercise A on pages 602–603 as a class activity. Have students identify subjects and verbs in each sentence to aid in determining if the sentence is simple, comlex, or compound.

3. Assign and discuss Exercise B on page 603.

Individualizing the Lesson

Less-Advanced Students

Have students copy the sentences from the Exercises. Have them underline each subordinate clause they find. Then have the students circle any coordinating conjunctions in the sentences.

Advanced Students

Have students rewrite the sentences from Exercises A and B. Tell them to change or expand simple sentences to compound sentences and compound sentences to complex sentences.

Optional Practice

Have students take each of the following simple sentences and expand and rewrite them twice, first as a compound sentence and then as a complex sentence. Answers will vary.

1. I wore my new boots.
2. *Nova* is Greg's favorite show.
3. Solar energy will be important in the future.
4. The airlines are raising their fares again.
5. Glenn will make a good salesman.

Extending the Lesson

Have students identify two examples of each of the three kinds of sentences in a newspaper or magazine article.

You have learned that a **compound sentence** consists of two simple sentences. These simple sentences are joined by a coordinating conjunction or by a semicolon. A compound sentence expresses two main ideas which are related in thought.

s.   v.   s. v.
The plane did a barrel roll; then it lost altitude.

s.   v.   v.   s.   v.
Our movie projector was not working well, and it scratched the film.

You have also learned that a **complex sentence** contains one main clause and one or more subordinate clauses. In the complex sentence the subordinate clause can act as a noun, an adjective, or an adverb. A complex sentence expresses only one main idea and one or more ideas that depend on the main idea.

s. v.   s. v.
The plane did a barrel roll *before it lost altitude.*

s.   s. v.   v.
Our movie projector, *which was not working well,* scratched the film.

Exercise A Number your paper from 1 to 10. For each sentence, write *Simple, Compound,* or *Complex* to show what kind it is.

S 1. Julia took the phone off the hook and forgot about it.

S 2. The Ferris wheel and the Eiffel Tower were both designed for world fairs.

S 3. Weather forecasters watch winds and clouds carefully.

Cx 4. When the tide came in, the beach disappeared.

Cx 5. The horse that he picked finished fourth.

S 6. Meredith and Keith were contestants on a game show.

C 7. Do you want to order pizzas, or shall we make them at home?

C 8. The old man feared muggers, and he walked cautiously.

Cx 9. The recreation center is the place where we can play various sports.

Cx 10. Pat Roberts was leading until the cars took the final turn.

Exercise B Follow the directions for Exercise A.

C 1. Darryl joined an exercise program, and he lost ten pounds.

Cx 2. Please rake the stones away before you cut the grass.

Cx 3. Vernon thought about the issues as he voted.

S 4. Mary Tyler Moore has starred in several TV series and specials.

Cx 5. Many companies advertise that they hire minorities.

C 6. Some popular songs last, but others are soon forgotten.

S 7. Amy and Alison warmed up and then ran the hurdles.

Cx 8. A roll bar protects riders when a car rolls over.

C 9. Terrorists took over an embassy, and they held three hostages.

S 10. We sat on the roof and watched the action below.

Exercise C: Writing Using the coordinating conjunctions (*and, or, but*) write three compound sentences. Then, using the subordinating conjunctions on page 588, write three complex sentences.

ADDITIONAL EXERCISES

Using Compound and Complex Sentences

A. Simple Sentences Label four columns *Subject, Verb, Object,* and *Predicate Word*. For each sentence fill in the appropriate columns. Not every sentence will contain each part. Some sentences may have compound parts.

1. Last month the landlord raised our rent.
2. Virgil and Eric are paddling the rubber raft.
3. Van wrote to Action Line and got quick results.
4. Samantha put on her coat and went to the library.
5. Dr. Early checked my throat and prescribed medicine.
6. The river was clean and clear.
7. Dancers and actors must often take temporary jobs.
8. We laughed at the chimps and admired the tigers.
9. Jenny bought ten raffle tickets but won nothing.
10. The loudspeaker was paging Elaine and Penny.

B. Simple and Compound Sentences Copy these sentences. Underline each subject once and each verb twice. After each sentence write *Simple* or *Compound* to show what kind it is.

C   1. Delia dreams each night, but she forgets her dreams.

S   2. Ms. Muller tied a rope to the branch and sawed it off.

S   3. Toby fell off the bike but got back on.

C   4. Betsy headed for the beach, and the dogs followed.

C   5. The city took bids for highway construction, and Quinlan got the contract.

C   6. Tom works in Dallas, but he is often out of town.

C   7. The flag went down, and a penalty was called.

C   8. Four players can place-kick, but only Dan is accurate.

C   9. The goalie dived, but the puck slid by.

S   10. Ed has a savings account but rarely adds to it.

C. Punctuation in Compound Sentences   Copy each sentence. Add the punctuation needed to make the sentence correct.

1. Someone flipped a switch, and the street lit up.
2. The manager asked the youths for identification, and they quickly left.
3. Most of the footage was destroyed, but some of the film was salvaged.
4. Japanese women sometimes wear kimonos; Indian women often wear saris.
5. This theater has an unusual policy; it books only G-rated movies.
6. Those laws are out of date, but they are still on the books.
7. I read my horoscope, and it predicted sudden wealth.
8. The starlet desperately wanted publicity, and she got it.
9. Sam carefully clipped the coupons; he forgot to take them to the store, though.
10. Nobody cheered; the crowd stood and stared.

D. Adverb Clauses   Copy each (adverb clause.) Underline its subject once and its verb twice. Circle the subordinating conjunction.

1. Jim grew a beard (because he wants to look older.)
2. The chair was damaged (when it sat out in the rain.)
3. Larry learned welding (when he was in the Marines.)
4. (Unless the Mets bounce back) they will finish in last place.
5. Eva got a social security card (before she got a job.)
6. (After Phil learned to swim,) he went canoeing.
7. (Although Mimi put on suntan oil,) she got a bad burn.
8. My sister had two jobs (while she was in college.)
9. (If the cans are dented,) don't buy them.
10. Hattie smiled (as she read the letter from Bob.)

E. Adjective Clauses
Copy the adjective clause from each sentence. Underline the subject once and the verb twice. After the clause, write the word it modifies.

1. This double album is the one (that I want.) one
2. This subdivision has rows of houses (that all look alike.) houses
3. Maya Angelou, (who is an author and a poet,) has received many honors. Maya Angelou
4. Parents (who work at the factory) started this day-care center. Parents
5. The number (that you dialed) has been disconnected. number
6. The store (where Jim had left his wallet) was closed. store
7. Do you remember the summer (when we went to Omaha?) summer
8. The counselor (whom Fred saw) seemed well informed. counselor
9. The pool is in Grove Park, (which is by the river.) Grove Park
10. The dormouse, (which is a rodent,) sleeps much of the time. dormouse

F. Noun Clauses
Copy the (noun clause) in each sentence. Write whether the clause is used as a subject, direct object, object of a preposition, or predicate noun.

DO 1. Coach Rock noticed (that the defense was tiring.)
DO 2. No one could understand (how the floodlight worked.)
DO 3. Sherry insisted (that the job would be easy.)
DO 4. Did you know (that the bus driver takes only exact change?)
DO 5. Your expression shows (what you are thinking.)
DO 6. The team protested (that the game had been rigged.)
S 7. (What Georgia had erased) still showed on the paper.
OP 8. Sometimes people dream about (what has happened during the day.)
DO 9. Ted didn't know (what to do.)
PN 10. This is (where Sal lives.)

G. Kinds of Subordinate Clauses Copy the subordinate clause in each sentence. Identify each clause as *Adverb*, *Adjective*, or *Noun*.

1. Marie Curie is the scientist (who won the Nobel Prizes in physics and chemistry.) Adj.
2. (Before she married,) her name was Marie Sklodowska. Adv.
3. Where did you put the wrench (that I lent to you last week?) Adj.
4. Carlos said (that he would get here before lunch.) N
5. How could Cheryl have known (where the house keys were?) N
6. (How birds fly) interests some engineers. N
7. (Whom did you say) was calling? N
8. Please stay (where you are.) Adv.
9. Jamaica was one island (where Columbus landed.) Adj.
10. Josh got nervous (when he looked down.) Adv.

H. Sentence Fragments Decide whether the groups of words below are sentences or fragments. Write *S* for *Sentence* or *F* for *Fragment*.

F 1. Because today is the first day of Angela's summer vacation
S 2. Where does this bolt go
S 3. Because I had missed the beginning I stayed for the next show
F 4. Where the audio-visual equipment is kept
F 5. Wherever the rest of you would like to go
S 6. Wherever Annette goes, she makes friends
S 7. Until today Francine had never missed practice
F 8. Until the groundhog comes out and looks around
S 9. What are some products made from petroleum
F 10. What Ernestine will make out of those torn scraps of cloth

I. Simple, Compound, and Complex Sentences For each sentence, write *Simple, Compound,* or *Complex* to tell what kind it is.

Cx 1. Ali announced that he was retiring.

C 2. Polly had trained hard, and she was confident.

S 3. All of the lights on the pinball machine flashed and flickered.

Cx 4. A sharecropper is a farmer who works another person's land.

C 5. Laurel winked at Tyrone, and he chuckled.

Cx 6. Tod was choking and gasping when he finally came up for air.

Cx 7. Whom you know is not important here.

C 8. Who told you, or did you just guess?

Cx 9. Plant those purple hyacinth bulbs before the ground freezes.

S 10. Virginia and Kate finished the tennis game before sundown.

MIXED REVIEW

Using Compound and Complex Sentences

A. Identifying sentences and fragments If a group of words is a sentence, write *S*. If a group is a fragment, write *F*. Then write whether each fragment is a *phrase* or a *clause*.

F 1. Who in the world P
S 2. Who knows
F 3. Which the disc jockey read over the radio C
S 4. Which of these spiders bite
F 5. The last game before the play-offs P
S 6. Pay me back before you run out of money
S 7. Although his shoelace was untied, Edwin Moses won the 1983 World Championship hurdles race
F 8. Although neither the North nor the South could, in honesty, claim victory in the Battle of Antietam C
F 9. The hockey stick that the Black Hawks autographed C
S 10. George looks around when he is nervous

B. Identifying kinds of sentences Read the following sentences. Write whether each is *Simple*, *Compound*, or *Complex*.

S 1. The path along the rocks is safe until dark.
S 2. Barb and Hilary tugged and then pulled.
Cx 3. Lenny should know that he needs a hall pass.
S 4. I did not really say that.
C 5. Harold found some bacon in the refrigerator; he couldn't find any eggs, though.
Cx 6. Although Franklin is a good batter, he is a slow runner.
Cx 7. The autumn leaves of the maple tree looked like a red cloud until the storm scattered them.
Cx 8. Erin and Jon carried furniture downstairs while Damon loaded the moving van.

609

c 9. Di could have played tennis, but she chose golf.

s 10. After the movie we clear the theater and clean the aisles.

C. Recognizing subordinate clauses Copy the (subordinate clause) from each of the following sentences. Underline its subject once and its verb twice. Then write *Adverb*, *Adjective*, or *Noun* to show what kind of clause it is.

1. The singer (that I like) has left the band. Adj.
2. The article states (that Samoa includes sixteen islands.) N
3. I heard (what you said.) N
4. What happened (while we were away?) Adv.
5. (If you wait any longer,) you will be late for the movie. Adv.
6. Do you know anyone (who needs a babysitter?) Adj.
7. Judy wondered (who had sent her the daisies.) N
8. Alicia asked (when the sidewalk café would open.) N
9. Nobody looks forward to the day (when summer is over.) Adj.
10. Why do you look so solemn (when you tell a joke?) Adv.

D. Using subordinate clauses correctly Copy the (subordinate clause) from each of the following sentences. Write *Noun*, *Adjective*, or *Adverb* to show what kind it is. If the clause is used as a noun, write *Subject*, *Direct Object*, *Object of Preposition*, or *Predicate Noun* to show what part of the sentence it is. If the clause is used as an adjective or adverb, write the word it modifies.

1. Lacey talks more (when he feels at ease.) Adv., talks
2. We will stop at (whatever restaurant we see first.) N., op
3. Breathe as slowly (as you can.) Adv., slowly
4. This is a job for someone (who likes people.) Adj., someone
5. Joaquin knows (who owns the car.) N. DO
6. A watch is (what Shelia needs.) N. predicate noun
7. That gray sweatshirt is the one (that I want.) Adj., one
8. (That the halfback had been injured) was obvious. N. Subject
9. Why don't you set the alarm (before you go to sleep?) Adv., set
10. He suddenly realized (why the alarm was sounding.) N. DO

USING GRAMMAR IN WRITING
Using Compound and Complex Sentences

A. Imagine that you are a student of veterinary medicine. You have volunteered for one evening on the Problem Pet Hot Line. Answer each of these problem calls with a compound sentence. Use the conjunction given for each sentence.

1. Due to a fondness for chocolate milk, my poodle is extremely overweight. (Use *and*.)
2. Our bulldog barks all night. He barks all day, too. (Use *or*.)
3. Are fleas a serious problem? (Use *but*.)
4. Our couches and chairs look like they've been through a shredder. How can we prevent our cat from clawing the furniture? (Use *or*.)
5. Are dogs and cats often compatible in the same house? (Use *but*.)
6. Visitors think our cat is a terrible snob. How can we encourage Lord Binghamton to be more outgoing and friendly? (Use *and*.)

B. You bought something that broke the first time you used it. Write a letter to the manufacturer, asking for a refund or a replacement. Explain what happened when you tried to use the item. Use several of these subordinate conjunctions in your letter of complaint:

after	because	so that	whatever
although	before	than	when
as	if	though	whenever
as if	in order that	till	where
as long as	provided	unless	wherever
as though	since	until	while

Using Grammar in Writing

These challenging and enjoyable activities allow the students to see how the concepts of grammar, usage, and mechanics may be applied in actual writing situations. Each exercise is designed to allow students practice in several of the skills they have acquired in this Section. The activities also provide opportunities for students to write creatively about a wide variety of interesting and unusual subjects.

611

Cumulative Review

These exercises are designed to cover broad areas of grammar, usage, and mechanics. They require the application of skills taught thus far in the text. The exercises may be used for testing purposes, or as an excellent resource for review.

CUMULATIVE REVIEW

The Sentence

A. Identifying kinds of sentences Copy the following sentences. Insert the correct punctuation. After each sentence, write *D* for declarative, *INT* for interrogative, *IMP* for imperative, or *E* for exclamatory. Underline each subject once and each verb twice.

IMP 1. Start your engines.
 D 2. The moose grazed on the new spring growth.
 E 3. Watch out for that truck! (or Imp.)
INT 4. Is that clock an antique?
IMP 5. Review your notes before the test.
 D 6. Heather memorized the poem.
 E 7. What a generous person she is!
INT 8. Who borrowed my fishing rod?
 D 9. Dr. Boraca is a pathologist.
IMP 10. Order the sale items from the catalog.

B. Understanding agreement in sentences Number your paper from 1 to 15. Write the correct word from the two given in parentheses.

1. None of the contestants (<u>seem</u>, seems) nervous.
2. You (is, <u>are</u>) the last guest to arrive.
3. There (is, <u>are</u>) twenty students in my music class.
4. The flowers and the shrubbery (<u>need</u>, needs) water.
5. Everyone carried (<u>his or her</u>, their) own backpack.
6. She (don't, <u>doesn't</u>) recognize me with my hat on.
7. The popcorn in the yellow cans (<u>is</u>, are) cheese-flavored.
8. Where (was, <u>were</u>) the lifejackets?
9. Either Katie or the twins (knows, <u>know</u>) the locker combination.
10. Here (is, <u>are</u>) the mustard and the catsup.

612

C. Correcting fragments and run-on sentences

The following paragraph contains fragments and run-on sentences. Rewrite the paragraph. Use capitalization and punctuation to correct the fragments and run-ons. Do not add or change any words.

The cockroach, a hardy creature, Has survived in the same form for millions of years. The cockroach can be found all over the globe, Except in polar regions. If the cockroach doesn't have food, It will eat glue, wallpaper, or soap. A cockroach can go without water for a month. One species can even survive freezing temperatures. One safeguard that cockroaches have, Is a set of sensory hairs that sample whatever the roach attempts to eat., Including poison. However, the most important safeguard is a vibration sensor in the cockroach's knee joints, it gets the cockroach moving. When a cockroach senses a footfall, it can get going in .054 second., Which is faster than humans can blink. With such remarkable abilities, The cockroach will probably be around for another million years or so.

D. Writing good sentences

Rewrite each of the following sentences. Follow the directions in the parentheses.

1. Cassie fell during gymnastics practice. (Add the prepositional phrase *from the balance beam.*)

2. Jim gathered the firewood. He made a campfire. (Combine these two simple sentences into one with a compound predicate.)

3. Mavis read during her break. (Change this NV sentence to one with a NVN pattern.)

4. Mr. McKinney tried to buy football tickets. The games were already sold out. (Combine these two simple sentences into a compound sentence using , *but.*)

5. Let's play tennis tomorrow. Would you rather go to the beach? (Combine these two simple sentences into one compound sentence using , *or.*)

Capitalization

There are many rules for the use of capital letters. You already know some of them well.

This section shows you the rules for capitalization. They are organized so that you can study them. They are also organized so that you can refer to them whenever you are writing.

614

Proper Nouns and Adjectives

Capitalize proper nouns and proper adjectives.

A **common noun** is a general name of a person, place, or thing.
A **proper noun** is the name of a particular person, place, or thing.
A **proper adjective** is an adjective formed from a proper noun.

Common Noun	Proper Noun	Proper Adjective
person	Elizabeth	Elizabethan
country	Spain	Spanish
city	Paris	Parisian

There are many different proper nouns. The following rules and examples will help you solve the capitalization problems that proper nouns present.

Names of Persons

Capitalize the names of persons and also the initials or abbreviations that stand for those names.

J. R. R. Tolkien   John Ronald Revel Tolkien
Elizabeth M. Grant   Elizabeth Mason Grant

Capitalize titles used with names of persons and also the initials or abbreviations that stand for those titles.

The titles *Mr.*, *Mrs.*, *Ms.*, and *Miss* are always capitalized.

Rev. M. R. Eaton   Judge Esther Falks
Lt. Patricia Smith   Dr. John J. DeBender
Mr. Edward Scott   Professor White

Do not capitalize titles used as common nouns:

Have you seen your doctor?
She is the company president.
The judge entered the courtroom.

615

Objective

To understand and apply the rules for capitalizing proper nouns and adjectives

Presenting the Lesson

1. Read pages 615–616 defining proper nouns and proper adjectives. Ask students to give proper nouns for these words:

boy   magazine   teacher
car   country   river

Ask students to form proper adjectives from these words:

Japan   England   France

2. Assign and discuss Exercises A and B on pages 616–617. In going over the Exercises, explain why capitalized words need to be capitalized.

3. Read pages 617–618. Go over rules and examples, again asking students to supply additional examples.

4. Assign and discuss Exercises A and B on page 619.

5. Read pages 620–621. Go over rules and examples. Have students suggest more names of locally familiar organizations and institutions which should be capitalized.

6. Assign and discuss Exercises A and B on pages 621–622.

Individualizing the Lesson

Less-Advanced Students

Have students tell which capitalization rule applies to each of the sentences in the Exercises.

Optional Practice

Have students capitalize words where necessary in the following paragraph. For each capital inserted, students should be prepared to tell what rule governs the capitalization.

My mother and father and I are going to visit aunt Esther in london, England, this summer. We will drive east to new york, stopping in the Ohio town where I was born. I hope to visit dawes school where I went to first and second grade. I think Dr. Sawyer, the principal, is still there. then we will fly on a Concorde. It will take us less time to cross the atlantic Ocean than to get from here to Ohio. We will spend all of july with my aunt, and then tour the english countryside in a rented car—probably a german Volkswagen—during august.

Extending the Lesson

Have students write a brief travelogue of a place they have been to or would like to visit. Tell them to use as many of the situations requiring capital letters as possible, but tell students not to capitalize any letters except for the first word in each sentence. Have the students exchange papers and capitalize the proper words.

Capitalize titles of very high importance, even when these titles are used without proper names.

the Pope

the President of the United States

a United States Senator

the Prime Minister of England

Family Relationships

Capitalize such words as *mother, father, aunt,* and *uncle* when these words are used as names. When the noun is modified by a possessive word, *a*, or *the*, it is not capitalized.

Hello, Mother. Is Dad home yet?

My aunt is going to visit my grandmother next week.

The Pronoun *I*

Capitalize the pronoun *I*.

Is he taller than I?   I am sure that he is.

The Supreme Being and Sacred Writings

Capitalize all words referring to God, the Holy Family, and religious scriptures.

the Gospel	Buddha	the Torah
God	the Lord	the Bible
Allah	the Virgin Mary	the Book of Exodus

Capitalize personal pronouns referring to God.

God spoke to His prophets.

Exercise A   Number your paper from 1 to 10. Copy the following sentences. Change small letters to capital letters wherever necessary.

1. Would you tell mom i'll be a little late for dinner?
2. The first book of the bible is the book of genesis.
3. The new teacher is from paris, france.

4. He is a parisian. [P]

5. I told my mother that i had a doctor's appointment. [I]

6. She said, "Please ask dr. hernandez to call me." [D] [H]

7. My mother asked aunt rose if tad and maria could stay for lunch. [A] [R] [T] [M]

8. Please take this message to the principal, lynn. [L]

9. She says that ms. holchak is not in her office. [M] [H]

10. Two names for god are jehovah and the almighty. [G] [J] [A]

Exercise B Follow the directions for Exercise A.

1. Which cairo do you mean? [C]

2. Is it the one in egypt or the one in illinois? [E] [I]

3. Our government is sometimes called a jeffersonian democracy. [J]

4. The new student is toshio kitagawa. His sister is mieko. [T] [K] [M]

5. Both of them were born in japan. [J]

6. There are seven cities named springfield. [S]

7. The largest is in massachusetts. [M]

8. Speakers were mrs. j. p. perez and ms. p. d. cardelo. [M] [J] [P] [P] [M] [P] [D] [C]

9. All my aunts and uncles live in california. [C]

10. It was captain sherman who gave sue and ted the booklets on bicycle safety. [C] [S] [S] [T]

Geographical Names

In a geographical name, capitalize the first letter of each word except articles and prepositions.

The article *the* appearing before a geographical name is not part of the geographical name and is therefore not capitalized.

Continents: Europe, Asia, Africa, Australia

Bodies of Water: the Pacific Ocean, Puget Sound, the Columbia River, Hudson Bay, the Straits of Magellan, Lake Superior, the English Channel

Landforms:	the Mississippi Delta, the Cape of Good Hope, the Mojave Desert, the Atlas Mountains, Pike's Peak, Dismal Swamp
Political Units:	Oak Park, Los Angeles, Commonwealth of Puerto Rico, First Congressional District, Utah, Great Britain, the Azores
Public Areas:	Badlands National Monument, Grant Park, Shawnee National Forest, the Battery, the Black Hills, Zion National Park
Roads and Highways:	Oregon Trail, Lincoln Highway, Broad Street, 34th Avenue, Tri-State Tollway, Riverside Freeway, Drury Lane, Route 23

Directions and Sections

Capitalize names of sections of the country.

Industrial production was high in the North.
The first English settlements were along the East Coast.
The Southwest is our fastest-growing region.

Capitalize proper adjectives derived from names of sections of the country.

Western dress   a New England town
Southern-style cooking   Midwestern twang

Do not capitalize directions of the compass.

We headed south for our vacation.
The pioneers moved west over the Oregon Trail.
The school is southwest of our home.

Do not capitalize adjectives derived from words indicating direction.

a north wind   the east side of the building

Exercise A   Number your paper from 1 to 10. Find the words in the following sentences that should be capitalized. Write the words after the proper number, using the necessary capital letters.

1. Many wagon trains left from independence, missouri.
2. The trail took them first to fort kearney, nebraska.
3. Then they followed the north platte river to fort laramie.
4. The pioneers crossed the rocky mountains at south pass, wyoming.
5. After the trail crossed the rockies, it split into three parts.
6. The oregon trail went to the pacific northwest.
7. The mormon trail went to salt lake city, utah.
8. A third trail crossed the great basin of nevada and utah.
9. It crossed the sierra nevada mountains at donner pass.
10. Many american pioneers followed these trails westward.

Exercise B   Follow the directions for Exercise A.

1. Lake baikal is the world's deepest freshwater lake.
2. The lake is in siberia, in the soviet union.
3. Next week we elect the representative from the eighth congressional district.
4. The track championships will be held in morton township.
5. The island of capri is in the bay of naples.
6. The blue grotto is a famous tourist attraction on capri.
7. The trans-canada highway crosses the entire width of canada.
8. Of the seven continents, asia and africa are the two largest.
9. We had our family picnic at the lincoln park zoo last week.
10. Last summer, we drove along the gulf of mexico to new orleans and then north to memphis.

Names of Organizations and Institutions

Capitalize the names of organizations and institutions, including political parties, governmental bodies or agencies, schools, colleges, churches, hospitals, clubs, businesses, and abbreviations of these names.

Gillette Company	Children's Hospital
Oakwood High School	St. Mark's Church
University of Southern California	U.S.C.

Do not capitalize such words as *school, college, church,* and *hospital* when they are not used as names:

This fund drive benefits the hospital.

Names of Events, Documents, and Periods of Time

Capitalize the names of historical events, documents, and periods of time.

Battle of Hastings	Treaty of Paris	Age of Discovery
World War II	Bill of Rights	Middle Ages

Months, Days, and Holidays

Capitalize names of months, days, holidays, but not the names of seasons.

March	Labor Day	summer
Friday	Feast of the Passover	spring

Races, Languages, Nationalities, Religions

Capitalize the names of races, languages, nationalities, and religions and adjectives derived from them.

Caucasian	African	Lutheranism
French	Buddhism	Catholic

School Subjects

Do not capitalize the names of school subjects, except course names followed by a number.

physical education   History of Civilization II
social studies   Algebra I

Remember that the names of languages are always capitalized.

English   Spanish   Hebrew   German

Ships, Trains, Airplanes, Automobiles

Capitalize the names of ships, trains, airplanes, and automobiles.

U.S.S. Constitution   Santa Fe Chief
Cutlass   *Spirit of St. Louis*

B.C., A.D.

Capitalize the abbreviations *B.C.* and *A.D.*

The first Olympic Games were held in 776 **B.C.**
The Norman Conquest took place in **A.D.** 1066.

Exercise A Write the words in each sentence that should be capitalized. Use the necessary capital letters.

1. The fourth of july is an important date in american history.
2. The declaration of independence was signed on july 4, 1776.
3. My sister is a class president at pulaski high school.
4. I registered for ancient history I, business math II, social studies, english, and music.
5. In 1898 the treaty of paris ended the spanish-american war.
6. Our car was made by american motors corporation.

7. They own a ford pinto and a buick skylark.
8. My favorite subjects are home economics and shop.
9. The first woman to fly solo across the atlantic ocean was amelia earhart.
10. In 44 b.c. julius caesar was assassinated.

Exercise B Follow the directions for Exercise A.

1. The prophet muhammad founded the religion of islam.
2. His followers are called moslems or muslims.
3. The island of hispaniola was discovered in a.d. 1492.
4. The *u.s.s. constitution* is also called "*old ironsides.*"
5. The *broadway limited* runs between new york and chicago.
6. The new head of brookston hospital is dr. margaret allen.
7. The new social studies teacher is from munich, germany.
8. She is a nurse in the emergency room at st. luke's hospital.
9. He has studied spanish, russian, french, and german.
10. My sister is studying russian at u.c.l.a.

First Words

Sentences and Poetry

Capitalize the first word of every sentence and the first word in most lines of poetry.

My sister likes tennis. She is the captain of her team.

Listen my children, and you shall hear
Of the midnight ride of Paul Revere . . .
—from "Paul Revere's Ride" HENRY WADSWORTH LONGFELLOW

622

First Words

Objective

To understand and apply the rules for capitalizing the first words in sentences, poems, direct quotations, greetings in letters, outlines, and titles

Presenting the Lesson

1. Read pages 622–624. Go over rules and examples. Be sure students understand what a divided

Sometimes, especially in modern poetry, the lines of a poem do not begin with capital letters.

Quotations

When you write the exact words of a speaker or writer, you are giving a **direct quotation.**

Capitalize the first word of a direct quotation.

Ralph Waldo Emerson said, "Hitch your wagon to a star."

Sometimes a direct quotation is interrupted by explaining words like *she said.* This is called a **divided quotation.** Do not capitalize the first word of the second part of a divided quotation unless it starts a new sentence.

"Well," he said, "what you say is quite true."
"I agree," he said. "What you say is quite true."

Letters

Capitalize the first word, words like *Sir* and *Madam*, and the name of the person addressed in the greeting of a letter.

Dear Mrs. Gomez   Dear Ms. Perkins   Dear Mr. Castillo

In the complimentary close, capitalize the first word only.

Yours very truly   Sincerely yours

Outlines

Capitalize the letters and the first word of each line of an outline.

I. Improve your handwriting.
  A. Form letters carefully.
    1. Watch *a, e, r, l,* and *t.*
    2. Watch *u, v,* and *o.*
  B. Proofread your work.

---

quotation is and that the second part is capitalized only when it begins a new sentence.

2. Assign and discuss Exercises A and B on pages 624–625.

Individualizing the Lesson

Less-Advanced Students

1. Explain to students that the Exercises apply rules from the preceding Part as well as the rules to be learned in this Part.

2. Have students identify which rule applies to each capitalization they make in the Exercises.

Advanced Students

Have students investigate examples of contemporary poetry that do not use capitalization. Ask them to explore the reasons for and the effects of this lack of capitalization.

Optional Practice

Have students insert capital letters where necessary in the following outline.

readings in english literature
I. works by william shakespeare
  A. romeo and juliet
  B. the taming of the shrew
  C. a comedy of errors
II. works by dr. samuel johnson
III. works by thomas hardy
  A. novels
    1. the mayor of casterbridge
    2. the return of the native
  B. poems
    1. "ah, are you digging on my grave?"
    2. "during wind and rain"

Extending the Lesson

Have students clip out an article from a newspaper or magazine and underline all capitalized words. On

Titles

Capitalize the first word and all important words in chapter titles; titles of magazine articles; titles of short stories, essays, or single poems; and titles of songs or short pieces of music.

Chapter:	Chapter 5, "The Undersea World"
Magazine article:	"Sleep and Dreams"
Short story:	"The Last Leaf"
Essay:	"Nature"
Poem:	"O Captain! My Captain!"
Song:	"America the Beautiful"

Capitalize the first word and all important words in titles of books, newspapers, magazines, plays, movies, television programs, works of art, and long musical compositions.

Underline these titles. (When these titles are printed, they are *italicized*.)

Book title:	*Brian's Song*
Newspaper:	*Miami Herald*
Magazine:	*People*
Play:	*A Christmas Carol*
Movie:	*Breaking Away*
Television Program:	*The Evening News*
Work of art:	Gainsborough's *Blue Boy*
Long musical composition:	*Peter and the Wolf*

Exercise A   Number your paper from 1 to 10. Write the words that should be capitalized. Use the correct capital letters.

1. the last chapter of the sherlock holmes book *valley of fear* is "danger."
2. steve martin hosted *saturday night live* last week on TV.
3. the famous humorist will rogers said, "all i know is just what i read in the papers."
4. I. american history
   A. the war for independence
      1. battle of bunker hill

624

5. "^Ddon't go," he said. "^Ii haven't explained yet."
6. ^Ffor my birthday ^Ii got a subscription to ^S*seventeen.*
7. ^Tthe morning paper is the ^H*herald* ^T*tribune.*
8. ^Vvery sincerely yours,
9. "^Hhurry up!" father said. "^Iif we don't leave soon, we'll be late."
10. ^Ddid you enjoy the movie *the* ^T*right* ^R*stuff*^S?

Exercise B Follow the directions for Exercise A.

1. ^Ddear ^Mms. ^Wweiss:
2. ^Rrobert ^Ffrost wrote "^Tthe ^Ddeath of the ^Hhired ^Mman."
3. I. ^Bbusiness letters
    A. ^Ccorrect business letter form
        1. ^Hheading
4. ^Tthe recent issue of *^Ssports* ^I*illustrated* has complete coverage of all the ^{AFL}afl teams.
5. ^Ii come from ^Ssalem ^Ccounty
        ^Wwhere the silver melons grow,
    ^Wwhere the wheat is sweet as an angel's feet
        ^Aand the zithering zephyrs blow.
                                        —CHARLES CAUSLEY
6. ^Tthe article "^Iimages of ^Yyouth ^Ppast" appeared last fall in an issue of ^L*life* magazine.
7. "^Ooh, no!" said ^Mmeg. "^Hhas the plane left?"
8. "^Ii'm afraid so," ^Jjanet replied. "^Wwe're too late."
9. ^Ii have always enjoyed *the* ^T*wizard* ^Wof ^O*oz,* but ^Ii was thoroughly entertained by the movie *the* ^T*wiz.* ^W
10. ^Ii enjoyed the book *the* ^T*call* ^C*of the* ^W*wild* by jack ^J ^Llondon.

Additional Exercises

These Additional Exercises may be used for additional practice of the concepts presented in this Section. Each exercise focuses on a single concept, and should be used after the page number indicated in parentheses.

Review

If you have not assigned these Additional Exercises before this time, you can also use them as an excellent Section Review.

ADDITIONAL EXERCISES

Capitalization

A. Capital Letters Number your paper from 1 to 10. Find the words in the following sentences that should be capitalized. Write the words beside the proper numbers and capitalize them correctly.

1. The umpire threatened to oust don baylor from the game.
2. That legislation was sponsored by senator paula hawkins.
3. After the beatles broke up, george harrison sang solo.
4. The president held a White House reception.
5. My mother and i gave dad a mexican sombrero.
6. Hasn't v. s. naipaul written a novel with an african setting?
7. The king read from the koran over the first telephone in Saudi Arabia.
8. Is ms. koh the president of the company?
9. The head juror, mr. vernon wills, announced the verdict to judge martha schultz.
10. Which psalm is rabbi gruber quoting?

B. Capital Letters Copy the following sentences, changing small letters to capital letters wherever necessary.

1. The jet took off for athens, greece, but landed in rome.
2. Go south on lake shore drive.
3. I will visit new york to see the catskill mountains.
4. Ascension island is in the middle of the atlantic ocean.
5. An american scientist explored the jungles of venezuela.
6. The capital of zambia is lusaka.
7. Isn't acapulco warmer than mexico city?
8. The caspian sea is actually a lake.
9. Is his accent english or irish?

10. Heather strolled through rock creek park.

11. Last sunday a baptist minister gave the sermon.

12. The national aeronautics and space administration is located in houston.

13. On veteran's day, november 11, we honor soldiers who fought for this country.

14. Many european schools teach english.

15. On April 8, 1974, hank aaron hit his 715th home run.

16. Are you taking an algebra course or business math 300?

17. Last fall my sister and i had a party on halloween.

18. Patrick davis was recruited by georgetown university.

19. The only warship to survive the attack on pearl harbor in world war II was the *phoenix*.

20. The first roman gladiators fought in 264 b.c.

C. Capital Letters Find the words in the following sentences that should be capitalized. Write the words after the proper numbers, using the necessary capital letters.

1. "the catbird seat" was written by the author of "the secret life of walter mitty."

2. chuck read *people* magazine in the waiting room.

3. dad asked, "will you stop at the newsstand and get *the new york times*?"

4. "how would i know," asked willie, "when the movie was made?"

5. "the issue is settled," said kit. "our school play will be *the glass menagerie*."

6. my english class read "the invisible man."

7. dear dr. lucenti:

8. the irish national anthem is "a soldier's song."

9. II. popular songs
       a. humorous songs

10. For the program, ann recited the poem, "birches."

628

MIXED REVIEW

Capitalization

A. Using capitalization correctly Copy the following sen-tences. Use correct capitalization.

1. my friend mr. brown teaches english to vietnamese refugees.
2. from 27 b.c. to a.d. 14, emperor augustus ruled rome.
3. the feast of tabernacles is a jewish celebration that be-gan as a harvest festival.
4. "on monday," said dr. cova, "students in literature II will discuss the novel *the outsiders* by s. e. hinton."
5. "yes, sgt. walker is a veteran," said aunt julia. "she served in the korean war."
6. didn't you give your aunt a bible last christmas, dad?
7. the cawley computer center gave carver high school equipment for its computer class; however, the school still needs software.
8. do i board the ferry to liberty island at battery park?
9. the words on the statue of liberty were written by emma lazarus.
10. every winter, midwesterners want to travel to an island in the caribbean sea; in july, people in florida long to go north.

B. Using capitalization correctly in proofreading Proof-read the following letter. Rewrite it, using correct capitalization.

march 15, 1985

dear ms. harmon:

in february, the *evening star* ran an ad for your auto-wrecking business, compacted cars company. after reading the ad, i had an idea. i wonder if your company would donate any used inner tubes to camp lone pine. our campers could then go tubing on red mill river.

you may be asking yourself, "what is tubing?" let me explain that tubing is a simple water sport in which swimmers put on inner tubes and float down the river.

your generosity would make a better summer for the children at our camp. also, i would encourage their parents to take their old fords, chevrolets, and other cars to your company.

i could pick up the inner tubes on any tuesday after 1:00 p.m.

thank you for your consideration.

respectfully yours,
roger m. glass

629

These challenging and enjoyable activities allow the students to see how the concepts of grammar, usage, and mechanics may be applied in actual writing situations. Each exercise is designed to allow students practice in several of the skills they have acquired in this Section. The activities also provide opportunities for students to write creatively about a wide variety of interesting and unusual subjects.

USING MECHANICS IN WRITING
Capitalization

A. You have entered a nationwide competition. The rules of the competition are given below. Follow the rules as fully and creatively as you can. Capitalize your paragraph correctly.

Why should the next Olympic Games be held in your home town? Write a paragraph to explain what is attractive about the town. Refer to historical landmarks, bodies of water, landforms, and public areas. Make your paragraph an enthusiastic pitch for your section of the United States.

B. Think about a movie that you have recently seen. Write a review of the movie, giving its strong points and weak points. Be sure to mention the names of the lead actors and actresses. Also tell where the story takes place. If you can find a newspaper ad for the movie, include the director's name. If the director has done other well-known movies, include them in your review. Finally, mention a line or two of dialogue that made an impression on you. Capitalize all necessary words.

C. A few of the many different religions practiced today are Judaism, Christianity, Islam, Hinduism, Buddhism, and Baha'i. Choose a religion other than your own, and do some research on it. Write about the religion. Include the countries where it is most widely practiced, the name or names of its founder, a brief explanation of its teachings, the name of its holy book, and the special holidays that the believers celebrate. Be sure to capitalize all necessary words.

Punctuation

When you read, you probably do not think much about the punctuation used. However, if it were not there, you would be confused. You might not be sure, for example, where one sentence ends and another begins.

Punctuation marks are signals for a reader. They indicate pauses and show points of emphasis. If you want your readers to understand the exact meaning of what you write, give them the right signals by using punctuation marks correctly.

Section Objectives

1. To use end marks—periods, question marks, exclamation points —correctly

2. To use the comma correctly

3. To use the semicolon and the colon correctly

4. To use the hyphen correctly

5. To use the apostrophe correctly

6. To use quotation marks correctly

Preparing the Students

Tell students that good driving depends upon understanding and obeying road signs. Road signs tell the driver to stop, to go slowly, to be wary. Good written communication depends upon proper use and understanding of punctuation. Punctuation functions as "road signs" for the reader, telling him or her when to stop, pause, or be prepared for a quotation. Since a reader can't rely on your voice, intonation, or facial gestures, you must use punctuation properly to help convey your meaning fully.

Additional Resources

Diagnostic Test — page 9 in the test booklet

Mastery Test — pages 70–71 in the test booklet

Additional Exercises — pages 656–663 in the student text

Practice Book — pages 243–256

Duplicating Masters — pages 243–256

Special Populations — See special section at the back of this Teacher's Edition.

Objective

To use end marks—periods, question marks, exclamation points —correctly

Presenting the Lesson

1. Read "The Period" on pages 632–633. Go over rules for using the period. Study examples of the uses of the period. Be certain that students understand the meaning of *declarative sentence, imperative sentence, indirect question, abbreviation,* and *initials.*

2. Read pages 633–634 covering the use of the question mark and the exclamation point. Be certain that students understand the meaning of: *interrogative sentence, exclamatory sentence,* and *interjection.* Stress the difference between *direct questions* and *indirect questions.* Ask students for examples of each kind of question.

3. Assign and discuss Exercises A and B on page 634.

Individualizing the Lesson

Less-Advanced Students

Do Exercise A orally. Assign Exercise B.

Advanced Students

Have students write five original examples of declarative, interrogative, and exclamatory sentences. Tell them to end the sentences with the proper punctuation.

632

End Marks

The punctuation marks that show where sentences end are called **end marks.** They include **periods, question marks,** and **exclamation points.**

The Period

Use a period at the end of a declarative sentence.

A **declarative sentence** is a sentence that makes a statement. It is the kind of sentence you use when you want to tell something.

My brother plays the guitar.

Use a period at the end of an imperative sentence.

An **imperative sentence** is a sentence that requests or orders someone to do something.

Please close the door.

If the imperative sentence also expresses excitement or emotion, an exclamation point is used after it.

Watch out!

Use a period at the end of an indirect question.

An **indirect question** tells what someone asked. However, it does not give the exact words of the person who asked the question.

She asked us whether we liked strawberries.

Use a period after an abbreviation or after an initial.

An **abbreviation** is a shortened form of a word. An **initial** is a single letter that stands for a word.

Dr. Marla E. Corona   Trenton, N. J.

Rev. John L. Haeger, Jr.   2:30 P.M.

632

Periods are omitted in some abbreviations. If you are not sure whether or not to use periods, look up the abbreviation in your dictionary.

FM (*frequency modulation*)
UN (*United Nations*)
FBI (*Federal Bureau of Investigation*)

Use a period after each number or letter that shows a division of an outline or that precedes an item in a list.

An Outline	A List
I. Poets	1. eggs
A. American	2. milk
1. Robert Frost	3. butter

Use a period in numerals between dollars and cents and before a decimal.

$18.98   2.853

The Question Mark

Use a question mark at the end of an interrogative sentence.

An **interrogative sentence** is a sentence that asks a question.

Has anyone brought a flashlight?

The above sentence gives the exact words of the person who asked the question. It is called a **direct question.** A question mark is used only with a direct question.

Do not use a question mark with an indirect question. Instead use a period.

Kelly asked whether anyone had brought a flashlight.

The Exclamation Point

Use an exclamation point at the end of an exclamatory sentence.

How great that looks!

Use an exclamation point after an interjection or after any other exclamatory expression.

An **interjection** is a word or group of words used to express strong feeling. It may be a real word or simply a group of letters used to represent a sound. It is one of the eight parts of speech.

Hurrah! Wow! Ugh!

Exercise A Copy the following sentences, adding the necessary punctuation.

1. I was supposed to meet Tom at 10:30 AM.
2. Dr. James Coogan, Jr. is going to talk about lifesaving.
3. What is Dr Harrigan's phone number?
4. Where is Sgt Leslie's office located?
5. Help! I can't get this door open!
6. Where did I put my new sweater?
7. Wow! That was quite a football game!
8. Mary, look out!
9. Our art supplies will cost less than ten dollars, but they'll be more than $825.
10. My appointment with Dr. Wagner is at 11:15 AM.

Exercise B Follow the directions for Exercise A.

1. My parents were born in Cincinnati, Ohio.
2. Rev. James M. Butler, Jr. will be the guest speaker.
3. While in Washington, DC, where did you stay?
4. One mile is equal to 16 kilometers.
5. Luis asked if he could help me with my homework.
6. I have two broadcast bands on my radio: AM and FM.
7. UNICEF is the children's organization of the UN.
8. Dr. Elizabeth McMinn is our school principal.
9. Please send your requests to Franklin's, Ltd, P.O. Box 552, New York, NY.
10. Will you mail these coupons to the Clark Company, Inc; 301 E. Walton Place, Miami, Florida 33152?

The Comma

Commas are used to separate words that do not belong together. In speaking, you can keep words apart by pausing. In writing, you must use commas.

Commas in a Series

Use a comma after every item in a series except the last.

The items in a series may be single words, or phrases, or clauses.

Words: The flag is red, white, and blue.

Phrases: The dog ran out the door, down the steps, and across the lawn.

Clauses: How kangaroos run, what jumps they can take, and how they live are explained in this book.

Use commas after the adverbs *first, second, third,* and so on, when these adverbs introduce a series of parallel items.

There are three ways to get good marks: first, pay attention; second, take notes; third, study.

When two or more adjectives come before a noun, use a comma after each adjective except the last one.

They drove away in a bright, shiny, expensive car.

Sometimes two adjectives are used together to express a single idea made up of two closely related thoughts. Adjectives so used are not usually separated by a comma.

Kim's dog is the small brown one.
Many young children go to that large elementary school.

635

Objective

To use the comma correctly

Presenting the Lesson

1. Read page 635. Go over the rules and examples showing commas used in series.

2. Assign and discuss Exercises A and B on pages 636–637.

3. Read page 637. Be certain that students understand what is meant by *introductory words, phrases, clauses,* and *interrupters.*

4. Assign and discuss Exercises A and B on pages 637–638.

5. Read pages 638–640. Be certain that students understand the meaning of a *noun of direct address,* an *appositive,* a *direct quotation,* and a *divided quotation.* Go over rules for punctuating divided quotations carefully. Review the compound sentence and the use of a comma before the conjunction. Stress that a comma does not precede the conjunction in compound sentence parts.

6. Assign and discuss Exercises A and B on pages 640–641.

7. Read pages 641–642.

8. Assign and discuss Exercises A and B on pages 642–643.

Individualizing the Lesson

Less-Advanced Students

1. Read the first half of the Exercises aloud. Have students indicate where they think commas should go. Then have them complete the Exercises independently.

2. Have students explain why each comma is placed where it is.

635

3. Have the students find an example of each use of commas discussed in this Section in a magazine or newspaper article.

Advanced Students

Have students write two sentences applying each use of commas discussed in this Section.

Optional Practice

Present the following sentences on the board or on a worksheet. Number the commas as indicated. Have students number their papers from 1–10 and write an explanation for the use of each comma.

1. I don't like disco music,[1] but I like rock,[2] jazz,[3] and classical music.

2. Yes,[4] Kathy,[5] the inscription read June 16,[6] 1985,[7] the day of her graduation.

3. "The problems of the past decade,[8] I predict,[9] will be solved by our youth,[10]" said the senator.

Extending the Lesson

Have students write and punctuate sentences which do the following: Answers will vary.

1. Two sentences describing the contents of your purse or pocket and your locker

2. Two sentence giving the birthdates of members of your family and important dates in your life

3. Two quotations spoken by a politician or movie star

4. Two addresses of out-of-town friends or relatives

5. Two compound sentences telling what you do in your spare time

Exercise A Number your paper from 1 to 10. Copy the following sentences and add commas where necessary.

1. Red, white, and blue bunting decorated the speaker's stand.

2. We went to the store and bought peanuts, potato chips, pretzels, and root beer.

3. A northerly wind swept the wet, thick snow against the front door.

4. That green TR7 has worn tires, brakes, and shocks.

5. The race car skidded, did a complete turnaround, and blew out its right front tire.

6. At the movies, I like fresh, hot, buttery popcorn.

7. Strong, gusty winds blew across the lake.

8. My sister can play the guitar, the banjo, and the mandolin.

9. In order to finish the scenery, do the following: first, nail the supports together; second, paint the backdrop; and third, put away all unnecessary tools and paint.

10. Sue finished her homework, made a telephone call, and went to bed.

Exercise B Follow the directions for Exercise A.

1. James, Joan, and Greg helped design the posters.

2. We need crepe paper, balloons, and tape to decorate the gym.

3. A small rabbit scooted across our doorstep, through the evergreens, and under our back porch.

4. Wool, silk, and cotton are natural cloths.

5. Bowling, skating, and running are my favorite activities.

6. A long, sleek, black limousine pulled up in front of the bank.

7. The committee discussed, debated, and accepted the proposal.

8. The baffled, worn-out mail carrier slumped on our porch swing.
9. The speaker stated the hard, clear facts.
10. The salesclerk pulled a green scarf off the shelf, spread it flat on the counter, and told us the price.

Commas After Introductory Words, Phrases, or Clauses

Use a comma to separate an introductory word, phrase, or clause from the rest of the sentence.

Yes, I will go.

After circling twice, the airplane landed.

Although Dick needed help, he said nothing.

The comma may be omitted if there would be little pause in speaking.

At first I didn't know what to do.

Commas with Interrupters

Use commas to set off words or groups of words that interrupt the flow of thought in a sentence.

Anne, to tell the truth, was quite happy.

The report, moreover, is altogether wrong.

Some other examples of interrupters are *however, I suppose, I think,* and *nevertheless.*

Exercise A Number your paper from 1 to 10. Copy the following sentences and add commas where necessary.

1. Yes, I have finished the dishes.
2. The exam, however, will be given as scheduled.

637

3. Although the game was postponed until Friday, we had practice every morning.
4. No, I don't think the library is open on Sundays.
5. After circling the airport for an hour, we finally landed.
6. Ms. Cassini, to tell the truth, was quite pleased with our panel discussion.
7. Since the Hawks lost their last ten games, they will not be in the play-offs.
8. The results of the student survey, however, will not be revealed until next week.
9. No, the mail has not been delivered.
10. Even though we arrived early, we still didn't get good seats for the basketball game.

Exercise B Follow the directions for Exercise A.

1. Yes, the intramural track meet is tomorrow.
2. Since Mardi Gras is such a celebrated occasion in New Orleans, most schools there take a holiday.
3. The game, consequently, was postponed.
4. The latest weather report, however, has predicted rain.
5. Although the heavy snow tied up the morning traffic, most companies and businesses were open as usual.
6. After we went on the hayride, we had a barbecue.
7. Yes, the garage has been cleaned out.
8. It is doubtful, however, that we will change our plans.
9. No, the garage sale isn't until next week.
10. If you look carefully at these old advertisements, you will see how different clothes and housing used to be.

Commas with Nouns of Direct Address

Use commas to set off nouns of direct address.

The name of someone directly spoken to is a **noun of direct address**.

638

If you look, Peggy, you will see the book I mean.

Sarah, you won the election!

I'll be right back, Cathy.

Commas with Appositives

Use commas to set off most appositives.

An **appositive** is a word or group of words used directly after another word to explain it.

The speaker, a famous explorer, told about New Guinea.

An appositive phrase may have a prepositional phrase within it.

The leader, the person *on horseback*, moved away.

Nouns used as appositives are called **nouns in apposition.** When the noun in apposition is a short name, it is not usually set off by commas.

This is my friend Rhoda.

Commas with Quotations

Use commas to set off the explaining words of a direct quotation.

The explaining words used in giving a direct quotation are such brief statements as *Tina said, Christie answered,* or *Bill asked.*

The pilot said, "We will land in a few minutes."

In the sentence above, the explaining words come *before* the quotation. A comma is then placed after the last explaining word.

Now look at this quotation:

"We will land in a few minutes," the pilot said.

639

If the explaining words come *after* the quotation, as in the example above, place a comma within the quotation marks after the last word of the quotation.

Sometimes a quotation is separated into two parts by the explaining words. This is often done to add variety to the sentence construction. Here is an example:

"We will land," the pilot said, "in a few minutes."

The sentence above is an example of a *divided quotation*. A comma is used after the last word of the first part. Another comma is used after the last explaining word.

Do not confuse direct and indirect quotations. Indirect quotations are *not* set off from the rest of the sentence by commas.

The pilot said that the plane would land in a few minutes.

Commas in Compound Sentences

Use a comma before the conjunction that joins the two main clauses in a compound sentence.

Kimberly seemed to agree, and no one else objected.

Sometimes very short compound sentences have clauses joined by *and*. It is not necessary to use a comma if there is no change in the thought. Always use a comma before *or* or *but*. These words do change the direction of the thought.

Pete finally arrived *and* we started off.

Pete finally arrived, *but* it was too late to go anywhere.

Do not use a comma before the *and* that joins a compound subject or a compound predicate.

Sally turned on the radio *and* sat down to read a magazine.

Exercise A Copy these sentences. Add commas where needed.

1. Ms. Leoni, our new science teacher, was born in Italy.
2. Sir Georg Solti, the famous conductor, directs the Chicago Symphony Orchestra.

3. I read *Roots*, but I preferred the television series.
4. I enjoy reading science fiction novels, but I also enjoy reading mysteries.
5. She ran down the stairs and raced down the sidewalk. c
6. "Cheerleading tryouts will be held tonight," began the announcement, "and all students are invited to take part."
7. The team captain, the player in the blue jersey, is a good student.
8. When you are finished, Kurt, will you help with this project?
9. Maria had supper and then went to play rehearsal. c
10. John Hancock, one of the signers of the Declaration of Independence, was from Massachusetts.

Exercise B   Follow the directions for Exercise A.

1. Andrés Segovia, the classical guitarist, will play at Orchestra Hall in May.
2. Will you come with me, or would you rather stay here?
3. I will wash the car, but I don't have time to wax it.
4. I asked Ms. Wright, our science teacher, about lasers.
5. The governor's aide, Deputy Chief Roseanna Ruhl, visited Latin America.
6. Linda showed me her present, a cassette tape recorder.
7. Ms. Watkins, our P.E. teacher, was an Olympic gymnast.
8. We saw the end of the special, and then we watched the *ABC Movie of the Week*.
9. "Please take the dog for a walk," said Dad.
10. Pam, this is my brother Paul.

Commas in Dates

In dates, use a comma between the day of the month and the year.

July 4, 1776   December 7, 1787

641

In a sentence, a comma follows the year.

The postmark read September 10, 1985, Chicago, Illinois.

Commas in Locations and Addresses

Use a comma between the name of a city or town and the name of its state or country.

Tucson, Arizona

Munich, Germany

In writing an address as part of a sentence, use a comma after each item.

Forward our mail to 651 Sentinel Drive, Milwaukee, Wisconsin 53203, where we will be moving next month.

Note that you do *not* place a comma between the state and the ZIP code.

Commas in Letter Parts

Use a comma after the salutation of a friendly letter and after the complimentary close of a friendly letter or a business letter.

Dear Tim,   Yours sincerely,

Commas To Prevent Misreading

When no specific rule applies, but there is danger of misreading, use a comma.

Who she is, is a mystery.   Inside, it was warm and cozy.

Exercise A Copy the following sentences. Add commas where necessary.

1. Whatever happens, happens.
2. Whatever you do, do it well.

3. The stock market crash on October 29, 1929, began the Great Depression.

4. The first state, Delaware, entered the Union on December 7, 1787.

5. The bombing of Pearl Harbor on December 7, 1941, marked the beginning of World War II for the United States.

6. On August 14, 1945, Japan surrendered to the Allies.

7. The first Transcontinental Railroad was completed on May 10, 1869, in Promontory, Utah.

8. In 1874, Joseph Glidden invented barbed wire.

9. Send your requests to Mr. R. Joseph Laya, 180 North Capitol Avenue, Denver, Colorado 80202.

10. George Washington was inaugurated in New York City on April 30, 1789, at Federal Hall.

Exercise B   Follow the directions for Exercise A.

1. My sister was born in Tokyo, Japan, on January 1, 1965, and I was born in Frankfurt, Germany, on January 1, 1968.

2. On August 26, 1920, the amendment that gave women the right to vote was adopted.

3. John H. Glenn, Jr. became the first American to orbit the earth on February 20, 1962, aboard the *Friendship 7*.

4. We ordered our uniforms from the J. C. Wood Company, P. O. Box 5835, Richmond, Virginia 23220.

5. Whatever it is, it is a strange-looking creature.

6. The flight will visit Helsinki, Finland and Stockholm, Sweden.

7. Because my parents work for the government, I have lived in Fairbanks, Alaska, and Madrid, Spain.

8. The Lewis and Clark expedition began on May 14, 1804, in St. Louis, Missouri, and returned there on September 23, 1806.

9. The Great Chicago Fire of 1871 supposedly started in Mrs. O'Leary's barn at 558 DeKoven Street, Chicago, Illinois.

10. Dear Jill,

Would you please send me the Harrisons' new address? I'd appreciate it.

Your friend,
Tom

The Semicolon

Use a semicolon to join the parts of a compound sentence when no coordinating conjunction is used.

Dan has finished his homework; Darcy has not begun hers.

When there are commas in the first part of a compound sentence, use a semicolon to separate the main clauses.

McCurdy of Illinois made the most spectacular shot of the game, a toss from mid-court; and Indiana, which had been favored to win, went down to defeat.

When there are commas within items in a series, use semicolons to separate the items.

Hartford, New Haven, and Norwich, Connecticut; Springfield, Lowell, and Worcester, Massachusetts; and Pine Bridge, Mt. Kisco, and Chappaqua, New York, have all tried this experiment.

Use a semicolon before a word that joins the main clauses of a compound sentence.

Such joining words are *therefore, however, hence, so, then, moreover, besides, nevertheless, yet,* and *consequently.*

It was a sunny day; however, it was quite cool.

Objective

To use the semicolon and the colon correctly

Presenting the Lesson

1. Read page 644. Go over rules and examples of the use of semicolons.

2. Read page 645. Go over rules and examples of the use of colons.

3. Assign and discuss Exercises A and B on pages 645–646.

Individualizing the Lesson

Less-Advanced Students

1. Have students identify the compound sentences in the Exercises before adding punctuation.

2. Tell students to identify which rule applies in each instance where punctuation is added to a sentence.

Advanced Students

Have students write two sentences for each semicolon and colon rule.

The Colon

Use a colon after the greeting in a business letter.

Dear Sir or Madam: Ladies and Gentlemen:

Use a colon between numbers indicating hours and minutes.

10:00 P.M.   6:30 A.M.

Use a colon to introduce a list of items.

If you are trying out for the team, bring the following things: a pair of gym shoes, your P.E. uniform, and your consent form.

Do not use a colon if the list immediately follows a verb or a preposition.

If you are trying out for the team, bring a pair of gym shoes, your P.E. uniform, and your consent form.

Exercise A Copy the word before and after each missing punctuation mark and add the correct punctuation mark.

1. Allen, fold the laundry;Jenny, clean up the yard;Joan, take the dog for a walk.
2. New animals in the collection include a cheetah, an okapi, and a harpy eagle from Africa;a tiger, two peacocks, and a rhinoceros from India;a snow leopard from Tibet;and two caribou, a Kodiak bear, and an arctic fox from Alaska.
3. San Francisco, Los Angeles, and Oakland, California; Dallas and Houston, Texas;and New York and Buffalo, New York, have professional teams.
4. It was a clear day;moreover, it was perfect for swimming.
5. Jon prepared dinner;Brian set the table.

645

Optional Practice

Have students insert semicolons, colons, and commas where needed in the following sentences. Students should be prepared to explain why each added mark is required.

1. I found the first movie fascinating; the second one I didn't care for.
2. The box contained the following items/: gauze, iodine, adhesive tape, splints, and elastic bandages.
3. Strep bacteria are very contagious; moreover, they can lead to heart damage.
4. Dear Sirs:I will arrive in your city at 10:00 A.M. Sunday;however, I will be leaving at 2:00 P.M.
5. Kate's travels took her to Denver, Colorado Springs, and Aspen, Colorado;Albuquerque and Sante Fe, New Mexico;and Flagstaff,Phoenix , and Tucson,Arizona.

Extending the Lesson

Have students start a bulletin board with published examples of all forms of punctuation.

6. Grinning broadly, Lee crossed the finish line ten feet ahead of the others;however, the grin faded when the judges told her she had been disqualified.

7. Bring three things to class tomorrow:your text, paper, and a blue or black pen.

8. You will need to meet me between 8:30 and 8:45 A.M.

9. Dear Madam:
   This letter will confirm your reservation.

10. Yesterday was a cold autumn day;however, it was quite sunny.

Exercise B   Follow the directions for Exercise A.

1. Mother's plane arrives at 6:55 P.M.; Dad's will land at 7:15 P.M.

2. Jim studied hard for the test; yet he thought it was one of the hardest ones he'd ever taken.

3. I know that there is not much time; nevertheless, the work must be finished by 5:30 P.M.

4. Please stop at the store and bring these items home:a gallon of milk, a can of tomatoes, and a box of crackers.

5. Tracy was reading a mystery;Sandy was talking on the phone.

6. The Pep Club will handle ticket sales; the cheerleaders will help with the ushering.

7. Our bus leaves at 7:15 A.M.; my sister's bus doesn't leave until 8:30 A.M.

8. The snow was blinding;however, the school bus arrived on time at 8:15 A.M.

9. The running back made a spectacular drive to the goal, a 47-yard run; and the defense, which couldn't get organized, was stunned.

10. Bring these items to sewing class on Monday: tracing paper, your pattern, thread, and pins.

The Hyphen

Use a hyphen if a syllable of a word must be carried over from one line to the next.

In the library you will find several authorita-
tive books on solar energy.

Only words of two or more syllables can be divided at the end of a line. Never divide words of one syllable, such as *worse*.

A single letter must not be left at the end of a line. For example, this division would be wrong: *a-waken*. A single letter must not appear at the beginning of a line, either. It would be wrong to divide *dictionary* like this: *dictionar-y*.

Use a hyphen in compound numbers from twenty-one through ninety-nine.

twenty-three cents   forty-two students

Use a hyphen in fractions.

We won a two-thirds majority.

Use a hyphen or hyphens in such compound nouns as *great-aunt* and *commander-in-chief*.

A Portuguese man-of-war stung the swimmer.

Use a hyphen or hyphens between words that make up a compound adjective used before a noun.

It was a school-sponsored dance.
But: The dance was school sponsored.

When compound adjectives are used after the noun, they usually are not hyphenated. When unsure, use a dictionary.

Exercise   Add the necessary hyphens to the following sentences.

1. Thirty-two students were chosen to go to the contest.
2. Chester A. Arthur was the twenty-first President.

647

The Hyphen

Objective

To use the hyphen correctly

Presenting the Lesson

1. Read page 647. Go over rules and examples of the use of the hyphen. Stress that the dictionary should be consulted to check the proper syllable divisions of words. Be certain that students understand the meaning of compound nouns and compound adjectives. Again, students should check the dictionary for the correct use of hyphens in compound nouns and adjectives.

2. Assign and discuss the Exercise on pages 647–648.

Individualizing the Lesson

Less-Advanced Students

Have students identify the rule that covers the use of the hyphen in each sentence in the Exercise.

Advanced Students

1. Have students write three sentences demonstrating the use of each hyphen rule.

2. Show students how to locate and interpret syllabification in a dictionary entry.

Optional Practice

Have students insert hyphens correctly in the following sentences. Students should consult the dictionary as necessary.

1. Bus fare is ninety-five cents.
2. Gloria won three-fourths of the games she played.
3. Two thirds of the voters were under forty-five years of age.

647

4. The ready-to-use frosting isn't nearly as creamy as the home-made kind.
5. Our typing teacher told us to divide the word *instructions* in this way: in-struc-tions.

Extending the Lesson

Have the students find ten new words from their science or math books, then have them write each word and its definition on their paper. Tell them to use hyphens to break the word into its syllables. Then have them use each word in a sentence.

The Apostrophe

Objective

To use the apostrophe correctly

Presenting the Lesson

1. Read pages 648–649. Go over rules and examples of the use of the apostrophe to form possessives. Study examples of contractions formed with the use of an apostrophe. Go over rules and examples for using an apostrophe to show omission of numbers in a date and to form plurals of letters, figures, and words used as words.

2. Assign and discuss Exercises A and B on pages 649–650.

Individualizing the Lesson

Less-Advanced Students

1. Have students identify the words that make up each contraction in the Exercises.

3. We had several out-of-town guests this weekend.
4. One-sixth of the students voted for Pam.
5. Ninety-three students in all voted in the election.
6. Maurita won the election by a three-fourths majority.
7. You must write out the amount of the check: one hundred twenty-three dollars and fifty-six cents.
8. My grandmother celebrated her ninety-fifth birthday.
9. The postage for this package is sixty-two cents.
10. About sixty-eight percent of the residents voted in the special election.
11. When were your great-grandparents born?
12. The woman had a well-to-do look about her.
13. We received the store's new, up-to-date catalog.
14. In ten years I will be twenty-six years old.
15. The President of the United States is the Commander-in-Chief of the Armed Forces.

The Apostrophe

One of the most frequent uses of the apostrophe is its use in forming the possessive of nouns. Before you form the possessive of a noun, be sure to notice whether the noun is singular or plural.

To form the possessive of a singular noun, add an apostrophe and an s.

girl + **'s** = girl's   man + **'s** = man's
boy + **'s** = boy's   Ross + **'s** = Ross's

To form the possessive of a plural noun that does not end in s, add an apostrophe and an s.

men + **'s** = men's   children + **'s** = children's

To form the possessive of a plural noun that ends in s, add only an apostrophe.

drivers + **'** = drivers'   pilots + **'** = pilots'

Use an apostrophe and an s to form the possessive of indefinite pronouns.

someone + **'s** = someone's   anybody + **'s** = anybody's

Never use an apostrophe in a personal pronoun.

ours   yours   its   hers   theirs

The game reached *its* high point in the second quarter.

Use an apostrophe in a contraction.

In a contraction, the apostrophe simply replaces one or more omitted letters.

he's = he is	aren't = are not	I'm = I am
it's = it is	isn't = is not	I've = I have
won't = will not	don't = do not	we've = we have

Use an apostrophe to show the omission of numbers in a date.

the class of '84 (*the class of 1984*)

Use an apostrophe and s to form the plurals of letters, figures, and words used as words.

two *m*'s   four *6*'s   *and*'s and *but*'s

Exercise A Copy these sentences, inserting apostrophes where they are needed.

1. All of the teachers' meetings are held in the library.
2. Babe Didrikson Zaharias's autobiography reveals her intense love for athletics and her zest for life.
3. Her writings and illustrations are well known in childrens' literature.
4. Jim's father drove us to their family's cottage in Iowa.
5. Wasnt that Ross's original plan?
6. Soichiro Honda's company has been producing motorcycles and cars in Japan since the 1940's.
7. Ive always liked the silent movies of Mary Pickford and Charlie Chaplin.

8. We've heard that there won't be an assembly until next week.
9. Beatrix Potter's most famous work is *Peter Rabbit*.
10. *The Miracle Worker* is a play about Helen Keller's childhood and Annie Sullivan's efforts to help the blind and deaf Helen.

Exercise B   Follow the directions for Exercise A.

1. Someone's moped is parked in the Burton's driveway.
2. Isn't the girls' gymnastics meet on Saturday?
3. Although she was the first woman to go into space, Valentina Tereshkova's name is not well known.
4. Wasn't that Rosemary's bike in the alley?
5. The *I*'s and the *7*'s in the ledger are difficult to tell apart.
6. The graduating classes of '84 and '85 are buying a new digital scoreboard for the school.
7. Clara Barton's dedication in a volunteer nurse corps led to her founding of the American Red Cross.
8. S. E. Hinton's novel, *That Was Then, This Is Now*, is one of the best books we've read this year.
9. Jenny's sister and Paula's brother are both interns at St. Mary's Hospital.
10. Nurses' training programs are thorough and demanding.

Quotation Marks

Quotation marks tell your reader that you are quoting directly the exact spoken or written words of another person.

Use quotation marks at the beginning and at the end of a direct quotation.

Sarah said, "My feelings were hurt."

Quotation marks are *not* used with indirect quotations:

Sarah said *that her feelings were hurt*.

Explaining words at the beginning of a sentence are followed by a comma *before* the quotation marks. At the end of a sentence a period is placed *inside* the quotation marks.

My sister announced, "There is someone to see you."

A quotation that begins the sentence is followed by a comma *inside* the quotation marks. A period follows the explaining words at the end of a sentence.

"There is someone to see you," my sister announced.

Divided Quotations Sometimes the explaining words break into the middle of a direct quotation. In that case, each part of the quotation is enclosed in quotation marks.

"Do you think," Don asked, "that you will like alfalfa sprouts?"

The second part of a divided quotation starts with a small letter, as in the last example. The only exceptions are the beginning of a new sentence and proper nouns or adjectives.

"We got drenched," said Sheila. "Our car roof leaks."

The first part of a divided quotation is followed by a comma *inside* the quotation marks.

"I want to see you," said Ms. Lazar, "before you leave."

The punctuation after the explanatory words in a divided quotation depends on the second part of the quotation. If the second part does not start a new sentence, a comma is used. If the second part does start a new sentence, a period is used.

"When you arrive," said Ben, "beep your horn."

"I can't go," said Janet. "I have to study."

651

placement of commas, periods, and capitals, as well as quotation marks.

2. Do the Exercise on page 652 as a class activity. Have quotations written on the board and discuss correct punctuation for each.

3. Read page 652. Study rules and examples of placement of question marks and exclamation points in quotations.

4. Assign and discuss Exercise A on page 653.

5. Assign Exercise B on page 653. Have students volunteer to put their quotations on the board. Try to have several versions for each quote written on the board.

6. Assign and discuss Exercise C on pages 653–654.

7. Read page 654. Study rules and examples of other uses of quotation marks.

8. Assign and discuss Exercises A and B on page 655.

Individualizing the Lesson

Less-Advanced Students

1. Read Exercises A and C, pages 653–654, aloud before students try to punctuate them. Exaggerate the inflections and pauses to help the students recognize the quoted parts in each sentence.

2. Have students write ten sentences that include titles of songs, books, movies, poems, etc. Tell students to underline and use quotation marks where necessary.

Advanced Students

1. Have students write five indirect quotations, then exchange papers and change sentences into direct quotations.

652

2. Have students write original titles for each category listed on page 654. Tell them their titles may be humorous.

Optional Practice

Have students write a brief dialogue about any topic they choose. Remind them to use proper punctuation and to put the punctuation in its correct place.

Extending the Lesson

Have students write quotations that do the following: Answers will vary.

1. Two quotations that ask a friend if he or she likes a particular song or television program

2. Two quotations that ask directions to a local restaurant

3. Two or more quotations of a dialogue between parents who are upset by something their teen-ager did

Exercise   Write each of the following sentences three ways as a direct quotation. Answers will vary.

Example: Be sure that you're on time.
   a. "Be sure that you're on time," he said.
   b. He said, "Be sure that you're on time."
   c. "Be sure," he said, "that you're on time."

1. Watch out for broken glass.
2. I'm sure that I am right.
3. On Monday summer vacation begins.
4. Did you know that a jaeger is a bird?

Place question marks and exclamation points inside quotation marks if they belong to the quotation itself.

Dad asked, "Is Cindy working in the garage?"

"Look out!" Terry shouted.

Place question marks and exclamation points outside quotation marks if they do not belong to the quotation.

Did she say, "I'll be home at midnight"?
The man said, "You've won the contest"!

Occasionally, two or more sentences of a single speaker are quoted. Notice the punctuation of such a quotation:

"Is the council going to meet tomorrow?" asked Carly. "I wasn't sure whether we had decided to meet tomorrow or the next day. We have important things to discuss."

Dialogue, which is conversation between two or more people, is punctuated differently. Begin a new paragraph every time the speaker changes.

"Do you like horror movies?" asked Clyde.
"I don't," said Ted. "Real life can be horrifying enough. I don't understand why anyone needs any more fright."
"Well," said JoAnn, "maybe a few fake scares can help prepare you for real ones."

Exercise A Copy the following sentences. Punctuate them correctly. If a sentence is correct, write *Correct*.

1. Did the teacher say, "We'll meet in the gym"?
2. The speaker said that inflation must be stopped.
3. Nicole said that I deserve better treatment.
4. "Have the committee members arrived yet?" asked Marka.
5. "Would you mind," asked Doug, "if I borrowed your jacket?"
6. "Jeff, have you see that movie?" asked Debbie.
7. "The best part," she added, "is the ending."
8. "That's the game!" yelled the announcer. "The Yankees have won!"
9. The receptionist asked us what we wanted.
10. "I never heard of such a thing," said my mother quietly. "Are you sure that is what he said?"

Exercise B Write each of the following sentences as a direct quotation. In some examples, put the quotation first. In others, put the quotation last. Also, for variety, divide some quotations.

Sentences will vary.

1. Watch me while I hop this fence.
2. I will drive you all the way home.
3. Are you curious about your new teacher?
4. Every day I check the mail.
5. I like that shirt, but I can't afford it.
6. Behind every good athlete is a lot of training.
7. Next week I will turn sixteen.
8. When did you begin studying Spanish?
9. You can do it!
10. Will you join us for lunch?

Exercise C: Writing Rewrite the following conversation. Make correct paragraph divisions, and use the right punctuation.

"What is your biggest fault?" Cecily asked, hoping to start a good discussion. "I don't have any faults," joked Brian.

"Come on, everybody," Karen said. "Answer her question."

Steve thought a minute and finally said, "I'm too quick-tempered. I get angry much too easily." "My biggest fault," Gloria said, "is that I'm selfish and don't consider other people enough." Quietly, Chris added, "My big fault is that I'm terribly lazy." "Yes," Brian said with a big grin, "I agree totally with what all of you have said." "And your main fault," Cecily said, "is that you're much too kind."

Using Quotation Marks for Titles

Use quotation marks to enclose the titles of magazine articles, chapters, titles of short stories, essays, or single poems, songs and short pieces of music.

Chapter:	Chapter 3, "Americans in London"
Magazine article:	"Images of Youth Past"
Short story:	"The Lottery"
Essay:	"My First Article"
Poem:	"The Raven"
Song:	"The Star-Spangled Banner"

Underline the titles of books, newspapers, magazines, plays, television programs, movies, works of art, and long musical compositions.

In writing or typewriting, these titles are underlined, like this: The Right Stuff.

In print, these titles appear in italics instead of being underlined.

Book:	*Native Son*
Newspaper:	*Des Moines Register*
Magazine:	*Time*
Play:	*You Can't Take It With You*
Television program:	*Good Morning America*
Movie:	*It's a Mad, Mad, Mad, Mad World*
Work of art:	Rembrandt's *The Night Watch*
Long musical composition:	*Nutcracker Suite*

Exercise A Copy the following sentences, adding quotation marks around titles or underlining titles where necessary.

1. The television program <u>Hill Street Blues</u> deals with life in an urban police precinct.
2. Two of James Thurber's stories are "The Very Proper Gander" and "The Shrike and the Chipmunks."
3. Read the first chapter, "Discovery in the New World."
4. I liked the story "The Monkey's Paw."
5. For my poetry assignment, I read "Ex-Basketball Player."
6. The band played music from <u>Camelot</u> and the theme from <u>Chariots of Fire</u>.
7. Charlie Chaplin's <u>The Gold Rush</u> and Harold Lloyd's <u>Safety Last</u> are two well-known silent films.
8. Did you see the movie?
9. Read Chapter 2, "How We Came to the River."
10. This is Judy Bass's painting <u>Jump out of Darkness</u>.

Exercise B Follow the directions for Exercise A.

1. "Old Man River" is a song from the musical <u>Showboat</u>.
2. Last week's editorial was entitled "The Mess in City Government—What Are *You* Doing about It?"
3. We read the novel <u>The Call of the Wild</u> and the short story "Brown Wolf" by Jack London.
4. "Adjö Means Good-Bye" by Carrie A. Young is a story of friendship.
5. My essay entitled "Youth Today" won an honorable mention in the poetry and prose contest.
6. <u>Gandhi</u> won the Oscar for the best picture in 1982.
7. "God Save the Queen" and "America" have the same melody.
8. Jack's favorite program is <u>Sixty Minutes</u>.
9. Barry Manilow recorded such songs as "I Write the Songs" and "Dancin' in the Streets."
10. My favorite poem is "Birches" by Robert Frost.

Additional Exercises

These Additional Exercises may be used for additional practice of the concepts presented in this Section. Each exercise focuses on a single concept, and should be used after the page number indicated in parentheses.

Review

If you have not assigned these Additional Exercises before this time, you can also use them as an excellent Section Review.

ADDITIONAL EXERCISES

Punctuation

A. End Marks Copy these sentences, adding the necessary punctuation.

1. Make my appointment with Dr. Stern at 3:00 PM.
2. How right you are!
3. When was Justice Sandra D. O'Connor appointed to the US Supreme Court?
4. Ty asked if the school was named after St. Francis of Assisi.
5. Wow! That's Gary Coleman, isn't it?
6. The album cost $898; so I gave the clerk a ten-dollar bill.
7. Mt. Vesuvius erupted and buried Pompeii in AD 79.
8. I. Modern American heroes
   A. Dr. Martin Luther King, Jr.
9. Is that an FM radio?
10. I wonder if I can wake up at 6 AM.?

B. Commas Copy the following sentences. Add commas where necessary.

1. Lily Tomlin, Carol Burnett, and Gilda Radner are comedians.
2. The pet store sold kittens, rabbits, hamsters, and mice.
3. Jill rolled the car window down, stuck her head out, and asked for directions.
4. Ed checked the hens' nests for eggs, picked some berries, and made breakfast.
5. Fran called, Joan stopped by, and Terri is here now.
6. First, she learned to operate the telegraph; second, she memorized the secret code; third, she parachuted behind enemy lines.

7. Soft, sweet breezes were blowing across the meadow.

8. His face had a hard, suspicious, and unpleasant look.

9. Kay tapped her fingers on the desk, frowned, and then laughed.

10. The long, brutal winter hurt farmers, ranchers, truckers, and builders.

C. Commas
Copy the following sentences. Add commas where necessary.

1. In addition, you have a terrific sense of humor.

2. Delia, of course, will take the photographs.

3. No, there is no mail for you.

4. After she had dug for half an hour, Nina was tired.

5. Mac, I suppose, is practicing his yoga.

6. When Sara pays attention, she remembers what she hears.

7. The ham in the refrigerator, however, is for the picnic.

8. During the six-month training period, the workers get paid less.

9. Consequently, Todd spent the night on the front porch.

10. Yes, if you see Suzanne, invite her to the party.

D. Commas
Copy the following sentences. Add commas where necessary.

1. Did you meet Carmella Rubens, our new coach?

2. "Small incidents cause big conflicts, and the result is sometimes war," our history teacher said.

3. Rachel, did you say that you had to leave early?

4. The speaker, a fire inspector, talked about arson.

5. Tim said, "My friend Ty wrote my campaign speech."

6. Nobody had dressed warmly, and the weather turned chilly.

7. "It's time," said Sloan, "to bail out."

8. The car, a rusty old Chevy, had sat in the lot for weeks.
9. Your backhand needs some work, but your serve is excellent, Michelle.
10. The table, a rare antique, was very fragile.

E. Commas Copy the following sentences. Add commas wherever necessary. If no commas are necessary, write *Correct*.

1. On Monday, April 15, 1912, the *Titanic* sank.
2. Visit the auto plants in Detroit, Michigan.
3. My new address, one which is easy to remember, is 123 Fourth Street, Cleveland, Ohio.
4. Write to the National Baseball Hall of Fame, Main Street, Cooperstown, New York 13326, for the information.
5. Above, the stars twinkled.
6. The conference was held in Cancun, Mexico, in October 1981.
7. Beyond, Steve could see the ocean.
8. Dear Julia,
   We'll see you in Portland, Oregon, on June 14.
   Affectionately,
   Lorene
9. Aretha Franklin was born on March 25, 1942, in Memphis, Tennessee.
10. The soldiers who remained, remained until the end.

F. Semicolons and Colons Copy the word before and after each missing punctuation mark and add the correct punctuation mark.

1. TV, radio, newspapers, and magazines reach the masses of people; therefore, they are called mass media.
2. The fire destroyed the dining room, living room, and bedroom; but it appears to have started in the kitchen.

3. The wrestling squad works out from 3:30 until 5:00 P.M. each day.

4. The following tools are used in carpentry: saws, hammers, drills, planes, and levels.

5. Dear Madam:
   The item that you ordered is not in stock; however, we expect a new shipment by the end of this month.

6. Rae opened the package and found a silk blouse, adorned with tiny bells, from Calcutta, India; long, delicate earrings from Mexico; and a ring from Athens, Greece.

7. Al followed the diet faithfully; he lost no weight, though.

8. I took the 6:30 A.M. bus, so I arrived before I was expected.

9. Here are some energy-saving substitutes: use a towel instead of hair dryer; use warm water instead of hot; use a forty-watt bulb instead of a sixty-watt bulb.

10. Some of the tallest players in professional basketball are Abdul-Jabbar, who plays for the Lakers; Parrish, a Celtics player; Caldwell Jones, one of the Philadelphia '76ers; and Donaldson of the Supersonics.

G. Hyphens Copy the following sentences. Add hyphens wherever necessary.

1. My great-grandfather gave a party when he turned ninety-two.

2. A hard-working crew finished the new road in a week.

3. A baton-twirling majorette led the parade.

4. Isn't the speed limit fifty-five miles per hour?

5. How many Vice-Presidents have become President of the United States?

6. The canal is twenty-six feet deep and one hundred feet wide.

7. One-half the children are from low-income households.
8. The castle had stood for five-and-a-half centuries.
9. Great-Aunt Lucy will be eighty-five this month.
10. After I got a part-time job, I bought a ten-speed bike.

H. Apostrophes Copy the following sentences. Add apostrophes where they are needed.

1. We collected everyone's donation to the children's hospital.
2. Vanessa's name is spelled with one *n* and two *s*s.
3. The two owners' goal is to expand the store.
4. Don't you wonder who's on the phone?
5. Julius Erving's team is the 76ers.
6. You've used too many *I*'s in your essay.
7. Carlos's *a*'s look like *o*'s.
8. There's an 80 Chevette like ours.
9. Isn't the Taylors' water meter in their basement?
10. Those dogs' leashes are tangled, aren't they?

I. Quotation Marks Copy the following sentences. Add the necessary quotation marks and other punctuation marks. Use capital letters where necessary. If a sentence needs no punctuation, write *Correct*.

1. "My driver's license," Val said, "is a learner's permit."
2. A harsh voice yelled, "Get out!"
3. "Hasn't the telephone company been here yet?" Julie asked. "The storm knocked down our wires."
4. "Did you know," asked Carla, "that horses' hoofs must be cleaned?"
5. The sign on Coach John Thompson's desk says "To err is human. To forgive is not my policy."
6. "Goats do not eat tin cans," said Trudy. "They eat the paste from the labels."
7. Did Ms. Chan say, "The make-up test is on Tuesday"?

8. Clyde told me that he is working at McDonald's._{Correct}
9. Marvin said, "A cultivator tractor is needed for that field."
10. "Didn't Charlie Chaplin once enter a Chaplin look-alike contest," asked Syd, "and come in third?"

J. Quotation Marks and Underlining Copy the following sentences. Add quotation marks around titles or underline titles where necessary.

1. The essay that won was entitled "Losers I Have Known."
2. Our teacher assigned the tenth chapter, "Credit Buying," in the book The Modern Consumer.
3. Isn't the Washington Post a morning newspaper?
4. Margot Kidder played Lois Lane in Superman III, as well as in the first two movies of the series.
5. Earl Hines played Duke Ellington's song, "Don't Get Around Much Anymore."
6. I gave Dad a cookbook, Fast Vegetarian Feasts.
7. Do you ever watch Today on television?
8. I read the poem "Macavity the Mystery Cat" from TS Eliot's book Old Possum's Book of Practical Cats.
9. Beethoven's "Moonlight Sonata" is one of his best-known musical compositions.
10. One UNICEF card shows a reproduction of Mother and Child by the Navajo artist R. C. Gorman.

MIXED REVIEW

Punctuation

A. Using punctuation correctly Copy these sentences, adding the correct punctuation.

1. Wow Whatever fell fell hard
2. Oh Im sure that the movie starts at 9:30 P.M. Carl
3. Jody asked Won't there be prizes music and fireworks?
4. My sister said that the five-subject notebook costs $1.49.
5. I cant open my backpack its zipper is stuck.
6. Its true that fifty-two runners entered the marathon.
7. "Do you know asked Pat if Jess's friend is from San Pablo?"
8. Mr. Kedir who is the school librarian asked if Id read Nobody Else Can Walk It for You by PJ. Petersen.
9. "Have you ever been to Taos New Mexico Ann?"
10. Mary were you born on July 15 1969?

B. Using punctuation in proofreading Proofread the following paragraph. Rewrite it, adding correct punctuation.

Danny's hobby is collecting old blues records. His collection began accidently. When his sister, Laura, moved away, she gave him hers. She said Take care of these, Danny. They're an important part of the past. He thanked her politely, but it took him a while to appreciate the records. After listening closely to them, he became an ardent blues fan. He liked the stories in the songs the emotion in the singers' voices and the heavy, rhythmical beat of the music. Danny started adding to the collection. He browsed at record stores, second-hand shops, and garage sales. His interest in the blues gave him a new awareness of music. For Laura's birthday, Danny taped some hits from the 80s that showed the influence of the blues. He wanted her to know that the past was an important part of the present.

USING MECHANICS IN WRITING
Punctuation

A. Over three hundred years ago, a great Spanish galleon sank in an Atlantic storm. Ever since then, its tons of treasure have lain on the ocean floor. Your diving team has succeeded in bringing that treasure to the surface. Your job is to write an article about the treasure for the magazine *Down Under*. Start by listing all the things you helped find. Estimate the price of several of the items. Make up the names of royalty who once wore the jewelry and used the silverware to dine. Include the dates when the ship sank and when the team found the treasure. When you turn your pre-writing notes into an article, be sure to follow punctuation rules for items in a series and for numbers.

B. Write a dialogue between two people, using the correct punctuation for quotations. Choose one of the following subjects for your dialogue, or make up your own.

1. You and a friend are arguing about which movie to see.

2. You and Michael Jackson are discussing his successful career.

3. A coach is talking to his team during a time out of an NBA playoff game. The team is losing by three points in the last minute.

4. A customer is arguing with a sales clerk. The customer is trying to return damaged merchandise to the store.

5. You are speaking to a possible employer. You are being interviewed for a job.

1. To develop an effective method to improve spelling skills

2. To develop an effective method to master the spelling of particular words

3. To understand and apply common spelling rules

4. To become familiar with the use and spelling of words often confused

Preparing the Students

Ask students if they know what the saying "Clothes make the man" means. Explain that often people judge other people by appearance. First impressions say a lot. Poor spelling makes a statement about the writer. To make the best impression possible, good spelling habits should be developed. Some people are better spellers than others, but everyone can benefit from paying closer attention to developing good spelling habits. Read the introduction on page 664.

Additional Resources

Diagnostic Test — page 10 in the test booklet

Mastery Test — pages 72–73 in the test booklet

Additional Exercises — pages 674–677 in the student text

Practice Book — pages 257–262

Duplicating Masters — pages 257–262

Special Populations — See special section at the back of this Teacher's Edition.

Spelling

It is important for you to have good spelling skills. You will need these skills when you write letters. You will need them when you write reports at school. You will use them when you fill out job applications. If you care what others think of you, you will want to be able to spell words correctly.

There is no simple way to teach you how to spell. However, there are several methods you can use to attack your spelling problems. These methods are discussed in this section.

How To Become a Better Speller

1. Find out what your personal spelling demons are and conquer them. Go over your written assignments and make a list of the words you misspelled on them. Keep this list and master the words on it.

2. Pronounce words carefully. It may be that you misspell words because you don't pronounce them carefully. For example, if you write *probly* for *probably*, you are no doubt mispronouncing the word.

3. Get into the habit of seeing the letters in a word. Many people have never really looked at many everyday words. As a result, even simple words are misspelled.

Take a good look at new words, or difficult words. You'll remember them better. Copy the correct spelling several times.

4. Proofread everything you write. In order to learn how to spell, you must learn to carefully examine everything you write.

To proofread a piece of writing, you must read it slowly, word for word. Otherwise, your eyes may play tricks on you and let you skip over misspelled words.

5. Use a dictionary to check troublesome words.

6. Learn the few important spelling rules given in this chapter.

How To Master the Spelling of Particular Words

1. Look at the word and say it to yourself. Be sure you pronounce it correctly. If it has more than one syllable, say it again, one syllable at a time. Look at each syllable as you say it.

2. Look at the letters and say each one. If the word has more than one syllable, divide the word into syllables when you say the letters.

How To Become a Better Speller

Objective

To develop an effective method to improve spelling skills

Presenting the Lesson

Discuss the six steps to becoming a better speller on page 665.

Individualizing the Lesson

Less-Advanced Students

Work with students to compile a class list of words that they frequently misspell.

Advanced Students

Have students exchange first drafts of their next writing assignment to edit for spelling errors.

Optional Practice

Have students follow steps 1–5 as they look at one of their recently written and graded composition assignments.

How To Master the Spelling of Particular Words

Objective

To develop an effective method to master the spelling of particular words

Presenting the Lesson

Read and discuss the five steps listed on pages 665–666.

Individualizing the Lesson

Less-Advanced Students

Have students apply the five steps to the list of words compiled in the previous **Less-Advanced Students.**

Advanced Students

Have students apply the five-step system to ten new words they find in a magazine article.

Optional Practice

Have the students practice the five-step system with the following words: *resistance, attendance, committee, condemn, height, whether,* and *government.*

Extending the Lesson

Have students apply the five-step approach to five or more of their own spelling demons.

Rules for Spelling

Objective

To understand and apply common spelling rules

Presenting the Lesson

1. The rules in this Section should be presented as separate lessons over several days' time. Practice with words that apply to each rule as frequently as possible. Before introducing new words and rules, review the previous ones.

3. Write the word without looking at your book or list.

4. Now look at your book or list and see whether you spelled the word correctly. If you did, write it again and compare it with the correct form again. Do this once more.

5. If you made a mistake, note exactly what it was. Then repeat 3 and 4 above until you have written the word correctly three times.

Rules for Spelling

The Addition of Prefixes

When a prefix is added to a word, the spelling of the word remains the same.

re- + elect = reelect
mis- + spell = misspell
im- + moderate = immoderate
il- + legible = illegible

mis- + direct = misdirect
re- + enter = reenter
dis- + satisfy = dissatisfy
ir- + regular = irregular

The Final Silent e

When a suffix beginning with a vowel is added to a word ending in a silent e, the e is usually dropped.

create + -ion = creation
graze + -ing = grazing
fame + -ous = famous

grieve + -ing = grieving
relate + ive = relative
continue + -ing = continuing

When a suffix beginning with a consonant is added to a word ending in a silent e, the e is usually retained.

spite + -ful = spiteful
state + -ment = statement
voice + -less = voiceless

taste + -ful = tasteful
move + -ment = movement
wide + -ly = widely

The following words are exceptions:

truly   argument   ninth   wholly

Exercise A Find the misspelled words in these sentences and spell them correctly.

1. The misspellings in your writing are unacceptable.
2. Let's end the argument before leaving.
3. I have spent money unnecessarily.
4. Who is driving us home today?
5. The cast immobilized my leg.
6. You had me almost believing your story!
7. That shiny new car is almost as noisy as our old one.
8. Do you truly understand the statement?
9. Hitchhiking is illegal in our state.
10. The teacher reemphasized her point about irregular verbs.

Exercise B Add the prefixes and suffixes as shown and write the new word.

1. joke + -ing — joking
2. store + -age — storage
3. re- + enter — reenter
4. relate + -ion — relation
5. care + -ful — careful
6. pre- + pay — prepay
7. use + -ful — useful
8. take + -ing — taking
9. mis- + place — misplace
10. un- + natural — unnatural
11. in- + born — inborn
12. co- + operate — cooperate
13. hope + -less — hopeless
14. space + -ious — spacious
15. pave + -ment — pavement
16. mis- + trust — mistrust
17. un- + known — unknown
18. hike + -ing — hiking
19. amaze + -ment — amazement
20. name + -less — nameless

Words Ending in y

When a suffix is added to a word ending in y preceded by a consonant, the y is usually changed to i.

crazy + -ly = crazily
seventy + -eth = seventieth
hilly + -est = hilliest

puppy + -es = puppies
silly + -ness = silliness
marry + -age = marriage

667

2. Read the rules governing the addition of prefixes and the final silent e on page 666. Go over examples of words used to illustrate each rule. Be certain that students know the meanings of words before and after the addition of prefixes and suffixes. Check that students can distinguish between suffixes beginning with vowels and those beginning with consonants. Look at and discuss exceptions to the rule regarding retention of the silent e.

3. Assign and discuss Exercises A and B on page 667.

4. Read the rules governing words ending in y on pages 667–668. Stress that the addition of -ing constitutes an exception to the rule for changing y to i. Go over examples of words which conform to the rules and their exceptions. Have students suggest other words ending in y. Write them on the board. Add suffixes to each and rewrite the newly formed words in two columns: those in which y changes to i and those in which y does not change. Have students relate the rules to the examples on the board.

5. Assign and discuss the Exercise on page 668.

6. Read the rules on pages 668–669 governing the suffixes -ness and -ly and the doubling of final consonants. Go over examples. Have students suggest more examples and apply the rules to each.

7. Assign and discuss Exercises A and B on page 669. As students correct misspelled words, have them state the rule which governs the correction.

8. Read the rules on page 670 governing words with the "seed" sound and words with *ie* and *ei*. Study examples.

9. Assign and discuss the Exercise on page 670.

Individualizing the Lesson

Less-Advanced Students

1. Do a portion of Exercise B, page 667, orally. Then have the students complete the Exercises independently.

2. Have students tell which rule applies to each word they spell or correct in the A Exercises on pages 667 and 669.

Advanced Students

Have the students write two additional examples for each spelling category. Have them check their spelling of the words in the dictionary.

Optional Practice

Dictate the following words to the class. Have them spell the words correctly.

1. tripping	13. equally
2. succeed	14. thinness
3. niece	15. easily
4. hurrying	16. slipped
5. marrying	17. shining
6. marriage	18. famous
7. lazier	19. silliest
8. relation	20. reelect
9. hateful	21. unnatural
10. skating	22. naturally ·
11. misspell	23. hopping
12. truly	24. hoping

Note the following exception: When *-ing* is added, the *y* does not change:

scurry + -ing = scurrying   carry + -ing = carrying
ready + -ing = readying   worry + -ing = worrying

When a suffix is added to a word ending in y preceded by a vowel, the y usually does not change.

employ + -ed = employed   stay + -ing = staying
play + -er = player   relay + -ing = relaying

Exercise   Add the suffixes as shown and write the new word.

1. dirty + -er — *dirtier*	11. skinny + -er — *skinnier*
2. happy + -ly — *happily*	12. mystery + -ous — *mysterious*
3. stay + -ing — *staying*	13. thirty + -eth — *thirtieth*
4. spray + -er — *sprayer*	14. duty + -ful — *dutiful*
5. hurry + -ing — *hurrying*	15. sleepy + -er — *sleepier*
6. glory + -ous — *glorious*	16. merry + -ment — *merriment*
7. pray + -er — *prayer*	17. joy + -ous — *joyous*
8. lazy + -est — *laziest*	18. silly + -est — *silliest*
9. shiny + -ness — *shininess*	19. carry + -age — *carriage*
10. enjoy + -ment — *enjoyment*	20. employ + -er — *employer*

The Suffixes -*ness* and -*ly*

When the suffix -*ly* is added to a word ending in *l*, both *l*'s are kept. When -*ness* is added to a word ending in *n*, both *n*'s are kept.

normal + -ly = normally   open + -ness = openness

Doubling the Final Consonant

In words of one syllable that end in one consonant preceded by one vowel, double the final consonant before adding -*ing*, -*ed*, or -*er*.

hit + -ing = hitting   spot + -ed = spotted
nod + -ed = nodded   rob + -er = robber

The following words do not double the final consonant because *two* vowels precede the final consonant:

$$near + -ing = nearing$$
$$look + -ed = looked$$
$$cool + -er = cooler$$
$$meet + -ing = meeting$$

Exercise A Number your paper from 1 to 10. Find the misspelled words in these sentences and spell them correctly. If there are no misspelled words in a sentence, write *Correct*.

1. That garden is carefuly tended.
2. The uneveness of the road is annoying.
3. This painting is beautifuly framed.
4. A strong wind faned the fire.
5. FBI agents nearred the cornered spy.
6. Ilona wraped the package and mailed it.
7. Is the boiler running?
8. Practicaly all the batters are striking out.
9. Joanna's openess makes her an easy person to talk to.
10. Mike is actualy siting on the stage.

Exercise B Add the suffixes as shown and write the new word.

1. even + -ness
2. cruel + -ly
3. plug + -ing
4. plan + -ed
5. remit + -ance
6. slim + -er
7. tug + -ing
8. loan + -ed
9. treat + -ing
10. sleep + -ing
11. bashful + -ly
12. trim + -ed
13. swim + -er
14. merry + -ly
15. fat + -er
16. heat + -ing
17. lean + -ness
18. soon + -er
19. slug + -er
20. drag + -ing

Extending the Lesson

Play the following game with students. Have students number their papers from 1–10. Tell them you will read the name of a rule and a sentence containing a blank. After the proper number, students should write the correct word which fills the blank. The winner is the student who supplies and correctly spells all ten words.

Words with the "seed" sound

1. The price of gasoline cannot _____ a certain price posted on the pump. (exceed)

Words with *ie* and *ei*

2. In order to wear certain earrings, you must _____ your ears. (pierce)

3. People retire to the sunbelt to spend their _____ time enjoying warm weather. (leisure)

4. You must have a cash register _____ in order to return your gift. (receipt)

Words ending in *y*

5. Do the _____ problems first and save the hardest ones for later. (easiest)

The suffixes *-ness* and *-ly*

6. Mother never gets angry; she always displays _____ of temper. (evenness)

Doubling the final consonant

7. The tire marks showed that the car _____ before it hit the guard rail. (skidded)

The addition of prefixes

8. It is _____ to drive through a red light. (illegal)

The final silent *e*

9. The pitcher is the _____, or last, batter in the batting order. (ninth)

10. Write a thank-you note to show how _____ you are for the kindness shown to you. (grateful)

Words with the "Seed" Sound

Only one English word ends in *sede: supersede.*
Three words end in *ceed: exceed, proceed, succeed.*
All other words ending in the sound of *seed* are spelled *cede:*

| concede | precede | recede | secede |

Words with *ie* and *ei*

When the sound is long *e* (*ē*), the word is spelled *ie* except after *c.*

I before E

relieve grieve field pierce
belief piece pier reprieve

Except after C

conceit conceive perceive deceive receive

The following words are exceptions:

either weird species neither seize leisure

Exercise Find the misspelled words in these sentences and spell them correctly.

1. When was Louisiana <u>ceeded</u> to the United States? ceded
2. The chief's shield was made of gold. c
3. There's one <u>peice</u> of pecan pie left. piece
4. Ford <u>preseeded</u> Carter as president. preceded
5. Will aspirin <u>releive</u> this headache? relieve
6. The city was <u>siezed</u> after a fierce battle. seized
7. The clerk <u>proceded</u> to write a receipt. proceeded
8. My leisure hours <u>excede</u> my work hours. exceed
9. The paint on the <u>cieling</u> is chipped. ceiling
10. I babysit for my <u>neice</u> every weekend. niece

Words Often Confused

capital means chief, most serious, or most important. It is also the official seat of government.

capitol is a building in which a state legislature meets.

the Capitol is the building in Washington, D.C., where the United States Congress meets.

> Murder is a *capital* crime.
> The state *capitol* building is in Springfield.
> The nation's laws are made in the *Capitol*.

des'·ert means a barren, dry region

de·sert' means to leave or to abandon

dessert (note the different spelling) is a sweet food, the last course of a meal.

> Lizards thrive in the *desert*.
> One soldier *deserted* his company.
> Order the cheesecake for *dessert*.

hear means to listen to or to take notice of.

here means in this place.

> Did you *hear* the news on the radio?
> The fire hose is kept *here*.

its is a word that shows possession by *it*.

it's is a contraction for *it is* or *it has*.

> The violin has *its* own case.
> *It's* time for a break.

loose means free, not fastened, not tight.

lose means to mislay or to fail to find or keep.

> Runners wear *loose* clothing.
> Did you *lose* track of time?

Words Often Confused

Objective

To become familiar with the use and spelling of words often confused

Presenting the Lesson

1. Explain that this Part presents sets of words which are often confused, and consequently misspelled, because they sound the same. They are called *homonyms*. Tell the students that the key to proper usage and spelling of these words is to understand the differences in meaning and spelling in each set.

2. For each of the twelve sets of words, read the definitions and carefully note the differences in spelling. Have students use each word of each set in a sentence.

3. Offer certain tricks to help students distinguish between words often confused. For example:

> a capitol is a building with a dome
> a principal is your pal
> stationery is made out of paper

Ask students to think up some helpful sayings of their own to help with the words in this Part.

4. Assign and discuss Exercises A and B on page 673.

Individualizing the Lesson

Less-Advanced Students

1. For each of the Exercises have students write not only the correct word, but its definition.

2. Help students memorize the definitions of the words often misspelled. Then have them quiz each

671

other on the words and their meaning.

Advanced Students

Have students write definitions and sentences for these words that are often confused: *peek-peak, advise-advice, council-counsel,* and *sight-cite-site.*

Optional Practice

Have students fill the blanks in the following sentences with the correct homonyms.

1. Dan will __lose__ the race because his skates are too __loose__ . (loose, lose)
2. __They're__ running as fast as __their__ legs can carry them. (they're, their, there)
3. The group did not want to __desert__ their friend in the __desert__ . (dessert, desert)
4. Can everyone __here__ __hear__ the speaker? (hear, here)
5. I don't know __whether__ the __weather__ will improve or not. (weather, whether)
6. As a matter of __principle__, the student took his complaint to the __principal__. (principle, principal)
7. Do you want __to__ swim or is it __too__ cold? (too, two, to)
8. In the __capitol__ building in Texas they are debating __capital__ punishment. (capital, Capitol, capitol)
9. __It's__ easy to see why the restaurant lost __its__ steady customers. (it's, its)
10. __Who's__ going to decide __whose__ turn it is? (whose, who's)

Extending the Lesson

Conduct a spelling bee using words from this Section.

principal refers to something which is chief or of highest importance. It is also the name for the head of an elementary or high school.

principle is a basic truth, rule, or policy.

> The *principal* speaker is the mayor.
> The Bill of Rights states basic *principles*.

stationary means fixed or unmoving.

stationery refers to paper and envelopes used for writing letters.

> The boat in the distance looks *stationary*.
> Cindy has *stationery* with her name on it.

their is a possessive word meaning belonging to *them*.

there means in that place.

they're is the contraction for *they are*.

> The children rode *their* bicycles.
> The trail begins *there*.
> Plants turn yellow when *they're* watered too often.

to means toward or in the direction of.

too means also or extremely.

two is the number.

> This bus goes *to* the civic center.
> Marla wears glasses, and Dave does *too*.
> We reserved *two* tickets.

weather refers to the state of the atmosphere, including temperature, wind, and moisture.

whether introduces choices or alternatives.

> Bad *weather* spoiled the picnic.
> The player must decide *whether* to pass or kick the ball.

who's is a contraction for *who is* or *who has*.

whose is the possessive form of *who*.

> *Who's* going to Sue's party?
> *Whose* locker is that?

your means belonging to *you*.

you're is the contraction for *you are*.

Do *your* new boots feel comfortable?
You're taking the bus, aren't you?

Exercise A   Write the correct word.

1. Camels trudged across the sandy (<u>desert</u>, dessert).
2. Ray pulled a (<u>loose,</u> lose) thread and ripped his shirt.
3. "My (<u>principal</u>, principle) aim," the politician said, "is to halt inflation."
4. We'll meet you (hear, <u>here</u>) at the corner at 8:00 P.M.
5. The spacecraft followed (<u>its</u>, it's) plotted course.
6. "(Its, <u>It's</u>) a girl!" said the nurse.
7. Engine trouble made the plane (loose, <u>lose</u>) altitude.
8. Choose between fortune cookies and almond cookies for (desert, <u>dessert</u>).
9. The President spoke in the House chamber at the (capital, capitol, <u>Capitol</u>).
10. When I took archery, we practiced with both moving and (<u>stationary</u>, stationery) targets.

Exercise B   Follow the directions for Exercise A.

1. (<u>Who's</u>, Whose) going to the youth center tonight?
2. Yvonne wondered (who's, <u>whose</u>) cat it was.
3. Gene is aiming (to, <u>too</u>, two) far to the right.
4. (To, Too, <u>Two</u>) of the spark plugs misfired.
5. We expect good (<u>weather</u>, whether) this spring.
6. We'll have a good time (weather, <u>whether</u>) or not Jeff comes to the party.
7. Drew and Lucy closed (<u>their</u>, there, they're) shop.
8. We left our bicycle right (their, <u>there</u>, they're).
9. (<u>Your</u>, You're) voice is trembling.
10. (Your, <u>You're</u>) nervous about this meeting, aren't you?

ADDITIONAL EXERCISES

Spelling

A. Prefixes Find the misspelled words in these sentences. Spell the words correctly.

1. What an unnusual message that was!
2. Did I missunderstand your proposeal?
3. Lois's reeaction was intense dissappointment.
4. The search party is hoplessly lost.
5. That dull ax you're carrying is usless.
6. Holding dog fights is ilegal.
7. You're misstaken about the topic of the argument.
8. Hank's amusment seemed imoderate.
9. Missmatched socks are hardly tastful.
10. The bus company is disscontinueing some routes.

B. Suffixes Add the suffixes as shown. Write the new word.

1. busy + -est — busiest
2. city + -es — cities
3. beauty + -ful — beautiful
4. lovely + -er — lovelier
5. rely + -ant — reliant

6. twenty + -eth — twentieth
7. injury + -ous — injurious
8. alley + -s — alleys
9. hurry + -ing — hurrying
10. frisky + -ly — friskily

C. Suffixes Find the misspelled words in these sentences. Spell the words correctly.

1. Shana was carefuly choping wood.
2. Rick is known for his meaness.
3. She repeatted the joke with a totaly straight face.
4. The mayor is siting beside the podium.
5. Craig eventualy caught the bigest trout of all.
6. The drain's stoper is usualy on a shelf by the tub.
7. Even the best players fearred that batter.

8. The engine is runing beautifuly.

9. Ireland is called the Emerald Isle because of its greeness.

10. Juanita casualy fliped a coin to decide.

D. Spelling Find the misspelled words. Write them correctly.

1. Mrs. Avery <u>recieved</u> a compliment from her niece. received

2. Dana <u>sucedes</u> because she believes in herself. succeeds

3. The winds <u>exceded</u> fifty miles per hour. exceeded

4. Armando <u>beleives</u> in <u>siezing</u> the moment. believes, seizing

5. <u>Niether</u> of the winners proceeded to the stage. Neither

6. Other people's beliefs sometimes seem <u>wierd</u> to us. weird

7. The <u>reciept</u> was written on a piece of scrap paper. receipt

8. James <u>conceeded</u> and left the field to Harry. conceded

9. The states that <u>seseded</u> from the Union <u>decieved</u> themselves about their strength. seceded, deceived

10. The waves, which had covered the pier, <u>receeded</u>. receded

E. Words Often Confused Choose the correct word from those given.

1. Did you (<u>hear</u>, here) the outdoor concert last night?

2. The (<u>principal</u>, principle) characters in the play are Laura and her mother.

3. The pilots checked (<u>their</u>, there, they're) flight pattern.

4. These streetlights are much (to, <u>too</u>, two) dim.

5. Are (<u>your</u>, you're) friends in the work-study program?

6. The (<u>capital</u>, capitol) of Indiana is Indianapolis.

7. A bear (<u>deserts</u>, desserts) her cubs suddenly when they know enough to survive without her.

8. Gene wondered (weather, <u>whether</u>) to use a fork or a spoon.

9. The jockey had to (<u>lose</u>, loose) five pounds.

10. A snapping turtle wiggles (it's, <u>its</u>) tongue to attract prey.

These exercises provide review of the concepts presented in this Section. Each exercise challenges the students to apply several of the skills they have acquired during previous study. Because the "mixed" feature of these activities makes them more difficult, the teacher may wish to have less-advanced students do them orally or in small groups.

MIXED REVIEW

Spelling

A. Spelling words correctly Pick out the words that are spelled incorrectly in these sentences. Write them correctly. If a sentence is already correct, write *Correct*.

1. Butterflies were <u>peacefuly</u> flying around the field. peacefully
2. Sitting up too quickly can cause <u>dizzyness</u>. dizziness
3. Swimmers stayed away from the <u>peir</u>. pier
4. <u>Their</u> has been an unfortunate mistake. There
5. We are relieved that <u>your</u> here. you're
6. <u>Its</u> clear that you're really joking. It's
7. Vincent <u>tryed</u> using a bigger piece of stationery. tried
8. The weather is <u>geting</u> hotter as the days get longer. getting
9. Kate felt <u>thiner</u> after skipping dessert for a week. thinner
10. My niece <u>siezed</u> her new toys greedily. seized
11. <u>Whose</u> running the water in the basement? Who's
12. <u>Actualy</u>, she was exceeding her duties. Actually
13. I <u>conceed</u> that you're winning the argument. concede
14. All day the puppies were digging a tunnel and now they're <u>lose</u>. loose
15. The two <u>dissappeared</u> with surprising suddenness. disappeared

B. Using spelling in proofreading Proofread the following paragraph. Rewrite it, spelling all the words correctly.

It's ~~usualy~~ usually true that people dislike being stared at. In some weird way, ~~there~~ they're able to ~~percieve~~ perceive that they're being looked at, too. ~~Weather~~ Whether or not they're ~~faceing~~ facing away from whoever is staring, people glance around nervously or ~~angryly~~ angrily. They ~~loose~~ lose their calmness. Finally, if the rudeness ~~continus~~ continues, you're ~~likly~~ likely to ~~here~~ hear them ask, "What do you want? Why are you staring at me?"

USING MECHANICS IN WRITING
Spelling

A. Some of the words in the list below are misspelled. Read the list several times to get a story idea from them. Then use the words in the list, correctly spelled, to write the first paragraph of a mystery story. Underline each word from the list.

mysteryous	scurriing	imagination
unknown	wierd	movement
nameless	dareing	windowes
carefully	creeppy	
renter	unnatural	

B. Make a crossword puzzle. This one will be full of spelling demons. The clues are given below. Write the words. Be sure to spell them correctly. Then put the words in a crossword form. On a separate sheet of paper, make the corresponding empty boxes. Number them and the clues. Challenge a friend with your puzzle.

1. To go before: p_____
2. The opposite of *here:* t_____
3. Another word for *mourn:* g_____
4. Where boats are docked: p_____
5. The feeling of being superior to others: c_____
6. To lie: d_____
7. Another word for *fetch:* r_____
8. Strange: w_____
9. A government building: c_____
10. End of a meal: d_____
11. To misplace something: l_____
12. Another word for *if:* w_____

677

Section Objectives

1. To use legible handwriting and to produce a neat, correct final copy

2. To become acquainted with accepted forms for headings, titles, margins, and spacing

3. To use numbers correctly in writing

4. To use abbreviations correctly in writing

Preparing the Students

Read the introduction on page 678. Stress that while *what* you say is most important, *how* you present your material also affects communication with your reader.

Additional Resources

Mastery Test — pages 74–75 in the test booklet

Additional Exercises — pages 684–687 in the student text

Special Populations — See special section at the back of this Teacher's Edition.

Legible Writing

Objective

To use legible handwriting and to produce a neat, correct final copy

Presenting the Lesson

Read page 679. Discuss the advantages of writing a first draft, doing revisions of that draft, and proofreading.

678

The Correct Form for Writing

What you say in your compositions and reports can be made clearer to your readers if you put it in the correct form. The correct form is neat, precise, and consistent. Such form also makes a good impression. It shows your reader that you care about what you have to say.

There are several ways to give your papers polish. Some schools provide their own guidelines for correct form. The form explained in this section is accepted by many schools.

678

Legible Writing

Good form requires neat, legible papers. Typewritten papers are easier to read than handwritten ones. However, few schools require typewritten papers.

For handwritten papers, use a pen. Dark blue or black ink is easiest to read. Letters should be formed carefully so that they can be distinguished from letters that they look like (*a*'s and *o*'s, *i*'s and *e*'s, for instance).

Preparing a Final Copy

It is nearly impossible to write one draft of a paper and have it turn out just as you want it. Revise and correct your first draft. Only then should you make a final copy. Proofread this copy to find and correct errors.

If you find words left out, insert them neatly above the line by using a caret (∧) to show their placement. If you want to change a word, cross it with a line and write the correction above it. If you find that you have made more than three corrections on a page, you should recopy it.

The Correct Form

As you can see, there are several important ways to make your paper look attractive. There are also accepted forms for headings, titles, margins, and spacing. In addition, you will learn the correct form for using numbers and abbreviations in writing.

Proper Labeling

Usually, a heading is placed in the upper right-hand corner of the first page. On the first line is your name. On the second line

679

Show students examples of several properly arranged pages alongside examples of poorly arranged pages. (Use an overhead projector.) Have students comment on the differences and on what the differences might mean to a reader.

Advanced Students

Discuss with students the importance of following the correct form when writing a paper. Explain that labeling helps the teacher identify the author and that proper spacing makes a paper easier to read.

Optional Practice

Have students write a composition on a topic of their own choosing. Tell them to make sure to follow the proper form throughout. Stress that every paper should have a title.

Extending the Lesson

Have students read a book and write a book report. Tell them to be sure to follow the correct form when writing the report.

is the name of the class. On the third line is the date.

Beginning with page two, number each page. A good spot for the number is the upper right-hand corner. To prevent pages from being lost or confused, you might want to place your name under the page number.

Many teachers have special requirements for the labeling of a paper. Follow those instructions.

Placement of Title

The title of a paper appears only on page one near the top of the page. A good rule to follow is to center the title several lines below the last line of your heading. The heading identifies your name and course and the date. Then skip two lines between the title and the first line of your paper.

As with all titles, the first word and all important words should be capitalized. If you are typing, do not capitalize every letter but only the first letters. Do not underline the title or place it in quotation marks.

For long papers of more than three or four pages, a title page is often used. This is a separate page, preceding page one of the paper. It contains the title centered on the page.

Margins and Spacing

To achieve a neat appearance, leave margins of one inch at the top, bottom, and left side of the paper.

If you are typing, try to keep the right-hand margin even. However, do not use too many hyphens to break words at the margin. A general guideline is not to have more than two lines in a row ending with hyphens.

Typewritten papers should be double-spaced. Paragraph indentation is usually five spaces. Leave two spaces following the end punctuation of a sentence.

Numbers in Writing

Numbers under 100 are usually spelled out. Numbers over 100 are written in figures.

> I get *fifty-two* paychecks a year.
> A train ticket costs *eighteen* dollars.
> A standard typewriter has *forty-four* keys.
> The thieves stole $3,450.

A number beginning a sentence is spelled out.

> *Six hundred and fifty-two* students graduated.
> *Nine and one-half* minutes is the record.
> *Forty-five* minutes later, Kent appeared.

Figures rather than words are used to express dates, street and room numbers, telephone numbers, temperatures, the time, page numbers, decimals, percentages, and fractions.

> On July 20, 1969, a man stepped on the moon.
> The studio is at 55 West Division Street.
> Jim is in room 459 at the hospital.
> Call me at 555-6756.
> Water freezes at 32 degrees Fahrenheit.
> Did you read the editorial on page 12?
> The wood is 1.75 inches thick.
> The cost of food rose 12 percent last year.
> The meeting began at 10:00 A.M.

Note: Commas are used to separate the figures in sums of money or expressions of large quantities. They are not used in dates, serial numbers, page numbers, addresses, or telephone numbers.

> Correct: The charity collected over $35,750.
> Correct: The population of our town is 30,875.
> Incorrect: One famous date is July 4, 1,776.
> Correct: One famous date is July 4, 1776.

Numbers in Writing

Objective

To use numbers correctly in writing

Presenting the Lesson

1. Read page 681. Go over rules for the use of numbers. Study sample sentences illustrating when figures are used and when numbers are spelled out.
2. Assign and discuss the Exercise on page 682.

Individualizing the Lesson

Less-Advanced Students

Do the first few sentences in the Exercise orally with students.

Advanced Students

Have students find examples of numbers in writing in the financial and sports sections of a newspaper. Discuss their findings in class.

Optional Practice

Have students write ten sentences of their own using as many numbers as possible. Students should be prepared to explain why each number is written as it is.

Extending the Lesson

Give students a quiz using numbers in sentences. Read each sentence aloud, emphasizing each number. Then repeat just the number and have students write it on their paper as it should appear in the sentence. Correct the quiz in class.

Exercise Copy these sentences, correcting any errors in the writing of figures.

1. The 1st postage stamp sold on July one, 1,847, for 5 cents. First; 1; 1847; five
2. The bike Jake wanted cost $80. eighty dollars
3. Check page forty-two for the answer to the question.
4. Our doctor's office is at 60 West 7th Street in Room 2
5. San Diego's average temperature for January is fifty-six degrees. 56
6. Kristen drove 600 miles and spent only $19 on gasoline. nineteen dollars
7. 126 beds were added in the new wing of the hospital. One hundred and twenty-six
8. Earth, the 5th largest planet, revolves around the sun at a rate of 17.5 miles per minute. fifth
9. I called the weather service at WE6-1660 and found out that the temperature is eighty degrees. 80
10. 2 percent of the people in the United States are farmers. Two

Abbreviations in Writing

Abbreviations may be used for most titles before and after proper names, for names of government agencies, and for time.

Titles before proper names:	Dr., Mr., Mrs., Ms., Rev., Hon., Capt., Lt., Gov.
Titles after proper names:	Jr., Ph.D., M.D.
Government agencies:	FDA, CIA, FCC, FAA
Dates and time:	A.D., B.C., A.M., P.M.

You will notice that there are no periods after the abbreviations of government agencies.

The abbreviations of titles are acceptable only when they are used with names. For instance, the following is not acceptable: The secy. went to the dr.

Abbreviations are not used for the President and Vice-President of the United States. Likewise, abbreviations are not used for *Honorable* and *Reverend* when they are preceded by *the: the Honorable Monica Stevens*. They appear with the person's full name, not just the last name.

In ordinary writing, abbreviations are not acceptable for names of countries and states, months, and days of the week. They are also not acceptable for words that are part of addresses or company names.

Incorrect: Denver, Colo., has a high altitude.
Correct: Denver, Colorado, has a high altitude.

Incorrect: Are you moving to Wash.?
Correct: Are you moving to Washington?

Incorrect: The dance is set for Sat., Oct. 4.
Correct: The dance is set for Saturday, October 4.

Incorrect: McDonald's Corp. runs a school.
Correct: McDonald's Corporation runs a school.

In most writing, do not use abbreviations for the following: *page, chapter, Christmas,* and the names of school courses. Abbreviations standing for measurements, such as *bu., in., hr., min., sec.,* should also be avoided.

Exercise   Correct the errors in abbreviation in these sentences.

1. Mr. Rhodes explained Mon.'s assignment of pp. 66 to 69 in the soc. studies textbook. Monday's, pages, social studies
2. Wounded Knee, S.D., was the site of a major conflict. South Dakota
3. Lt. Reilly saluted the capt. captain
4. In Dec., basketball season begins for the yr. December, year
5. On Tues., November 4, the polls will open at 6 A.M. Tuesday
6. The address of the White House is 1600 Penn. Ave. Pennsylvania Avenue
7. The cactus in Ariz. often reach fifty ft. in height. Arizona, feet
8. The Dept. of Energy building in Md. is hard to find. Department of Energy, Maryland
9. The F.C.C. granted a license to a new radio station in Eugene, Ore. FCC, Oregon
10. I introduced Calvin Olby, Jr., the pres. of Dixie Co. President, Company

683

ADDITIONAL EXERCISES

The Correct Form for Writing

A. Numbers in Writing Copy these sentences, correcting any errors in the writing of figures.

1. 16th century spelling was not standardized. Sixteenth
2. John Lennon was killed on December eighth, 1980. 8
3. *Grease* ran for 3388 Broadway performances. 3,388
4. In 1,980, female teenagers watched television an average of 22 hours and nineteen minutes a week. 1980, twenty-tw
5. Male teenagers watched television an average of twenty-three hours and 40 minutes per week. forty
6. Shirley's motorcycle gets fifty point two miles per gallon. 50.2
7. The movie starts at seven and ends at 9:00. 7:00
8. The 5 pages of classified ads start on page sixty-five. five, 65
9. Even thirty degrees felt warm in January. 30
10. *Star Wars* made $175685000 in its first 3 years. $175,685,000, three

B. Abbreviations in Writing Copy these sentences, correcting any errors in abbreviations. If a sentence contains no errors, write *Correct*.

1. Xmas vacation starts on Dec. 20. Christmas, December
2. Why did you read Chap. 2 1st? Chapter Two, first
3. Is she Lynn Rollins, M.D., or Lynn Rollins, Ph.D.? C
4. Dr. Hayes and the Rev. Harold Ryan are in town. C
5. Naval Medical Hosp. is in Bethesda, Md. Hospital, Maryland
6. In 1958, NASA was established. C
7. Mr. Hill shook hands with the dr. doctor
8. When Kay was thirteen yrs. old, she was six ft. tall. years, fee
9. Was Pres. Hoover related to J. Edgar Hoover of the FBI? President
10. The phys. ed. class was canceled last Tues. physical education, Tuesda

MIXED REVIEW

The Correct Form for Writing

Using the correct form for writing   Copy the following composition, correcting any errors in writing form.

"TAKING A BREAK"

The 1st 2 weeks of Jan. need not be dull for Roosevelt H. S. students. A list outside Dr. Romero's office describes activities available to students during the break.

One project introduces students to various kinds of jobs. For instance, one day can be spent watching govt. workers inspect chickens. These inspectors stand for 8 hrs. watching chickens pass by on hooks at the rate of about one thousand, two hundred an hr. The inspectors have 3 seconds to check each chicken for twenty different problems and then decide whether it passes or fails.

The next day could be spent following drs. around a hosp. On the 3rd day, students can observe police officers. This day might include chasing a stolen car down Main St. at 80 m.p.h., listening to an interview between a police lieut. and an FBI agent, or watching a sgt. rescue somebody from the river in 20° weather.

After observing these and other workers, students write a ten pg. essay in which they describe the stresses and responsibilities of each job. Page ten must state which job seems most stressful. Incidentally, last yr. ninety percent of the students agreed that chicken inspectors were under the most pressure.

If this particular interim project does not appeal to you, take a look at the others on the list. Some projects cost $5; others are free. Some take place at home; others take you miles away. They offer an escape from the stress of boredom. Don't get listless! Look at the list.

Mixed Review

These exercises provide review of the concepts presented in this Section. Each exercise challenges the students to apply several of the skills they have acquired during previous study. Because the "mixed" feature of these activities makes them more difficult, the teacher may wish to have less-advanced students do them orally or in small groups.

685

These challenging and enjoyable activities allow the students to see how the concepts of grammar, usage, and mechanics may be applied in actual writing situations. Each exercise is designed to allow students practice in several of the skills they have acquired in this Section. The activities also provide opportunities for students to write creatively about a wide variety of interesting and unusual subjects.

USING MECHANICS IN WRITING
The Correct Form for Writing

A. Imagine that you are a reporter on the campaign trail. You are traveling with a candidate for the governorship of your state. Write a report for your newspaper about one campaign stop that your candidate made. Include the following abbreviations and numbers in your news story. Remember that some of the abbreviations and numbers must be written out. Give your story a title or headline, and place it correctly on the page.

10,000 votes	Fri., Oct. 11
FBI	Wash., D.C.
2 o'clock P.M.	NBC television
Sen. Carey	45 degree weather
Dem. candidate	20 minute speech
3 senators	

B. The following report contains 10 errors in form. Number your paper from 1 to 10. List the errors and show how they can be corrected.

> Brett Adams
> English II
> April 25, 1985

BIKING FOR DOLLARS, NOT SENSE

15 cyclists entered the Mem. Day bicycle race. My goal was to beat them all and win the 75 dollar prize. Never had I trained so hard for an event. The race was scheduled to begin at two o'clock P.M. but at that time I was at the corner of Elm St. and Grove with a flat tire on my bike. I had done what no serious cyclist should ever do: I had ridden my bike to the event. A stray nail had punctured the tire and my ego as well. Next yr. I'll go the right way, with my bike mounted majestically on the top of our VW.

CUMULATIVE REVIEW
Capitalization, Punctuation, and Spelling

A. Using capitalization, punctuation, and spelling correctly Copy the following sentences, correcting the errors in capitalization, punctuation, and spelling.

1. The spanish ship santa margarita sank off the florida keys in 1622
2. "I beleive said myra that you're time is up on the dryer
3. mr. allen had beautyful whether when he visited jasper national park in canada.
4. The Birkebeiner also called the Birkie is a fifty-five kilometer cross-country ski race.
5. carl is makeing twenty-five posters for Evan's campaign.

B. Using proofreading skills Copy this paragraph, correcting the errors in capitalization, punctuation, and spelling.

Do you wear glasses? Well, although many people have worn glasses over the ages, no one realy knows who invented them. According to an article in the smithsonian magazine, the substance of glass was used as early as 2500 bc and magnifying lenses dating to 1200 bc have been found in crete. Scholars beleive that glasses were probably invented in venice, italy by a 13th century glassworker. The first glasses probably looked like too small magnifying glasses with there handles riveted together. The problem with that style was that it didnt stay on well. The spanish used loops of ribbon tied to the spectacles to hold them on there ears. Instead of using loops the chinese used ribbons with weights on the ends to drape over the ears and hold they're glasses in place. Finaly in 1730 an englishman perfectted the use of rigid sidepeices for glasses. This style is the one that's been used since that time. What an interesting history eyeglasses have.

Cumulative Review

These exercises are designed to cover broad areas of grammar, usage, and mechanics. They require the application of skills taught thus far in the text. The exercises may be used for testing purposes, or as an excellent resource for review.

of titles in card catalog, 276
Anecdotes in paragraphs, 70–71,
  86–87
Announcements, 348, 350
Antecedents, 437–438
Antonyms, 6–7, 27
Apostrophe
  in contractions, 649
  to form plurals, 648–649
  in possessives, 648–649
Articles, 276, 484
Assignments, understanding,
  286–287
Atlas, 281
Audience
  of a composition, 166–167
  of a paragraph, 82–83
  of a speaker, 352–353
Author card, 275
Auxiliaries, *See* Helping Verbs.

B

bad/badly, 501
Bar graph, 300–301
Base words, 8–9
be, forms of, 386–387, 456,
  459. *See also* Irregular verbs
  and Linking verbs.
Bibliography cards, 236–238
Bibliographies, 253–254
Biographical references, 281
Body
  of a business letter, 315–317
  of a composition, 160–161,
    166–167, 184–185,
    196–197, 218–219,
    228–229
  of a friendly letter, 310–312
  of a report, 247–249
  of a speech, 356
Books, finding and using in the

library. *See* Library, using
  the.
Brainstorming, 78–79, 86–87
Bread-and-butter notes,
  310–311
Business letters, 315–317

C

Call numbers, 272
can/may, 472–473
capital/capitol, 671
Capitalization, 614–630
  abbreviations, 615,
    632–633
  A. D., 621
  airplanes, 621
  automobiles, 621
  B. C., 621
  days, 620
  directions, 618
  direct quotations, 639–640,
    651
  events, 620
  family relationships, 616
  first words
    in letters, 623
    of outlines, 623
    of poetry lines, 622
    of quotations, 623
    of sentences, 622–623
  geographical names,
    617–618
  holidays, 620
  I, 616
  initials, 615, 632–633
  languages, 620
  in letters, 623
  months, 620
  names, 615–616
  nationalities, 620

organizations and institutions, 620

periods (of time), 620

proper adjectives, 615

proper nouns, 615

races, 620

religions, 620

school subjects, 621

sections of the country, 618

sentences, 622–623

ships, 621

Supreme Being and sacred writings, 616

titles of persons, 615–616

titles of written works, 624

trains, 621

Card catalog, 275–276

Characters, 178–179

Charts, 298–299

Chronological order
  in narrative compositions, 180–181
  in paragraphs, 88–89, 108–109, 112–113

Circle graph, 300–301

Circular reasoning, 266–267

Clauses
  adjective, 592–595
  adverb, 590–592
  dependent, 587
  main, 586–587
  noun, 595–598
  relative, 593
  subordinate, 587–588, 598

Closing of letters, 310–312, 315–317
  colons with, 315–316
  commas with, 310

Colon, 315, 645

Combining sentence parts, 56–57

Combining sentences, 53–61

Command words, 262–263

Commas, 635–644
  with adjectives, 635
  with adverbs, 635
  with appositives, 639
  to avoid confusion, 583, 642
  with city, state and country, 642
  in combined sentences, 54–55
  in compound constructions, 578–579
  in compound predicates, 581–582
  in compound sentences, 578–580, 640–641
  with dates, 641–642
  with direct address, 638–639
  with direct quotations, 639–640, 651
  with divided quotations, 640
  with interrupters, 637–638
  with indirect quotations, 640
  with introductory words, 637
  in letters, 642
  with a semicolon, 644
  in a series, 635
  to set off names, 638–639
  after *yes, no,* 637

Common nouns, 410–411

Comparison and contrast, 88–89

Comparisons
  using adjectives, 487–489
  using adverbs, 494–496
  as context clue, 2

Complete predicate, 371–373

Complete sentence, 368–369, 400–403

Complete subject, 371–373

Completing applications and work-related forms, 321–323

topic sentence in, 160, 214
transitions in, 188–189,
208–209, 218–219
See also Writing, Pre-writing,
Revising, *and* Transitions.
Compound direct object, 390,
576
Compound object of prep-
osition, 390–576
Compound object of verb, 390,
576
Compound personal pronouns,
439–440
Compound predicate, 389, 576,
581–582
Compound predicate adjective,
390, 485–486
Compound predicate noun, 390
Compound sentences, 578–586
commas in, 578–579
or compound predicate,
581–582
definition of, 578
diagraming of, 579–580
punctuation of, 583–584
Compound subjects, 565–566,
576, 389
diagraming, 389
Compound verbs, 389, 576
Conclusions
in compositions, 160–161,
166–167, 184–185,
196–197, 218–219,
228–229
in paragraphs, 92–93
in reports, 247–249
in speeches, 356–357
Conflict in stories, 178–179
Conjunctions, 517–520
to combine sentences, 54–55
in compound sentence parts,
578–580

coordinating, 518
correlative, 519
definition of, 517–518
subordinating, 587
Connectives, 510–511
Context
clues, 1–5
definition of, 2
learning word meanings from
comparison, 2
contrast, 2–3
definition, 2
examples, 2
inference, 4–5
restatement, 2
Contractions
apostrophe in, 649
list of, 649
negatives, 501–503
n't not included in verb,
376
and possessive pronouns,
444–445
Cross-reference card, 276
Cumulative review
capitalization, punctuation
and spelling, 687
parts of speech, 561
sentences, 612–613
usage, 574

D

Dates
capitalization of, 620
commas in, 641–642
Declarative sentences
definition of, 369
periods in, 370
Definition
as context clue to meaning of
word, 2

in dictionary, 27
in explanatory *what* paragraph, 150–153
Demonstrations, 348, 350
Demonstrative adjectives, 484–485
Demonstrative pronouns, 440, 484–485
Descriptions 117–127
Descriptive compositions
  ending description in, 198–199
  first draft of, 196–197
  revising, 200–201
  using sensory details, 194–195
Descriptive paragraphs, 72–73, 117–127
  first draft of, 124–125
  gathering sensory details for, 118–119
  mood in, 122–123
  revising, 126–127
  using spatial order, 120–121
  using transitional words, 124–125
desert/dessert, 671
Details
  descriptive, in paragraphs, 86–87, 106–107
  organizing, 88–89
  sensory, 16–17, 70, 86–87, 118–119, 194–195
Dewey Decimal System, 272–274
Diagraming, 374–375
  adjectives, 485–486
  adverbs, 492
  compound sentences, 579–580
  compound subjects and verbs, 389–390

direct objects, 384
exclamatory sentences, 378
imperative sentences, 380
indirect objects, 384
interrogative sentences, 380
possessive nouns, 419–421
predicate adjectives, 485
predicate nouns, 485
prepositional phrases, 516–517
questions. *See* Interrogative sentences.
sentences, 374
subjects in unusual word order, 378–379
verbs and their subjects, 374–375
Diagrams, 298–299
Dialogue, 186–187
Dialogue tags, 186–187
Dictionary, 23–31
  abridged, 24
  accent marks in, 26
  alphabetical order in, 24
  abbreviations and symbols in, 24–26
  antonyms in, 27
  colloquial meaning in, 27
  definition of, 24
  definitions in, 27
  entries, information in, 26–31
  entry word, 26
  guide words, 24–25
  irregular verbs in, 464
  meaning, choosing right one, 29–31. *See also* Context clues.
  origin of word in, 26
  part of speech listed in, 26
  plurals in, 26
  principal parts in, 464
  pronunciation in, 26

slang in, 27
special forms or endings in,
　26
syllables in entries, 26
synonyms in, 27
types of, 24
unabridged, 24
See also Words *and*
　Vocabulary.
Directions
　following, 288–289
　giving (in a speech), 348, 350
　for reading forms, 321–323
Direct objects, 381–383,
　413–414
　compound, 390
　definition of, 382
　diagraming, 384
　nouns as, 413–414
　predicate words or, dis-
　　tinguishing, 388–389
　pronouns as, 430, 432–433
　recognizing, 382–383
Direct quotations, 639–640, 651
Discovery draft. *See* First draft.
Double negatives, 501–503

E
Empty sentences, 46–47
Encyclopedia, 278–279
Ending compositions. *See* Con-
　clusions in compositions *and*
　Compositions, conclusions.
Ending sentences in paragraphs,
　92–93
English language
　jargon, 38–39
　nonstandard, 34–35
　number of words in, 20
　slang, 36–37
　standard, 34–35

English language words. *See*
　Words.
Entry words in dictionary, 26
Envelope, addressing, 313–314
Essay tests, 306–307
Examples
　as context clues to word
　　meaning, 2
　to develop a paragraph,
　　70–71
Exclamation mark, or point,
　with exclamatory sentences,
　　370, 633–634
　with interjections,
　　526–527
　with quotation marks, 652
Exclamatory sentences
　definition of, 369
　diagraming, 378
　punctuation of, 370
Explanatory compositions,
　203–231
　how, 203–211
　　revising, 210–211
　　step-by-step order in,
　　　206–207
　　using transitional words in,
　　　208–209
　what, 223–231
　　developing a definition,
　　　224–225
　　first draft of, 228–229
　　organizing a definition in,
　　　226–227
　　revising, 230–231
　why, 213–221
　　developing an opinion,
　　　214–215
　　first draft of, 218–219
　　organizing an opinion,
　　　216–217
　　revising, 220–221

Geographical names, capitalization of, 617–618
Gerunds, 543–546, 549–550, 554–556
Goals for study, 290–291
good/well, 500–501
Graphic aids, 298–299
Graphs, 298–301
Guidelines for writing compositions, 162–163
Guide words
in dictionary, 24–25
in encyclopedia, 279

H

have as helping verb, 459, 461–462
Heading in letters, 310, 315
Hearing words, 18
Helping verbs, 375–377, 458–460, 461–462, 463–465
here/there, 378–381, 500
How compositions, 203–211. *See also* Explanatory compositions, *how.*
How paragraphs, 129–137. *See also* Explanatory paragraphs, *how.*
Hyphen, 647–648

I

I
capitalization of, 616
with first-person point of view, 110–111, 182–183
ie/ei, 670
Illustrations, 298–299

Imaginary narrative compositions (stories), 178–179
Imaginary subjects for paragraphs, 106–107
Imperative sentences
definition of, 360, 369
diagraming, 380
period with, 370
you as understood subject in, 380–381
Importance of reasons as method of organization, 88–89, 142–143
Indefinite pronouns, 441–442, 566–568
Indenting first-line of paragraphs in letters, 310–315
Indirect object, 383–385, 414–415
Inference, drawing word meaning from, 4–5
Infinitive, 550–556
phrase, 550–552
split, 552–554
Initials
capitalization of, 615, 632–633
periods with, 632–633
Inside address of business letters, 315–317
Interjections, 526–527
Interrogative pronouns, 491
Interrogative sentences
definition of, 369
diagraming, 380
question mark with, 370
subjects and verbs in, 379–380
Interviews and discussions, 78–79, 86–87
Intransitive verbs, 457–458

699

plural forms of, 417–419
possessive forms of, 419–421
predicate, 415–416
proper, 410–411
in sentence patterns, 534–538
singular forms of, 417–419
as subject of the verb,
373–374, 412
no words, *See* Negatives.
Number of the verb, 563
Numbers in writing, 681–682
N LV Adj. sentence pattern,
538
N LV N sentence pattern, 537
N V sentence pattern, 534
N V N sentence pattern, 535
N V N N sentence pattern, 536

comparison and contrast, 88–89
general-to-specific, 88–89,
152–153, 226–227
importance, 88–89, 142–143,
216–217
most familiar to least familiar,
164
spatial, 88–89, 120–121,
193–194
step-by-step, 132–133,
206–207
Outlines
capitalization in, 623
periods in, 633
Outside sources, 260–261,
281–282, 354
Overloaded sentences, 50–51

O

Objective tests, 304–305
Object of the preposition,
513–517
Object of the verb, 381–385
Object pronouns, 430, 432–433
Observations, 86, 260–261
Omniscient point of view,
182–183
Opinion
definition of, 262
and facts, 262–263
supporting, 262–263
in *why* composition, 214–215
in *why* paragraph, 140–141
Order of importance as method
of organization, 88–89,
142–143, 216–217
Order of writing
chronological, 88–89,
108–109, 112–113,
180–181

P

Padded sentences, 48–49
Paragraphs, 63–157
anecdotes in, 70–71, 86–87
audience of, 82–83
chronological order in, 88–89,
108–109
coherence in, 94–95
definition of, 64–65
descriptive, 72–73, 117–127
details in, 70–71, 86–87,
106–107, 118–119. *See also*
Details.
developing, 70–71, 86–87
ending sentence in, 92–93
examples in, 70–71, 86–87
explanatory, 72–73, 129–157.
See also Explanatory
paragraphs.
facts and statistics in, 70–71,
86–87
final copy of, 103

first drafts of, 90–93, 101, 112–113, 124–125, 134–135, 144–145, 154–155

first-person point of view in, 110–111

general-to-specific order in, 88–89, 152–153

incidents in, use of, 70–71, 86–87

kinds of, 72–73

logical order in. *See* Logical order in paragraphs.

main idea in, 66–69

narrative, 72–73, 105–115. *See also* Narrative paragraphs.

order of importance in, 88–89, 142–143

organizing, 88–89, 142–143. *See also* Order of writing.

point of view in, 110–111

purpose of, 82–83

revising, 76–77, 94–95, 114–115, 126–127, 156–157

sensory details in, 70–71, 86–87, 118–119

spatial order in, 88–89, 120–121

step-by-step order in, 132–133

third-person point of view, 110–111

time sequence in, 88–89

topic for, narrowing, 80–81

topic sentence in, 68–69, 84–85

transitions in, 112–113, 124–125, 132–133, 144–145

unity in, 66–67, 94–95

Participles, 546–550, 554–556

Participial phrase, 547–548

Parts of speech, 26, 525–531
definition of, 525
as shown in dictionary entries, 26
using words as different, 527–528
See also particular parts of speech.

Past participle of verbs, 462–463

Past tense of verbs, 461–462

Perfect tense of verbs, 461–462

Period, 632–633
with quotation marks, 651

Personal observation to obtain information, 86–87

Personal point of view. *See* First-person point of view.

Persuasian, 268–269

Phrases and clauses, 587–588

Phrases, transitional
in compositions, 188–189
in paragraphs, 112–113, 124–125, 132–133, 144–145

Picture graph, 300–301

Pictures, 298–299

Plagiarism, 237

Plot in stories, 178–179

Plural forms
of nouns, 417–419
of pronouns, 428
of verbs, 563, 565

Poetry lines, capitalization of, 622

Point of view
first-person, 110–111, 182–183
omniscient, 182–183
third-person limited, 182–183

third-person, 110–111,
182–183
Possessive nouns, 419–421
Possessive pronouns, 430,
433–434, 444–445
Predicate
complete, 371–373
compound, 389–390, 485–486
definition of, 372
simple, 371–373
Predicate adjectives, 380, 484,
498–499
compound, 485–486
definition of, 386, 484
diagraming, 485
Predicate noun, 386, 415–416
compound, 390
definition of, 386
diagraming, 485
Predicate pronouns, 386,
431–432
Predicate words, 386–387
Prefixes, 10–11, 666
Prepositional phrases, 511,
514–517
Prepositions, 510–517
adverbs or, distinguishing,
513–514
compound objects, 390, 576
definition of, 511
list of, 512
objects of, 513–517
Present tense of verbs, 461–462
Pre-writing
as part of a process, 76–77,
98–99
choosing point of view,
110–111, 182–183
choosing a subject, 78–79,
140–141, 162–163
choosing a topic, 78–79
for compositions, 162–165

creating mood, 122–123
definition of, 76, 98
for descriptive writing,
118–121, 194–197
developing a definition,
152–153
developing an opinion,
140–141, 214–215
developing a paragraph,
86–87
for explanatory writing,
130–133, 140–143,
150–153, 204–207,
214–217, 224–227
gathering ideas, 86–87,
162–163
gathering sensory details,
118–119
guidelines, 162–163
for narrative writing,
106–107, 178–183
narrowing a topic, 80–81,
106–107
notes, 106–107, 164–165
organizing paragraphs
chronological order, 88–89,
108–111
comparison and contrast,
88–89
general-to-specific order,
88–89
order of importance,
88–89, 142–143
spatial order, 88–89,
120–121
step-by-step order,
132–133
stating definitions, 150–151
using sensory details, 194–195
and purpose, 82–83
topic sentence in, 68–69,
84–85

Principal parts of verbs,
462–463
principal/principle, 672
Process of writing
pre-writing, 76–77, 98–99.
See also Pre-writing.
proofreading, 102
revising, 76–77, 100–101. *See
also* Revising.
steps in, 76–77
writing the first draft, 76–77,
99–100. *See also* First
draft.
See also Writing.
Pronouns, 427–454
as adjectives, 484–485
and antecedents, 437–438
as compound objects of
preposition, 435–436
compound personal,
439–440
in compound sentence parts,
435–436
definition of, 427–428
demonstrative, 440, 484–485
indefinite, 441–443, 566–568
interrogative, 441
as objects, 430, 432–433
of prepositions, 513–517
of verbs, 432–433
plural, 428
possessive, 430, 433–434,
444–445
predicate, 431–432
relative, 593–594
singular forms of, 428
as subjects, 430–432
agreement with verbs, 568
with point of view,
110–111, 182–183
substituting nouns, 428
them/those, 446–447

we/us, 446
who/whom, 445–446
Pronunciation of words, as
shown in dictionary, 26
Proofreading, 102
Proper adjectives, 483–484,
515
Proper nouns, 410–411, 515
Punctuation, 631–663
accent mark, 26
apostrophe, 648–650
to avoid confusion, 642
colon, 315–317, 645
comma, 635–644. *See also*
Comma.
in compound sentences,
54–55, 644
at end of sentence, 370,
632–634
exclamation mark, or point,
633–634
hyphen, 647–648
in letters, 309–323
period, 632–633
question mark, 633
quotation mark, 650–655
semicolon, 644
and underlining, 654
Purr words, 268–269

Q

Qualifiers, 264–265
Question mark, 370, 633
Questions. *See* Interrogative
sentences.
Quotations
capitalization in, 651
commas with, 639–640, 651
definition of, 650–651
direct, 639–640, 651
divided, 651

punctuation with, 639–640,
651
Quotation marks, 650–655
commas with, 639–640, 651
in dialogue, 652
with divided quotations, 651
exclamation marks with, 652
question marks with, 652
for titles, 654

R

raise/rise, 473
*Readers Guide to Periodical
Literature,* 282
Reading, 78–79
Real life narrative compositions,
178–179
Real life subjects for paragraphs, 106–107
Reference works, 281–282
Regular verbs, 463. *See also*
Verbs.
Relative clauses, 593–594
Religions, capitalization of,
620
Reports, 233–253
bibliography in, 252–254
body of, 247–249
conclusion of, 247–249
finishing, 252–254
footnotes in, 252–254
introduction in, 244–246
organizing information in,
239–240
outlines, 241–243
revising, 250–251
taking notes for, 236–238
thesis statement in, 234
Research, 86–87, 234–235. *See
also* Study and Research
Skills.

Restatement as key to context
clue to word meaning, 2
Résumés, 330–331
Return address on envelope,
313–314
Revision
definition of, 76–77
of compositions, 168–169,
175, 190–191, 200–201,
210–211, 220–221
of descriptive writing,
126–127, 200–201
of explanatory writing,
136–137, 146–147,
156–157, 210–211,
220–221
of first drafts, 94–95,
126–127, 200–201,
220–221
of narrative writing, 114–115
of paragraphs, 94–95,
100–101, 114–115,
126–127, 136–137,
146–147, 156–157
as part of a process, 76–77,
100–102
of a report, 250–251
rise/raise, 473
Roots, Latin, 14–15
Run-on sentences, 403–404

S

s'/'s, 419–421
Salutation in letters, 310, 315
Scanning, 296–297
Schedules for study, 290–291
Semicolon, 644
Senses, as basis for gathering
detail, 16–17
Sensory details, 16–17, 70,
118–119

Subject of the sentence
  agreement with verb,
    562–572
  complete, 371–373
  compound, 565–566
  definition of, 371
  diagraming, 374–375
  in exclamatory sentences,
    378–380
  in imperative sentences,
    380–381
  in interrogative sentences,
    379–380
  nouns as, 373–374, 412
  pronouns as, 430–432
  simple, 373–374
  understood (*you*), 380–381
    in unusual positions,
      377–381
    of the verb, 373–374, 412
Subordinate clauses, 587–589
Suffixes, 12–13, 666–668
Superlatives
  adjectives as, 488–489
  adverbs as, 404–495
Syllables
  as shown in dictionary
    entries, 26
  dividing words into, 647–648
Synonyms, 6–7, 27

T

Tables, 298–299
Talks. *See* Speech.
Taste words, 19
teach/learn, 471
Test taking, 302–307
Thank-you notes. *See* Letters.
their/they're, 672
them/those, 499–500
there/here, extra in sentence,
  500

there/here, when introducing
  sentence, 378–381
Thesis statement, 234
Third-person limited point of
  view, 182–183
Third-person point of view
  in compositions, 182–183
  in paragraphs, 110–111
those/them, 446–447, 499–500
Time sequence. *See* Chronological order.
Title card, 276
Titles
  capitalization of, 615–616,
    624
  of compositions, 170–172
  of persons, 615–616
  of written works
    quotation marks with, 624
    underlining for italics, 624
to/too/two, 703
Topic, choosing, 78–79
Topic, narrowing the
  in compositions, 162–163
  in paragraphs, 78–79, 80–81
Topic sentences
  in compositions, 214–215
  in paragraphs, 68–69, 84–85
Touch words, 19
Transitions
  showing chronological order,
    108–109, 112–113, 188–189
  in compositions, 188–189,
    208–209, 218–219
  showing order of importance
    of reasons, 218–219
  in paragraphs, 112–113,
    124–125, 132–133
  showing spatial order,
    124–125, 193–194
  showing step-by-step order,
    132–135, 208–209

Transitive verbs, 457–458
True-false tests, 304–305
two/to/too, 672

U

Underlining titles for italics, 624
Understood subject (*you*),
   380–381
Unity in paragraphs, 66–67
Using grammar in writing. *See*
   end of each lesson.
Using mechanics in writing
   capitalization, 630
   punctuation, 663
   spelling, 677

V

Verb (simple predicate),
   371–373
Verbals, 542–556. *See also*
   Gerunds, Participles *and*
   Infinitives.
Verbs, 455–480
   action, 456
   after there, 378
   agreement with subject,
     562–572
   be, 456. *See also* State-of-
     being verbs, Linking verbs
     and Irregular verbs.
   in a clause, 586–588
   compound, 389, 576
   with compound subjects,
     565–566
   contractions, 568, 649
   definition of, 456
   diagraming, 374–375
   using dictionary to find prin-
     cipal parts of, 464

direct objects of, 381–383
helping, 375–377, 458–460
in imperative sentences, 380
intransitive, 457–458
irregular, 463–470
linking, 386–388, 456,
   498–499
main, 375–377, 458–460
in negative contractions, 376,
   501–503
n't not part of, 376
number, definition of, 563
object of, 381–385
past participle of, 462–463
perfect tense, 461–462
plural forms of, 563, 565
present tense, 462–463
principal parts of, 462–463
regular, 463
in sentence patterns, 532–540
separated parts of, 376–377
singular forms of, 563, 656
state-of-being, 456
subjects of, 373–374, 562–565
tenses, 460–462
transitive, 457–458
troublesome, 471–474
using negatives, 376, 501–503
See also Irregular verbs.
Vertical file, 281–282
Vocabulary, 1–20. *See also*
   Words *and* Dictionary.

W

we/us, 446
weather/whether, 672
well/good, 501
whether/weather, 672
who/whom, 445–446, 593

Acknowledgments

Harold Ober Associates Inc.: For "Cats" by Eleanor Farjeon, from *The Children's Bells*; copyright
© 1957 by Eleanor Farjeon.

Photographs

Jim Whitmer, ii, 40, 62, 202; Donald Johnson/Hillstrom Stock, xviii; Jacqueline Durand, 22, 74,
116, 138, 148, 158, 232, 270, 346; Abigail Heyman/Magnum, 32; Ray Hillstrom, 52, 128; Don
Smetzer/Click Chicago, 96, 364; Don & Pat Valenti/Hillstrom Stock, 104; Brent Jones, 176, 308,
324; Michael Hayman/Click Chicago, 192; Tom McCarthy/Hillstrom Stock, 212; James L. Ballard,
222, 258, 284.

Cover

Sinjerli Variation III, 1977. Frank Stella. Petersburg Press, London and New York, © Vert Foncé,
1977.

Editorial Credits

Editor-in-Chief: Joseph F. Littell
Editorial Director: Joy Littell
Administrative Editor: Kathleen Laya
Managing Editor: Geraldine Macsai

Director of Secondary English: Bonnie Dobkin
Editors: James M. LiSacchi, Mary Schafer
Associate Editor: Robert D. Shepherd
Associate Designer: Mary E. MacDonald
Assistant Designer: Debbie Costello
Cover Design: Joy Littell, Mary E. MacDonald

Teaching Special Populations: Specific Suggestions

Section 1: The Sentence and Its Parts

LD   LD students will find it easier to distinguish sentences from fragments if you stress that a fragment contains only part of an idea. Demonstrate this by using, first, an incomplete request and then a complete request.

EXAMPLE: Look. (incomplete)
            Look at the chalkboard.

Explain that this request can be understood only when expressed in full.

You may want to limit your LD students to the simple subject-verb diagrams. Introduce other elements when and if your students are ready for them.

ESL   ESL students will have trouble distinguishing sentence fragments from sentences, as their command of syntax is likely to be poor. Provide extra practice using the diagram on page 371 and the questions *who?* and *what?* until the difference is clear. Use a scrambled sentence exercise; give sentences with scrambled word order (*is desk there notebook a on the*) and have students unscramble it (*there is a notebook on the desk*).

Stress word order in each of the four types of sentences. Demonstrate differences in intonation.

Practice with scrambled sentences and substitution drills. In the latter, the teacher provides a model sentence; students substitute cue words (from the teacher) to make new sentences.

MODEL: I walked to the store this morning.
CUES: ran bus
STUDENT RESPONSE: I ran to the bus this morning.

Stress the logic of punctuation, which is common to all languages.

ESL students will find the English verb system confusing. Demonstrate usage and correct form, and provide practice as needed. Give additional practice placing *who?* or *what?* before the verb in order to identify the subject. Stress the exercises in which the students must find the subject in unusual positions, and add to them if possible.

ESL students will find diagraming especially helpful because it provides visual representations of difficult syntactical patterns.

NSD   NSD students frequently have difficulty with the use of helping verbs and with the verb *be*. The lessons on *The Parts of a Verb* and *Linking Verbs and Predicate Words* can be used as diagnostic exercises, to determine where students' difficulties lie.

Section 2: Using Complete Sentences

LD and ESL   Because LD and ESL students will do a number of the exercises in this text orally, it will be helpful to spend some time on the lesson *Avoiding Run-on Sentences*. Run-on errors, which are readily apparent in written work, are not easy to detect in oral work.

When teaching ESL students, see comments in preceding section. Identifying fragments and run-ons requires comprehension of examples. Check for understanding of vocabulary. Do many exercises orally, encouraging the use of logic. ESL students may not be able to generate their own sentences. Provide them with native English-speaking partners, or help them yourself.

Section 3: Using Nouns

LD   LD students may have difficulty using dictionaries to find the plurals of nouns. Frequent repetition and reinforcement will be necessary when teaching singular and plural nouns, particularly for irregular examples.

ESL   ESL students will understand proper and common nouns and possessives more readily through comparisons and contrasts with their own languages. They will need extra practice with forming plurals, the irregular ones in particular. Using a dictionary may be beyond their skill; an English-speaking partner could help.

Word order will continue to be a problem. Be alert for negative transfer from the student's native language: for example, placing an adjective after a noun or not using article adjectives.

NSD NSD students will need to spend some additional time working on *Plural Forms of Nouns*. Encourage these students to use a dictionary. You may wish to work through or review the lesson **Using a Dictionary** (Writing Section 2) before attempting this Section.

Section 4: Using Pronouns

LD LD students should be allowed to do several exercises orally, to make sure that they understand the directions.

ESL ESL students will find this section difficult because pronouns are much more complicated in English than in many other languages. These students are likely to mistake case and gender and to omit pronouns. Review the rules, stressing that pronouns are not dropped in English. Provide extensive practice: scrambled sentences, cloze exercises, substitution drills.

ESL students cannot usually judge what "sounds natural." Encourage reference to the chart on page 430. Practice possessive pronouns, especially *its*, extensively.

Some ESL students will substitute a pronoun for the verb *be*, forming a double subject (*David, he sick*). Be aware of this problem, too, when teaching linking verbs.

NSD NSD students will have difficulty determining when to use the object form and when to use the subject form of pronouns. Pay particular attention to Parts 2 and 9 of this lesson.

Section 5: Using Verbs

LD LD students may require additional explanation and drill in order to master state-of-being verbs. Instructions for exercises will have to be more explicit.

LD students will require extensive practice while working on this Section. Additional exercises can be found in this book and in the Practice Book.

ESL ESL students frequently omit forms of *be*, drop *s* from third-person singular present tense, or drop *ed* from regular past tense. Go over rules very carefully and provide extra practice: scrambled sentences, fill-in sentences, substitution drills.

As far as possible, compare English forms with forms in other languages.

ESL students will have many difficulties with helping verbs. Emphasize practice and use additional examples.

ESL students may have trouble distinguishing between past and past participle forms. Provide extensive oral drills and substitution drills. These students will not be good judges of what "sounds right." Give supplementary oral practice before assigning written exercises, or do some written exercises together as a class.

Allow ESL students ample time for practice with confusing pairs of verbs. Review and practice with extra exercises.

NSD NSD students, as already noted, have many difficulties with main verbs and helping verbs. If you have already used Section 1 as a diagnostic test, use Part 2 of this section to concentrate on specific problems. Be especially aware of the faulty use of *be*.

Many NSD students will be more familiar with deviant than with standard usage of irregular verbs. They may not be able to distinguish aurally between standard and nonstandard usage. Repetition and patience will be essential when attempting to modify linguistic habits.

Part 6 is of particular importance to NSD students. Many non-standard dialects regularly substitute one verb for another similar verb. (Example: *lay* for *lie*). Remember that these are not eccentric habits in the student; rather, the student is obeying semantic rules acquired over many years. If necessary, spend extra time on this Part.

Section 6: Using Modifiers

LD LD students will have trouble generating and writing sentences as instructed in Exercise C on page 487. Either omit the exercise or do it as a group exercise.

ESL ESL students may have difficulty using articles and placing adjectives in the sentences correctly. Practice with scrambled sentences and expansion drills. In an expansion drill, the teacher gives a base sentence (*Our dog is brown*), the student repeats it, the teacher gives a new word (*large*), and the student inserts it in the correct place in the sentence (*Our large dog is brown*).

Make sure that these students know the vocabulary in this section, and also concepts like *what kind, how many, to what extent,* etc.

Agreement in gender and number between an adjective and the noun it modifies is much simpler in English than in many languages. Point out that English does not require distinct forms for gender and number (except for demonstratives *this, these, that,* and *those*).

Give many examples of predicate adjectives, and use arrows, as in the examples on page 484, to indicate the word modified.

ESL students may confuse adverbs and predicate adjectives, especially when they are used with linking verbs. Focus on the words modified. As you present the examples and the exercises on adverbs, ask the questions *how, when, where,* or *to what extent,* and encourage the students to do so. Give these students ample practice (scrambled sentences, fill-in sentences) using adjectives and adverbs before moving on to comparative forms.

Double negatives are required in some languages. Compare the form in the ESL student's language and mark out the extra negative to show the difference. Practice with substitution drills and fill-in sentences.

NSD NSD students often use *more* and *most* with adverbs as an emphatic statement (*most best, more sooner*). Provide extra examples of correct usage.

Many non-standard dialects use double negatives and incorrect modifiers. It will require repetition and patience to modify these linguistic habits.

Section 7: Using Prepositions and Conjunctions

LD Students may have trouble understanding relationships between sentence parts. Use extra examples to help recognition of correlative conjunctions.

ESL For ESL students the functions of prepositions and conjunctions in English may be very confusing because their native languages use them quite differently. Contrast the usages whenever possible, and emphasize memorizing the list on page 512. Pace this material very cautiously, as the concepts presented are numerous and difficult to see in relation to one another. Correct placement of prepositional phrases may require more sensitivity to English word order than these students have developed. Do many of the sentences orally, discussing the relationships among sentence parts and, when possible, the contrasts with the native language. You may need to review terminology and give additional examples. You may also have to review *and, but,* and *or.*

Section 8: Review of Parts of Speech

LD   LD students will require some review of parts of speech before they can do the first exercise. You can use the exercise as the basis for an oral review.

ESL   ESL students will find this review very helpful. Stress the material on multiple functions of words, which is very important for non-native speakers.

Section 9: Sentence Patterns

LD   LD students may have trouble completing pattern charts in exercises. Do them orally as class exercises.

ESL   This section will be helpful but difficult for ESL students. They will not know what word order makes sense, or how a word's position in a sentence changes the meaning of the sentence. Use word pictures to explain how ideas change with word order. Switch pictures to show who does action and who receives action (Example: *The suitcase filled the box* and *The box filled the suitcase*).

Pair ESL students with native English-speaking partners, or help them yourself.

NSD   Review verb forms with NSD students, specifically the use of *be*, before you begin *LV* patterns.

Section 10: Using Verbals

LD   You may wish to limit your LD students to just finding verbals in a sentence rather than identifying the kind of verbal and its uses. You will have to modify exercises to your students' abilities, and do most of the ʳexercises orally.

Review the concept of words being used in ʳthan one way before starting (Handbook Section ʳattention to spelling changes of verbs made into ʳnd participles. Give extra exercises and prac-

NSD   NSD students frequently drop the *-ing* ending of verbals to an *-in'* sound (*playin', singin'*). These students will need reinforcement of the spelling and pronunciation of participles and gerunds in order to recognize them aurally.

Section 11: Making Subjects and Verbs Agree

LD   For LD students, emphasize the rules. Use extra examples to illustrate conditional statements such as "Some indefinite pronouns can be used either as a singular or plural pronoun."

ESL   ESL students may need some review. The concepts *singular* and *plural* will be familiar, but the students may need to be reminded of their application to English words. Third person singular present tense verbs end in *s* as do plural nouns, a fact which may cause confusion. Practice with substitution drills and fill-in sentences. Compound subjects and indefinite pronouns may require extra practice; encourage their use in classroom conversation.

NSD   Stress the necessity of agreement between subject and verb, especially the state-of-being verbs. Use extra examples and practice for Part 4.

Section 12: Using Compound and Complex Sentences

LD   Work slowly through this section with LD students. Do all exercises orally with the class. You may want to review the definition of a sentence before trying to teach main and subordinate clauses. Present two simple sentences and show different ways they can be put together.

ESL   ESL students may need careful explanation of the nuances in the uncombined sentences before they can combine them with the correct conjunction. Review uses of *and, but,* and *or.*

If students find combining sentences difficult, present an add-on sentence exercise: start with a noun or verb and have students place additional words where they belong in a sentence. After building two related sentences, have students add a conjunction to join them.

Encourage ESL students to practice writing complex sentences. Additional exercises will be found at the end of this section and in the Practice Book.

Make sure students understand that a subordinate clause does not have only one position in a sentence, that it can appear first, last, or in the middle of a sentence. It is important to make ESL students aware of which subordinating words are to be used when referring to people (*who, whom,* etc.).

Section 13: Capitalization

LD LD students will have trouble copying all the sentences. Assign fewer sentences, or allow these students to complete them orally.

ESL ESL students will find some personal titles, proper nouns, outline/letter forms, and literary titles unfamiliar. Have these studens work with native speaking partners who can explain this material.

Section 14: Punctuation

LD LD students will have trouble copying all the sentences. Assign fewer sentences, or allow these students to complete them orally.

ESL ESL students will benefit from emphasis on the logic of punctuation. Point out any marks whose use may be unfamiliar, such as the hyphen or the apostrophe in possessives, and give extra practice in using them. A native English speaking partner may be helpful, especially in using the dictionary.

Section 15: Spelling

ESL ESL students must learn English spelling through written use and practice. Discuss the rules at a leisurely pace, using a multi-sensory approach: see, hear, say, write.

NSD NSD students will usually need additional work in spelling. Encourage the use of the dictionary through dictionary drills.

Section 16: The Correct Form for Writing

LD You may have to modify the guide lines for correct writing form according to students' physical abilities.

ESL This is an important section for ESL students. Not only does it give them an acceptable form model for their papers, but discusses writing conventions that are probably different than those of their native countries. Since most countries use the metric system, take time to go over the American numerical system. Also emphasize the acceptable form for dates, monetary amounts, and abbreviations, all of which vary from country to country.

Guidelines for Evaluating Composition

Adapted from Teaching and Evaluating Student Writing,
copyright © 1985 by McDougal, Littell & Company

Types of Evaluation

In order to give student writers the constant practice and feedback they need, teachers must have a practical method of evaluation. Obviously, if the student will be writing constantly, a teacher cannot be expected to evaluate each piece in a line-by-line, word-by-word manner. Nor would such an evaluation necessarily be useful to the developing writer. It is therefore suggested that a teacher learn to use two different evaluation methods—the holistic method and the more detailed analytic method.

Holistic evaluation of writing is a quick, guided method of rating pieces of writing. It can best be used to evaluate daily writing samples or first drafts of more complex pieces. With holistic evaluation, an evaluator reads the written piece as a whole, considers certain features, and immediately assigns a grade. The grade may be a single rating for the entire piece of writing or a set of ratings for the different features being considered.

Analytic evaluation should occur only when the student has turned in the clean, final copy of a piece of writing. In this detailed type of evaluation, the teacher analyzes each aspect of a piece of writing, including both content and mechanics.

Evaluators

The evaluation process can be utilized by three types of evaluators: the writer of the piece, other students, and the teacher. Each type of evaluation offers unique benefits to the developing writer.

1. Self-Evaluation. In this type of evaluation, a writer comments on his or her own work, noting which parts were successful and which unsuccessful.

2. Peer Evaluation. Evaluating the writing of others is often a strong learning experience. In peer evaluation, students work together in small groups to improve a piece of writing. Student evaluators should always be given a list of specific criteria that the writing is expected to meet, and should then comment on how well each paper succeeds.

3. Teacher Evaluation. The teacher's comments and suggestions may be incorporated at any point in the writing process. Studies indicate that evaluation by the teacher is most successful when it is done in combination with self- and peer evaluation. The evaluation that follows provides for such a combination of evaluation procedures.

Teacher evaluation should also involve direct communication with every student. Such help can be provided in student-teacher conferences.

Keeping a Record of Improvement

Both the teacher and students benefit when writing folders are maintained throughout the school year. A piece of writing from early in the year, along with its evaluations, can be compared with later pieces. Progress from one piece to the next will be erratic, as the writer takes risks using new techniques and appears to move backwards until gaining mastery of each new technique. However, over the course of the year, progress should be evident.

BIBLIOGRAPHY

Cooper, Charles R. and Lee Odell, eds. *Evaluating Writing: Describing, Measuring, Judging.* Urbana, Illinois: National Council of Teachers of English, 1977.

Graves, Donald H. *Balance the Basics: Let Them Write.* New York: The Ford Foundation, 1978.

Murray, Donald M. *A Writer Teaches Writing: A Practical Method of Teaching Composition.* Boston: Houghton Mifflin, 1968.

Payne, Lucile Vaughn, *The Lively Art of Writing.* Chicago: Follett, 1965.

Using the Evaluation Form

The following form for composition evaluation may be used at any stage of the writing process, and may be re-used after each revision.

The form should be filled out by the student and turned in with the writing. There is also space on the form for peer evaluation, if desired. The teacher may ask students to turn in only final copies, or may ask to see work in progress. The student states whether the submitted writing is the final copy.

On the evaluation form, content may be rated at any point; mechanics should be graded only on a final copy.

Self-Evaluation: Besides the questions on the form, the student can ask himself or herself the questions concerning revising listed in the relevant composition chapter. The student may use 1, 3, and 5 subjectively.

Peer Evaluation: Members of the peer group should rate each feature as objectively as possible. In order to focus on ideas and organization, the group should evaluate content only.

Teacher Evaluation: The following standards for evaluating composition are provided to assist the teacher in rating papers with objectivity and consistency. In a conference, the teacher might discuss one or two of these areas in detail.

Standards for Evaluation

Content	1—Low	3—Average	5—High
1	Unclear, unimaginative writing.	Understandable but unimaginative writing.	Imaginative, interesting writing.
2	Boring or poorly defined topic.	Topic adequately limited and defined.	Well-chosen, precisely developed topic.
3	Purpose unclear, or not achieved in the writing.	Purpose defined adequately. Not completely achieved.	Clear, well-defined purpose. Writing achieves purpose successfully.
4	Writing so lacking in detail that topic remains undeveloped.	Incomplete development. More information needed.	Topic thoroughly covered. Writing is rich in detail and supporting information.
5	Many irrelevant sentences or details.	Few irrelevant sentences or details.	Well-chosen, relevant sentences and details.
6	Disjointed ideas. No transitional words, phrases, or ideas.	Inconsistent flow. Some transitional devices.	Ideas flow well. Good use of transitional devices.
7	Lack of any logical organization of ideas.	Some organization of ideas evident.	Well-organized ideas. Type of organization suited to topic and purpose.
8	Dull, general words, poorly chosen. Inappropriate to audience.	Suitable but unimaginative language. Generally appropriate to audience.	Specific, vivid language. Appropriate to audience.

Mechanics

1	Many fragments and run-on sentences. Frequent mistakes in the use of nouns, verbs, pronouns, and subject-verb agreement.	Few fragments and run-ons. Some mistakes in the use of nouns, verbs, pronouns, and subject-verb agreement.	No fragments or run-ons. Few mistakes in the use of nouns, verbs, pronouns, and subject-verb agreement.
2	Frequent mistakes in capitalization.	Occasional mistakes in capitalization.	Infrequent mistakes in capitalization.
3	Punctuation marks frequently misused or missing.	Punctuation marks usually used correctly.	Infrequent mistakes in punctuation.
4	Frequent mistakes in spelling, without any indication of awareness of spelling patterns.	Occasional misspellings, usually indicating an approximation of the correct spelling and an awareness of spelling patterns.	Infrequent spelling mistakes.
5	Paragraphs not indented. Writing illegible. Incorrect headings or margins.	Some carelessness or inconsistency in form. Occasionally hard to read.	Correct form. Neat, legible handwriting.

Composition Evaluation Form

Writer _____ **Date** _____

Title _____

Circle one: Unfinished   Final Copy

Evaluation Symbols
1 Needs a great deal of work
3 Acceptable—could be improved
5 Very good. Needs no further revision.

Content

	Writer's Opinion	Peer Group Opinion	Teacher's Evaluation	Teacher's Comments
1. **Interest.** Is the writing interesting and understandable? Does it hold the reader's attention?				
2. **Topic.** Is the topic a good one? Has it been narrowed sufficiently?				
3. **Purpose.** Is the purpose of the writing clear? Has the writer accomplished this purpose?				
4. **Development.** Has the topic been developed well? Is there sufficient information?				
5. **Unity.** Are all ideas and details related to the topic? Do they all help to develop or strengthen the main idea?				
6. **Continuity.** Do ideas flow smoothly? Has the writer avoided any breaks in thought?				
7. **Organization.** Were ideas arranged in a logical order? Does this order suit the purpose of the writing?				
8. **Language.** Is the language appropriate to the writing? Does it suit the audience? Are the words vivid?				
Additional Guidelines				

Mechanics (to be graded by teacher on final copy only)

1. **Grammar and Usage.** Are there any fragments or run-ons? Is the correct form of every pronoun or verb used? Are adjectives and adverbs used correctly?				
2. **Capitalization.** Are all first words, initials, proper nouns, proper adjectives, and titles capitalized?				
3. **Punctuation.** Does each sentence have the proper end mark? Are all punctuation marks used correctly?				
4. **Spelling.** Are all words spelled correctly? Are plurals and possessive forms spelled correctly?				
5. **Form.** Is the writing legible? Is the heading correct? Are there sufficient margins?				